Mastering
VMware vSphere® 6.7

D1160135

Mastering
VMware vSphere® 6.7

Nick Marshall

Mike Brown

G. Blair Fritz

Ryan Johnson

SYBEX®
A Wiley Brand

Development Editor: Stephanie Barton

Technical Editor: Rebecca Fitzhugh

Production Editor: Athiyappan Lalith Kumar

Copy Editor: Kathryn Duggan

Content Enablement and Operations Manager: Pete Gaughan

Production Manager: Kathleen Wisor

Associate Publisher: Jim Minatel

Proofreader: Evelyn Wellborn

Indexer: Johnna VanHoose Dinse

Project Coordinator, Cover: Brent Savage

Cover Designer: Wiley

Cover Image: ©ColorBlind Images

I dedicate this book to my family. My wife Natalie, my son Ethan, and my daughters, Estelle and Eve.

You are the reason I do what I do.
—Nick Marshall

Acknowledgments

What a journey it has been the last few years since my previous Mastering vSphere book. When completing the last book, I had just moved to Palo Alto, California from Australia and was awaiting the arrival of my second child. The opportunity had come up to work out of VMware's headquarters on a beautiful campus not far from Stanford University. However, after a fantastic 2.5 years in the US, it was time to move back closer to our family in Australia.

When writing my last book, I spoke about my wife being my rock, and that has not changed. Our life is somehow even more chaotic with three kids, yet she amazingly handles it all in her stride. Nat, you are still my everything; I owe you more than I could possibly repay, but I hope a remote tropical holiday for two might be a good first step.

Thanks to my fellow authors, work mates and good friends, Mike Brown, Blair Fritz, and Ryan Johnson. You guys really knocked it out of the park with your contributions. Your dedication to refining and (re)writing your respective sections reinforces my respect for you as VMware authorities. The content of this book is so much better thanks to your involvement. . . even if you didn't know what you were getting yourselves into!

I'd also like to thank our technical editor, Rebecca Fitzhugh. Thanks for keeping us honest, Rebecca. Your technical review was most appreciated, and the feedback rightfully kept us on our toes.

Once again, the team at Wiley/Sybex have been so supportive. Jim Minatel, thank you for your guidance and direction. Stephanie Barton, thank you for graciously coming back and keeping our rambling streams of consciousness somewhat cohesive for a third time. Also, to Athiyappan Kumar and the rest of the team, thank you for all that you did to ensure the quality of this work. Your attention to detail is second to none.

As always, I'd like to thank the VMware community as a whole. To all the bloggers, speakers, tweeters, and podcasters: without you all, I would never have started down this virtual road.

—Nick Marshall

About the Author

Nick Marshall is a Senior Integration Architect with nearly 20 years of IT experience. He is currently working for VMware in the Integrated Systems Business Unit.

Previously, Nick has worked in a number of roles, ranging from computer assembler, to infrastructure architect, to product manager. Nick loves to solve business problems with technical solutions.

Nick's passion for virtualization is evident by his involvement in starting the most popular virtualization podcast, *vBrownBag*, and writing on his personal blog, at www.nickmarshall.com. au. You can also find him speaking at industry conferences such as VMworld, VMUG (VMware User Group), and PEX (Partner Exchange). To recognize his contributions to the VMware community, Nick has been awarded the vExpert award each year since 2012.

Outside of his day job, Nick has a budding interest in woodworking, professional audio and video production, and volunteering at his local church.

Nick lives in Melbourne, Australia with his wife, Natalie, and their three children, Ethan, Estelle, and Eve.

About the Contributors

The following individuals also contributed to this book.

Mike Brown (Chapters 5 and 6) is a Senior SDDC Integration Architect in VMware's Integrated Systems Business Unit. He currently focuses on Architecture and Design for the core vSphere, Networking, and NSX components of the VMware Validated Designs.

Mike is a double VMware Certified Design Expert (VCDX #71) in Datacenter and Network Virtualization. He also holds many other industry certifications. He has been awarded the VMware vExpert award each year since 2011.

Mike has been working in IT since 1997 where he worked for a small VAR. Since then he has worked both in a customer environment and also as a consultant for a few local companies before joining VMware's Professional Services team in 2012. Since joining VMware, Mike spent two years as a Senior Consultant before moving into the vCloud Suite Technical Marketing Team where he spent another two years before moving into the VMware Validated Design Architect's team.

Mike lives in Houston, Texas with his amazing wife, Courtney, and five children Brycen (11), Brennan (9), Bronson (6), Joy (3), and Joss (1).

G. Blair Fritz (Chapters 3, 4, and 8) is a SDDC Integration Architect in VMware's Integrated Systems Business Unit, alongside Mike, Ryan, and Nick, where he currently focuses on Architecture and Design for the core vSphere, Operation Management (including vRealize Operations and vRealize Log Insight), and Lifecycle Management of the VMware Validated Designs and VMware Cloud Foundation.

Blair has been working in IT since 2003 where he started his adventures by working at The Children's Museum of Indianapolis. Since then, he's had over 15 years of experience as a support engineer and technologist, ranging from systems engineer, staff escalation engineer, technical lead, and solutions architect roles.

Blair lives in Indianapolis, Indiana with his wonderful wife, Jenny, and their two dogs, Theo and Olive. When he isn't working, you'll likely find him bike riding, playing tennis, or playing Dungeons and Dragons.

Ryan Johnson (Chapters 11, 12, and 14) is a Senior Solutions Architect in the Integrated Systems Business Unit at VMware where he is an architect, author, and product owner for both the VMware Validated Designs and VMware Cloud Foundation.

Ryan has over 23 years of experience as a technologist, ranging from systems engineer, enterprise architect, and solutions architect roles.

Ryan lives in Tallahassee, Florida with his incredibly patient wife, Darcie, and their two creative boys, Nolan and Parker. You are likely to find him on one of many nearby trails.

Contents at a Glance

Contents

Foreword

When *Mastering VMware vSphere 6.0* was released in 2015, Nick Marshall stopped by my office for a chat. We discussed the vSphere 6.0 release, of course, but we also discovered we had a number of things in common. Obviously, we have a love for virtualization, some would be aware of our strong Christian faiths, but maybe more obscurely, we discovered that we have both written books for (Wiley) Sybex. During this meeting, Nick also asked me if I would write the foreword for the next Mastering VMware vSphere book. As you can see, he's been planning this one for a while!

Fast forward to 2018, and it brings us to a very exciting year in virtualization. VMware released vSphere 6.7, and Nick has now released the long-awaited *Mastering VMware vSphere 6.7* to accompany it. This is Nick's third revision of the best-selling vSphere book after being handed the mantle from Scott Lowe. Stepping back a little, there are some anniversaries to celebrate this year too. This is the 10-year mark from when Chris McCain released the very first Mastering VMware book, *Mastering VMware Infrastructure 3*. Also, VMware celebrates its 20th year since being founded by Diane Greene, Mendel Rosenblum, Scott Devine, Edward Wang, and Edouard Bugnion.

Looking back at these milestones gives us an opportunity to also consider where virtualization sits in today's IT environment. We've come a long way since IBM enabled multitasking by partitioning their mainframes into virtual machines. The days of traditional client/server workloads are definitely diminishing, and we are well and truly in the cloud era, a multi-cloud world. Even though we are moving into a new era, virtualization is still the foundation of both public and private clouds. And of course, the best, most advanced virtualization platform is still VMware vSphere.

With VMware vSphere 6.7, we have taken the world's best hypervisor, ESXi, and added improvements in scale, performance, and even more stability. VMware has enabled even more seamless cross-cloud mobility with features like Per-VM EVC, and we've doubled down on security with features like TPM, vTPM, and FIPS compliance.

In this book, you'll find all the features and functionality available to you in vSphere, not just the things that have changed in 6.7. Nick and his coauthors have made sure that both new and old features are covered so that you can understand everything there is to know.

Well done on another release of this bit of VMware history, Nick. I know the readers will appreciate your continued dedication to their understanding of vSphere and the value it can bring them.

—*Pat Gelsinger, VMware CEO*

Introduction

It seems like a lifetime ago, 2005. That was the year that I tried to convince my boss to use VMware GSX Server on our new DL385 and thus the start of my journey delving into the depths of virtualization. The world of information technology (IT) has definitely shifted a couple of times since then. The two most obvious changes are the proliferation of virtualization and the subsequent widespread adoption of cloud computing.

Virtualization—especially server virtualization—is readily embraced in datacenters worldwide. VMware has gone from being a relatively small vendor to having the commanding share of the server virtualization market. Over the years, other companies such as Microsoft, Red Hat, and Citrix have jumped into the server virtualization space, but after all this time, it's still VMware that's synonymous with virtualization. For all intents and purposes, VMware invented the market.

Cloud Computing is a somewhat natural evolution of virtualization. If virtualization is the abstraction of individual server hardware, cloud computing is the abstraction of entire datacenters' worth of hardware. The scale can be smaller or larger, but the abstraction type is the same. But I'm getting ahead of myself. If you're reading this, there's a chance you're just now starting to learn about virtualization. What is virtualization, and why is it important to you?

As I mentioned, I define *virtualization* as the abstraction of one computing resource from another computing resource. Consider storage virtualization—in this case, you are abstracting servers (one computing resource) from the storage to which they are connected (another computing resource). This holds true for other forms of virtualization, too, like application virtualization (abstracting applications from the operating system). When most IT professionals think of virtualization, they think of hardware (or server) virtualization: abstracting the operating system from the underlying hardware on which it runs and thus enabling multiple operating systems to run simultaneously on the same physical server. That is the technology on which VMware has built its market share.

Almost single-handedly, VMware's enterprise-grade virtualization solution has revolutionized how organizations manage their datacenters. Before VMware introduced its powerful virtualization solution, organizations bought a new server every time a new application needed to be provisioned. Over time, datacenters became filled with servers that were all using only a fraction of their overall capacity. Even though these servers were underutilized, organizations still had to pay to power them and to dissipate the heat they generated.

Now, using VMware's server virtualization products, organizations can run multiple operating systems and applications on their existing hardware, and new hardware is purchased only when capacity needs dictate. No longer must organizations purchase a new physical server whenever a new application needs to be deployed. By stacking workloads together using virtualization, organizations derive greater value from their hardware investments. They also reduce operational costs by reducing the number of physical servers and associated hardware in the datacenter, in turn decreasing power usage and cooling needs in the datacenter. In some cases, these operational cost savings can be quite significant.

But consolidation is only one benefit of virtualization; companies also realize greater workload mobility, increased uptime, streamlined disaster-recovery options, and a bevy of other benefits from adopting virtualization. And virtualization, specifically server virtualization, has created the foundation for a new way of approaching the computing model: cloud computing.

Cloud computing is built on the tenets of broad network access, resource pooling, rapid elasticity, on-demand self-service, and measured service. Virtualization, such as that provided by VMware's products, enables the IT industry to embrace this new operational model of more efficiently providing services to their customers, whether those customers are internal (their employees) or external (partners, end users, or consumers). That ability to efficiently provide services is the reason virtualization is important to you.

This book provides all the information you, as an IT professional, need to design, deploy, configure, manage, and monitor a dynamic virtualized environment built on VMware's enterprise-class server virtualization product: vSphere 6.7.

—*Nick Marshall, Author*

What Is Covered in This Book

This book is written with a start-to-finish approach to installing, configuring, managing, and monitoring a virtual environment using the VMware vSphere 6.7 product suite. The book begins by introducing the vSphere product suite and all of its great features. After introducing all of the bells and whistles, the book details an installation of the product and then moves into configuration. This includes configuring vSphere's extensive networking and storage functionality. We wrap up the configuration discussion with chapters on high availability, redundancy, and resource utilization. After completing the installation and configuration, we move into virtual machine creation and management and then into monitoring and troubleshooting. You can read this book from cover to cover to gain an understanding of the vSphere product suite in preparation for a new virtual environment, or you can use it as a reference if you are an IT professional who has begun your virtualization and wants to complement your skills with real-world tips, tricks, and best practices as found in each chapter.

This book, geared toward the aspiring as well as the practicing virtualization professional, provides information to help implement, manage, maintain, and troubleshoot an enterprise virtualization scenario.

Here is a glance at what's in each chapter and the appendix:

Chapter 1: Introducing VMware vSphere 6.7   We begin with a general overview of all the products that make up the vSphere 6.7 product suite. This chapter also covers vSphere licensing and provides some examples of benefits that an organization might see from adopting vSphere as its virtualization solution.

Chapter 2: Planning and Installing VMware ESXi   This chapter looks at the architecture of the VMware hypervisor, ESXi, along with selecting the physical hardware, choosing your version of VMware ESXi, planning your installation, and installing VMware ESXi, both manually and in an unattended fashion.

Chapter 3: Installing and Configuring vCenter Server   In this chapter, we dive deep into planning your vCenter Server environment. vCenter Server is a critical management component of vSphere, so this chapter discusses the proper design, planning, installation, and configuration for vCenter Server.

Chapter 4: vSphere Update Manager and the vCenter Support Tools   This chapter describes what is involved in planning, designing, installing, and configuring the vSphere Update Manager along with some of the other vCenter tools. You'll use vCenter Update Manager to keep your vSphere environment patched and up-to-date.

Chapter 5: Creating and Configuring a vSphere Network   This virtual-networking chapter covers the design, management, and optimization of virtual networks, including features like the vSphere Distributed Switch. In this chapter, we also initiate discussions and provide solutions on how to integrate the virtual networking architecture with the physical network architecture while maintaining network security.

Chapter 6: Creating and Configuring Storage Devices   This in-depth chapter provides an extensive overview of the various storage architectures available for vSphere. In this chapter, we discuss vSAN, Fibre Channel, iSCSI, and NAS storage design and optimization techniques as well as storage features like thin provisioning, multipathing, and round-robin load balancing.

Chapter 7: Ensuring High Availability and Business Continuity   This exciting chapter covers the hot topics regarding business continuity and disaster recovery. We provide details on building highly available server clusters in virtual machines. In addition, this chapter discusses the use of vSphere High Availability (HA) and vSphere Fault Tolerance (FT) as ways of providing failover for virtual machines running in a vSphere environment. We also discuss backup options using vSphere's Storage APIs.

Chapter 8: Securing VMware vSphere   Security is an important part of any implementation, and in this chapter, we cover different security management aspects, including managing direct ESXi host access and integrating vSphere with Active Directory. This chapter also covers how to manage user access for environments with multiple levels of system administration and how to employ Windows users and groups in conjunction with the vSphere security model to ease the administrative delegation that comes with enterprise-level deployments.

Chapter 9: Creating and Managing Virtual Machines   This chapter introduces the practices and procedures involved in provisioning virtual machines through vCenter Server. In addition, you're introduced to timesaving techniques, virtual machine optimization, and best practices that will ensure simplified management as the number of virtual machines grows larger over time.

Chapter 10: Using Templates and vApps   This chapter introduces the idea of templates, a mechanism for more rapidly deploying standardized virtual-machine images. We also discuss the different types of cloning and the concept of a vApp—a specialized container used by vSphere for the distribution of multi-VM applications. In addition, we discuss the Open Virtualization Format (OVF) standard used by VMware and other vendors for distributing virtual machines.

Chapter 11: Managing Resource Allocation   In this chapter, we provide a comprehensive look at managing resource allocation. From individual virtual machines to resource pools and clusters of ESXi hosts, this chapter explores how resources are consumed in vSphere and addresses the mechanisms you can use—reservations, limits, and shares—to manage and modify that resource allocation.

Chapter 12: Balancing Resource Utilization   Resource allocation isn't the same as resource utilization, and this chapter follows up the discussion of resource allocation in Chapter 11 with a look at some of the ways vSphere offers to balance resource utilization. In this chapter, you'll learn about vSphere vMotion, Enhanced vMotion Compatibility, vSphere Distributed Resource Scheduler (DRS), Storage vMotion, and Storage DRS.

Chapter 13: Monitoring VMware vSphere Performance   In this chapter, we look at some of the native tools in vSphere that give virtual infrastructure administrators the ability to track and troubleshoot performance issues. The chapter focuses on monitoring CPU, memory, disk, and network adapter performance across ESXi hosts, resource pools, and clusters in vCenter Server. In this chapter, you'll also learn about vCenter Operations Manager.

Chapter 14: Getting Started with vSphere Automation   Many tasks that VMware vSphere administrators face are repetitive, but automation can help. In this chapter, we close out the book by discussing several different ways to bring automation to your vSphere environment, including PowerCLI and the vSphere APIs.

Appendix: The Bottom Line   This appendix offers solutions to the Master It problems at the end of each chapter.

The Mastering Series

The *Mastering* series from Sybex provides outstanding instruction for readers with intermediate and advanced skills, in the form of top-notch training and development for those already working in their field and clear, serious education for those aspiring to become pros. Every *Mastering* book includes the following:

◆   Real-World Scenarios, ranging from case studies to interviews, that show how the tool, technique, or knowledge presented is applied in actual practice

◆   Skill-based instruction, with chapters organized around real tasks rather than abstract concepts or subjects

◆   Self-review test questions, so you can be certain you're equipped to do the job right

The Hardware Behind the Book

Starting out, it can seem difficult to build an environment in which you can learn by implementing the exercises and practices detailed in this book. It is possible to build a practice lab with minimal hardware, and we encourage you to follow along with the book. If you're just starting, we recommend that you build a nested virtual lab on your laptop or desktop computer. A nested lab runs the hypervisor itself, ESXi, as a virtual machine. It needs VMware Workstation or Fusion installed and at least 16 GB of RAM. Be sure to read Chapters 2 and 3 before you attempt to construct any type of environment for development purposes.

For the purpose of writing this book, we used multiple hardware configurations. When travelling, it was simple to spin up a simple nested lab on our laptops, but more often than not, we used a decent setup with a small number of servers and storage.

It's not impossible to set yourself up with a nice lab to follow along. But for some, this is not the sort of environment to which they have access. For entry-level NFS and iSCSI testing, a number of vendors, including DellEMC, HP, and NetApp, offer virtual storage appliances or simulators that you can use to gain some familiarity with shared storage concepts and the vendor's specific products. We encourage you to use these sorts of tools where applicable in your learning process. vSAN can also run in evaluation mode if you wish to use local disks.

In addition, the VMware Hands-on Labs (HOL) provide fully functioning environments, using nested virtualization at scale. You can find details on the HOL website: `labs.hol.vmware.com`. They're free to use, and you don't have to follow the guides associated with the labs if you don't want to.

Who Should Buy This Book

This book is for IT professionals looking to strengthen their knowledge of constructing and managing a virtual infrastructure on vSphere 6.7. While the book can also be helpful for those new to IT, a strong set of assumptions is made about the target reader:

- A basic understanding of networking architecture

- Experience working in a Microsoft Windows environment

- Experience managing DNS and DHCP

- A basic understanding of how virtualization differs from traditional physical infrastructures

- A basic understanding of hardware and software components in standard x86 and x64 computing

How to Contact the Authors

We welcome feedback from you about this book or about books you'd like to see from us in the future.

You can reach Nick by writing to **nick@nickmarshall.com.au**, by following him on Twitter (his username is **@nickmarshall9**), or by visiting his blog at www `.nickmarshall.com.au`.

You can reach out to Mike by following him on Twitter (his username is **@vcdx71**) or by visiting his personal blog at www.`vcdx71.com`.

You can reach out to Blair by following him on Twitter (his username is **@TheVMBlair**), or by visiting his blog at www.`vmblair.com`.

You can reach Ryan by writing to **ryan@tenthirtyam.org**, by following **@tenthirtyam** on Twitter, or by visiting `tenthirtyam.org` for his occasional hypertext fragments.

Chapter 1

Introducing VMware vSphere 6.7

VMware vSphere 6.7 builds on previous generations of VMware's enterprise-grade virtualization products that have been leading the industry since 2001. vSphere 6.7 gives greater control, performance, and extensibility with a focus on enabling workload security and mobility. With dynamic resource controls, high availability, and fault-tolerance features along with distributed resource management and operational tools included as part of the suite, IT administrators have all the tools they need to run an enterprise environment ranging from a few servers to tens of thousands of servers distributed among multiple clouds.

IN THIS CHAPTER, YOU WILL LEARN TO

◆ Identify the role of each product in the vSphere product suite

◆ Recognize the interaction and dependencies between the products in the vSphere suite

◆ Understand how vSphere differs from other virtualization products

Exploring VMware vSphere 6.7

VMware vSphere is a comprehensive collection of products and features that together provide a full array of enterprise virtualization functionality. The vSphere product suite includes the following products and main features:

◆ VMware ESXi

◆ VMware vCenter Server

◆ vSphere Update Manager (VUM)

◆ vSphere Virtual Symmetric Multi-Processing

◆ vSphere vMotion and Storage vMotion

◆ vSphere Distributed Resource Scheduler (DRS)

◆ vSphere Storage DRS (SDRS)

◆ Storage I/O Control (SIOC) and Network I/O Control (NIOC)

◆ Storage-Based Policy Management (SBPM)

◆ vSphere High Availability (HA)

- vSphere Fault Tolerance (FT)

- vSphere Storage APIs

- VMware Virtual SAN (vSAN)

- vSphere Replication

- vSphere Content Library

Rather than waiting to introduce these products and features in their own chapters, we will introduce each product or feature in the following sections. This will allow us to explain how each one affects the design, installation, and configuration of your virtual infrastructure. After w cover the features and products in vSphere, you'll have a better grasp of how each of them fits into the design and the big picture of virtualization.

Certain products outside the vSphere product suite extend the vSphere product line with new functionality. These additional products include VMware Horizon View, VMware vRealize Automation, and VMware vCenter Site Recovery Manager, just to name a few. VMware even offers bundles of vSphere and these other products in the vCloud Suite to make it easier for user to purchase and consume the products in their environments. However, because of the size and scope of these products, they are not covered in this book.

As of this writing, VMware vSphere 6.7 is the latest release of the VMware vSphere product family. This book covers functionality found in version 6.7. Where possible, we've tried to note differences between vSphere versions. For detailed information on other vSphere versions, refer to the previous books in the *Mastering VMware vSphere* series, also published by Sybex.

To help simplify navigation and to help you find information on the breadth of products and features in the vSphere product suite, we've prepared Table 1.1, which contains cross-references to where you can find more information about a particular product or feature elsewhere in the book.

TABLE 1.1: Product and Feature Cross-References

VMWARE VSPHERE PRODUCT OR FEATURE	CHAPTERS WHERE THIS IS COVERED
VMware ESXi	Installation:—Chapter 2 Networking:—Chapter 5 Storage:—Chapter 6
VMware vCenter Server	Installation:—Chapter 3 Networking:—Chapter 5 Storage:—Chapter 6 Security:—Chapter 8
vSphere Update Manager	Chapter 4
vSphere Host Client and vSphere Web Client	vSphere Host Client: Chapter 2 vSphere Web Client: Chapter 3
VMware vRealize Orchestrator and PowerCLI	Chapter 14

TABLE 1.1:   Product and Feature Cross-References *(CONTINUED)*

VMWARE vSPHERE PRODUCT OR FEATURE	CHAPTERS WHERE THIS IS COVERED
vSphere Virtual Symmetric Multi-Processing	Chapter 9
vSphere vMotion and Storage vMotion	Chapter 12
vSphere Distributed Resource Scheduler	Chapter 12
vSphere Storage DRS	Chapter 12
Storage I/O Control and Network I/O Control	Chapter 11
Profile-driven storage	Chapter 6
vSphere High Availability	Chapter 7
vSphere Fault Tolerance	Chapter 7
vSphere Storage APIs for Data Protection	Chapter 7
VMware Data Protection	Chapter 7
VMware Virtual SAN	Chapter 6
vSphere Replication	Chapter 7
vSphere Flash Read Cache	Installation:—Chapter 6 Usage:—Chapter 11
vSphere Content Library	Chapter 9

First we'll look at the products that make up the VMware vSphere suite, and then we'll examine the major features. Let's start with the products in the suite, beginning with VMware ESXi.

Examining the Products in the vSphere Suite

In the following sections, we'll describe and review the products found in the vSphere product suite.

VMWARE ESXI

The core of the vSphere product suite is the hypervisor, which is the virtualization layer that serves as the foundation for the rest of the product line. In vSphere 5 and later, including vSphere 6.7, the hypervisor comes solely in the form of VMware ESXi.

Longtime users of VMware vSphere will remember this as a shift in the way VMware provides the hypervisor. Prior to vSphere 5, the hypervisor was available in two forms: VMware ESX and VMware ESXi. Although both products shared the same core virtualization engine, supported the same set of virtualization features, leveraged the same licenses, and were considered bare-metal installation hypervisors (also referred to as Type 1 hypervisors; see the sidebar "Type 1 and Type 2 Hypervisors"), there were still notable architectural differences. In VMware ESX, VMware used a Red Hat Enterprise Linux (RHEL)-derived Service Console to provide an interactive environment through which users could interact with the hypervisor. The Linux-based Service Console also included services found in traditional operating systems, such as a firewall, Simple Network Management Protocol (SNMP) agents, and a web server.

TYPE 1 AND TYPE 2 HYPERVISORS

Hypervisors are generally grouped into two classes: Type 1 hypervisors and Type 2 hypervisors. Type 1 hypervisors run directly on the system hardware and thus are often referred to as *bare-metal* hypervisors. Type 2 hypervisors require a host operating system, and the host operating system provides I/O device support and memory management. VMware ESXi is a Type 1 bare-metal hypervisor. (In earlier versions of vSphere, VMware ESX was also considered a Type 1 bare-metal hypervisor.) Other Type 1 bare-metal hypervisors include KVM (part of the open source Linux kernel), Microsoft Hyper-V, and products based on the open source Xen hypervisor like Citrix Hypervisor (formally XenServer) and Oracle VM.

VMware ESXi, on the other hand, is the next generation of the VMware virtualization foundation. Unlike VMware ESX, ESXi installs and runs without the Linux-based Service Console. This gives ESXi an ultralight footprint of approximately 150 MB. Despite the lack of the Service Console, ESXi provides all the same virtualization features that VMware ESX supported in earlier versions. Of course, ESXi 6.7 has been enhanced from earlier versions to support even more functionality, as you'll see in this and future chapters.

The key reason that VMware ESXi is able to support the same extensive set of virtualization functionality as VMware ESX but without the Service Console is that the core of the virtualization functionality wasn't found in the Service Console. It's the *VMkernel* that is the foundation of the virtualization process. It's the VMkernel that manages the virtual machines' access to the underlying physical hardware by providing CPU scheduling, memory management, and virtual switch data processing. The section "VMware ESXi Architecture" in Chapter 2 will go into more detail on how the VMkernel supports and interacts with the rest of the hypervisor. Figure 1.1 shows the high level structure of VMware ESXi.

FIGURE 1.1
The VMkernel is the foundation of the virtualization functionality found in VMware ESXi.

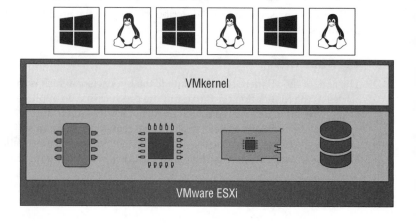

TABLE 1.2:   VMware ESXi Maximums

COMPONENT	VMWARE ESXI 6.7	VMWARE ESXI 6.5	VMWARE ESXI 6.0	VMWARE ESXI 5.5	VMWARE ESXI 5.0
Number of virtual CPUs per host	4,096	4,096	4,096	4,096	2,048
Number of logical CPUs (hyperthreading enabled)	768	576	480	320	160
Number of virtual CPUs per core	32	32	32	32	25
Amount of RAM per host	16 TB	12 TB	6 TB	4 TB	2 TB
Number of virtual machines per host	1,024	1,024	1,024	512	512
Number of virtual CPUs per virtual machine	128	128	128	64	32
Amount of RAM per virtual machine	6 TB	6 TB	4 TB	1 TB	1 TB

We mentioned earlier that VMware ESXi 6.7 is enhanced, and one such area of enhancement is in the configuration limits of what the hypervisor can support. Table 1.2 shows the configuration maximums for the last few versions of VMware ESXi.

These are just some of the configuration maximums. Where appropriate, future chapters will include additional values for VMware ESXi maximums for network interface cards (NICs), storage, virtual machines (VMs), and so forth.

Given that VMware ESXi is the foundation of virtualization within the vSphere product suite, you'll see content for VMware ESXi throughout the book. Table 1.1, earlier in this chapter, tells you where you can find more information about specific features of VMware ESXi.

VMWARE VCENTER SERVER

Stop for a moment to think about your current IT environment. Does it include Active Directory? There is a good chance it does. Now imagine your environment without Active Directory, without the ease of a centralized management database, without the single sign-on capabilities, and without the simplicity of groups. That's what managing VMware ESXi hosts would be like without using VMware vCenter Server. Not a very pleasant thought, is it? Now calm yourself down, take a deep breath, and know that vCenter Server, like Active Directory, is meant to provide a centralized management platform and framework for all ESXi hosts and their respective VMs. vCenter Server allows IT administrators to deploy, manage, monitor, automate, and secure a virtual infrastructure in a centralized fashion. To help provide scalability, vCenter Server leverages a backend database that stores all the data about the hosts and VMs.

In previous versions of VMware vSphere, vCenter Server was a Windows-only application. Version 6.7 of vSphere still offers this Windows-based installation of vCenter Server, but this will be the last release available for Windows. VMware offers a prebuilt vCenter Server Appliance (a virtual appliance, in fact, something you'll learn about in Chapter 10, "Using Templates and vApps") that is based on Photon, a thin and lightweight Linux distribution. The Linux-based vCenter Server appliance, or vCSA, is now a more feature-rich version of vCenter since development of new features has ceased on a Windows version. Chapter 3, "Installing and Configuring vCenter Server," will include more details on what is missing from the Windows version of vCenter Server. But for now, unless you already have an existing Windows-based installation, all new installations should use the Linux-based vCenter Server Appliance to ensure a supported future.

vCenter Server not only provides configuration and management capabilities—which include features such as VM templates, VM customization, rapid provisioning and deployment of VMs, role-based access controls, and fine-grained resource allocation controls—it also provides the tools for the more advanced features of vSphere vMotion, vSphere Distributed Resource Scheduler, vSphere High Availability, and vSphere Fault Tolerance. All of these features are described briefly in this chapter and in more detail in later chapters.

In addition to vSphere vMotion, vSphere Distributed Resource Scheduler, vSphere High Availability, and vSphere Fault Tolerance, using vCenter Server to manage ESXi hosts enables a number of other features:

♦ Enhanced vMotion Compatibility (EVC), which leverages hardware functionality from Intel and AMD to enable greater CPU compatibility between servers

♦ Host profiles, which allow you to bring greater consistency to host configurations across larger environments and to identify missing or incorrect configurations

♦ Storage I/O Control, which provides cluster-wide quality of service (QoS) controls so you can ensure critical applications receive sufficient storage I/O resources even during times of congestion

♦ vSphere Distributed Switches, which provide the foundation for networking settings and third-party virtual switches that span multiple hosts and multiple clusters

♦ Network I/O Control, which allows you to flexibly partition physical NIC bandwidth and provide QoS for different types of traffic

♦ vSphere Storage DRS, which enables VMware vSphere to dynamically migrate storage resources to meet demand, much in the same way that DRS balances CPU and memory utilization

vCenter Server plays a central role in any sizable VMware vSphere implementation. In Chapter 3, we discuss planning and installing vCenter Server as well as look at ways to ensure its availability. As previously mentioned, Chapter 3 will examine the differences between the Windows-based version of vCenter Server and the Linux-based vCenter Server virtual appliance. Because of vCenter Server's central role in a VMware vSphere deployment, we'll touch on vCenter Server in almost every chapter throughout the rest of the book. Refer to Table 1.1, earlier in this chapter, for specific cross-references.

vCenter Server is available in three packages:

◆ vCenter Server Essentials is integrated into the vSphere Essentials kits for small office deployment.

◆ vCenter Server Foundation provides all the functionality of vCenter Server, but for a limited number of ESXi hosts.

◆ vCenter Server Standard provides all the functionality of vCenter Server, including provisioning, management, monitoring, and automation.

You can find more information on licensing and product editions for VMware vSphere in the section "Licensing VMware vSphere."

vSphere Update Manager

vSphere Update Manager is a component of vCenter Server that helps users keep their ESXi hosts and select VMs patched with the latest updates. vSphere Update Manager provides the following functionality:

◆ Scans to identify systems that are not compliant with the latest updates

◆ User-defined rules for identifying out-of-date systems

◆ Automated installation of patches for ESXi hosts

◆ Full integration with other vSphere features like Distributed Resource Scheduler

vSphere Update Manager works as an installable package with the Windows-based installation of vCenter Server as well as the prepackaged feature pre-installed in the vCenter Server virtual appliance. Refer to Table 1.1 for more information on where vSphere Update Manager is described in this book.

VMware vSphere Client and vSphere Host Client

vCenter Server provides a centralized management framework for VMware ESXi hosts, but it's the web-based vSphere Client (like its predecessor, the Windows-based vSphere Desktop Client) where you will spend most of your time.

With the release of vSphere 5, VMware shifted its primary administrative interface to a web-based vSphere Client built on Adobe Flash. The "vSphere Web Client"provided a web-based user interface for managing a virtual infrastructure and enabled you to manage your infrastructure without needing to install the Windows-based vSphere Desktop Client on a system. Unfortunately, the Flash-based client was not well received and ultimately VMware decided to move to the HTML5 web standard. This transition took a number of releases, and as a result, multiple clients could be used to do some (but not all) administrative tasks.

Initially, the HTML5-based vSphere Web Client (simply known as the "vSphere Client") offered only a subset of the functionality available to the "Flash" vSphere Web Client. However, in subsequent releases—including the 6.7 release—the vSphere Client has been enhanced and expanded to include most of the functionality you need to manage a vSphere environment.

Further, VMware has stated that the Flash-based vSphere Web Client and the Windows-based vSphere Desktop Client are now end-of-life. Luckily, the step-by-step procedures for the Flash-based vSphere Web Client and the HTML5-based vSphere client are usually identical. For this reason, we'll use Flash-based vSphere Web Client screen shots and step-by-step guidance throughout this book to ensure each instruction can be completed with the same client.

Administering hosts without vCenter has also changed. You now access the user interface by browsing to the URL of each ESXi host. This loads an HTML5-based user interface (UI) but only for that particular host. No client installation is needed.

This can be a little confusing if this is your first foray into the VMware landscape, so let us recap. The vSphere Web Client, based on Flash, has been deprecated. The Windows-installable vSphere Desktop Client (for connecting to vCenter and hosts) has been deprecated. To administer vCenter, and hosts attached to a vCenter Server, use the new HTML5-based vSphere Client or the Flash-based vSphere Web Client. To administer ESXi hosts directly, without vCenter, use the HTML5-based vSphere Host Client.

Examining the Features in VMware vSphere

In the following sections, we'll take a closer look at some of the features available in the vSphere product suite. We'll start with Virtual SMP.

vSphere Virtual Symmetric Multi-Processing

The vSphere Virtual Symmetric Multi-Processing (vSMP or Virtual SMP) product allows you to construct VMs with multiple virtual processor cores and/or sockets. vSphere Virtual SMP is *not* the licensing product that allows ESXi to be installed on servers with multiple processors; it is the technology that allows the use of multiple processors *inside* a VM. Figure 1.2 identifies the differences between multiple processors in the ESXi host system and multiple virtual processors.

FIGURE 1.2
vSphere Virtual SMP allows VMs to be created with more than one virtual CPU.

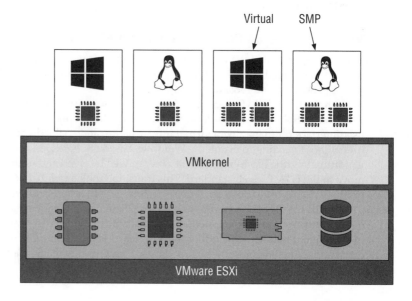

With vSphere Virtual SMP, applications that require and can actually use multiple CPUs can be run in VMs configured with multiple virtual CPUs. This allows organizations to virtualize even more applications without negatively impacting performance or being unable to meet service-level agreements (SLAs).

This functionality also allows users to specify multiple virtual cores per virtual CPU. Using this feature, a user could provision a dual "socket" VM with two cores per "socket" for a total of four virtual cores. This approach gives users tremendous flexibility in carving up CPU processing power among the VMs.

vSphere vMotion and vSphere Storage vMotion

If you have read anything about VMware, you have most likely read about the extremely useful feature called vMotion. vSphere vMotion, also known as *live migration*, is a feature of ESXi and vCenter Server that allows you to move a running VM from one physical host to another physical host without having to power off the VM. This migration between two physical hosts occurs with no downtime and with no loss of network connectivity to the VM. The ability to manually move a running VM between physical hosts on an as-needed basis is a powerful feature that has a number of use cases in today's datacenters.

Suppose a physical machine has experienced a nonfatal hardware failure and needs to be repaired. You can easily initiate a series of vMotion operations to remove all VMs from an ESXi host that is to undergo scheduled maintenance. After the maintenance is complete and the server is brought back online, you can use vMotion to return the VMs to the original server.

Alternately, consider a situation in which you are migrating from one set of physical servers to a new set of physical servers. Assuming that the details have been addressed—and we'll discuss the details of vMotion in Chapter 12, "Balancing Resource Utilization"—you can use vMotion to move the VMs from the old servers to the newer servers, making quick work of a server migration with no interruption of service.

Even in normal day-to-day operations, vMotion can be used when multiple VMs on the same host are in contention for the same resource (which ultimately causes poor performance across all the VMs). With vMotion, you can migrate any VMs facing contention to another ESXi host with greater availability for the resource in demand. For example, when two VMs contend with each other for CPU resources, you can eliminate the contention by using vMotion to move one VM to an ESXi host with more available CPU resources.

vMotion moves the execution of a VM, relocating the CPU and memory footprint between physical servers but leaving the storage untouched. Storage vMotion builds on the idea and principle of vMotion: you can leave the CPU and memory footprint untouched on a physical server but migrate a VM's storage while the VM is still running.

Deploying vSphere in your environment generally means that lots of shared storage—Fibre Channel or FCoE or iSCSI SAN or NFS—is needed. What happens when you need to migrate from an older storage array to newer storage hardware based on vSAN? What kind of downtime would be required? Or what about a situation where you need to rebalance utilization of the array, either from a capacity or performance perspective?

With the ability to move storage for a running VM between datastores, Storage vMotion lets you address all of these situations without downtime. This feature ensures that outgrowing datastores or moving to new storage hardware does not force an outage for the affected VMs and provides you with yet another tool to increase your flexibility in responding to changing business needs.

vSphere Distributed Resource Scheduler

vMotion is a manual operation, meaning that you must initiate the vMotion operation. What if VMware vSphere could perform vMotion operations automatically? That is the basic idea behind vSphere Distributed Resource Scheduler (DRS). If you think that vMotion sounds exciting, your anticipation will only grow after learning about DRS. DRS, simply put, leverages vMotion to provide automatic distribution of resource utilization across multiple ESXi hosts that are configured in a cluster.

Given the prevalence of Microsoft Windows Server in today's datacenters, the use of the term *cluster* often draws IT professionals into thoughts of Microsoft Windows Server Failover Clusters. Windows Server clusters are often active-passive or active-active-passive clusters. However, ESXi clusters are fundamentally different, operating in an active-active mode to aggregate and combine resources into a shared pool. Although the underlying concept of aggregating physical hardware to serve a common goal is the same, the technology, configuration, and feature sets are quite different between VMware ESXi clusters and Windows Server clusters.

Aggregate Capacity and Single Host Capacity

Although we say that a DRS cluster is an implicit aggregation of CPU and memory capacity, it's important to keep in mind that a VM is limited to using the CPU and RAM of a single physical host at any given time. If you have two small ESXi servers with 64 GB of RAM each in a DRS cluster, the cluster will correctly report 128 GB of aggregate RAM available, but any given VM will not be able to use more than approximately 64 GB of RAM at a time.

An ESXi cluster is an implicit aggregation of the CPU power and memory of all hosts involved in the cluster. After two or more hosts have been assigned to a cluster, they work in unison to provide CPU and memory to the VMs assigned to the cluster (keeping in mind that any given VM can only use resources from one host; see the sidebar "Aggregate Capacity and Single Host Capacity"). The goal of DRS is twofold:

◆   At startup, DRS attempts to place each VM on the host that is best suited to run that VM at that time.

◆   Once a VM is running, DRS seeks to provide that VM with the required hardware resources while minimizing the amount of contention for those resources in an effort to maintain balanced utilization levels.

The first part of DRS is often referred to as *intelligent placement.* DRS can automate the placement of each VM as it is powered on within a cluster, placing it on the host in the cluster that it deems to be best suited to run that VM at that moment.

DRS isn't limited to operating only at VM startup, though. DRS also manages the VM's location while it is running. For example, let's say three hosts have been configured in an ESXi cluster with DRS enabled. When one of those hosts begins to experience a high contention for CPU utilization, DRS detects that the cluster is imbalanced in its resource usage and uses an internal algorithm to determine which VM(s) should be moved in order to create the least imbalanced cluster. For every VM, DRS will simulate a migration to each host and the results will be compared. The migrations that create the least imbalanced cluster will be recommended or automatically performed, depending on the DRS configuration.

DRS performs these on-the-fly migrations without any downtime or loss of network connectivity to the VMs by leveraging vMotion, the live migration functionality we described earlier. This makes DRS extremely powerful because it allows clusters of ESXi hosts to dynamically rebalance their resource utilization based on the changing demands of the VMs running on that cluster.

FEWER BIGGER SERVERS OR MORE SMALLER SERVERS?

Recall from Table 1.2 that VMware ESXi supports servers with up to 768 logical CPU cores and up to 16 TB of RAM. With vSphere DRS, though, you can combine multiple smaller servers for the purpose of managing aggregate capacity. This means that bigger, more powerful servers might not be better servers for virtualization projects. These larger servers, in general, are significantly more expensive than smaller servers, and using a greater number of smaller servers (often referred to as "scaling out") may provide greater flexibility than a smaller number of larger servers (often referred to as "scaling up"). The key thing to remember is that a bigger server isn't necessarily a better server.

---

vSPHERE STORAGE DRS

vSphere Storage DRS takes the idea of vSphere DRS and applies it to storage. Just as vSphere DRS helps to balance CPU and memory utilization across a cluster of ESXi hosts, Storage DRS helps balance storage capacity and storage performance across a cluster of datastores using mechanisms that echo those used by vSphere DRS.

Earlier, we described vSphere DRS's feature called intelligent placement, which automates the placement of new VMs based on resource usage within an ESXi cluster. In the same fashion, Storage DRS has an intelligent placement function that automates the placement of VM virtual disks based on storage utilization. Storage DRS does this through the use of datastore clusters. When you create a new VM, you simply point it to a datastore cluster, and Storage DRS automatically places the VM's virtual disks on an appropriate datastore within that datastore cluster.

Likewise, just as vSphere DRS uses vMotion to balance resource utilization dynamically, Storage DRS uses Storage vMotion to rebalance storage utilization based on capacity and/or latency thresholds. Because Storage vMotion operations are typically much more resource-intensive than vMotion operations, vSphere provides extensive controls over the thresholds, timing, and other guidelines that will trigger a Storage DRS automatic migration via Storage vMotion.

STORAGE I/O CONTROL AND NETWORK I/O CONTROL

VMware vSphere has always had extensive controls for modifying or controlling the allocation of CPU and memory resources to VMs. Before the release of vSphere 4.1, however, vSphere could not apply extensive controls to storage I/O and network I/O. Storage I/O Control and Network I/O Control address that shortcoming.

Storage I/O Control (SIOC) allows you to assign relative priority to storage I/O as well as assign storage I/O limits to VMs. These settings are enforced cluster-wide; when an ESXi host detects storage congestion through an increase of latency beyond a user-configured threshold, it will apply the settings configured for that VM. The result is that you can help the VMs that need priority access to storage resources get more of the resources they need. In vSphere 4.1, Storage I/O Control applied only to VMFS storage; vSphere 5 extended that functionality to NFS datastores.

The same goes for Network I/O Control (NIOC), which provides you with more granular controls over how VMs use network bandwidth provided by the physical NICs. As the widespread adoption of 10 Gigabit Ethernet (10GbE) and faster continues, Network I/O Control provides you with a way to more reliably ensure that network bandwidth is properly allocated t VMs based on priority and limits.

POLICY-BASED STORAGE

With profile-driven storage, vSphere administrators can use storage capabilities and VM storage profiles to ensure VMs reside on storage that provides the necessary levels of capacity, performance, availability, and redundancy. Profile-driven storage is built on two key components:

◆ Storage capabilities, leveraging vSphere APIs for storage awareness (VASA)

◆ VM storage profiles

Storage capabilities are either provided by the storage array itself (if the array can use VASA and/or defined by a vSphere administrator. These storage capabilities represent various attributes of the storage solution.

VM storage profiles define the storage requirements for a VM and its virtual disks. You create VM storage profiles by selecting the storage capabilities that must be present for the VM to run. Datastores that have all the capabilities defined in the VM storage profile are compliant with the VM storage profile and represent possible locations where the VM could be stored.

This functionality gives you much greater visibility into storage capabilities and helps ensure that the appropriate functionality for each VM is indeed being provided by the underlying storage. These storage capabilities can be explored extensively by using VVOLs or vSAN.

Refer to Table 1.1 to find out which chapter discusses profile-driven storage in more detail.

vSphere High Availability

In many cases, high availability—or the lack of high availability—is the key argument used against virtualization. The most common form of this argument more or less sounds like this: "Before virtualization, the failure of a physical server affected only one application or workload. After virtualization, the failure of a physical server will affect many more applications or workloads running on that server at the same time. We can't put all our eggs in one basket!"

VMware addresses this concern with another feature present in ESXi clusters called vSphere High Availability (HA). Once again, by nature of the naming conventions (clusters, high availability), many traditional Windows administrators will have preconceived notions about this feature. Those notions, however, are incorrect in that vSphere HA does not function like a high-availability configuration in Windows. The vSphere HA feature provides an automated process for moving and restarting VMs that were running on an ESXi host at a time of server failure (or other qualifying infrastructure failure, as we'll describe in Chapter 7, "Ensuring High Availability and Business Continuity"). Figure 1.3 depicts the VM migration that occurs when an ESXi host that is part of an HA-enabled cluster experiences failure.

FIGURE 1.3
The vSphere HA feature
will restart any VMs
that were previously
running on an ESXi
host that experiences
server or storage
path failure.

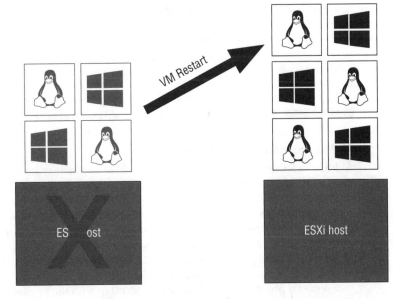

The vSphere HA feature, unlike DRS, does not always use the vMotion technology as a means of migrating servers to another host. vMotion applies only to planned migrations, where both the source and destination ESXi host are running and functioning. Let us explain what we mean. In a vSphere HA failover situation, there is no anticipation of failure; it is not a planned outage, which means there is no time to perform a vMotion operation. vSphere HA is intended to minimize unplanned downtime because of the failure of a physical ESXi host or other infrastructure components. We'll go into more detail in Chapter 7 on what kinds of failures vSphere HA helps protect against.

---

vSphere HA Improvements from vSphere 5

vSphere HA received a few notable improvements over the last few releases. Scalability was significantly improved, and it was closely integrated with the intelligent placement functionality of vSphere DRS, giving vSphere HA greater ability to restart VMs in the event of a host failure. However, perhaps the most significant improvement is the complete rewrite of the underlying architecture for vSphere HA; this newer architecture, known as Fault Domain Manager (FDM), eliminated many of the constraints found in earlier versions of VMware vSphere (before version 5.0).

By default, vSphere HA does not provide failover in the event of a guest OS failure, although you can configure vSphere HA to monitor VMs and restart them automatically if they fail to respond to an internal heartbeat. This feature is called VM Failure Monitoring, and it uses a combination of internal heartbeats and I/O activity to attempt to detect if the guest OS inside a VM has stopped functioning. If the guest OS has stopped functioning, the VM can be restarted automatically.

With vSphere HA in a failure scenario, it's important to understand that there will be an interruption of service. If a physical host or storage device fails, vSphere HA restarts the VM, an while the VM is restarting, the applications or services provided by that VM are unavailable. Th only time that this is not true is if Proactive HA is enabled on the host. Proactive HA uses hardware monitoring to proactively move VMs from a host that is suffering from hardware issues.

For users who need even higher levels of availability than can be provided using vSphere HA vSphere Fault Tolerance (FT), which is described in the next section, can help.

vSPHERE FAULT TOLERANCE

Although vSphere HA provides a certain level of availability for VMs in the event of physical host failure, this might not be good enough for some workloads. vSphere FT might help in these situations.

As we described in the previous section, vSphere HA protects against unplanned physical server failure by providing a way to automatically restart VMs upon physical host failure. This need to restart a VM in the event of a physical host failure means that some downtime—generally less than three minutes—is incurred. vSphere FT goes even further and eliminates any downtime in the event of a physical host failure. vSphere FT maintains a mirrored secondary VM on a separate physical host that is kept in lockstep with the primary VM. vSphere's newer Fast Checkpointing technology supports FT of VMs with one to four vCPUs. Everything that occurs on the primary (protected) VM also occurs simultaneously on the secondary (mirrored) VM, so that if the physical host for the primary VM fails, the secondary VM can immediately step in and take over without any loss of connectivity. vSphere FT will also automatically re-create the secondary (mirrored) VM on another host if the physical host for the secondary VM fails, as illustrated in Figure 1.4. This ensures protection for the primary VM at all times.

FIGURE 1.4
vSphere FT provides protection against host failures with no downtime experienced by the VMs.

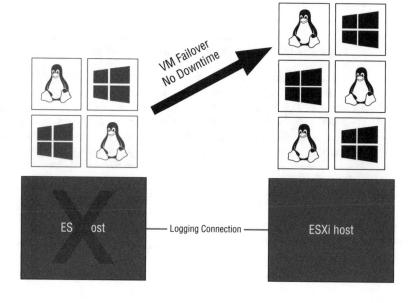

In the event of multiple host failures—say, the hosts running both the primary and secondary VMs failed—vSphere HA will reboot the primary VM on another available server, and vSphere FT will automatically create a new secondary VM. Again, this ensures protection for the primary VM at all times.

vSphere FT can work in conjunction with vMotion. As of vSphere 5.0, vSphere FT is also integrated with vSphere DRS, although this feature does require Enhanced vMotion Compatibility (EVC). VMware recommends that multiple FT virtual machines with multiple vCPUs have 10GbE networks between hosts.

vSphere Storage APIs for Data Protection and VMware Data Protection

One of the most critical aspects of any IT infrastructure, not just virtualized infrastructure, is a solid backup strategy as defined by a company's disaster recovery and business continuity plan. To help address organizational backup needs, VMware vSphere has a key component: the vSphere Storage APIs for Data Protection (VADP).

VADP is a set of application programming interfaces (APIs) that back up vendors leverage in order to provide enhanced backup functionality of virtualized environments. VADP enables functionality like file-level backup and restore; support for incremental, differential, and full-image backups; native integration with backup software; and support for multiple storage protocols.

On its own, though, VADP is just a set of interfaces, like a framework for making backups possible. You can't actually back up VMs with VADP. You'll need a VADP-enabled backup application. There are a growing number of third-party backup applications that are designed to work with VADP from vendors such as CommVault, DellEMC, and Veritas.

---

vSphere Data Protection

In vSphere 5.1, VMware phased out its earlier data protection tool, VMware Data Recovery (VDR), in favor of vSphere Data Protection (VDP). Although VDR was provided with vSphere 5.0, VDR is not supported with vSphere 5.1 and later. Subsequently, VMware has also discontinued VDP from vSphere 6.5. Backups of your vSphere environment now need to be handled by another vendor.

Virtual SAN (vSAN)

vSAN was a major new feature included with, but licensed separately from, vSphere 5.5 and later. It is the evolution of work that VMware has been doing for a number of years now. vSAN lets organizations leverage the internal local storage found in individual compute nodes and turn it into a *virtual SAN.*

vSAN requires a minimum of two ESXi hosts (or nodes) for some limited configurations, but it will scale to as many as 64. vSAN also requires solid-state (flash) storage in each of the compute nodes providing vSAN storage; this is done to help improve I/O performance given that most compute nodes have a limited number of physical drives present. vSAN pools the aggregate storage across the compute nodes, allowing you to create a datastore that spans multiple compute nodes. vSAN employs policies and algorithms to ensure performance or to help protect against data loss, such as ensuring that the data exists on multiple participating vSAN nodes at the same time.

There's more information on vSAN in Chapter 6, "Creating and Configuring Storage Devices."

vSphere Replication

vSphere Replication brings data replication, which is a feature typically found in hardware storage platforms, into vSphere itself. It's been around since vSphere 5.0, when it was only enabled for use in conjunction with VMware Site Recovery Manager (SRM) 5.0. In vSphere 5.1, vSphere Replication was decoupled from SRM and enabled for independent use without VMware SRM.

vSphere Replication enables customers to replicate VMs from one vSphere environment to another vSphere environment. Typically, this means from one data center (often referred to as the primary or production data center) to another datacenter (typically the secondary, backup, or disaster recovery [DR] site). Unlike hardware-based solutions, vSphere Replication operates on a per-VM basis, so it gives customers very granular control over which workloads will be replicated and which workloads won't be replicated.

You can find more information about vSphere Replication in Chapter 7.

vSphere Flash Read Cache

Since the release of vSphere 5.0 in 2011, the industry has seen tremendous uptake in the use of solid-state or "flash" storage across a wide variety of use cases. Because solid-state storage can provide massive numbers of I/O operations per second (IOPS) and very large bandwidth (Mbps) it can handle the increasing I/O demands of virtual workloads. However, depending on the performance, solid-state storage is still typically more expensive on a per-gigabyte basis than traditional, magnetic-disk-based storage and therefore is often first deployed as a caching mechanism to help speed up frequently accessed data.

Unfortunately, without support in vSphere for managing solid-state storage as a caching mechanism, vSphere architects and administrators have had difficulty fully leveraging solid-state storage in their environments. In vSphere 5.5 and later, VMware addresses that limitation through a feature called *vSphere Flash Read Cache.*

vSphere Flash Read Cache brings full support for using solid-state storage as a caching mechanism to vSphere. Using this feature, you can assign solid-state caching space to VMs in much the same way as you assign CPU cores, RAM, or network connectivity to VMs. vSphere manages how the solid-state caching capacity is allocated and assigned as well as how it is used by the VMs.

VMWARE vSPHERE COMPARED TO MICROSOFT HYPER-V AND CITRIX HYPERVISOR

It's not possible to compare some virtualization solutions to others, because they are fundamentally different in approach and purpose. Such is the case with VMware ESXi and some of the other virtualization solutions on the market.

To make accurate comparisons between vSphere and others, you must include only Type 1 ("baremetal") virtualization solutions. This would include ESXi, Microsoft Hyper-V, and Citrix Hypervisor.

It would not include products such as VMware Fusion or Workstation and Windows Virtual PC, all of which are Type 2 ("hosted") virtualization products. Even within the Type 1 hypervisors, there are architectural differences that make direct comparisons difficult.

For example, both Microsoft Hyper-V and Citrix Hypervisor route all the VM I/O through the "parent partition" or "dom0." This typically provides greater hardware compatibility with a wider range of products. In the case of Hyper-V, for example, as soon as Windows Server—the general-purpose operating system running in the parent partition—supports a particular type of hardware, Hyper-V supports it also. Hyper-V "piggybacks" on Windows' hardware drivers and the I/O stack. The same can be said for Citrix Hypervisor, although its "dom0" runs Linux and not Windows.

VMware ESXi, on the other hand, handles I/O within the hypervisor itself. This typically provides greater throughput and lower overhead at the expense of slightly more limited hardware compatibility. To add more hardware support or updated drivers, the hypervisor must be updated because the I/O stack and device drivers are in the hypervisor.

This architectural difference is fundamental, and nowhere is it more greatly demonstrated than in ESXi, which has a small footprint yet provides a full-featured virtualization solution. Both Citrix Hypervisor and Microsoft Hyper-V require a full installation of a general-purpose operating system (Windows Server for Hyper-V, Linux for Citrix Hypervisor) in the parent `partition/dom0` in order to operate.

In the end, each of the virtualization products has its own set of advantages and disadvantages, and large organizations may end up using multiple products. For example, VMware vSphere might be best suited in a large corporate datacenter, whereas Microsoft Hyper-V or Citrix Hypervisor might be acceptable for test, development, or branch office deployment. Organizations that don't require VMware vSphere's advanced features like vSphere DRS, vSphere FT, or Storage vMotion may also find that Microsoft Hyper-V or Citrix Hypervisor is a better fit for their needs.

As you can see, VMware vSphere offers some pretty powerful features that will change the way you view the resources in your datacenter. vSphere also has a wide range of features and functionality. Some of these features, though, might not be applicable to all organizations, which is why VMware has crafted a flexible licensing scheme for organizations of all sizes.

Licensing VMware vSphere

With each new version, VMware usually revises the licensing tiers and bundles intended to provide a good fit for every market segment. Introduced with vSphere 5.1 (and continuing on through vSphere 6.7), VMware refined this licensing arrangement with the vCloud Suite—a bundling of products including vSphere, vRealize Automation, vCenter Site Recovery Manager, and vRealize Operations Management Suite.

Although licensing vSphere via the vCloud Suite is likely the preferred way of licensing vSphere moving forward, discussing all the other products included in the vCloud Suite is beyond the scope of this book. Instead, we'll focus on vSphere and explain how the various features discussed so far fit into vSphere's licensing model when vSphere is licensed stand-alone.

One thing that you need to be aware of is that VMware may change the licensing tiers and capabilities associated with each tier at any time. You should visit the vSphere products web page (`www.vmware.com/products/vsphere.html`) or talk to your VMware representative before making any purchasing decisions.

---

vSphere vs vSphere With Operations Management

VMware sells "stand-alone" vSphere in one of two ways: as vSphere, with all the various kits and editions, and as vSphere with Operations Management. vSphere with Operations Management is the same as vSphere but adds the vRealize Operations Management product. In this section, we are focused on stand-alone vSphere only, but keep in mind that vSphere with Operations Management would be licensed and packaged in much the same way.

You've already seen how VMware packages and licenses VMware vCenter Server, but here's a quick review:

♦ VMware vCenter Server for Essentials is bundled with the vSphere Essentials kits (more on the kits in just a moment).

♦ VMware vCenter Server Standard includes all functionality and does not have a preset limit on the number of vSphere hosts it can manage (although normal sizing limits do apply). vRealize Orchestrator is included only in the Standard edition of vCenter Server.

In addition to the two editions of vCenter Server, VMware offers two editions of VMware vSphere:

♦ vSphere Standard Edition

♦ vSphere Enterprise Plus Edition

These editions are differentiated primarily by the features each edition supports, although there are some capacity limitations with the different editions.

Table 1.3 summarizes the features that are supported for each edition of VMware vSphere 6.7.

TABLE 1.3:   Overview of VMware vSphere Product Editions

	ESSENTIALS KIT	ESSENTIALS PLUS KIT	STANDARD	ENTERPRISE PLUS
vCenter Server compatibility	vCenter Server Essentials	vCenter Server Essentials	vCenter Server Standard	vCenter Server Standard
vCPUs per VM	128	128	128	128
Cross-Host / vSwitch vMotion		X	X	X
Cross-vCenter / Long Distance / Cross-Cloud vMotion				X
High Availability		X	X	X
Data Protection		X	X	X
vSphere Replication		X	X	X

TABLE 1.3: Overview of VMware vSphere Product Editions *(CONTINUED)*

	ESSENTIALS KIT	ESSENTIALS PLUS KIT	STANDARD	ENTERPRISE PLUS
vShield Endpoint		X	X	X
Hot Add			X	X
Fault Tolerance			2 vCPU	4 vCPU
Storage vMotion			X	X
Virtual Volumes and Storage Policy-based Management			X	X
Distributed Resource Scheduler and Distributed Power Management				X
Storage APIs for Array Integration, Multipathing				X
Big Data Extensions				X
Reliable Memory				X
Distributed Switch				X
I/O Controls (Network and Storage) and SR-IOV				X
Host Profiles				X
Auto Deploy				X
Storage DRS				X
Flash Read Cache				X
Content Library				X
Proactive High Availability				X
VM-level Encryption				X

Source: "VMware vSphere 6.7 Licensing, Pricing and Packaging" white paper published by VMware, available at www.vmware.com.

It's important to note that all editions of VMware vSphere 6.7 include support for thin provisioning, vSphere Update Manager, and the vSphere Storage APIs for Data Protection. We did not include them in Table 1.3 because these features are supported in all editions. Because prices change and vary depending on partner, region, and other factors, we have not included any pricing information here. Also, we did not include vSAN in Table 1.3, because it is licensed separately from vSphere.

For all editions of vSphere, VMware requires at least one year of Support and Subscription (SnS). The only exception is the Essential Kits, as we'll explain in a moment.

In addition to the different editions described previously, VMware offers some bundles, referred to as *kits*.

Essentials Kits are all-in-one solutions for small environments, supporting up to three vSphere hosts with two CPUs each. To support three hosts with two CPUs each, the Essentials Kits come with six licenses. All these limits are product-enforced. Two Essentials Kits are available:

◆ VMware vSphere Essentials

◆ VMware vSphere Essentials Plus

You can't buy these kits on a per-CPU basis; they are bundled solutions for three servers. vSphere Essentials includes one year of subscription; support is optional and available on a per-incident basis. Like other editions, vSphere Essentials Plus requires at least one year of SnS, which must be purchased separately and is not included in the bundle.

The Retail and Branch Offices (ROBO) Kits are differentiated from the "normal" Essentials and Essentials Plus Kits only by the licensing guidelines. These kits are licensed per pack of 25 virtual machines. Central management of all the sites via vCenter Server Standard is possible, though vCenter Server Standard must be purchased separately. vCenter Server Essentials is included.

Now that you have an idea of how VMware licenses vSphere, we'll review why an organization might choose to use vSphere and what benefits that organization could see as a result.

Why Choose vSphere?

Much has been said and written about the total cost of ownership (TCO) and return on investment (ROI) for virtualization projects involving VMware virtualization solutions. Rather than rehashing that material here, we'll instead focus, briefly, on why an organization should choose VMware vSphere as their virtualization platform.

ONLINE TCO CALCULATOR

VMware offers a web-based TCO calculator that helps you calculate the TCO and ROI for a virtualization project using VMware virtualization solutions. This calculator is available online at `https://www.vmware.com/go/tcocalculator/`.

You've already read about the various features that VMware vSphere offers. To help you understand how these features can benefit your organization, we'll apply them to the fictional XYZ Corporation. We'll walk you through several scenarios and show how vSphere helps in these scenarios:

Scenario 1   XYZ Corporation's IT team has been asked by senior management to rapidly provision six new servers to support a new business initiative. In the past, this meant ordering hardware, waiting on the hardware to arrive, racking and cabling the equipment once it arrived, installing the operating system and patching it with the latest updates, and then installing the application. The time frame for all these steps ranged anywhere from a few days to a few months and was typically a couple of weeks. Now, with VMware vSphere in place, the IT team can use vCenter Server's templates functionality to build a VM, install the operating system, and apply the latest updates, and then rapidly clone—or copy—this VM to create additional VMs. Now their provisioning time is down to hours, likely even minutes. Chapter 10 discusses this functionality in detail.

Scenario 2   Empowered by the IT team's ability to quickly respond to the needs of this new business initiative, XYZ Corporation is moving ahead with deploying updated versions of a line-of-business application. However, the business leaders are a bit concerned about upgrading the current version. Using the snapshot functionality present in ESXi and vCenter Server, the IT team can take a "point-in-time picture" of the VM so that if something goes wrong during the upgrade, it's a simple rollback to the snapshot for recovery. Chapter 9, "Creating and Managing Virtual Machines," discusses snapshots.

Scenario 3   XYZ Corporation is impressed with the IT team and vSphere's functionality and is now interested in expanding its use of virtualization. To do so, however, a hardware upgrade is needed on the servers currently running ESXi. The business is worried about the downtime that will be necessary to perform the hardware upgrades. The IT team uses vMotion to move VMs off one host at a time, upgrading each host in turn without incurring any downtime to the company's end users. Chapter 12 discusses vMotion in more depth.

Scenario 4   After the great success it has had virtualizing its infrastructure with vSphere, XYZ Corporation now finds itself in need of a new, larger shared storage array. vSphere's support for Fibre Channel, iSCSI, NFS, or vSAN gives XYZ room to choose the most cost-effective storage solution available, and the IT team uses Storage vMotion to migrate the VMs without any downtime. Chapter 12 discusses Storage vMotion.

These scenarios begin to provide some idea of the benefits that organizations see when virtualizing with an enterprise-class virtualization solution like VMware vSphere.

WHAT DO WE VIRTUALIZE WITH VMWARE vSPHERE?

Virtualization, by its very nature, means that you are going to take multiple operating systems—such as Microsoft Windows, Linux, Solaris, or Novell NetWare—and run them on a single physical server. While VMware vSphere offers broad support for virtualizing a wide range of operating systems, it would be almost impossible for us to discuss how virtualization impacts all the different versions of all the operating systems that vSphere supports.

VMware provides in-depth information on all the operating systems it supports and how vSphere interacts with those operating systems on its website at www.vmware.com. Also worth noting is that while VMware lists the operating systems it supports, many older operating systems still work when virtualized—they are just not on the "supported" list anymore, so your mileage may vary. As an example, we have virtualized MS-DOS and Windows 3.1 for the fun of it, but these are not listed on VMware's website.

The Bottom Line

Identify the role of each product in the vSphere product suite. The VMware vSphere product suite contains VMware ESXi and vCenter Server. ESXi provides the base virtualization functionality and enables features like Virtual SMP. vCenter Server provides management for ESXi and enables functionality like vMotion, Storage vMotion, vSphere Distributed Resource Scheduler (DRS), vSphere High Availability (HA), and vSphere Fault Tolerance (FT) Storage I/O Control and Network I/O Control provide granular resource controls for VMs. The vStorage APIs for Data Protection (VADP) provide a backup framework that allows for the integration of third-party backup solutions into a vSphere implementation.

Master It Which products are licensed features within the VMware vSphere suite?

Master It Which two features of VMware ESXi and VMware vCenter Server together aim to reduce or eliminate downtime due to unplanned hardware failures?

Recognize the interaction and dependencies between the products in the vSphere suite. VMware ESXi forms the foundation of the vSphere product suite, but some features require the presence of vCenter Server. Features like vMotion, Storage vMotion, vSphere DRS, vSphere HA, vSphere FT, SIOC, and NIOC require ESXi as well as vCenter Server.

Master It Name three features that are supported only when using vCenter Server along with ESXi.

Master It Name two features that are supported without vCenter Server but with a licensed installation of ESXi.

Understand how vSphere differs from other virtualization products. VMware vSphere's hypervisor, ESXi, uses a Type 1 bare-metal hypervisor that handles I/O directly within the hypervisor. This means that a host operating system, like Windows or Linux, is not required in order for ESXi to function. Although other virtualization solutions are listed as "Type 1 bare-metal hypervisors," most other Type 1 hypervisors on the market today require the presence of a "parent partition" or "dom0" through which all VM I/O must travel.

Master It One of the administrators on your team asked whether he should install the standard Red Hat Linux (RHEL) deployment on the new servers you purchased for ESXi. What should you tell him, and why?

Chapter 2

Planning and Installing VMware ESXi

Now that you've taken a close look at VMware vSphere and its suite of applications in Chapter 1, "Introducing VMware vSphere 6.7," it's easy to see that VMware ESXi is the foundation of vSphere.

Although the act of installation can be relatively simple, understanding the detailed ESXi hypervisor architecture will help not only your deployment but also configuration options and troubleshooting down the road.

IN THIS CHAPTER, YOU WILL LEARN TO

◆ Understand ESXi architecture

◆ Work with ESXi compatibility requirements

◆ Plan an ESXi deployment

◆ Deploy ESXi

◆ Perform post-installation configuration of ESXi

◆ Use the vSphere Host Client

VMware ESXi Architecture

Before we get too far into the implementation details of ESXi, you should understand how this software works and why it's the best-in-class hypervisor available. Once you have a good understanding of the software, you will be on your way to running a well-operated virtual IT environment with reduced troubleshooting effort.

Understanding the ESXi Hypervisor

ESXi, as a piece of software, is quite small in comparison to the average size of most software, weighing in at just a few hundred megabytes. The small footprint provides numerous advantages, such as reduced attack surface, less code to find bugs, shorter deployment times, and multiple deployment methods. While appearing small and simple from the outside, ESXi is actually a complex system with capabilities that have been refined over many years of vSphere releases. Let's dive into some of the inner workings of ESXi before you learn about how to actually deploy the software in your environment.

Examining the ESXi Components

There are a number of major components that make up VMware's ESXi hypervisor (see Figure 2.1). Let's start with the most important component of any operating system (OS): the kernel; or in this case, the VMkernel. This process is the heart of the ESXi OS and controls the majority of the other components. The VMkernel is responsible for resource management and scheduling, running virtual machines (VMs), and starting the processes needed for host management.

FIGURE 2.1
The VMware ESXi architecture.

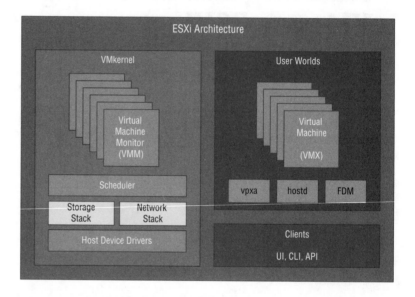

The Virtual Machine Monitor (VMM) is a process that runs inside the VMkernel. It virtualizes guest OS instructions and manages guest OS memory. The VMM sends storage and network requests to the VMkernel and passes all other requests to the VMX process. There is a VMM process for each virtual CPU in every virtual machine.

The resource scheduler also sits inside the VMkernel. Its job is to take hardware resource requests from the VMM and VMX processes and schedule them on to the underlying physical system. Considering that one ESXi physical server could have a large number of virtual machine running on it at any one time, the resource scheduler is a critical component. It has direct access to the underlying physical hardware through the storage and network stacks to the host device drivers.

Just like the majority of operating systems, in ESXi, the User World space is for non-kernel processes to execute. This allows non-privileged execution of tasks to help ensure the integrity of the OS. Only kernel-related tasks can run in the kernel space. ESXi has a number of processes that run in the User World; two of the most important are hostd and VMX.

Each VM that is running on an ESXi host has a single Virtual Machine Execution (VMX) helper process running in the User World space. It is not to be confused with the .VMX file that is explained in Chapter 9, "Creating and Managing Virtual Machines." The VMX process controls the VM's keyboard, mouse, and screen (KMS); remote console; and some non-critical I/O operations like CD-ROM. This process works in conjunction with the VMM processes to provide each VM's functionality to the administrator.

Finally, each ESXi host also has a single process running called hostd. Hostd is a proxy service for the VMkernel. All graphical and command-line interface (CLI) and application programming interface (API) calls are routed to the appropriate VMX or kernel process through hostd. These might come from the vSphere Host client, a PowerCLI instruction, or vCenter Server itself. All instructions reach the VMkernel through hostd.

Now that you understand how ESXi is put together, let's have a look at what is required to deploy the software in an environment.

Planning a VMware vSphere Deployment

Deploying VMware vSphere is more than just virtualizing servers. Storage, networking, and security in a vSphere deployment are equally as significant as they are with the physical servers. As a result, the process of planning the vSphere deployment becomes even more important. Without appropriate planning, you run the risk of configuration problems, instability, incompatibilities, and diminished return on investment.

To plan a vSphere deployment, you must answer a number of questions (please note that this list is far from comprehensive):

◆ What types of servers will I use for the underlying physical hardware?

◆ What kinds of storage will I use, and how will I connect that storage to my servers?

◆ How will the networking be configured?

In some cases, the answers to these questions will determine the answers to other questions. After you have answered these questions, you can then move on to more difficult issues. These issues center on how the vSphere deployment will impact your staff, your business processes, and your operational procedures. Although such areas are still important, you won't answer those sorts of questions here; instead, we'll just focus on the technical issues.

---

vSphere Design Is a Topic All Its Own

This chapter barely scratches the surface of what is involved in planning and designing a vSphere deployment. The topic of vSphere design warranted its own book: *VMware vSphere Design, Second Edition* (Sybex, 2013). If you are interested in a more detailed discussion of design decisions and design impacts, or you are studying for the certification "VMware Advanced Professional—Data Center Virtualization Design," that's the book for you.

The next few sections discuss the three major questions outlined earlier for planning your vSphere deployment: compute platform, storage, and network.

Choosing a Server Platform

The first major decision when you're planning to deploy vSphere is choosing a hardware, or "compute," platform. Compared to traditional operating systems like Windows or Linux, ESXi has more stringent hardware restrictions. ESXi won't necessarily support every storage controller or every network adapter chipset available on the market. When we talk about Virtual SAN (vSAN) in Chapter 6, "Creating and Configuring Storage Devices," you will find this especially true. Although these hardware restrictions limit the options for deploying a supported virtual infrastructure, they also ensure that the hardware has been tested and will work as expected with ESXi. As stated within the ESXi installer: "VMware ESXi installs on most systems but only systems on VMware's Compatibility Guide are supported." All the major hardware vendors continue to test their new hardware models to be certified to run ESXi when they are released, however, some of the smaller, white-box or consumer hardware vendors do not.

You can check for hardware compatibility using the searchable Compatibility Guide available on VMware's website at `www.vmware.com/resources/compatibility/`. A quick search returns dozens of systems from major vendors such as Hewlett-Packard, Cisco, IBM, and Dell. For example, as of this writing, searching the guide for *HP* or *Dell* both returned hundreds of individual results, including blades and traditional rack-mount servers supported across several different versions of vSphere. Within the major vendors like HP, Dell, Cisco, and IBM, you should easily find a tested and supported platform to run ESXi, especially their newer models of hardware. When you expand the list to include other vendors, you can choose from a substantial base of compatible servers supported by vSphere.

THE RIGHT SERVER FOR THE JOB

Selecting the appropriate server is undoubtedly the first step in ensuring a successful vSphere deployment. In addition, it is the only way to ensure that VMware will provide the necessary support. Remember the discussion from Chapter 1, though—a bigger server isn't necessarily a better server!

Finding a supported server is only the first step. It's also important to find the *right* server— the server that strikes the correct balance of capacity, scalability, availability, and affordability. Do you use larger servers, such as servers that support four or more CPU sockets and over 512 GB of RAM? Or would smaller servers, such as servers that support dual physical CPUs and 256 GB of RAM, be a better choice? There is a point of diminishing returns when it comes to adding more physical CPUs and more RAM to a server. Once you pass that point, the servers get more expensive to acquire and support, but the number of VMs the servers can host doesn't increase enough to offset the increase in cost. You may have a requirement to host a small number of very large (or "monster") VMs. Or, depending on the purpose of the servers you are selecting, you may find that the acceptable levels of risk are lower than the maximum achievable consolidation ratio with some servers. The challenge, therefore, is finding server models that provide enough expansion for growth and then fitting them with the right amount of resources to meet your needs.

Fortunately, a deeper look into the server models available from a specific vendor, such as Dell, reveals server models of all types and sizes (see Figure 2.2). Looking through the results of a search will reveal a number of common systems including:

- Half-height blades, such as the M630 or M640

- Full-height blades, such as the M830

- Single-socket 1U servers, such as the R230

- Dual-socket 2U servers, such as the R740

- Quad-socket 3U servers, such as the R940

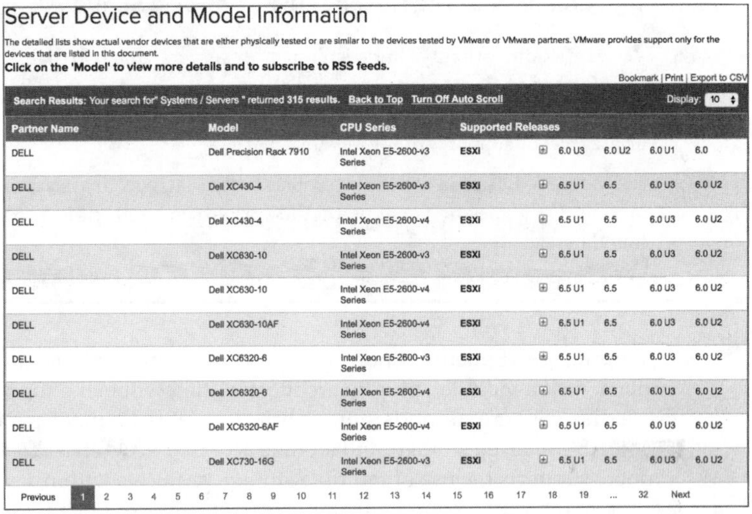

FIGURE 2.2

Servers listed in the Compatibility Guide come in various sizes and models.

Server Device and Model Information

The detailed lists show actual vendor devices that are either physically tested or are similar to the devices tested by VMware or VMware partners. VMware provides support only for the devices that are listed in this document.

Click on the 'Model' to view more details and to subscribe to RSS feeds.

Bookmark | Print | Export to CSV

Search Results: Your search for° Systems / Servers ° returned 315 results. Back to Top Turn Off Auto Scroll   Display: 10

Partner Name	Model	CPU Series	Supported Releases				
DELL	Dell Precision Rack 7910	Intel Xeon E5-2600-v3 Series	ESXi	6.0 U3	6.0 U2	6.0 U1	6.0
DELL	Dell XC430-4	Intel Xeon E5-2600-v3 Series	ESXi	6.5 U1	6.5	6.0 U3	6.0 U2
DELL	Dell XC430-4	Intel Xeon E5-2600-v4 Series	ESXi	6.5 U1	6.5	6.0 U3	6.0 U2
DELL	Dell XC630-10	Intel Xeon E5-2600-v3 Series	ESXi	6.5 U1	6.5	6.0 U3	6.0 U2
DELL	Dell XC630-10	Intel Xeon E5-2600-v4 Series	ESXi	6.5 U1	6.5	6.0 U3	6.0 U2
DELL	Dell XC630-10AF	Intel Xeon E5-2600-v4 Series	ESXi	6.5 U1	6.5	6.0 U3	6.0 U2
DELL	Dell XC6320-6	Intel Xeon E5-2600-v3 Series	ESXi	6.5 U1	6.5	6.0 U3	6.0 U2
DELL	Dell XC6320-6	Intel Xeon E5-2600-v4 Series	ESXi	6.5 U1	6.5	6.0 U3	6.0 U2
DELL	Dell XC6320-6AF	Intel Xeon E5-2600-v4 Series	ESXi	6.5 U1	6.5	6.0 U3	6.0 U2
DELL	Dell XC730-16G	Intel Xeon E5-2600-v3 Series	ESXi	6.5 U1	6.5	6.0 U3	6.0 U2

Previous **1** 2 3 4 5 6 7 8 9 10 11 12 13 14 15 16 17 18 19 ... 32 Next

You can easily view compatibility with the latest version using VMware's website. Keep in mind that hardware is added to the list as it is certified, not just at major vSphere releases, so check the list whenever making hardware purchases to ensure you have compatible hardware.

Which server is the right server? The answer to that question depends on many factors. The number of CPU cores is often used as a determining factor, but you should also consider the total number of RAM slots. A higher number of RAM slots means that you can use lower-cost, lower-density RAM modules and still reach high memory configurations. You should also consider server expansion options, such as the number of available Peripheral Component Interconnect Express (PCIe) buses, expansion slots, and the types of expansion cards supported in the server. If you are looking to use converged storage in your environment, such as vSAN, the number of local drive bays and the type of storage controller are other considerations. Finally, be sure to consider the server form factor; blade servers have advantages and disadvantages when compared to rack-mount servers.

Determining a Storage Architecture

Selecting the right storage solution is the second major decision you must make before you proceed with your vSphere deployment. The lion's share of advanced features within vSphere—features like vSphere DRS, vSphere HA, and vSphere FT—depend on the presence of a shared storage architecture. Although we won't talk in depth about a particular brand of storage *hardware*, VMware has a storage solution: Virtual SAN (vSAN), which we'll discuss more in Chapter 6. As stated earlier, vSphere's dependency on shared storage makes choosing the correct storage architecture for your deployment as critical as choosing the server hardware on which to run ESXi.

THE COMPATIBILITY GUIDE ISN'T JUST FOR SERVERS

VMware's Compatibility Guide isn't just for servers. The searchable guide also provides compatibility information on storage arrays and other storage components. Be sure to use the searchable guide to verify the compatibility of your host bus adapters (HBAs) and storage arrays to ensure the appropriate level of support from VMware.

VMware also has the Product Interoperability Matrixes to assist with software compatibility information. Only specific versions of VMware's own products can be used together; details can be found here:

http://www.vmware.com/resources/compatibility/sim/interop_matrix.php

---

Fortunately, vSphere supports a number of storage architectures out of the box and has implemented a modular, plug-in architecture that will make supporting future storage technologies easier. vSphere supports storage based on Fibre Channel and Fibre Channel over Ethernet (FCoE), iSCSI-based storage, and storage accessed via Network File System (NFS). In addition, vSphere supports the use of multiple storage protocols within a single solution so that one portion of the vSphere implementation might run over Fibre Channel while another portion runs over NFS. This provides a great deal of flexibility in choosing your storage solution. Finally, vSphere provides support for software-based initiators as well as hardware initiators (also referred to as HBAs or converged network adapters), so this is another option you must consider when selecting your storage solution.

WHAT IS REQUIRED FOR FIBRE CHANNEL OVER ETHERNET SUPPORT?

Fibre Channel over Ethernet (FCoE) is a somewhat hybrid storage protocol. However, because FCoE was designed to be compatible with Fibre Channel, it looks, acts, and behaves like Fibre Channel to ESXi. As long as drivers for the FCoE converged network adapter (CNA) are available—and this is where you would go back to the VMware Compatibility Guide again—support for FCoE should not be an issue.

When determining the correct storage solution, you should consider additional questions such as:

♦ What type of storage will best integrate with your existing storage or network infrastructure?

♦ Do you have experience or expertise with some types of storage?

♦ Can the storage solution provide the necessary performance to support your environment?

♦ Does the storage solution offer any form of advanced integration with vSphere?

♦ Will your backup or disaster recovery (DR) solution work with all types of storage?

The procedures involved in creating and managing storage devices are discussed in detail in Chapter 6.

Integrating with the Network Infrastructure

The third and final major decision of the planning process is how your vSphere deployment will integrate with the existing network infrastructure. In part, this decision is driven by the choice of server hardware and the storage protocol.

For example, an organization selecting a blade form factor may run into limitations on the number of physical network interface cards (NICs) that can be supported in a given blade model. Of course, the opposite could also be true, as some blade manufacturers offer virtual network adapters as part of their rack and chassis solution. These configuration options affect how the vSphere implementation will integrate with the network. Similarly, organizations choosing to use iSCSI or NFS instead of Fibre Channel will typically have to deploy more NICs in their ESXi hosts to accommodate the additional network traffic or use 10 Gigabit Ethernet (10GbE). Organizations also need to account for network interfaces for vMotion and vSphere FT.

Until 10GbE became common, ESXi hosts in many vSphere deployments had a minimum of 6 NICs and often 8, 10, or even more NICs. So, how do you decide how many NICs to use? We'll discuss some of this in greater detail in Chapter 5, "Creating and Configuring a vSphere Network," but here are some general guidelines:

♦ The ESXi management network needs at least one NIC. We strongly recommend adding a second NIC for redundancy. In fact, some features of vSphere, such as vSphere HA, will note warnings if the hosts do not have redundant network connections for the management network.

♦ vMotion needs a NIC. Again, we heartily recommend a second NIC for redundancy. These NICs should be at least Gigabit Ethernet. In some cases, this traffic can be safely combined with ESXi management traffic, so you could assume that two NICs will handle both ESXi management and vMotion.

♦ vSphere FT (if you will be using that feature) needs a NIC. A second NIC would provide redundancy and is recommended. This should be at least a Gigabit Ethernet NIC; it can require a 10GbE NIC depending on how many vCPUs the FT-enabled VM has.

♦ For deployments using iSCSI, NFS, or VSAN, at least one more NIC, preferably two, is needed. Gigabit Ethernet or 10GbE is necessary here. Although you can get by with a single NIC, we strongly recommend at least two.

♦ Finally, at least two NICs are needed for traffic originating from the VMs themselves. Gigabit Ethernet or faster is strongly recommended for VM traffic.

This adds up to eight NICs per server (again, assuming management and vMotion share a pair of NICs). You'll want to ensure that you have enough network ports available, at the appropriate speeds, to accommodate the needs of this sort of vSphere deployment. This is only a rudimentary discussion of networking design for vSphere. It does not incorporate any discussion on the use of speeds over 10GbE, storage protocols sharing network links, or what type of virtual switching infrastructure you will use. All of these other factors would affect your networking setup.

How About 10GbE NICs?

Lots of factors go into designing how a vSphere deployment will integrate with the existing network infrastructure. For example, only in the last few years has 10GbE networking become pervasive in the datacenter. This bandwidth change fundamentally changes how virtual networks are designed.

In one particular case, a company wished to upgrade its existing rack-mount server clusters with six NICs and two Fibre Channel HBAs to two dual-port 10GbE CNAs. Not only physically was there a stark difference from a switch and cabling perspective, but the logical configuration was significantly different. Obviously this allowed greater bandwidth to each host but it also allowed more design flexibility.

The final design used vSphere Network I/O Control (NOIC) and Load-Based Teaming (LBT) to share available bandwidth between the necessary types of traffic but only restricted bandwidth when the network was congested. This resulted in an efficient use of the new bandwidth capability without adding too much configuration complexity. Networking is discussed in more detail in Chapter 5.

With these major questions answered, you at least have the basics of a vSphere deployment established. As mentioned previously, this discussion on designing a vSphere solution is far from comprehensive. You should find a good resource on vSphere design and consider performing a comprehensive design exercise before deploying vSphere.

Deploying VMware ESXi

After you've established the basics of your vSphere design, you must decide exactly how you will deploy ESXi. You have three options:

♦ Interactive installation of ESXi

♦ Unattended (scripted) installation of ESXi

♦ Automated provisioning of ESXi

Of these, the simplest is an interactive installation of ESXi. The most complex—but perhaps the most powerful, depending on your needs and your environment—is automated provisioning of ESXi. In the following sections, we describe all three of these methods for deploying ESXi in your environment.

Let's start with the simplest method first: interactively installing ESXi.

Installing VMware ESXi Interactively

VMware has done a great job of making the interactive installation of ESXi as simple and straightforward as possible. It takes just minutes to install, so let's walk through the process.

Perform the following steps to interactively install ESXi:

1. Ensure that your server hardware is configured to boot from the CD-ROM/DVD drive.

   This will vary from manufacturer to manufacturer and will also depend on whether you are installing locally or remotely via an IP-based keyboard, video, mouse (KVM), or other remote management facility.

2. Ensure that VMware ESXi installation media is available to the server.

   Again, this will vary based on a local installation (which involves simply inserting the VMware ESXi installation media into the optical drive) or a remote installation (which typically involves mapping an image of the installation media, known as an ISO image, to a virtual optical drive).

OBTAINING VMware ESXi INSTALLATION MEDIA

You can download the installation files from VMware's website at www.vmware.com/download/.

Physical boxed copies of VMware products are no longer sold, but if you hold a valid license, all products can be downloaded directly from VMware. These files are typically ISO files that you can mount to a server or burn to a physical CD or DVD.

---

3. Power on the server.

   After it boots from the installation media, the initial boot menu screen appears. If the boot menu does not appear, you may need to check your servers boot device order. This will vary from vendor to vendor, but ensure the device you intend on booting from is the first boot device.

4. Press Enter to boot the ESXi installer.

   The installer will boot the vSphere hypervisor and eventually stop at a welcome message. Press Enter to continue.

5. At the End User License Agreement (EULA) screen, press F11 to accept the EULA and continue with the installation.

6. Next, the installer will display a list of available disks on which you can install or upgrade ESXi.

Potential devices are identified as either local devices or remote devices. Figure 2.3 and Figure 2.4 show two different views of this screen: one with a local device and one with remote devices.

FIGURE 2.3
The installer offers options for both local and remote devices; in this case, only local devices were detected.

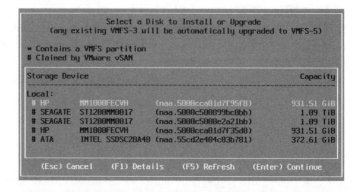

FIGURE 2.4
Although local SAS devices are supported, they are listed as remote devices.

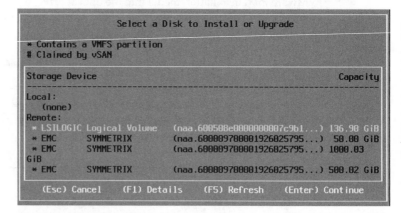

RUNNING ESXi AS A VM

You might be able to deduce from Figure 2.3 that we're actually running ESXi 6.7 as a virtual machine. Yes, that's right—you can virtualize ESXi! In this particular case, we're using VMware's desktop virtualization solution for MacOS, VMware Fusion, to run an instance of ESXi as a VM. As of this writing, the latest version of VMware Fusion is v10, and it includes ESXi as an officially supported guest OS. This is a great way to test out the latest version of ESXi without the need for server class hardware. You can also run ESXi as a VM on ESXi itself, but remember it is not supported for running production workloads inside these "nested" or virtual hypervisors.

Storage area network logical unit numbers, or SAN LUNs, are listed as remote, as you can see in Figure 2.4. Local serial attached SCSI (SAS) devices are also listed as remote. Figure 2.4 shows a SAS drive connected to an LSI Logic controller; although this device is physically local to the server on which we are installing ESXi, the installation routine marks it as remote.

If you want to create a boot-from-SAN environment, where each ESXi host boots from a SAN LUN, then you'd select the appropriate SAN LUN here. You can also install directly to your own USB or Secure Digital (SD) device—simply select the appropriate device from the list.

WHICH DESTINATION IS BEST?

Local device, SAN LUN, or USB? Which destination is the best when you're installing ESXi? Those questions truly depend on the overall vSphere design you are implementing, and there is no simple answer. Many variables affect this decision. Are you using an iSCSI SAN and you don't have iSCSI hardware initiators in your servers? That would prevent you from using a boot-from-SAN setup. Are you installing into an environment like Cisco UCS, where booting from SAN is highly recommended? Is your storage larger than 2 GB? Although you can install ESXi on a 2 GB partition, no log files will be stored locally so you'll receive a warning in the UI advising you to set an external logging host. Be sure to consider all the factors when deciding where to install ESXi.

---

7. To get more information about a device, highlight the device and press F1.

The information about the device includes whether it detected an installation of ESXi and what Virtual Machine File System (VMFS) datastores, if any, are present on it, as shown in Figure 2.5. Press Enter to return to the device-selection screen when you have finished reviewing the information for the selected device.

FIGURE 2.5
Checking to see if there are any VMFS datastores on a device can help you avoid accidentally overwriting data.

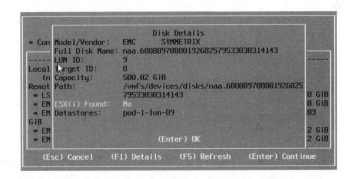

8. Use the arrow keys to select the device on which you are going to install ESXi, and press Enter.

9. If the selected device includes a VMFS datastore or an installation of ESXi, you'll be prompted to choose what action you want to take, as illustrated in Figure 2.6. Select the desired action and press Enter.

FIGURE 2.6
You can upgrade or install ESXi as well as choose to preserve or overwrite an existing VMFS datastore.

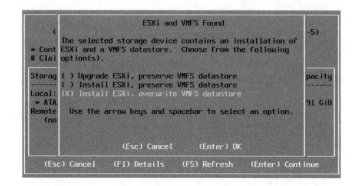

These are the available actions:

◆ Upgrade ESXi, Preserve VMFS Datastore: This option upgrades to ESXi 6.7 and preserves the existing VMFS datastore.

◆ Install ESXi, Preserve VMFS Datastore: This option installs a fresh copy of ESXi 6.7 and preserves the existing VMFS datastore.

◆ Install ESXi, Overwrite VMFS Datastore: This option overwrites the existing VMFS datastore with a new one and installs a fresh installation of ESXi 6.

10. Select the desired keyboard layout and press Enter.

11. Enter (and confirm) a password for the root account. Press Enter when you are ready to continue with the installation. Be sure to make note of this password—you'll need it later

12. At the final confirmation screen, press F11 to proceed with the installation of ESXi.

After the installation process begins, it takes only a few minutes to install ESXi onto the selected storage device.

13. Press Enter to reboot the host at the Installation Complete screen.

After the host reboots, ESXi is installed. ESXi is configured by default to obtain an IP address via Dynamic Host Configuration Protocol (DHCP). Depending on the network configuration, you might find that ESXi will not be able to obtain an IP address via DHCP. Later in this chapter in the section "Reconfiguring the Management Network," we'll discuss how to correct networking problems after installing ESXi by using the Direct Console User Interface (DCUI).

VMware also provides support for scripted installations of ESXi. As you've already seen, there isn't a lot of interaction required to install ESXi, but support for scripting the installation of ESXi reduces the time to deploy even further.

INTERACTIVELY INSTALLING ESXi FROM USB OR ACROSS THE NETWORK

As an alternative to launching the ESXi installer from the installation CD/DVD, you can install ESXi from a USB flash drive or across the network via Preboot Execution Environment (PXE). More details on how to use a USB flash drive or how to PXE boot the ESXi installer are found in the *vSphere Installation and Setup Guide*, available from `https://docs.vmware.com/en/VMware-vSphere/`. Note that PXE booting the installer is not the same as PXE booting ESXi itself, something that we'll discuss later in the section "Deploying VMware ESXi with vSphere Auto Deploy."

Performing an Unattended Installation of VMware ESXi

ESXi supports the use of an installation script (often referred to as a kickstart, or KS, script) that automates the installation routine. By using an installation script, users can create unattended installation routines that make it easy to quickly deploy multiple instances of ESXi.

Listing 2.1 shows the default installation script that ships as part of ESXi.

LISTING 2.1:   The default installation script provided by ESXi

```
#
# Sample scripted installation file
#
# Accept the VMware End User License Agreement
vmaccepteula
# Set the root password for the DCUI and Tech Support Mode
rootpw mypassword
# Install on the first local disk available on machine
install—firstdisk—overwritevmfs
# Set the network to DHCP on the first network adapter
network—bootproto=dhcp—device=vmnic0
# A sample post-install script
%post—interpreter=python—ignorefailure=true
import time
stampFile = open('/finished.stamp', mode='w')
stampFile.write( time.asctime() )
```

If you want to use this default install script to install ESXi, you can specify it when booting the VMware ESXi installer by adding the `ks=file://etc/vmware/weasel/ks.cfg` boot option. We'll show you how to specify that boot option shortly.

Of course, the default installation script is useful only if the settings work for your environment. Otherwise, you'll need to create a custom installation script. The installation script commands are much the same as those supported in previous versions of vSphere. Here's a breakdown of some of the commands supported in the ESXi installation script:

accepteula or vmaccepteula   These commands accept the ESXi license agreement.

Install   The `install` command specifies that this is a fresh installation of ESXi, not an upgrade. You must also specify the following parameters:

-firstdisk This specifies the disk on which ESXi should be installed. By default, the ESXi installer chooses local disks first, then remote disks, and then USB disks. You can change the order by appending a comma-separated list to the -firstdisk command, like this:

-firstdisk=remote,local This would install to the first available remote disk and then to the first available local disk. Be careful here—you don't want to inadvertently overwrite something (see the next set of commands).

-overwritevmfs or -preservevmfs These commands specify how the installer will handle existing VMFS datastores. The commands are pretty self-explanatory.

Keyboard This command specifies the keyboard type. It's an optional component in the installation script.

Network This command provides the network configuration for the ESXi host being installed. It is optional but generally recommended. Depending on your configuration, some additional parameters are required:

-bootproto This parameter is set to dhcp for assigning a network address via DHCP or to static for manual assignment of an IP address.

-ip This sets the IP address and is required with –bootproto=static. The IP address should be specified in standard dotted-decimal format.

-gateway This command specifies the IP address of the default gateway in standard dotted-decimal format. It's required if you specified –bootproto=static.

-netmask The network mask, in standard dotted-decimal format, is specified with this command. If you specify –bootproto=static, you must include this value.

-hostname This specifies the hostname for the installed system.

-vlanid If you need the system to use a VLAN ID, specify it with this command. Without a VLAN ID specified, the system will respond only to untagged traffic.

-addvmportgroup This parameter is set to either 0 or 1 and controls whether a default VM Network port group is created. 0 does not create the port group; 1 does create the port group.

Reboot This command is optional and, if specified, will automatically reboot the system at the end of installation. If you add the —noeject parameter, the CD is not ejected.

Rootpw This is a required parameter and sets the root password for the system. If you don't want the root password displayed in the clear, generate an encrypted password and use the –iscrypted parameter.

Upgrade This specifies an upgrade to ESXi 6. The upgrade command uses many of the same parameters as install and also supports a parameter for deleting the ESX Service Console VMDK for upgrades from ESX to ESXi. This parameter is the –deletecosvmdk parameter.

This is by no means a comprehensive list of all the commands available in the ESXi installation script, but it does cover the majority of the commands you'll see in use.

Looking back at Listing 2.1, you'll see that the default installation script incorporates a %pos section, where additional scripting can be added using either the Python interpreter or the

BusyBox interpreter. What you don't see in Listing 2.1 is the `%firstboot` section, which also allows you to add Python or BusyBox commands for customizing the ESXi installation. This section comes after the installation script commands but before the `%post` section. Any command supported in the ESXi shell can be executed in the `%firstboot` section, so commands such as `esxcfg-vswitch`, `esxcfg-vmknic`, and others can be combined in the `%firstboot` section of the installation script.

A number of commands that were supported in previous versions of vSphere (by ESX or ESXi) are no longer supported in installation scripts for ESXi 6.7. For an updated list of supported commands, please check `docs.vmware.com`.

Once you have created the installation script you will use, you need to specify that script as part of the installation routine.

Specifying the location of the installation script as a boot option is not only how you would tell the installer to use the default script but also how you tell the installer to use a custom installation script that you've created. This installation script can be located on a USB flash drive or in a network location accessible via NFS, HTTP, HTTPS, or FTP. Table 2.1 summarizes some of the supported boot options for use with an unattended installation of ESXi.

TABLE 2.1: Boot Options For an Unattended ESXi Installation

BOOT OPTION	BRIEF DESCRIPTION
`ks=cdrom:/path`	Uses the installation script found at path on the CD-ROM. The installer checks all CD-ROM drives until the file matching the specified path is found.
`ks=usb`	Uses the installation script named `ks.cfg` found in the root directory of an attached USB device. All USB devices are searched as long as they have a FAT16 or FAT32 file system.
`ks=usb:/path`	Uses the installation script at the specified path on an attached USB device. This allows you to use a different filename or location for the installation script.
`ks=protocol:/serverpath`	Uses the installation script found at the specified network location. The protocol can be NFS, HTTP, HTTPS, or FTP.
`ip=XX.XX.XX.XX`	Specifies a static IP address for downloading the installation script and the installation media.
`nameserver=XX.XX.XX.XX`	Provides the IP address of a Domain Name System (DNS) server to use for name resolution when downloading the installation script or the installation media.
`gateway=XX.XX.XX.XX`	Provides the network gateway to be used as the default gateway for downloading the installation script and the installation media.
`netmask=XX.XX.XX.XX`	Specifies the network mask for the network interface used to download the installation script or the installation media.
`vlanid=XX`	Configures the network interface to be on the specified VLAN when downloading the installation script or the installation media.

NOT A COMPREHENSIVE LIST OF BOOT OPTIONS

The list found in Table 2.1 includes only some of the more commonly used boot options for performing a scripted installation of ESXi. For the complete list of supported boot options, refer to the *vSphere Installation and Setup Guide*, available from `https://docs.vmware.com/en/ VMware-vSphere/`.

To use one or more of these boot options during the installation, you'll need to specify them the boot screen for the ESXi installer. The bottom of the installer boot screen states that you can press Shift+O to edit the boot options.

The following code line is an example that could be used to retrieve the installation script from an HTTP URL; this would be entered at the prompt at the bottom of the installer boot screen:

```
<ENTER: Apply options and boot> <ESC: Cancel>
> runweasel ks=http://192.168.1.1/scripts/ks.cfg ip=192.168.1.200
netmask=255.255.255.0 gateway=192.168.1.254
```

Using an installation script to install ESXi not only speeds up the installation process but also helps to ensure the consistent configuration of all your ESXi hosts.

The final method for deploying ESXi—using vSphere Auto Deploy—is the most complex, but it also offers administrators a great deal of flexibility.

Deploying VMware ESXi with vSphere Auto Deploy

vSphere Auto Deploy is a network deployment service that enables ESXi hosts to be built off an image template over a network connection. No mounting of installation media is required to get an ESXi host up and running if it is installed using Auto Deploy, but you will need to address a number of prerequisites before using Auto Deploy. They are listed here, but before we get too far into this section, we wanted to mention the requirement for a vCenter Server. Auto Deploy requires vCenter Server to operate, but we won't start discussing this until Chapter 3, "Installing and Configuring vCenter Server" and further to this, we won't discuss the add-ons available to vCenter Server, such as Auto Deploy, until Chapter 4 "Maintaining VMware vSphere." We'll cover the overview of Auto Deploy here but will leave getting your hosts deployed with it for once your vCenter Server is up and running.

vSphere Auto Deploy can be configured with one of three different modes:

♦   Stateless

♦   Stateless Caching

♦   Statefull Install

In the Stateless mode, you deploy ESXi using Auto Deploy directly into server memory, there is no need for the server's local disk or SAN boot LUN. In the event that the Auto Deploy infrastructure is not available, the host will not be able to boot the image. It is not too hard to see why this is not necessarily the most desirable outcome, especially if you don't have a resilient setup for the Auto Deploy service.

In the Stateless Caching mode, you deploy ESXi using Auto Deploy directly into server memory, but the image is cached on the server's local disk or SAN boot LUN. In the event that the Auto Deploy infrastructure is not available, the host boots from a local cache of the image. In this mode, ESXi is still *running* in memory but it's loaded from the local disk instead of directly from the Auto Deploy server on the network.

The third mode, Stateful Install, is similar to Stateless Caching except the server's boot order is reversed: local disk first and network second. Unless the server is specifically told that it needs to network boot again, the Auto Deploy service is no longer needed. This mode is effectively just a mechanism for network installation.

Auto Deploy Dependencies

This chapter deals with ESXi host installation methods; however, vSphere Auto Deploy is dependent on host profiles, a feature of VMware vCenter. More information about installing vCenter and configuring host profiles can be found in Chapter 3.

Auto Deploy uses a set of rules (called *deployment rules*) to control which hosts are assigned a particular ESXi image (called an *image profile*). Deploying a new ESXi image is as simple as modifying the deployment rule to point that physical host to a new image profile and then rebooting with the PXE/network boot option. When the host boots up, it will receive a new image profile.

Sounds easy, right? Maybe not. In theory, it is—but there are several steps you have to accomplish before you're ready to deploy ESXi in this fashion:

1. You must set up a vCenter Server and enable the vSphere Auto Deploy service. This is the service that stores the image profiles.

2. You must set up and configure a Trivial File Transfer Protocol (TFTP) server on your network.

3. A DHCP server is required on your network, configured to pass the correct TFTP information to hosts booting up.

4. You must create an image profile using the new AutoDeploy UI.

5. Finally, you must also create a deployment rule that assigns the image profile to a particular subset of hosts.

As we mentioned at the start of this section, the specifics on configuring these settings are detailed in Chapter 4. After these requirements are configured, you can then build hosts in a standardized and repeatable way, with very little interaction.

Performing Post-installation Configuration

Whether you are installing interactively from a mounted ISO or performing an unattended installation of ESXi using a kickstart script, when the installation is complete, several post-installation steps are necessary, depending on your specific configuration. We discuss these tasks in the following sections.

Reconfiguring the Management Network

During the installation of ESXi, the installer creates a virtual switch—also known as a *vSwitch*—bound to a physical NIC. The tricky part, depending on your server hardware, is that the installer might select a different physical NIC than the one you need for correct network connectivity. Consider the scenario shown in Figure 2.7. If, for whatever reason, the ESXi installer doesn't link the correct physical NIC to the vSwitch it creates, then you won't have network connectivity to that host. We'll talk more about why ESXi's network connectivity must be configured with the correct NIC in Chapter 5, but for now just understand that this is a requirement for connectivity. Since you need network connectivity to manage the host from the vSphere Client, how do you fix this?

FIGURE 2.7
Network connectivity won't be established if the ESXi installer links the wrong NIC to the management network.

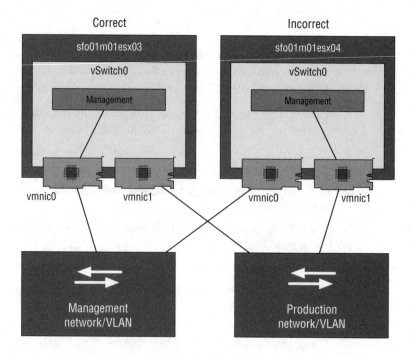

The simplest fix for this problem is to unplug the network cable from the current Ethernet port in the back of the server and continue trying the remaining ports until the host is accessible, but that's not always possible or desirable. The better way is to use the DCUI to reconfigure the management network so that it is converted the way you need it to be configured.

Perform the following steps to fix the management NIC in ESXi using the DCUI:

1. Access the console of the ESXi host, either physically or via a remote console solution such as an IP-based KVM.

2. On the ESXi home screen, shown in Figure 2.8, press F2 for Customize System/View Logs. If a root password has been set, enter that root password.

FIGURE 2.8

The ESXi home screen provides options for customizing the system and restarting or shutting down the server.

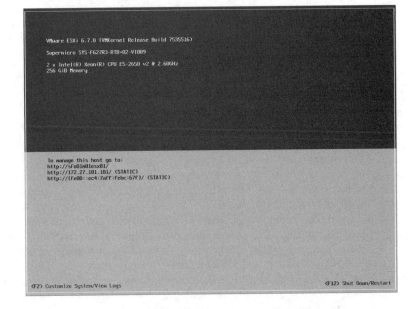

3. From the System Customization menu, select Configure Management Network and press Enter.

4. From the Configure Management Network menu, select Network Adapters and press Enter.

5. Use the spacebar to toggle which network adapter or adapters will be used for the system's management network, as shown in Figure 2.9. Press Enter when finished.

FIGURE 2.9

In the event the incorrect NIC is assigned to ESXi's management network, you can select a different NIC.

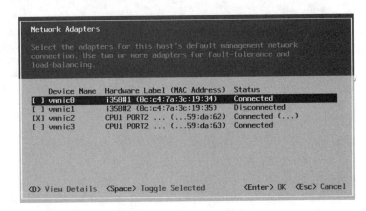

6. Press Esc to exit the Configure Management Network menu. When prompted to apply changes and restart the management network, press Y.

    After the correct NIC has been assigned to the ESXi management network, the System Customization menu provides a Test Management Network option to verify network connectivity.

7. Press Esc to log out of the System Customization menu and return to the ESXi home screen.

The other options within the DCUI for troubleshooting management network issues are covered in detail in Chapter 5.

At this point, you should have management network connectivity to the ESXi host, and from now on, you can use the vSphere Host Client to perform other configuration tasks, such as configuring time synchronization and name resolution. Simply put in the IP address or FQDN of the host into a web browser to bring up the new HTML5-based vSphere Host Client.

Using the vSphere Host Client

This might come as a bit of a shock for IT professionals who have grown accustomed to managing Microsoft Windows–based servers from the server's console (even via Remote Desktop), but ESXi wasn't designed for you to manage it from the server's console. Instead, you should use the vSphere Host Client.

In earlier versions, both stand-alone ESXi hosts and vCenter servers were administered with the C# Client, which is now known as the "legacy desktop client." vSphere 5.0 introduced the Web Client, but that was only for administering vCenter Server, not ESXi hosts directly.

Things have come a long way since the move to web-based clients, and now each ESXi host has a built-in web-based UI called the vSphere Host Client. There is no client to install, and there's nothing to set up; it's running as soon as the host is online. Using the vSphere Host Client to administer an ESXi host requires authentication with a user account that exists on that specific host, whereas connecting to a vCenter Server installation relies on Single Sign-On (explained in Chapter 3) users for authentication (see Figure 2.10). Additionally, a number of significant features—such as initiating vMotion, for example—are available only when you're connecting to a vCenter Server installation.

LEARNING A NEW USER INTERFACE

For those accustomed to the legacy vSphere Desktop Client, things are not too different in the new HTML5-based vSphere Host Client. Visually, the vSphere Host Client is fairly close to the original C# vSphere Client. The examples in this book primarily use the vSphere Web Client logged into a vCenter Server, unless you are directly administering the hosts (as in this chapter).

FIGURE 2.10
You can initially authenticate directly to the host using "root" and the password set during installation of ESXi.

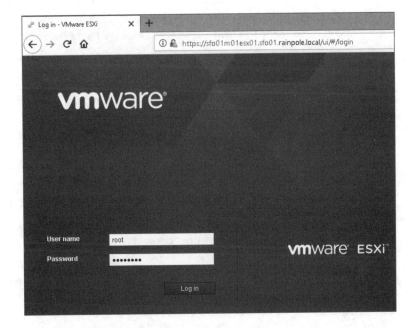

Configuring Time Synchronization

Time synchronization in ESXi is an important configuration because the ramifications of incorrect time run deep. Although ensuring that ESXi has the correct time seems trivial, time-synchronization issues can affect features such as performance charting, SSH key expirations, NFS access, backup jobs, authentication, and more.

After the installation of ESXi or during an unattended installation of ESXi using an installation script, the host should be configured to perform time synchronization with a reliable time source. This source could be another server or device on your network or, alternatively, a time source located on the Internet. For the sake of managing time synchronization, it is easiest (and most secure) to synchronize all your servers against one reliable *internal* time server and then synchronize the internal time server with a reliable *external* Internet time server. ESXi provides a Network Time Protocol (NTP) implementation to provide this functionality.

AUTOMATING BASIC CONFIGURATION

Although configuring Time Synchronization or Name Resolution is quite simple, if your environment has a large number of hosts, configuration can become tedious. These kinds of changes can be scripted. You can find a number of examples on VMware community member blogs.

The simplest way to configure time synchronization for ESXi involves the vSphere Host Client. Perform the following steps to enable NTP using the vSphere Host Client:

1. Use a web browser and navigate to your ESXi host IP address of FQDN.

2. The host is already selected in the Navigator tree on the left, simply click on the Manage label beneath your host.

3. Select Time & Date from the System tab on the right side of the UI.

4. Click the Edit Settings link.

5. In the Edit Time Configuration dialog box, select Use Network Time Protocol (enable NTP client).

6. Still in the Time Configuration dialog box, select "Start and Stop with Host." This will ensure the NTP client loads every time ESXi boots up.

7. Within the NTP Servers dialog box, add one or more NTP servers to the list, as shown in Figure 2.11.

FIGURE 2.11
Specifying NTP servers allows ESXi to automatically keep time synchronized.

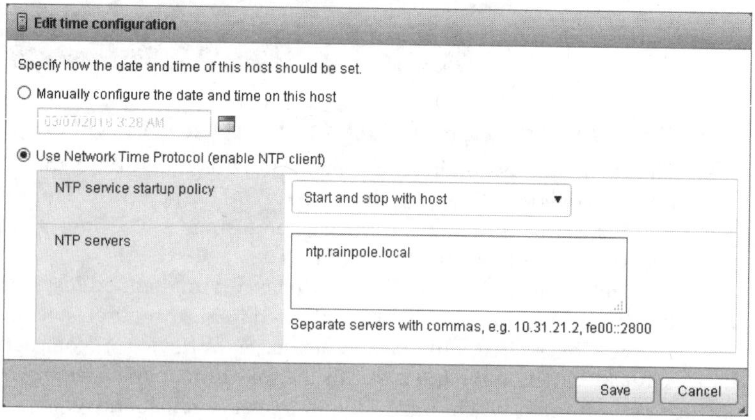

8. Click OK to return to the vSphere Host Client. The Time & Date Configuration area will update to show the new NTP server(s).

You'll note that using the vSphere Client to enable NTP this way also automatically enables NTP traffic through the firewall. You can verify this by noting an Open Firewall Ports entry in the Tasks pane or by clicking Security Profile under the Software menu and seeing an entry for NTP Client listed under Outgoing Connections.

WINDOWS AS A RELIABLE TIME SERVER

You can configure an existing Windows server as a reliable time server by using Group Policy, or if you have the Active Directory Domain Controller role already configured, this server can already be used as a time source.

Configuring Name Resolution

Just as time synchronization is important for your vSphere environment, so is name resolution. Although the vSphere dependency on name resolution is less than it was, there is still some functionality that may not work as expected without proper name resolution.

Configuring name resolution is a simple process in the vSphere Client (see Figure 2.12):

1. Use the vSphere Desktop Host Client to connect directly to the ESXi host.

2. With the hostname already selected in the inventory tree on the left, click the Networking label in the Navigator.

3. Click on the TCP/IP stacks tab from the right side of the UI.

4. Select the TCP/IP stack called "Default TCP/IP stack" and then click the Edit settings button.

5. In the Edit TCP/IP configuration dialog box, add the IP address(s) of your DNS server(s), and any relevant search domain(s).

FIGURE 2.12
Configuring DNS servers allows ESXi to resolve other hostnames on the network.

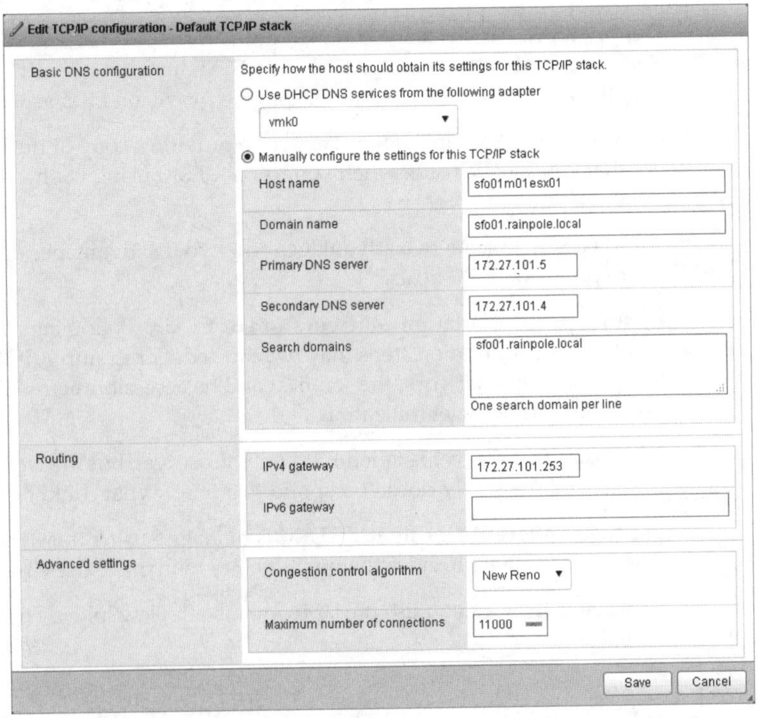

Edit TCP/IP configuration - Default TCP/IP stack	
Basic DNS configuration	Specify how the host should obtain its settings for this TCP/IP stack.
	○ Use DHCP DNS services from the following adapter
	vmk0 ▼
	● Manually configure the settings for this TCP/IP stack
	Host name — sfo01m01esx01
	Domain name — sfo01.rainpole.local
	Primary DNS server — 172.27.101.5
	Secondary DNS server — 172.27.101.4
	Search domains — sfo01.rainpole.local
	One search domain per line
Routing	IPv4 gateway — 172.27.101.253
	IPv6 gateway —
Advanced settings	Congestion control algorithm — New Reno ▼
	Maximum number of connections — 11000
	Save Cancel

In this chapter, we've discussed some of the decisions that you'll have to make as you deploy ESXi in your datacenter, and we've shown you how to deploy these products using both interactive and unattended methods. In the next chapter, we'll show you how to deploy VMware vCenter Server, a key component in your virtualization environment.

The Bottom Line

Understand ESXi compatibility requirements.   Unlike traditional operating systems like Windows or Linux, ESXi has much stricter hardware compatibility requirements. This helps ensure a stable, well-tested product line that can support even the most mission-critical applications.

Master It   You have some older servers onto which you'd like to deploy ESXi. They aren't on the Compatibility Guide. Will they work with ESXi?

Plan an ESXi deployment.   Deploying ESXi will affect many different areas of your organization—not only the server team but also the networking team, the storage team, and the security team. There are many issues to consider, including server hardware, storage hardware, storage protocols or connection types, network topology, and network connections. Failing to plan properly could result in an unstable and unsupported implementation.

Master It   Name three areas of networking that must be considered in a vSphere design.

Master It   What are some of the different types of storage that ESXi can be installed on?

Deploy ESXi.   ESXi can be installed onto any supported and compatible hardware platform. You have three different ways to deploy ESXi: install it interactively, perform an unattended installation, or use vSphere Auto Deploy to provision ESXi as it boots up.

Master It   Your manager asks you to provide a copy of the unattended installation script that you will be using when you roll out ESXi using vSphere Auto Deploy. Is this something you can give?

Master It   Name two advantages and two disadvantages of using vSphere Auto Deploy to provision ESXi hosts.

Perform post-installation configuration of ESXi.   Following the installation of ESXi, some additional configuration steps may be required. For example, if the wrong NIC is assigned to the management network, the server won't be accessible across the network. You'll also need to configure time synchronization.

Master It   You've installed ESXi on your server, but the welcome web page is inaccessible, and the server doesn't respond to a ping. What could be the problem?

Use the vSphere Host Client.   "ESXi is managed using the vSphere Host Client, a HTML5-based web UI that provides the functionality to manage the virtualization platform.

Master It   Can you use the VMware installable vSphere client to manage your new ESXi 6.7 hosts?

Chapter 3

Installing and Configuring vCenter Server

In the majority of today's information systems, the client-server architecture is king. This standing is because the client-server architecture can centralize resource management and give end users and client systems simplified access to those resources. Information systems used to exist in a flat, peer-to-peer model, when user accounts were required on every system where resource access was needed and when significant administrative overhead was needed simply to make things work. That's how managing a large infrastructure with many ESXi hosts feels without vCenter Server. vCenter Server brings the advantages of the client-server architecture to the ESXi host and to virtual machine (VM) management.

IN THIS CHAPTER, YOU WILL LEARN TO

◆ Understand the components and role of vCenter Server and Platform Services Controller

◆ Plan a vCenter Server deployment

◆ Install and configure the Platform Services Controller

◆ Install and configure vCenter Server

◆ Use the vSphere Web Client's System Configuration to view all vCenter Server nodes

◆ Use the vSphere Web Client's System Configuration to export a log bundle from vCenter Server

◆ Use vCenter Server's Virtual Appliance Management Interface to view service status

Introducing vCenter Server

As the size of a virtual infrastructure grows, managing the infrastructure from a central location becomes significantly more important. vCenter Server is an application that serves as a centralized management tool for ESXi hosts and their respective VMs. vCenter Server acts as a proxy that performs tasks on the individual ESXi hosts that have been added as members of a vCenter Server installation. As discussed in Chapter 1, "Introducing VMware vSphere 6.7," VMware includes vCenter Server licensing in every kit and every edition of vSphere, underscoring the importance of vCenter Server. Although VMware does offer a few different editions of vCenter Server (vCenter Server Essentials, vCenter Server Foundation, and vCenter Server Standard), we'll focus only on vCenter Server Standard in this book.

VMware has a number of other products, but vCenter Server is considered the central integration point tying them all together. Software such as vRealize Automation, Site Recovery Manager, and its often-paired vSphere Replication, as well as vRealize Operations Manager all depend on an instance of vCenter Server to integrate into the VMware environment. Not only this, but as you will see, much of the advanced functionality that vSphere offers comes only when vCenter Server is present. Specifically, vCenter Server offers core services in the following areas:

- ◆ Resource management for ESXi hosts and VMs

- ◆ Template management

- ◆ VM deployment

- ◆ VM management

- ◆ Scheduled tasks

- ◆ Statistics and logging

- ◆ Alarms and event management

- ◆ ESXi host management

Figure 3.1 illustrates the core services available through vCenter Server.

FIGURE 3.1
vCenter Server provides a full spectrum of virtualization management functions.

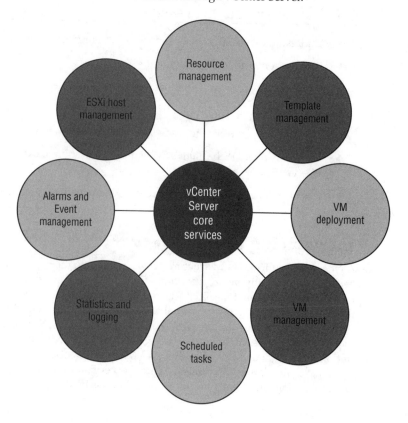

vCenter Server can be installed in two ways. The historic approach is an application installed on a Windows Server, but as of vSphere 6.7, this will be the last release of this deployment type; the other format is as a Linux-based virtual appliance. You'll learn more about virtual appliances in Chapter 10, "Using Templates and vApps," but for now, suffice it to say that the vCenter Server virtual appliance (which you may see referred to as VCVA or VCSA) offers an option to quickly and easily deploy a full installation of vCenter Server and Platform Services on VMware's open source Photon OS.

Because of the breadth of features included in vCenter Server, most of these core services are discussed in later chapters. For example, Chapter 9, "Creating and Managing Virtual Machines," discusses VM deployment, VM management, and template management. Chapter 11, "Managing Resource Allocation," and Chapter 12, "Balancing Resource Utilization," deal with resource management for ESXi hosts and VMs. Chapter 13, "Monitoring VMware vSphere Performance," discusses alarms. In this chapter, we'll focus primarily on ESXi host management, but we'll also discuss scheduled tasks, statistics and logging, event management, and appliance management.

There are other key items about vCenter Server that you can't really consider core services. Instead, these underlying features support core services. To help you more fully understand the value of vCenter Server in a vSphere deployment, let's take a closer look at the following:

◆ Centralized user authentication

◆ Web Client server

◆ Extensible framework

Centralizing User Authentication Using vCenter Single Sign-On

Centralized user authentication is not listed as a core service of vCenter Server, but it is essential to how vCenter Server and many other VMware products operate. In Chapter 2, "Planning and Installing VMware ESXi," we discussed a user's authentication to an ESXi host under the context of a user account created and stored locally on that host. Generally speaking, without vCenter Server, you would need a separate user account on each ESXi host for each administrator who needed access to the server. As the number of ESXi hosts and required administrators grows, the number of accounts to manage grows exponentially. There are workarounds for this overhead; one such workaround is integrating your ESXi hosts into Active Directory, a topic we'll discuss in more detail in Chapter 8, "Securing VMware vSphere." In this chapter, we'll assume the use of local accounts, but be aware that using Active Directory integration with your ESXi hosts does change the picture somewhat. In general, though, the centralized user authentication that vCenter Server offers is easier to manage than other available methods.

In a virtualized infrastructure with only one or two ESXi hosts, administrative effort is not a major concern. Administering one or two servers would not incur incredible effort on the part of the administrator, and creating user accounts for administrators would not be too much of a burden.

In situations like this, you may not miss vCenter Server from a management perspective, but you may certainly miss its feature set. In addition to its management capabilities, vCenter Server can perform vMotion, configure vSphere Distributed Resource Scheduler (DRS), establish vSphere High Availability (HA), and use vSphere Fault Tolerance (FT). These features are not accessible using ESXi hosts without vCenter Server. You also lose key functionality such as vSphere Distributed Switches, host profiles, policy-driven storage, VM encryption, and vSphere Update Manager. vCenter Server is a requirement for any enterprise-level virtualization project.

---

vCenter Server Requirement

Strictly speaking, vCenter Server is not a requirement for a vSphere hypervisor deployment. You can create and run VMs without it. However, to use the advanced features of the vSphere product suite—features such as vSphere Update Manager, vMotion, Storage vMotion, vSphere DRS, vSphere HA, vSphere Distributed Switches, host profiles, vSphere FT, VM encryption—vCenter Server must be licensed, installed, and configured accordingly.

But what happens when the environment grows? What happens when there are 10 ESXi hosts and 5 administrators? Now the administrative effort of maintaining all these local accounts on the ESXi hosts becomes a significant burden. If a new account is needed to manage the ESXi hosts, you must create the account on 10 different hosts. If an account password needs to change, you must change it on 10 different hosts. Then add into this equation other VMware components such as vRealize Automation or vRealize Orchestrator, with their own possible accounts and passwords.

The Platform Services Controller (PSC)—or more accurately, the medley of components that comprise the service of vCenter Single Sign-On (SSO), including the Secure Token Service (STS) and Identity Management Service (IDM)—addresses this problem. It is a prerequisite for installing vCenter Server—that is, vCenter Server cannot be installed without SSO being available first. We'll explain briefly how SSO works and what other software it interacts with (both VMware and non-VMware).

Prior to vSphere 5.1, when you logged onto vCenter your authentication request was forwarded to either the local security authority on vCenter Server's OS or Active Directory. In versions up through vSphere 6.7, with SSO the request can still end up going to Active Directory but it can also go to a list of locally defined users within SSO itself or to another Security Assertion Markup Language (SAML) 2.0–based authority. Generally speaking, SSO is a more secure way of authenticating to VMware products. Notice we said *products* and not vSphere? That's because SSO has hooks into other VMware products, not just vCenter Server. vRealize Orchestrator, vRealize Operations Manager, and vCloud Director are just a few. Why is this important? It means that SSO can take a single user and provide them with access to everything they need through the virtual infrastructure with a single username and password, and it can do so securely.

The following steps outline what happens when a user logs on using the vSphere Web Client or any other VMware product that is integrated with SSO (see Figure 3.2):

1. The vSphere Web Client presents a secure web page to log into.

2. The username and password are issued to the SSO server (in the form of a SAML 2.0 token).

3. The SSO server sends a request to the relevant authentication mechanism (local, AD, or another SAML 2.0–based authority).

4. Once authentication succeeds, SSO passes a token to the vSphere Web Client.

5. This token can now be used to authenticate directly with vCenter, or any other SSO integrated VMware products.

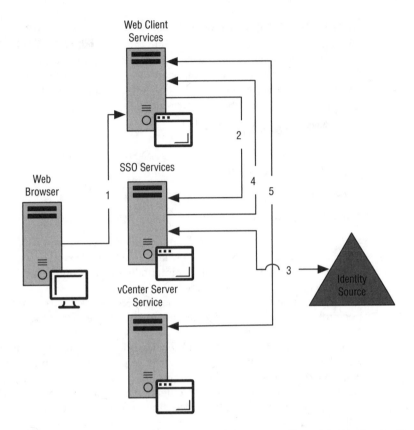

FIGURE 3.2
The steps taken to issue an authenticated session with the SSO component.

As you can see, the authentication procedure can sound more complicated than other traditional methods; however, the process is seamless to the end administrators who get access as they always have.

Before we talk about some of the more visible components of vCenter Server, let's discuss some of the unseen aspects inside the Platform Services Controller of vCenter.

AUTHENTICATION WITH THE VMWARE HOST CLIENT

Generally speaking, logging onto an ESXi host using the VMware Host Client requires an account created and stored locally on that host. That is to say, ESXi does not have integration with SSO. So, even though you use the vSphere Web Client to connect to vCenter Server, generating a session token that can traverse multiple VMware products, this does not extend to ESXi—each session of authentication to ESXi will be independent. Keep in mind that SSO and ESXi hosts do not make any attempt to reconcile the user accounts in their respective account databases.

Using the VMware Host Client to connect directly to an ESXi host that is currently managed by vCenter Server can cause negative effects in vCenter Server. A successful logon to a managed host will display an info icon indicating that it is managed and provide you a link to the associated vCenter Server.

Understanding the Platform Services Controller

vSphere 6.0 introduced a new component called the Platform Services Controller (PSC). This component has remained in the vSphere architecture up through vSphere 6.5, and now vSphere 6.7. It is used to run common components for VMware products in a central or in distributed location(s). The PSC offers multiple services; let's step through them so you can understand why the PSC is vital to your vSphere environment:

◆ Single Sign-On (SSO)

◆ Licensing

◆ Certificate Authority

◆ Certificate Store

◆ Service Registry

As you read over the paragraph preceding this list, you may have noticed that we said "for VMware products." The PSC is not solely for vCenter Server, or vSphere for that matter. These services can be located externally or internally to the vCenter Server and provide a common service across your entire VMware environment.

As we mentioned in the previous section, SSO is a service offered via the PSC for authentication brokering and secure token exchange, and can be shared to multiple vCenter instances or other VMware products.

The Licensing Service holds all licensing information for the vSphere environment and potentially other products, too, when they ship with PSC support. It removes the dependency where vCenter must be available for licensing operations to occur. This is especially important when you're installing multiple vCenter Servers in a geographically wide environment—older vCenter versions didn't replicate licensing information between them unless they were in a linked mode group.

The Certificate Authority and Store is the SSL certificate mint and wallet for your vSphere Environment. These services will allow you to create your own or store and assign third-party certificates for both vCenter and ESXi hosts. You'll find more details on how this service is used in Chapter 8.

The Service Registry works as the name suggests: it is a registration index of all VMware services available in this environment. This index will be particularly powerful when all VMware products also register their existence with the PSC, or more specifically, the Service Registry. No longer will you need to provide the details of each component to every other component; the Service Registry will do this automatically on your behalf.

During the installation of the PSC, which we'll detail later in this chapter, you see options for the installation type. Depending on the availability requirements of your vCenter Server installation, you may wish to make the PSC embedded on the vCenter Server; alternately, you may choose to make the PSC externally available from multiple sites, highly available in a single cluster, or even highly available across multiple sites. When you're installing a PSC for the first time, the first instance will always be a single node. Installing additional PSCs then allows you to join nodes to suit your environment. They can be external to the vCenter Server or embedded, as you can see in Figure 3.3. We'll discuss the pros and cons of the different PSC models in the section "Protecting the Platform Services Controller," later in this chapter We will also go through configuring the more complex installation model, a vCenter Server using an external Platform Services Controller, later in this chapter. After you've wrapped your head around each configuration, the simpler, embedded Platform Services Controller model will be quite intuitive.

FIGURE 3.3
The Platform Services Controller can be installed as an embedded or external component of vCenter Server, just like a database.

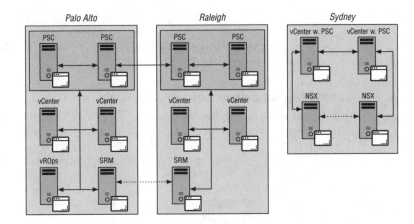

Using the vSphere Web Client for Administration

In the months that preceded and followed the release of vSphere 6.5, VMware made deprecation announcements to both their Flash-based vSphere Web Client and vSphere Client, the latter often referred to as C# Client or Thick Client, ushering in a new HTML5-based vSphere Client. The new HTML5 Client, like its Flash-based predecessor, is a server-side service for administering vSphere from a web browser. The following browsers are certified and supported with the vSphere Web Client and the HTML5 Client:

◆ Microsoft Internet Explorer—versions 10 and later (Windows only)

◆ Microsoft Edge—versions 39 and later (Windows only)

◆ Mozilla Firefox—versions 39 and later

◆ Google Chrome—versions 34 and later

Additionally, to use the vSphere Web Client, you must have Adobe Flash Player version 16 or later, up to and including version 23 installed.

WHICH CLIENT SHOULD YOU USE?

Now that there are two possible client choices to manage your vCenter Server, you need to decide which client to use day to day. For the time being, any new features that are part of the vSphere 6.7 release will be available in both the Flash-based vSphere Web Client as well as the HTML5-based vSphere Client; however, VMware has made it abundantly clear that they are shifting all work to make the HTML5 Client's experience *the* interface in which you interact with your environment, introducing more functionality with each iteration. So that would indicate that the HTML5 Client is the one to use. But what happens if your storage vendor has a vSphere Web Client plug-in that has not been updated to work with the HTML5 Client? In some cases, you may not have a choice other than to use the older client, but over time, the crossover period will fade away and only the HTML5 Client will be used. Prior to vSphere 6.5, we would have stated that the vSphere Web Client was still the one to use, and while we are heading up the curve of innovation and adoption with vendors rolling out features presented through the HTML5 Client, it's our opinion that we haven't yet reached the point for a full transition.

As stated in Chapter 2, the HTML5-based vSphere Client is not as feature-rich as the Flash-based vSphere Web Client. As you read through the rest of this book, you can assume that unless we specify the HTML5 Client, the Flash-based vSphere Web Client is the default choice and the one you should be using.

Providing an Extensible Framework

Just as centralized authentication is not a core vCenter Server service, we don't include vCenter Server's extensible framework as a core service. Rather, this extensible framework provides the foundation for vCenter Server's core services and enables third-party developers to create applications built around vCenter Server. Figure 3.4 shows some of the components that revolve around the core services of vCenter Server.

FIGURE 3.4
Other applications can extend vCenter Server's core services to provide additional management functionality.

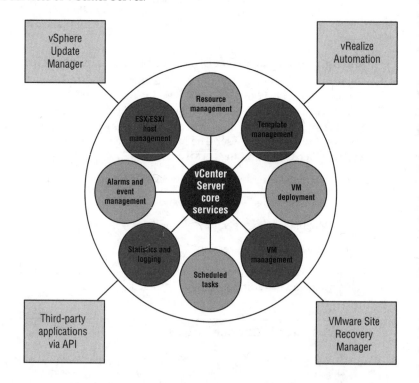

A key aspect for successful virtualization is the ability to allow third-party companies to provide products that add value, ease, and functionality to existing products. By building vCenter Server in an extensible fashion and providing an application programming interface (API) to it, VMware has shown its interest in allowing third-party software developers to play an integral part in virtualization. The vCenter Server API allows companies to develop custom applications that can take advantage of the virtual infrastructure created in vCenter Server. For example, numerous companies have created backup utilities that work off the exact inventory created inside vCenter Server to allow for advanced backup options of VMs. Storage vendors use the vCenter API to create plug-ins that expose storage details, and other third-party applications use the vCenter Server APIs to provide management, monitoring, life-cycle management, or automation functionality.

You can find more information on vCenter Server functionality in Chapter 10, which provides a detailed look at templates along with VM deployment and management, and in Chapter 8, which goes deeper into vCenter Server's access controls. Chapter 11 discusses resource management, and Chapter 13 offers an in-depth look at ESXi host and VM monitoring as well as alarms.

You're almost ready to take a closer look at installing, configuring, and managing vCenter Server. First, however, we'll discuss how to choose which version of vCenter Server you should deploy in your environment.

Choosing the Version of vCenter Server

As mentioned in the previous section, vSphere 6.7 marks the last release in which vCenter Server comes available as an installable Windows-based application, and all future releases will be the Photon OS Linux–based virtual appliance. As a result, while appearing straightforward on the surface, a critical decision you must make as you prepare to deploy vCenter Server is which version you will use. Will you use the Windows Server–based version, and later use the vCenter Server Appliance Migration utility, or go with the virtual appliance from the get-go?

There are advantages and disadvantages to each approach:

◆ If your experience is primarily with Windows Server, you may not be familiar with the Linux underpinnings of the vCenter virtual appliance. This introduces a learning curve that you should consider.

◆ If you need support for Microsoft SQL Server or Oracle RDBMS, the Linux-based vCenter Server virtual appliance won't work; you'll have to deploy the Windows Server–based version of vCenter Server. The vCenter Server virtual appliance supports only an embedded Postgres database, which, if you and/or your staff are only familiar with the aforementioned databases, may also introduce a learning curve that you should consider.

◆ If your experience is primarily with Linux or you manage a "Linux only by policy" datacenter, then deploying a Windows Server–based application will require some learning and acclimation for you and/or your staff.

◆ Because the vCenter Server virtual appliance naturally runs only as a VM, you are constrained to that particular design decision. If you want or are required to run vCenter Server on a physical system, you cannot use the vCenter Server virtual appliance.

As you can see, a number of considerations will affect your decision to deploy vCenter Server as a Windows Server–based installation or as a Linux-based virtual appliance.

OUR VIEW ON THE vCENTER SERVER APPLIANCE

Some of the early support limitations around the SUSE Linux–based vCenter Server virtual appliance led people to believe that this solution was more appropriate for smaller installations. This may have been because the virtual appliance was certified to support only 100 hosts and 3,000 VMs or because deploying a virtual appliance that handles all the various services required would appeal more to a smaller implementation. However, VMware has now certified this solution to support up to 2,000 hosts and/or 25,000 powered-on VMs, so the former argument is no longer valid. The way we see it, you should always use the right tool for the job (with proper planning), and the vCenter Server virtual appliance is now the right tool for most vCenter jobs.

Something we like to point out when people have concerns with the virtual appliance is that VMware itself uses the vCenter Server Virtual Appliance internally for large-scale environments. A specific example is VMware's Hands-On Labs (HOL)—even with this very large environment and intensive workloads, the virtual appliance is used.

In the next section, we'll discuss some of the planning and design considerations that have to be addressed if you plan to deploy the Linux–based version of vCenter Server. Most of these issues apply to the Linux–based version of vCenter Server, but some may also apply to the Windows Server-based installation; we'll point those out where applicable.

Planning and Designing a vCenter Server Deployment

vCenter Server is a critical application for managing your virtual infrastructure. Its implementation should be carefully designed and executed to ensure availability and data protection. When discussing the deployment of vCenter Server and its components, the following questions are among the most common questions to ask:

◆ How much hardware do I need to power vCenter Server?

◆ How do I provide high availability for vCenter Server?

◆ How do I prepare vCenter Server for disaster recovery?

◆ If I run vCenter Server in a VM, do I need a separate management cluster?

◆ Should I use a vCenter Server with an embedded Platform Services Controller or with an external Platform Services Controller?

Many of the answers to these questions are dependent on each other, but we have to start somewhere, so let's start with the first topic: figuring out how much hardware you need for vCenter Server.

Sizing Hardware for vCenter Server

The amount of hardware that vCenter Server requires is directly related to the number of hosts and VMs it will be managing. This planning and design consideration applies not only to the appliance–based version of vCenter Server but also the Windows Server–based version. Because it is a prepackaged virtual appliance, the virtual hardware of the vCenter Server virtual appliance is predefined and established before it is deployed.

As a starting point, the minimum hardware requirements for the Linux–based version of vCenter Server are as follows:

◆ Two vCPUs

◆ 10 GB of RAM

◆ 300 GB of disk space

◆ A network adapter (Gigabit Ethernet is strongly recommended)

Keep in mind these are *minimum* system requirements that an appliance can be deployed with, only allowing you to run up to approximately 10 hosts and 100 VMs. Large enterprise environments with many ESXi hosts and VMs must scale the vCenter Server system accordingly.

SIZING DISKS ON A VCENTER SERVER APPLIANCE

Due to the prepackaged nature of the appliance, disk storage allocation is distributed across multiple virtual disks with standard sizes. Unlike the Windows Server–based vCenter Server install that can be deployed across 2 virtual disks, the appliance contains 13 individual virtual disks that provide granular storage for such items as application logs, the vPostgres database along with its logs, and SEAT (stats, events, alarms, and tasks) data, to name a few. This can be both beneficial and problematic in production because you'll need to keep a close eye on each of these disks, particularly application logs.

Unlike the prepackaged Linux-based vCenter Server virtual appliance, the minimum requirements for the Windows Server–based edition of vCenter Server do not account for running a database server, which vCenter Server requires. Although vCenter Server is the application that manages your ESXi hosts and VMs, vCenter Server uses a database for storing all of its configuration, permissions, statistics, and other data. Figure 3.5 shows the relationship between vCenter Server and the separate database server.

FIGURE 3.5
vCenter Server acts as a proxy for managing ESXi hosts, but all of the data for vCenter Server is stored in a database.

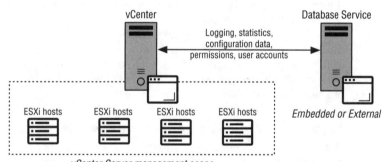

Although you can run vCenter Server and its dependencies on the same machine, it's usually not recommended, because it creates a single point of failure for key aspects of your virtual infrastructure. However, sometimes you don't have a choice, especially in smaller environments where capacity is at a premium. Keep in mind that VMware recommends 10 GB of RAM if vCenter Server is installed with an embedded Platform Services Controller, but only for environments with up to 10 ESXi hosts or 100 VMs. This would be the case if you use the Embedded option when installing vCenter Server.

VMware suggests vCenter hardware requirements depending on the size of the environment that vCenter will be managing. Table 3.1 shows these recommendations.

TABLE 3.1: vCenter sizing

ESXi HOSTS	POWERED-ON VMs	CPU CORES	RAM GB	STORAGE GB
10	100	2	10	300
100	1,000	4	16	340
400	4,000	8	24	525
1,000	10,000	16	32	740
2,000	35,000	24	48	1180

> **CPU CORES**
>
> Most modern physical servers ship with at least quad-core CPUs. As you can see, based on VMware's recommendations, vCenter Server will leverage multiple CPU cores when necessary.

Should you choose to run the separate database server on the same physical or virtual computer as vCenter Server, if you're opting for a Windows-based deployment, you'll need to consult the documentation for your chosen database server. Without a doubt, the database serve requires additional CPU capacity, RAM, and disk storage just like other co-located services, so you will need to plan accordingly. With the vCenter Server virtual appliance, this has been taker care of for you with the embedded Postgres database and the removal of external databases available in previous versions, so you just need to account for inventory size and other integrating components that you plan on deploying to the environment. That brings us to the next topic planning for availability.

Planning for vCenter Server Availability

Planning for a vCenter Server deployment is more than just accounting for CPU and memory resources. You must also create a plan for business continuity and disaster recovery. Remember, features such as vSphere vMotion, vSphere Storage vMotion, vSphere DRS, and, to a certain extent, vSphere HA stop functioning or are significantly impacted when vCenter Server is unavailable. While vCenter Server or any component it depends on is down, you won't be able to clone VMs or deploy new VMs from templates. You also lose centralized authentication and role-based administration of the ESXi hosts. Clearly, there are reasons why you might want vCenter Server to be highly available.

Keep in mind, too, that the heart of the vCenter Server and its components are stored in backend databases. Although the Linux-based vCenter Server virtual appliance obfuscates this from you with the use of an embedded database, with a Windows-based deployment, this need to be high on the list of considerations. Any good disaster-recovery or business-continuity plan must also include instructions on how to handle data loss or corruption, especially so in the backend databases, and if you're running external backend databases on separate physical computers or VMs, they must be designed and deployed to be resilient and highly available. Th is especially true in larger or mission-critical environments.

There are a few different ways to approach this concern. First, we'll discuss how to protect the vCenter Server components, then the vCenter Server itself, and finally, we'll talk about protecting the separate database server.

PROTECTING THE PLATFORM SERVICES CONTROLLER

The Platform Services Controller (PSC) is an integral part of vCenter Server. Without it there is no ability to log in and administer vCenter. Therefore, it is imperative that your protection strategy encompass the whole of vCenter Server and its components. There are three methods for ensuring you have a PSC node available to you with little or no downtime: deploying in an HA-enabled cluster, deploying multiple nodes, and having a solid backup plan.

During the PSC installation, you can join an existing deployment—specifically, the same site as a pre-existing PSC—and configure an HA cluster—often dubbed PSC HA. With this configuration, all PSC instances must sit behind a load balancer. Deploying PSC in this way protects you from an outage of the SSO application or server. Keep in mind, however, that just because you have deployed multiple PSCs into the same site, you do not have to configure a load balancer; being in the same site is purely a prerequisite for high availability.

If the complexity of configuring a highly available PSC configuration is too much for you or your organization, consider the secondary model of high redundancy. Instead of using a load balancer for near-seamless failover between nodes, by using a site with multiple PSCs, you are able to repoint the vCenter Server to a secondary PSC. This process does require downtime for the vCenter Server, unlike PSC HA, so if your environment must abide to a strict service level agreement (SLA) with any of your customers, this needs to be taken into account.

The last installation option for PSCs is called Multisite. This mode lets you install PSCs with multiple physical locations. This is usually deployed when you need to be able to sign in from multiple locations, but, like having multiple PSCs in the same site, it can also be used to facilitate a protection mechanism, allowing for an administrator to repoint vCenter to a separate site. Multisite can be used in conjunction with PSC HA to provide per-site high availability; however, we consider multisite PSC HA to be the most complex and intricate of the methods available, which should really only be considered when you are faced with the strictest of uptime requirements.

However, with all of these models in mind, there is no substitute for a properly configured, companywide backup solution that covers the PSC deployment. Having a solid backup plan that covers all of your nodes is critical to the integrity of your vSphere environment.

PROTECTING vCENTER SERVERS

If the vCenter Server computer is a physical server, one way to provide availability is to create a standby vCenter Server system that you can turn on in the event of a failure of the online vCenter Server computer. After failure, you bring the standby server online and attach it to the existing SQL Server database, and then the hosts can be added to the new vCenter Server computer. In this approach, you'll need to find mechanisms to keep the primary and secondary/standby vCenter Server systems synchronized with regard to file system content and configuration settings. The use of the Linux-based virtual appliance might make this approach easier because it is a VM; it therefore can be cloned (a process you'll see in more detail in Chapter 10).

A variation on that approach, which is applicable to both a physical deployment and a virtual deployment (Windows-based or Linux-based), is to keep the standby vCenter Server system as a

VM. You can use physical-to-virtual (P2V) conversion tools to regularly "back up" the physical vCenter Server instance to a standby VM. This method reduces the amount of physical hardware required and leverages the P2V process as a way of keeping the two vCenter Servers synchronized. Obviously, this sort of approach is viable for a Windows Server–based installation on a physical system but is not applicable to the virtual appliance version of vCenter Server.

Finally, if you are using the Linux-based vCenter Server virtual appliance, vSphere 6.5 introduced a native solution called vCenter High Availability (vCHA). This solution uses a cluster of three vCenter Server nodes—an Active, a Passive, and a Witness node—to provide an automated process of synchronization and failover between the Active and Passive nodes. The Witness node provides a quorum—the tie-breaking entity—in the event of network isolation between the Active and Passive nodes, often referred to as a split-brain event. Setting up this solution gives you the most consistent experience with documented performance overhead and recovery time objective (RTO), unlike the previously mentioned solutions that require their own bit of creativity to provide synchronization, failover initiation, and maintenance. However, like vCenter Server Heartbeat, vCHA comes at the expense of utilizing much more active resources. As mentioned previously, in environments where resources come at a premium, justifying this solution may be a struggle.

Ultimately, the most important part of the vCenter Server recovery plan is to ensure that the application server and its associated database server, be it embedded or external, is redundant and protected. Although this will get you up and running from a vCenter perspective, remember that other products (SRM, Horizon View, vRealize Operations Manager, etc.) also rely on vCenter Server and need to be accounted for. Recovery can get complicated, so test your recovery plan often.

PROTECTING THE vCENTER DATABASE

For high availability of the database server supporting the Windows-based vCenter Server, you can configure the backend database on a cluster. Figure 3.6 illustrates using a SQL Server cluster for the backend database. This figure also shows a standby vCenter Server system. Methods used to provide high availability for the database server are in addition to whatever steps you might take to protect vCenter Server itself. Other options might include using SQL log shipping or database mirroring to create a database replica on a separate system. If clustering or log shipping/database replication is not available or is not within fiscal reach, you should strengthen your database backup strategy to support easy recovery in the event of data loss or corruption. Using the native SQL Server tools, you can create a backup strategy that combines full, differential, and transaction log backups. This strategy allows you to restore data up to the minute when the loss or corruption occurred.

The suggestion of using a VM as a standby system for a physical computer running vCenter Server naturally brings us to the last topic surrounding architecture: Should you run vCenter Server in a VM? That's quite a question, and it's what we'll answer next.

Running vCenter Server and Its Components as VMs

As touched on earlier, you certainly have the option of skipping a physical server entirely and running vCenter Server and its components as a VM or even multiple VMs. This is actually the VMware recommendation. Running vCenter on a VM gives you several advantages, including snapshots, clones, vMotion, vSphere HA, Fault Tolerance, and vSphere DRS.

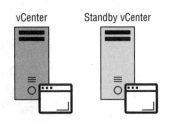

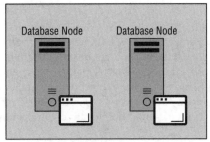

Database cluster

Running vCenter Server and the PSC as VMs on an HA-enabled cluster makes perfect sense. In fact, even with regular backups, clones, or snapshots, running vCenter Server on an HA-enabled cluster should be your default platform. Remember, the VMs running on your ESXi hosts, the storage, and the networking all continue to operate normally even with vCenter down. There are no dependencies on vCenter for these VMs to keep running. If the ESXi host that's running these VMs becomes unavailable, HA will kick in and restart the vCenter VM(s) on another available host. You might not even know it's happened unless your monitoring systems tell you!

Another feature that's available with vSphere 6 is Fault Tolerance (FT). Previously FT could only support one vCPU on a protected Virtual Machine. This meant that vCenter was not a possible candidate as it requires a minimum of two vCPUs to operate. As of vSphere 6.7 and later, FT supports eight vCPUs, vCenter and the PSC can be protected to avoid downtime altogether if an individual host goes down. You can read more about both HA and FT in Chapter 7, "Ensuring High Availability and Business Continuity."

Snapshots are a feature we'll discuss in detail in Chapter 9. At a high level, snapshot functionality lets you return to a specific point in time for your VM—in this case, your vCenter Server VM. vMotion gives you the portability to move the server from host to host without experiencing server downtime. But what happens when a snapshot is corrupted or the VM is damaged to the point it will not run? With vCenter Server as your VM, you can make regular copies of the virtual disk file and keep a "clone" of the server ready to go in the event of server failure. The clone will have the same system configuration used the last time the virtual disks were copied. Given that the bulk of the data processing by vCenter Server ends up in a backend database running on a different server, this should not be very different. Additionally, if you are using the vCenter Server virtual appliance with the embedded database, you could run into issues with snapshots and reverting to snapshots. This might or might not be an issue, but be sure to plan accordingly. Figure 3.7 illustrates the setup of a manual cloning of a vCenter Server VM.

FIGURE 3.7
If vCenter Server is a
VM, its virtual disk
file can be copied
regularly and used as
the hard drive for a
new VM, effectively
providing a point-in-
time restore in the
event of complete
server failure or loss.

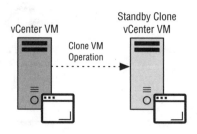

Some organizations may have a "virtualize first" or a "100 percent virtual" policy; although
this may give all the advantages of virtualization, you need to consider other issues in the design
of the infrastructure. Having a separate management cluster to host all the vCenter Server
components, along with any dependencies such as database servers and Active Directory, is fast
becoming commonplace. This separate management cluster will ensure that a production
workload incident would not negatively impact the manageability of the environment.

SEPARATING MANAGEMENT FROM WORKLOADS

As mentioned, separating the management VMs from the rest of the workload VMs is fast becoming
commonplace. The reason behind this is the increased dependency on the virtual infrastructure and
its management. VMware itself recommends this design practice in its vCloud Architecture Toolkit
(vCAT), VMware Validated Design (VVD), and VMware Cloud Foundation (VCF). Think of this
design best practice as similar to the way we separate the management network in physical designs.
Ensuring that this environment is highly secure and available goes a long way toward decreasing the
downtime in the event of a problem.

Delving into design best practices is outside the scope of this book, just as with physical
infrastructure design, but there are certain things you must consider to ensure that your virtual
infrastructure is designed to meet business requirements. Like any "best practice," it's a recommendation when there are no requirements that would point you in a different direction. For
more information on vSphere design, we recommend you read *VMware vSphere Design*
(Sybex, 2013).

By now, you have a good understanding of the importance of vCenter Server in a large
enterprise environment and some of the considerations that go into planning for a vCenter
Server deployment. You also have a good idea of the components, features, functions, and role of
vCenter Server. With this information in mind, let's deploy vCenter Server. The next section
mainly focuses on the installation of the vCenter Server and Platform Services Controller virtual
appliances; for information on the Windows-based vCenter Server, refer to older versions of
this book.

Installing vCenter Server and Its Components

Depending on the size of the environment to be managed, installing vCenter Server can be simple. In small environments, the vCenter Server Installer can install and configure all the necessary components. For larger environments, installing vCenter Server in a scalable and resilient fashion is a bit more involved and requires a few different steps. For example, supporting more than 2,000 ESXi hosts or more than 25,000 VMs requires installing multiple vCenter Server instances in a linked mode group, a scenario that we'll discuss later in this chapter in the section "Installing vCenter Server in an Enhanced Linked Mode Group."

Most of this discussion applies only to installing vCenter Server and its components as a Linux–based virtual appliance. However, some tasks—such as those required for configuring the SSO portion of the PSC—apply to the use of the Windows-based vCenter Server (physical or virtual) as well.

INSTALLING THE vCENTER SERVER COMPONENTS

The vCenter Server virtual appliance is a Photon OS–based VM that comes prepackaged and preinstalled with vCenter Server. It is commonly referred to as the vCSA, vCVA, or sometimes just the vCenter appliance. Rather than creating a new VM, installing a guest OS, and then installing vCenter Server, you only need to deploy the virtual appliance using a special deployment application. We discussed the vCenter Server virtual appliance earlier in this chapter in the section "Choosing the Version of vCenter Server."

The vCenter Server virtual appliance comes as a packaged VM that requires its own deployment tool, both of which are packed together on the installation media. We'll discuss OVF templates in great detail in Chapter 10, but for now we'll simply explain them as an easy way to distribute "prepackaged VMs."

USE THE LATEST VERSION OF vCENTER SERVER

Remember that the latest version of vCenter Server is available for download from www.vmware.com/download. It is often best to install the latest version of the software to ensure the highest levels of compatibility and security. You can also use a newer version of vCenter with older versions of ESXi. vCenter Server 6.7 can manage hosts from version 6.0 and later. The VMware interoperability matrix should also be referenced when using other VMware products together.

The vCenter Server virtual appliance deployment and configuration takes only a few minutes and is not too administratively intensive, assuming you've completed all the pre-installation tasks. Once mounted, you can start the vCenter Server installation by double-clicking the OS-specific installer inside the vCenter Server installation directory.

The vCenter Server Appliance Installer, shown in Figure 3.8, is the central point for freshly deploying, upgrading, migrating, and even restoring your vSphere environment. But before we get too carried away, let's focus on getting your first environment deployed and take you through what the Install option provides. Once the Install tile is clicked, this option enables you to deploy the following:

◆ vCenter Server with an embedded Platform Services Controller

◆ vCenter Server that uses an External Platform Services Controller

◆ External Platform Services Controller

FIGURE 3.8
The VMware vCenter Server Appliance Installer has become one of the central places for install, upgrade, migration, and restore operations within your environment.

Unlike the a la carte style of installation that came with vSphere 5.x, with vSphere 6.0 and later, nearly all of the auxiliary components shipped with vCenter Server are now bundled together, and you will have full access to them once the system has been setup. These auxiliary components include the following:

◆ vCenter Authentication Proxy

◆ vSphere Web Clients (Flash-based and HTML5-based)

◆ vSphere Update Manager

◆ vSphere Auto Deploy

◆ vSphere Syslog Collector

◆ vSphere ESXi Dump Collector

In addition, the ISO that packages the vCenter Server Appliance Installer contains the binaries necessary to set up Update Manager Download Service (UMD). Chapter 4, "vSphere Update Manager and the vCenter Support Tools," provides more detail on vSphere Update Manager. For now, we'll focus just on vCenter Server and its components.

INSTALLING A PLATFORM SERVICES CONTROLLER

Earlier in this chapter, we explained that vCenter Single Sign-On (SSO) is a prerequisite for vCenter and is part of the Platform Services Controller. Not only must it be installed for vCenter to run, it must also be running before the vCenter Server itself is installed.

We'll assume that you've already downloaded the files for the vCenter Server virtual appliance from VMware's website at my.vmware.com. You'll need these files before you can proceed with deploying either the Platform Services Controller virtual appliance or vCenter Server virtual appliance.

Use the following steps to install a PSC running SSO:

1. Mount the ISO (or burn it to a CD).

2. Once mounted, launch the vCenter Server Appliance Installer. To begin, navigate to x:\ vcsa-ui-installer, where x is the drive or mount point, depending on your operating system. There will be three directories available to you, allowing you to run installer on Mac OS X (/mac/installer.app), Microsoft Windows (\win32\installer.exe), or Linux (/lin64/installer).

3. The vCenter Server Appliance Installer should appear. Click Install, review the Introduction screen, which explains the two-stage appliance deployment operation, and then click Next.

4. On the End User License Agreement (EULA) page, select the check box to accept and click Next.

5. On the Select Deployment Type page, as shown in Figure 3.9, we'll choose the second option, Platform Services Controller, and click Next.

   The list of options available allow you to craft your environment's architecture given the set of requirements we covered previously.

   ◆ The first option, vCenter Server With An Embedded Platform Services Controller, allows you to install a combined vCenter Server installation with a PSC on the same system.

   ◆ The second option, which we've used for this walkthrough, installs a stand-alone/ external PSC. The Platform Services Controller option installs only the components required for the PSC and will not install vCenter Server itself. This is a precursor to PSC HA, if needed.

   ◆ Finally, the third option, vCenter Server (Requires External Platform Services Controller), will install just vCenter Server and, as the option details, not the PSC components. This option should only be used if you already have a stand-alone, external PSC installed that you wish to join a new vCenter installation to.

6. You'll need a running ESXi host to deploy the vCSA to. At a minimum, the host needs to be running version 6.0 to work for this installation. Provide the ESXi hostname or IP address, a username (in this case, **root**), and the appropriate password. Click Next.

7. A pop-up box will prompt you with an SSL certificate warning, which will be the certificate thumbprint of the ESXi host. Click Yes to proceed to the next screen.

8. Supply a VM (or display) name for the Platform Services Controller virtual appliance. You will also need to provide a password for the root account of this VM. Click Next to continue.

FIGURE 3.9
The Platform Services controller can be installed either embedded with or separately from vCenter Server.

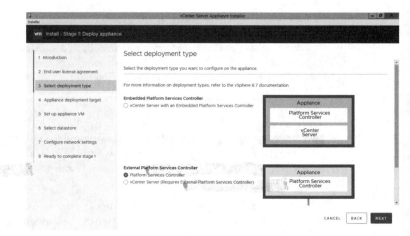

9. Select the datastore that you want the Platform Services Controller to reside on, and then click Next.

   Chapter 6 and Chapter 9 provide more details on the different disk provisioning types. In all likelihood, you'll want to use Thin Provision to help you conserve disk space.

10. The final steps of Stage 1 are to provide the network information for the VM deployment. Working from top to bottom of the screen, first you must choose a network. On the ESXi host, this could also be called a port group, which you can read more about in Chapter 5, "Creating and Configuring a vSphere Network."

11. Second, select between IPv4 or IPv6 as the protocol. You'll most likely want to use a static IP address for Platform Services Controller—so on the third field, IP Address, select Static. However, if DHCP is available on the selected network, you can use that option. You'll need to provide a hostname, the associated IP address, a subnet mask, a gateway, and at least one DNS server. The hostname established in this step will be used to sign the SSL certificate generated upon deployment.

12. Finally, new in vSphere 6.7 for appliance deployments, you have the option to provide unique ports that the Platform Services ontroller will use. Leave these as default, and click Next.

   Unless there is a conflict in your environment, we recommend not changing the default port numbers. It can make configuration and troubleshooting more difficult later on.

13. On the last page of Stage 1, review all the configuration details, as shown in Figure 3.10, make sure there are no errors. Click Finish to deploy the virtual appliance.

   A progress window like the one shown in Figure 3.11 will appear while the Platform Services Controller virtual appliance is being deployed to the ESXi host.

14. After the appliance has been successfully deployed, you'll begin Stage 2 to finalize the Platform Services Controller's configuration. Review the Introduction page, which explains the two-stage appliance deployment operation, and then click Next.

FIGURE 3.10

Ensure that everything has been configured before clicking Finish. Once committed, you can't make any grandiose changes like changing the Fully Qualified Domain Name.

FIGURE 3.11

You can monitor each component being deployed and installed via the installation progress bar.

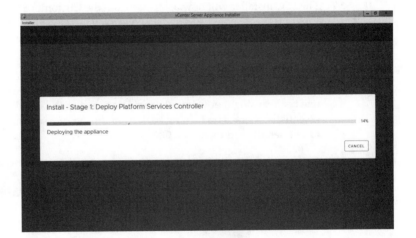

15. In the Appliance Configuration section, provide an NTP source. Unless necessary, due to a lack of NTP server availability in your environment, avoid using the VMware time sync tool because a time-drift can occur unless it's set up in a specific way.

For troubleshooting purposes, enable SSH access, and then click Next.

16. On the following screen, shown in Figure 3.12, you're asked if you would like to configure a new Single Sign-On instance or join an existing one. Again, choose to configure a new SSO instance. You'll need to create a domain name, an SSO administrator password, and a site name. Click Next to continue.

It is worth noting that these domain and site names have nothing to do with Active Directory domain or site names. In fact, we suggest that you use different names to avoid namespace conflicts in the future.

FIGURE 3.12
To instantiate your first SSO domain, use the top radio button. For subsequent PSCs you want to join to the SSO domain, use the bottom radio button.

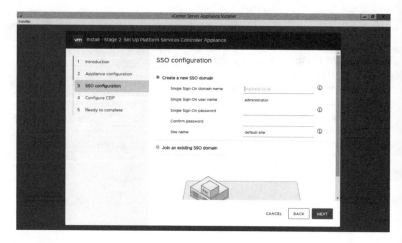

17. The PSC installer will now ask you to join the Customer Experience Improvement Program that enabled VMware to collect telemetry data from your environment. Depending on your security requirements, either check the box to join or uncheck it to opt-out. Then click Next.

18. Finally, review all configuration details for errors, as shown in Figure 3.13. Click Finish to proceed with configuring the Platform Services Controller virtual appliance. You'll receive one last warning that you will be unable to pause the installation after you proceed—essentially, there is no turning back from this point—so double-check those final configuration details, and then click OK.

FIGURE 3.13
Reviewing configuration details for errors.

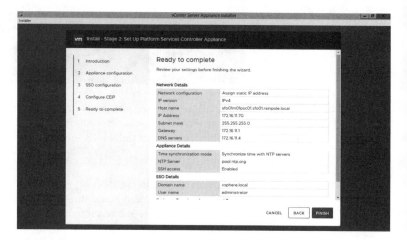

19. When installation is complete, click Close to close the installer.

After you complete the installation of Platform Services Controller, a link to the Platform Services Controller Getting Started page is displayed (`https://<server name>:443` or `https://<server ip address>:443`). Unlike the previous version of vSphere, the administrator no longer has access to the Platform Services Controller UI, where the Login Banners, Smart Card Authentication, and certificate management were handled. All of these items have been relocated into vCenter Server HTML5-based Web Client.

THE RELATIONSHIP BETWEEN vCENTER AND THE PSC

In previous versions of vCenter, the component architecture called for scaling out the services among a number of servers to achieve a vCenter instance capable of supporting a large number of hosts and VMs. With the introduction of the Platform Services Controller, VMware has significantly simplified the potential installation variants.

Think of the PSC just like you do vCenter's supporting database. It can be embedded or external. If you need to scale your environment past a few hundred VMs for your vCenter Server(s), we suggest having an external PSC to accompany them. Also, remember that you only get the "single pane of glass" with linked mode if you join your PSC SSO instances to the same SSO domain.

INSTALLING vCENTER SERVER

After you've completed deploying the Platform Services Controller, you are now in a position to install the vCenter Server virtual appliance. If you have installed vCenter any number of times with a previous release, be it on Windows or using the appliance, this process should feel very familiar. Further, due to the nature of the two-stage operation for deploying the appliances, Stage 1 is largely a repeat of the same process you followed to deploy the Platform Services Controller.

Perform the following steps to install vCenter Server virtual appliance:

1. Mount the ISO (or burn it to a CD).

2. Once mounted, launch the vCenter Server Appliance Installer. To begin, navigate to *x*:\vcsa-ui-installer, where *x* is the drive or mount point, depending on your operating system. There will be three directories available for you, allowing you to run installer on Mac OS X (`/mac/installer.app`), Microsoft Windows (`\win32\installer.exe`), or Linux (`/lin64/installer`).

3. The vCenter Server Appliance Installer should appear. Click Install, review the Introduction screen, which explains the two-stage appliance deployment operation, and then click Next.

4. On the End User License Agreement (EULA) page, select the check box to accept and click Next.

5. For Select Deployment Type, you have the same options outlined in the previous section. Since we showed you how to do a stand-alone/external Platform Services Controller, we'll now step you through a stand-alone vCenter Server and join them together. The result will functionally be the same as the Embedded Platform Services Controller

option, but you'll have seen both sides of the installation process. This is important because if you want to add new vCenter Servers (or PSCs) in the future, the chances are you'll separate them. Select the third option, vCenter Server (Requires External Platform Services Controller), and click Next.

6. Identical to the Platform Services Controller process, you'll need a running ESXi host to deploy the vCSA to. At a minimum, the host needs to be running version 6.0 to work for this installation. Provide the ESXi hostname or IP address, a username (in this case, **root**) and the appropriate password. Click Next.

7. A pop-up box will prompt you with an SSL certificate warning, which will be the certificate thumbprint of the ESXi host. Click Yes to proceed to the next screen.

8. Supply a VM (or display) name for the vCenter Server virtual appliance. You will also need to provide a password for the root account of this VM. Click Next to continue.

9. Select the datastore that you want the vCenter Server to reside on, and then click Next.

10. The following screen, shown in Figure 3.14, is where we see the first big divergence from the Platform Services Controller installation: you'll be asked to define the appliance's size. Select Tiny vCenter Server from the Deployment Size drop-down and Default from the Storage Size drop-down, and then click Next to continue.

Though we selected Tiny, the drop-down menus for Deployment Size and Storage Size allow you to configure the number of vCPUs and Memory along with Storage Space, respectively. The former drop-down defines the number of hosts and virtual machines the appliance can handle, while the latter drop-down defines the retention time of non-persistent items stored on disk, such as logs. These choices will dictate what the appliance will receive upon deployment.

FIGURE 3.14

Depending on the initial number of hosts and VMs in your environment, choose the appropriate size. You can increase the vCenter Server's resources as your environment grows.

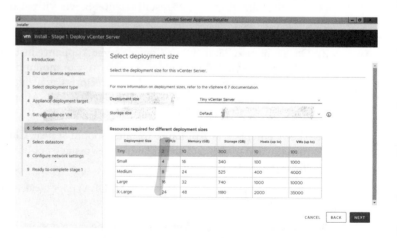

Deployment Size	vCPUs	Memory (GB)	Storage (GB)	Hosts (up to)	VMs (up to)
Tiny	2	10	300	10	100
Small	4	16	340	100	1000
Medium	8	24	525	400	4000
Large	16	32	740	1000	10000
X-Large	24	48	1180	2000	35000

11. The final steps of Stage 1 are to provide the network information for the VM deployment. Working from top to bottom of the page, first you must choose a network. On the ESXi host, this could also be called a port group. Since you've already performed this activity for your PSC deployment, select the port group you previously used.

12. Second, select between IPv4 or IPv6 as the protocol. You'll most likely want to use a static IP address for vCenter Server so in the third field, IP Address, select Static; however, you have the option to use DHCP if it is available on the selected Network. You'll need to provide a hostname, the associated IP address, a subnet mask, a gateway, and at least one DNS server. The hostname established in this step will be used to sign the SSL certificate generated upon deployment.

13. Finally, new in vSphere 6.7 for appliance deployments, you have the option to provide unique ports that the vCenter Server will use. Leave these as default values. Click Next.

Unless there is a conflict in your environment, we recommend not changing the default port numbers. It can make configuration and troubleshooting more difficult later on.

14. On the last page of Stage 1, review all the configuration details to make sure there are no errors. Click Finish to deploy the virtual appliance.

A progress window like the one shown earlier in Figure 3.11 will appear while the vCenter Server virtual appliance is being deployed to the ESXi host.

You can use the VM console from the Host Client to watch the virtual appliance boot up. Eventually, it will display a virtual appliance management screen, as shown in Figure 3.15. The vCenter Virtual Appliance console looks very similar to an ESXi host console. You can perform some limited configuration and troubleshooting from here, but the vast majority of vCenter configuration will be performed using the vSphere Web Client. The next section will show you what that looks like.

FIGURE 3.15
Until your first vCenter Server has been instantiated, using the ESXi Host Client's virtual machine consoles gives you visibility into their boot activities.

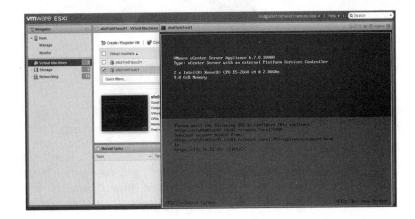

15. When the appliance has been successfully deployed, you'll be greeted with a Success screen. This screen displays a web address you can use in the event that you need to continue the installation of this vCenter at a later time. That is, from the web address, you can continue the Stage 2 operation. For the sake of continuity, let's keep using the Installer click Continue to move to Stage 2.

16. Begin Stage 2 of the deployment that finalized the vCenter Server's configuration by reviewing the Introduction page, which again explains the two-stage appliance deployment operation, and then click Next.

17. In the Appliance Configuration section, you'll also need to provide an NTP source. Like with the PSC install, unless necessary, such as a lack of NTP server in your environment, avoid using the VMware time sync tool because it can cause time-drift unless it's set up in a specific way.

    For troubleshooting purposes, enable SSH access, and then click Next

18. The following screen, shown in Figure 3.16, is where we see the second noticeable divergence from the Platform Services Controller installation. Enter the Platform Services Controller name you previously installed, along with the SSO domain name and the password to the Administrator account. Note that there is no mention of the Site as that is defined at the Platform Services Controller level; the vCenter Server simply inherits the site that is associated with the Platform Services Controller you join it to. Click Next to continue.

FIGURE 3.16
Joining multiple PSCs to the same SSO domain enables redundancy and scale out of your environment.

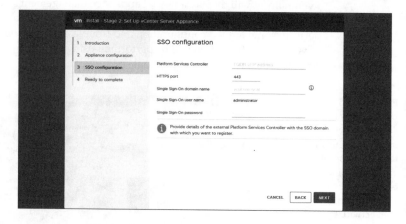

19. On the last page of Stage 2, review the configuration details for errors, as shown in Figure 3.17. Click Finish to proceed with configuring the vCenter Server virtual appliance You'll receive one last warning that you will be unable to pause the installation once you proceed, so double-check those final configuration details, and then click Finish.

20. When the installation is complete, click Close to close the installer.

FIGURE 3.17
The vCenter Server
installation program
will ask for all the
configuration options
up front, before
installing
the software.

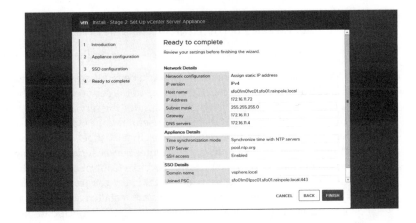

FIGURE 3.17
The vCenter Server
installation program
will ask for all the
configuration options
up front, before
installing
the software.

After you complete the installation of vCenter Server, a link to the vCenter Server Getting Started page is displayed (`https://<vcenter.domain.name>: 443` or `https://<vcenter ip address>:443`). Unlike the Platform Services Controller, on the Getting Started for vCenter Server, you'll have the option to launch either the HTML5-based Web Client (`https://<vcenter.domain.name>/ui`) or the Flash-based Web Client (`https://<vcenter .domain.name>/vsphere-client`). If you click the latter link, your default web browser will launch to this page. Before we dive into this area, we want to cover a few details regarding user interfaces and services.

The Flash-based vSphere Web Client connected to vCenter Server should be the primary management tool for managing vCenter. However, in the event that vCenter Server becomes unavailable, the HTML5-based Host Client will allow you to connect to each of the managed ESXi hosts, and give you visibility into their respective VMs. As we've mentioned, the Host Client can connect directly to ESXi hosts only under the context of a local user account defined on each ESXi host. That's not to say you cannot log in with an Active Directory account, but ESXi does not have any integration with the Platform Services Controller, so while you can authenticate to each host independently, once the vCenter Server services have been restored, your token won't allow you to seamlessly log in.

After you install vCenter Server, a number of new services will be installed to facilitate the operation of vCenter Server. Depending on whether you have installed both the PSC and vCenter on the same server, the services you may see will differ. Here are some of the most important ones:

◆ VMware vCenter Server, the core of vCenter Server that provides centralized management of ESX/ESXi hosts and VMs

◆ VMware Services Lifecycle Manager API, the interface to the VMware Lifecycle Manager (vMon) that provides the watchdog service to the Platform Services Controllers and vCenter Server, ensuring each node has healthy services and proper start order

◆ VMware Postgres, the embedded database on vCenter Server where configuration and historical data from the environment is preserved

◆ VMware vSphere Web Client, the web server that runs the user interface

As a vSphere administrator, you should be familiar with the default states of these services. I● times of troubleshooting, check the status of the services to see whether they've changed. Later i● this chapter, we'll show you where to monitor the services within the VMware Appliance Management Interface, but that's only useful if your vCenter is working enough to see that user interface. Keep in mind the dependencies that exist between vCenter Server and other services on the network. For example, if the vCenter Server service is failing to start, be sure to check tha● the system has access to the Platform Services Controller. If vCenter Server cannot access the PS● because of a lack of connectivity or the PSC services are not running, it will not start.

As additional features and extensions are installed, additional services will also be installed t● support those features. For example, installing vSphere Update Manager will install an additional service called VMware Update Manager Service. You'll learn more about vSphere Update Manager in Chapter 4.

In Chapter 2, you learned that there are two clients that can be used to administer a vCenter Server installation: the old vSphere Desktop Client and the newer vSphere Web Client. We guided you through installing the older client. In previous versions of vSphere, the Web Client required a separate install, but with vSphere 6, the vSphere Web Client is installed with every vCenter Server installation.

Now that you've successfully installed vCenter Server, you'll probably want to log in and get started. Unless you also wish to know how to deploy for enhanced linked mode, feel free to skip to the section "Exploring vCenter Server."

Installing vCenter Server in an Enhanced Linked Mode Group

What is an enhanced linked mode (ELM) group, and why might you want to install multiple instances of vCenter Server into such a group? If you need more ESXi hosts or more VMs than a single vCenter Server instance can handle, or if you need more than one instance of vCenter Server, you can install multiple instances of vCenter Server to scale outward or sideways and have those instances share licensing and permission information. The multiple instances of vCenter Server that share information among them are referred to as an *enhanced linked mode group*, or simply *enhanced linked mode*. In an enhanced linked mode environment, there are multiple vCenter Server instances, and each of the instances has its own set of hosts, clusters, an● VMs. They are all registered back to the same PSC and SSO instance.

Prior to vSphere 6, vCenter Server *linked mode*, as it was previously called, used Microsoft Active Directory Application Mode (ADAM) to replicate the information between vCenter instances. Because of this architecture, it was limited to only the Windows version of vCenter. Now, with the re-architecting that was introduced in vSphere 6, the PSC is used to replicate the following information between the instances:

◆ Connection information (IP addresses and ports)

◆ Certificates and thumbprints

◆ Licensing information

◆ User roles and permissions

◆ Policies and tags

There are a few reasons you might need multiple vCenter Server instances running in an enhanced linked mode group. With vCenter Server 4.0, one common reason was the size of the environment. With the dramatic increases in capacity incorporated into vCenter Server 4.1 and later, and with vSphere 6.7 nearly doubling capacity maximums, the need for multiple vCenter Server instances due to size is reduced. However, you might still use multiple vCenter Server instances. You might prefer to deploy multiple vCenter Server instances in enhanced linked mode to accommodate organizational or geographic constraints, or you might want to manage multiple vCenter Servers from a single user interface. You can have up to 15 vCenter Servers participating in a linked mode group.

Before you install additional vCenter Server instances, you must verify the following prerequisites:

◆ All computers that you wish to run vCenter Server in an enhanced linked mode group must be registered to the same SSO domain, sometimes referred to as a vSphere domain. The servers can exist in different Active Directory domains only if a two-way trust relationship exists between the domains.

◆ DNS must be operational. Also, the DNS name of the servers must match the server name.

◆ You must use the same version of vSphere when deploying additional Platform Services Controllers and vCenter Servers; you cannot combine vCenter Server 6 instances in an enhanced linked mode group with earlier versions of vCenter Server via fresh installation.

◆ Enhanced Linked Mode is supported between the Linux-based vCenter virtual appliance and the installable Windows version of vCenter.

◆ Each vCenter Server instance must have its own backend (Windows) or embedded (Appliance) database.

USING MULTIPLE vCENTER SERVER INSTANCES WITH ORACLE

If you're using Oracle, you'll need to make sure that each vCenter Server instance has a different schema owner or uses a dedicated Oracle server for each instance.

After you've met the prerequisites, installing vCenter Server in an enhanced linked mode group is straightforward, though you have two choices to achieve this: deploying an additional Platform Services Controller for your new vCenter Server to use or connecting the new vCenter Server to the already-deployed Platform Services Controller. As previously discussed, depending on your availability requirements, the former operation provides higher redundancy within your vSphere environment at the cost of an increase in resources and administrative overhead, while the latter raises the risk of availability by introducing a single point of failure for multiple vCenters while reducing your resources and additional administrative overhead.

For the former operation, in which you deploy a new Platform Services Controller, you follow the steps outlined previously in "Installing a Platform Services Controller" until you get to step 14. In the previous instructions, you installed the Platform Services Controller as a new instance in step 14. This time, however, you simply select the option Join An Existing SSO Domain.

When you select to install into an existing SSO domain, you will be prompted for the name and port number of the existing SSO instance on a Platform Services Controller. The new Platform Services Controller instance uses this information to replicate data from the PSC server's repository. After you've provided the information to connect to a remote Platform Services Controller instance, the rest of the installation follows the same steps.

Next, you follow the steps outlined previously in "Installing vCenter Server" until you reach step 16. Instead of providing the first Platform Services Controller you deployed in this step, you'll provide the newest Platform Services Controller deployed.

This operation also applies to using vCenter Servers with Embedded Platform Services Controllers. However, rather than configuring the vCenter Server and Platform Services Controller separately, these operations have been joined together. So as you want to scale out and add more vCenter Servers to your ELM group, you simply use the option Join an existing SSO domain as you would for an External Platform Services Controller.

For the latter operation in which you want to re-use your original Platform Services Controller, nothing in the installation process changes for the vCenter Server installation outlined previously in "Installing vCenter Server."

If, however, you are nervous about only having a single PSC servicing multiple vCenter Servers, don't fret. You can install PSCs later using the process mentioned previously and manually redistribute the vCenter Servers via repoint scripts covered in VMware Knowledge Base article 2113917.

When the additional vCenter Server is up and running in the enhanced linked mode group, logging in via the vSphere Client displays all the linked vCenter Server instances in the inventory view, as you can see in Figure 3.18.

FIGURE 3.18
In an enhanced linked mode environment, the vSphere Client shows all the vCenter Server instances for which a user has permission.

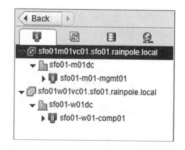

One quick note about enhanced linked mode: although the licensing and permissions are shared among all the enhanced linked mode group members, each vCenter Server instance is managed separately. Prior to vSphere 6, each vCenter Server instance represented a vMotion domain. This meant that you couldn't perform a vMotion migration between vCenter Server instances, even in a linked mode group. In vSphere 6 and later, this is no longer a limitation—you can now migrate vMotion VMs between vCenters joined in enhanced linked mode. This certainly blurs the line between managing vCenter Servers as single entities and managing your vCenter Servers together. We'll discuss vMotion in detail in Chapter 12. As you'll see, joining vCenter instances together by specifying an existing SSO domain is quite straightforward. Most vSphere administrators will likely now install their vCenters in enhanced linked mode by default.

Exploring vCenter Server

As explained, you can access vCenter Server through either of the vSphere Web Clients, be it the Flash-based or HTML-based version. Previously, the HTML5-based Web Client was not as feature-rich compared with the Flash-based Web Client, but starting with vSphere 5.5, and through the vSphere 6.0 and vSphere 6.5 releases, the Flash-based Web Client has become quite feature-rich by comparison. Therefore, this is the client we'll use to demonstrate the majority of features throughout this book. There's a lot to cover, so let's start out at the beginning: logging in.

To run the vSphere Web Client, all you need is a compatible web browser with Adobe Flash installed. While the legacy Windows vCenter Server has a shortcut in the Start ➤ All Programs ➤ VMware ➤ VMware vSphere Web Client folder, since we're focusing on the vCenter Server Appliance, accessing the vCenter Web Client can only be done via another computer. Go to `https://<vcenter.domain.name>/vsphere-client`. For our vSphere Web Client, this address is `https://sfo01m01vc01.rainpole.local/vsphere-client`.

When you connect to a vCenter Server instance with the vSphere Web Client, you may receive a security warning message that differs slightly depending on your web browser. This security warning appears because the vSphere Web Client uses HTTP over Secure Sockets Layer (HTTPS) to connect to vCenter Server but the vCenter Server is using a Secure Sockets Layer (SSL) certificate from an "untrusted" source.

To correct this error, you have the following two options:

◆ You can choose the Do Not Prompt For Security Warnings option (again, the option depends on your browser). This option tells your browser to ignore that there's an untrusted certificate.

◆ You can install your own SSL certificate from a trusted certification authority on the vCenter Server. We recommend this, and we'll step you through this process in Chapter 8 when we discuss security in greater detail.

If you simply browse to HTTPS on the vCenter Server's hostname or IP address, you'll be prompted with a splash screen with a link to the `/vsphere-client` URL. After the vSphere Web Client connects and authenticates to the vSphere Web Client, you'll notice a Getting Started tab that explains the various sections of the user interface. Closing this tab reveals the home screen, which is the starting point for the vSphere Web Client.

REMOVING THE GETTING STARTED PAGES

If you prefer not to see the Getting Started pages in the vSphere Client, you can turn them off either individually or all at once. Individually, you can simply click the close button at the top right of each one. To turn them all off at once, from the vSphere Web Client Help menu select Hide All Getting Started Pages.

The vSphere Web Client Home Screen

So far, you've seen only the Hosts And Clusters inventory view within the traditional vSphere Client, but it's very similar in the Web Client. The Hosts And Clusters view is where you manage ESXi hosts, clusters, and VMs. You already understand hosts and VMs; and we'll discuss clusters in the section "Creating and Managing a vCenter Server Inventory," later in this chapter. To see the rest of what vCenter Server has to offer, click the house icon on the top of the browser next to the VMware vSphere Web Client name.

As shown in Figure 3.19, the interface is divided into five main areas and a search bar appears in the upper-right corner.

FIGURE 3.19

The vSphere Web Client home screen shows the full selection of features within vCenter Server as well as both services that hook into the vSphere Web Client.

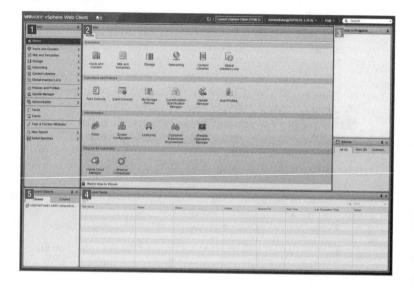

Navigator (1)   The leftmost column is used for showing inventory and for navigation. It is the primary item selection tool.

Content Area (2)   Once an item is selected, the larger middle column shows the content or configuration options for that item.

Alarms and Work In Progress (3)   On the right is a column that brings potential problems to your attention and also shows any current wizards that are in progress but put to the side for completion at a later time.

Recent Tasks (4)   The Recent Tasks bar shows anything that is currently or has recently occurred within vCenter. Recent Tasks can be swapped between My Tasks and All Users.

Recent Objects (5)   The Recent Objects bar shows the last 10 objects that you have recently viewed or created within vCenter. The Recent Viewed Objects can be swapped with Recent Created Objects by clicking on the opposite tab.

A DIFFERENT LAYOUT

The layout for the improved vSphere Web Client in vSphere 6 can be highly customized. Simply drag any of the Alarms, Work In Progress, or Recent Items title bars to move them around. You can pin areas to the bottom or close them completely. Play around to find a layout that best suits your workflow if the default is not sufficient. You can always revert back to the default by clicking on the username at the top of the user interface, selecting Customize Global Panels, and then clicking Reset To Default Layout.

The home screen lists all the various features that the vSphere Web Client has to offer within the content area in managing ESXi hosts and VMs:

◆ Under Inventories, the Web Client offers several views, including Hosts And Clusters, VMs And Templates, Storage, Networking, Content Library, and Global Inventory Lists.

◆ Under Operations And Policies, the Web Client has screens for viewing tasks, events, host profiles, storage service classes, and customization specifications.

◆ Under Administration are areas for managing roles, configuring the system, and licensing.

◆ Under Plug-ins For Installation, the Web Client has screens to access Hybrid Cloud and vRealize Orchestrator.

Many of these features are explored in other areas of the book. For example, networking is discussed in Chapter 5, and storage is discussed in Chapter 6. Chapter 10 discusses templates and customization specifications, and Chapter 8 discusses roles and permissions. Under Administration, you'll also see a link to vCenter Operations Manager, which is outlined in Chapter 13. A large portion of the rest of this chapter is spent just on vCenter Server's inventory views.

CONTINUED IMPROVEMENTS TO THE WEB CLIENT

It's no secret that the first iterations of the vSphere Web Client were not well received by VMware administrators. However, with this version of the vSphere Web Client, major rework directly addresses some of the faults in the previous versions.

There are two significant areas of improvement that we would like to point out. First, the performance has been improved, especially in larger environments with hundreds of hosts and thousands of VMs. Second, the UI has reverted to look a little closer to the vSphere Desktop Client. Recent Tasks are down at the bottom, and the right-click menus are more traditional, too.

These changes, along with the new linked mode, should prove to be popular with those of you not as comfortable with the older vSphere Web Clients. Those of you who have yet to make the switch will be in more familiar territory when you do.

From the home screen, you can click any of the icons to navigate to the corresponding area. There may or may not be additional icons here, depending on the plug-ins you have installed. The vSphere Web Client also has another way to navigate quickly and easily, and that's called th navigator.

Using the Navigator

The left-hand column of the vSphere Web Client is the navigator. As stated on the Getting Starte tab, the navigator is an "aggregated view of all objects in the inventory." The top of the navigato shows you exactly where you are in the various screens that vCenter Server provides and also displays a chronological history so you can jump back to a prior screen.

If you click any item in the navigation bar with an arrow next to it, the menu changes and displays just the subitems of the selected item. When you click an item without the arrow, the Navigator menu doesn't change, but it does change the content area. A key point about the vSphere Web Client and vCenter Server is that many of the menu options and tabs that appear within the application are context sensitive, meaning they change depending on what object is selected or active. You'll learn more about this topic throughout the chapter.

Now that you understand how to navigate using the vSphere Web Client, you're ready to sta creating and managing the vCenter Server inventory.

Creating and Managing a vCenter Server Inventory

As a vSphere administrator, you'll spend a significant amount of time using the vSphere Web Client. You will spend a great deal of that time working with the various inventory views available in vCenter Server, so it's quite useful to first explain them.

Understanding Inventory Views and Objects

Every vCenter Server has one or more root objects; these are datacenter objects, which serve as a container for all other objects. Prior to adding an object to the vCenter Server inventory, you must create at least one datacenter object (you can have multiple datacenter objects in a single vCenter Server instance). The objects found within the datacenter object depend on which inventory view is active. The navigator provides a quick and easy reminder of which inventory view is currently active by displaying the four main inventory trees as tabs at the top. In the Hosts And Clusters view, you'll work with ESXi hosts, clusters, resource pools, and VMs. In the VMs And Templates view, you'll work with folders, VMs, and templates. In the Storage view, you'll work with datastores and datastore clusters; in the Networking view, you'll work with vSphere Standard Switches and vSphere Distributed Switches.

---

vCenter Server Inventory Design

If you're familiar with objects used in Microsoft Windows Active Directory (AD), you may recognize a strong similarity in the best practices of AD design and the design of a vCenter Server inventory. A close parallel can even be drawn between a datacenter object and an organizational unit because both are the building blocks of their respective infrastructures.

You organize the vCenter Server inventory differently in different views. The Hosts And Clusters view is primarily used to determine or control where a VM is executing or how resources are allocated to a VM or group of VMs. You would not, typically, create your logical administrative structure in the Hosts And Clusters inventory view. This would be a good place, though, to provide structure for resource allocation or to group hosts into clusters according to business rules or other guidelines.

In VMs And Templates view, though, you can place VMs and templates within folders irrespective of the specific host on which that VM is running. Thus you can create a logical structure for VM administration that remains, for the most part, independent of the physical infrastructure on which those VMs are running. There is one very important tie between the VMs And Templates view and the Hosts And Clusters view: datacenter objects are shared between them. Datacenter objects span both the Hosts And Clusters view and the VMs And Templates view.

The naming strategy you provide for the objects in vCenter Server should complement existing datacenter design and management. For example, if you have qualified IT staff at each of your three datacenters across the country, you would most likely create a hierarchical inventory that mirrors that management style. If your IT management was set by the various departments in your company, the datacenter objects might be named after each respective department. In most enterprise environments, the vCenter Server inventory will be a hybrid that involves management by geography, department, server type, and even project title.

The vCenter Server inventory can be structured as needed to support a company's IT management needs. Folders can be created above and below the datacenter object to provide higher or more granular levels of control that can propagate to lower-level child objects. In Chapter 8, we'll discuss the details of vCenter Server permissions and how you can use them in a vCenter Server hierarchy. Figure 3.20 shows a Hosts And Clusters view of a vCenter Server inventory that is based on a geographical management style.

FIGURE 3.20

Users can create folders above the datacenter object to grant permission at a level that can propagate to multiple datacenter objects or to create folders beneath a datacenter to manage the objects within the datacenter object.

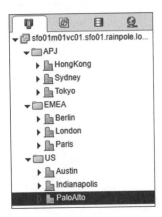

If a company uses more of a departmental approach to IT resource management, the vCenter Server inventory can be shifted to match that management style. Figure 3.21 reflects a Hosts And Clusters inventory view based on a departmental management style.

FIGURE 3.21

A departmental vCenter
Server inventory
allows the IT adminis-
trator to implement
controls within each
organizational
department.

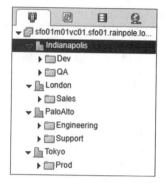

In most enterprise environments, the vCenter Server inventory will be a hybrid of the
different topologies. Perhaps one topology might be a geographical top level, followed by
departmental management, followed by project-based resource configuration.

Folders can be used to organize all different object types within vCenter Server. Figure 3.22
shows how you can create folders designated for the various objects, such as hosts and clusters
or VMs and templates.

FIGURE 3.22

Create folders to
organize objects and
delegate permissions
within the vCenter
Web Client.

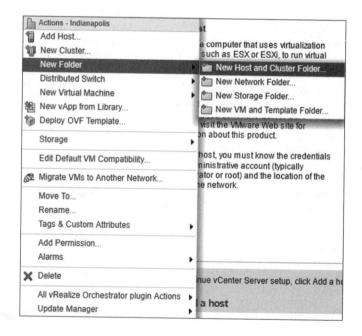

These inventory views are mostly separate and independent, although as we pointed out
earlier, they do share datacenter objects. For example, the Hosts And Clusters view may reflect a
physical or geographical focus, whereas the VMs And Templates view may reflect a departmental or functional focus. Because permissions are granted based on these structures, organizations
can build inventory structures that properly support their administrative structures. Chapter 8
will describe the security model of vCenter Server that will work hand in hand with the manage-
ment-driven inventory design.

With that basic understanding of vCenter Server inventory views and the hierarchy of inventory objects behind you, it's time for you to build your inventory structure and start creating and adding objects in vCenter Server.

Creating and Adding Inventory Objects

Before you can build your inventory—in either Hosts And Clusters view or VMs And Templates view—you must get your ESXi hosts into vCenter Server. And before you can get your ESXi hosts into vCenter Server, you need to have a datacenter object.

CREATING A DATACENTER OBJECT

You might have created the datacenter object as part of the Getting Started Wizard, but if you didn't, you must create one now. Don't forget that you can have multiple datacenter objects within a single vCenter Server instance.

Perform the following steps to create a datacenter object:

1. Launch the vSphere Web Client, if it is not already running, and connect to a vCenter Server instance.

2. On the home screen, select Hosts And Clusters.

3. In the navigator, right-click the vCenter Server object and select New Datacenter.

4. Type a name for the new datacenter object and click OK.

MAKE SURE NAME RESOLUTION IS WORKING

Name resolution—the ability for one computer to match the hostname of another computer to its IP address—is a key component for a number of ESXi functions. We've witnessed many problems resolved by making sure name resolution was working properly.

We strongly recommend that you ensure name resolution is working in a variety of directions. You'll want to do the following:

◆ Ensure that the vCenter Server computer can resolve the hostnames of every ESXi host added to the inventory.

◆ Ensure that every ESXi host can resolve the hostname of the vCenter Server computer by which it is managed.

◆ Ensure that every ESXi host can resolve the hostnames of the other ESXi hosts in the inventory, especially if those hosts might be combined into a vSphere HA cluster.

We also recommend that you enable reverse lookup functionality for your name resolution too—that is, the ability to turn an IP address back into a hostname. This helps especially when dealing with SSL certificates. For the most scalable and reliable solution, ensure that your Domain Name System (DNS) infrastructure is robust and functional, and make sure the vCenter Server computer and all ESXi hosts are configured to use DNS for name resolution. You'll save yourself a lot of trouble later by investing a bit of effort in this area now.

Once you create at least one datacenter object, you're ready to add your ESXi hosts to the vCenter Server inventory, as described in the next section.

ADDING ESXI HOSTS

In order for vCenter Server to manage an ESXi host, you must first add the ESXi host to vCenter Server. The process of adding an ESXi host to vCenter Server automatically installs a vCenter agent on the ESXi host through which vCenter Server communicates and manages the host.

Note that vCenter Server 6.7 supports adding and managing only ESXi 6.x hosts to the inventory; vCenter Server 6.7 no longer supports managing ESXi 5.x hosts. We'll only describe adding ESXi 6.7 hosts to vCenter Server, but the process is nearly identical for other versions.

Perform the following steps to add an ESXi host to vCenter Server:

1. Launch the vSphere Web Client, if it is not already running, and connect to a vCenter Server instance.

2. From the navigator, select vCenter Hosts And Clusters, or simply click the Hosts And Clusters icon on the home screen.

3. In the navigator, right-click the datacenter object and select Add Host.

4. In the Add Host Wizard, supply the IP address or fully qualified hostname and user account information for the host being added to vCenter Server. This will typically be the root account.

   Although you supply the root password when adding the host to the vCenter Server inventory, vCenter Server uses the root credentials only long enough to establish a different set of credentials for its own use moving forward. This means that you can change the root password without worrying about breaking the communication and authentication between vCenter Server and your ESXi hosts. In fact, regularly changing the root password is considered a security best practice.

5. When you're prompted to decide whether to trust the host, and an SHA1 fingerprint is displayed, click Yes.

   Strictly speaking, security best practices dictate that you should verify the SHA1 fingerprint before accepting it as valid. ESXi provides the SHA1 fingerprint in the View Support Information screen at the console.

6. The next screen displays a summary of the ESXi host being added, along with information on any VMs currently hosted on that server. Click Next.

7. On the next screen, you need to assign a license to the host being added (see Figure 3.23). The option to add the host in evaluation mode is also available.

   Choose evaluation mode, or assign a license; then click Next.

8. The next screen offers the option to enable lockdown mode. There are two lockdown mode options. Normal lockdown mode ensures that the management of the host occurs via vCenter Server, not through the vSphere Client connected directly to the ESXi host. Strict lockdown mode takes normal mode one step further and disables the Direct Console User Interface (DCUI). For now, leave this disabled and click Next.

FIGURE 3.23

Licenses can be assigned to an ESXi host as they are added to vCenter Server or at a later time.

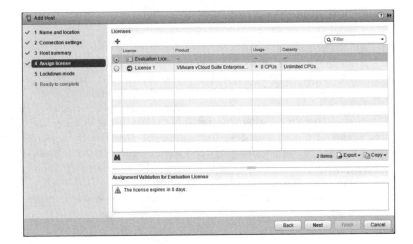

9. On the VM location screen, you will be asked where you want to move any existing VMs running on this host. If you have folders set up within the VMs And Templates view, these folders will be displayed under the datacenter object here. For now, simply select the datacenter you already have created and click Next.

10. Review your host details and click Finish at the summary screen.

11. Repeat this process for all the ESXi hosts you want to manage using this instance of vCenter Server.

Now compare the tabs in the content area in the middle of the vSphere Web Client for the vCenter Server, datacenter, and host objects. You can see that the tabs presented to you look the same, but if you select them, their subsections change depending on the object selected in the inventory tree. This is yet another example of how vCenter Server's user interface is context sensitive and changes the options available to the user depending on what is selected.

You can add hosts to vCenter Server and manage them as separate, individual entities, but you might prefer to group these hosts together into a cluster, another key object in the vCenter Server inventory. We'll describe clusters in the next section.

CREATING A CLUSTER

We've made a few references to clusters here and there, and now it's time to take a closer look at them. Clusters are not just administrative groupings of ESXi hosts but a way to pool resources. After you group hosts into a cluster, you can enable some of vSphere's most useful features. vSphere High Availability (HA), vSphere Distributed Resource Scheduler (DRS), and vSphere Fault Tolerance (FT) all work only with clusters. We'll describe these features in later chapters; Chapter 7 discusses vSphere HA and vSphere FT, and Chapter 12 discusses vSphere DRS.

Perform the following steps to create a cluster:

1. Launch the vSphere Web Client, if it is not already running, and connect to a vCenter Server instance.

2. Right-click a datacenter object in the Hosts And Clusters view.

3. Select New Cluster to open the New Cluster Wizard.

4. Supply a name for the cluster.

Don't select Turn ON vSphere DRS, Turn ON vSphere HA, or Turn ON Virtual SAN. We'll explore those options later in the book (Chapter 12, Chapter 7, and Chapter 6, respectively).

Also, leave EVC set to Disable (the default), and click OK.

When the cluster is created, adding hosts to it is a matter of simply dragging the ESXi host object onto the cluster object within the navigator; vCenter Server will add the host to the cluster There are other avenues—using the right-click menu or scripting—but dragging host objects is the simplest, provided you don't have a large number of hosts to add. You may be prompted about resource pools; refer to Chapter 11 for more information on what resource pools are and how they work.

Adding ESXi hosts to vCenter Server enables you to manage them with vCenter Server. You' explore some of vCenter Server's management features in the next section.

Exploring vCenter Server's Management Features

After your ESXi hosts are managed by vCenter Server, you can take advantage of some of vCenter Server's management features:

◆ Basic host management tasks in Hosts And Clusters view

◆ Basic host configuration

◆ Scheduled tasks

◆ Events

◆ Host profiles

◆ Tags

In the next few sections, you'll examine each of these areas in a bit more detail.

Understanding Basic Host Management

A great deal of the day-to-day management tasks for ESXi hosts in vCenter Server occur in the Hosts And Clusters view. From this area, the context (right-click) menu for an ESXi host shows some of the options available. This menu has changed from the previous versions of the vSphere Web Client; it is now more closely aligned to the menus that exist within the deprecated vSphere Desktop Client and Host Client, as shown in Figure 3.24.

The majority of these options are described in later chapters. Chapter 9 describes creating VMs, and Chapter 11 discusses resource pools. Chapter 8 covers permissions, and Chapter 13 discusses alarms and reports. The remaining actions—shutting down, rebooting, powering on, standing by, disconnecting, and removing from vCenter Server—are self-explanatory.

Additional commands may appear on this context menu as extensions or are installed into vCenter Server depending on the ESXi host's configuration. For example, after you install vSphere Update Manager, several new commands appear on the context menu for an ESXi host. ESXi hosts in a cluster enabled for vSphere HA would have additional options. You'll learn more about vSphere HA in Chapter 7.

FIGURE 3.24
The right-click menu in the vSphere Web Client is now very similar to the vSphere Desktop Client.

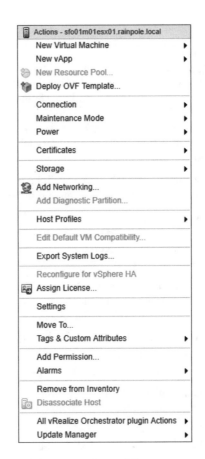

In addition to the context menu, the tabs across the middle content area of the vSphere Web Client also provide some host-management features. Figure 3.25 shows some of the tabs.

FIGURE 3.25
When a host is selected in the inventory view, the tabs across the top also provide host-management features.

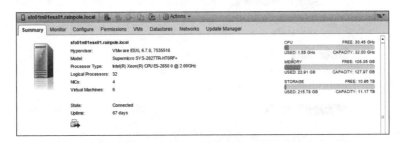

Within each of these tabs are subsections that further divide the settings into appropriate areas. For the most part, these tabs correspond closely to the commands on the context menu.

Here are the tabs and subsections that are displayed when a host is selected in the inventory view, along with a brief description of what each does:

Summary The Summary tab gathers and displays information about the underlying physical hardware, the storage devices that are configured and accessible, the networks that are configured and accessible, and the status of certain features such as vMotion, vSphere FT, and Host Profiles. The content within this tab is somewhat configurable. You can drag the different boxes around, change their size, and expand categories to reveal more information. There are no subsections of the Summary tab, but it does provide links to commonly per-formed host- management tasks.

Monitor The Monitor tab displays all the monitoring information available about the selected host and breaks it down into a number of subsections.

Issues The Issues subsection lists any current configuration problems with the selected host; this could be any number of things, from a cluster configuration to a network issue. The triggered alarms area relates to alarms on this host that have not been acknowledged or reset.

Performance The Performance subsection displays performance information for the host, such as overall CPU utilization, memory utilization, disk I/O, and network throughput. We'll discuss this area in more detail in Chapter 13.

Tasks All tasks related to the selected host are displayed here. The Tasks subsection shows all tasks, the target object, which account initiated the task, which vCenter Server was involved, and the result of the task.

Events Similar to the Tasks subsection, the Events subsection lists all events related to the selected host, such as a triggered alarm. If a host is using almost its entire RAM or if a host's CPU utilization is very high, you may see some triggered alarms.

Scheduled Tasks The scheduled tasks subsection lists any pending tasks that you may have scheduled, while also letting you set up a scheduled job of creating a new virtual machine.

Hardware Status The Hardware Status subsection displays sensor information on hardware components such as fans, CPU temperature, power supplies, network interface cards (NICs) and NIC firmware, and more.

Configure The Configure tab is where you will make configuration changes to the host. Tasks such as configuring storage, configuring the network, changing security settings, configuring hardware, and so forth are all performed here.

Permissions The Permissions tab displays all of the permissions that may have been established above the ESXi host—at the cluster, datacenter, or vCenter level—and allows you to add permissions directly on the ESXi host. Keep in mind that any permissions added to th ESXi from vCenter Server do not propagate to the ESXi host's local permissions store.

VMs The VMs tab displays all of the virtual machines and templates that currently reside on the ESXi host, giving you quick insight into the specifications of the virtual machines such as their power state, their resource allocation, and their vSphere HA status. You can add additional columns that can provide more details across the VMs and templates.

Datastores The Datastores tab displays all the mounted datastores available on the selected host and information about each, such as the type—NFS, VMFS 5, VMFS 6, Virtual SAN (vSAN), or Virtual Volume (VVOL)—overall capacity, free space, and whether or not the datastore is in a datastore cluster. As with other sections, you can add columns that provide more details across the different datastores.

Networks The Networks tab displays all the networking information available about the selected host and breaks it down into two subsections: Networks and Distributed Switches. The Networks subsection lists all of the port groups associated with the selected host, displaying information such as the port group types, how many virtual machines reside on which port group, and how many hosts have access to the port group. The other subsection, Distributed Switches, gives you a cursory look at any Distributed Virtual Switches that are associated with the selected host; this will give you information such as the DVS's version, the version of Net IO Control, and what vCenter Server owns the DVS.

Update Manager The Update Manager tab, often referred to as the Update Manager Compliance view, is where you will coordinate updates and patches to the selected host, which includes managing the baselines, managing the compliance against said baselines along with staging patches, and scheduling remediation operations. We'll discuss this area in more detail in Chapter 4.

Before showing you some of vCenter Server's other management features, we want to walk you through the Manage tab in detail. This is where you'll perform almost all of the ESXi host-configuration tasks and where you're likely to spend a fair amount of time, at least in the beginning.

Examining Basic Host Configuration

You've already seen the Configuration tab of an ESXi host, when in Chapter 2 you learned how to configure Network Time Protocol (NTP) time synchronization. We'll spend a bit more time on it; however, in the Web Client, the System subsection is under the Configure tab, along with others. You'll be visiting this area quite often throughout this book. In Chapter 5, you'll use the Configure tab for networking configuration, and in Chapter 6, you'll use the Configure tab for storage configuration.

CONFIGURE TAB

Figure 3.26 shows the commands available on the Configure tab for an ESXi host that has just been added to vCenter Server.

FIGURE 3.26

The Configure tab of an ESXi host offers a number of commands to view or modify the host's configuration.

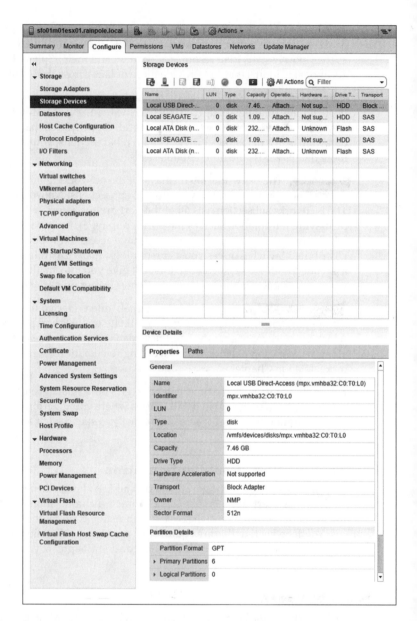

There are a lot of options here, so let's quickly run through them and provide a brief explanation of each. Let's start by going from top to bottom.

Storage Subsection   The following areas are available in the Storage subsection of the Configure tab:

Storage Adapters   This area provides information on the various storage adapters installed in the ESXi host as well as information on storage resources connected to those adapters.

Storage Devices   The Storage Devices area shows storage LUN and device mapping along with their relative paths to the host. Devices in here generally have a datastore on top of them that can be viewed in the Storage view. This is more of a logical view of storage, whereas the Storage Adapters area described earlier is more physical in nature.

Host Cache Configuration   The Host Cache Configuration area displays how the host's Flash-based datastores are configured. You are able to see what space is reserved for Host Cache and how much space is available on a per-host level.

Protocol Endpoints   The Protocol Endpoints area directly relates to the endpoints that this host can see with the Virtual Volume (VVOL) storage configuration. VVOLs are explained in detail in Chapter 6.

I/O Filters   The I/O Filters area directly relates to the storage filters that this host has been configured with. By default, you should see spm and vmwarevmcrypt, which are for VMware's default Storage Policies and VM Encryption, respectively. We'll talk more about VM Encryption in Chapter 8, and talk about Storage Policies and I/O Filters are explained in detail in Chapter 6.

Networking Subsection   The following areas are available in the Networking subsection of the Configure tab:

Virtual Switches   In Chapter 5, we'll explore the functionality found in this area. You'll configure network connectivity to both standard and distributed virtual switches here and in the Network view.

Virtual Adapters   The Virtual Adapters area is where you can configure different VMkernel network interfaces to the ESXi host to use for Management, vMotion, and Fault Tolerance, for example.

Physical Adapters   The Network Adapters area provides read-only information on the network adapters that are installed in the selected ESXi host. It also allows you to add networking to the ESXi host along with changing the network speed of any network adapter. We'll talk more about the Physical Adapters section in Chapter 5.

TCP/IP Configuration   In this area, you can view and change the DNS and routing configuration for the selected ESXi host.

Advanced   In this area, you can view advanced options such as IPv6 configuration.

Virtual Machines Subsection   The following areas are available in the Virtual Machines subsection of the Configure tab:

VM Startup/Shutdown   If you want VMs to start up or shut down automatically with the ESXi host, you configure those settings in this area. You can also define the startup order of VMs that are set to power on with the host.

Agent VM Settings   Agent VMs add specific supporting functionality to the virtual environment. Although they are VMs, they are considered part of the infrastructure and should be started before all others. For example, NSX Edge Gateway uses agent VMs to help supply its functionality.

Swap File Location   This area is where you'll configure the location of the swap files fo running VMs on the host. By default, the swap file is stored in the same directory as the VM itself. When an ESXi host is in a cluster, the cluster setting overrides the per-host configuration.

Default VM Compatibility   When a VM is created, it is created with a specific VM hardware version. Each VM hardware version has a certain level of features available to based on the version of the vSphere host, and with each new revision of vSphere, new V hardware versions are introduced and new features are added. This may cause backward compatibility issues when you want to migrate VMs with newer VM hardware versions from a newer environment to an older one. You'll learn more about VM compatibility in Chapter 9; for now, just know that this is the area where you can set the default level wh a VM is created.

System Subsection   The following areas are available in the System subsection of the Configure tab:

Licensing   This area allows you to view the currently licensed features as well as assigr or change the license for the selected ESXi host.

Time Configuration   From here, you can configure time synchronization via NTP for th selected ESXi host. You saw this area within the vSphere Client in Chapter 2.

Authentication Services   This area allows you to configure how ESXi hosts authenticate users; we'll discuss it in more detail in Chapter 8.

Certificate   SSL certificates are managed by the PSC but can be updated on a per-host basis from this area. More details about the PSC Certificate Authority can be found in Chapter 8.

Power Management   If you want to use Distributed Power Management (DPM), you'll need to configure the ESXi hosts appropriately. This area is where that configura- tion occurs.

Advanced System Settings   The Advanced System Settings area provides direct access detailed configuration settings on the selected ESXi host. In the majority of instances, this is not an area you'll visit on a regular basis, but it is helpful to know where it is in the event you need to change a setting.

System Resource Allocation   The System Resource Allocation area allows you to fine-tune the resource allocation for the selected ESXi host.

Security Profile   This area allows you to configure which daemons (services) should ru on the host.

System Swap   In this area, you can disable or specify which datastore should be used fc host swap files. We'll explain host swapping and how it differs from VM swapping in Chapter 11.

Host Profile   Although there is a Host Profiles area accessible from the home screen, thi area lets you attach a host profile as well. See the section "Working with Host Profiles," later in this chapter.

Hardware and Virtual Flash Subsections   The following areas are available in the Hardware and Virtual Flash subsections of the Configure tab:

Processors   In this area, vCenter Server provides details about the processors in the selected ESXi host as well as the ability to enable or disable hyperthreading on that ESXi host.

Memory   This area shows you the amount of memory installed in an ESXi. It only provides information about the memory in the host, how much is allocated to the system (ESXi), and how much is allocated to VMs—there are no options to configure.

Graphics   Within the Graphics area, you can see what type of GPU is in the system and how much memory it has. In Chapter 9, you'll read about use cases for sharing the GPU of an ESXi host to the guest VMs in certain circumstances.

PCI Devices   The PCI Devices area allows you to mark available devices on the ESXi host that can then be allocated to one of the virtual machines in the host's inventory. This allows for the virtual machines to directly access the physical device on the host.

Power Management   The Power Management area in the Hardware subsection differs from the area under the System subsection above it. This area allows you to set various power-management policies on the selected ESXi host.

Virtual Flash Resource Management   Solid State Drive (SSD)–backed datastores can be allocated to the flash resource type in this area. You can then further allocate this resource in the Cache Configuration described next.

Virtual Flash Host Swap Cache Configuration   This area allows you to specify or view the amount of space on Solid State Drive (SSD)–backed datastores (or flash) that can be used for swapping. Swapping to SSD as opposed to traditional disks is much faster, and this area allows you to control which SSD-backed datastores may be used for swapping.

As you can see, vCenter Server provides all the tools that most administrators will need to manage ESXi hosts. Although these host-management tools are visible in the Hosts And Clusters view, several of vCenter Server's other management features are found in the multiple views.

Using Scheduled Tasks

Earlier in this chapter, you learned how the vSphere Web Client often displayed the UI depending on the context of the item selected. Scheduled Tasks is a feature that's available from many areas, including vCenter.

From the Navigator, select Manage Scheduled Tasks to display the Scheduled Tasks area of vCenter Server.

Here, you can create jobs to run based on a defined logic. You can schedule the following list of tasks:

◆   Change the power state of a VM.

◆   Clone a VM.

◆   Deploy a VM from a template.

◆   Move a VM with vMotion.

◆ Move a VM's virtual disks with Storage vMotion.

◆ Create a VM.

◆ Make a snapshot of a VM.

◆ Add a host.

◆ Change the power settings for a cluster.

◆ Change resource settings for a resource pool or VM.

◆ Check compliance for a profile.

As you can see, vCenter Server supports quite a list of tasks you can schedule to run automatically. Because the information required for each scheduled task varies, the wizards are different for each of the tasks. Let's take a look at one task that you might find quite useful to schedule: adding a host.

Why might you want to schedule a task to add a host? Perhaps you know that you'll be adding a host to vCenter Server but you want to add it after hours. You can schedule a task to add the host to vCenter Server at a later time, although keep in mind that the host must be reachable and responding when the task is created.

Follow these steps to create a scheduled task to add a host to vCenter Server:

1. Launch the vSphere Web Client, if it is not already running, and connect to a vCenter Server instance.

2. After you connect to vCenter Server, navigate to the Scheduled Tasks area of the Hosts And Clusters view by selecting a cluster and then choosing Manage Scheduled Tasks. Th example will also work by selecting a datacenter instead of a cluster.

3. Select Schedule A New Task from within the content area.

4. From the list of tasks to schedule, select Add Host.

   The Add Host Wizard starts.

5. Supply the hostname, username, and password to connect to the host, just as if you were adding the host manually.

6. When prompted to accept the host's SHA1 fingerprint, click Yes.

7. The next four steps in the wizard are the same as adding the host manually. Click Next after each step until you come to the point of scheduling the task.

8. Supply a task name and task description, and click the Change button. The Configure Scheduler pop-up is fairly self-explanatory, but you can run the task now, after startup, o at a later time of your choosing. There's also an option for setting a recurring schedule, b for adding a host, the recurring option doesn't make sense. Click OK once your schedule is configured.

9. Specify that you want to receive email notification of the scheduled task when it completes by supplying an email address. Note that vCenter Server must be configured with the name of an SMTP server it can use.

Scheduling the addition of an ESXi host is of fairly limited value. However, the ability to schedule tasks such as powering off a group of VMs, moving their virtual disks to a new datastore, and then powering them back on again is quite useful.

Using the Events and Events Consoles in vCenter Server

The consoles for Tasks and Events in vCenter Server bring together all the events and tasks that have been logged by vCenter Server. Figure 3.27 shows the Events console with an event selected.

FIGURE 3.27
The Events console lets you view event details, search events, and export events (highlighted).

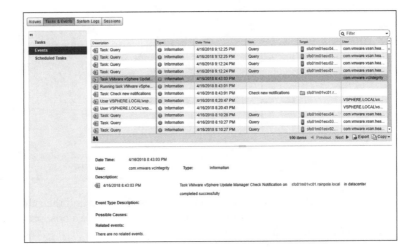

You can view the details of an event by simply clicking it in the list. Any text highlighted in blue is a link; clicking that text will take you to that object in vCenter Server. You can search through the events using the search box in the upper-right corner of the vSphere Web Client content window. Right below the event list is a button that you can click to export the events to a text file. Figure 3.28 shows the dialog box for exporting events.

Working with Host Profiles

Host profiles are a powerful feature of vCenter Server. As you'll see in upcoming chapters, a bit of configuration is involved in setting up an ESXi host. Although vCenter Server and the vSphere Web Client make it easy to perform these configuration tasks, it's easy to overlook something. Additionally, making all these changes manually for multiple hosts can be time consuming and even more error prone. That's where host profiles can help.

A host profile is essentially a collection of all the various configuration settings for an ESXi host. This includes settings such as NIC assignments, virtual switches, storage configuration, date and time, and more. By attaching a host profile to an ESXi host, you can compare the compliance of that host with the settings outlined in the host profile. If the host is compliant, you know its settings are the same as the settings in the host profile. If the host is not compliant, you can enforce the settings in the host profile to make it compliant. This provides you with a way not only to verify consistent settings across ESXi hosts but also to quickly and easily apply settings to new ESXi hosts.

FIGURE 3.28
Users have a number of
options when
exporting events out
of vCenter Server to
a CSV file.

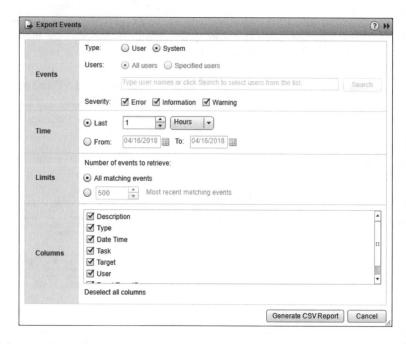

FIGURE 3.28
Users have a number of
options when
exporting events out
of vCenter Server to
a CSV file.

To work with host profiles, click the Home button and then click Host Profiles. Figure 3.29 shows the Host Profiles view in vCenter Server, where a host profile has been created but not yet attached to any hosts.

FIGURE 3.29
Host profiles provide a
mechanism for
checking and
enforcing compliance
with a specific
configuration.

As you can see in Figure 3.29, the toolbar contains a number of buttons. These buttons allow you to perform the following tasks:

♦ Extract a profile from a host.

♦ Import a host profile.

♦ Duplicate a host profile.

♦ Copy settings from a host.

♦ Check the host profile compliance.

♦ Attach/detach host profiles from hosts or clusters.

♦ Remediate a host based on its host profile.

To create a new profile, you must either create one from an existing host or import a profile that was already created somewhere else. Creating a new profile from an existing host requires only that you select the reference host for the new profile. vCenter Server will then compile the host profile based on that host's configuration.

After you create a profile, you can edit the profile to fine-tune the settings contained in it. For example, you might need to change the IP addresses of the DNS servers found in the profile because they've changed since the profile was created.

Follow these steps to edit the DNS server settings in a host profile:

1. If the vSphere Web Client isn't already running, launch it and connect to a vCenter Server instance.

2. On the home screen, select Host Profiles.

3. Right-click the host profile to be edited, and select Edit Settings.

4. Click Next to move past the Name And Description page onto Edit Host Profile.

5. From the tree menu on the left side of the Edit Host Profile window, navigate to Networking Configuration ➤ Netstack Instance ➤ defaultTcpipStack ➤ DNS Configuration.

   Figure 3.30 shows this area.

FIGURE 3.30

To make changes to a number of ESXi hosts at the same time, put the settings into a host profile, and attach the profile to the hosts.

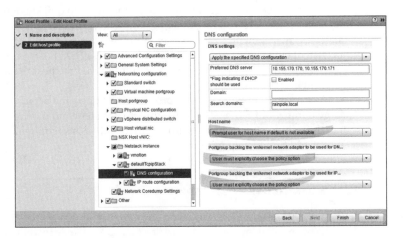

6. Change the values shown in the host profile.

7. Click Next and then click Finish to save the changes to the host profile.

Although this procedure describes only how to change DNS settings, the steps for changing other settings within a host profile are similar. This allows you to quickly create a host profile based on a reference host and then customize the host profile until it represents the correct "golden configuration" for your hosts.

Host profiles don't do anything until they are attached to ESXi hosts. Click the Attach/Detach A Host Profile To Hosts And Clusters button just below the Objects tab in the vSphere Web Client to open a dialog box that allows you to select one or more ESXi hosts to which the host profile should be attached.

After a host profile has been attached to an ESXi host, checking for compliance is as easy as right-clicking that host on the Hosts And Clusters tab and selecting Host Profile Check Compliance from the context menu.

If an ESXi host is found noncompliant with the settings in a host profile, you can then place the host in Maintenance mode and apply the host profile. When you apply the host profile, the settings found in the host profile are enforced on that ESXi host to bring it into compliance. No that some settings require a reboot to take effect.

To truly understand the power of host profiles, consider a group of ESXi hosts in a cluster. V haven't discussed clusters yet, but as you'll see elsewhere in the book—especially in Chapter 5 and Chapter 6—ESXi hosts in a cluster need to have consistent settings. Without a host profile, you would have to manually review and configure these settings on each host in the cluster. W a host profile that captures the settings, adding a new host to the cluster is a simple two-step process:

1. Add the host to vCenter Server and to the cluster.

2. Attach the host profile and apply it.

That's it. The host profile will enforce all the settings on this new host that are required to bring it into compliance with the settings on the rest of the servers in the cluster. This approach a great timesaver for larger organizations that need to quickly deploy new ESXi hosts.

Host profiles are also hugely important when you're using vSphere Auto Deploy to create a stateless environment. In stateless environments using Auto Deploy, configuration settings are persistent between reboots. To keep your stateless ESXi hosts properly configured, you'll want use host profiles to apply the proper settings so that the host retains a consistent configuration over time, even when it's rebooted.

As explained previously, host profiles start to become beneficial when your environment ha large number of ESXi hosts to keep things consistent and manageable. However, host profiles a not the only feature included with vSphere that assists with management; tags are a relatively recent addition to help with these tasks.

WHEN TO USE HOST PROFILES

While helping a business resolve a Host Profiles adoption issue, moving them away from exhaustively maintaining their configuration runbooks, the discussion of host uniformity within their clusters became one of the biggest deciding factors. Over time, their initial compute clusters had grown with the demands of their customers—existing clusters were expanded, new clusters were created, and new hardware was sequestered. Though Enhanced vMotion Compatibility (EVC) proved to be extremely handy when scaling out a cluster to handle the increasing load, this put the administrators into quite a pickle—while they were able to bring in newer hosts over time as demand grew, this resulted in a mixture of different underlying host hardware, and maintaining configuration runbooks was becoming quite expensive and slowing down their overall adoption of new technologies. As previously discussed, when a profile is extracted from a host, it captures a *highly* detailed snapshot of the host's configuration, which includes everything from the physical NIC ordering and daemon enablement down to the specific queue depth of the host's storage adapter. You can probably connect the dots on how each cluster behaved when the customer started applying the profiles to the non-uniform hosts!

The customer was faced with a few tough decisions—short term, medium term, and long term—in order to move the project forward. Short term, the administrators were going to work towards disabling a few sections of host profiles that were found to result in the most noncompliance in the cluster in order to perform the initial bootstrapping of the hosts and keep a minimized runbook for configuration verification—not the grandest of solutions, but one where they could start bringing in some automated configuration management into their environment. In the medium term, the administrators were going to begin auditing each of their clusters to find matching hardware across each, and during their monthly scheduled maintenance windows, begin shifting around each of their clusters in order to match up identical hosts, bringing each cluster slowly but surely to a uniform state (where possible). Finally, long term, with a better understanding of host profiles, the administrators aimed at better organizing their clusters and working closer with their hardware vendors to ensure that new, bulk hardware purchases would yield identical hosts.

Tags and Custom Attributes

Nearly every item within a vCenter inventory can have a label and metadata added to it by way of tags or custom attributes. Tags let you group related items together using categories, and they help sort and manage your vCenter objects. Tags can be both exclusive and inclusive, which gives you great flexibility when you design your metadata structure. They also can extend outside the confines of a single vCenter Server; if multiple vCenter Servers are configured in enhanced linked mode the tags and categories you create will be accessible and searchable across all of their inventories. We'll explain how this might be useful with an example. Say that you want to know which VMs belong to the engineering team, as well as which VMs are production, test, or development. In the section "Understanding Inventory Views and Objects," earlier in this chapter, you saw how to use folders to organize objects for management and security. The problem with folders is that a VM can reside in only one folder, and a folder can only exist within a single vCenter Server; taking this example, you cannot put a VM in both the Engineering folder and the Production folder. With tags, this problem is solved. Although you can specify that only a single tag can be applied to a certain object at any one time, you can also specify multiple tags against a single object.

Using tags to build metadata around your ESXi hosts, VMs, and other objects is quite powerful, and the integration with the vSphere Web Client's search functionality makes large inventories much more manageable. As your environment grows, and your engineering team begins deploying more virtual machines across multiple vCenter Servers, object tracking can quickly become a tedious task. With the potential of VMs, Templates, hosts of varying hardware, and a myriad of other items spread across multiple clusters and multiple vCenter Servers, leveraging the shared tags and categories quickly enables you to search out logical relationships, allowing you to quantify and locate specific objects.

Custom Attributes provide a similar role within your vCenter inventory.

We'll now show you how to create some tags and how they can be used. Each tag must belo to a category (and only a single category), and because of this requirement, you must create a category before or at the same time you create any tags. Here are the steps:

1. If the vSphere Web Client isn't already running, launch it and connect to a vCenter Server instance.

2. From the home screen within the navigator, select Tags & Custom Attributes.

3. From the Tags tab, click the New Tag icon to open the New Tag dialog box.

4. Enter the name of the tag and a description.

5. Change the category to New Category, and the window will expand to show more fields

6. Give the Category a name and a description.

7. Decide whether this category should allow a single tag or multiple tags per object, and then select what object type(s) are associated with this category, as shown in Figure 3.31.

FIGURE 3.31
You are able to create both tags and tag categories in the New Tag dialog box.

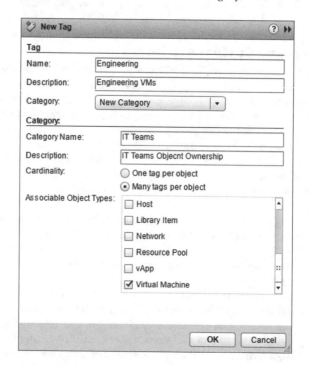

8. Click OK to save the new tag and category.

Tags let you define custom identification or information options for nearly every object type within vCenter, including the following:

◆ Clusters

◆ Datacenters

◆ Datastores

- Distributed switches

- Folders

- Hosts

- Networks

- Resource pools

- vApps

- Virtual machines

TAGS FLOW THROUGH INTO OTHER VMWARE PRODUCTS

Custom tags within vCenter are used not just within this one product. VMware also exposes your custom tags within its API and allows other VMware (or non-VMware) software to utilize this metadata. One such use of this data lies within vCenter Operations Manager. Although it is technically a separate product, it has deep integration with vSphere and vCenter. The tags created within the vSphere Web Client can also be used for creating monitored applications or groups of VMs within vCenter Operations Manager.

After you create this tag, you can attach the tag to an object. After the tag is added, it appears in the Tags section of the content area Summary tab. You can use the Assign Tag option in the right-click menu to add tags to various objects, as shown in Figure 3.32.

FIGURE 3.32
You can add metadata to objects by creating and assigning tags.

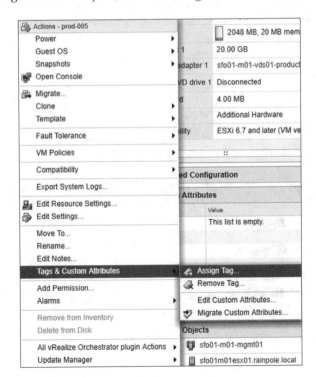

With the tags clearly defined for various objects, you can then search based on that data. Figure 3.33 shows a custom search for all objects whose tag contains the text *Production, Engineering,* and *Windows.*

FIGURE 3.33
After you've defined a category and a tag, you can use it as search criteria for quickly finding objects with similar tags.

At this point, you have installed vCenter Server, added at least one ESXi host, and explored some of vCenter Server's features for managing settings on ESXi hosts. Now we'll cover how to manage some of the settings for vCenter Server itself.

Managing vCenter Server Settings

To make it easier for vSphere administrators to find and change the settings that affect the behavior or operation of a vCenter Server instance, VMware centralized these settings into a single area within the vSphere Web Client user interface. You'll see this Settings area on the Manage tab when you have a vCenter Server selected in the vSphere Web Client navigator. Here you can configure vCenter Server after installation with options that are not provided during installation. The Administration menu contains these items:

◆ General

◆ Licensing

◆ Message Of The Day

◆ Advanced Settings

The vCenter Server Settings area lets you change the settings that control how vCenter Server operates, as you'll see in the next section.

General vCenter Server Settings

The General vCenter Server Settings area contains 10 vCenter Server settings:

◆ Statistics

◆ Database

◆ Runtime Settings

◆ User Directory

- ◆ Mail
- ◆ SNMP Receivers
- ◆ Ports
- ◆ Timeout Settings
- ◆ Logging Settings
- ◆ SSL Settings

When you have vCenter Server instances running in a linked mode group, be sure to select the correct vCenter Server instance within the navigator.

Each of these settings controls a specific area of interaction or operation for vCenter Server, which we briefly discuss next:

Statistics On the Statistics page, shown in Figure 3.34, you can configure the collection intervals and the system resources for accumulating statistical performance data in vCenter Server. In addition, it provides a database-sizing calculator that can estimate the size of a vCenter Server database based on the configuration of statistics intervals. By default, the following four collection intervals are available.

- ◆ Past day: 5 minutes per sample at statistics level 1
- ◆ Past week: 30 minutes per sample at statistics level 1
- ◆ Past month: 2 hours per sample at statistics level 1
- ◆ Past year: 1 day per sample at statistics level 1

FIGURE 3.34
You can customize statistics collection intervals to support broad or detailed logging.

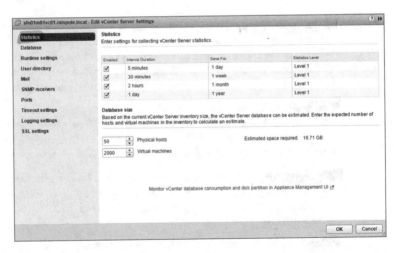

By selecting an interval and clicking the drop-down list, you can customize the interval configuration. You can set the interval, how long to keep the sample, and what statistics level (level 1 through level 4) vCenter Server will use.

Four Statistics Collection levels are defined in the user interface:

Level 1   Has the basic metrics for average usage of CPU, memory, disk, and network. It als includes data about system uptime, system heartbeat, and DRS metrics. Statistics for device are not included.

Level 2   Includes all the average, summation, and rollup metrics for CPU, memory, disk, a network. It also includes system uptime, system heartbeat, and DRS metrics. Maximum and minimum rollup types as well as statistics for devices are not included.

Level 3   Includes all metrics for all counter groups, including devices, except for minimum and maximum rollups.

Level 4   Includes all metrics that vCenter Server supports.

DATABASE ESTIMATES

By editing the statistics collection configuration, you can see the estimated database size change accordingly. For example, when you reduce the 1-day collection interval to 1 minute as opposed to 5 minutes, the database size jumps from an estimated 16.71 GB to an estimated 30.87 GB. Similarly, if the collection samples taken once per day are kept for 5 years instead of 1 year, the database size jumps from an estimated 16.71 GB to an estimated 34.78 GB. Changing all of these settings to their most aggressive values (For Example Statistics Level 4, Save For 5 years) results in an estimated size of 1.45 TB. The collection intervals and retention durations should be set to a level required by your company's audit policy.

Runtime Settings   The Runtime Settings area lets you configure the vCenter Server unique ID, the IP address used by vCenter Server, and the server name of the computer running vCenter Server. The unique ID will be populated by default, and changing it requires a resta of the vCenter Server service. These settings would normally require changing only when running multiple vCenter Server instances in the same environment.

Database   The Database page lets you configure the maximum number of connections to th backend database. To limit the growth of the vCenter Server database, you can configure a retention policy. vCenter Server offers options for limiting the length of time that both tasks and events are retained in the backend database.

User Directory   On this page you can set the user directory (usually Active Directory) time-out value, a limit for the number of users and groups returned in a query against the user directory database, and the validation period (in minutes) for synchronizing users and groups used by vCenter Server.

Mail   The Mail page might be the most commonly customized page because its configuration is crucial to the sending of alarm results, as you'll see in Chapter 13. The mail SMTP server name or IP address and the sender account will determine the server and the account from which alarm results will be sent.

SNMP Receivers   The SNMP Receivers configuration page is where you would configure vCenter Server for integration with a Systems Network Management Protocol (SNMP) management system. The receiver URL should be the name or IP address of the server with the appropriate SNMP trap receiver. The SNMP port, if not configured away from the default, should be set at 162, and the community string should be configured appropriately (Public is the default). vCenter Server supports up to four receiver URLs.

Ports The Ports page is used to configure the HTTP and HTTPS ports used by vCenter Server.

Timeout Settings This area, the Timeout Settings area, is where you configure client connection time-outs. The settings by default allow for a 30-second time-out for normal operations or 120 seconds for long operations.

Logging Settings The Logging Settings area customizes the level of detail accumulated in vCenter Server logs. The logging options include the following:

- None (Disable Logging)
- Errors (Errors Only)
- Warning (Errors And Warnings)
- Information (Normal Logging)
- Verbose (Verbose)
- Trivia (Trivia)

By default, the Windows-based vCenter Server stores its logs at `C:\ProgramData\VMware\VMware VirtualCenter\Logs` (on Windows Server 2008 R2, Windows Server 2012 and later) while the Linux-based vCenter Server virtual appliance stores its logs at `/var/log/vmware.`

SSL Settings On this page, you can configure a certificate validity check between vCenter Server and the vSphere Client. If enabled, both systems will check the trust of the SSL certificate presented by the remote host when performing tasks such as adding a host to inventory or establishing a remote console to a VM. You'll learn more about SSL certificates in Chapter 8.

Licensing

The Licensing configuration area of the vCenter Server Settings dialog box, shown in Figure 3.35, provides the parameters for how this specific vCenter Server instance is licensed. The options include using an evaluation mode or assigning a license key to this instance of vCenter Server.

FIGURE 3.35
Licensing vCenter Server is managed through the vCenter Server Settings dialog box.

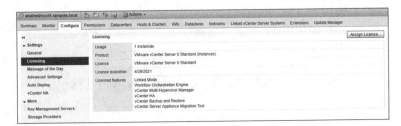

When an evaluation of vSphere and vCenter Server is no longer required and the appropriate licenses have been purchased, you must deselect the evaluation option and add a license key. Evaluation licenses are only valid for 60 days after installation.

Message of the Day

As the name suggests, you can edit the message of the day (MOTD) from this area. The MOTD displayed to users each time they log into vCenter Server. This provides an excellent means of distributing information regarding maintenance schedules or other important information.

Advanced Settings

The Advanced Settings area provides for an extensible configuration interface. These settings should be changed only under specific circumstances, usually at VMware's direction.

Auto Deploy

We'll take you through Auto Deploy as another method of rapidly deploying and configuring ESXi hosts in Chapter 4, but for now, just know that this area provides access to some of the underlying components necessary for configuring this service, including iPXE boot loader, a keystone to the image streaming process.

vCenter HA

Touched on earlier in the chapter, the vCenter HA configuration area is where you'll setup and maintain a highly available configuration of your Linux-based vCenter Server virtual appliance. In its out-of-the-box form, you'll simply see a splash page, but we'll take you through vCenter HA more in-depth in Chapter 7.

Key Management Servers

We'll touch on this more in in Chapter 8, but for now, just know that the Key Management Servers area allows you to establish a trust between the vCenter Server and the local key management server (KMS). This is a prerequisite if you ever plan on enabling encryption in your virtual infrastructure in order to provide an extra level of security within the environment.

Storage Providers

The Storage Providers area provides insight into the existing storage entities and their capabilities within your environment, including external physical storage and abstracted storage, such as VMware Virtual SAN (vSAN) or Virtual Volumes (VVols), leveraging the vSphere APIs for Storage Awareness (VASA). This can be a powerful component within your environment, allowing vCenter Server and its ESXi hosts to obtain information about your storage configuration, its status, and storage data services offered, which enables you to make more informed decisions about workload placement.

We'll talk more about Storage Providers and Storage Policy-Based Management (SPBM) in Chapter 6.

vSphere Web Client Administration

As we explained when outlining the home screen of the vSphere Web Client, there are three distinct areas: Inventories, Monitoring, and Administration. So far, we've explained a number of features of the Inventories and Monitoring areas, but let's also briefly touch on the third category of features, Administration.

There are three areas under the Administration banner: Roles, Licensing, and vCenter Solutions Manager. There is some overlap between these areas and those that come under Inventories.

Roles

The Roles option from the Administration menu is available only when the view is set to Administration and the Roles tab is selected. This menu works like a context menu where you can add, edit, rename, or remove roles based on what object is selected. Although you set up the roles and accounts within this area, you apply those roles for permissions against vCenter objects within the various inventory views. Chapter 8 describes vCenter Server's roles in detail.

Licensing

In the previous section, you saw how to go about setting a license for a specific vCenter Server through the inventories vCenter view. There are also licensing options when you select individual hosts in the Hosts And Clusters view. However, the Licensing area of the vSphere Web Client home screen gives you a broad view of all your licenses within the environment and indicates to which component those licenses are allocated.

Within Licensing, you can also report on your license usage over time and export this data. Depending on how complex your environment and license agreement is with VMware, you will seldom use this area, or only dedicated licensing staff will look at this section. Standard (Perpetual) licenses or VMware Service Provider Program (VSPP) licensing agreements are all managed through the overall licensing area.

vCenter Solutions Manager

As extensions—such as vSphere Update Manager or vSphere Auto Deploy—are added to vCenter Server, additional icons, tabs, and features may appear throughout the vSphere Web Client. The extensions themselves that enable these new features are managed through this vCenter Solutions Manager area.

Chapter 4 discusses one such extension to vCenter Server: vSphere Update Manager.

System Configuration

The System Configuration feature falls under the Administration banner on the vSphere Web Client home screen, and just like the Licensing section, this feature gives you an aerial view of all vCenter Servers and Platform Services Controller within your environment. In the earlier sections "Understanding Basic Host Management" and "Understanding Inventory Views and Objects," you learned to interact with and address the different objects' services and settings within the management domain of vCenter Server, such as ESXi hosts, clusters, or data centers; however, although we touched upon some of the Advanced Settings you can configure on vCenter, you may have noticed we are missing actual visibility into the vCenter Server's and Platform Services Controller's services, health, and domain. While there is some overlap with what is available in the VMware Appliance Management Interface (VAMI), System Configuration allows for you to see all vCenter Servers and Platform Services Controllers deployed in the same vSphere domain in one place. This area allows you to do the following:

◆ View and browse all nodes in a vSphere domain, quickly observing their aggregate health at either the Node or Services level.

◆ Monitor the networking, storage, and performance (memory and CPU usages) of each node.

◆ Manage settings such as SSH or DCUI access, change networking settings, and add Firewall rules.

◆ Check the health of individual services that belong to a specific node.

◆ Manage the startup type as well as the start, stop, and restart of individual services.

◆ Manage service-specific settings of individual services, such as Content Library, vSphere Authentication Proxy, or vSphere Update Manager.

◆ Export the logs from vCenter Server or Platform Services Controller.

When you select System Configuration from the Administration section on the home screen, you can observe the overall health for all nodes and services within your vSphere domain, as shown in Figure 3.36.

FIGURE 3.36

You can view the health of vCenter Server or Platform Services Controller easily from the System Configuration.

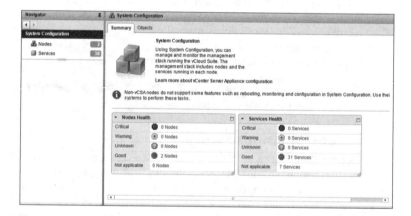

Perform the following tasks to export system logs out of vCenter Server and Platform Service Controller:

1. With the vSphere Web Client running and connected to a vCenter Server instance, on the home screen, select System Configuration.

2. In the Navigator pane, select Nodes, and let the pane load your Platform Services Controller and vCenter Server.

3. Right-click on your Platform Services Controller, and select Export Support Bundles.

4. Select the log(s) you want to export. By default, neither of the bundles is selected, so go ahead and select both. Use the drop-down menu to select a specific, desired log if needed.

5. Click the Export Support Bundle button.

6. A new browser window will appear where you can specify a local path in which to save the logs. Allow for the export to finish.

> **MORE OPTIONS FOR EXPORTING LOGS**
>
> On the File menu, you'll see an Export System Logs option. If you select the vCenter Server object and then choose this option, you'll get the same dialog box as if you'd selected Administration Export System Logs. If, however, you select an ESXi host or a VM, the dialog box changes to show you log export options that are specific to the currently selected inventory object.

In the location you selected, the Platform Services Controller will download VMware-vCenter-Support-<Date>@<Time>.zip, which contains another compressed file: <Hostname>-supportbundle<date>@<time>.tgz. If you decompress both files, you'll find the system logs for the Platform Services Controller system. Figure 3.37 shows some log files exported from the Platform Services Controller.

FIGURE 3.37
These logs are for the Platform Services Controller.

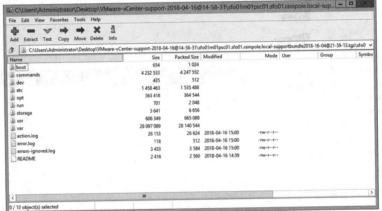

We'll continue to explore vCenter Server's functionality in the coming chapters. Chapter 4 explores the functionality added to vCenter Server by the vSphere Update Manager extension.

VMware Appliance Management Administration

If you've ever taken any of the other VMware appliance-based products for a spin, you may have had some hands-on time with the Virtual Appliance Management Interface (VAMI). The VAMI is your view into the host operating system—often referred to as the Host OS—that runs the VMware application services. In this case, the VAMI on the vCenter Server virtual appliance gives you visibility into the underpinnings of Photon OS and provides you with administrative features that don't necessarily fit into the vSphere Web Client's virtual infrastructure management-oriented user interface. Unlike the vSphere Web Client, which can only be accessed from the vCenter Server, VAMI is available for both vCenter Servers and External Platform Services Controllers, and can be accessed from https://<server.domain.com>:5480.

These underpinnings and administrative features are broken down into the following 10 area within the VAMI, as shown in Figure 3.38:

◆ Summary

◆ Monitor

◆ Access

◆ Networking

◆ Time

◆ Services

◆ Update

◆ Administration

◆ Syslog

◆ Backup

FIGURE 3.38
The VAMI, similar to Explorer and Task Manager on a Windows OS, allows for insight into the Host OS and application state of the vCenter Server or Platform Services Controller virtual appliances.

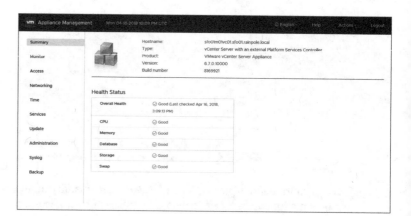

There is some overlap between these areas and those that come under the vSphere Web Client's System Configuration. Let's jump in and have a look around.

Summary

The Summary screen is the first part of the VAMI you'll see. It contains two main areas for the vCenter Server with External Platform Services Controller, and three main areas for vCenter Servers with Embedded Platform Services Controllers and External Platform Services Controllers.

For a vCenter Server with External Platform Services Controllers, the two main areas are

◆ An upper section detailing the Host OS's Hostname, Type (in Figure 3.38, 'it's *vCenter Server with an external Platform Services Controller*), the Version, and the Build Number of the system.

◆ A lower section that provides a high-level overview of the health status of the Host OS's virtual hardware, which includes CPU, Memory, Database (only available on your vCenter Server with an external or embedded Platform Services Controller), Storage, and Swap, which all bubble up into Overall Health.

For a vCenter Server with Embedded Platform Services Controllers or External Platform Services Controllers, you'll see a new section that covers the Single Sign-On Status for the node, giving you the domain name and whether the SSO-related services discussed earlier in this chapter are running. The other two sections, as shown in Figure 3.39, are nearly identical with the following exceptions in the upper section:

◆ The Node Type will reflect whether it's an External Platform Services Controller or a vCenter Server with an Embedded Platform Services Controller.

◆ The bottom health section lacks a Database monitor for External PSCs as they do not come with a database.

We'll discuss accessing more of the health monitoring details in the next couple of sections.

FIGURE 3.39
The Summary screen, along with some of the subsections, will be contextualized around what deployment architecture you chose for your vCenter Server.

Monitor

In the previous section, you were given a high-level view of the vCenter Server virtual appliance's Host OS health, but with the Monitor area, you can drill down into these individual components' health. In the middle pane, you'll see four distinct items: CPU & Memory, Disks, Network, and Database. Again, the Database monitor is only available on a vCenter Server with an external or embedded Platform Services Controller.

CPU & Memory   The CPU & Memory page allows you to report on your CPU and Memory usage over time. The drop-down menus include the following options for increasing windows of time:

◆ Last Hour

◆ Last Day

◆ Last Week

♦ Last Month

♦ Last Quarter

♦ Last Year

As with other performance charts available within the different vSphere UIs, due to the u of rollup jobs, you lose granularity with the metrics displayed as you go further back in time For example, the Last Hour option gives you extreme granularity into the CPU and memory activities of the appliance—you can look at the statistics in 5-minute increments. By contrast the Last Year option provides the least amount of granularity and can only report on the aggregated statistics of the appliance by the day.

Disks On the Disks page, you can look at the usage across all 13 disks within the appliance Hovering over the bar graphs under the Utilization column will give you more details on the Used Space and Available Space that aren't readily perceivable from the graph itself.

Network In the Network area, you can review the inbound and outbound traffic utilization on the appliance over time. In the bottom section, you can choose from a medley of options c the virtual NIC (vNIC) interfaces, which will dictate what's shown in the graph. The options include the following generalized vNIC statistics:

♦ Receive Bytes

♦ Received Packets

♦ Received Errors Detected

♦ Received Packets Dropped

♦ Transmitted Bytes

♦ Transmitted Packets

♦ Transmitted Errors Detected

♦ Transmitted Packets Dropped

As previously mentioned, the time period drop-down menu enables you to select a time increment, from last hour up to the last year, with decreased granularity as you increase your time period being monitored.

Database And finally, on the Monitor page, you are provided visibility into the capacity of the database, split into two graphs:

♦ One graph depicts the SEAT (Stats, Events, Alarms, and Tasks) data generated from activities from your virtual infrastructure, which is often referred to as historical data.

♦ One graph depicts the overall space of the database, with individual lines for SEAT, Database Logging. and Core statistics.

As with the CPU & Memory and Network areas, these statistics are graphed over time, and you have the ability to use the drop-down menu to select a time interval between the last hou up to the last year, with decreased granularity as you increase your time period.

Access

In the unlikely event that you need to log into the Appliance—either to view something or when working with your support group to perform troubleshooting—the Access area allows you to manipulate the different methods to logging in. This includes enabling or disabling SSH, the Direct Console User Interface (DCUI), the Console CLI, and Bash Shell.

We'll discuss these different access methods in more detail in Chapter 4.

Networking

On this page, you can set and view the DNS server settings (usually defined during install), the virtual NIC settings (such as MAC address, IP address, subnet mast, default gateway, and whether the NIC is enabled), and Proxy settings used by vCenter Server.

Time

The Time area, as the name implies, allows you to manipulate the time configuration of the appliance. The top section in this area allows you to change the Time Zone on the appliance from its default Coordinated Universal Time (UTC), though we recommend against changing this unless your company policy requires you to do so. The bottom section allows you to update the Time settings, including setting the appliance's time mode to either use NTP or rely on the underlying host's time, as well as managing the Time Servers. The current Time Server will be identical to what was used during the appliance's deployment (covered earlier in this chapter).

Services

The services area is your one-stop shop for reviewing service health as well as which services are started or stopped within your appliances, with the caveat that the service has been integrated with VMware Service Lifecycle Manager—referred to as vMon. vMon serves as the watchdog engine for both the vCenter Server and Platform Services Controller, and monitors the services under its domain. If the service is found to be in a defunct state, vMon will attempt to cycle the service and bring it back into a health state. The Services section plugs directly into vMon, and therefore gives you visibility into the state of these services. What this means is that while all of the vCenter Server's services have been integrated, and thus you can monitor and cycle them within the VAMI, some of the services from the Platform Services Controller—such as the VMware Identity Management Service, Security Token Service, and VMware Directory Service—are not integrated and must be cycled from command line.

You'll notice that most of the services have been configured with the Startup Type of automatic, while some have been set to Manual or Disabled. This indicates the behavior of the services under the domain of vMon:

Automatic   This enables the service to start up on successful boot of the OS, following vMon's instantiation. If the service has been configured with a startup dependency—such as the vCenter Server Service (VPXD) starting after vPostgres or the vSphere Update Manager service (VUM) starting after VPXD—this will be orchestrated by vMon.

Manual   This marks the service as eligible for manual startup from the UI or CLI, but it does not start after boot of the OS and vMon.

Disabled   This marks the service as ineligible for manual startup from the UI and CLI, or after the bootup of the OS or vMon.

vPostgres → VPXD → VUM

It's best not to toggle any of these settings unless explicitly told to do so by product documentation or support as incorrectly modifying one of the services in a chain of dependencies could result in multiple services not starting—often referred to as a catastrophic event. If a service is configured for Disabled or Manual, all dependent items will not automatically start. Oftentimes the services marked as Manual or Disabled are auxiliary to the core management components of vCenter Server—such as Image Builder or vCenter High Availability—which will be toggled on and off when enabled elsewhere, such as in the vSphere Web Client.

Update

As patches and updates are released for vCenter Server, and, due to their conjoined nature, the Platform Services Controller, the Update page is the area in which you'll stage and install the bundles into the appliance. You are providing two means of updating your appliances:

♦ Manually downloading the upgrade ISO from MyVMware's Product Patches microsite and mounting them to the individual appliances as a virtual CD-ROM.

♦ Via a repository that's hosted either by VMware or your own internal web server. By default, the Upgrade framework is set to query the VMware's public repository.

In environments where vCenter Server does not have direct access to the Internet, you'll need to configure the system to either use a proxy or set up an Internet web server to host the upgrade bundles. In an environment where bandwidth is limited, such as a remote or branch office, downloading the upgrade ISO manually and attaching it to each of the components may prove to be the most reliable form of transport.

Administration

The Administration area allows you to change the password for your Root account on the appliance, or any other local account that may have been created. It also lets you set the password requirements for the local account as well as an expiry period.

Remember, the VAMI, like the HTML5 Host Client, does not hook into SSO, so the password policies configured within the vSphere Web Client do not propagate to the VAMI or to the local accounts.

Syslog

Having visibility into the state of your environment both immediately and over time is key, but it just may not be possible based on the number of vCenter Servers and Platform Services Controllers that have been deployed. Further, if you are in an industry where auditing is required for compliance purposes, streaming logs from your environment is key. In the Syslog area, you have the ability to configure log streaming to a remote syslog server to preserve logs as well as vCenter Server events that the environment has generated. While this feature was available in previous versions, with vSphere 6.7, you can now configure up to three forwarders to remote syslog servers. This may prove to be extremely useful if you have discreet syslog servers in your environment that provide different functions, such as a long-term auditing archive for auditors, a security response system monitoring for questionable activity, or a site reliability system keeping a watchful eye on service health. As with the previous version of vSphere, you can configure the log-forwarding protocol using UDP, TCP, TLS (encrypted over TCP), or RELP—depending on what your syslog server can support.

Chapter 8 discusses the use of Syslog in more depth and under the context of Security.

Backup

As touched upon in the "Planning for vCenter Server Availability" section, having solid backups for your vCenter Server and Platform Services Controllers is key to an enterprise ready environment. In the Backup area, you can configure the vCenter Server or Platform Services Controller to create file-based backups to an external location, using FTP, FTPS, HTTP, HTTPS, or SCP. While this functionality is not new in vSphere 6.7, the ability to schedule is! Gone are the days of using customized scripts to manually run a backup of the vCenter Server or PSC., You can now pick the schedule and retention of file-based backups of your systems.

Chapter 7 discusses how to configure and use the file-based backup functionality to preserve your environment in the event of a corruption or disaster.

The Bottom Line

Understand the components and role of vCenter Server.   vCenter Server plays a central role in the management of ESXi hosts and VMs. Key features such as vMotion, Storage vMotion, vSphere DRS, vSphere HA, and vSphere FT are all enabled and made possible by vCenter Server. vCenter Server provides scalable authentication and role-based administration based on integration with Active Directory.

> **Master It**   Specifically with regard to authentication, what are three key advantages of using vCenter Server?

Plan a vCenter Server deployment.   Planning a vCenter Server deployment includes selecting a backend database engine, choosing an authentication method, sizing the hardware appropriately, and providing a sufficient level of high availability and business continuity. You must also decide whether you will run vCenter Server as a VM or on a physical system. Finally, you must decide whether you will use the Windows Server–based version of vCenter Server or deploy the vCenter Server virtual appliance.

> **Master It**   What are some of the advantages and disadvantages of running vCenter Server as a VM?

> **Master It**   What are some of the advantages of using the vCenter Server virtual appliance?

Install and configure a vCenter Server database.   vCenter Server supports several enterprise-grade database engines, including Oracle and Microsoft SQL Server. Depending on the database in use, there are specific configuration steps and specific permissions that must be applied in order for vCenter Server to work properly.

> **Master It**   Why is it important to protect the database engine used to support vCenter Server?

Install and configure the Platform Services Controller.   The Platform Services Controller is an architectural change in vCenter Server 6. Along with SSO, it allows the vSphere Client to present multiple solutions interfaces within a single console provided the authenticated user has access.

> **Master It**   After installing vCenter 6.7 and all the appropriate components, you cannot log into the vCenter Server Web Client with your local credentials and gain access to vCenter. What could be missing from the configuration of SSO?

Install and configure vCenter Server. vCenter Server is installed using the VMware vCen Server Appliance Installer. You can install vCenter Server as a stand-alone instance or join a linked mode group for greater scalability.

> **Master It** When preparing to install multiple vCenter Servers, are there any concerns about using a single Platform Services Controller versus multiple? Can this be handled later?

Use vCenter Server's management features. vCenter Server provides a wide range of management features for ESXi hosts and VMs. These features include scheduled tasks, host profiles for consistent configurations, tags for metadata, and event logging.

> **Master It** Your department just merged vSphere environments with another departme and your manager has asked for you to find a way of easily tracking both departments' virtual machines. How would you go about accomplishing that task?

Provide Visibility into vCenter Server's settings. vCenter Server's Appliance Managemer Interface provides insight into its health, configuration, and settings.

> **Master It** Your manager has asked you why the vCenter Server recently came back on audit report saying that SSH is enabled. What section in vCenter Server's VAMI will hel; you in this task?

> **Master It** You recently added a few more Active Directory domain controllers within your environment after a recent refresh and configured them to replace your older time server. How can you update the NTP servers on your vCenter Servers and Platform Services Controllers?

Chapter 4

vSphere Update Manager and the vCenter Support Tools

Software and firmware updates are a fact of life in today's IT departments. Most organizations recognize that software updates are necessary to correct problems or flaws, to address security-related vulnerabilities, and to add new features. Fortunately, VMware offers a tool to help centralize, automate, and manage these patches for vSphere. This tool is called vSphere Update Manager (VUM). The remainder of the vCenter Support Tools assist in centrally deploying and managing hosts.

IN THIS CHAPTER, YOU WILL LEARN TO

- ◆ Review the vSphere Update Manager plug-in within the vSphere Web Client
- ◆ Determine which ESXi hosts or VMs need to be patched or upgraded
- ◆ Use VUM to upgrade VM hardware or VMware Tools
- ◆ Apply patches to ESXi hosts
- ◆ Upgrade hosts and coordinate large-scale datacenter upgrades
- ◆ Use alternative approaches to VUM updates when required
- ◆ Start and configure vSphere Auto Deploy and vSphere ESXi Image Builder services
- ◆ Import and create a software depot
- ◆ Create an image profile and map it to a vSphere Auto Deploy deployment rule
- ◆ Configure vSphere ESXi Dump Collector
- ◆ Configure hosts for centralized logging

vSphere Update Manager

VUM is a tool designed to help VMware administrators automate and streamline the process of applying updates—patches or upgrades—to their vSphere environment. VUM is fully integrated with vCenter Server and offers the ability to scan and remediate ESXi hosts, host extensions (such as EMC's PowerPath/VE Multipathing software), older ESXi hosts (6.0 and 6.5), and some virtual appliances. Further, with VUM, administrators can upgrade VMware Tools and virtual machine (VM) hardware.

VUM integrates tightly with vSphere's inherent cluster features. It can use the Distributed Resource Scheduler (DRS) for nondisruptive updating of ESXi hosts by moving its VMs between hosts in the cluster and avoiding downtime. It can coordinate with the cluster's Distributed Power Management (DPM), High Availability (HA), and Fault Tolerance (FT) settings to ensure that they don't prevent VUM from updating at any stage. Introduced in vSphere 5, the cluster can even calculate if it can remediate multiple hosts at once while still appeasing its cluster constraints, thus speeding up the overall patching process.

VUM's Host-Patching Capabilities in vSphere 6.7

As covered in previous chapters, vSphere 6.7 has only the ESXi variant of the hypervisor, with vCenter being able to manage only hosts that are running vSphere 6.0 and later. With no direct upgrade path of vSphere 5.x to vSphere 6.7, VUM 6.0 and 6.5 can migrate ESXi 5.x hosts across to the respective ESXi 6.x version. In these cases, a fresh install is required, so you'll need to consider how you want to migrate their settings. If you are licensed for vSphere at the Enterprise Plus level, you could use the Host Profiles feature discussed in Chapter 3 to help in the migration of existing settings. At the time of writing ESXi 5.x is approaching being unsupported by VMware; therefore these older hosts should be upgraded as soon as possible.

VUM and the vSphere Web Clients

As vSphere has matured, the Web Client has become the primary user and administrator client. However, as discussed in Chapter 3, with both the older Windows-only C#-based vSphere Desktop Client and Flash-based vSphere Web Client being deprecated—the former no longer shipping with vSphere at all—all new features are being moved to the vSphere HMTL5 Client to make it a true successor. Again, this chapter will primarily focus on the vSphere Web Client to avoid swapping between clients.

Since the release of vSphere 5.5 (and Update 1 to 5.1), VUM includes a small Web Client plug-in that enables rudimentary capabilities. It allows you to attach baselines to objects and to initiate scans, and it displays compliance levels. The Web Client can't administer VUM, configure or make changes to it, or remediate objects—for that, you have to go back to the VUM Client. But the Web Client is useful. It's far more visible to the average user. How compliant the object is with your baseline is now front and center on the summary page. Users now realize how up-to-date their VMs are and can see the hosts on which their VMs run.

The Web Client's VUM abilities are limited, and the vSphere Desktop Client can do it all, but we'll use the Web Client to demonstrate anything that can be done in both tools. The workflow for these tasks is similar, so it should be straightforward to follow along in either. In general, because you'll spend most of your time in the Web Client, it seems appropriate to favor that tool where possible.

In the vSphere Web Client, VUM uses two views: the administrative view, where you can configure VUM settings and manage baselines, and a compliance view, where you can scan and remediate vSphere objects. When you're applying updates to VMs, VUM can apply snapshots to them to enable a simple rollback in the event of problems. It can identify when hardware upgrades and VMware Tools are needed and combine them into a single, actionable task.

To help keep your vSphere environment patched and up-to-date, VUM uses your company's Internet connection to download information about available updates, the products to which those updates apply, and the actual updates themselves. Based on rules and policies the VMware administrator defines and applies using the vSphere Web Client, VUM will then apply updates to hosts and VMs. You can schedule update installations and even apply automated updates to VMs that are powered off or suspended.

UPGRADING, PATCHING, AND UPDATING WITHOUT FRUSTRATION

Commonly used terms sometimes lead to confusion. *Upgrading* refers to the process of bringing the object to a new version, which often includes new features and capabilities. For example, for hosts, this can mean moving from 5.0 to 6.0 or, when the next minor version is available, from 6.5 to 6.7. VM hardware, virtual appliances, and host extensions all tend to be associated with upgrades because they are usually rip-and-replace-type software changes.

The term *patching* is reserved for applying remedial software changes to individual host components. This will change the host's build number but not its version number. Often these are rolled up into host *updates*, so expect ESXi 6.7 to receive 6.7 Update 1 before you see another 6.x or even 7.x version change. However, and certainly somewhat confusingly, the term *updates* is often used to explain the generic process of both patching and upgrading. So applying updates might include host patches (some of which might be rolled into a host update) and various upgrades.

Regardless of the terminology used, it is useful to think about updating in terms of how routine it is—in fact, this is the way this chapter splits it up. Routine updates would include applying host patches and updates and upgrading a VM's VMware Tools. These are the sort of remediation tasks you could expect to perform on, say, a monthly basis because many guest operating system (OS) patches are, and should be, more trivial to test and apply. Non-routine updates are the upgrades to hosts and VM hardware. These updates will often change the functionality of the object, so they need to be tested in your environment to make sure they are fully compatible and to determine how best to take advantage of the new capabilities that the upgrades are likely to bring.

The one gray area is upgrading host extensions and virtual appliances, because they need to be evaluated on a case-by-case basis. Some of their upgrades will be simple improvements; others can bring significant changes to the way they work. Some of their upgrades will be highly coupled to the versioning of ESXi, down to the Update being used; others will simply cover the entire version of vSphere. You need to evaluate each extension and appliance upgrade and decide for yourself how much testing is required before you deploy it.

Putting VUM to work in your vSphere deployment involves installing and configuring VUM, setting up baselines, scanning hosts and VMs, and applying patches.

vSphere Update Manager and the vCenter Server Appliance

In previous editions of vSphere, the end-to-end installation of vSphere Update Manager used either a Windows-based vCenter Server or on a standalone Microsoft Windows Server. This included setting up the VUM database, creating an Open Database Connectivity (ODBC) data source name (DSN) and, finally, installing the vSphere Update Manager application. VMware is transitioning vCenter to use the vCenter Server Appliance, without Windows. While Windows still an option, as we covered in Chapter 3, again, we will focus on vSphere Update Manager an how it now functions with the vCenter Server Appliance. Though some of these topics will overlap with the Windows-based version, we will primarily focus on vSphere Update Manager and how it currently functions with the vCenter Server Appliance.

VUM now comes pre-installed with the vCenter Server appliance, and once your appliance has been fully deployed and configured, the service will automatically start like any other services on the system. Due to this paradigm shift, VUM inherited some key architecture chang that are worthy of mention:

Watchdog Monitoring The VUM service is now under the watchful eye of the VMware Lifecycle Manager (vMON), discussed in Chapter 3. In the event that the VUM service falls into a defunct state, vMON will intervene and restart the service as a corrective action.

Simplified Database The database is co-located with the vCenter Server service's database in the appliance's Postgres database, although they reside in separate instances. This remove the need for an administrator to maintain VUM's ODBC DSN and database.

Certificates Administrators no longer need to worry about procuring a certificate for VUM because it now shares vCenter Server's certificate. When you cycle the certificates on vCente Server, VUM will inherit these changes.

Lifecycle The lifecycle management of the service is now coupled with vCenter Server. When you apply a patch or perform an upgrade of your vCenter Server appliance, this will automatically upgrade VUM.

VUM has a one-to-one relationship with vCenter. That is, for every vCenter instance, you wi have a separate VUM instance, and each VUM can provide update services to only one vCenter The one exception to this is that you can share the job of downloading patches among multiple VUMs (and therefore multiple vCenters) with an ancillary component known as the Update Manager Download Service (UMDS), which is discussed in the section "Installing the Update Manager Download Service (Optional)."

If you have multiple vCenters connected via linked mode, you can use VUM, but a separate instance is still required for each vCenter. All the installation, configuration, permissions, updat scanning, and remediation are done on a per-VUM basis, because each vCenter operates independently.

As discussed briefly at the beginning of the chapter, there are two deployment options for vCenter: the conventional Windows installation and the newer Linux-based prebuilt vCenter

Server Appliance (vCSA). As of vSphere 6.5, VUM has been ported into the vCSA with all the functionality available from its Windows-based counterpart. However, similar to the shift that was made in using an embedded-only database on the appliance, VUM can now only be run embedded. Alternately, when you're running a Windows-based vCenter Server, you can easily connect VUM to it, either by installing it on the same server instance as vCenter, or by using a separate Windows install—both deployment models provide the same functionality.

CONFIGURING PROXY SETTINGS DURING INSTALLATION

If you forget to select the box to configure proxy settings during installation, fear not! All is not lost. After you install VUM, you can use the vSphere Desktop Client to set the proxy settings accordingly. Just be aware that VUM's first attempt to download patch information will fail because it can't access the Internet.

Installing the Update Manager Download Service (Optional)

An optional step in the deployment of VUM is to install the Update Manager Download Service (UMDS). UMDS provides a centralized download repository. Installing UMDS is especially useful in two situations. First, UMDS is beneficial when you have multiple VUM servers. Using UMDS prevents you from consuming more bandwidth than necessary, because the updates need to be downloaded only once. Instead of each VUM server downloading a full copy, multiple VUM servers can leverage the centralized UMDS repository.

UMDS is also beneficial in environments where the VUM servers do not have direct Internet access. Internet access is required to download the updates and update metadata, so you can use UMDS to download and distribute the information to the individual VUM servers.

To install UMDS on a server, select Download Service from the vCenter media installation media. Like Windows-based VUM, UMDS can only be installed on 64-bit servers. After stepping through the UMDS installation process (which is almost identical to the VUM installation process), you can start using it.

UMDS is a command-line tool. By default, the UMDS tool is installed in either `C:\Program Files (x86)\VMware\Infrastructure\Update Manager` for Windows installations or `/usr/local/vmware-umds/bin/` for Linux installations.

You can configure many options in UMDS, but to start using it, you need to configure the following three settings.

1. Specify the updates to download using the **-S** switch.

2. Download the updates with the **-D** switch.

3. Export the updates and metadata with the **-E** switch.

To view the full details of all the command's switch options from the built-in help, run **vmware-umds -h**. Figure 4.1 shows the UMDS utility being run from the command prompt. Along with the basic switches, the full help file provides all the arguments as well as a series of examples of common usage tasks.

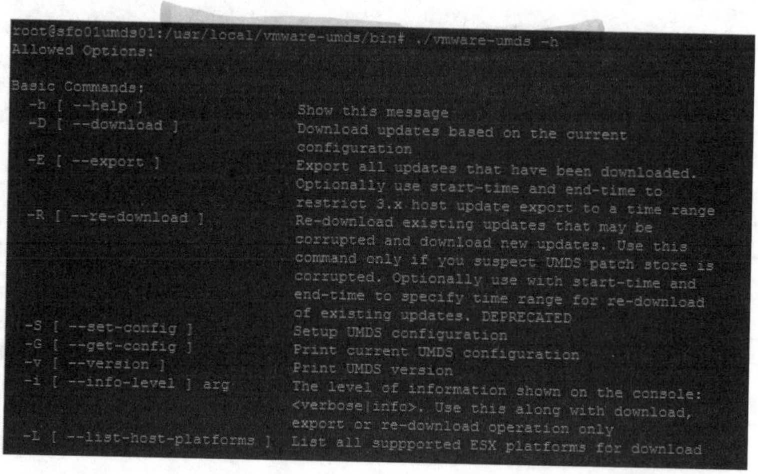

FIGURE 4.1

You must configure the UMDS utility at the command prompt.

There are two different designs for using UMDS:

♦ The VUM server does not have network connectivity to the UMDS server. In this case, need to move the downloaded patches and metadata to a removable media drive and physically transfer the data via old-fashioned "sneakernet."

♦ The VUM server can connect to the UMDS server. Although the VUM server may not b allowed to connect directly to the Internet, if it can hit the UMDS, then it can effectively use it as a web proxy. You need to configure a web server, such as IIS or Apache, on the UMDS server. Then the VUM server can connect to the UMDS server and download its patches. This is also typically the approach you would take if you wanted to use UMDS a centralized download server for several VUM instances.

At this point, VUM is installed, but you have no way to manage it. In order to manage VUM you must install the vSphere Desktop Client and the VUM plug-in for vCenter Server, as we discuss in the next section.

The vSphere Update Manager Plug-in

The tools to manage and configure VUM are implemented as a vCenter Server plug-in and are completely integrated into vCenter Server and the vSphere Clients. By default, no configuratio is needed to enable the VUM plug-in for the vSphere Web Client or the vSphere HTML5 Client Furthermore, with the release of vSphere 6.7, both the vSphere HTML5 Client and the older Flex-based vSphere Web Client have near-feature parity with regard to VUM; however, for the sake of consistency, we suggest you use the vSphere Web Client for VUM activities. Don't worr that you are missing out on the latest and greatest features by using the older Flash-based client—the workflows performed in this chapter are nearly identical between the two clients.

To access these tools, you just need to log into one of the clients and have the proper permis-sions within vCenter Server—it's as easy as that. With the server-side plug-in architecture of th Flex- and HTML5-based clients, once VUM is registered with vCenter Server—or any solution for that matter—the plug-ins will then be accessible to everyone. This enables the vSphere Web Clients to manage and configure VUM by adding an Update Manager tab (or just Update in the HTML5 Client) and some extra context-menu commands to objects within the client.

Perform the following steps to review the state of the VUM plug-in for the vSphere Web Client:

1. Launch the vSphere Web Client, if it is not already running, and connect to a vCenter Server instance.

2. Navigate to the Client Plug-Ins by using the Navigator pane ➤ Administration ➤ Client Plug-Ins.

3. From the Client Plug-Ins area, find the vSphere Update Manager extension, as shown in Figure 4.2.

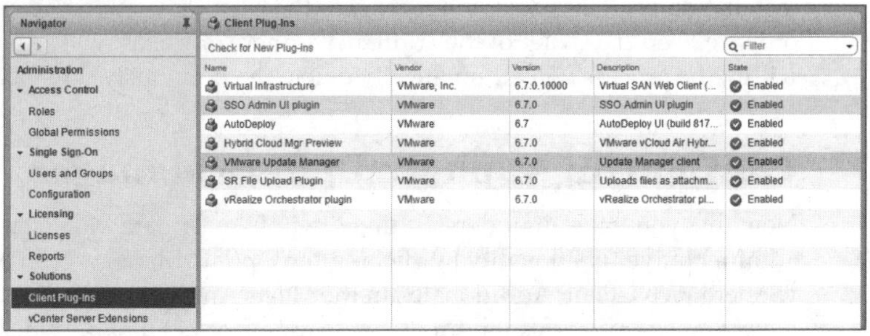

FIGURE 4.2
From the Client Plug-ins area, you can see all available plug-ins, scan for new plug-ins, and disable plug-ins on the vSphere Web Client.

Reconfiguring the VUM or UMDS Installation with the Update Manager Utility

Once the vCenter Server appliance has been deployed and vSphere Update Manager has been instantiated, as part of VUM's integration you have access to a small utility within the Appliance shell: `updatemgr-util`. In previous versions of vSphere, this utility allowed you to change some of the fundamental installation settings without needing to reinstall either VUM. With the current vSphere version's porting of the utility into the PI shell, you have access to this same functionality.

This utility allows you to change the following settings are as follows:

◆ Proxy settings

◆ Database username and password

◆ vCenter Server IP address

◆ SSL certificate (provides a set of instructions to follow)

Perform the following steps to run the Update Manager Utility:

1. SSH to the vCenter Server appliance and log in.

2. From the default Appliance shell, execute the following command in order to see all of the settings at your disposal:

```
com.vmware.updatemgr-util -h
```

3. The utility will present you with three options: re-registering the VUM instance with vCenter, resetting the database, and modifying the configuration of VUM.

As for UMDS, unfortunately the available configuration tools are a bit more complicated, an it's spread across multiple utilities if you chose to go with the Linux route, including `vmware-vciInstallUtils` for database maintenance and directly modifying `downloadConfig.xml` for proxy settings. If you go the Windows Server route to run UMDS, you still have access to the `VMwareUpdateManagerUtility.exe` located in `C:\Program Files (x86)\VMware\Infrastructure\Update Manager`.

Upgrading VUM from a Previous Version

As mentioned previously, with VUM now ported into the vCenter Server Appliance, upgrading from earlier versions of VUM is greatly simplified. When the vCenter Server upgrade starts the installation of VUM 6.7, it will recognize the existing version and automatically upgrade it. In order to keep the sizing of the appliance under control as well as potentially save some bandwidth, the process will automatically delete the previously downloaded patches and start afresh.

Configuring vSphere Update Manager

Now that you have an understanding of vSphere Update Manager, you can access all of its administrative functionality by clicking the Update Manager icon on the Home screen within th vSphere Web Client. Additionally, in the Hosts And Clusters or VMs And Templates inventory view, you'll see a corresponding Update Manager tab that provides you access to the operational-side of Upgrade Manager—allowing you to scan for patches, create and attach baselines, stage patches to hosts, and remediate hosts and guests.

Clicking the Update Manager icon at the vSphere Web Client home page takes you to the main VUM administration screen. Figure 4.3 shows that this area is divided into two main sections: Monitor and Manage. These two sections are further divided: under the Monitor tab, you can see Events and Notifications; under the Manage tab, you can see Settings, Hosts Baselines, VMs Baselines, Patch Repository, and ESXi Images. Initially, as in many other areas o the vSphere Web Client, you will also see a leading Getting Started tab.

FIGURE 4.3
The Update Manager Administration tabs in the vSphere Web Client

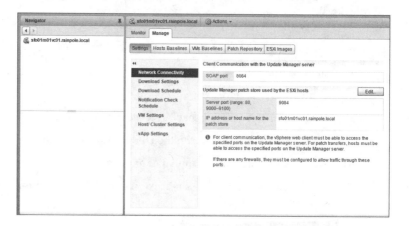

Under the Monitor tab, there are two buttons that provide visibility into the activities of VUM, letting you keep track of what operations are being performed at any one time. Here's a quick look at both areas:

Events The Events tab lists the VUM-specific events logged. As shown in Figure 4.4, the Events tab lists actions taken by administrators as well as automatic actions taken by VUM. Administrators can sort the list of events by clicking the column headers, as well as use the filter to sort specific events they want to see. As we discussed in Chapter 3, you can also export events from here instead of having to go to vCenter's holistic Events area and sort through activities.

FIGURE 4.4
The Events tab lists events logged by VUM during operation and can be a good source of information for troubleshooting.

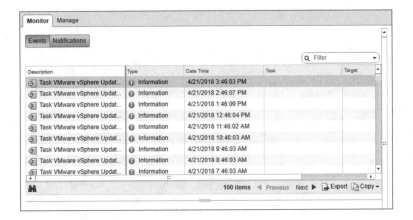

Notifications This tab displays any notifications gathered by VUM regarding patch recalls, patch fixes, and other alerts issued by VMware.

For example, if VMware recalled a patch, VUM would mark the patch as recalled. This prevents you from installing the recalled patch. A notification that the patch was recalled would be displayed in the Notifications area. Similarly, if a patch is fixed, VUM would update the new patch and include a notification that the patch has been updated.

Under the Manage tab are five sections that represent the major areas of configuration for VUM. Here's a closer look at each of the Manage sections:

Settings The bulk of the configuration of VUM is performed in the Settings section. From here, administrators can configure the full range of VUM settings, including network connectivity, download settings, download schedule, notification check schedule, VM settings, ESXi host settings, and vApp settings. Here are some of the various options that you can configure:

Network Connectivity Under Network Connectivity, you can change the ports on which VUM communicates. In general, there is no need to change these ports, and you should leave them at the defaults.

Download Settings In the Download Settings area, you can specify the types of patches that VUM will download and store. You can also add custom URLs to download third-party patches by adding sources, as shown in Figure 4.5.

FIGURE 4.5

Select patch sources so
that VUM downloads
only certain types
of patches.

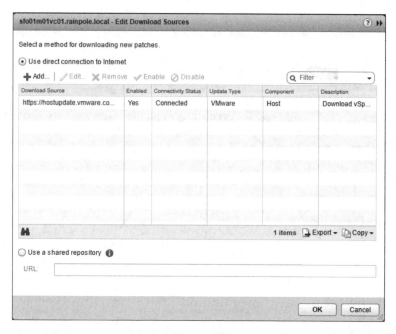

This is also the area in the settings where you can point to a web server configured on a UMDS instance if you are centralizing your downloads. You set VUM to use a download server by choosing the Use A Shared Repository radio button. You can also import offline patch bundles, distributed as zip files, to add collections of VMware or third-party patch and updates.

The Download Settings area is also where you would set the proxy configuration, if a proxy server is present on your network. VUM needs access to the Internet in order to download the patches and patch metadata, so if a proxy server controls Internet access, you must configure the proxy settings here in order for VUM to work.

Download Schedule   The Download Schedule area allows you to control the timing an frequency of patch downloads. Click the Edit Download Schedule link in the upper-right corner of this area to open the Schedule Update Download Wizard, where you can specif the schedule for patch downloads as well as configure email notifications.

EMAIL NOTIFICATIONS REQUIRE SMTP SERVER CONFIGURATION

To receive any email notifications that you might configure in the Schedule Update Download Wizard, you must also configure the SMTP server in the vCenter Server settings, accessible from the Administration menu of either the vSphere Web or the HTML5-base vSphere Client.

Notification Check Schedule   In this area, you configure the schedule to check for VUM notifications about patch recalls, patch fixes, and other alerts. As in the Download Schedule area, you can click the Edit Notifications link in the upper-right corner of the window to edit the schedule that VUM uses to check for notifications.

VM Settings   Under VM Settings, vSphere administrators configure whether to use VM snapshots when applying upgrades to VMs, as shown in Figure 4.6. As you'll see in Chapter 7, "Ensuring High Availability and Business Continuity," you can use snapshots to capture a VM's state at a given point and then roll back to that captured state if so desired. Having this ability to use a snapshot to undo the installation of a driver from a VMware Tools upgrade can be incredibly valuable. However, be careful not to keep the snapshot for an unnecessary length of time, because it can affect the VM's performance and, more important, cause storage issues—it can grow and fill your datastore unexpectedly.

FIGURE 4.6
By default, VM snapshots are enabled for use with VUM.

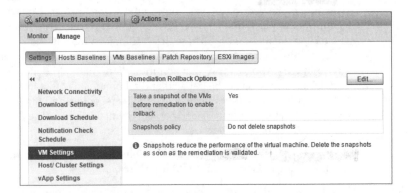

Host/Cluster Settings   The Host/Cluster Settings area provides controls for fine-tuning how VUM handles Maintenance mode operations. Before an ESXi host is patched or upgraded, it is first placed into Maintenance mode. When the ESXi host is part of a cluster that has VMware Distributed Resource Scheduler (DRS) enabled, this will also trigger automatic vMotions of VMs to other hosts in the cluster. These settings allow you to control what happens if a host fails to go into Maintenance mode and how many times VUM retries the Maintenance mode operation. The default settings specify that VUM will retry three times to place a host in Maintenance mode.

You can configure whether VUM will disable certain cluster features in order to perform remediation. Otherwise, VUM may not perform updates on the hosts with these features enabled. The features that VUM can control are Distributed Power Management (DPM), High Availability Admission Control, and Fault Tolerance (FT). You can opt to let the cluster determine if more than one host can be updated simultaneously while safely maintaining compliance with the rest of the cluster settings. If so, then multiple hosts can be patched or upgraded at once.

Last, you can select whether to patch any PXE-booted ESXi hosts.

PATCHING STATELESS PXE-BOOTED SERVERS

When you patch a PXE-booted server, those changes won't survive the host's next reboot, because the host will revert to the network image. You should apply these patches to the image itself for them to remain persistent.

So why apply patches to the hosts?

VUM can live install most patches, which do not require a host reboot. This means that you can quickly apply a patch to a fleet of PXE-booted ESXi hosts without needing to reboot them, or without needing to update and test the images, in order to pick up an important patch. If you do this, make sure you go back and patch your image to ensure patch consistency for when your ESXi hosts *do* need rebooting.

vApp Settings The vApp Settings allow you to control whether VUM's Smart Reboot feature is enabled for vApps. You can think of vApps as teams of VMs. Consider a multitier application that consists of a front-end web server, a middleware server, and a backend database server. These three different VMs and their respective guest OSs could be combined into a vApp. The Smart Reboot feature simply restarts the different VMs within the vApp in a way that accommodates inter-VM dependencies. For example, if the database server has to be patched and rebooted, it is quite likely that the web server and the middleware server will also need to be rebooted, and they shouldn't be restarted until after the database server is back up and available again. The default setting is to leverage Smart Reboot.

Hosts Baselines and VMs Baselines Baselines are a key part of how VUM works. To keep ESXi hosts and VMs updated, VUM uses *baselines*.

VUM uses several different types of baselines. First, baselines are divided into host baselines which are designed to update ESXi hosts, and VM baselines, which are designed to update VMs. These are split out into two separate subtabs for easy identification.

IMPORTANCE OF BASELINES

As vSphere becomes more central to an organization's infrastructure, baselines become increasingly important. Host baselines provide a stable platform for ever intertwined components. Many datacenter tools take advantage of vSphere APIs, such as the storage arrays via vSphere APIs for Array Integration (VAAI) and backup tools via vSphere APIs for Data Protection (VADP), and interact with vCenter and the hosts in a significant way. Keeping all hosts at the same build level is crucial to maintaining a reliable environment. Additionally, keeping your VMs at a standardized hardware level with the same VMware Tools guest drivers minimizes the variances that can create support issues and troubleshooting headaches.

Hosts Baselines are further subdivided into Patch Baselines, Host Extension Baselines, Upgrade Baselines, and System Managed Baseline. Patch Baselines define lists of patches to applied to an ESXi host. Extension Baselines define the extensions—any additional software packages that can run on an ESXi host—to be applied to an ESXi host. Upgrade Baselines define how to upgrade an ESXi host. System-managed Baselines are a unique construct with VUM in that they are dictated by a solution, such as VSAN or NSX, and can be a combination of defined patches, extensions (for example, drivers) or even imaged-based upgrades to be applied to an ESXi host. Some items to note about these different baselines: while the Patch

Baseline and Extension Baseline can have many items mapped to a single baseline, the Upgrade Baseline is a one-to-one mapping of the baseline to the fixed ESXi image; while you can associate a Patch, Extension, or Upgrade baseline to any of the clusters you choose, the System Managed baselines will only be associated with the hosts or clusters which have the managing solution enabled on them.

Finally, Patch baselines are divided again into dynamic baselines and fixed baselines. Dynamic baselines can change over time—for example, all security host patches since a certain date; while fixed baselines remain constant—for example, a specific host patch that you want to ensure is applied to your hosts.

VMs Baselines are subdivided into VM Hardware upgrade baselines and VMware Tools upgrade baselines. VM Hardware upgrade baselines define how to upgrade the associated VMs to the latest version of VM hardware supported by the underlying host that they reside on. VMware Tools upgrade baselines define how to upgrade the associated VMs to the latest version of VMware Tools supported by the underlying host. Unlike the Hosts Baselines, where you can create your own custom baselines, all of the available baselines for VMs are predefined and dynamic.

HOW TO DETERMINE WHETHER TO USE A FIXED OR DYNAMIC

Fixed baselines are best used to apply a specific fix to a group of hosts. For example, let's say that VMware released a specific fix for ESXi and you wanted to be sure that it was installed on all your hosts. By creating a fixed baseline that included just that patch and attaching that baseline to your hosts, you could ensure that your hosts had that specific fix installed. Another use for fixed baselines is to establish the approved set of patches that you have tested and are now ready to deploy to the environment as a whole.

Dynamic baselines, on the other hand, are best used to keep systems current with the latest sets of patches. Because these baselines evolve over time, attaching them to your hosts can help you understand just how current your systems are (or aren't!).

Patch Repository The Patch Repository tab shows all the patches that are currently in VUM's patch repository. From here, you can also view the details of any specific patch by right-clicking the patch and selecting Show Patch Detail or by double-clicking a patch. Figure 4.7 shows the additional information displayed about a patch when you select Show Patch Detail from the context menu (right-click).

The item shown in Figure 4.7 is the roll-up upgrade bundle for ESXi 6.5 Update 1. The Import Patches link in the upper-left corner of the Patch Repository area allows you to upload patches directly into the repository. Importing patches here is the same as importing them on the Settings ➤ Download Settings page.

ESXi Images This is the area where you will upload ISO files for upgrading ESXi. These ISO files are the same images used to create the CD installation media for a base ESXi install. You can find more information on this task in the section "Upgrading Hosts with vSphere Update Manager," later in this chapter.

FIGURE 4.7
The Patch Repository tab offers detailed information about each of the items in the repository.

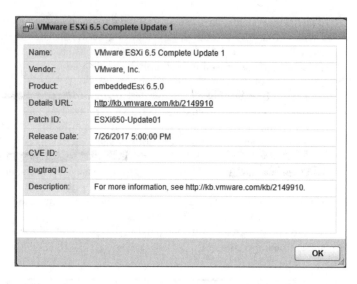

Name:	VMware ESXi 6.5 Complete Update 1
Vendor:	VMware, Inc.
Product:	embeddedEsx 6.5.0
Details URL:	http://kb.vmware.com/kb/2149910
Patch ID:	ESXi650-Update01
Release Date:	7/26/2017 5:00:00 PM
CVE ID:	
Bugtraq ID:	
Description:	For more information, see http://kb.vmware.com/kb/2149910.

Creating Baselines

VMware provides a few baselines with VUM when it's installed. The following baselines are present upon installation:

♦ Two dynamic host patch baselines named Critical Host Patches and Non-Critical Host Patches

♦ A dynamic baseline for upgrading VMware Tools to match the host

♦ A dynamic baseline for upgrading VM hardware to match the host

♦ A dynamic VA upgrade baseline named VA Upgrade To Latest

Although these baselines provide a good starting point, many administrators will need to create additional baselines that better reflect their organizations' specific patching policy or procedures. For example, organizations may want to ensure that ESXi hosts are kept fully patched with regard to security patches but not necessarily critical nonsecurity patches. You ca do this by creating a custom dynamic baseline.

Perform the following steps to create a new dynamic host patch baseline for security-relate ESXi host patches:

1. Launch the vSphere Web Client, if it is not already running, and connect to a vCenter Server instance.

2. On the Home screen, select Update Manager. In the Navigator pane, select your vCenter Server.

If you have multiple vCenter Servers in Enhanced Linked Mode, and they have VUM associated, each VUM instance will be displayed here. If VUM is local to vCenter Server as it is on the appliance, it will share the same name; if VUM is external to vCenter Serv a choice you have with windows, it will have its own unique name displayed. You can s the vCenter-to-VUM mapping under the Objects tab.

Figure 4.8 shows an example of multiple VUM instances being displayed when multiple vCenters are in Enhanced Linked Mode.

FIGURE 4.8

Using Enhanced Linked Mode across your vCenters will also let you see all of their associated Update Managers.

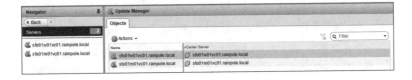

3. Click the Manage tab to navigate to the Administrative area of Update Manager.

4. Just under the tab bar, you need to select the correct baseline type: Hosts or VMs/VAs. In this case, click the Hosts Baselines button.

5. Click the New Baseline button just above the Host Baselines Administration area (not the New Baseline Group button above the Baseline Groups area on the far right). This launches the New Baseline Wizard.

6. Supply a name and description for the new baseline, and select Host Patch as the baseline type. Click Next.

7. Select Dynamic, and click Next.

8. On the next screen, you define the criteria for the patches to be included in this baseline. Select the correct criteria for the baseline you are defining, and then click Next.

   Figure 4.9 shows a sample selection set—in this case, all security-related patches.

FIGURE 4.9

Dynamic baselines contain a set of criteria that determine which patches are included in the baseline and which are not.

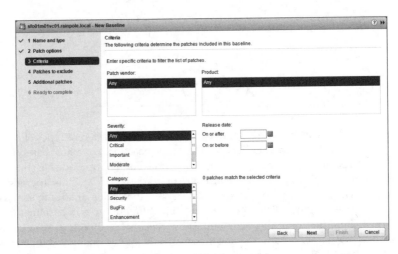

9. Select any patches that match the selection criteria but that you want to exclude from the baseline.

   Use the up/down arrows to move patches out of or into the exclusion list in the lower pane, respectively. In this case, don't exclude any patches and just click Next.

10. Now you have the option to permanently include any patches that are available but that were not automatically included by the selection criteria.

Once again, use the up/down arrows to remove patches or add patches to be included, respectively. Don't add any additional patches; just click Next.

11. Click Finish to create the baseline.

You can now use this baseline to determine which ESXi hosts are not compliant with the late security patches by attaching it to one or more hosts, a procedure you'll learn later in this chapt in the section "Routine Updates."

Groups, or baseline groups, are simply combinations of nonconflicting baselines. You might use a baseline group to combine multiple dynamic patch baselines, like the baseline group shown in Figure 4.10. In that example, a baseline group is defined that includes the built-in Critical Host Patches and Non-Critical Host Patches baselines. By attaching this baseline group to your ESXi hosts, you would be able to ensure that your hosts had *all* available patches installed.

FIGURE 4.10
Combining multiple dynamic baselines into a baseline group provides greater flexibility in managing the deployment and compliance of patches.

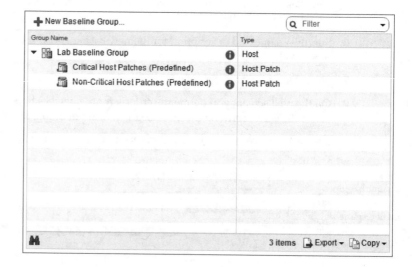

You can also use baseline groups to combine different types of baselines. Each baseline group can include one of each type of upgrade baseline. For a host baseline group, there is only one type of upgrade baseline: a host upgrade. For VM upgrade baselines, as previously discussed, there are two types: VM Hardware upgrades and VM Tools upgrades. When you are working with a host baseline group, you also have the option of adding a host extension baseline into the baseline group. This ability to combine different types of baselines together into a baseline group simplifies the application of multiple baselines to objects in your vCenter Server hierarchy.

Another use for baseline groups would be to combine a dynamic patch policy and a fixed patch policy into a baseline group. For example, there might be a specific fix for your ESXi hosts and you want to ensure that all your hosts have all the critical patches—easily handled by the built-in Critical Host Patches dynamic baseline—as well as the specific fix. To do this, create a fixed baseline for the specific patch you want included, and then combine it in a baseline group with the built-in Critical Host Patches dynamic baseline.

Figure 4.11 shows an example of a host baseline group that combines different types of host baselines. In this example, a baseline group is used to combine a host upgrade baseline and dynamic patch baselines. This would allow you to upgrade an ESXi host and then ensure that the host has all the applicable updates for the new version.

FIGURE 4.11
Use baseline groups to combine host upgrade and dynamic host patch baselines.

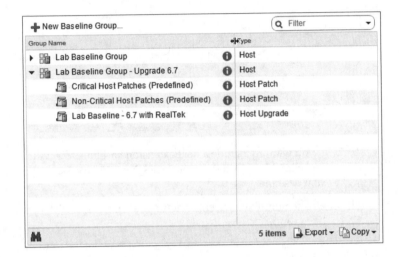

Perform the following steps to create a host baseline group that combines multiple host baselines:

1. Launch the vSphere Web Client, if it is not already running, and connect to a vCenter Server instance.

2. Navigate to the Update Manager Administration area, and make sure the Hosts Baselines button is selected.

3. In the upper-right corner of the Host Baselines Administration area, click the New Baseline Group button. This starts the New Baseline Group Wizard.

4. Select Host Baseline Group as the baseline type and enter a name for the new baseline group. Click Next.

5. Because we haven't yet discussed how to create a host upgrade baseline, you probably don't have an upgrade baseline listed. Instead, for this procedure, you will combine a dynamic and a fixed-host patch baseline.

   Select None and click Next to skip attaching an upgrade baseline to this host baseline group.

6. Place a check mark next to each individual baseline you want to include in this baseline group, as shown in Figure 4.12, and click Next.

FIGURE 4.12
A baseline group combines multiple individual baselines for a more comprehensive patching capability.

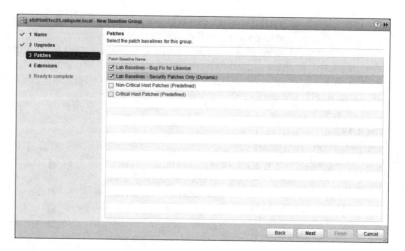

7. If you want to include a host extension baseline, select the desired host extension baseline and click Next. Otherwise, just click Next to proceed without adding a host extension baseline.

8. On the Summary screen, review the settings, and click Finish to create the new baseline group.

The new baseline group you just created is now included in the list of baseline groups, and you can attach it to ESXi hosts or clusters to identify which of them are not compliant with the baseline.

You'll see more about host upgrade baselines in the section "Upgrading Hosts with vSphere Update Manager" later in this chapter.

Having examined the different areas present within VUM, let's now take a look at using VUM to patch hosts and VMs.

Routine Updates

VUM uses the term *remediation* to refer to the process of applying patches and upgrades to a vSphere object that is not in compliance. As described in the previous section, VUM uses baselines to create lists of patches based on certain criteria. By attaching a baseline to a host or VM and performing a scan, VUM can determine whether that object is compliant or noncompliant with the baseline. Compliance with the baseline means that the host or VM has all the patches included in the baseline currently installed and is up-to-date; noncompliance means that one or more patches are missing and the target is not up-to-date compared to the current baseline.

After noncompliance with one or more baselines or baseline groups has been determined, you can remediate—or *patch*—the hosts or VMs. Optionally, you can stage patches to ESXi hosts before remediation.

The first step in this process is creating the baselines that you will attach to your ESXi hosts or VMs. The process for creating a host patch baseline was covered earlier. The next step is attaching a baseline to—or detaching a baseline from—ESXi hosts or VMs. Let's take a closer look at how to attach and detach baselines.

Attaching and Detaching Baselines or Baseline Groups

Before you patch a host or guest, you must determine whether an ESXi host or VM is compliant or noncompliant with one or more baselines or baseline groups. Defining a baseline or baseline group alone is not enough. To determine compliance, you must first attach the baseline or baseline group to a host or VM. After it is attached, the baseline or baseline group becomes the "measuring stick" that VUM uses to determine compliance. Attaching and detaching baselines is performed in one of vCenter's inventory views. To attach or detach a baseline or baseline groups for ESXi hosts, you need to be in the Hosts And Clusters view; for VMs, you need to be in the VMs And Templates view. In both cases, you'll use the Update Manager tab to attach or detach baselines or baseline groups.

In both views, baselines and baseline groups can be attached to a variety of objects. In the Hosts And Clusters view, baselines and baseline groups can be attached to datacenters, clusters, or individual ESXi hosts. In the VMs And Templates view, baselines and baseline groups can be attached to datacenters, folders, or specific VMs. Because of the hierarchical nature of the vCenter Server inventory, a baseline attached at a higher level will automatically apply to eligible child objects as well. You may also find yourself applying different baselines or baseline groups at different levels of the hierarchy; for example, there may be a specific baseline that applies to all hosts in the environment and another baseline that applies only to a specific subset of hosts.

Let's look at attaching a baseline to a specific ESXi host. The process is much the same, if not identical, for attaching a baseline to a datacenter, cluster, folder, or VM.

Perform the following steps to attach a baseline or baseline group to an ESXi host:

1. Launch the vSphere Web Client, if it is not already running, and connect to a vCenter Server instance.

NOTE   Because VUM is integrated with and depends on vCenter Server, you cannot manage, attach, or detach VUM baselines when connected directly to an ESXi host via the Host Client.

2. On the Web Client's home screen, select Hosts and Clusters.

3. In the inventory tree on the left, select the ESXi host to which you want to attach a baseline or baseline group.

4. From the contents pane in the middle, select the Update Manager tab.

5. Click the Attach Baseline link in the upper-left corner. This link opens the Attach Baseline Or Baseline Group dialog box, shown in Figure 4.13.

6. Select the baselines and/or baseline groups that you want to attach to this ESXi host, and then click OK.

The steps for attaching a baseline or baseline group to a VM with a guest OS installed are similar, but let's walk through the process anyway. A useful baseline to point out is named VMware Tools Upgrade To Match Host. This baseline is a default baseline that is defined upon installation of VUM, and its purpose is to help you identify which VMs have guest OSs running outdated versions of VMware Tools. As you'll see in Chapter 7, using VMware Tools is an important piece of optimizing your guest OSs to run in a virtualized environment, and it's great that VUM can help identify which VMs have guest OSs with an outdated version of VMware Tools installed.

FIGURE 4.13

The Attach Baseline or Baseline Group dialog box

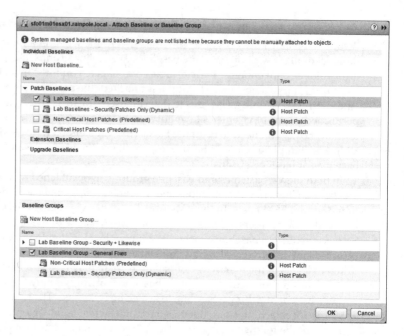

Perform the following steps to attach a baseline to a datacenter so that it applies to all the objects under the datacenter:

1. Launch the vSphere Web Client, if it is not already running, and connect to a vCenter Server instance.

2. Switch to the VMs And Templates inventory view from the Web Client's home screen.

3. Select a datacenter object from the inventory on the left.

4. From the contents pane in the middle, click the Update Manager tab.

5. Click the Attach button in the top right-hand corner of the Update Manager tab's panel. This opens the Attach Baseline Or Baseline Group dialog box.

6. Click to select the VMware Tools Upgrade To Match Host upgrade baseline, and then click OK.

In the event that you need to detach a baseline from an object, you can highlight the baseline in question and use either the Detach Baseline or Detach Baseline Group button, depending on the type of baseline you selected, just above the left corner of the list. Figure 4.14 shows the Detach Baseline Group button about halfway down on the left. This link is visible only when a baseline is highlighted.

Clicking the Detach Baseline button then takes you to a screen that also allows you to detach the baseline from other objects to which it is attached. Figure 4.15 shows how VUM allows you to detach the selected baseline or baseline group from other objects at the same time (it does not allow you to detach baselines from objects that have inherited the baseline, only those that have been explicitly attached to each child object—if an object has inherited the baseline, then this can be detached only at the point it was applied).

FIGURE 4.14
Detaching baselines

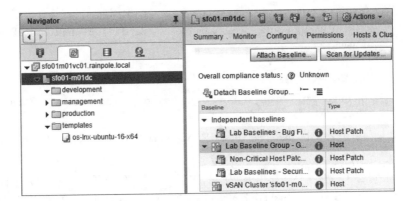

FIGURE 4.15
When you're detaching a baseline or baseline group, VUM offers the option to detach it from other objects at the same time.

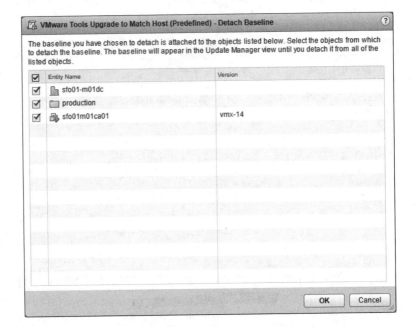

In much the same way that simply defining a baseline or baseline group wasn't enough, simply attaching a baseline or baseline group to an ESXi host or VM isn't enough to determine compliance or noncompliance. To determine compliance or noncompliance with a baseline or baseline group, you need to perform a scan.

Performing a Scan

The next step after attaching a baseline is to perform a scan. The purpose of a scan is to determine the compliance or noncompliance of an object with the baseline. If the object being scanned matches what's defined in the baseline, then the object—be it an ESXi host, a VM, or a virtual appliance instance—is compliant. If something is missing from the object, then it's noncompliant.

Although the process of scanning these objects within vCenter Server is essentially the same there are enough differences in the processes and requirements to make it worthwhile to examine each one.

SCANNING VMs

You might perform any of three different types of scans against a VM and virtual appliances using VUM:

◆ Scan the installed version of VMware Tools to see if it's the latest version in relation to its host.

◆ Scan the VM hardware to see if it's the latest version in relation to its host.

◆ Scan a virtual appliance to see if a new version is available and if it can be upgraded.

The process for actually conducting a scan is identical in all three instances except for the check box that indicates what type of scan you'd like to perform, as shown in Figure 4.16.

FIGURE 4.16
Different types of scans are initiated depending on the check boxes selected at the start of the scan.

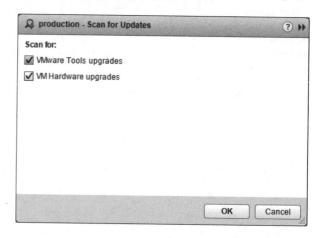

Here is a brief description of what's required to perform each type of scan:

Scanning for VMware Tools Upgrades   If you scan a VM for VMware Tools upgrades and that VM does not have VMware Tools installed, the scan will succeed but VUM will report the VM as Incompatible. To get a Compliant or Non-Compliant report, some version of the VMware Tools needs to already be running within the guest OS installed in the VM. Other than that requirement, VUM has no other restrictions. VUM can scan both online and offline VMs and templates.

Scanning for VM Hardware Upgrades   Scanning for VM hardware upgrades requires that the latest version of VMware Tools be installed in the VM first. This, of course, means that a guest OS is installed in the VM. You can perform VM hardware upgrade scans on both online as well as offline VMs and templates.

UNMANAGED VMWARE TOOLS

Creators of virtual appliances have the option of installing operating system–specific packages (OSPs) for VMware Tools. Because installing VMware Tools through the vSphere Clients is mutually exclusive to using the OSP VMware Tools, the OSP VMware Tools will report Unmanaged as the status in the vSphere Clients. In addition, scans of virtual appliances for VMware Tools upgrades will report the virtual appliance as Incompatible. This is not something you need to be concerned about—it just allows the virtual appliance creators to use the native OS packaging tools to more effectively manage the driver updates.

SCANNING ESXi HOSTS

As with VMs, the requirements for being able to scan an ESXi host vary depending on the type of scan VUM is performing. In all cases, the ESXi hosts need to be online and reachable via the network from the VUM server. VUM 6.7 can scan the hosts of versions 6.0 and above for updates to patches and extensions or for potential upgrades.

Let's look at the steps involved to perform a scan. Keep in mind that the process for performing a scan on a VM and the process for performing a scan on a virtual appliance are very similar.

Perform the following steps to initiate a scan of an ESXi host for patches, extensions, or upgrades after a baseline is attached:

1. Launch the vSphere Web Client, if it is not already running, and connect to a vCenter Server instance.

2. Go to the Hosts And Clusters inventory view from the Web Client's home screen.

3. Select an ESXi host from the inventory tree on the left.

4. From the contents pane on the right, click the Update Manager tab.

5. Click the Scan Of Updates link in the upper-right corner.

6. Select whether you want to scan for patches and extensions, upgrades, or both, and then click Scan.

When the scan is complete, the Update Manager tab will update to show whether the object is compliant or noncompliant. Compliance is measured on a per-baseline basis. In Figure 4.17, you can see that the selected ESXi host is compliant with both the Critical Host Patches baseline and the Non-Critical Host Patches baseline, as well as the vSAN-generated System Managed baseline. This means the host is compliant overall. If a host is noncompliant with at least one attached baseline, the host is considered noncompliant.

When you are viewing the Update Manager tab for an object that contains other objects—such as a datacenter, cluster, or folder—then compliance might be mixed. That is, some objects might be compliant and other objects might be noncompliant. Figure 4.18 shows a datacenter with mixed compliance reports. In this particular case, you're looking at a compliance report for VMware Tools upgrades to match the host. The compliance report shows objects that are compliant (VMware Tools is up-to-date), noncompliant (VMware Tools is outdated), and incompatible (VMware Tools cannot be installed for some reason).

FIGURE 4.17

When multiple baselines are attached to an object, compliance is reflected on a per-baseline basis.

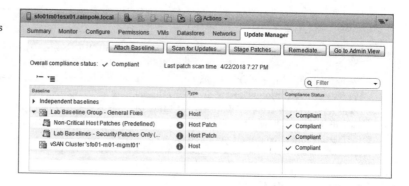

FIGURE 4.18

VUM can display partial compliance when viewing objects that contain other objects.

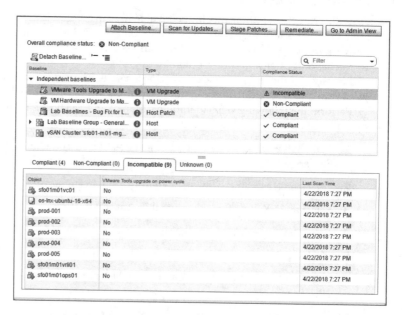

VUM can report an object as Incompatible for a number of reasons. In this particular case, VUM is reporting nine objects as Incompatible when scanning for VMware Tools. Taking a closer look at Figure 4.18—you can see that these objects comprise five VMs named prod-00#, our vCenter Server virtual appliance, our template for creating linux VMs, and two other virtual appliances named sfo01m01vrli01 and sfo01m01ops01 (vRealize Log Insight and vRealize Operations, respectively). The VMs named prod-00# are reported as Incompatible because this is a fresh VM with no guest OS installed yet, and the appliances are reporting Incompatible because they are virtual appliances running the OSP VMware Tools, which is not intended to be managed by the vSphere Clients.

Depending on the type of scan you are performing, scans can be fairly quick. Scanning a large group of VMs for VMware Tools upgrades or VM hardware upgrades may also be fairly quick. Scanning a large group of hosts for patches, on the other hand, might be more time-consuming and more resource-intensive. Combining several tasks at the same time can also slow down scans while they run concurrently. You can consult VMware's latest web application, the VMware Configuration Maximum, which lists the maximum number of concurrent VUM operations possible.

After the scanning is complete and compliance is established, you are ready to fix the noncompliant systems. Before we discuss remediation, let's first look at staging patches to ESXi hosts.

Staging Patches

If the target of remediation—that is, the object within vCenter Server that you are trying to remediate and make compliant with a baseline—is an ESXi host, an additional option exists. With VUM, you can stage patches to ESXi hosts. Staging a patch copies the files across to the host to speed up the actual time of remediation. Staging is not a required step; you can update hosts without staging the updates first, if you prefer. VUM won't stage patches to a PXE-booted ESXi host such as a host provisioned via standard Auto Deploy (although it will stage patches to hosts using *stateful* Auto Deploy).

Staging host patches is particularly useful for companies whose VUM-connected hosts are spread across slow WAN links. This can substantially reduce the outage required on such sites, especially if the WAN link is particularly slow or the patches themselves are very large. Hosts do not need to be in Maintenance mode while patches are being staged, but they do during the remediation phase. Staging patches reduces the Maintenance mode period associated with remediation. Staging patches also allows the uploads to be scheduled for a time when heavy WAN utilization is more appropriate, allowing you to remediate the host at a more agreeable time.

Perform the following steps to stage patches to an ESXi host using VUM:

1. Launch the vSphere Web Client, if it is not already running, and connect to a vCenter Server instance.

2. Navigate to the Hosts And Clusters view by selecting Home ➢ Hosts And Clusters, by pressing Ctrl+Alt+3, or by using the Navigator bar.

3. From the inventory list on the left, select an ESXi host.

4. From the contents pane on the right, scroll through the tabs and select the Update Manager tab.

5. Click the Stage Patches button in the top-right corner of the contents pane, or right-click the host and select Update Manager ➢ Stage Patches. Either method activates the Stage Wizard.

6. Select the baselines for the patches you want to be staged, and click Next to proceed.

7. The next screen allows you to deselect any specific patches you do not want to be staged. If you want all the patches to be staged, leave them all selected, and click Next.

8. Click Finish at the Summary screen to start the staging process.

After the staging process is complete, the Recent Tasks pane at the bottom of the vSphere Web Client reflects this, as shown in Figure 4.19.

FIGURE 4.19
The vSphere Web Client reflects when the process of staging patches is complete.

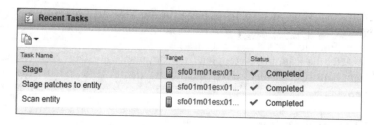

After you stage patches to the ESXi hosts, you can begin the task of remediating immediately or defer to a later or more appropriate time window.

Remediating Hosts

After you have attached a baseline to a host, scanned the host for compliance, and optionally staged the updates to the host, you're ready to remediate, or update, the ESXi host.

REMEDIATION

The term *remediation* is simply VMware parlance to mean the process of applying patches or upgrades to an object to bring it up to a compliant level. This cannot be performed through the Web Client but only through the stand-alone VUM Client.

Perform the following steps to patch an ESXi host:

1. Launch the vSphere Web Client, if it is not already running, and connect to a vCenter Server instance.

2. Switch to the Hosts And Clusters view by using the Navigator pane, by pressing Ctrl+Alt+3, or by selecting Home ➢ Hosts and Clusters.

3. Select an ESXi host from the inventory tree on the left.

4. From the contents pane on the right, select the Update Manager tab.

5. In the upper-right corner of the window, click the Remediate button. You can also right-click the ESXi host and select Update Manager ➢ Remediate from the context menu.

6. The Remediate dialog box opens, as shown in Figure 4.20. From here, select the baselines or baseline groups that you want to apply. Click Next.

7. Ensure that your ESXi host has been selected. Click next.

   If you performed the previous operation of staging, observe the number of patches the Remediation operation is going to apply versus how many are staged. Some patches won't be staged if they are obsoleted by patches in the baselines or baseline groups used during the same staging operation; VUM will only stage the highest version patch available to optimize the upgrade operations.

   Figure 4.21 shows the differences between staged patches and available patches to be applied during this remediation.

FIGURE 4.20
The Remediate dialog box allows you to select the baselines or baseline groups against which you would like to remediate an ESXi host.

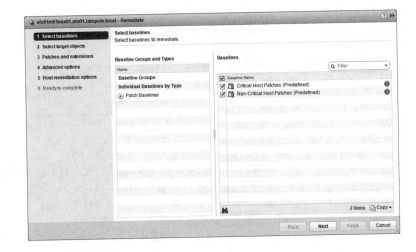

FIGURE 4.21
Some patches available between baselines will obsolete others when applied during the same remediation process, so not all patches will be staged.

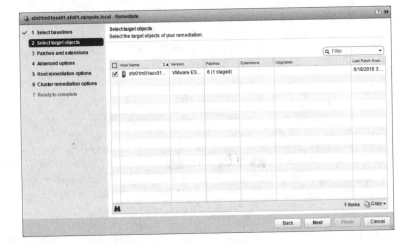

8. Deselect any patches or extensions that you don't want applied to the ESXi host.

   This allows you to customize the exact list of patches. Click Next after you've deselected any patches to exclude.

9. Specify whether you want the remediation to occur immediately or run at a specific time and whether the Remediation Process should ignore warnings about deprecated hardware or VMFS volumes, and then click Next.

   Figure 4.22 shows these options.

10. The Host Remediation Options page gives you the option to modify the default settings for how VUM should handle a host's VMs if it has to enter Maintenance mode. It also lets you patch PXE-booted ESXi hosts but warns you that those changes will be lost on the next power cycle. Figure 4.23 shows the options available during this stage. Make any changes required and click Next.

FIGURE 4.22
When remediating a host, you need to specify a name for the remediation task and a schedule for the task.

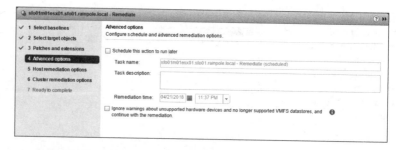

FIGURE 4.23
Host remediation options available if the host has to enter Maintenance mode

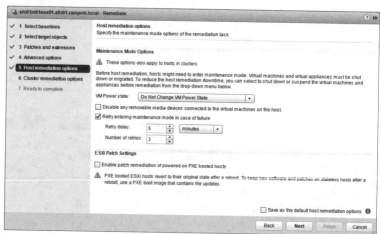

11. If the host is a member of a cluster, you can choose whether to disable any of the cluster settings for DPM, HA, and FT if you think they may interfere with the remediation process. Starting with version 5, VUM offers the option to remediate hosts in parallel if the cluster has sufficient compute resources to meet the other cluster controls. In Figure 4.24 you can see the full gamut of cluster options.

FIGURE 4.24
Cluster options during host remediation

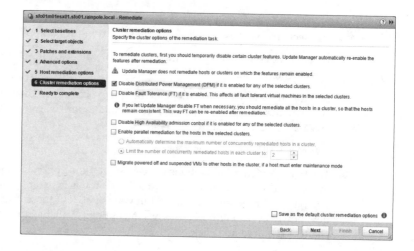

12. Review the Summary screen, and click Finish if everything is correct. If there are any errors, use the Back button to double-check and change the settings.

If you selected to have the remediation occur immediately, which is the default setting, VUM initiates a task request with vCenter Server. You'll see this task, as well as some related tasks, in the Recent Tasks pane at the bottom of the vSphere Web Client.

If necessary, VUM automatically puts the ESXi host into Maintenance mode. If the host is a member of a DRS-enabled cluster, putting the host into Maintenance mode will, in turn, initiate a series of vMotion operations to migrate all VMs to other hosts in the cluster. It's common to see the remediation task pause for an extended time at the 22% point. This is normal and it often takes about 15 minutes to complete the migrations before progressing further. Designing vMotion networks for rapid host evacuation by using 10 Gbps networking or Multi-NIC vMotion can considerably speed up this task. The higher the compute consolidation ratio, the more pronounced the wait to enter Maintenance mode, which may call for more efficient vMotion network design. See Chapter 5, "Creating and Configuring Virtual Networks," for more information. After the patching is complete, VUM automatically reboots the host, if required, and then takes the host out of Maintenance mode.

KEEPING HOSTS PATCHED IS IMPORTANT

We all know that keeping your ESXi hosts patched is important, but too often, VMware administrators forget to incorporate this key task into their operations.

VUM makes it easy to keep your hosts patched, but you still need to actually do it! Be sure to take the time to establish a regular schedule for applying host updates and take advantage of VUM's integration with vMotion, vCenter Server, and VMware Distributed Resource Scheduler (DRS) to avoid downtime for your end users during the patching process.

Upgrading VMware Tools

VUM can scan and remediate not only ESXi hosts but also the VMware Tools package running inside your VMs. VMware Tools is an important part of your virtualized infrastructure. The basic idea behind VMware Tools is to provide a set of virtualization-optimized drivers for all guest OSs that VMware supports with VMware vSphere. These virtualization-optimized drivers help provide the highest levels of performance for guest OSs running on VMware vSphere, and it's considered a best practice to keep VMware Tools up-to-date whenever possible. (You can find a more thorough discussion of VMware Tools in Chapter 9, "Creating and Managing Virtual Machines.")

To help with that task, VUM comes with a prebuilt upgrade baseline named VMware Tools Upgrade To Match Host. This baseline can't be modified or deleted from within the vSphere Desktop Client, and its sole purpose is to help vSphere administrators identify VMs that are not running a version of VMware Tools that is appropriate for the host on which it is currently running.

In general, follow the same order of operations for remediating VMware Tools as you did for ESXi hosts:

1. Attach the baselines to the VMs you want to scan and remediate.

2. Scan the VMs for compliance with the attached baseline.

3. Remediate VMware Tools inside the VMs if it is noncompliant.

The procedure for attaching a baseline was described in the section "Attaching and Detaching Baselines or Baseline Groups," earlier in this chapter, and the process of performing a scan for compliance with a baseline was described in the section "Performing a Scan."

If you have attached a baseline to a VM and scanned VMware Tools on that VM for compliance, the next step is remediating VMware Tools inside the VM.

Perform these steps to remediate VMware Tools:

1. Launch the vSphere Web Client if it is not already running, and connect to an instance of vCenter Server.

2. From Home, navigate to the VMs And Templates by selecting Home ➤ VMs And Templates. You can also use the Navigator pane or the Ctrl+Alt+4 keyboard shortcut.

3. Right-click the VM that you want to remediate, and select Update Manager ➤ Remediate from the context menu. To remediate several VMs, select an object further up the hierarchy. This displays the Remediate dialog box.

4. In the Remediate dialog box, select the VMware Tools Upgrade To Match Host baseline, and then click Next.

5. Ensure that your virtual machine has been selected. Click next

6. Provide a name for the remediation task, and select a schedule for the task. Different schedules are possible for powered-on VMs, powered-off VMs, and suspended VMs, as shown in Figure 4.25.

FIGURE 4.25

VUM supports different schedules for remediating powered-on VMs, powered-off VMs, and suspended VMs.

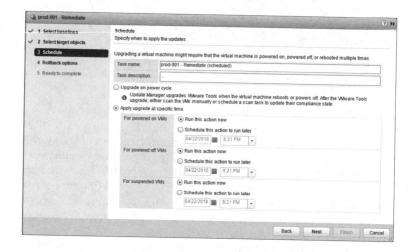

7. Select an appropriate schedule for each of the different classes of VMs, and then click Next.

8. If you want to take a snapshot of the VM, supply a name for the snapshot and a description.

   You may also specify a maximum age for the snapshot and whether to snapshot the VM's memory. The default settings, as shown in Figure 4.26, are Do Not Delete Snapshots and Take A Snapshot Of The Virtual Machines Before Remediation To Enable Rollback.

FIGURE 4.26
VUM integrates with vCenter Server's snapshot functionality to allow remediation operations to be rolled back in the event of a problem.

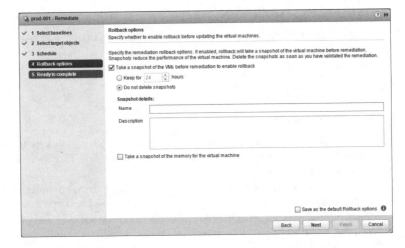

Depending on the scale of virtual machines you are remediating at any one time, this may dictate your choice for automated snapshot remediation. For instance, if you are using an environment to test a small batch of virtual machines for stability until rolling these changes out to production, keeping the snapshot indefinitely for you to clean up later may not be a big undertaking; however, applying this to tens or hundreds of virtual machines (or more) can turn snapshot cleanup into a time-intensive task, so setting a timer for snapshot cleanup may be a better choice.

9. Review the information in the Summary screen. If anything is incorrect, use the Back button to double-check and change the settings. Otherwise, click Finish to start the remediation.

A reboot of the guest OS is often required after the VMware Tools upgrade is complete, although this varies from guest OS to guest OS. Windows guests with a version of VMware Tools prior to 5.1 will require a reboot, so plan accordingly. vSphere 5.1 introduced the "zero downtime" tools upgrade, which is designed to minimize guest reboots after the tools have been updated. Updates to certain device drivers still mean a reboot is necessary, but the incidence has been significantly reduced. The Knowledge Base article at http://kb.vmware.com/kb/2015163 details the circumstances that still require a reboot, but simplistically, if the drivers for storage or networking must be updated then the virtual machine must be rebooted.

Where multiple VMs are in a vApp, VUM and vCenter Server will coordinate restarting the VMs within the vApp to satisfy inter-VM dependencies unless you turned off Smart Reboot in the VUM configuration.

When you are dealing with VMs brought into a VMware vSphere environment from previous versions of VMware Infrastructure, you must be sure to first upgrade VMware Tools to the latest version and then deal with upgrading VM hardware. This process is explained at the end of the section "Upgrading Hosts with vSphere Update Manager" later in this chapter. By upgrading the VMware Tools first, you ensure that the appropriate drivers are already loaded into the guest OS when you upgrade the VM hardware.

Upgrading Host Extensions

Once again, you follow the same overall procedure to upgrade host extensions in VUM as you did with VMware Tools in the previous section:

1. Attach the baseline.

2. Scan for compliance.

3. Remediate.

However, it is worth noting that host extensions are less likely to be upgraded quite so routinely. When upgraded, they are replaced wholesale, and their settings are migrated across the new version.

Host extensions often come from third-party hardware or software providers. Each vendor will make its own decisions regarding what changes to functionality are included in these upgrades. For some, you may find that the upgrade includes only minor bug fixes but no chang in the way the appliance or extension works. Another upgrade might bring significant changes how it operates.

For this reason, it is prudent to treat each upgrade to a host extension as something that nee to be tested thoroughly before running a wide-scale upgrade.

Now let's look at the last major piece of VUM's functionality: upgrading vSphere hosts.

Upgrading Hosts with vSphere Update Manager

Upgrading vSphere ESXi to the newest versions when they become available is principally a three-stage process. Although ESXi 5.x and 6.x are fundamentally the same hypervisors, VUM 6 has been designed to only upgrade 6.x hosts to 6.7. You can upgrade either version of ESXi, but you will need to perform an additional step to get older 5.x hosts upgraded all the way to 6.0 or 6.5 and then on to 6.7. It's a process that requires a VUM 6.x server to get the 5.x hosts upgraded to 6.x prior to upgrading VUM itself to 6.7. You may then update any 6.x to 6.7 with ease.

Perform the following steps to upgrade a host server with VUM 6.0:

1. Import an ESXi image and create a host upgrade baseline.

2. Upgrade the host by remediating with the upgrade baseline.

3. Upgrade the VMs' VMware Tools and hardware.

Strictly speaking, the last point is not part of the host upgrade procedure. However, most of the time when you upgrade VMs' hardware, it is immediately following a host upgrade (at leas you *should* be upgrading them at that time!).

Importing an ESXi Image and Creating the Host Upgrade Baseline

Previous versions of vSphere used Update Bundles to upgrade hosts. These offline bundle zip files are still used by vSphere to patch hosts and third-party software but not for host upgrades. In VUM 6.0, all host upgrades use the same image file that is used to install ESXi.

Perform the following steps to import the ISO file into VUM and create the baseline:

1. Launch the vSphere Web Client if it is not already running, and connect to an instance of vCenter Server.

2. Navigate to the Update Manager Administration area by using the Home menu ➢ Updat Manager, and selecting the vCenter's associated Update Manager.

3. Click the ESXi Images tab.

4. Click the orange-and-green Import ESXi Image link in the top-left corner of this area.

5. Use the Browse button, shown in Figure 4.27, to select the new ESXi ISO file. This will immediately start the upload of the ISO and display a progress bar that can be monitored as shown in Figure 4.28. This might take a few minutes to complete.

FIGURE 4.27

Select the ESXi image to use for the host upgrade.

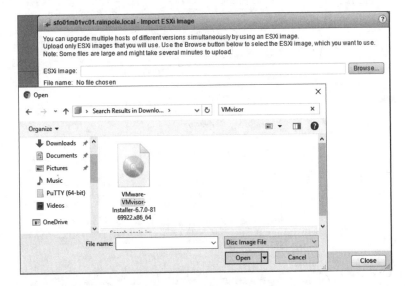

FIGURE 4.28

Monitoring the import time of your ESXi image

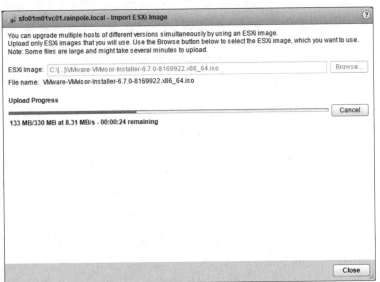

6. Once the file import is complete, as shown in Figure 4.29, verify the summary information and click Close.

7. Click your newly imported image in the list, and to the right of the Import ESXi Image, click Create Baseline. Give the baseline a name and appropriate description, and then click OK. Figure 4.30 shows an image uploaded into the list of imported images. When a image is selected, the lower pane lists all the software packages included in the image ar their version numbers.

FIGURE 4.29

ESXi image imported and summarized

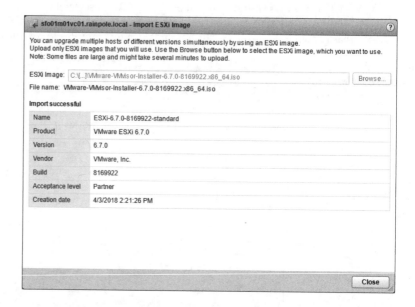

FIGURE 4.30

All the packages contained in the imported ESXi image are shown.

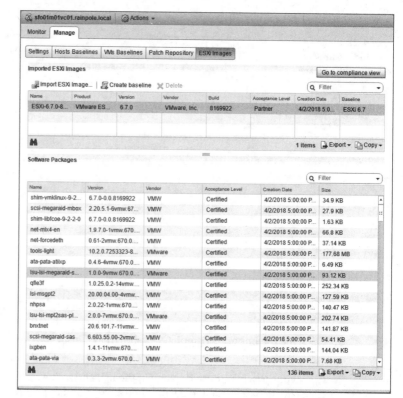

Upgrading a Host

After you've created a host upgrade baseline, you can use this baseline to upgrade an ESXi host following the same basic sequence of steps outlined previously to remediate other vSphere objects:

1. Attach the baseline to the ESXi hosts that you want to upgrade. Refer to the previous section, "Attaching and Detaching Baselines or Baseline Groups," for a review of how to attach a baseline to an ESXi host or several hosts.

2. Scan the ESXi hosts for compliance with the baseline. Don't forget to select to scan for upgrades when presented with the scan options.

3. Remediate the host.

BACK UP YOUR HOST CONFIGURATION AS REQUIRED

Unlike with previous host upgrade methods, VUM no longer supports rollbacks after a problematic upgrade. Before you start the upgrade, make sure you have sufficient information about the state of the host to restore or rebuild it if necessary.

The Remediate Wizard is similar to the process previously discussed in the section "Remediating Hosts," but there are enough differences to warrant reviewing the process. Perform the following steps to upgrade an ESXi host with a VUM host upgrade baseline:

1. Launch the vSphere Web Client, if it is not already running, and connect to a vCenter Server instance.

2. Switch to the Hosts And Clusters view by using the Navigator pane, by pressing Ctrl+Alt+3, or by selecting Home ➤ Hosts And Clusters.

3. Select the ESXi host from the inventory tree on the left.

4. From the contents pane on the right, select the Update Manager tab.

5. In the upper-right corner of the window, click the Remediate button. You can also right-click the ESXi host and select Remediate from the context menu.

6. The Remediate dialog box opens (Figure 4.31). Ensure that the Upgrade Baselines radio button is selected in the Baseline Groups And Types frame, and then choose the baseline that you want to apply. Click Next.

7. Ensure that your ESXi host has been selected, and then click Next.

8. Select the check box to accept the license terms, and then click Next.

9. If you are upgrading the hosts from vSphere 6.x that have come from 5.x, the next screen gives you the option to explicitly ignore any third-party software on the host that might prevent a host upgrade, as shown previously in Figure 4.22. Either select the check box or leave it unchecked. Additionally, specify whether you want the remediation to occur immediately or whether it should run at a specific time, and click Next.

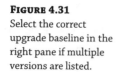

FIGURE 4.31
Select the correct upgrade baseline in the right pane if multiple versions are listed.

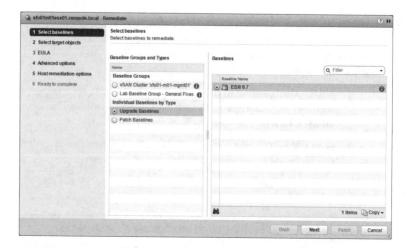

10. Choose how the host's VMs should react to the host entering Maintenance mode, and click Next.

11. The next page gives you the same cluster options shown in Figure 4.24. You can control how the host's cluster should conform to its own DPM, HA, and FT settings and whether to allow multiple hosts to be upgraded at the same time if the cluster has sufficient resources. Select the options required and click Next.

12. Review the summary, and use the Back button if any settings need to be changed. Click Finish when the settings are correct.

VUM then proceeds with the host upgrade at the scheduled time (Immediately is the default setting in the wizard). The upgrade will be an unattended upgrade, and at the end of the upgrade, the host will automatically reboot.

After upgrading all the hosts in a cluster, you should consider upgrading VMware Tools on the VMs and then their virtual hardware versions. Upgrading a VM's hardware can prevent the VM from running on older hosts, which is why you should ensure that all the hosts in the same cluster are upgraded first. Otherwise, you can restrict the efficiency of fundamental cluster operations such as DRS and HA.

Keeping in mind that you should upgrade VMware Tools on the VMs first, as discussed in the earlier section "Upgrading VMware Tools," let's look at how to upgrade the virtual hardware.

Upgrading VM Hardware

So far, the idea of VM hardware hasn't been discussed, but the topic is covered in Chapter 9. For now, suffice it to say that VMs brought into a VMware vSphere environment from previous versions of ESXi will have outdated VM hardware. You'll see outdated hardware most often after you upgrade a host. In order to use all the latest functionality of VMware vSphere with these VMs, you will have to upgrade the VM hardware. To help with this process, VUM lets you scan for and remediate VMs with out-of-date VM hardware.

VUM already comes with a VM upgrade baseline that addresses this: the VM Hardware Upgrade To Match Host baseline. This baseline is predefined and can't be changed or deleted from within the vSphere Desktop Client. The purpose of this baseline is to determine whether a VM's hardware is current. vSphere 6.7 VMs use hardware version 14 by default. Hardware version 13 is the version used by vSphere 6.5, version 11 was used by 6.0, and version 10 was used by 5.5.

To upgrade the virtual VM version, you again follow the same general sequence:

1. Attach the baseline.

2. Perform a scan.

3. Remediate.

To attach the baseline, follow the same procedures outlined earlier in the section "Attaching and Detaching Baselines or Baseline Groups." Performing a scan is much the same as well, but make sure you select the VM Hardware upgrade option when initiating a scan so VUM will detect outdated VM hardware. Even if the correct baseline is attached, outdated VM hardware won't be detected during a scan unless you select this box.

PLANNING FOR DOWNTIME

Remediation of VMs found to be noncompliant—for example, found to have outdated VM hardware—is again much like the other forms of remediation that have already been discussed. The important thing to note is that VM hardware upgrades are done while the VM is powered off. This means you must plan for downtime in the environment to remediate this issue.

VUM performs VM hardware upgrades only when the VM is powered off. It's also important to note that VUM might not be able to conduct an orderly shutdown of the guest OS to do the VM hardware upgrade. To avoid an unexpected shutdown of the guest OS when VUM powers off the VM, specify a schedule in the dialog box shown previously in Figure 4.25 that provides you with enough time to perform an orderly shutdown of the guest OS first.

Depending on which guest OS and which VMware Tools version is running inside the VM, the user may see prompts for "new hardware" after the VM hardware upgrade is complete. If you've followed the recommendations, and the latest version of VMware Tools is installed, then all the necessary drivers should already be present, and the "new hardware" should work without any real issues.

KEEP A RECORD OF YOUR VM's IP ADDRESSES

The most common problem faced with upgrading VM hardware is losing the VM's IP address. This occurs if VMware Tools has not been upgraded properly before you start the hardware upgrade process. Normally, the new version of VMware Tools can record the VM's IP settings, and if a new VM hardware upgrade changes the network card's driver, VMware Tools can migrate the IP settings across automatically. However, VMware Tools can drop the settings for several reasons—for example, it does not recognize an issue with VMware Tools before it proceeds with the hardware upgrade, you may not have allowed for enough reboots after the VMware Tools upgrade, there may be OS issues caused by the new drivers, and so forth.

Although this shouldn't happen, it is seen often enough that a quick plan B is in order. One simple approach, prior to initiating the remediation step, is to list all the VMs to be upgraded in the VMs And Templates view. Right-click one of the columns, and add the IP address to the view. Then from the File menu, select Export List To A Spreadsheet. This way, should one or more VMs lose their IP settings in the upgrade, you have a quick reference you can pull up. It's not foolproof, but this 30-second action might just save you some time trawling through DNS records if things go awry.

Although you might find virtual appliances with old versions of virtual hardware, it's advisable to treat these as special cases and wait for the software vendors to include the hardware upgrade in the next version. Virtual appliances are custom built and tuned by the vendor for their purpose. They are often released with older hardware so they are compatible with as many versions of vSphere as possible. If a new version of VM hardware is available that would benefit the vendor's appliance, the vendor will likely provide a new version of its appliance to take advantage of the new hardware version.

By combining some of the different features of VUM, you can greatly simplify the process o upgrading your virtualized infrastructure to the latest version of VMware vSphere through an orchestrated upgrade.

Performing an Orchestrated Upgrade

A specific use case for baseline groups is the *orchestrated upgrade*. For an orchestrated upgrade, you run a host baseline group and a VM/VA baseline group sequentially to help automate the process of moving an organization's environment fully into VMware vSphere 6.0. Quite simply upgrades your hosts and then your VMs in one job.

Consider this sequence of events:

1. You create a host baseline group that combines a host upgrade baseline with a dynamic host patch baseline to apply the latest updates.

2. You create a VM baseline group that combines two different VM upgrade baselines—the VMware Tools upgrade baseline and the VM hardware upgrade baseline.

3. You schedule the host baseline group to execute, followed at some point by the VM baseline group.

4. The host baseline group upgrades the hosts from ESXi 6.0/6.5 to ESXi 6.7 and installs all applicable patches and updates.

5. The VM baseline group upgrades VMware Tools and then upgrades the VM hardware to version 14.

When these two baseline groups have completed, all the hosts and VMs affected by the baselines will be upgraded and patched. Most, if not all, of the tedious tasks surrounding the VMware Tools and VM hardware upgrade have been automated. Congratulations! You've just simplified and automated the upgrade path for your virtual environment.

Investigating Alternative Update Options

In most circumstances, using the VUM tools in the vSphere Desktop Client is the easiest and most efficient method of keeping your hosts, VMs, and virtual appliances patched and at the latest, greatest level. However, there are sometimes circumstances where you want to look beyond the standard tools and investigate the alternatives. As you'll learn, vSphere can be updated in several other ways.

Using vSphere Update Manager PowerCLI

vSphere takes advantage of Microsoft's PowerShell scripting environment with the PowerCLI extensions that are discussed in Chapter 14, "Automating VMware vSphere."

Without getting ahead of ourselves, it's worth noting the PowerCLI tools that are available to script many of VUM's functions. The VUM PowerCLI cmdlets cover the most common tasks, like working with baselines and scanning, staging, and remediating vSphere objects. Figure 4.32 shows the list of cmdlets currently available.

FIGURE 4.32
VUM PowerCLI
cmdlets available

To use the VUM PowerCLI, you need to first install VMware PowerCLI, which comes pre-packaged with the Update Manager PowerCLI package. You can get more information about this package from VMware's *VMware vSphere Update Manager PowerCLI Installation and Administration Guide* for VUM 6.0.

Get-PowerCLIVersion

Upgrading and Patching without vSphere Update Manager

You can maintain your vSphere environment, keeping the elements patched and upgraded, without resorting to the use of VUM. Also, you may want to use VUM for certain updating tas but take an alternative approach for others. For example, you might not want to use VUM in th following situations:

◆ You are using the free stand-alone vSphere ESXi hypervisor, which does not come with vCenter Server. Without a licensed vCenter Server, you can't use VUM.

◆ You have only a small environment with one or two small host servers. To maximize the use of your server hardware for VMs, you don't want the infrastructure overhead of another application and another database running.

◆ You rely heavily on scripting to manage your environment, and you would like to take advantage of tools that don't need PowerShell, such as the PowerCLI toolset that VMware offers.

◆ You don't want to use VUM for host upgrades, because you choose to always run fresh host rebuilds when required.

◆ You already have kickstart scripts, PowerShell postinstall scripts, host profiles, and EDA UDA tools, or you want to set up an Auto Deploy server to control the installation and upgrading of your hosts.

So, what alternatives are available?

Upgrading and Patching Hosts To upgrade your legacy ESXi 5.x and 6.x hosts to vSphere 6.7, you have two non-VUM options. You can run through an interactive install from the ES. 6.x ISO media, choosing an in-place upgrade, and then perform the same process with the 6. media. Or you can run a kickstart scripted upgrade along with the same ESXi 6.x and 6.7 media to perform an unattended upgrade. No command-line utility can upgrade an older ESXi 5.5 host directly to 6.7.

For upgrades from ESXi 5.0 or 5.1 to newer versions, you can likewise use an interactive or unattended upgrade. If you have used VMware's Auto Deploy technology to roll out vSphe you will be able to leverage this tool to upgrade or patch it to the latest updates. ESXi 5.x ho can also be patched and upgraded to 6.x and then to 6.7 with the vCLI command-line `esxcl` `software vib` tool.

The `esxupdate` and `vihostupdate` tools are no longer supported for ESXi 5.x or 6.x updates

Upgrading VMs Without VUM, upgrading VM hardware can be done via the VMware H Client or directly in vCenter via the vSphere Web Client. If the hosts are connected to vCent then your connected client can manually upgrade the hardware. Even without vCenter, you can still upgrade each VM by connecting via the host client straight at the host. You must sh down the VMs yourself and initialize each upgrade. Similarly, VMware Tools can be upgraded in each guest OS manually from within the VM's console. You must mount VMware Tools from one of the vSphere Clients. You can also use the Host Client to perform the upgrade from outside the VM.

The older `vmware-vmupgrade.exe` tool should not be used to upgrade VMs anymore.

vSphere Auto Deploy

vSphere Auto Deploy—often just referred to as Auto Deploy—is, like vSphere Update Manager, a tool designed to help VMware administrators rapidly automate and streamline the process of deploying ESXi images to physical hosts within their vSphere environment. By combining the boot infrastructure abilities of PXE (Preboot eXecution Environment) with vSphere Host Profiles, discussed previously in Chapter 3, an administrator is no longer required to build a kickstart file or directly install ESXi on each individual host. Auto Deploy provides a centralized configuration plane for the state of the hosts. Each time a host is rebooted, its image and configuration will be picked up from the Auto Deploy services and the associated Host Profile, respectively, and loaded into memory, resulting in no physical state being preserved on the hosts.

The following requirements must be met before you can use Auto Deploy to install ESXi on your hosts:

- PXE and TFTP boot environment
- ESXi Image Profiles created with Image Builder
- Host Profiles to attach to newly deployed hosts
- Deployment Rule to help the hosts get the right image and configuration

We'll step you through the process of getting these things up and running so you can see the level of configuration and speed that can be achieved if you need to deploy a large number of hosts.

Deploying Hosts with Auto Deploy

Autodeploy is split into five steps in order to achieve stateless boot of an ESXi host. With each operation configured and in place, the process looks something like this:

1. When the physical server boots, the server starts a PXE boot sequence. The DHCP server assigns an IP address to the host and provides the IP address of the TFTP server as well as a boot filename to download.

2. The host contacts the TFTP server and downloads the specified filename, which contains the iPXE boot file and an iPXE configuration file.

3. iPXE executes, which causes the host to make an HTTP boot request to the Auto Deploy server. This request includes information about the host, the host hardware, and the host network. This information is written to the server console when iPXE is executing, as you can see in Figure 4.33.

4. Based on the information passed to it from iPXE (the host information shown in Figure 4.33), the Auto Deploy server matches the server against a deployment rule and assigns the correct image profile. The Auto Deploy server then streams the assigned ESXi image across the network to the physical host.

5. Once the image has been received on the physical host, the host will store this in memory and then begin the boot process.

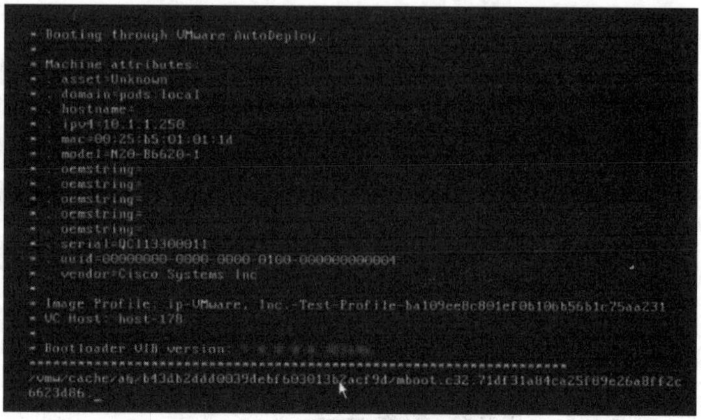

FIGURE 4.33
Host information is
echoed to the server
console when it
performs a
network boot.

When the host has finished executing, you have a system running ESXi. The Auto Deploy
server can also automatically join the ESXi host to vCenter Server and assign a host profile
(which we discussed in more detail in Chapter 3) for further configuration. As you can see, this
system offers administrators tremendous flexibility and power.

Ready to get started with provisioning ESXi hosts using Auto Deploy? Let's start with setting
up the vSphere Auto Deploy server.

FINDING THE vSPHERE AUTO DEPLOY AND vSPHERE ESXI IMAGE BUILDER SERVER

The vSphere Auto Deploy server is where the various ESXi image profiles are stored. This works
in conjunction with the vSphere ESXi Image Builder service, which gives you the user interface
(UI) functionality to construct and manage image profiles that Auto Deploy can then consume
and serve to hosts. The image profile is transferred from this server via HTTP to a physical host
when it boots. The image profile is the actual ESXi image, and it consists of multiple vSphere
Installation Bundle (VIB) files. VIBs are ESXi software packages; these could be drivers, Common
Information Management (CIM) providers, or other applications that extend or enhance the ESX
platform. Both VMware and VMware's partners could distribute software as VIBs.

The vSphere Auto Deploy and vSphere ESXi Image Builder services are installed but not
enabled by default with vCenter Server. Previous versions of vSphere required a separate install
of Auto Deploy, while Image Builder was only full introduced into the vSphere Web Client in
vSphere 6.5.

Perform the following steps to enable the vSphere Auto Deploy and vSphere ESXi Image
Builder services and set their startup configuration to Automatic:

1. Launch the vSphere Web Client, if it is not already running, and connect to a vCenter
   Server instance.

2. Navigate to Administration ➤ System Configuration ➤ Nodes and select your vCenter in
   the Navigator Pane ➤ Related Objects.

3. Right-click on Auto Deploy, and select Edit Startup Type from the context menu. Change
   the default setting of Manual to Automatic and click OK. Repeat this process on the
   ImageBuilder Service.

4. After both services have been set to start with the OS, click on each service and then click the Start link in the upper-left corner of the content area.

5. Log out and back into the Web Client in order to load the new Auto Deploy plugin.

6. Now that the Auto Deploy and ImageBuilder have started and the plugins have loaded, click Home ➤ Global Inventory Lists, open the Navigator pane and click Configure ➤ Auto Deploy, and select your vCenter.

You'll see information about the registered Auto Deploy service. Figure 4.34 shows the Auto Deploy screen after we enabled the service.

FIGURE 4.34
This screen provides information about the Auto Deploy server that is registered with vCenter Server.

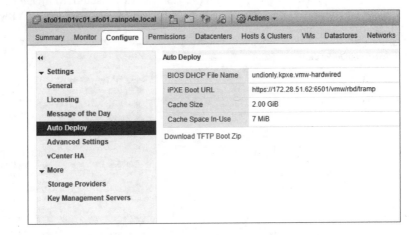

After you have started and allowed the plug-ins to register with vCenter, a new vSphere Auto Deploy icon appears on the home page. From this icon, you will have access to both the Auto Deploy and ESXi Image Builder features, enabling you to build your image profiles and hand them over to Auto Deploy relatively seamlessly.

Clicking the vSphere Auto Deploy icon at the vSphere Web Client home page takes you to the main Auto Deploy management screen. Figure 4.35 shows that this area is divided into four main sections: Software Depots, Deploy Rules, Deployed Hosts, and Discovered Hosts.

FIGURE 4.35
The tabs in the vSphere Auto Deploy area of the vSphere Web Client

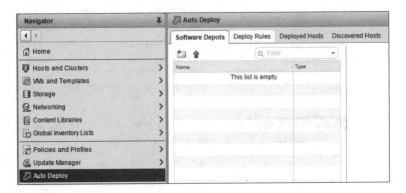

These four tabs make up the major areas of managing Auto Deploy, so let's take a quick look at each section:

Software Depots   The Software Depots tab shows the collection of software depots that currently in the Image Builder's repository. From here, you can add, remove, and update online or offline depots, made available through either an HTTP URL (online depot) or through uploaded ZIP files supplied from your workstation (offline depot). You can view the details of any specific software depot by clicking the depot in the left pane, and by using either the Image Profiles or Software Packages button in the right pane, you can see the associated image profile (if it's available) and the VIBs (software packages) that are contained within the image. Figure 4.36 shows the standard image that's packaged with the generally available release of ESXi 6.7 and all of its associated VIBs.

FIGURE 4.36
The Software Depots tab offers detailed information about each of the items in the repository.

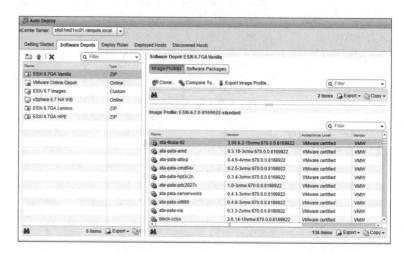

Deploy Rules   Deployment rules are a key to how Auto Deploy works, and from the Deploy Rules tab, the administrator will perform the bulk of configuring Auto Deploy. From here, administrators can configure and fine-tune the deployment rules that are used to breathe life into the PXE hosts, the order in which these rules are executed against the hosts, and the rule overall enablement status.

Once a deployment rule has been defined and added to the list, you can also see the details any specific rule, including what patterns it will use to identify the hosts, what image profile and host profile it will use, the location where the hosts will reside after a successful boot, and whether the rule is active.

Figure 4.37 shows our environment running multiple rules in order to account for a variety hardware, the IP ranges that the hosts are booting on and clusters we expect the hosts to reside in.

Deployed Hosts   The Deployed Hosts tab allows you to see what hosts have been successfully booted and, due to their association with one of your rules, their attached image profile host profiles, and locations.

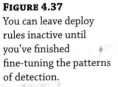

FIGURE 4.37
You can leave deploy rules inactive until you've finished fine-tuning the patterns of detection.

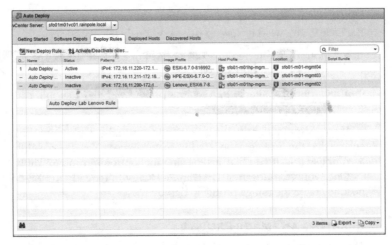

Discovered Hosts If one of your deploy rules fails to capture the specifics of a host, or if this is your first time using Auto Deploy and there are not any rules for your host yet, this tab will provide the specifics of each of the hosts that have been found. This will allow an administrator to construct new deployment rules or adapt existing ones in order to capture the host on its next reboot.

Once the Auto Deploy server has been enabled to start automatically and is up and running, there's very little additional work or configuration required, except configuring TFTP and DHCP on your network to support vSphere Auto Deploy. The next section provides an overview of the required configurations for TFTP and DHCP.

CONFIGURING TFTP AND DHCP FOR AUTO DEPLOY

The procedures for configuring TFTP and DHCP will vary based on the specific TFTP and DHCP servers you are using on your network. For example, configuring the ISC DHCP server to support vSphere Auto Deploy is dramatically different from configuring the DHCP Server service provided with Windows Server. Therefore, we can provide only high-level information in this section. Refer to your specific vendor's documentation for details on how the configuration is carried out.

Configuring TFTP

For TFTP, you need only upload the appropriate TFTP boot files to the TFTP directory. The Download TFTP Boot Zip link shown earlier in Figure 4.34 provides the necessary files. Simply download the zip file using that link, unzip the file, and place the contents of the unzipped file in the TFTP directory on the TFTP server.

Configuring DHCP

For DHCP, you need to specify two additional DHCP options:

◆ Option 66, referred to as next-server or as Boot Server Host Name, must specify the IP address of the TFTP server.

◆ Option 67, called boot-filename or Bootfile Name, should contain the value `undionly` `.kpxe.vmw-hardwired`.

If you want to identify hosts by IP address in the deployment rules, then you'll need a way ensure that the host gets the IP address you expect. You can certainly use DHCP reservations t accomplish this, if you like; just be sure that options 66 and 67 apply to the reservation as well

Once you've configured TFTP and DHCP, you're ready to PXE-boot your server, but you st need to create the image profile to deploy ESXi.

CREATING AN IMAGE PROFILE

The process for creating an image profile may seem counterintuitive at first. Creating an image profile involves first adding at least one *software depot*. A software depot could be a directory structure of files and folders on an HTTP server, or (more commonly) it could be an offline dep in the form of a zip file. You can add multiple software depots.

Some software depots will already have one or more image profiles defined, and you can define additional image profiles (usually by cloning an existing image profile). You'll then hav the ability to add software packages (in the form of VIBs) to the image profile you've created. Once you've finished adding or removing software packages or drivers from the image profile you can export the image profile (either to an ISO or as a zip file for use as an offline depot).

All image profile tasks can be accomplished using either the Image Builder UI contained within the vSphere Web Client or through PowerCLI, the latter of which has been the tradition method for many releases leading up to vSphere 6.5. We'll describe PowerCLI, along with othe automation tools, in more detail in Chapter 14, "Automating VMware vSphere," but for now, we'll walk you through creating an image profile using the Image Builder within the Auto Deploy UI. This workflow will use the ESXi 6.7 offline depot zip file available for downloading by registered customers.

Perform the following steps to create an image profile:

1. Launch the vSphere Web Client, if it is not already running, and connect to a vCenter Server instance.

2. On the Web Client's home screen, select Auto Deploy. You can also select Auto Deploy from the Navigator or Home menu. Click the Software Depots tab.

3. Click the Add Software Depots in the upper-left of the content area and then click the Custom Depot radio button. Input a name for the software depot that will serve as a pla to store all of your images (as shown in Figure 4.38), and then click OK.

    You can also use the Add Software Depots button to add *online* depots, such as VMware online depot (Figure 4.39) or the local vCenter's hosted repository that contains the VIB for vSphere HA (Figure 4.40), which we covered in Chapter 3.

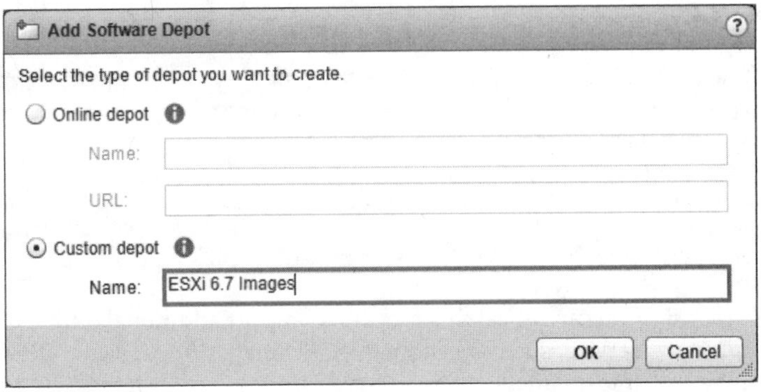

FIGURE 4.38
The first step to building any custom images is creating your first software depot.

Add Software Depot

Select the type of depot you want to create.

○ Online depot ⓘ

Name:

URL:

⦿ Custom depot ⓘ

Name: ESXi 6.7 Images

OK   Cancel

FIGURE 4.39
VMware and its partners provide public repositories giving you access to all of their ESXi images, which can then be leveraged for the purposes of Auto Deploy or host provisioning.

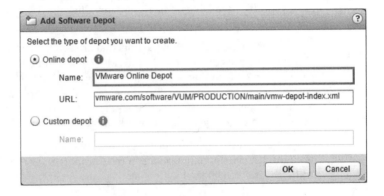

Add Software Depot

Select the type of depot you want to create.

⦿ Online depot ⓘ

Name: VMware Online Depot

URL: vmware.com/software/VUM/PRODUCTION/main/vmw-depot-index.xml

○ Custom depot ⓘ

Name:

OK   Cancel

FIGURE 4.40
Even your local vCenter provides a local repository, allowing you to inject the VIBs for vSphere HA into an image profile.

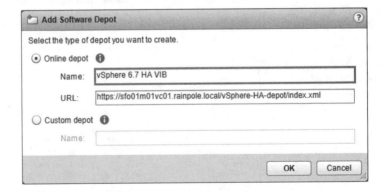

Add Software Depot

Select the type of depot you want to create.

⦿ Online depot ⓘ

Name: vSphere 6.7 HA VIB

URL: https://sfo01m01vc01.rainpole.local/vSphere-HA-depot/index.xml

○ Custom depot ⓘ

Name:

OK   Cancel

4. Now that you have a place to store your image profiles, click the Import Software Depots button to the right of the Add Software Depots button.

5. In the Import Software Depots dialog box, give your depot a name, and then use the Browse button (shown in Figure 4.41) to select the ESXi 6.7 offline depot file. Click Upload, and allow this operation to complete (this might take a few minutes). Then click Close.

FIGURE 4.41
You can import a variety
of software depots into
your environment,
with some containing
image profiles while
others contain
only software
packages (VIBs).

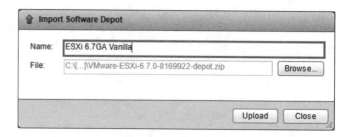

6. You can repeat this process to import additional offline depots into your Image Builder service, such as vendor-specific images or packaged VIBs that can be later built into an image.

7. Once your ESXi 6.7 depot has been imported, click on the depot in the left pane to list all image profiles available in the right pane. Click the Software Packages button in the right pane to show all of the VIBs associated with this image.

As with ESXi ISOs, the offline depots that are available from different vendors will contain images that have different VIBs, providing added functionality to your hosts (as discussed in Chapter 2, "Planning and Installing VMware ESXi". When using Auto Deploy, it is recommended that you use the offline depot that complements the hardware so as to reduce the need for customization and the administrative overhead that might otherwise be required to get the images to work properly.

Figure 4.42 shows the differences between two image depots from two different vendors. You can use the different options in the Compare Image profile dialog box to review the differences between the two images.

FIGURE 4.42
Software depots and
their image providers
will have different
VIBs, enabling vendor-
specific functionality or
hardware that comes
with your hosts.

Lenovo_ESXi6.7-8169922_20180404 - Compare Image Profile

Image profile:	Lenovo_ESXi6.7-8169922_20180404	Image profile: HPE-ESXi-6.7.0-OS-Releas... Change...
Software depot:	ESXi 6.7GA Lenovo	Software depot: ESXi 6.7GA HPE
Acceptance level:	Partner supported	Acceptance level: Partner supported
Vendor:	Lenovo	Vendor: Hewlett Packard Enterprise

Software packages:

All | Upgraded | Downgraded | Additional | Missing | Same

The following software packages are only present in HPE-ESXi-6.7.0-OS-Release-Gen9plus-670.10.2.0.35:

Name	Version	Acceptance Level	Vendor
amsd	670.11.2.0-12.7535516	Partner supported	HPE
bootcfg	6.7.0.02-04.00.4.7535516	Partner supported	HPE
conrep	6.7.0.03-01.00.2.7535516	Partner supported	HPE
cru	670.6.7.10.14-1OEM.670.0.0.7535516	Partner supported	HPE
fc-enablement	670.3.20.12-7535516	Partner supported	HPE
hponcfg	6.7.0.5.0-3.8.7535516	Partner supported	HPE
ilo	670.10.1.0.16-1OEM.670.0.0.7535516	Partner supported	HPE
intelcim-provider	0.5-3.3	VMware accepted	Intel
net-ixgbe	3.7.13.7.14iov-20vmw.670.0.0.8169922	VMware certified	VMW
oem-build	670.10.2.0-7535516	Partner supported	HPE
scsi-hpdsa	5.5.0.60-1OEM.550.0.0.1331820	Partner supported	Hewlett-Packard
smx-provider	670.03.13.00.5-7535516	VMware accepted	HPE
ssacli	3.25.4.0-6.5.0.4240417	Partner supported	HPE
testevent	6.7.0.02-00.01.12.7535516	Partner supported	HPE

OK

8. To create a new image profile, clone an existing profile (existing profiles are typically read-only) by clicking on one of the available images and click the Clone image profile button to the upper-left of the expanded software depots area to begin the cloning process, as shown in Figure 4.43.

FIGURE 4.43

Since most software depots you import will be read-only, cloning an image profile allows you to further tailor the final image.

9. In the Clone Image Profile dialog box, the fields are self-explanatory and. with the exception of the short description. they are all required. Fill in each field, and ensure that the Software Depot drop-down menu is set to the depot you created in step 3. Click Next.

10. On the next screen, you define the software packages (VIBs) that will be bundled in your final image. Make sure that all of the default software packages from your image profile are included. You can use the Software Depot drop-down menu, shown in Figure 4.44, to filter between your different depots, which can be extremely useful once you get more than a few depots imported. If there are any additional packages you'd like to include, such as the vSphere HA software depot, select them, then click next

FIGURE 4.44

When building your final image, you can browse all of your available software depots to select any additional VIBs that are required for your hosts to successfully boot.

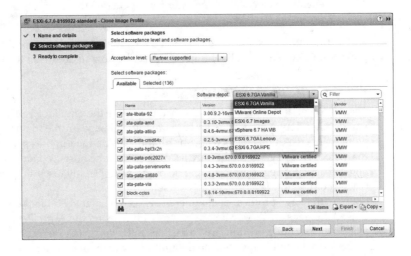

11. Review the image profile summary screen and ensure all of the fields are accurate. Click Finish.

12. Once the new image has been compiled, click on the custom software depot that you created in step 3 to review it, and click Edit if additional customization is needed.

If you have more VIBs that you'd like to add after you've already established an image profile, don't panic—you can customize the image by adding VIBs, or you can export it. You can use the export function to either export the image as a ZIP file or an ISO file. The former output can be used for transferring built image profiles between vCenters, especially if you plan on using Auto Deploy in multiple environments and would like to use a standard image. Unfortunately, the Image Builder service is not currently shared between multiple systems. The latter output can be used to do manual, full installs as discussed in Chapter 2—which is quite useful if you find that the original image you tried installing is missing some critical VIBs.

All of your images and software depots will be preserved on your vCenter Server, so you can always revisit your profiles if further customization is needed. However, if you chose to do this operation via PowerCLI, you might want to export the image profile at this point because after you exit a PowerCLI session, the image profiles will not be available when you start a new session. If you export an image profile as an offline-depot zip file, you can easily add it back in when you start a new session.

To export an image profile as an offline-depot zip file, perform the following steps:

1. Launch the vSphere Web Client, if it is not already running, and connect to a vCenter Server instance.

2. On the Web Client's home screen, select Auto Deploy. You can also select Auto Deploy from the Navigator or Home menu. Click the Software Depots tab.

3. In the left pane of available depots, click your depot, and in the right pane, select the image profile and click Export Image Profile (the last button in the upper-left area of the right pane).

4. Decide between exporting as a ZIP or ISO (we selected ZIP for this example), and then click Generate Image. Allow the vCenter to generate the image; then click the Download Image link, and click Close.

The final step is establishing deployment rules that link image profiles to servers in order to provision ESXi to them at boot time. We describe how to do this in the next section.

ESTABLISHING DEPLOYMENT RULES

The deployment rules are where the "rubber meets the road" for vSphere Auto Deploy. When you define a deployment rule, you are linking an image profile to one or more hosts. At this point, vSphere Auto Deploy will copy all the VIBs defined in the specified image profile up to the Auto Deploy server so they are accessible from the hosts. When a deployment rule is in place, you can actually begin provisioning hosts via Auto Deploy (assuming all the other pieces are in place and functioning correctly, of course).

As with image profiles, deployment rules can be managed via the Auto Deploy UI or via PowerCLI. Let's create our first deployment rule using the Auto Deploy UI, since once you master the overall workflow, this translates to PowerCLI quite nicely.

Perform the following steps to define a new deployment rule:

1. Launch the vSphere Web Client, if it is not already running, and connect to a vCenter Server instance.

2. On the Web Client's home screen, select Auto Deploy. You can also select Auto Deploy from the Navigator or Home menu. Click the Deploy Rules tab.

3. Click the New Deploy Rule button to define an image profile, and define a new deployment rule that matches the image profile to a physical host.

   Give the deploy rule a name, and under the Rules area, define the pattern (or patterns) the rule should look for with the PXE booting hosts. In the example shown in Figure 4.45, the defined rules will assign the image profile to all hosts with "Lenovo" in the vendor string and an IP address that's between 172.16.11.200–172.16.11.200 (using a hyphen to separate the start and end of the IP address range).

FIGURE 4.45
Deployment rules let you be as specific or as general as you'd like when capturing hosts.

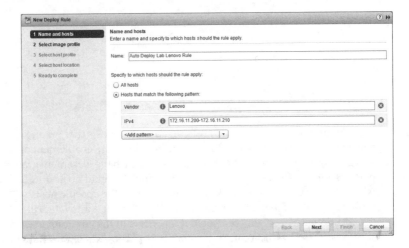

4. Assign an image profile that complements the rules you previously defined. Use the Software Depot drop-down menu to toggle between your available images.

5. Skip the assigning of a host profile to the deploy rule for now. You can circle back around to this once your first host has booted, been added to vCenter, and configured.

6. Select the cluster in which you want the ESXi host assigned to within vCenter Server. Click Next.

   In the example shown in Figure 4.46, this rule puts all hosts into the cluster named sfo01-m01-mgmt02 in the vCenter Server with which the Auto Deploy server is registered. (Recall that an Auto Deploy server has a one-to-one relationship with a vCenter Server instance.)

7. Verify that the patterns, image, and cluster have been set correctly for the new rule, and then click Finish.

8. The rule will be created, but it will be in an inactive state. This prevents administrators from creating new rules and accidentally impacting existing ones. Since this is our only rule at the moment, go ahead and click the Activated/Deactivate Rules button.

9. Select your new rule in the bottom area of the Activate And Reorder dialog box, and then click Activate. Click Next and Finish.

FIGURE 4.46
A deployment rule
can only place hosts into
a single cluster, but a
single cluster can be
used by multiple
deployment rules.

FIGURE 4.46
A deployment rule
can only place hosts into
a single cluster, but a
single cluster can be
used by multiple
deployment rules.

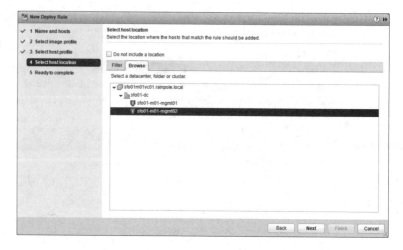

As your environment grows and you add more hosts that map to different image profiles and clusters, you can use this area to manage how both the enablement of rules as well as their sequencing for booting hosts. Some rule sets may have extremely granular patterns in them—perhaps for specific use cases where only a specific set of hosts are eligible—while other rule sets will be broader. This will allow you to ensure that the specific hosts will be captured by a higher order rule, while other, more generalized hosts will fall into later rules.

Additionally, once you've booted a few hosts in the environment, you can utilize the Test Rules Before Activation feature, located in the Activate And Reorder dialog box covered in the workflow above, and run this against the available hosts to ensure that they do, in fact, fall into the pattern(s) you defined.

Now that a deployment rule is in place, you're ready to provision via Auto Deploy. Boot the physical host that matches the patterns you defined in the deployment rule, and it should follow the boot sequence described at the start of this section. Figure 4.47 shows how it looks when a host is booting ESXi via vSphere Auto Deploy.

FIGURE 4.47
Note the differences in
the ESXi boot process
when using Auto
Deploy versus a
traditional installation
of ESXi.

Once the host is fully booted, you can use the Deployed Hosts tab to review all Auto Deploy hosts and their associated image profile, host profile, and the cluster in which they reside. If you fail to see one of your hosts, and fear that you may have failed at your shepherding duties, there's no need to worry—you can use the Discovered Hosts tab, which will list all hosts that failed to find an appropriate rule. You can then review these hosts, and adjust your different rules, using the Test Rules Before Activation functionality in the Activation And Reordering dialog box discussed previously.

By now, you should be seeing the flexibility Auto Deploy offers. If you have to deploy a new ESXi image, you need only define a new image profile (using a new software depot, if necessary), assign that image profile with a deployment rule, and reboot the physical servers. When the servers come up, they will boot the newly assigned ESXi image via PXE.

Of course, there are some additional concerns that you'll need to address should you decide to go this route:

◆ The image profile doesn't contain any ESXi configuration state information, such as virtual switches, security settings, advanced parameters, and so forth. Host profiles are used to store this configuration state information in vCenter Server and pass that configuration information down to a host automatically. You can use a deployment rule to assign a host profile, or you can assign a host profile to a cluster and then use a deployment rule to join hosts to a cluster. We described host profiles in greater detail in Chapter 3.

◆ State information—such as log files, generated private keys, and so forth—is stored in host memory and is lost during a reboot. Therefore, you must configure additional settings such as setting up syslog for capturing the ESXi logs. Otherwise, this vital operational information is lost every time the host is rebooted. The configuration for capturing this state information can be included in a host profile that is assigned to a host or cluster.

In the Auto Deploy Stateless mode, the ESXi image doesn't contain the configuration state and doesn't maintain dynamic state information, thus the hosts are therefore considered *stateless ESXi hosts*. All the state information is stored elsewhere instead of on the host itself.

ENSURING AUTO DEPLOY IS AVAILABLE

When helping a business deploy a large number of ESXi hosts, we had to ensure that all Auto Deploy components were highly available. This meant that designing the infrastructure responsible for booting and deploying ESXi hosts was more complicated than normal. Services such as PXE, DHCP, and the vCenter VMs were all deployed on hosts that were not provisioned using Auto Deploy in a separate management cluster.

Building a separate cluster for vSphere infrastructure-management purposes will ensure there is no chicken-and-egg situation. You need to ensure that in a completely virtualized environment that the VMs used to provision ESXi hosts with Auto Deploy are not running on the ESXi hosts they need to build.

STATELESS CACHING MODE

Unless your ESXi host hardware is purchased without any local storage or you plan on using bootable SAN storage, we recommend that you consider one of the two other Auto Deploy modes. These modes offer resiliency for your hosts if at any time the Auto Deploy services become unavailable.

To configure stateless caching, follow the previous procedure for stateless ESXi with these additions:

1. If the vSphere Web Client isn't already running, launch it and connect to a vCenter Server instance.

2. On the Home screen, select Host Profiles.

3. Create a new host profile or edit the existing one attached to your host.

4. Navigate to System Image Cache Configuration under Advanced Configuration Settings.

5. Select either "Enable stateless caching on the host" or "Enable stateless caching to a USB disk on the host."

6. If you chose the first option in step 5, input the disk configuration details, using the same disk syntax as described in the section "Performing an Unattended Installation of VMwar ESXi" in Chapter 2, such as *mptsas*, *remote*, or *local*. By default, this process will use the fir available disk containing ESXi as you can see in Figure 4.48.

FIGURE 4.48
Editing the host profile to allow Stateless Caching on a local disk

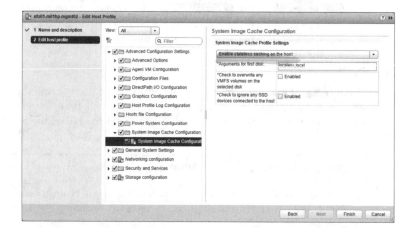

7. Click Finish to end the Host Profile Wizard.

8. Next, you need to configure the boot order in the host BIOS to boot from the network firs and the local disk second. This procedure will differ depending on your server type.

9. Reboot the host to allow a fresh Auto Deploy image, and the new host profile will be attached.

This configuration tells the ESXi host to take the Auto Deploy image loaded in memory and save it to the local disk after a successful boot. If, for some reason, the network or Auto Deploy server is unavailable when your host reboots, it will fall back and boot the cached copy on its local disk.

STATEFUL MODE

Just like Stateless Caching mode, the Auto Deploy Stateful mode is configured by editing host profiles within vCenter and the boot order settings in the host BIOS. Follow these steps to use the Stateful install:

1. If the vSphere Web Client isn't already running, launch it and connect to a vCenter Server instance.

2. On the Home screen, select Host Profiles.

3. Create a new host profile or edit the existing one attached to your host.

4. Navigate to System Image Cache Configuration under Advanced Configuration Settings.

5. Select either "Enable stateful installs on the host" or Enable stateful installs to a USB disk on the host."

6. If you chose the first option in step 5, input the disk configuration details, using the same disk syntax as described in the section "Performing an Unattended Installation of VMware ESXi"in Chapter 2 as well as in the "Stateless Caching Mode" covered above. Again, by default, this process will use the first available disk containing ESXi (see Figure 4.49).

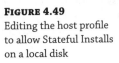

FIGURE 4.49
Editing the host profile to allow Stateful Installs on a local disk

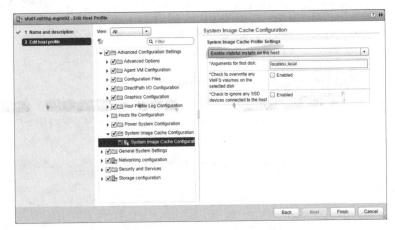

7. Click Finish to end the Host Profile Wizard.

8. Next, you need to configure the boot order in the host BIOS to boot from the local disk first, and the network second. This procedure will differ depending on your server type.

9. The host will boot into Maintenance mode, and you must apply the host profile by clicking Remediate Host on the host's Summary tab.

10. Provide IP addresses for the host, and then reboot the host.

   Upon this reboot, the host is now running off the local disk like a "normally provisioned" ESXi host.

vSphere Auto Deploy offers some great advantages, especially for environments with lots o ESXi hosts to manage, but it can also add complexity. As mentioned earlier, it all comes down t the design and requirements of your vSphere deployment.

vCenter Support Tools

In addition to VUM, vCenter includes a few other useful support tools. Let's go through them before we finish up this chapter and move out of vCenter specifics and on to networking.

ESXi Dump Collector

The ESXi Dump Collector is a centralized service that can receive and store memory dumps fro ESXi servers should they crash unexpectedly. These memory dumps occur when an ESXi host suffers what is known as a purple screen of death (PSOD), analogous to the Windows blue scre of death (BSOD) or a Linux kernel panic. The kernel grabs the contents of memory and *dumps* them to nonvolatile disk storage before the server reboots. This allows VMware support service to investigate the cause of the PSOD and hopefully recommend an action to prevent the issue from occurring again.

Ordinarily, these dumps are sent to the host's local storage in a separate partition not nor- mally mounted to the running filesystem, known as vmkDiagnostic. If the host has been deployed to a USB key/SD card, or via Auto Deploy, then a core dump partition isn't available. For these hosts, it is important to redirect these dumps to a central dump collector. Even if your hosts are not installed or deployed in this way, it can be beneficial, particularly in larger enviror ments, to manage this potentially valuable data in one place.

ESXI DUMP COLLECTOR SERVICE

The ESXi Dump Collector service is installed but not running by default on both Windows and Virtual Appliance vCenter Server versions. Figure 4.50 shows the service in the vSphere Web Client.

FIGURE 4.50
Dump Collector services not running by default

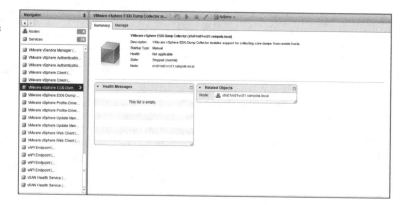

Here are the steps to check the service status from vCenter, or to restart or stop it:

1. Log into the vSphere Web Client.

2. On the vCenter Home screen, select Administration from the Navigation pane.

3. Open System Configuration ➤ Services and select VMware vSphere ESXi Dump Collector.

4. From the Actions menu, you can select Restart, Start, or Stop.

The list of services and their status is available on the first screen in the bottom left. If you have navigated away from this screen, it can be found under the vCenter Server tab, and then the Summary tab.

Only two configuration options are available on the ESXi Dump Collector. First, you can change the amount of storage reserved for all dumps. Core dumps can be anywhere from 100 MB to 5 GB, so size this space appropriately depending on how many hosts are configured, how frequently you might expect them to PSOD, and how long you need to retain the information. If you have a large environment, are experiencing frequent PSODs, or have to keep troubleshooting data for extended periods, then you should consider increasing this level. By default, vCenter needs 2 GB of space for the ESXi Dump Collector. Figure 4.51 shows the service's Manage tab.

FIGURE 4.51
ESXi Dump Collector
Manage tab

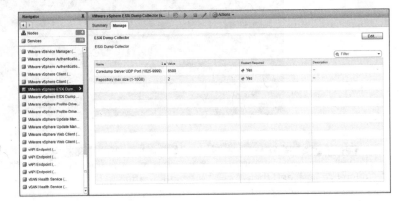

Second, you can configure the port number that the ESXi Dump Collector listens on. By default, this is port 6500. If this or the storage space size changes, a restart of the service is required to apply the changes.

CONFIGURING ESXi HOSTS TO REDIRECT THEIR CORE DUMPS

The primary method for configuring hosts to redirect their core dumps to your newly minted ESX Dump Collector is to use the `esxcli` command-line tool:

1. Log into your host via SSH, via the local ESXi shell, or using a vCLI installation (vCLI usage requires additional context switches to identify the host).

2. Review the existing Dump Collector configuration:

```
esxcli system coredump network get
```

3. Configure the host's dump redirection settings (management VMkernel interface and collector's IP and port):

```
esxcli system coredump network set -v vmk0 -i 172.16.11.62 -o 6500
```

4. Turn on dump redirection:

```
esxcli system coredump network set -e true
```

5. Confirm that the settings are configured correctly:

```
esxcli system coredump network get
```

Figure 4.52 shows the process in a console session.

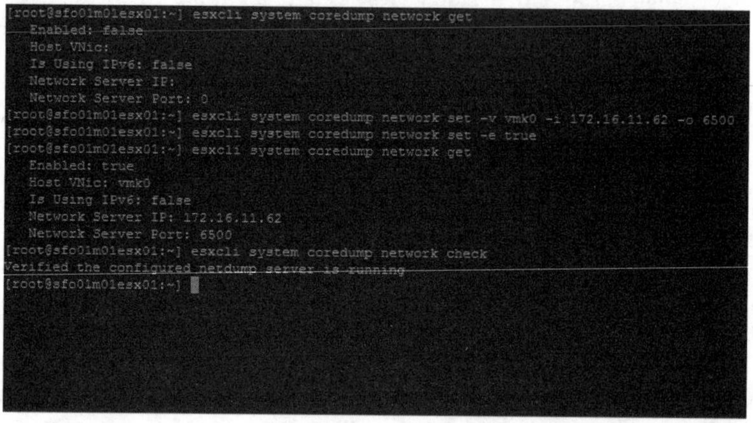

FIGURE 4.52

Configuring a host to redirect dumps to a Dump Collector

Hosts can also be configured for a centralized dump collector via the Host Profiles feature or PowerCLI. The recommended approach is to configure one host via the command line, use it as reference host, and then apply that configuration to the remaining hosts.

It is possible to set the configuration directly by editing a host profile, selecting Network Configuration and then Network Coredump Settings, and selecting the Enabled check box. From here, specify the NIC, server IP, and port details. This is shown in Figure 4.53.

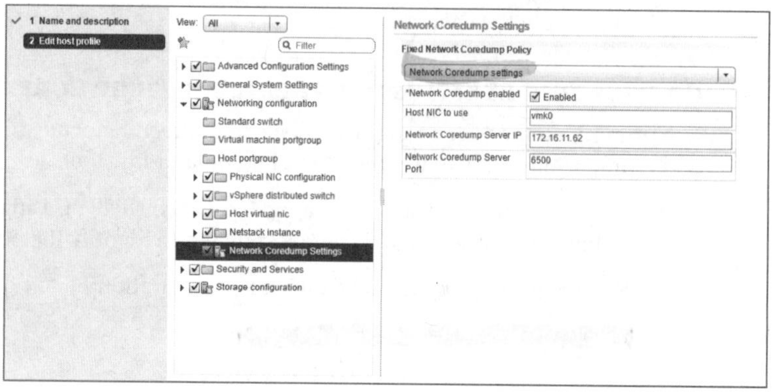

FIGURE 4.53

Configuring a host to a Dump Collector via its host profile

TESTING THE ESXi DUMP COLLECTOR

You should check that each host is configured correctly and can communicate with the Dump Collector:

1. Log into your host via SSH, via the local ESXi shell, or using a vCLI installation (vMA or vCLI usage requires additional context switches to identify the host).

2. Send a test dump to the collector:

   ```
   esxcli system coredump network check
   ```

3. Connect to the Dump Collector server and check that success is reported in the logs (located on the appliance in /var/log/vmware/netdumper/netdumper.log). On a vCSA, the dumps are put in /var/core/netdumps/ and are organized into directories named after the sending hosts' IP address.

Other vCenter Support Tools

In addition to VUM, Auto Deploy, and the ESXi Dump Collector, several other vCenter Support Tools exist. We've discussed each of these tools in previous chapters as they were pertinent to the deployment of ESXi or vCenter.

Authentication Proxy   The Authentication Proxy allows hosts to join an Active Directory domain without needing to include domain credentials in deployment tools such as Auto Deploy depots or scripted install files. Authentication Proxy was covered in Chapter 2.

Host Agent Check   The Host Agent Check tool is a pre-upgrade solution that checks that hosts connected to vCenter are suitable to be connected to vCenter 6.0. This verification prevents host issues after a vCenter upgrade. Host Agent Check was covered in Chapter 3.

DCUI   Those that are familiar with ESXi and the previous versions of the vCenter Server Appliance, when accessing the vCenter Server Appliance virtual machine within either the vSphere Web Client or VMware Host Client, the Direct Console User Interface (DCUI) is how you'll interact with the system. The DCUI allows administrators to change the networking configuration, change the root account password, and toggle SSH and BASH shell enablement on the vCenter Server and Platform Services Controller appliances.

SSH   While some readers may get a good chuckle out of this inclusion, Secure Socket Shell (SSH) is one of the key support tools when working with the appliance. By default, when you log into the vCenter Server or Platform Services Controller appliance, you'll enter into the Appliance Shell. The Appliance Shell provides you access to a collection of services designed for managing and monitoring your installations in the form of CLI commands. This list is divided into Plug-Ins (PI) and APIs, with the former providing you with a collection of tools—such as the vSphere Update Manager Utility or vCenter Top—while the latter is a collection of queries about the state of the appliances' individual components, though there is some overlap between the two. Linux administrators also have access to the BASH shell of the appliance where you can troubleshoot and interact with the appliance.

Now you're ready to start taking advantage of the new networking functionality available in VMware vSphere in Chapter 5.

The Bottom Line

Determine which ESXi hosts or VMs need to be patched or upgraded. Baselines are the "measuring sticks" whereby VUM knows whether an ESXi host or VM instance is up-to-date. VUM compares the ESXi hosts or VMs to the baselines to determine whether they need to be patched and, if so, what patches need to be applied. VUM also uses baselines to determine which ESXi hosts need to be upgraded to the latest version or which VMs need to have their VM hardware upgraded. VUM comes with some predefined baselines and allows administrators to create additional baselines specific to their environments. Baselines can be fixed—the contents remain constant—or they can be dynamic, where the contents of the baseline change over time. Baseline groups allow administrators to combine baselines and apply them together.

> **Master It** In addition to ensuring that all your ESXi hosts have the latest critical and security patches installed, you need to ensure that all your ESXi hosts have another specific patch installed. This additional patch is noncritical and therefore doesn't get included in the critical patch dynamic baseline. How do you work around this problem?

Use VUM to upgrade VM hardware or VMware Tools. VUM can detect VMs with outdated VM hardware versions and guest OSs that have outdated versions of VMware Tools installed. VUM comes with predefined baselines that enable this functionality. In addition, VUM has the ability to upgrade VM hardware versions and upgrade VMware Tools inside guest OSs to ensure that everything is kept up-to-date. This functionality is especially helpful after upgrading your ESXi hosts to version 6.7 from a previous version.

> **Master It** You've just finished upgrading your virtual infrastructure to VMware vSphere. What two additional tasks should you complete?

Apply patches to ESXi hosts. Like other complex software products, VMware ESXi needs software patches applied from time to time. These patches might be bug fixes or security fixes. To keep your ESXi hosts up-to-date with the latest patches, you can have VUM apply patches to your hosts on a schedule of your choosing. In addition, to reduce downtime during the patching process or perhaps to simplify the deployment of patches to remote offices, VUM can stage patches to ESXi hosts before the patches are applied.

> **Master It** How can you avoid VM downtime when applying patches (for example, remediating) to your ESXi hosts?

Upgrade hosts and coordinate large-scale datacenter upgrades. Upgrading hosts manually, with each host having dozens of VMs on it, is burdensome and doesn't scale well once you have more than a handful to deal with. Short outage windows, host reboots, and VM downtime mean that coordinating upgrades can involve complex planning and careful execution.

> **Master It** Which VUM functionality can simplify the process of upgrading vSphere across a large number of hosts and their VMs?

Use alternative approaches to VUM updates when required. VUM presents the simplest and most efficient method to upgrade your vSphere hosts. However, sometimes VUM may not be available. For example, VUM is reliant on vCenter, so if the host isn't connected to a licensed vCenter, an alternate method to upgrade the host must be used.

Master It Without using VUM, how else can you upgrade an existing host?

Configure hosts for centralized logging. To make use of the ESXi Dump Collector, you must configure each host to point to the centralized loggers.

Master It You have just started a new job as the vSphere administrator at a company. The company hasn't previously centralized the hosts' core dumps and you decide you want to collect them, and so you want to setup the ESXi Dump Collector tool. How do you go about setting this up on the company's vCSA instance?

Chapter 5

Creating and Configuring a vSphere Network

Eventually, it all comes back to the network. Having servers running VMware ESXi with virtual machines stored on a highly redundant storage is great, but they're ultimately useless if the virtual machines can't communicate across the network. What good is the ability to run 10, 20, 30, or more production servers on a single ESXi host if those production servers aren't available to clients on the network? Clearly, vSphere networking within ESXi is a key area for every vSphere administrator to understand fully.

IN THIS CHAPTER, YOU WILL LEARN TO

◆ Identify the components of vSphere networking

◆ Create vSphere Standard Switches and vSphere Distributed Switches

◆ Create and manage NIC teaming, VLANs, and private VLANs

◆ Configure virtual switch security policies

Putting Together a vSphere Network

Designing and building vSphere networks with ESXi and vCenter Server bears some similarities to designing and building physical networks, but there are enough significant differences that an overview of components and terminology is warranted. Before addressing some of the factors that affect network design in a virtual environment, let's define the components that may be used to build your virtual network.

vSphere Standard Switch A software-based switch that resides in the VMkernel and provides traffic management for virtual machines. Users must manage vSphere Standard Switches independently on each ESXi host. In this book, the term *vSwitch* also refers to a vSphere Standard Switch.

vSphere Distributed Switch A software-based switch that resides in the VMkernel and provides traffic management for virtual machines and the VMkernel. vSphere Distributed Switches are shared by and managed across ESXi hosts and clusters within a vSphere datacenter. You might see *vSphere Distributed Switch* abbreviated as *VDS*; this book will use *VDS*, *vSphere Distributed Switch*, or just *distributed switch*.

Port/Port Group A logical object on a vSphere Standard or Distributed Switch that provide specialized services for the VMkernel or virtual machines. A virtual switch can contain a VMkernel port or a Virtual Machine Port Group. On a vSphere Distributed Switch, these are called distributed port groups.

VMkernel Port A specialized virtual switch port type that is configured with an IP address to allow hypervisor management traffic, vMotion, VMware vSAN, iSCSI storage, Network File System (NFS) storage, vSphere Replication, and vSphere Fault Tolerance (FT logging. VMkernel ports are also created for VXLAN tunnel endpoints (VTEPs) as used by the VMware NSX network virtualization and security platform. These VMkernel ports are created with the VXLAN TCP/IP stack rather than using the default stack. TCP/IP stacks are covered a bit later in the chapter. A VMkernel port is also referred to as a *vmknic*.

Virtual Machine Port Group A group of virtual switch ports that share a common configuration and allow virtual machines to access other virtual machines that are configured on the same port group or accessible PVLAN or on the physical network.

Virtual LAN (VLAN) A logical local area network configured on a virtual or physical switch that provides efficient traffic segmentation, broadcast control, security, and efficient bandwidth utilization by providing traffic only to the ports configured for that particular VLAN.

Trunk Port (Trunking) A port on a physical switch that listens for and knows how to pass traffic for multiple VLANs. It does so by maintaining the 802.1q VLAN tags for traffic movin through the trunk port to the connected device(s). Trunk ports are typically used for switch-to-switch connections to allow VLANs to pass freely between switches. Virtual switches support VLANs, and using VLAN trunks enables the VLANs to pass freely into the virtual switches.

TRUNKING VS. LINK AGGREGATION

Depending on your networking vendor, you might also see the term *trunk* used to describe an aggregation of multiple individual links into a single logical link. In this book, the word *trunk* describes a connection that passes multiple VLAN tags. *Link aggregation* refers to the practice of bonding multiple individual links together.

Access Port A port on a physical switch that passes traffic for only a single VLAN. Unlike a trunk port, which maintains the VLAN identification for traffic moving through the port, an access port strips away the VLAN information for traffic moving through the port.

Network Interface Card Team The aggregation of physical network interface cards (NICs) to form a single logical communication channel. Different types of NIC teams provide varyin levels of traffic load balancing and fault tolerance.

VMXNET Adapter A virtualized network adapter operating inside a guest operating system (guest OS). The VMXNET adapter is optimized for performance in a virtual machine. VMware Tools are required to be installed in the guest OS to provide the VMXNET driver. Th VMXNET adapter is sometimes referred to as a *paravirtualized* driver.

VMXNET 2 Adapter   The VMXNET 2 adapter is based on the VMXNET adapter but provides some high-performance features commonly used on modern networks, such as jumbo frames and hardware offloads. VMware Tools are required to be installed in the guest OS to provide the VMXNET driver.

VMXNET 3 Adapter   The VMXNET 3 adapter is the next-generation paravirtualized NIC, designed for performance, and is not related to VMXNET or VMXNET 2. It offers all the features available in VMXNET 2 and adds several new features like multiqueue support (also known as Receive Side Scaling in Windows), IPv6 offloads, and MSI/MSI-X interrupt delivery. VMXNET 3 requires virtual machine hardware version 7 or later as well as VMware Tools installed in the guest OS to provide the VMXNET driver.

E1000 Adapter   A virtualized network adapter that emulates the Intel 82545EM Gigabit network adapter. Typically, the guest OS provides a built-in driver.

E1000e Adapter   A virtualized network adapter that emulates the Intel 82574 Gigabit network adapter. The E1000e requires virtual machine hardware version 8 or later. The E1000e adapter is available for Windows 8 and newer operating systems and is not available for Linux.

Now that you have a better understanding of the components involved and the terminology that you'll see in this chapter, let's examine how these components work together in support of virtual machines, IP-based storage, and ESXi hosts.

Your answers to the following questions will, in large part, determine the design of your vSphere network:

- Do you have or need a dedicated network for management traffic, such as for the management of physical switches?

- Do you have or need a dedicated network for vMotion traffic?

- Do you have an IP storage network? Is this IP storage network a dedicated network? Are you running iSCSI or NFS? Are you planning on implementing VMware vSAN?

- How many NICs are standard in your ESXi host design?

- Do the NICs in your hosts run 1 Gb Ethernet, 10 Gb Ethernet, 25 Gb Ethernet, or 40 Gb Ethernet?

- Do you need extremely high levels of fault tolerance for virtual machines?

- Is the existing physical network composed of VLANs?

- Do you want to extend the use of VLANs into the virtual switches?

- Will you be introducing an overlay, such as VXLAN or Geneve, into your network through the use of NSX?

As a precursor to setting up a vSphere networking architecture, you need to identify and document the physical network components and the security needs of the network. It's also important to understand the architecture of the existing physical network because that also greatly influences the design of the vSphere network. If the physical network can't support the use of VLANs, for example, then the vSphere network's design has to account for that limitation.

Throughout this chapter, as we discuss the various components of a vSphere network in mc detail, we'll also provide guidance on how the various components fit into an overall vSphere network design. A successful vSphere network combines the physical network, NICs, and vSwitches, as shown in Figure 5.1.

FIGURE 5.1
Successful vSphere networking is a blend of virtual and physical network adapters and switches.

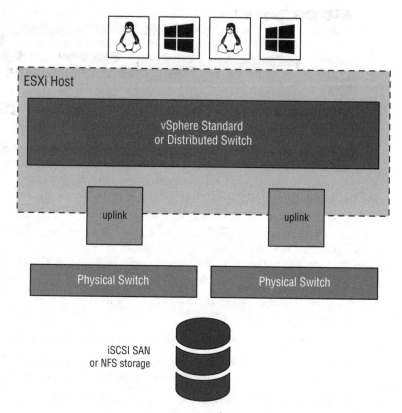

Because the vSphere network implementation makes virtual machines accessible, it is essential that the vSphere network be configured in a way that supports reliable and efficient communication around the various network infrastructure components.

Working with vSphere Standard Switches

The networking architecture of ESXi revolves around creating and configuring virtual switches. These virtual switches are either a vSphere Standard Switch or a vSphere Distributed Switch. First, we'll discuss the vSphere Standard Switch, and then we'll discuss the vSphere Distributed Switch.

You create and manage vSphere Standard Switches through the vSphere Web Client or through the vSphere CLI using the `esxcli` command, but they operate within the VMkernel. Virtual switches provide the connectivity for network communications, such as:

◆ Between virtual machines within an ESXi host

◆ Between virtual machines on different ESXi hosts

◆ Between virtual machines and other virtual or physical network identities connected via the physical network

◆ For VMkernel access to networks for Management, vMotion, VMware vSAN, iSCSI, NFS, vSphere Replication, or fault tolerance logging

Take a look at Figure 5.2, which shows the vSphere Web Client depicting a vSphere Standard Switch on an ESXi host. In this figure, the vSphere Standard Switch isn't depicted alone; it also depicts port groups and uplinks for communication external to the host. Without uplinks, a virtual switch can't communicate with the upstream network; without port groups, a vSphere Standard Switch can't provide connectivity for the VMkernel or the virtual machines. It is for this reason that most of our discussion on virtual switches centers on port groups and uplinks.

FIGURE 5.2

vSphere Standard Switches alone don't provide connectivity; they need port groups and uplinks to provide connectivity external to the ESXi host.

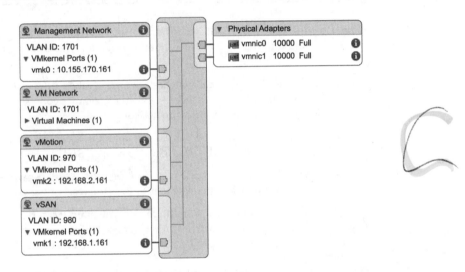

First, though, let's take a closer look at virtual switches and how they are similar to, and yet different from, physical switches in the network.

Comparing Virtual Switches and Physical Switches

Virtual switches in ESXi are constructed by and operate in the VMkernel. Virtual switches are not managed switches and do not provide all the advanced features that many new physical switches provide. You cannot, for example, telnet into a vSwitch to modify settings. There is no command-line interface (CLI) for a vSwitch, apart from vSphere CLI commands such as `esxcli` or PowerCLI commands such as `New-VirtualPortGroup`. Even so, a vSwitch operates like a physical switch in some ways. Like its physical counterpart, a vSwitch functions at Layer 2, maintains MAC address tables, forwards frames to other switch ports based on the MAC address, supports VLAN configurations, can trunk VLANs using IEEE 802.1q VLAN tags, and can establish port channels. A vSphere Distributed Switch also supports PVLANs, providing there is PVLAN support on the upstream physical switches. Similar to physical switches, vSwitches are configured with a specific number of ports.

Despite these similarities, vSwitches do differ somewhat from physical switches. A vSphere Standard Switch does not support the use of dynamic negotiation protocols for establishing 802.1q trunks or port channels, such as Dynamic Trunking Protocol (DTP) or Link Aggregation

SS - no DTP, LACP

Control Protocol (LACP). Although the vSphere Distributed Switch does support LACP in bot
Active and Passive modes. A vSwitch cannot be connected to another vSwitch, thereby elimin
ing a potential loop configuration. Because there is no possibility of looping, the vSwitches do
not run Spanning Tree Protocol (STP).

SPANNING TREE PROTOCOL

In physical switches, Spanning Tree Protocol (STP) offers redundancy for paths and prevents loops
in the network topology by locking redundant paths in a standby state. Only when a path is no
longer available will STP activate the standby path.

It is possible to link vSwitches together using a virtual machine with Layer 2 bridging
software and multiple virtual NICs, but this is not an accidental configuration and would requ
some effort to establish.

◆ vSwitches and physical switches have some other differences: A vSwitch authoritatively
knows the MAC addresses of the virtual machines connected to it, so there is no need to
learn MAC addresses from the network.

◆ Traffic received by a vSwitch on one uplink is never forwarded out another uplink. This
yet another reason why vSwitches do not run STP.

◆ A vSwitch does not need to perform Internet Group Management Protocol (IGMP)
snooping, because it knows the multicast interests of the virtual machines attached to it.

As you can see from this list of differences, you simply can't use virtual switches in the sam
way you can use physical switches. You can't use a virtual switch as a transit path between two
physical switches, for example, because traffic received on one uplink won't be forwarded out
another uplink.

With this basic understanding of how vSwitches work, let's now take a closer look at ports
and port groups.

Understanding Ports and Port Groups

As described earlier, a vSwitch allows several different types of communication, including comm
nication to and from the VMkernel and between virtual machines. To help distinguish between
these different types of communication, ESXi hosts use ports and port groups. A vSphere Standar
Switch without any ports or port groups is like a physical switch that has no physical ports; there
no way to connect anything to the switch, and it therefore serves no purpose.

Port groups differentiate between the types of traffic passing through a vSwitch, and they al
operate as a boundary for communication and/or security policy configuration. Figure 5.3 and
Figure 5.4 show the two different types of ports and port groups that you can configure on
a vSwitch:

◆ VMkernel port

◆ Virtual machine port group

FIGURE 5.3
Virtual switches can contain two connection types, a VMkernel port and a virtual machine port group.

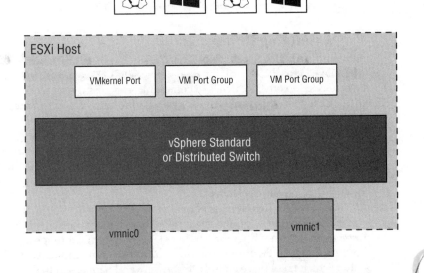

FIGURE 5.4
You can create virtual switches with both connection types on the same switch.

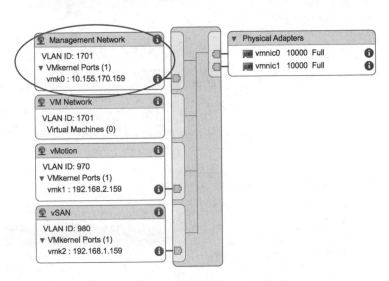

Because a vSwitch cannot be used in any way without at least one port or port group, you'll see that the vSphere Web Client combines the creation of new vSwitches with the creation of new ports or port groups.

As previously shown in Figure 5.2, though, ports and port groups are only part of the overa solution. The uplinks are the other part of the solution that you need to consider, because they provide external network connectivity to the vSwitches.

Understanding Uplinks

Although a vSwitch allows communication between virtual machines connected to the vSwitc it cannot communicate with the physical network without uplinks. Just as a physical switch m be connected to other switches to communicate across the network, vSwitches must be connec to the ESXi host's physical NICs as uplinks to communicate with the rest of the network.

Unlike ports and port groups, uplinks aren't required for a vSwitch to function. Physical systems connected to an isolated physical switch with no uplinks to other physical switches in the network can still communicate with each other—just not with any other systems that are n connected to the same isolated switch. Similarly, virtual machines connected to a vSwitch without any uplinks can communicate with each other but not with virtual machines on other vSwitches or physical systems.

This sort of configuration is known as an *internal-only* vSwitch. It can be useful to allow virtual machines to communicate only with each other. Virtual machines that communicate through an internal-only vSwitch do not pass any traffic through a physical adapter on the ES host. As shown in Figure 5.5, communication between virtual machines connected to an intern only vSwitch takes place entirely in software and happens at the speed at which the VMkernel can perform the task.

FIGURE 5.5
Virtual machines communicating through an internal-only vSwitch do not pass any traffic through a physical adapter.

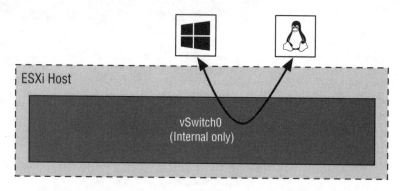

No Uplink, No vMotion?

In older versions of vSphere, virtual machines connected to an internal-only vSwitch were not vMotion capable. Although the requirement for uplinks was relaxed in more recent versions of vSphere, the workflow to vMotion a machine changed in vSphere 6. When requesting a vMotion, you can select a destination port group. This port group can be either on a standard or distributed virtual switch, and it is a valid destination regardless of whether the associated virtual switch has any uplinks. The full requirements for vMotion are covered in Chapter 12, "Balancing Resource Utilization."

For virtual machines to communicate with resources beyond the virtual machines hosted on the local ESXi host or when PVLAN is enabled, a vSwitch must be configured to use at least on physical network adapter, or uplink. A vSwitch can be bound to a single network adapter or bound to two or more network adapters.

A vSwitch bound to at least one physical network adapter allows virtual machines to establish communication with physical servers on the network or with virtual machines on other ESXi hosts. That's assuming, of course, that the virtual machines on the other ESXi hosts are connected to a vSwitch that is bound to at least one physical network adapter. Just like a physical network, a virtual network requires connectivity from end to end. Figure 5.6 shows the communication path for virtual machines connected to a vSwitch bound to a physical network adapter. In the diagram, when vm1 on sfo01m01esx01 needs to communicate with vm2 sfo-01m01esx02, the traffic from the virtual machine passes through vSwitch0 (via a virtual machine port group) to the physical network adapter to which the vSwitch is bound. From the physical network adapter, the traffic will reach the physical switch (PhySw1). The physical switch (PhySw1) passes the traffic to the second physical switch (PhySw2), which will pass the traffic through the physical network adapter associated with the vSwitch on sfo01m01esx02. In the last stage of the communication, the vSwitch will pass the traffic to the destination virtual machine vm2.

FIGURE 5.6
A vSwitch with a single network adapter allows virtual machines to communicate with physical servers and other virtual machines on the network.

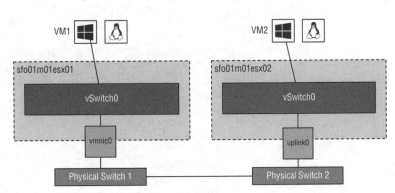

The vSwitch associated with a physical network adapter provides virtual machines with the amount of bandwidth the physical adapter is configured to support. All the virtual share this bandwidth when communicating with physical machines or ESXi hosts. In this way, a vSwitch is once again similar to vSwitch with a single 1 Gbps network adapte virtual machines connected to it; similarly, a p physical switch provides up to 1 Gbps of band attached to the physical switches.

A vSwitch can also be configured with multi

UPLINK LIMITS

Although a single vSwitch can be configured with adapter cannot be configured to multiple vSwitches. with varying speeds. The number of network adapt *vSphere Maximums* guide (https://configmax.vm ported with your chipset(s).

Figure 5.7 and Figure 5.8 show a vSwitch configured with multiple physical network adapters. A vSwitch can have a maximum of 32 uplinks. In other words, a single vSwitch can use up to 32 physical network adapters to send and receive traffic to and from the physical network. Configuring multiple physical network adapters on a vSwitch offers the advantage of redundancy and load distribution. In the section "Configuring NIC Teaming," later in this chapter, we'll dig deeper into this sort of vSwitch configuration.

NOTE It's important to note that NIC teaming is a policy for how traffic is handled on multiple uplinks and not necessarily a type link aggregation such as LACP.

FIGURE 5.7
A vSwitch using NIC teaming has multiple available adapters for data transfer. NIC teaming offers redundancy and load distribution.

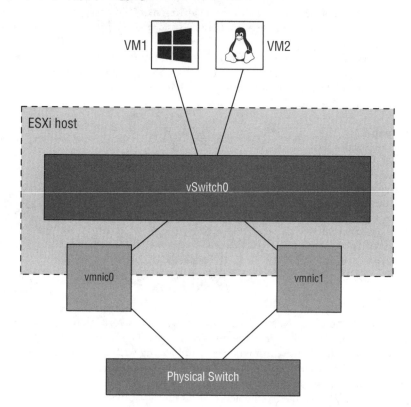

We've examined vSwitches, ports and port groups, and uplinks, and you should have a basic understanding of how these pieces begin to fit together to build a virtual network. The next step is to delve deeper into the configuration of the various types of ports and port groups, because they are essential to vSphere networking. We'll start with a discussion on the management network.

FIGURE 5.8

Virtual switches using NIC teaming are identified by the multiple physical network adapters assigned to the vSwitch.

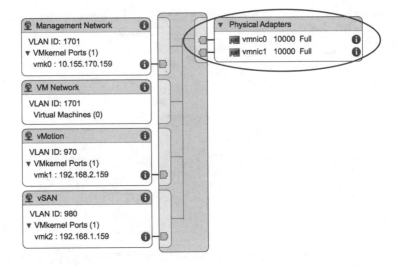

Configuring the Management Network

Management traffic is a special type of network traffic that runs across a VMkernel port. VMkernel ports provide network access for the VMkernel's TCP/IP stack, which is separate and independent from the network traffic generated by virtual machines. The ESXi hosts management network, however, is treated a bit differently than other VMkernel ports in two ways:

◆ First, the ESXi management VMkerel port is automatically created when you install ESXi. In order for the ESXi host to be reachable across the network, a management VMkernel port must be configured and working.

◆ Second, the Direct Console User Interface (DCUI)—the user interface that exists when you're working at the physical console of a server running ESXi—provides a mechanism for configuring or reconfiguring the management network (Management VMKernel port) but not any other forms of networking on that host, apart from a few options for resetting network configuration.

Although the vSphere Web Client offers an option to enable management traffic when configuring networking, as you can see in Figure 5.9, it's unlikely that you'll use this option very often. After all, for you to configure management networking from within the vSphere Web Client, the ESXi host must already have functional management networking in place (vCenter Server communicates with ESXi hosts over the management network). You might use this option if you were creating additional management interfaces. To do this, you would use the procedure described later (in the section "Configuring VMkernel Networking") to create VMkernel ports with the vSphere Web Client, simply enabling Management Traffic in the Enable Services section while creating the VMkernel port.

In the event the ESXi host is unreachable—and therefore cannot be configured using the vSphere Web Client—you'll need to use the DCUI to configure the management network.

FIGURE 5.9
The vSphere Web Client offers a way to enable Management networking when configuring networking.

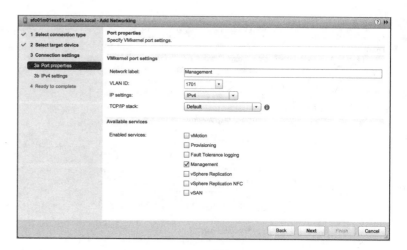

Perform the following steps to configure the ESXi management network using the DCUI:

1. At the server's physical console or using a remote console utility such as HP iLO, or Dell DRAC, press F2 to enter the System Customization menu.

   When prompted to log in, enter the appropriate credentials.

2. Use the arrow keys to highlight the Configure Management Network option, as shown in Figure 5.10, and press Enter.

FIGURE 5.10
Configure ESXi's Management Network using the Configure Management Network option in the System Customization menu.

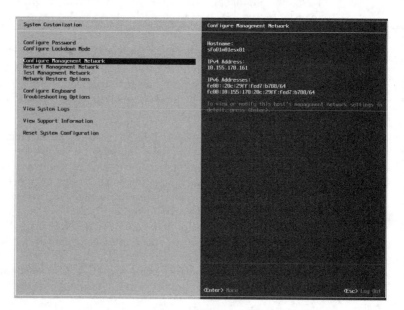

3. From the Configure Management Network menu, select the appropriate option for configuring ESXi management networking, as shown in Figure 5.11.

FIGURE 5.11
From the Configure
Management Network
menu, users can
modify assigned
network adapters,
change the VLAN ID,
IP address, DNS Servers,
and DNS search
configuration.

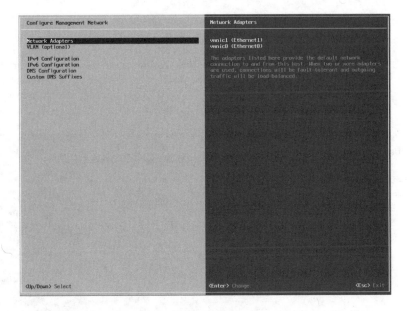

You cannot create additional management network interfaces from here; you can only
modify the existing management network interface.

4. When finished, follow the screen prompts to exit the management networking
configuration.

If prompted to restart the management networking, select Yes; otherwise, restart the management networking from the System Customization menu, as shown in Figure 5.12.

FIGURE 5.12
The Restart Management
Network option restarts
ESXi's management
networking and applies
any changes that
were made.

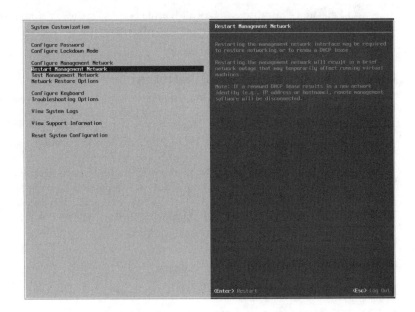

In looking at Figure 5.10 and Figure 5.12, you'll also see options for testing the management network, which lets you verify that the management network is configured correctly. This is invaluable if you are unsure of the VLAN ID or network adapters that you should use.

Also notice the Network Restore Options screen, shown in Figure 5.13. This screen lets you restore the network configuration to defaults, restore a vSphere Standard Switch, or even restore a vSphere Distributed Switch—all very handy options if you are troubleshooting management network connectivity to your ESXi host.

FIGURE 5.13

Use the Network Restore Options screen to manage network connectivity to an ESXi host.

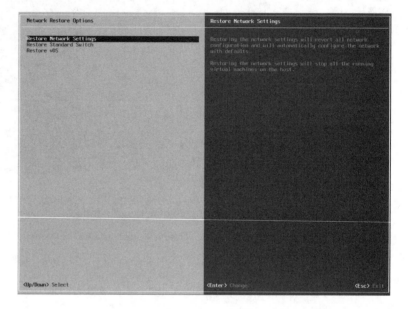

Let's move our discussion of VMkernel networking away from just management traffic and take a closer look at the other types of VMkernel traffic, as well as how to create and configure VMkernel ports.

Configuring VMkernel Networking

VMkernel networking carries management traffic, but it also carries all other forms of traffic that originate with the ESXi host itself (i.e., any traffic that isn't generated by virtual machines running on that ESXi host). As shown in Figure 5.14 and Figure 5.15, VMkernel ports are used for Management, vMotion, vSAN, iSCSI, NFS, vSphere Replication, and vSphere FT, basically, all types of traffic that are generated by the hypervisor itself. Chapter 6, "Creating and Configuring Storage Devices," details the iSCSI and NFS configurations as well as vSAN configurations. Chapter 12 provides details on the vMotion process and how vSphere FT works. These discussions provide insight into the traffic flow between VMkernel and storage devices (iSCSI/NFS/vSAN) or other ESXi hosts (for vMotion or vSphere FT). At this point, you should be concerned only with configuring VMkernel networking.

FIGURE 5.14
A VMkernel adapter is assigned an IP address for accessing iSCSI or NFS storage devices or for other management services.

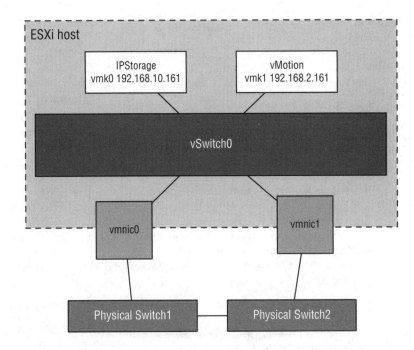

FIGURE 5.15
It is recommended to add only one type of traffic to a VMkernel interface.

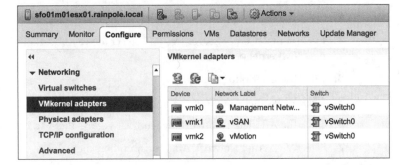

In vSphere 6.0, a number of services that were previously the responsibility of management traffic have been split into discrete services that can be attached to a unique VMkernel interface. These services, as shown in Figure 5.16, are Provisioning, vSphere Replication, and vSphere Replication NFC (Network File Copy).

Provisioning handles the data transfer for virtual machine cloning, cold migration, and snapshot creation. This can be a traffic-intensive process, particularly when VMware vSphere Storage APIs – Array Integration (VAAI) is not leveraged. There are a number of situations where this can occur, as referenced in the VMware KB Article 1021976.

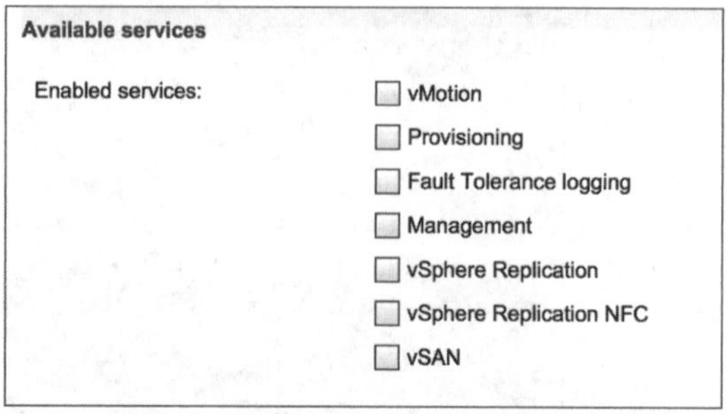

FIGURE 5.16

VMkernel traffic types in vSphere 6.7. Starting with vSphere 6.0, VMkernel ports can now also carry Provisioning traffic, vSphere Replication traffic, and vSphere Replication NFC traffic.

vSphere Replication transmits replicated blocks from an ESXi host to a vSphere Replication Appliance, whereas vSphere Replication NFC handles the Network File Copy from the vSphere Replication Appliance to the destination datastore through an ESXi host.

A VMkernel port consists of two components: a port group on a vSwitch and a VMkernel network interface, also known as a vmknic.

Perform the following steps to add a VMkernel port to an existing vSwitch using the vSphere Web Client:

1. If not already connected, open a supported web browser and log into a vCenter Server instance. For example, if your vCenter Server instance is called "vcenter," then you'll connect to `https://vcenter.domain.name/vsphere-client` and then log in with appropriate credentials.

2. From the vSphere Web Client, select Hosts And Clusters.

3. Expand the vCenter Server tree and select the ESXi host on which you'd like to add the new VMkernel port.

4. Click the Configure tab.

5. Click VMkernel Adapters.

6. Click the Add Host Networking icon. This starts the Add Networking wizard.

7. Select VMkernel Network Adapter, and then click Next.

8. Because you're adding a VMkernel port to an existing vSwitch, make sure Select An Existing Standard Switch is selected; then click Browse to select the virtual switch to which the new VMkernel port should be added. Click OK in the Select Switch dialog box and click Next to continue.

9. Type the name of the port in the Network Label text box.

10. If necessary, specify the VLAN ID for the VMkernel port.

11. Select whether this VMkernel port will be enabled for IPv4, IPv6, or both.

12. Select the TCP/IP stack that this VMkernel port should use. Unless you have already created a custom TCP/IP stack, the only options listed here will be Default, Provisioning, and vMotion. (We discuss TCP/IP stacks later in this chapter in the section titled "Configuring TCP/IP Stacks.")

13. Select the various services that will be enabled on this VMkernel port, and then click Next. For a VMkernel port that will be used only for iSCSI or NFS traffic, all the Services check boxes should be deselected. For a VMkernel port that will act as an additional management interface, only Management Traffic should be selected.

14. For IPv4 (applicable if you selected IPv4 or IPv4 And IPv6 for IP Settings in the previous step), you may elect to either obtain the configuration automatically (via DHCP) or supply a static configuration.

OVERRIDING THE DEFAULT GATEWAY ON AN ADAPTER

When you choose to enter a static IPv4 address, you now have the option to override the default gateway and provide a gateway specifically for this VMkernel adapter. This, however, does not add an entry to the ESXi hosts routing table. Only the services that specify this VMkernel as an egress interface use this gateway. This provides additional Layer 3 connectivity options for services that need multiple gateways. This can be useful for a service like vSphere Replication where you do not wish to have the traffic go over the management network or create static routes on the ESXi hosts.

DNS SERVERS AREN'T EDITABLE

Note that DNS server addresses are controlled by the TCP/IP stack configuration and can't be changed here. To change the DNS server settings, you'll need to edit the TCP/IP stack settings, as described in the section "Configuring TCP/IP Stacks."

---

15. For IPv6 (applicable if you selected IPv6 or IPv4 And IPv6 for IP Settings earlier), you can choose to obtain configuration automatically via DHCPv6, obtain your configuration automatically via Router Advertisement, and/or assign one or more IPv6 addresses. Use the green plus symbol to add an IPv6 address that is appropriate for the network to which this VMkernel interface will be connected.

16. Click Next to review the configuration summary, and then click Finish.

After you complete these steps, you can use the `Get-VMHostNetworkAdapter` PowerCLI command to show the new VMkernel port and the new VMkernel NIC that was created:

```
Connect-VIServer <ESXi hostname> ↵
```

When prompted to log in, enter the appropriate credentials.

```
Get-VMHostNetworkAdapter -VMkernel | Format-list ↵
```

To help illustrate the different parts, the VMkernel port, and the VMkernel NIC or vmknic that are created during this process, let's again walk through the steps for creating a VMkernel port using PowerCLI.

Perform the following steps to create a VMkernel port on an existing vSwitch using the command line:

1. Open PowerCLI and connect to the ESXi host by entering the following command:

```
Connect-VIServer <ESXi hostname> ↵
```

When prompted to log in, enter the appropriate credentials.

2. Enter the following command to add a port group named VMkernel to vSwitch0:

```
New-VirtualPortGroup -Name VMkernel -VirtualSwitch vSwitch0 ↵
```

3. Use the command to list the port groups on vSwitch0. Note that the port group exists but nothing has been connected to it (the Port column is blank).

```
Get-VirtualSwitch -Name vSwitch0 | Get-VirtualPortGroup | Select Name,
Port, VLanId ↵
```

4. Enter the following command to create the VMkernel port with an IP address and attach it to the port group created in step 2:

```
New-VMHostNetworkAdapter -PortGroup VMkernel -VirtualSwitch vSwitch0 -IP
<IP Address> -SubnetMask <Subnet Mask> ↵
```

5. Repeat the command from step 3, noting now that the Port column displays {host}.

This indicates that a VMkernel adapter has been connected to a virtual port on the port group. Figure 5.17 shows the output of the PowerCLI command after completing step 5.

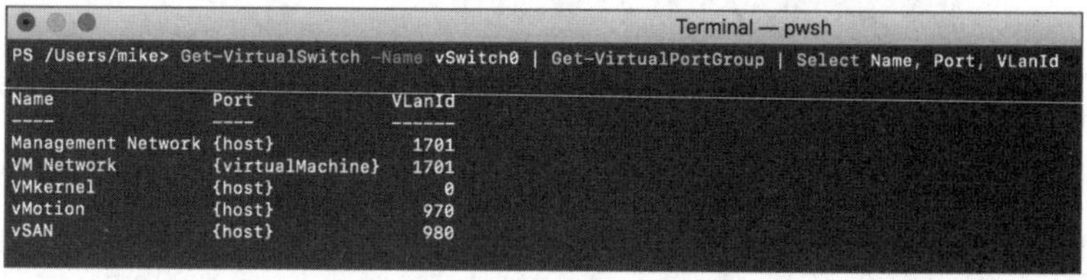

FIGURE 5.17

Using the CLI helps drive home the fact that the port group and the VMkernel port are separate objects.

Aside from the default ports required for the management network, no VMkernel ports are created during the installation of ESXi, so you must create VMkernel ports for the required services in your environment, either through the vSphere Web Client or via CLI.

In addition to adding VMkernel ports, you might need to edit a VMkernel port or even remove a VMkernel port. You can perform both tasks in the same place you added a VMkernel port: the Networking section of the Configure tab for an ESXi host.

To edit a VMkernel port, select the desired VMkernel port from the list and click the Edit Settings icon (it looks like a pencil). This will bring up the Edit Settings dialog box, where you can change the services for which this port is enabled, change the maximum transmission unit (MTU), and modify the IPv4 and/or IPv6 settings. Of particular interest here is the Analyze Impact section, shown in Figure 5.18, which helps point out dependencies on the VMkernel port in order to prevent unwanted side effects that might result from modifying the VMkernel port's configuration.

To delete a VMkernel port, select the desired VMkernel port from the list and click the Remove Selected Virtual Network Adapter button (it looks like a red X). In the resulting confirmation dialog box, you'll see the option to analyze the impact (same as with modifying a VMkernel port). Click OK to remove the VMkernel port.

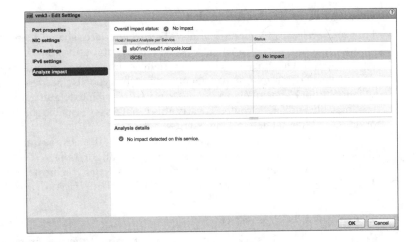

FIGURE 5.18
The Analyze Impact section shows administrators' dependencies on VMkernel ports.

Enabling Enhanced Multicast Functions

Two new multicast filtering modes were added to the vSphere Virtual Switches in vSphere 6.0: basic multicast filtering and multicast snooping.

The vSphere Standard Switch supports only basic multicast filtering, so multicast snooping will be covered in "Working with vSphere Distributed Switches," later in the chapter.

In basic multicast filtering mode, a standard switch will pass multicast traffic for virtual machines according to the destination MAC address of the multicast group. When a virtual machine joins a multicast group, the operating system running inside the virtual machine sends the multicast MAC address of the group to the standard switch. The standard switch saves the mapping between the port that the virtual machine is attached to and the destination multicast MAC address in a local forwarding table.

The standard switch is responsible for sending IGMP messages directly to the local multicast router, which then interprets the request to join the virtual machine to the group or remove it.

There are some restrictions to consider when evaluating basic multicast filtering:

◆ The vSwitch does not adhere to the IGMP version 3 specification of filtering packets according to its source address.

◆ The MAC address of a multicast group can be shared by up to 32 different groups, which can result in a virtual machine receiving packets in which it has no interest.

◆ Due to a limitation in the forwarding model, if a virtual machine is subscribed to more than 32 multicast MAC addresses, it will receive unwanted packets.

The best part about basic multicast filtering is that it is enabled by default, so there is no work for you to configure it!

Configuring TCP/IP Stacks

Prior to the release of vSphere 5.5, all VMkernel interfaces shared a single instance of a TCP/IP stack. As a result, they all shared the same routing table and same DNS configuration. This created some interesting challenges in certain environments. For example, what if you needed a default gateway for your management network but you also needed a default gateway for your vMotion traffic? The only workaround was to use a single default gateway and then populate the routing table with static routes. Clearly, this is not a very scalable solution for those with robust or unique VMkernel networking requirements.

vSphere now allows the creation of multiple TCP/IP stacks as introduced in vSphere 5.5. Each stack has its own routing table and its own DNS configuration.

Let's take a look at how to create TCP/IP stacks. After you create at least one additional TCP/IP stack, you'll learn how to assign a VMkernel interface to a specific TCP/IP stack.

CREATING A TCP/IP STACK

Creating new TCP/IP stack instances can only be done from the command line using the esxcli command.

To create a new TCP/IP stack, use this command:

```
esxcli network ip netstack add --netstack=<Name of new TCP/IP stack>
```

For example, if you wanted to create a separate TCP/IP stack for your NFS traffic, the command might look something like this:

```
esxcli network ip netstack add --netstack=NFS
```

You can get a list of all the configured TCP/IP stacks with a very similar esxcli command:

```
esxcli network ip netstack list
```

Once the new TCP/IP stack is created, you can, if you wish, continue to configure the stack using the esxcli command. However, you will probably find it easier to use the vSphere Web Client to do the configuration of the new TCP/IP stack, as described in the next section.

ASSIGNING PORTS TO A TCP/IP STACK

Before you can edit the settings of a TCP/IP stack, a VMkernel port must be assigned to it. Unfortunately, you can assign VMkernel ports to a TCP/IP stack only at the time of creation. In other words, after you create a VMkernel port, you can't change the TCP/IP stack to which it has been assigned. You must delete the VMkernel port and then re-create it, assigning it to the desired TCP/IP stack. We described how to create and delete VMkernel ports earlier, so we won't go through those tasks again here.

Note that in step 12 of creating a VMkernel port in the Configuring VMkernel Networking section, you can select a specific TCP/IP stack to bind this VMkernel port. This is illustrated in Figure 5.19, which lists the system default stack, the vMotion stack, the Provisioning stack, and the custom NFS stack created earlier.

FIGURE 5.19
VMkernel ports can be
assigned to a TCP/IP
stack only at the time
of creation.

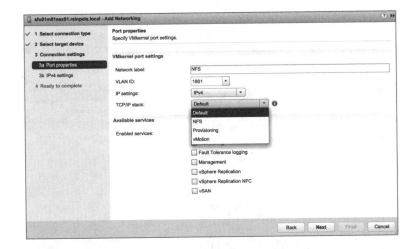

CUSTOM vMOTION STACKS

vSphere 6.0 was the first release to include a System TCP/IP stack for vMotion. Unfortunately, custom TCP/IP stacks aren't supported for use with fault tolerance logging, management traffic, VMware vSAN traffic, vSphere Replication traffic, or vSphere Replication NFC traffic. When you select a custom TCP/IP stack, you'll see that the check boxes to enable these services automatically disable themselves. You can only use custom TCP/IP stacks for IP-based storage, such as iSCSI and NFS.

CONFIGURING TCP/IP STACK SETTINGS

The settings for the TCP/IP stacks are found in the same place where you create and configure other host networking settings: in the Networking section of the Configure tab for an ESXi host object, as shown in Figure 5.20.

FIGURE 5.20
TCP/IP stack settings
are located with other
host networking
configuration options.

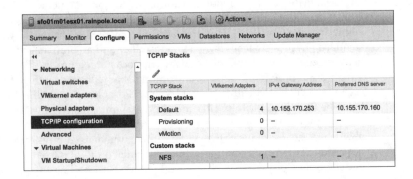

In Figure 5.20, you can see the new TCP/IP stack, named NFS, that was created in the previous section. To edit the settings for that stack, select it from the list and click the Edit TCP/IP Stack Configuration icon (it looks like a pencil above the list of TCP/IP stacks). That brings up the Edit TCP/IP Stack Configuration dialog box, shown in Figure 5.21.

FIGURE 5.21

Each TCP/IP stack can have its own DNS configuration, routing information, and other advanced settings.

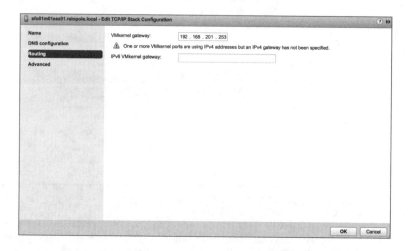

In the Edit TCP/IP Stack Configuration dialog box, make the changes you need to make to the name, DNS configuration, routing, or other advanced settings. Once you're finished, click OK.

It's now time to shift focus from host networking to virtual machine networking.

Configuring Virtual Machine Networking

The second type of port group to discuss is the Virtual Machine Port Group, which is responsible for all virtual machine networking. The Virtual Machine Port Group is quite different from a VMkernel port. With VMkernel networking, there is a one-to-one relationship with an interface: each VMkernel NIC, or vmknic, requires a matching VMkernel port group on a vSwitch. In addition, these interfaces require IP addresses for management or VMkernel network access.

A Virtual Machine Port Group, on the other hand, does not have a one-to-one relationship, and it does not require an IP address. For a moment, forget about vSwitches and consider standard physical switches. When you install or add an unmanaged physical switch into your network environment, that physical switch does not require an IP address; you simply install the switches and plug in the appropriate uplinks that will connect them to the rest of the network.

A vSwitch created with a Virtual Machine Port Group is no different. A vSwitch with a Virtual Machine Port Group acts just like an additional unmanaged physical switch. You need only plug in the appropriate uplinks—physical network adapters, in this case—that will connect that vSwitch to the rest of the network. As with an unmanaged physical switch, an IP address does not need to be configured for a Virtual Machine Port Group to combine the ports of a vSwitch with those of a physical switch. Figure 5.22 shows the switch-to-switch connection between a vSwitch and a physical switch.

FIGURE 5.22

A vSwitch with a Virtual Machine Port Group uses associated physical network adapters to establish switch-to-switch connections with physical switches.

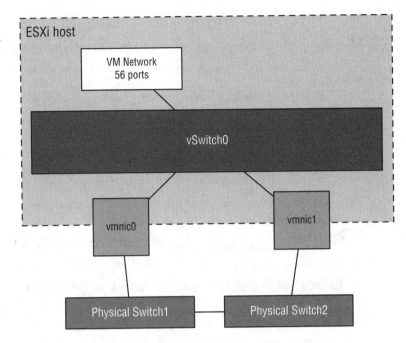

Perform the following steps to create a vSwitch with a Virtual Machine Port Group using the vSphere Web Client:

1. Connect to a vCenter Server instance using the vSphere Web Client.

2. From the Hosts And Clusters view, expand the vCenter Server tree.

3. Select the ESXi host on which you'd like to add a vSwitch, click the Configure tab, and under Networking, click Virtual Switches.

4. Click the Add Host Networking icon (a small globe with a plus sign) to start the Add Networking wizard.

5. Select the Virtual Machine Port Group For A Standard Switch radio button and click Next.

6. Because you are creating a new vSwitch, select the New Standard Switch radio button. Click Next.

7. Click the green plus icon to add physical network adapters to the new vSwitch you are creating. From the Add Physical Adapters To The Switch dialog box, select the NIC or NICs that can carry the appropriate traffic for your virtual machines.

8. Click OK when you're done selecting physical network adapters. This returns you to the Create A Standard Switch screen, where you can click Next to continue.

9. Type the name of the Virtual Machine Port Group in the Network Label text box.

10. Specify a VLAN ID, if necessary, and click Next.

11. Click Next to review the virtual switch configuration, and then click Finish.

If you are a command-line junkie, you can create a Virtual Machine Port Group using PowerCLI as well.

Perform the following steps to create a vSwitch with a Virtual Machine Port Group using the command line:

1. Open PowerCLI and connect to vCenter Server:

```
Connect-VIServer <vCenter host name> ↵
```

When prompted to log in, enter the appropriate credentials.

2. Enter the following command to add a virtual switch named vSwitch1 to the ESXi host sfo01m01esx01:

```
New-VirtualSwitch -VMhost sfo01m01esx01 -Name vSwitch1 ↵
```

3. Enter the following command to add the physical NIC vmnic1 to vSwitch1:

```
Set-VirtualSwitch -VirtualSwitch vSwitch1 -Nic vmnic1 ↵
```

By adding a physical NIC to the vSwitch, you provide physical network connectivity to the rest of the network for virtual machines connected to this vSwitch. Again, remember that you can assign any given physical NIC to only one vSwitch at a time (but a vSwitch may have multiple physical NICs at the same time).

4. Enter the following command to create a Virtual Machine Port Group named ProductionLAN on vSwitch1:

```
New-VirtualPortGroup -VirtualSwitch vSwitch1 -Name ProductionLAN ↵
```

Of the different connection types—VMkernel ports and Virtual Machine Port Groups—vSphere administrators will spend most of their time creating, modifying, managing, and removing Virtual Machine Port Groups.

Configuring VLANs

A virtual LAN (VLAN) is a logical LAN that provides efficient segmentation, security, and broadcast control while allowing traffic to share the same physical LAN segments or same physical switches. Figure 5.23 shows a typical VLAN configuration across physical switches.

VLANs use the IEEE 802.1q standard for *tagging* traffic as belonging to a particular VLAN. The VLAN tag, also known as the VLAN ID, is a numeric value between 1 and 4094, and it uniquely identifies that VLAN across the network. Physical switches such as the ones depicted in Figure 5.23 must be configured with ports to trunk the VLANs across the switches. These ports are known as *trunk* ports. Ports not configured to trunk VLANs are known as *access* ports and can carry traffic only for a single VLAN at a time.

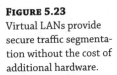

FIGURE 5.23
Virtual LANs provide secure traffic segmentation without the cost of additional hardware.

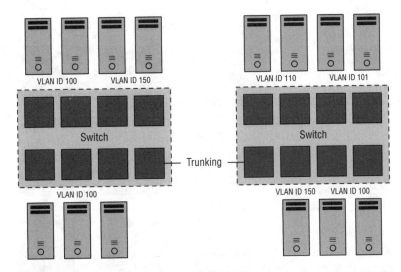

USING VLAN ID 4095

Normally the VLAN ID will range from 1 to 4094. In a vSphere environment, however, a VLAN ID of 4095 is also valid. Using this VLAN ID with ESXi causes the VLAN tagging information to be passed through the vSwitch all the way up to the guest OS. This is called *virtual guest tagging* (VGT) and is useful only for guest OSs that support and understand VLAN tags.

VLANs are an important part of ESXi networking because of the impact they have on the number of vSwitches and uplinks required. Consider this configuration:

♦ The management network needs access to the network segment carrying management traffic.

♦ Other VMkernel ports, depending on their purpose, may need access to an isolated vMotion segment or the network segment carrying iSCSI and NFS traffic.

♦ Virtual Machine Port Groups need access to whatever network segments are applicable for the virtual machines running on the ESXi hosts.

Without VLANs, this configuration would require three or more separate vSwitches, each bound to a different physical adapter, and each physical adapter would need to be physically connected to the correct network segment, as illustrated in Figure 5.24.

Add in an IP-based storage network and a few more virtual machine networks that need to be supported, and the number of required vSwitches and uplinks quickly grows. And this doesn't even take into account uplink redundancy.

FIGURE 5.24
Supporting multiple networks without VLANs can increase the number of vSwitches, uplinks, and cabling that is required.

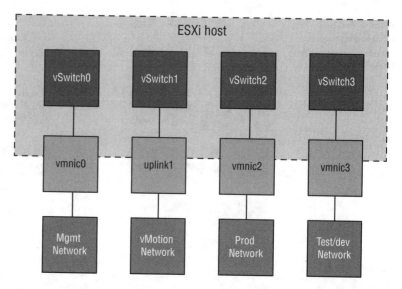

VLANs are the answer to this dilemma. Figure 5.25 shows the same network as in Figure 5.24, but with VLANs this time.

FIGURE 5.25
VLANs can reduce the number of vSwitches, uplinks, and cabling required.

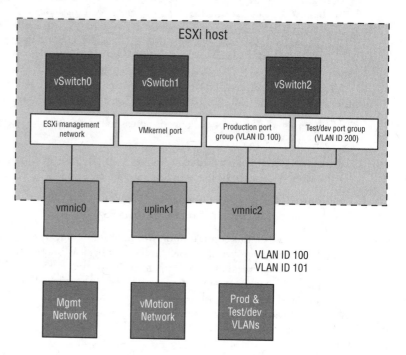

Although the reduction from Figure 5.24 to Figure 5.25 is only a single vSwitch and a single uplink, you can easily add more virtual machine networks to the configuration in Figure 5.25 by simply adding another port group with another VLAN ID. Blade servers provide an excellent example of when VLANs offer tremendous benefit. Because of the small form factor of the blade casing, blade servers have historically offered limited expansion slots for physical network adapters. VLANs allow these blade servers to support more networks than they could otherwise.

No VLAN Needed

Virtual switches in the VMkernel do not need VLANs if an ESXi host has enough physical network adapters to connect to each of the different network segments. However, VLANs provide added flexibility in adapting to future network changes, so the use of VLANs where possible is recommended.

As shown in Figure 5.25, VLANs are handled by configuring different port groups within a vSwitch. The relationship between VLANs and port groups is not a one-to-one relationship; a port group can be associated with only one VLAN at a time, but multiple port groups can be associated with a single VLAN. In the section "Configuring Virtual Switch Security," later in this chapter, you'll see some examples of when you might have multiple port groups associated with a single VLAN.

To make VLANs work properly with a port group, the uplinks for that vSwitch must be connected to a physical switch port configured as a trunk port. A trunk port understands how to pass traffic from multiple VLANs simultaneously while also preserving the VLAN IDs on the traffic. Figure 5.26 shows a snippet of configuration from a Cisco Nexus 9000 series switch for a port configured as a trunk port.

FIGURE 5.26

The physical switch ports must be configured as trunk ports in order to pass the VLAN information to the ESXi hosts for the port groups to use.

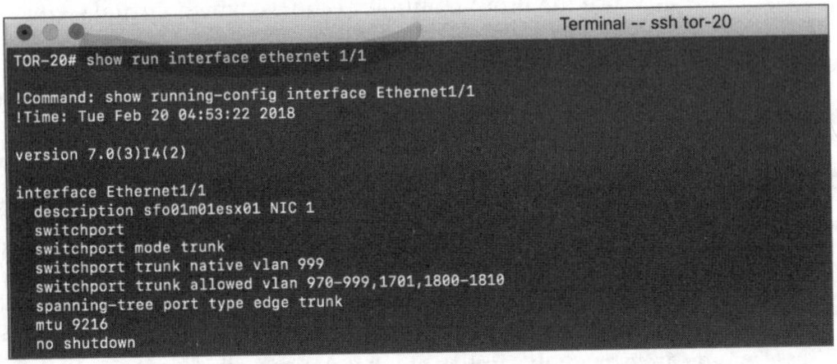

```
                                                    Terminal -- ssh tor-20

TOR-20# show run interface ethernet 1/1

!Command: show running-config interface Ethernet1/1
!Time: Tue Feb 20 04:53:22 2018

version 7.0(3)I4(2)

interface Ethernet1/1
  description sfo01m01esx01 NIC 1
  switchport
  switchport mode trunk
  switchport trunk native vlan 999
  switchport trunk allowed vlan 970-999,1701,1800-1810
  spanning-tree port type edge trunk
  mtu 9216
  no shutdown
```

The configuration for switches from other manufacturers will vary, so be sure to check with your particular switch manufacturer for specific details on how to configure a trunk port.

THE NATIVE VLAN

In Figure 5.26, you might notice the `switchport trunk native vlan 999` command. The default native VLAN (also known as the untagged VLAN) on most switches is VLAN 1. If you need to pass traffic on VLAN 1 to the ESXi hosts, you should designate another VLAN as the native VLAN using this command (or its equivalent). We recommend creating a dummy VLAN, like 999, and setting that as the native VLAN. This ensures that all VLANs will be tagged with the VLAN ID as they pass into the ESXi hosts. Keep in mind that this might affect behaviors like PXE booting, which generally requires untagged traffic.

When the physical switch ports are correctly configured as trunk ports, the physical switch passes the VLAN tags to the ESXi server, where the vSwitch directs the traffic to a port group with that VLAN ID assigned. If there is no port group configured with that VLAN ID, the traffic is discarded.

Perform the following steps to configure a Virtual Machine Port Group using VLAN ID 971:

1. Connect to a vCenter Server instance using the vSphere Web Client.

2. Navigate to the ESXi host to which you want to add the Virtual Machine Port Group, click the Configure tab, and then select Virtual Switches under Networking.

3. Select the vSwitch where the new port group should be created.

4. Click the Add Host Networking icon (it looks like a globe with a plus sign in the corner) to start the Add Networking wizard.

5. Select the Virtual Machine Port Group For A Standard Switch radio button and click Next.

6. Make sure the Select An Existing Standard Switch radio button is selected and, if necessary, use the Browse button to choose which virtual switch will host the new Virtual Machine Port Group. Click Next.

7. Type the name of the Virtual Machine Port Group in the Network Label text box.

8. Type **971** in the VLAN ID (Optional) text box, as shown in Figure 5.27.

   You will want to substitute a value that is correct for your network.

9. Click Next to review the vSwitch configuration, and then click Finish.

As you've probably gathered by now, you can also use PowerCLI to create or modify the VLAN settings for ports or port groups. We won't go through the steps here because the commands are extremely similar to what we've shown you already.

Although VLANs reduce the costs of constructing multiple logical subnets, keep in mind that they do not address traffic constraints. Although VLANs logically separate network segments, all the traffic still runs on the same physical network underneath. To accommodate bandwidth-intensive network operations, ensure the physical network adapters and switches are capable of sustaining the required throughput.

FIGURE 5.27

You must specify the correct VLAN ID in order for a port group to receive traffic intended for a particular VLAN.

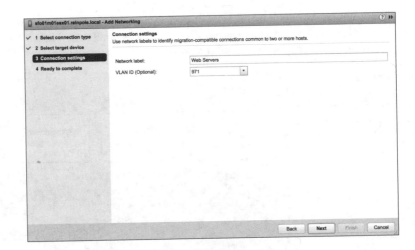

CONTROLLING THE VLANs PASSED ACROSS A VLAN TRUNK

You might see the `switchport trunk allowed vlan` command in some Cisco switch configurations as well. This command allows you to control which VLANs are passed across the VLAN trunk to the device at the other end of the link—in this case, an ESXi host. You will need to ensure that all the VLANs that are defined on the vSwitches are also included in the `switchport trunk allowed vlan` command, or those VLANs not included in the command won't work.

Configuring NIC Teaming

For a vSwitch and its associated ports or port groups to communicate with other ESXi hosts or with physical systems, the vSwitch must have at least one uplink. An *uplink* is a physical network adapter that is bound to the vSwitch and connected to a physical network switch. With the uplink connected to the physical network, there is connectivity for the VMkernel and the virtual machines connected to that vSwitch. But what happens when that physical network adapter fails, when the cable connecting that uplink to the physical network fails, or the upstream physical switch to which that uplink is connected fails? With a single uplink, network connectivity to the entire vSwitch and all of its ports or port groups is lost. This is where NIC teaming comes in.

NIC teaming involves connecting multiple physical network adapters to a single vSwitch. NIC teaming provides redundancy and load balancing of network communications to the VMkernel and virtual machines.

Figure 5.28 illustrates NIC teaming conceptually. Both of the vSwitches have two uplinks, and each of the uplinks connect to a different physical switch. Note that NIC teaming supports all the different connection types, so it can be used with ESXi management networking, VMkernel networking, and networking for virtual machines.

Figure 5.29 shows what NIC teaming looks like from within the vSphere Web Client. In this example, the vSwitch is configured with an association to multiple physical network adapters (uplinks). As mentioned previously, the ESXi host can have a maximum of 32 uplinks; these uplinks can be spread across multiple vSwitches or all tossed into a NIC team on one vSwitch. Remember that you can connect a physical NIC to only one vSwitch at a time.

FIGURE 5.28
Virtual switches with multiple uplinks offer redundancy and load balancing.

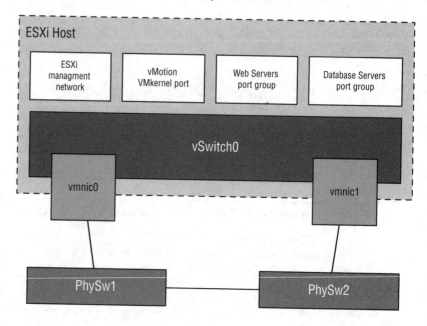

Building a functional NIC team requires that all uplinks be connected to physical switches in the same broadcast domain. If VLANs are used, all the switches should be configured for VLAN trunking, and the appropriate subset of VLANs must be allowed across the VLAN trunk. In a Cisco switch, this is typically controlled with the `switchport trunk allowed vlan` statement.

FIGURE 5.29
The vSphere Web Client shows when multiple physical network adapters are associated with a vSwitch using NIC teaming.

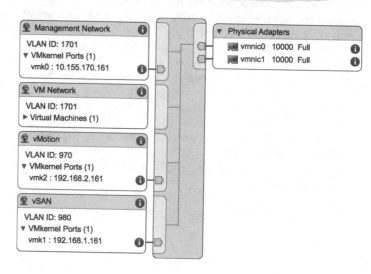

In Figure 5.30, the NIC team for vSwitch0 will work, because both of the physical switches share VLAN 100. The NIC team for vSwitch1, however, will not work because the physical switches the network adapters are connected to do not carry the same VLAN's, in this case VLAN 200.

FIGURE 5.30
All the physical network adapters in a NIC team must carry the same VLANs.

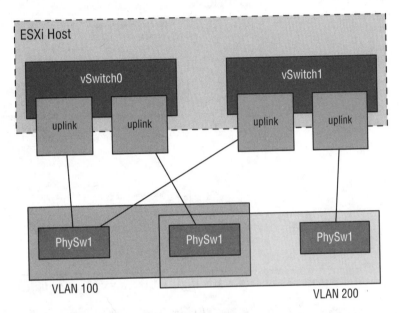

CONSTRUCTING NIC TEAMS

NIC teams should be built on physical network adapters located on separate bus architectures. For example, if an ESXi host contains two onboard network adapters and a PCI Express–based quad-port network adapter, a NIC team should be constructed using one onboard network adapter and one network adapter on the PCI bus. This design eliminates a single point of failure.

Perform the following steps to create a NIC team with an existing vSwitch using the vSphere Web Client:

1. Connect to a vCenter Server instance using the vSphere Web Client.

2. Navigate to the Networking section of the Configure tab for the ESXi host where you want to create the NIC team.

3. Select Virtual Switches; then select the virtual switch that will be assigned a NIC team and click the Manage The Physical Adapters Connected To The Selected Virtual Switch icon (it looks like a NIC with a wrench).

4. In the Manage Physical Network Adapters dialog box, click the green Add Adapters icon.

5. In the Add Physical Adapters To The Switch dialog box, select the appropriate adapter (or adapters) from the list, as shown in Figure 5.31.

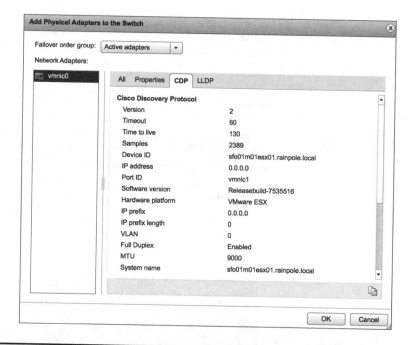

FIGURE 5.31
Create a NIC team by adding network adapters that belong to the same layer 2 broadcast domain as the original adapter.

PUTTING NEW ADAPTERS INTO A DIFFERENT FAILOVER GROUP

The Add Physical Adapters To The Switch dialog box shown in Figure 5.31 allows you to add adapters to the list of active adapters and to the list of standby or unused adapters. Simply change the desired group using the Failover Order Group drop-down list.

6. Click OK to return to the Manage Physical Network Adapters dialog box.

7. Click OK to complete the process and return to the Virtual Switch section of the selected ESXi host. Note that it might take a moment or two for the display to update with the new physical adapter.

After a NIC team is established for a vSwitch, ESXi can then perform load balancing for that vSwitch. The load-balancing feature of NIC teaming does not function like the load-balancing feature of advanced routing protocols. Load balancing across a NIC team is not a product of identifying the amount of traffic transmitted through a network adapter and shifting traffic to equalize data flow through all available adapters. The load-balancing algorithm for NIC teams in a vSwitch is a balance of the number of connections—not the amount of traffic. NIC teams on a vSwitch can be configured with one of the following four load-balancing policies:

◆ Originating virtual port-based load balancing (default)

◆ Source MAC-based load balancing

◆ IP hash-based load balancing

◆ Explicit failover order

The last option, explicit failover order, isn't really a "load-balancing" policy; instead, it uses the administrator-assigned failover order whereby the highest order uplink from the list of active adapters that passes failover detection criteria is used. You'll learn more about failover order in the section "Configuring Failover Detection and Failover Policy," later in this chapter. Also note that the list I've supplied here applies only to vSphere Standard Switches; vSphere Distributed Switches, covered later in this chapter in the section "Working with vSphere Distributed Switches," have additional options for load balancing and failover.

NOTE The load-balancing feature of NIC teams on a vSwitch applies only to the outbound traffic.

REVIEWING ORIGINATION VIRTUAL PORT-BASED LOAD BALANCING

The default load-balancing policy route is based on the originating virtual port and uses an algorithm that ties (or pins) each virtual switch port to a specific uplink associated with the vSwitch. The algorithm attempts to maintain an equal number of port-to-uplink assignments across all uplinks to achieve load balancing. As shown in Figure 5.32, this policy setting ensures that traffic from a specific virtual network adapter connected to a virtual switch port will consistently use the same physical network adapter. In the event that one of the uplinks fails, the traffic from the failed uplink will fail over to another physical network adapter.

FIGURE 5.32
The virtual port-based load balancing policy assigns each virtual switch port to a specific uplink. Failover to another uplink occurs when one of the physical network adapters experiences failure.

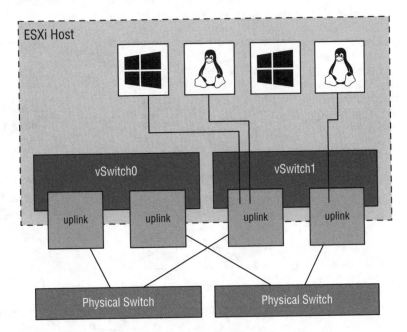

Although this policy does not provide dynamic load balancing, it does provide redundancy. Because the port for a virtual machine does not change, each virtual machine is tied to a physical network adapter until failover or vMotion occurs regardless of the amount of network traffic. Looking at Figure 5.32, imagine that the Linux virtual machine and the Windows virtual machine on the far left are the two most network intensive virtual machines. In this case, the virtual port-based policy has assigned both ports for these virtual machines to the same physical network adapter. In this case, one physical network adapter could be much more heavily used than other network adapters in the NIC team.

The physical switch passing the traffic learns the port association and therefore sends replies back through the same physical network adapter from which the request initiated. The virtual port-based policy is best used when you have more virtual network adapters than physical network adapters, which is almost always the case for virtual machine traffic. When there are fewer virtual network adapters, some physical adapters will not be used. For example, if five virtual machines are connected to a vSwitch with six uplinks, only five vSwitch ports will be assigned to exactly five uplinks, leaving one uplink with no traffic to process.

REVIEWING SOURCE MAC-BASED LOAD BALANCING

The second load-balancing policy available for a NIC team is the source MAC-based policy, shown in Figure 5.33. This policy is susceptible to the same pitfalls as the virtual port-based policy simply because the static nature of the source MAC address is the same as the static natu of a virtual port assignment. The source MAC-based policy is also best used when you have more virtual network adapters than physical network adapters. In addition, virtual machines st cannot use multiple physical adapters unless configured with multiple virtual network adapter Multiple virtual network adapters inside the guest OS of a virtual machine will provide multipl source MAC addresses and allow multiple physical network adapters.

FIGURE 5.33

The source MAC-based load balancing policy, as the name suggests, ties a virtual network adapter to a physical network adapter based on the MAC address.

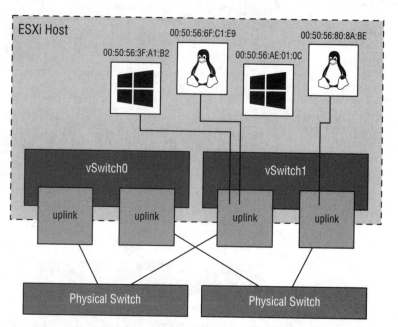

VIRTUAL SWITCH TO PHYSICAL SWITCH

To eliminate a single point of failure, you can connect the physical network adapters in NIC teams set to use the virtual port-based or source MAC-based load balancing policies to different physical switches. Link aggregation using 802.3ad teaming is not supported with either of these load-balancing policies.

REVIEWING IP HASH-BASED LOAD BALANCING

The third load-balancing policy available for NIC teams is the IP hash-based policy, also called the *out-IP* policy. This policy, shown in Figure 5.34, addresses the static-like limitation of the other two policies. The IP hash-based policy uses the source and destination IP addresses to calculate a hash. The hash determines the physical network adapter to use for communication. Different combinations of source and destination IP addresses will, quite naturally, produce different hashes. Based on the hash, then, this algorithm could allow a single virtual machine to communicate over different physical network adapters when communicating with different destinations, assuming that the calculated hashes select a different physical NIC.

FIGURE 5.34
The IP hash-based policy is a more scalable load-balancing policy that allows virtual machines to use more than one physical network adapter when communicating with multiple destination hosts.

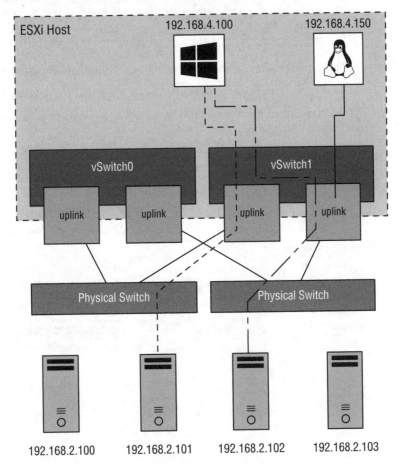

The vSwitch with the NIC-teaming load-balancing policy set to use the IP-based hash must have all physical network adapters connected to the same physical switch or switch stack. In addition, the switch must be configured for link aggregation. ESXi configured to use a vSphere Standard Switch supports standard 802.3ad link aggregation in static (manual) mode, sometimes referred to as EtherChannel, but does not support dynamic-mode link-aggregation protocols such as LACP. Link aggregation may increase overall aggregate throughput by potentially combining the bandwidth of multiple physical network adapters for use by a single virtual network adapter of a virtual machine.

Also consider when using the IP hash-based load-balancing policy that all physical NICs mu be set to active. This is because of the way IP hash-based load balancing works between the virtual switch and the physical switch.

BALANCING FOR LARGE DATA TRANSFERS

Although the IP hash-based load-balancing policy can spread traffic more evenly for a single virtual machine, it does not provide a benefit for large data transfers occurring between the same source and destination systems. Because the source-destination hash will be the same for the duration of the session, the session data will flow through only a single physical network adapter, rather than round-robin alternating through all available adapters servicing the port group.

Perform the following steps to alter the NIC-teaming load-balancing policy of a vSwitch:

1. Connect to a vCenter Server instance using the vSphere Web Client.

2. Navigate to the specific ESXi host that has the vSwitch whose NIC teaming configuration you wish to modify.

3. With an ESXi host selected, go to the Configure tab and select Virtual Switches.

4. Select the name of the virtual switch from the list of virtual switches, and then click the Edit icon (it looks like a pencil).

5. In the Edit Settings dialog box, select Teaming And Failover, and then select the desired load-balancing setting from the Load Balancing drop-down list, as shown in Figure 5.35.

6. Click OK to save the changes.

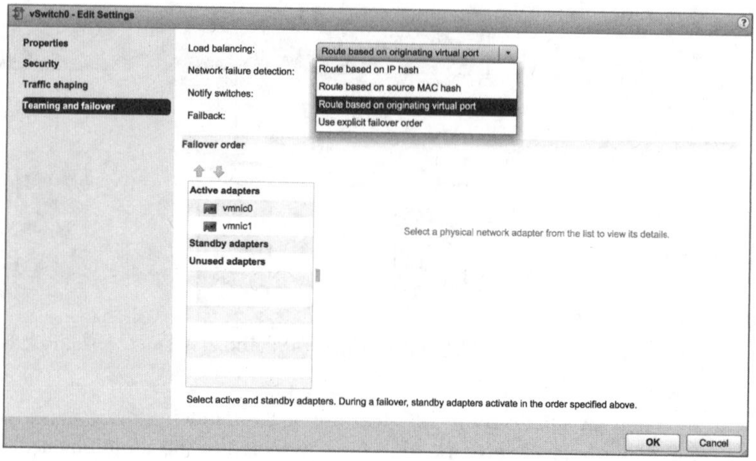

FIGURE 5.35

Select the load-balancing policy for a vSwitch in the Teaming And Failover section.

Now that we've explained the load-balancing policies, and before we explain explicit failover order, let's take a deeper look at the failover and failback of uplinks in a NIC team. There are two parts to consider: failover detection and failover policy. We'll cover both of these in the next section.

CONFIGURING FAILOVER DETECTION AND FAILOVER POLICY

Failover detection with NIC teaming can be configured to use either a link status method or a beacon probing method.

The link status failover detection method works just as the name suggests. The link status of the physical network adapter identifies the failure of an uplink. In this case, failure is identified for events like removed cables or power failures on a physical switch. The downside to the setting for link status failover detection is its inability to identify misconfigurations or pulled cables that connect the switch to other networking devices (for example, a cable connecting one switch to an upstream switch).

The beacon probing failover detection setting, which includes link status as well, sends Ethernet broadcast frames across all physical network adapters in the NIC team. These broadcast frames allow the vSwitch to detect upstream network connection failures and will force failover when STP blocks ports, when ports are configured with the wrong VLAN, or when a switch-to-switch connection has failed. When a beacon is not returned on a physical network adapter, the vSwitch triggers the failover notice and reroutes the traffic from the failed network adapter through another available network adapter based on the failover policy.

Consider a vSwitch with a NIC team consisting of three physical network adapters, where each adapter is connected to a different physical switch, each of which is connected to an upstream switch as shown in Figure 5.36. When the NIC team is set to the beacon-probing failover-detection method, a beacon will be sent out over all three uplinks.

FIGURE 5.36
The beacon-probing failover-detection policy sends beacons out across the physical network adapters of a NIC team to identify upstream network failures or switch misconfigurations.

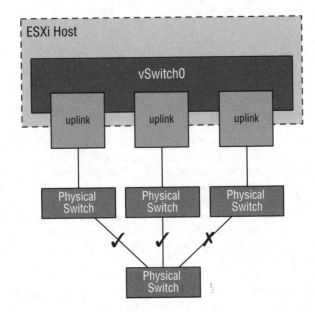

OTHER WAYS OF DETECTING UPSTREAM FAILURES

Some network switch manufacturers have added features into their network switches that assist in detecting upstream network failures. In the Cisco product line, for example, there is a feature known as *link state tracking* that enables the switch to detect when an upstream port has gone down and react accordingly.

After a failure is detected, either via link status or beacon probing, a failover will occur. Traff from any virtual machines or VMkernel ports is rerouted to another member of the NIC team. Exactly which member that might be, though, depends primarily on the configured failover order.

Figure 5.37 shows the failover order configuration for a vSwitch with two adapters in a NIC team. In this configuration, both adapters are configured as active adapters, and either adapter both adapters may be used at any given time to handle traffic for this vSwitch and all its associated ports or port groups.

FIGURE 5.37

The failover order helps determine how adapters in a NIC team are used when a failover occurs.

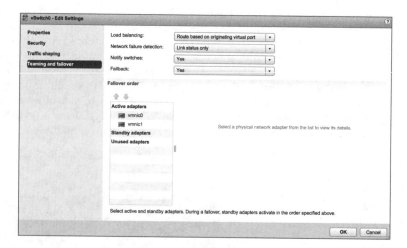

Now look at Figure 5.38. This figure shows a vSwitch with three physical network adapters in a NIC team. In this configuration, one of the adapters is configured as a standby adapter. Any adapters listed as standby adapters will not be used until a failure occurs on one of the active adapters, at which time the standby adapters activate in the order listed.

It should go without saying, but adapters that are listed in the Unused Adapters section will not be used in the event of a failure.

Now take a quick look back at Figure 5.35. You'll see an option there labeled Use Explicit Failover Order. This is the explicit failover order policy mentioned toward the beginning of the earlier section "Configuring NIC Teaming." If you select that option instead of one of the other load-balancing options, traffic will move to the next available uplink in the list of active adapters If no active adapters are available, traffic will move down the list to the standby adapters. Just as the name of the option implies, ESXi will use the order of the adapters in the failover order to determine how traffic will be placed on the physical network adapters. Because this option does not perform any sort of load balancing whatsoever, it's generally not recommended and one of the other options is used instead.

FIGURE 5.38
Standby adapters
automatically activate
when an active
adapter fails.

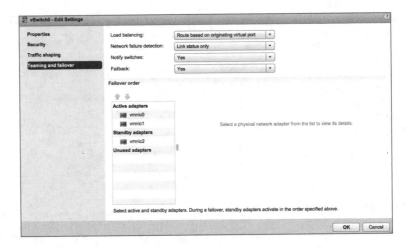

The Failback option controls how ESXi will handle a failed network adapter when it recovers from failure. The default setting, Yes, as shown in Figure 5.37 and Figure 5.38, indicates that the adapter will be returned to active duty immediately upon recovery, and it will replace any standby adapter that may have taken its place during the failure. Setting Failback to No means that the recovered adapter remains inactive until another adapter fails, triggering the replacement of the newly failed adapter.

Perform the following steps to configure the Failover Order policy for a NIC team:

1. Connect to a vCenter Server instance using the vSphere Web Client.

2. Navigate to the ESXi host that has the vSwitch for which you'd like to change the failover order. With an ESXi host selected, select the Configure tab and click Virtual Switches.

3. Select the virtual switch you want to edit and click the Edit Settings icon.

4. Select Teaming And Failover.

5. Use the Move Up and Move Down buttons to adjust the order of the network adapters and their location within the Active Adapters, Standby Adapters, and Unused Adapters lists, as shown in Figure 5.39.

6. Click OK to save the changes.

When a failover event occurs on a vSwitch with a NIC team, the vSwitch is obviously aware of the event. The physical switch that the vSwitch is connected to, however, will not know immediately. As you can see in Figure 5.39, a vSwitch includes a Notify Switches configuration setting, which, when set to Yes, will allow the physical switch to immediately learn of any of the following changes:

◆ A virtual machine is powered on (or any other time a client registers itself with the vSwitch).

◆ A vMotion occurs.

◆ A MAC address is changed.

◆ A NIC team failover or failback has occurred.

FIGURE 5.39

Failover order for a NIC team is determined by the order of network adapters as listed in the Active Adapters, Standby Adapters, and Unused Adapters lists.

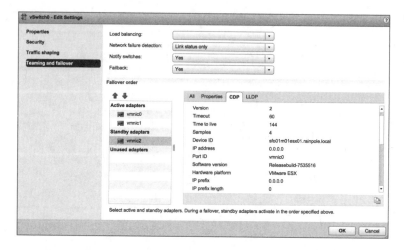

In any of these events, the physical switch is notified of the change using the Reverse Address Resolution Protocol (RARP). RARP updates the lookup tables on the physical switches and offers the shortest latency when a failover event occurs.

TURNING OFF NOTIFY SWITCHES

The Notify Switches option should be set to No when the port group has virtual machines using Microsoft Network Load Balancing (NLB) in Unicast mode. This prevents the vSwitch or port group from sending a RARP packet.

Although the VMkernel works proactively to keep traffic flowing from the virtual networking components to the physical networking components, VMware recommends taking the following actions to minimize networking delays:

- Disable PAgP and LACP on the physical switches.
- Disable DTP or trunk negotiation.
- Disable STP.

VIRTUAL SWITCHES WITH CISCO SWITCHES

VMware recommends configuring Cisco devices to use PortFast mode for access ports or PortFast trunk mode for trunk ports.

Using and Configuring Traffic Shaping

By default, all virtual network adapters connected to a vSwitch have access to the full amount of bandwidth on the physical network adapter with which the vSwitch is associated. In other words, if a vSwitch is assigned a 10 Gbps network adapter, each virtual machine configured to use the vSwitch has access to 10 Gbps of bandwidth. Naturally, if contention becomes a bottle-neck hindering virtual machine performance, NIC teaming will help. However, as a complement to NIC teaming, you can also enable and configure traffic shaping. Traffic shaping establishes hard-coded limits for peak bandwidth, average bandwidth, and burst size to reduce a virtual machines outbound bandwidth capability.

As shown in Figure 5.40, the Peak Bandwidth value and the Average Bandwidth value are specified in kilobits per second, and the Burst Size value is configured in units of kilobytes. The value entered for Average Bandwidth dictates the data transfer per second across the virtual switch. The Peak Bandwidth value identifies the maximum amount of bandwidth a vSwitch can pass without dropping packets. Finally, the Burst Size value defines the maximum amount of data included in a burst. The burst size is a calculation of bandwidth multiplied by time. During periods of high utilization, if a burst exceeds the configured value, packets are dropped in favor of other traffic; however, if the queue for network traffic processing is not full, the packets are retained for transmission at a later time.

FIGURE 5.40

Traffic shaping reduces the outbound (or egress) bandwidth available to a port group.

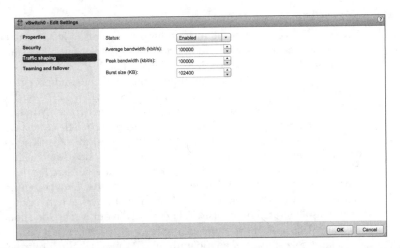

TRAFFIC SHAPING AS A LAST RESORT

Use the traffic shaping feature sparingly. Traffic shaping should be reserved for situations where virtual machines are competing for bandwidth and the opportunity to add physical network adapt-ers isn't available. With the low cost of network adapters, it is more worthwhile to spend time building vSwitch devices with NIC teams as opposed to cutting the bandwidth available to a set of virtual machines. Network I/O Control is also much easier to manage and provides fairness across both virtual machine and VMkernel port groups.

Perform the following steps to configure traffic shaping:

1. Connect to a vCenter Server instance using the vSphere Web Client.

2. Navigate to the ESXi host on which you'd like to configure traffic shaping. With an ESXi host selected, go to the Virtual Switch section of the Configure tab.

3. Select the virtual switch where you want to enable traffic shaping, and then click the Edit Settings icon.

4. Select Traffic Shaping.

5. Select the Enabled option from the Status drop-down list.

6. Adjust the Average Bandwidth value to the desired number of kilobits per second.

7. Adjust the Peak Bandwidth value to the desired number of kilobits per second.

8. Adjust the Burst Size value to the desired number of kilobytes.

Keep in mind that traffic shaping on a vSphere Standard Switch applies only to outbound (or egress) traffic.

Bringing It All Together

By now, you've seen how all the various components of ESXi virtual networking interact with each other, vSwitches, ports and port groups, uplinks and NIC teams, and VLANs. But how do you assemble all these pieces into a usable whole?

The number and the configuration of the vSwitches and port groups depend on several factors, including the number of network adapters in the ESXi host, the number of IP subnets, the existence of VLANs, and the number of physical networks. With respect to the configuration of the vSwitches and Virtual Machine Port Groups, no single correct configuration will satisfy every scenario. However, the greater the number of physical network adapters in an ESXi host, the more flexibility you will have in your virtual networking architecture.

Later in the chapter, we'll discuss some advanced design factors, but for now, let's stick with some basic design considerations. If the vSwitches will not be configured with VLANs, you must create a separate vSwitch for every IP subnet or physical network to which you need to connect. This was illustrated previously in Figure 5.24 in our discussion about VLANs. To understand the concept, let's look at two more examples.

Figure 5.41 shows a scenario with five IP subnets that your virtual infrastructure components need to reach. The virtual machines in the production environment must reach the production LAN, the virtual machines in the test environment must reach the test LAN, the VMkernel needs to access the IP storage and vMotion LANs, and finally, the ESXi host must have access to the management LAN. In this scenario, without VLANs and port groups, the ESXi host must have five different vSwitches and five different physical network adapters. (Of course, this doesn't account for redundancy or NIC teaming for the vSwitches.)

FIGURE 5.41
Without VLANs, each
IP subnet will require a
separate vSwitch with
the appropriate
connection type.

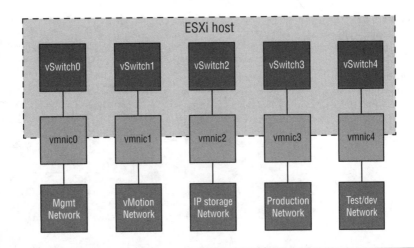

WHY DESIGN IT THAT WAY?

During the virtual network design process, people often ask questions such as why virtual switches should not be created with the largest number of ports to leave room to grow, or why multiple vSwitches should be used instead of a single vSwitch (or vice versa). Some of these questions are easy to answer; the answers to others are a matter of experience and, to be honest, personal preference.

Consider the question about why vSwitches should not be created with the largest number of ports. As you'll see in Table 5.1, later in this chapter, the maximum number of virtual network switch ports per host is 4,096. This means that if virtual switches are created with 1,024 ports, only 4 virtual switches can be created. Calculate 1,024 × 4, and you'll arrive at the per-host maximum of 4,096 ports. (Keep in mind that virtual switches actually have 8 reserved ports, so a 1,016-port switch actually has 1,024 ports.)

Other questions aren't necessarily so clear-cut. Using multiple vSwitches can make it easier to shift certain networks to dedicated physical networks; for example, if a customer wants to move their management network to a dedicated physical management network for greater security, this is more easily accomplished by using a dedicated management vSwitch instead of a single vSwitch. The same can be said for using VLANs. That said, keeping the number of vSwitches to the absolute minimum will keep your implementation simpler and easier to maintain.

In the end, though, many areas of virtual networking design are simply areas of personal preference or dictated by a network infrastructure team policy and not technical necessity. Learning to determine which areas are which will go a long way to helping you understand your virtualized networking environment.

Figure 5.42 shows the same configuration, but this time using VLANs for the Management, vMotion, Production, and Test/Dev networks. The IP storage network is still a physically separate network (a common configuration for iSCSI in many environments).

FIGURE 5.42
The use of the physically separate IP storage network limits the reduction in the number of vSwitches and uplinks.

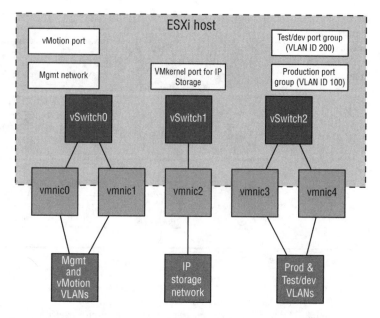

The configuration in Figure 5.42 still uses three network adapters, but this time you're able to provide NIC teaming for all the networks.

If the IP storage network were configured as a VLAN, the number of vSwitches and uplinks could be further reduced. Figure 5.43 shows a possible configuration that would support this so of scenario.

FIGURE 5.43
With the use of port groups and VLANs in the vSwitches, even fewer vSwitches and uplinks are required.

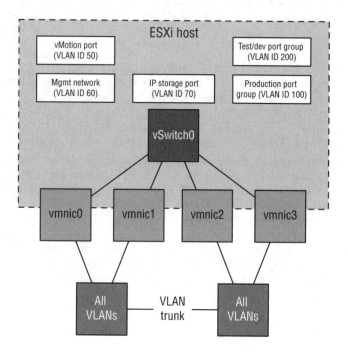

This time, you're able to provide NIC teaming to all the traffic types involved—Management, vMotion, IP storage, and virtual machine traffic—using only a single vSwitch with multiple uplinks.

Clearly, there is a tremendous amount of flexibility in how vSwitches, uplinks, and port groups are assembled to create a virtual network capable of supporting your infrastructure. Even given all this flexibility, though, there are limits. Table 5.1 lists some of the limits of ESXi networking.

TABLE 5.1: Configuration maximums for ESXi networking components (vSphere Standard Switches)

CONFIGURATION ITEM	MAXIMUM
Ports per vSwitch	4,088
Maximum ports per host (vSS/vDS)	4,096
Port groups per vSwitch	512
Uplinks per vSwitch	32
Maximum active ports per host (vSS/vDS)	1,016

VIRTUAL SWITCH CONFIGURATIONS: DON'T GO TOO BIG OR TOO SMALL

Although you can create a vSwitch with a maximum of 4,088 ports (really 4,096), we don't recommend doing so if you anticipate growth. Because ESXi hosts can't have more than 4,096 ports, if you create a vSwitch with 4,088 ports, you're limited to a single vSwitch on that host. With only a single vSwitch, you may not be able to connect to all the networks that you need. In the event you do run out of ports on an ESXi host and need to create a new vSwitch, you can reduce the number of ports on an existing vSwitch. That change requires a reboot to take effect, but vMotion allows you to move the virtual machines to a different host to prevent virtual machine downtime.

Also be sure to account for scenarios such as a host failure, when virtual machines will be restarted on other hosts using vSphere HA (described in more detail in Chapter 7, "Ensuring High Availability and Business Continuity"). In this case, if you make your vSwitch too small (for example, not enough ports), then you could run into an issue there also.

The key takeaway: virtual switch sizing is the factor of multiple variables that you need to consider, so plan carefully! We recommend creating virtual switches with enough ports to cover existing needs, projected growth, and failover capacity.

With all the flexibility provided by the different vSphere networking components, you can be assured that whatever the physical network configuration might hold in store, there are several ways to integrate the vSphere networking. What you configure today may change as the infrastructure changes or as the hardware changes. ESXi provides enough tools and options to ensure a successful communication scheme between the vSphere and physical networks.

Working with vSphere Distributed Switches

So far, our discussion has focused solely on vSphere Standard Switches (just vSwitches). Starting with vSphere 4.0 and continuing with the current release, there is another option: vSphere Distributed Switches.

Whereas vSphere Standard Switches are managed per host, a vSphere Distributed Switch functions as a single virtual switch across all the associated ESXi hosts within a datacenter object. There are a number of similarities between a vSphere Distributed Switch and a Standard Switch.

◆ A vSphere Distributed Switch provides connectivity for virtual machines and VMkernel interfaces.

◆ A vSphere Distributed Switch leverages physical network adapters as uplinks to provide connectivity to the external physical network.

◆ A vSphere Distributed Switch can leverage VLANs for logical network segmentation.

◆ Most of the same load balancing, failback, security, and traffic shaping policies are available, with a few additions in the vSphere Distributed Switch that increase functionality over the vSphere Standard Switch.

Of course, differences exist as well, but the most significant of these is that a vSphere Distributed Switch can span multiple hosts in a vSphere Datacenter instead of each host having its own set of independent vSwitches and port groups. This greatly reduces complexity in clustered ESXi environments and simplifies the addition of new servers to an ESXi cluster.

VMware's official abbreviation for a vSphere Distributed Switch is VDS. In this chapter, we'll use the full name (vSphere Distributed Switch), VDS, or sometimes just distributed switch to refer to this feature.

Creating a vSphere Distributed Switch

The process of creating and configuring a distributed switch is twofold. First, you create the distributed switch at the datacenter object level, and then you add ESXi hosts to it.

Perform the following steps to create a new vSphere Distributed Switch:

1. Launch the vSphere Web Client and connect to a vCenter Server instance.

2. On the vSphere Web Client home screen, select Networking from the Navigator.

3. Right-click the datacenter object, navigate to Distributed Switch, and select New Distributed Switch.

    This launches the New Distributed Switch wizard.

4. Supply a name for the new Distributed Switch and click Next.

5. Select the version of the Distributed Switch you'd like to create. Figure 5.44 shows the options for distributed switch versions.

FIGURE 5.44

If you want to support all the features included in vSphere 6.7, you must use a version 6.6.0 distributed switch.

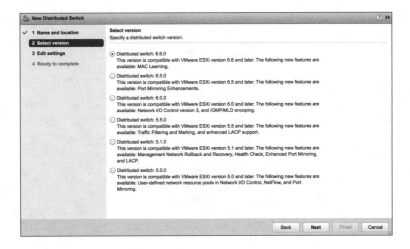

Six options are available:

◆ Distributed Switch 5.0.0: This version is compatible only with vSphere 5.0 and later and adds support for features such as user-defined network resource pools in Network I/O Control, NetFlow, and port mirroring.

◆ Distributed Switch 5.1.0: Compatible with vSphere 5.1 or later, this version of the Distributed Switch adds support for Network Rollback and Recovery, Health Check, Enhanced Port Mirroring, and LACP.

◆ Distributed Switch 5.5.0: This version is supported on vSphere 5.5 or later. This Distributed Switch adds traffic filtering and marking and enhanced support for LACP.

◆ Distributed Switch 6.0.0: This version is supported on vSphere 6.0 or later. This version of the Distributed Switch adds NIOC3 support, multicast snooping, and multicast filtering.

◆ Distributed Switch 6.5.0: This version is supported on vSphere 6.5 or later. This version of the Distributed Switch supports the ERSPAN port-mirroring protocol.

◆ Distributed Switch 6.6.0: This is the latest version and is only supported on vSphere 6.7. This version of the Distributed Switch supports MAC Learning.

In this case, select vSphere Distributed Switch Version 6.6.0 and click Next.

6. Specify the number of uplink ports, as illustrated in Figure 5.45.

7. On the same screen shown in Figure 5.45, select whether you want Network I/O Control enabled or disabled. Also specify whether you want to create a default port group and, if so, what the name of that default port group should be. For this example, leave Network I/O Control enabled, and create a default port group with the name of your choosing. Click Next.

FIGURE 5.45

The number of uplinks controls how many physical adapters from each host can serve as uplinks for the distributed switch.

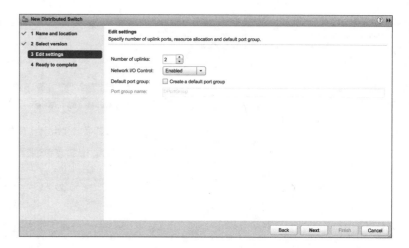

8. Review the settings for your new distributed switch. If everything looks correct, click Finish; otherwise, use the Back button to go back and change settings as needed.

After you complete the New Distributed Switch wizard, a new distributed switch will appear in the vSphere Web Client. You can click the new distributed switch to see the ESXi hosts connected to it (none yet), the virtual machines hosted on it (none yet), the distributed ports groups on (only one—the one you created during the wizard), and the uplink port groups (of which there is also only one).

All this information is also available using the vSphere CLI or PowerCLI, but due to the nature of how the `esxcli` command is structured, you'll need to have an ESXi host added to the distributed switch first. Let's look at how that's done.

---

vSphere Distributed Switches Require vCenter Server

This may seem obvious, but it's important to point out that because of the shared nature of a vSphere Distributed Switch, vCenter Server is required. In other words, you cannot create or manage a vSphere Distributed Switch in an environment that is not being managed by vCenter Server; however, traffic will continue to flow in the event of a vCenter outage. Apart from this requirement, you will also need Enterprise Plus licensing.

Once you've created a distributed switch, it is relatively easy to add an ESXi host. When the ESXi host is added, all of the distributed port groups will automatically be propagated to the host with the correct configuration. This is the distributed nature of the distributed switch, as configuration changes are made via the vSphere Web Client, vCenter Server pushes those changes out to all participating ESXi hosts. VMware administrators who are used to managing large ESXi clusters and having to repeatedly create vSwitches and port groups and maintain consistency of these port groups across hosts will be pleased with the reduction in administrative overhead that distributed switches offer.

Perform the following steps to add an ESXi host to an existing distributed switch:

1. Launch the vSphere Web Client and connect to a vCenter Server instance.

2. In the Navigator, click Networking.

3. Select an existing distributed switch, and then select Add And Manage Hosts from the Actions menu.

   This launches the Add And Manage Hosts wizard, shown in Figure 5.46.

FIGURE 5.46

When you're working with distributed switches, the vSphere Web Client offers a single wizard to add hosts, remove hosts, or manage host networking.

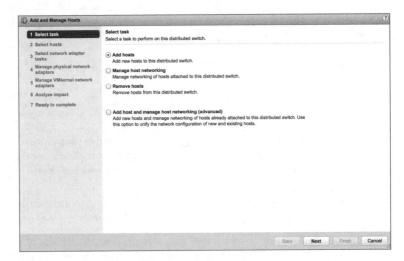

4. Select the Add Hosts radio button and click Next.

5. Click the green plus icon to add an ESXi host. This opens the Select New Host dialog box.

6. From the list of new hosts to add, place a check mark next to the name of each ESXi host you'd like to add to the distributed switch. Click OK when you're done, and then click Next to continue.

7. The next screen offers three different adapter-related tasks to perform, as shown in Figure 5.47. In this case, make sure only Manage Physical Adapters is selected. Click Next to continue.

   The Manage VMkernel Adapters option allows you to add, migrate, edit, or remove VMkernel adapters (VMkernel ports) from this distributed switch.

   The Migrate Virtual Machine Networking option enables you to migrate virtual machine network adapters to this distributed switch.

8. The next screen lets you choose the physical adapters on the hosts that should be connected to the uplinks port group for the distributed switch. For each physical adapter you'd like to add, click the adapter and then click Assign Uplink. You'll be prompted to confirm the uplink to which this physical adapter should be connected. Repeat this process to add as many physical adapters as you have uplinks configured for the distributed switch.

FIGURE 5.47

All adapter-related changes to distributed switches are consolidated into a single wizard.

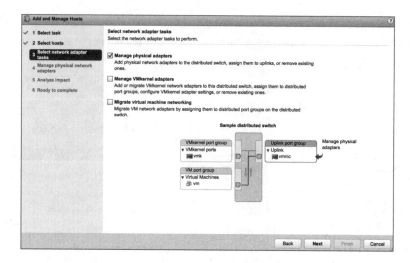

NOTE Leave at least one physical adapter connected to your vSphere Standard Switch until you have migrated the management VMkernel port. If you attempt to move them all at this point, the operation will fail because there will be no connectivity to the ESXi hosts.

9. Repeat step 8 for each ESXi host you're adding to the distributed switch. Click Next when you're finished adding uplinks for all ESXi hosts.

10. The Analyze Impact screen displays the potential effects of the changes proposed by the wizard. If everything looks okay, click Next; otherwise, click Back to go back and change the settings.

11. Click Finish to complete the wizard.

You'll have an opportunity to see this wizard again in later sections. For example, we'll discuss the options for managing physical and VMkernel adapters in more detail in the section "Managing VMkernel Adapters," later in this chapter.

We mentioned earlier in this section that you could use the vSphere CLI to see distributed switch information after you'd added a host to the distributed switch. The following command will show you a list of the distributed switches that a particular ESXi host is a member of:

```
esxcli network vswitch dvs vmware list
```

The output will look similar to the output shown in Figure 5.48.

Use the --help parameter with the network vswitch dvs vmware namespace command to see some of the other tasks that you can perform with the vSphere CLI related to vSphere Distributed Switches.

Now, let's take a look at a few other tasks related to distributed switches. We'll start with removing an ESXi host from a distributed switch.

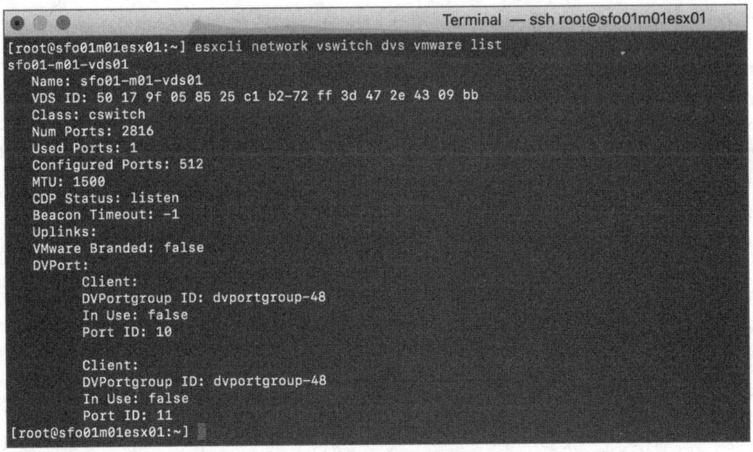

FIGURE 5.48

The `esxcli` command shows full details on the configuration of a distributed switch.

```
●  ●  ●                          Terminal — ssh root@sfo01m01esx01
[root@sfo01m01esx01:~] esxcli network vswitch dvs vmware list
sfo01-m01-vds01
   Name: sfo01-m01-vds01
   VDS ID: 50 17 9f 05 85 25 c1 b2-72 ff 3d 47 2e 43 09 bb
   Class: cswitch
   Num Ports: 2816
   Used Ports: 1
   Configured Ports: 512
   MTU: 1500
   CDP Status: listen
   Beacon Timeout: -1
   Uplinks:
   VMware Branded: false
   DVPort:
         Client:
         DVPortgroup ID: dvportgroup-48
         In Use: false
         Port ID: 10

         Client:
         DVPortgroup ID: dvportgroup-48
         In Use: false
         Port ID: 11
[root@sfo01m01esx01:~]
```

Removing an ESXi Host from a Distributed Switch

Naturally, you can also remove ESXi hosts from a distributed switch. You can't remove a host from a distributed switch if it still has virtual machines connected to a distributed port group on that switch. This is analogous to trying to delete a standard switch or a port group while a virtual machine is still connected; this, too, is prevented. To allow the ESXi host to be removed from the distributed switch, you must move all virtual machines to a standard switch or a different distributed switch.

Perform the following steps to remove an individual ESXi host from a distributed switch:

1. Launch the vSphere Web Client and connect to a vCenter Server instance.

2. Navigate to the list of distributed switches and select the specific distributed switch from which you'd like to remove an individual ESXi host.

3. From the Actions menu, select Add And Manage Hosts. This will bring up the Add And Manage Hosts dialog box, shown earlier in Figure 5.47.

4. Select the Remove Hosts radio button. Click Next.

5. Click the green plus icon to select hosts to be removed from the distributed switch.

6. In the Select Member Hosts dialog box, place a check mark next to each ESXi host you'd like to remove from the distributed switch. Click OK when you're done selecting hosts.

7. Click Finish to remove the selected ESXi hosts.

8. If any virtual machines are still connected to the distributed switch, the vSphere Web Client will display an error similar to the one shown in Figure 5.49.

FIGURE 5.49

The vSphere Web Client won't allow a host to be removed from a distributed switch if a virtual machine is still attached.

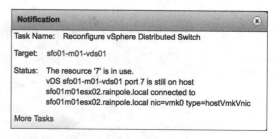

To correct this error, reconfigure the virtual machine(s) to use a different distributed switch or standard switch. Then proceed with removing the host from the distributed switch.

If there were no virtual machines attached to the distributed switch, or after all virtual machines are reconfigured to use a different standard switch or distributed switch, the host is removed.

In addition to removing individual ESXi hosts from a distributed switch, you can remove the entire distributed switch.

Removing a Distributed Switch

Removing the last ESXi host from a distributed switch does not remove the distributed switch itself. Even if all the virtual machines and/or ESXi hosts have been removed from the distributed switch, the distributed switch still exists in the vCenter inventory. You must still remove the distributed switch object itself.

You can only remove a distributed switch when no virtual machines are assigned to a distributed port group on the distributed switch. Otherwise, the removal is blocked with an error message similar to the one shown earlier in Figure 5.49. Again, you'll need to reconfigure the virtual machine(s) to use a different standard switch or distributed switch before the operation can proceed. Refer to Chapter 9, "Creating and Managing Virtual Machines," for more information on modifying a virtual machine's network settings.

Follow these steps to remove the distributed switch if no virtual machines are connected to any distributed port group on it:

1. Launch the vSphere Web Client and connect to a vCenter Server instance.

2. From the Navigator, select Networking.

3. Select an existing vSphere Distributed Switch.

4. From the Actions menu, select Delete.

   The distributed switch and all associated distributed port groups are removed from the inventory and from any connected hosts.

The bulk of the configuration for a distributed switch isn't performed for the distributed switch itself but rather for the distributed port groups on that distributed switch. Nevertheless, let's first take a look at managing distributed switches themselves.

Managing Distributed Switches

As stated earlier, the vast majority of tasks a VMware administrator performs with a distributed switch involve working with distributed port groups. We'll explore distributed port groups later, but for now, let's discuss managing the distributed switch.

The Configure tab is an area you've already seen and will see again throughout this chapter; in particular, you've been working in the Settings section of the Configure tab quite a bit. You'll continue to do so as you start creating distributed port groups. The Configure tab also includes the Resource Allocation section.

The Resource Allocation section is where you'll allocate resources for system traffic and create network resource pools for use with Network I/O Control, a topic discussed in Chapter 11, "Managing Resource Allocation."

On the Monitor tab, there are three sections:

◆ The Issues section shows issues and/or alarms pertaining to a distributed switch.

◆ The Tasks and Events sections provide insight into recently performed tasks and a list of events that have occurred and could be the result of either user or system action. You could use these sections to see which user performed a certain task or to review various events pertaining to the selected distributed switch.

◆ The Health section centralizes health information for the distributed switch, such as VLAN checks, MTU checks, and other health checks.

The Health section contains some rather important functionality, so let's dig a little deeper into that section in particular.

USING HEALTH CHECKS AND NETWORK ROLLBACK

The vSphere Distributed Switch Health Check feature was added in vSphere 5.1 and is available only when you're using a version 5.1.0 or above distributed switch. The idea behind the health check feature is to help VMware administrators identify mismatched VLAN configurations, mismatched MTU configurations, and mismatched NIC teaming policies, all of which are common sources of connectivity issues.

You should know the requirements for using the health check feature:

◆ You must be using a version 5.1.0 or above distributed switch.

◆ VLAN and MTU checks require at least two NICs with active links.

◆ The teaming policy check requires at least two NICs with active links and at least two hosts.

By default, vSphere Distributed Switch Health Check is turned off; you must enable it in order to perform checks.

To enable vSphere Distributed Switch Health Check, perform these steps:

1. Connect to a vCenter Server instance using the vSphere Web Client.

2. From the Navigator, select Networking and select the distributed switch you wish to enable the Health Check feature on.

3. Click the Configure tab and then select Health Check.

4. Click the Edit button.

5. In the Edit Health Check Settings dialog box, you can independently enable checks for VLAN and MTU, teaming and failover, or both. Click OK when finished.

After the health checks are enabled, you can view the health check information on the Monitor tab of the distributed switch. Figure 5.50 shows the health check information for a distributed switch once health checks have been enabled.

FIGURE 5.50

The vSphere Distributed Switch Health Check helps identify potential problems in configuration.

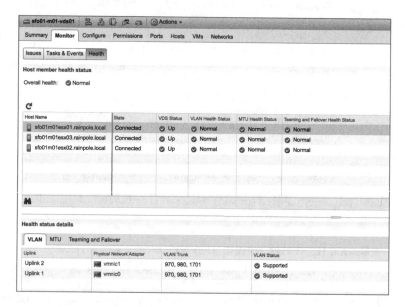

Closely related to the health check functionality is a feature called vSphere Network Rollback. The idea behind network rollback is to automatically protect environments against changes that would disconnect ESXi hosts from vCenter Server by rolling back changes if they are invalid. For example, changes to the speed or duplex of a physical NIC, updating teaming and failover policies for a switch that contains the ESXi host's management interface, or changing the IP settings of a host's management interface are all examples of changes that are validated when they occur. If the change would result in a loss of management connectivity to the host, the change is reverted, or rolled back, automatically.

Rollbacks can occur at two levels: at the host networking level or distributed switch level. Rollback is enabled by default.

In addition to automatic rollbacks, VMware administrators have the option of performing manual rollbacks. You learned how to do a manual rollback at the host level earlier, in the section "Configuring the Management Network," which discussed the Network Restore Options area of an ESXi host's DCUI. To perform a manual rollback of a distributed switch, you use the same process as restoring from a saved configuration, which will be discussed in the next section.

Importing and Exporting Distributed Switch Configuration

vSphere 5.1 added the ability to export (save) and import (load) the configuration of a distributed switch. This functionality can serve a number of purposes; one purpose is to manually "roll back" to a previously saved configuration.

To export (save) the configuration of a distributed switch to a file, perform these steps:

1. Log into a vCenter Server instance using the vSphere Web Client.

2. Navigate to the distributed switch whose configuration you'd like to save.

3. From the Actions menu, select Settings ➢ Export Configuration. This opens the Export Configuration dialog box.

4. Select the appropriate radio button to export either the configuration of the distributed switch and all the distributed ports groups or just the configuration of the distributed switch.

5. Optionally, supply a description of the exported (saved) configuration; then click OK.

6. When prompted to specify whether you want to save the exported configuration file, click Yes.

7. Use your operating system's File Save dialog box to select the location where the exported configuration file (named `backup.zip`) should be saved.

Once you have the configuration exported to a file, you can then import this configuration back into your vSphere environment at a later date to restore the saved configuration. You can also import the configuration into a different vSphere environment, such as an environment being managed by a separate vCenter Server instance.

To import a saved configuration, perform these steps:

1. Log into a vCenter Server instance using the vSphere Web Client.

2. Navigate to the distributed switch whose configuration you'd like to restore.

3. From the Actions menu, select Settings ➢ Restore Configuration. This opens the Restore Configuration wizard.

4. Use the Browse button to select the saved configuration file created earlier by exporting the configuration.

5. Select the appropriate radio button to restore either the distributed switch and all distributed port groups or just the distributed switch configuration.

6. Click Next.

7. Review the settings that the wizard will import. If everything is correct, click Finish; otherwise, click Back to go back and make changes.

Both vSphere Network Rollback and the ability to manually export or import the configuration of a distributed switch are major steps forward in managing distributed switches in a vSphere environment.

Most of the work that a VMware administrator needs to perform will revolve around distributed port groups, so let's turn our attention to working with them.

Working with Distributed Port Groups

With vSphere Standard Switches, port groups are the key to connectivity for the VMkernel and for virtual machines. Without ports and port groups on a vSwitch, nothing can be connected to that vSwitch. The same is true for vSphere Distributed Switches. Without a distributed port group, nothing can be connected to a distributed switch, and the distributed switch is, therefore, unusable. In the following sections, you'll take a closer look at creating, configuring, and removing distributed port groups.

CREATING A DISTRIBUTED PORT GROUP

Perform the following steps to create a new distributed port group:

1. Log into a vCenter Server instance using the vSphere Web Client.

2. Select Networking in the navigator.

3. Select an existing vSphere Distributed Switch, and then choose Distributed Port Group ➤ New Distributed Port Group from the Actions menu.

4. Supply a name for the new distributed port group. Click Next to continue.

5. The Configure Settings screen, shown in Figure 5.51, allows you to specify a number of settings for the new distributed port group.

FIGURE 5.51
The New Distributed Port Group wizard gives you extensive access to customize the new distributed port group's settings.

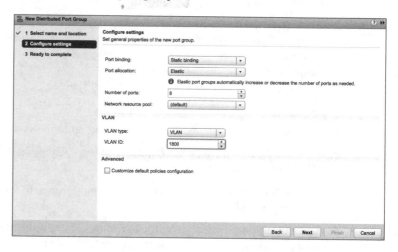

The Port Binding and Port Allocation options allow you more fine-grained control over how ports in the distributed port group are allocated to virtual machines.

◆ With Port Binding set to the default value of Static Binding, ports are statically assigned to a virtual machine when a virtual machine is connected to the distributed switch. You may also set Port Allocation to be either Elastic (in which case, the distributed port group starts with 8 ports and adds more in 8-port increments as needed) or Fixed (in which case, it defaults to 128 ports).

- With Port Binding set to Dynamic Binding, you specify how many ports the distributed port group should have (the default is 128). Note that this option is deprecated and not recommended; the vSphere Web Client will post a warning to that effect if you select it.

- With Port Binding set to Ephemeral Binding, you can't specify the number of ports or the Port Allocation method.

The Network Resource Pool option allows you to connect this distributed port group to a Network I/O Control resource pool. Network I/O Control and network resource pools are described in more detail in Chapter 11.

Finally, the options for VLAN Type might also need a bit more explanation:

- With VLAN Type set to None, the distributed port group will receive only untagged traffic. In this case, the uplinks must connect to physical switch ports configured as access ports or they will receive only untagged/native VLAN traffic.

- With VLAN Type set to VLAN (i.e., 802.1Q VST), you'll need to specify a VLAN ID. The distributed port group will receive traffic tagged with that VLAN ID. The uplinks must connect to physical switch ports configured as VLAN trunks.

- With VLAN Type set to VLAN Trunking (i.e., 802.1Q VGT), you'll need to specify the range of allowed VLANs. The distributed port group will pass the VLAN tags up to the guest OSs on any connected virtual machines.

- With VLAN Type set to Private VLAN, you'll need to specify a Private VLAN entry. Private VLANs are described in detail later in the section "Setting Up Private VLANs."

6. Select the desired port binding settings (and port allocation, if necessary), the desired network resource pool, and the desired VLAN type, and then click Next.

7. On the summary screen, review the settings and click Finish if everything is correct. If you need to make changes, click the Back button to go back and make the necessary edits.

After a distributed port group has been created, you can select that distributed port group in the virtual machine configuration as a possible network connection, as shown in Figure 5.52.

After you create a distributed port group, it will appear in the Topology view for the distributed switch that hosts it. In the vSphere Web Client, this view is accessible from the Settings area of the Configure tab for the distributed switch. From there, clicking the Info icon (the small *i* in the blue circle) will provide more information about the distributed port group and its current state. Figure 5.53 shows some of the information provided by the vSphere Web Client about a distributed port group.

EDITING A DISTRIBUTED PORT GROUP

To edit the configuration of a distributed port group, use the Edit Distributed Port Group Settings link in the Topology View for the distributed switch. In the vSphere Web Client, you can locate this area by selecting a distributed switch and then going to the Settings area of the Configure tab. Finally, select Topology to produce the Topology view shown in Figure 5.54.

FIGURE 5.52
A distributed port group is selected as a network connection for virtual machines, just like port groups on a vSphere Standard Switch.

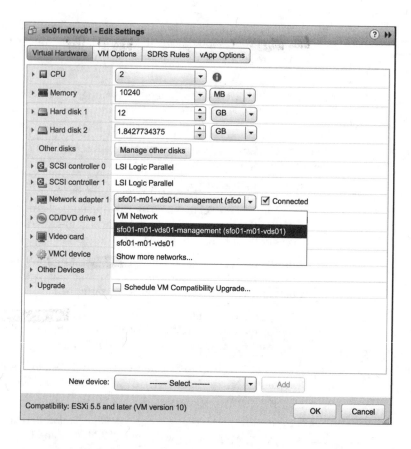

FIGURE 5.53
The vSphere Web Client provides a summary of the distributed port group's configuration.

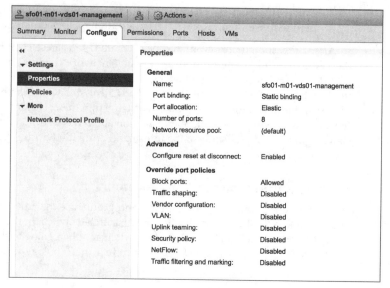

FIGURE 5.54

The Topology view for a distributed switch provides easy access to view and edit distributed port groups.

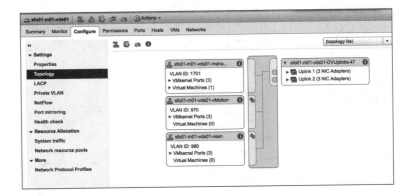

For now, let's focus on modifying VLAN settings, traffic shaping, and NIC teaming for the distributed port group. Policy settings for security and monitoring are discussed later in this chapter.

DIFFERENT OPTIONS BASED ON vSPHERE DISTRIBUTED SWITCH VERSION

Recall that you can create different versions of distributed switches in the vSphere Web Client. The configuration options available are dependent on the vSphere Distributed Switch version.

Perform the following steps to modify the VLAN settings for a distributed port group:

1. Connect to a vCenter Server instance using the vSphere Web Client.

2. Navigate to the distributed port group you want to edit.

3. Click the Edit Distributed Port Group Settings icon.

4. In the Edit Settings dialog box, select the VLAN option from the list of options on the left.

5. Modify the VLAN settings by changing the VLAN ID or by changing the VLAN Type setting to VLAN Trunking or Private VLAN.

6. Click OK when you have finished making changes.

Follow these steps to modify the traffic-shaping policy for a distributed port group:

1. Connect to a vCenter Server instance using the vSphere Web Client.

2. Navigate to the distributed port group you want to edit.

3. Click the Edit Distributed Port Group Settings icon.

4. Select the Traffic Shaping option from the list of options on the left of the distributed port group settings dialog box, as illustrated in Figure 5.55.

FIGURE 5.55

You can apply both ingress (inbound) and egress (outbound) traffic-shaping policies to a distributed port group on a distributed switch.

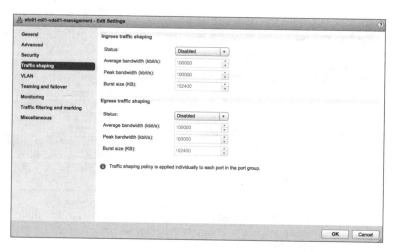

Traffic shaping was described in detail earlier, in the section "Using and Configuring Traffic Shaping." The big difference here is that with a distributed switch, you can apply traffic shaping policies to both ingress and egress traffic. With vSphere Standard Switches, you could apply traffic-shaping policies only to egress (outbound) traffic. Otherwise, the settings here are for a distributed port group function as described earlier.

5. Click OK when you have finished making changes.

Perform the following steps to modify the NIC teaming and failover policies for a distributed port group:

1. Connect to a vCenter Server instance using the vSphere Web Client.

2. Navigate to the distributed port group you want to edit.

3. Click the Edit Distributed Port Group Settings icon.

4. Select the Teaming And Failover option from the list of options on the left of the Edit Settings dialog box, as illustrated in Figure 5.56.

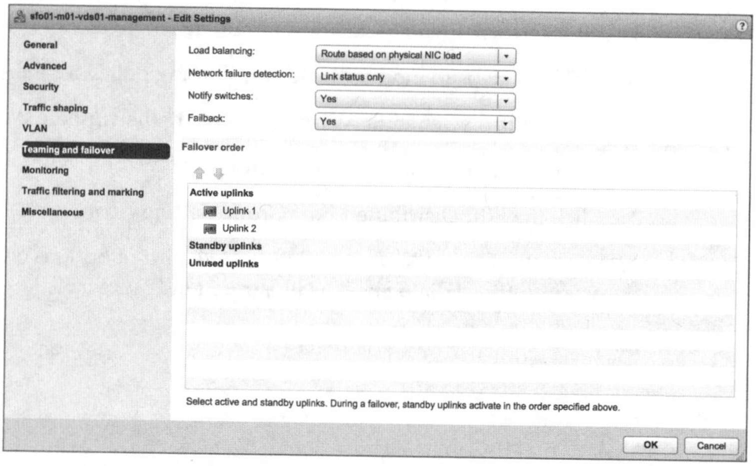

FIGURE 5.56

The Teaming And Failover item in the Edit Settings dialog box for the distributed port group provides options for modifying how a distributed port group uses uplinks.

These settings were described in detail in the section "Configuring NIC Teaming," with one notable exception—version 4.1 and higher distributed switches support Route Based On Physical NIC Load. When this load-balancing policy is selected, ESXi checks the utilization of the uplinks every 30 seconds for congestion. In this case, congestion is defined as either transmit or receive traffic greater than a mean utilization of 75% over a 30-second period. If congestion is detected on an uplink, ESXi will dynamically reassign the virtual machine or VMkernel traffic to a different uplink.

REQUIREMENTS FOR LOAD BASED TEAMING

Load Based Teaming (LBT) requires that all upstream physical switches be part of the same Layer 2 (broadcast) domain. In addition, VMware recommends that you enable the PortFast or PortFast Trunk option on all physical switch ports connected to a distributed switch that is using LBT.

---

5. Click OK when you have finished making changes.

Later in this chapter, the section "Configuring LACP" provides more detail on vSphere's support for Link Aggregation Control Protocol (LACP), including how you would configure a distributed switch for use with LACP. That section also refers back to some of this information on modifying NIC teaming and failover.

If you browse through the available settings, you might notice a Blocked Policy option. This is the equivalent of disabling a group of ports in the distributed port group. Figure 5.57 shows that the Block All Ports setting is set to either Yes or No. If you set the Block Policy to Yes, all traffic to and from that distributed port group is dropped.

FIGURE 5.57

The Block policy is set to either Yes or No. Setting the Block policy to Yes disables all the ports in that distributed port group.

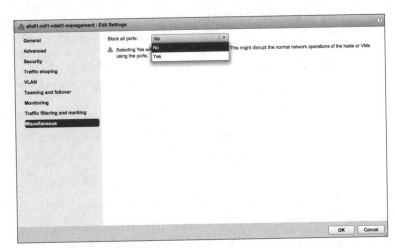

EFFECTS OF SETTING BLOCK POLICY TO YES

Don't change the Block policy to Yes unless you are prepared for network downtime for all virtual machines attached to that distributed port group!

A HELPFUL FEATURE

Suppose you accidentally set Block to Yes on a distributed port group that contains the management interface. Is there a feature you've already encountered that might help in this situation? Yes! The vSphere Network Rollback would help here.

REMOVING A DISTRIBUTED PORT GROUP

To delete a distributed port group, first select the distributed port group. Then, click Delete from the Actions menu. Click Yes to confirm that you do want to delete the distributed port group.

If any virtual machines are still attached to that distributed port group, the vSphere Web Client prevents its deletion and logs an error notification.

To delete the distributed port group to which a virtual machine is attached, you must first reconfigure the virtual machine to use a different distributed port group on the same distributed switch, a distributed port group on a different distributed switch, or a vSphere standard switch. You can use the Migrate Virtual Machines To Another Network command on the Actions menu, or you can just reconfigure the virtual machines network settings directly.

Once all virtual machines have been moved off a distributed port group, you can delete the distributed port group using the process described in the previous paragraphs.

The next section will focus on managing adapters, both physical and virtual, when working with a vSphere Distributed Switch.

Managing VMkernel Adapters

With a distributed switch, managing VMkernel and physical adapters is handled quite differently than with a vSphere standard switch. VMkernel adapters are VMkernel interfaces, so by managing *VMkernel adapters*, we're really talking about managing *VMkernel traffic*. Management, vMotion, IP-based storage, vSAN, vSphere Replication, vSphere Replication NFC, and Fault Tolerance logging are all types of VMkernel traffic. Physical adapters are, of course, the physical network adapters that serve as uplinks for the distributed switch. Managing physical adapters involves adding or removing physical adapters connected to ports in the uplinks distributed port group on the distributed switch.

Perform the following steps to add a VMkernel adapter to a distributed switch:

1. Connect to a vCenter Server instance using the vSphere Web Client.

2. Select Networking in the navigator.

3. Select the distributed switch you want to add the VMkernel adapter to.

4. Select Add And Manage Hosts from the Actions menu.

5. Select the Manage Host Networking radio button, and then click Next.

6. On the Select Hosts screen, use the green plus icon to add hosts to the list of hosts that will be modified during this process. Though it seems the wizard is asking you to add hosts to the distributed switch, you're really adding hosts to the list of hosts that will be modified. Click Next when you're ready to move to the next step.

7. In this case, we're modifying VMkernel adapters, so make sure only the Manage VMkernel adapters check box is selected. Click Next.

8. With an ESXi host selected, click the New Adapter link near the top of the Manage VMkernel Network Adapters screen, shown in Figure 5.58. This opens the Add Networking wizard.

FIGURE 5.58

The Manage VMkernel Network Adapters screen of the wizard allows you to add new adapters as well as migrate existing adapters.

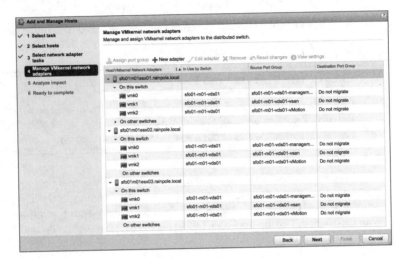

9. In the Add Networking wizard, click the Browse button to select the existing distributed port group to which this new virtual adapter should be added. (Refer to the sidebar "Create the Distributed Port Group First" for an important note.) Click OK once you've selected an existing distributed port group, and then click Next.

10. On the Port Properties screen, select whether you want to enable IPv4 only, IPv6 only, or both protocols.

11. Enable the desired services—like vMotion, v SAN, vSphere Replication, or Fault Tolerance Logging—that should be enabled on this new virtual adapter. Click Next.

12. Depending on whether you selected IPv4, IPv6, or IPv4 and IPv6, the next few screens ask you to configure the appropriate network settings.

♦ If you selected only IPv4, then supply the desired IPv4 settings.

♦ If you selected only IPv6, then supply the correct IPv6 settings for your network.

♦ If you selected both IPv4 and IPv6, then there will be two configuration screens in the wizard, one for IPv4 and a separate screen for IPv6.

13. Once you've entered the correct network protocol settings, the final screen of the wizard presents the settings that will be applied. If everything is correct, click Finish; otherwise, click the Back button to go back and change settings as necessary.

14. This returns you to the Add And Manage Hosts wizard, where you'll now see the new virtual adapter that will be added. Repeat steps 8 through 13 if you need to add a virtual adapter for another ESXi host at the same time; otherwise, click Next.

15. The Analyze Impact screen will show you the potential impact of the changes you're making. If necessary, click the Back button to go back and make changes to mitigate any negative impacts. When you're ready to proceed, click Next.

16. Click Finish to commit the changes to the selected distributed switch and ESXi hosts.

CREATE THE DISTRIBUTED PORT GROUP FIRST

When you are adding new VMkernel adapters to a distributed switch, make sure you've created the distributed port group you'd like this new virtual adapter to use first. The wizard for adding a new virtual adapter does not provide a way to create a distributed port group as part of the process.

Migrating an existing virtual adapter, such as a VMkernel port on an existing vSphere standard switch, is done in exactly the same way. The only real difference is that in step 8, you'll select an existing virtual adapter, and then click the Assign Port Group link across the top. Select an existing port group and click OK to return to the wizard, where the screen will look similar to what's shown in Figure 5.59.

FIGURE 5.59

Migrating a virtual adapter involves assigning it to an existing distributed port group.

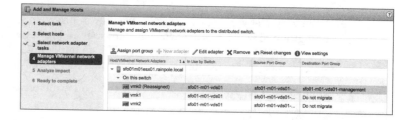

After you create or migrate a virtual adapter, you use the same wizard to make changes to the virtual port, such as modifying the IP address, changing the distributed port group to which the adapter is assigned, or enabling features such as vMotion or Fault Tolerance logging. To edit an existing virtual adapter, you'd select the Edit Adapter link seen in Figure 5.59. You would remove VMkernel adapters using this wizard as well, using the Remove link on the Manage Virtual Network Adapters screen of the Add And Manage Hosts wizard.

Not surprisingly, the vSphere Web Client also allows you to add or remove physical adapters connected to ports in the uplinks port group on the distributed switch. Although you can specify physical adapters during the process of adding a host to a distributed switch, as shown earlier, it might be necessary at times to connect a physical NIC to the distributed switch after the host is already participating in it.

Perform the following steps to add a physical network adapter in an ESXi host to a distributed switch:

1. Connect to a vCenter Server instance using the vSphere Web Client.

2. From the vSphere Web Client home screen, navigate to the distributed switch you'd like to modify.

3. From the Actions menu, select Add And Manage Hosts.

4. Select the Manage Host Networking radio button, and then click Next.

5. Use the green plus icon to add ESXi hosts to the list of hosts that will be affected by the changes in the wizard. Click Next when you're finished adding ESXi hosts to the list.

6. Make sure only the Manage Physical Adapters option is selected, as shown in Figure 5.60, and click Next.

FIGURE 5.60

To manage uplinks on a distributed switch, make sure only the Manage Physical Adapters option is selected.

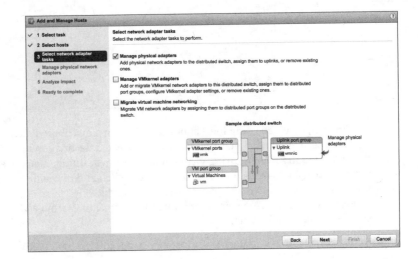

7. At the Manage Physical Network Adapters screen, you can add or remove physical network adapters to the selected distributed switch.

   ◆ To add a physical adapter as an uplink, select an unassigned adapter from the list and click the Assign Uplink link. You can also use the Assign Uplink link to change the uplink to which a given physical adapter is assigned (for example, to move it from uplink 2 to uplink 3).

   ◆ To remove a physical adapter as an uplink, select an assigned adapter from the list and click the Unassign Adapter link.

   ◆ To migrate a physical adapter from another switch to this distributed switch, select the already assigned adapter and use the Assign Uplink link. This will automatically remove it from the other switch and assign it to the selected switch.

   Repeat this process for each host in the list. Click Next when you're ready to proceed.

8. At the Analyze Impact screen, the vSphere Web Client will provide feedback on the anticipated impact of the changes. If the impact of the changes is undesirable, use the Back button to go back and make any necessary changes. Otherwise, click Next.

9. Click Finish to complete the wizard and commit the changes.

In addition to migrating VMkernel adapters and modifying the physical adapters, you can use vCenter Server to assist in migrating virtual machine adapters, that is, migrating a virtual machines networking between vSphere standard switches and vSphere distributed switches, as shown in Figure 5.61.

FIGURE 5.61

The Migrate Virtual Machine Networking wizard automates the process of migrating virtual machines between a source and a destination network.

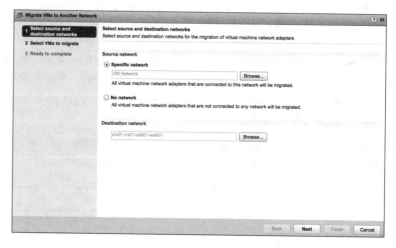

This tool, accessed using the Actions menu when a distributed switch is selected, will reconfigure all selected virtual machines to use the selected destination network. This is much easier than individually reconfiguring virtual machines! In addition, this tool allows you to easily migrate virtual machines both *to* a distributed switch and *from* a distributed switch. Let's walk through the process so that you can see how it works.

Perform the following steps to migrate virtual machines from a vSphere Standard Switch to a vSphere Distributed Switch:

1. Connect to a vCenter Server instance using the vSphere Web Client.

2. Select Networking in the navigator.

3. Select a distributed switch from the inventory tree on the left, and then select Migrate VM To Another Network from the Actions menu. This launches the Migrate Virtual Machine Networking wizard.

4. Use the Browse button to select the source network that contains the virtual machines you'd like to migrate. You can use the Filter and Find search boxes to limit the results if you need to. Click OK once you've selected the source network.

5. Click the Browse button to select the destination network to which you'd like the virtual machines to be migrated. Again, use the Filter and Find search boxes, where needed, to make it easier to locate the desired destination network. Click OK to return to the wizard once you've selected the destination network.

6. Click Next after you've finished selecting the source and destination networks.

7. A list of matching virtual machines is generated, and each virtual machine is analyzed to determine if the destination network is accessible or inaccessible to the virtual machine.

Figure 5.62 shows a list with both accessible and inaccessible destination networks. A destination network might show up as inaccessible if the ESXi host on which that virtual machine is running isn't part of the distributed switch. Select the virtual machines you want to migrate; then click Next.

FIGURE 5.62

You cannot migrate virtual machines matching your source network selection if the destination network is listed as inaccessible.

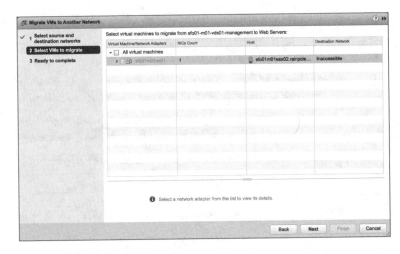

8. Click Finish to start the migration of the selected virtual machines from the specified source network to the selected destination network.

   You'll see a Reconfigure Virtual Machine task spawn in the Tasks pane for each virtual machine that needs to be migrated.

Keep in mind that this tool can migrate virtual machines from a vSphere standard switch to a distributed switch or from a distributed switch to a standard switch—you only need to specify the source and destination networks accordingly.

Now that we've covered the basics of distributed switches, let's delve into a few advanced topics. First up is network monitoring using NetFlow.

Using NetFlow on vSphere Distributed Switches

NetFlow is a mechanism for efficiently reporting IP-based traffic information as a series of *traffic flows*. Traffic flows are defined as the combination of source and destination IP addresses, source and destination TCP or UDP ports, IP, and IP Type of Service (ToS). Network devices that support NetFlow will track and report information on the traffic flows, typically sending this information to a NetFlow collector. Using the data collected, network administrators gain detailed insight into the types and amount of traffic flows across the network.

In vSphere 5.0, VMware introduced support for NetFlow with vSphere Distributed Switches (only on distributed switches that are version 5.0.0 or higher). This allows ESXi hosts to gather detailed per-flow information and report that information to a NetFlow collector.

Configuring NetFlow is a two-step process:

1. Configure the NetFlow properties on the distributed switch.

2. Enable or disable NetFlow (the default is disabled) on a per–distributed port group basis.

To configure the NetFlow properties for a distributed switch, perform these steps:

1. Connect to a vCenter Server instance using the vSphere Web Client.

2. Navigate to the list of distributed switches and select the distributed switch where you want to enable NetFlow.

3. With the desired distributed switch selected, from the Actions menu, select Settings ➢ Edit NetFlow.

   This opens the Edit NetFlow Settings dialog box.

4. As shown in Figure 5.63, specify the IP address of the NetFlow collector, the port on the NetFlow collector, and an IP address to identify the distributed switch.

FIGURE 5.63
You'll need the IP address and port number for the NetFlow collector in order to send flow information from a distributed switch.

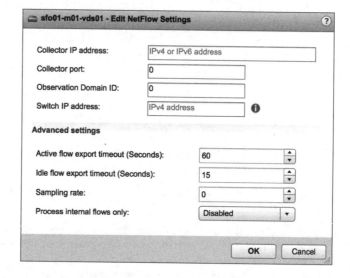

5. You can modify the Advanced Settings if advised to do so by your NetFlow collector.

6. If you want the distributed switch to process only internal traffic flows, that is, traffic flows from virtual machine to virtual machine on the same ESXi host—set Process Interna Flows Only To Enabled.

7. Click OK to commit the changes and return to the vSphere Web Client.

After you configure the NetFlow properties for the distributed switch, you then enable NetFlow on a per–distributed port group basis. The default setting is Disabled. Perform these steps to enable NetFlow on a specific distributed port group:

1. In the vSphere Web Client, navigate to the distributed switch hosting the distributed port group where you want to enable NetFlow. You must have already performed the previous procedure to configure NetFlow on that distributed switch.

2. From the Actions menu, select Distributed Port Groups ➢ Manage Distributed Port Groups. This opens the Manage Distributed Port Groups wizard. This can also be accomplished by right-clicking the distributed port group and selecting Edit Settings.

3. Place a check mark next to Monitoring, and then click Next.

4. In the Select port groups window, click the Select Distributed Port Groups icon, select the distributed ports groups to edit, and click OK.

   Click Next once you've selected the desired distributed port groups.

5. At the Monitoring screen, shown in Figure 5.64, set NetFlow to Enabled; then click Next.

FIGURE 5.64

NetFlow is disabled by default. You enable NetFlow on a per–distributed port group basis.

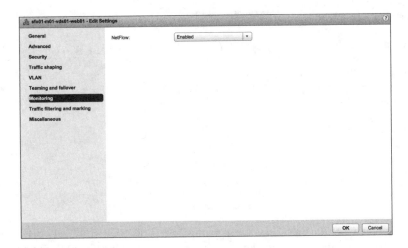

6. Click Finish to save the changes to the distributed port group.

This distributed port group will start capturing NetFlow statistics and reporting that information to the specified NetFlow collector.

Another feature that is quite useful is vSphere's support for switch discovery protocols, like Cisco Discovery Protocol (CDP) and Link Layer Discovery Protocol (LLDP). The next section shows you how to enable these protocols in vSphere.

Enabling Switch Discovery Protocols

Previous versions of vSphere supported Cisco Discovery Protocol (CDP), a protocol for exchanging information between network devices. However, it required using the command line to enable and configure CDP.

In vSphere 5.0, VMware added support for Link Layer Discovery Protocol (LLDP), an industry standard discovery protocol, and provided a location within the vSphere Client where CDP/LLDP support can be configured.

Perform the following steps to configure switch discovery support:

1. Connect to a vCenter Server instance using the vSphere Web Client.

2. With the distributed switch selected, select the Configure tab.

3. Under Settings, select Properties.

4. Click the Edit button and then select Advanced in the Edit Settings dialog box to configure the distributed switch for CDP or LLDP support, as shown in Figure 5.65.

This figure shows the distributed switch configured for LLDP support, both listening (receiving LLDP information from other connected devices) and advertising (sending LLDP information to other connected devices).

5. Click OK to save your changes.

FIGURE 5.65

LLDP support enables distributed switches to exchange discovery information with other LLDP-enabled devices over the network.

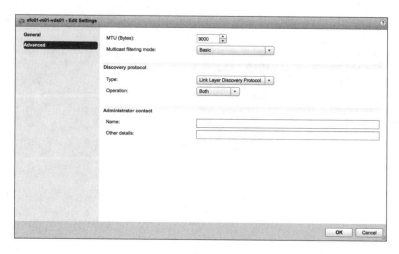

Once the ESXi hosts participating in this distributed switch start exchanging discovery information, you can view that information from the physical switch(es). For example, on most Cisco switches, the show cdp neighbor command will display information about CDP-enabled network devices, including ESXi hosts. Entries for ESXi hosts will include information on the physical NIC used and the vSwitch involved.

vSphere Standard Switches also support CDP, though not LLDP, but there is no GUI for configuring this support; you must use esxcli. This command will set CDP to Both (listen and advertise) on vSwitch0:

```
esxcli network vswitch standard set --cdp-status=both --vswitch-name=vSwitch0
```

Enabling Enhanced Multicast Functions

On top of basic multicast filtering supported by the vSphere Standard Switch, the vSphere Distributed Switch also supports multicast snooping.

In this mode, the distributed switch learns about the membership of a virtual machine dynamically. This is achieved by monitoring virtual machine traffic and capturing IGMP or multicast listener discovery (MLD) details when a virtual machine sends a packet containing this information. The distributed switch then creates a record of the destination IP address of the group, and for IGMPv3 it also records the source IP address from which the virtual machine prefers to receive traffic. The distributed switch will remove the entry containing the group details if a virtual machine does not renew its membership within a certain period of time.

STICKING TO STANDARDS

Multicast snooping in vSphere 6 has been implemented according to RFC 4541, and supports IGMPv1, IGMPv2, and IGMPv3 for IPv4 multicast groups as well as MLDv1 and MLDv2 for IPv6 multicast groups.

Perform the following steps to enable multicast snooping on a vSphere Distributed·Switch:

1. Connect to a vCenter Server instance using the vSphere Web Client.

2. Select Networking in the navigator.

3. Select an existing distributed switch, right-click the distributed switch, and select Settings ➤ Edit Settings.

4. In the dialog box, select Advanced and then change the multicast filtering mode to IGMP/ MLD snooping, as shown in Figure 5.66.

FIGURE 5.66

The vSphere Distributed Switch supports both basic multicast filtering and IGMP/ MLD snooping.

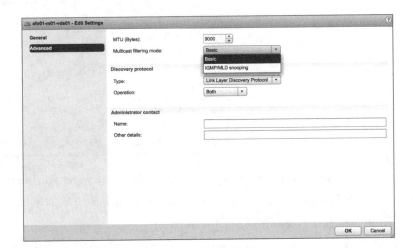

Setting Up Private VLANs

Private VLANs (PVLANs) are an advanced networking feature of vSphere that build on the functionality of vSphere Distributed Switches. Within the vSphere environment, PVLANs are possible only when using distributed switches and are not available to use with vSphere Standard Switches. Further, you must ensure that the upstream physical switches to which your vSphere environment is connected also support PVLANs.

Here is a quick overview of private VLANs. PVLANs are a way to further isolate ports within a given VLAN. For example, consider the scenario of hosts within a demilitarized zone (DMZ). Hosts within a DMZ rarely need to communicate with each other, but using a VLAN for each host quickly becomes unwieldy for a number of reasons. By using PVLANs, you can isolate hosts from each other while keeping them on the same IP subnet. Figure 5.67 provides a graphical overview of how PVLANs work.

PVLANs are configured in pairs: the primary VLAN and any secondary VLANs. The primary VLAN is considered the *downstream* VLAN; that is, traffic to the host travels along the primary VLAN. The secondary VLAN is considered the *upstream* VLAN; that is, traffic from the host travels along the secondary VLAN.

To use PVLANs, first configure the PVLANs on the physical switches connecting to the ESXi hosts, and then add the PVLAN entries to the distributed switch in vCenter Server.

FIGURE 5.67
Private VLAN entries consist of a primary VLAN and one or more secondary VLAN entries.

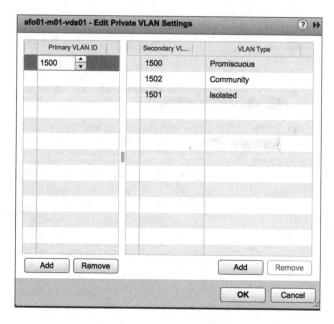

Perform the following steps to define PVLAN entries on a distributed switch:

1. Connect to a vCenter Server instance using the vSphere Web Client.

2. Select Networking in the navigator.

3. Select an existing distributed switch and click the Configure tab.

4. Select Private VLAN; then click the Edit button.

5. In the Edit Private VLAN Settings dialog box, click Add to add a primary VLAN ID to th list on the left.

6. For each primary VLAN ID in the list on the left, add one or more secondary VLANs to the list on the right, as shown previously in Figure 5.67.

   Secondary VLANs are classified as one of the two following types:

   ◆ Isolated: Ports placed in secondary PVLANs configured as isolated are allowed to communicate only with promiscuous ports in the same secondary VLAN. (We'll explain promiscuous ports later in this chapter.)

   ◆ Community: Ports in a secondary PVLAN are allowed to communicate with other ports in the same secondary PVLAN as well as with promiscuous ports.

   Only one isolated secondary VLAN is permitted for each primary VLAN. Multiple secondary VLANs configured as community VLANs are allowed.

7. When you finish adding all the PVLAN pairs, click OK to save the changes and return to the vSphere Web Client.

After you enter the PVLAN IDs for a distributed switch, you must create a distributed port group that takes advantage of the PVLAN configuration. The process for creating a distributed port group was described earlier. Figure 5.68 shows the New Distributed Port Group wizard for a distributed port group that uses PVLANs.

FIGURE 5.68
When a distributed port group is created with PVLANs, the distributed port group is associated with both the primary VLAN ID and a secondary VLAN ID.

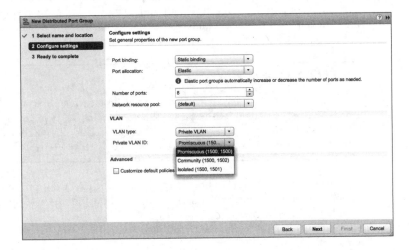

In Figure 5.68, you can see the term *promiscuous* again. In PVLAN parlance, a promiscuous port is allowed to send and receive Layer 2 frames to any other port in the VLAN. This type of port is typically reserved for the default gateway for an IP subnet—for example, a Layer 3 router.

PVLANs are a powerful configuration tool but also a complex configuration topic and one that can be difficult to understand, let alone troubleshoot when communications issues occur. For additional information on PVLANs, we recommend that you visit https://kb.vmware.com/s/article/1010691.

As with vSphere Standard Switches, vSphere Distributed Switches provide a tremendous amount of flexibility in designing and configuring a virtual network. But, as with all things, there are limits to the flexibility. Table 5.2 lists some of the configuration maximums for vSphere Distributed Switches.

TABLE 5.2: Configuration maximums for ESXi networking components (vSphere Distributed Switches)

CONFIGURATION ITEM	MAXIMUM
Switches per vCenter Server	128
Maximum ports per host (vSS/vDS)	4,096
vDS ports per vCenter instance	60,000
ESXi hosts per vDS	2,000
Static port groups per vCenter instance	10,000
Ephemeral port groups per vCenter instance	1,016

Configuring LACP

Link Aggregation Control Protocol (LACP) is a standardized protocol for supporting the aggregation, or joining, of multiple individual network links into a single, logical network link. Note that LACP support is available only when you are using a vSphere Distributed Switch; vSphere Standard Switches do not support LACP.

IS LACP THE ONLY WAY?

It's possible to use link aggregation without LACP. When you use either a vSphere Standard Switch or a vSphere Distributed Switch, setting the NIC teaming policy to Route Based on IP Hash enables link aggregation. Although it enables link aggregation, this configuration does not use LACP. This is the only way to use link aggregation with a vSphere Standard Switch.

We'll start with a review of how to configure basic LACP support on a version 5.1.0 vSphere Distributed Switch; then we'll show you how the LACP support has been enhanced in vSphere 5.5 and above.

Using a version 5.1.0 vSphere Distributed Switch, you must configure the following four areas:

◆ Enable LACP in the properties for the distributed switch's uplink group.

◆ Set the NIC teaming policy for all distributed port groups to Route Based On IP Hash.

◆ Set the network detection policy for all distributed port groups to link status only.

◆ Configure all distributed port groups so that all uplinks are active, not standby or unused.

Figure 5.69 shows the Edit Settings dialog box for the uplink group on a version 5.1.0 vSphere Distributed Switch. You can see here the setting for enabling LACP as well as the reminder of the other settings that are required.

FIGURE 5.69
Basic LACP support in a version 5.1.0 vSphere Distributed Switch is enabled in the uplink group but requires other settings as well.

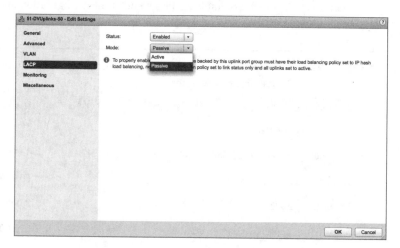

You must configure LACP on the physical switch to which the ESXi host is connected; the exact way you enable LACP will vary from vendor to vendor. The Mode setting shown in Figure 5.69—which is set to either Active or Passive—helps dictate how the ESXi host will communicate with the physical switch to establish the link aggregate:

◆ When LACP Mode is set to Passive, the ESXi host won't initiate any communications to the physical switch; the switch must initiate the negotiation.

◆ When LACP Mode is set to Active, the ESXi host will actively initiate the negotiation of the link aggregation with the physical switch.

You can probably gather from this discussion of using LACP with a version 5.1.0 vSphere Distributed Switch that only a single link aggregate (a single bundle of LACP-negotiated links) is supported and LACP is enabled or disabled for the entire vSphere Distributed Switch.

When you upgrade to a version 5.5.0 or 6.0.0 vSphere Distributed Switch, though, the LACP support is enhanced to eliminate these limitations. Version 5.5.0 and later distributed switches support multiple LACP groups, and how those LACP groups are used (or not used) can be configured on a per–distributed port group basis. Let's take a look at how you'd configure LACP support with a version 6.6 distributed switch.

As was introduced with the version 5.5.0 distributed switch, a new LACP section appears in the Settings area of the Configure tab, as shown in Figure 5.70. From this area, you'll define one or more link aggregation groups (LAGs), each of which will appear as a logical uplink to the distributed port groups on that distributed switch. vSphere 5.5 and later support multiple LAGs on a single distributed switch, which allows administrators to dual-home distributed switches (connect distributed switches to multiple upstream physical switches) while still using LACP. There are a few limitations, which are described near the end of this section.

FIGURE 5.70

Enhanced LACP support in vSphere 5.5 and later eliminates many of the limitations of the support found in vSphere 5.1.

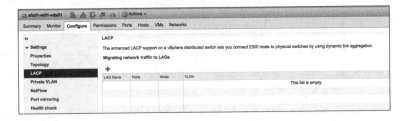

To use LACP with a version 5.5.0 or later distributed switch, you must follow three steps:

1. Define one or more LAGs in the LACP section of the Settings area of the Manage tab.

2. Add physical adapters into the LAG(s) you've created.

3. Modify the distributed port groups to use those LAGs as uplinks in the distributed port groups' teaming and failover configuration.

Let's take a look at each of these steps in a bit more detail.

To create a LAG, perform these steps:

1. Connect to a vCenter Server instance using the vSphere Web Client.

2. Navigate to the specific distributed switch for which you want to configure a LACP link aggregation group.

3. With the distributed switch selected, click the Configure tab, and then click LACP. This displays the screen shown earlier in Figure 5.70.

4. Click the green plus symbol to add a LAG. This displays the New Link Aggregation Group dialog box, shown in Figure 5.71.

FIGURE 5.71

With a version 5.5.0 or newer distributed switch, the LACP properties are configured on a per-LAG basis instead of for the entire distributed switch.

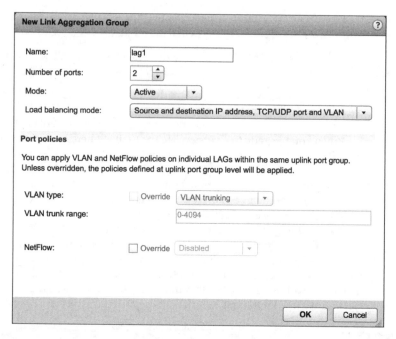

5. In the New Link Aggregation Group dialog box, specify a name for the new LAG.

6. Specify the number of physical ports that will be included in the LAG.

7. Specify the LACP mode—either Active or Passive, as we described earlier—that this LAG should use.

8. Select a load-balancing mode. Note that this load-balancing mode affects only outbound traffic; inbound traffic will be load balanced according to the load-balancing mode configured on the physical switch. (For best results and ease of troubleshooting, the configuration here should match the configuration on the physical switch where possible.

9. If you need to override port policies for this LAG, you can do so at the bottom of this dialog box.

10. Click OK to create the new LAG and return to the LACP area of the vSphere Web Client.

Now that at least one LAG has been created, you need to assign physical adapters to it. To do this, you'll follow the process outlined earlier for managing physical adapters (see the section "Managing VMkernel Adapters" for the specific details). The one change you'll note is that when you click the Assign Uplink link for a selected physical adapter, you'll now see an option to assign that adapter to one of the available uplink ports in the LAG(s) that you created. Figure 5.72 shows the dialog box for assigning an uplink for a distributed switch with two LAGs.

FIGURE 5.72
Once a LAG has been created, physical adapters can be added to it.

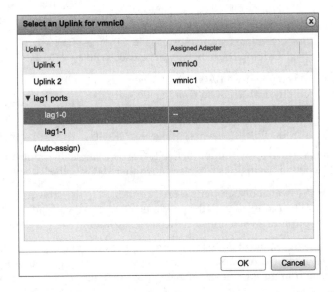

Once you've added physical adapters to the LAG(s), you can proceed with the final step: configuring the LAG(s) as uplinks for the distributed port groups on that distributed switch. Specific instructions for this process were given earlier, in the section "Editing a Distributed Port Group." Note that the LAG(s) will appear as physical uplinks in the teaming and failover configuration, as you can see in Figure 5.73. You can assign the LAG as an active uplink, a standby uplink, or an unused uplink.

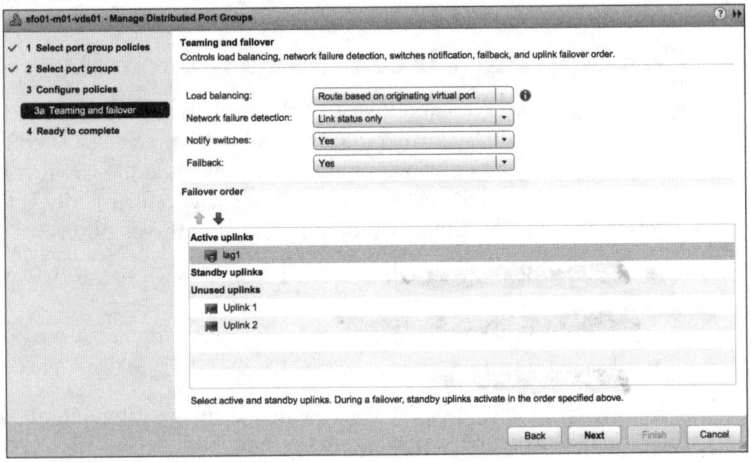

FIGURE 5.73
LAGs appear as physical uplinks to the distributed port groups.

When using LAGs, you should be aware of the following limitations:

◆ Some vSphere features such as Host Profiles, Port Mirroring, teaming Health Check, and the Netdump collector cannot be used with a LAG. See VMware KB 2051307.

◆ When you use a LAG, you lose benefits of the distributed switch such as the Route based on physical NIC load teaming algorithm.

◆ You can't mix LAGs and physical uplinks for a given distributed port group. Any physical uplinks must be listed as unused adapters.

◆ You can't use multiple active LAGs on a single distributed port group. Place one LAG in the active uplinks list; place any other LAGs in the list of unused uplinks.

◆ VMware only supports a LAG connected to the same physical switch, or switch stack. When coupled with the previous bullet point, you can see that traffic can only use one physical switch until a switch or LAG failure. See VMware KB 1001938.

Note that some of these limitations are per distributed port group; you can use different active LAGs or stand-alone uplinks with other distributed port groups because the teaming and failover configuration is set for each individual distributed port group.

IGNORE THE LOAD BALANCING SETTING WITH LAGS

When using LACP and LAGs with a version 5.5 or newer distributed switch, you can ignore the Load Balancing setting seen earlier in Figure 5.73. It is overridden by the load-balancing policy set on the LAG(s).

Configuring Virtual Switch Security

Even though vSwitches and distributed switches are considered to be "dumb switches," you can configure them with security policies to enhance or ensure Layer 2 security. For vSphere Standard Switches, you can apply security policies at the vSwitch or at the port group level. For vSphere Distributed Switches, you apply security policies only at the distributed port group level. The security settings include the following three options:

◆ Promiscuous mode

◆ MAC address changes

◆ Forged transmits

Applying a security policy to a vSwitch is effective, by default, for all connection types within the switch. However, if a port group on that vSwitch is configured with a competing security policy, it will override the policy set at the vSwitch. For example, if a vSwitch is configured with a security policy that rejects MAC address changes, but a port group on the switch is configured to accept MAC address changes, then any virtual machines connected to that port group will be allowed to communicate even though it is using a MAC address that differs from what is configured in its VMX file.

The default security profile for a vSwitch, shown in Figure 5.74, is set to reject Promiscuous mode and to accept MAC address changes and forged transmits. Similarly, Figure 5.75 shows the default security profile for a distributed port group on a distributed switch.

FIGURE 5.74

The default security profile for a standard switch prevents Promiscuous mode but allows MAC address changes and forged transmits.

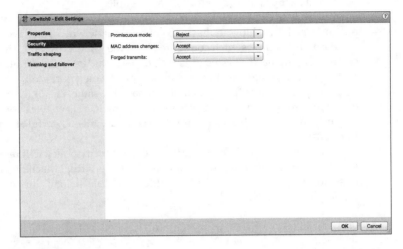

FIGURE 5.75

The default security profile for a distributed port group on a distributed switch also denies MAC address changes and forged transmits.

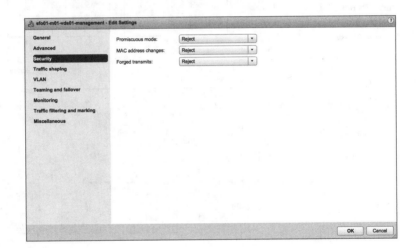

Each of these security options is explored in more detail in the following sections.

Understanding and Using Promiscuous Mode

The Promiscuous Mode option is set to Reject by default to prevent virtual network adapters from observing any of the traffic submitted through a vSwitch or distributed switch. For enhanced security, allowing Promiscuous mode is not recommended, because it is an insecure mode of operation that allows a virtual adapter to access traffic other than its own. Despite the security concerns, there are valid reasons for permitting a switch to operate in Promiscuous mode. An intrusion-detection system (IDS) must be able to identify all traffic to scan for anomalies and malicious patterns of traffic, for example.

Previously in this chapter, we talked about how port groups and VLANs did not have a one-to-one relationship and that occasions may arise when you have multiple port groups on a standard/distributed switch configured with the same VLAN ID. This is exactly one of those situations—you need a system, the IDS, to see traffic intended for other virtual network adapters. Rather than granting that ability to all the systems on a port group, you can create a dedicated port group for just the IDS system. It will have the same VLAN ID and other settings but will allow Promiscuous mode instead of rejecting it. This enables you, the administrator, to carefully control which systems are allowed to use this powerful and potentially security-threatening feature.

As shown in Figure 5.76, the virtual switch security policy will remain at the default setting Reject for the Promiscuous Mode option, while the Virtual Machine Port Group for the IDS will be set to Accept. This setting will override the virtual switch, allowing the IDS to monitor all traffic for that VLAN.

FIGURE 5.76
Promiscuous mode, though it reduces security, is required when using an intrusion-detection system.

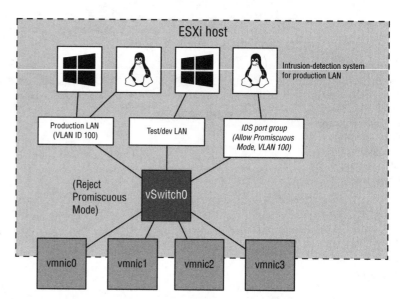

Allowing MAC Address Changes and Forged Transmits

When a virtual machine is created with one or more virtual network adapters, a MAC address is generated for each virtual adapter. Just as Intel, Broadcom, and others manufacture network adapters that include unique MAC address strings, VMware is a network adapter manufacturer that has its own MAC prefix to ensure uniqueness. Of course, VMware doesn't actually manufacture anything, because the product exists as a virtual NIC in a virtual machine. You can see the 6-byte, randomly generated MAC addresses for a virtual machine in the configuration file (VMX) of the virtual machine as well as in the Settings area for a virtual machine within the vSphere

Web Client, shown in Figure 5.77. A VMware-assigned MAC address begins with the prefix 00:50:56 or 00:0C:29. The fifth and sixth sets (YY:ZZ) are generated randomly based on the universally unique identifier (UUID) of the virtual machine that is tied to the location of the virtual machine. For this reason, when a virtual machine location is changed, a prompt appears prior to successful boot. The prompt inquires about keeping the UUID or generating a new UUID, which helps prevent MAC address conflicts.

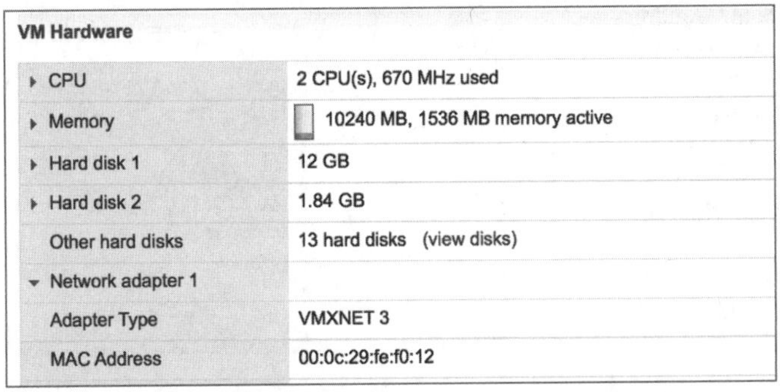

FIGURE 5.77

A virtual machine's initial MAC address is automatically generated and listed in the configuration file for the virtual machine and displayed within the vSphere Web Client.

VM Hardware	
▸ CPU	2 CPU(s), 670 MHz used
▸ Memory	▯ 10240 MB, 1536 MB memory active
▸ Hard disk 1	12 GB
▸ Hard disk 2	1.84 GB
Other hard disks	13 hard disks (view disks)
▾ Network adapter 1	
Adapter Type	VMXNET 3
MAC Address	00:0c:29:fe:f0:12

MANUALLY SETTING THE MAC ADDRESS

Manually configuring a MAC address in the configuration file of a virtual machine does not work unless the first three bytes are VMware-provided prefixes and the last three bytes are unique. If a non-VMware MAC prefix is entered in the configuration file, the virtual machine will not power on.

All virtual machines have two MAC addresses: the initial MAC and the effective MAC. The initial MAC address is the MAC address discussed in the previous paragraph that is generated automatically and resides in the configuration file. The guest OS has no control over the initial MAC address. The effective MAC address is the MAC address configured by the guest OS that is used during communication with other systems. The effective MAC address is included in network communication as the source MAC of the virtual machine. By default, these two addresses are identical. To force a non-VMware-assigned MAC address to a guest operating system, change the effective MAC address from within the guest OS, as shown in Figure 5.78.

The ability to alter the effective MAC address cannot be removed from the guest OS. However, you can deny or allow the system to function with this altered MAC address through the security policy of a standard switch or distributed port group. The remaining two settings of a virtual switch security policy are MAC Address Changes and Forged Transmits. These security policies allow or deny differences between the initial MAC address in the configuration file and the effective MAC address in the guest OS. As noted earlier, the default security policy is to accept the differences and process traffic as needed.

The difference between the MAC Address Changes and Forged Transmits security settings involves the direction of the traffic. MAC Address Changes is concerned with the integrity of incoming traffic. If the option is set to Reject, traffic will not be passed through the standard switch or distributed port group to the virtual machine (incoming) if the initial and the effective MAC addresses do not match. Forged Transmits oversees the integrity of outgoing traffic, and if this option is set to Reject, traffic will not be passed from the virtual machine to the standard switch or distributed port group (outgoing) if the initial and the effective MAC addresses do no match. Figure 5.79 highlights the security restrictions implemented when MAC Address Chang and Forged Transmits are set to Reject.

FIGURE 5.78
A virtual machine's source MAC address is the effective MAC address, which by default matches the initial MAC address configured in the VMX file. The guest OS, however, may change the effective MAC address.

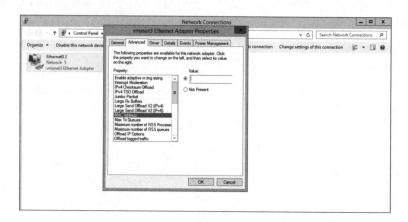

FIGURE 5.79
The MAC Address Changes and Forged Transmits security options deal with incoming and outgoing traffic, respectively.

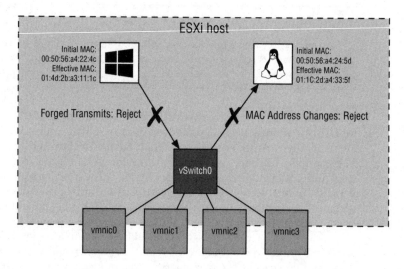

For the highest level of security, VMware recommends setting MAC Address Changes, Forge Transmits, and Promiscuous Mode on each standard switch or distributed port group to Reject. When warranted or necessary, use port groups to loosen the security for a subset of virtual machines to connect to the port group.

VIRTUAL SWITCH POLICIES FOR MICROSOFT NETWORK LOAD BALANCING

As with anything, there are, of course, exceptions to the general recommendations for how a virtual switch should be configured. The recommendations for allowing MAC address changes and forged transmits are great examples. For virtual machines that will be configured as part of a Microsoft Network Load Balancing (NLB) cluster set in Unicast mode, the virtual machine port group must allow MAC address changes and forged transmits. Systems that are part of an NLB cluster will share a common IP address and virtual MAC address.

The shared virtual MAC address is generated by using an algorithm that includes a static component based on the NLB cluster's configuration of Unicast or Multicast mode plus a hexadecimal representation of the four octets that make up the IP address. This shared MAC address will certainly differ from the MAC address defined in the VMX file of the virtual machine. If the Virtual Machine Port Group does not allow for differences between the MAC addresses in the VMX and guest OS, NLB will not function as expected. VMware recommends running NLB clusters in Multicast mode because of these issues with NLB clusters in Unicast mode.

Perform the following steps to edit the security profile of a vSwitch:

1. Connect to a vCenter Server instance using the vSphere Web Client.

2. Navigate to the specific ESXi host that has the vSphere Standard Switch you'd like to edit.

3. With an ESXi host selected in the inventory list on the left, click the Configure tab, and then click Virtual Switches.

4. From the list of virtual switches, select the vSphere Standard Switch you'd like to edit, and click the Edit link (it looks like a pencil). This opens the Edit Settings dialog box for the selected vSwitch.

5. Click Security on the list on the left side of the dialog box and make the necessary adjustments.

6. Click OK.

Perform the following steps to edit the security profile of a port group on a vSwitch:

1. Connect to a vCenter Server instance using the vSphere Web Client.

2. Navigate to the specific ESXi host and vSphere Standard Switch that contains the port group you wish to edit.

3. Click the name of the port group under the graphical representation of the virtual switch, and then click the Edit link.

4. Click Security and make the necessary adjustments. You'll need to place a check mark in the Override box to allow the port group to use a different setting than its parent virtual switch.

5. Click OK to save your changes.

Perform the following steps to edit the security profile of a distributed port group on a vSphere Distributed Switch:

1. Connect to a vCenter Server instance using the vSphere Web Client.

2. Select Networking in the navigator.

3. Select an existing distributed port group, and then click the Edit Distributed Port Group sSettings icon.

4. Select Security from the list of policy options on the left side of the dialog box.

5. Make the necessary adjustments to the security policy.

6. Click OK to save the changes.

If you need to make the same security-related change to multiple distributed port groups, yo can use the Manage Distributed Port Groups command on the Actions menu to perform the same configuration task for multiple distributed port groups at the same time.

Managing the security of a virtual network architecture is much the same as managing the security for any other portion of your information systems. Security policy should dictate that settings be configured as secure as possible to err on the side of caution. Only with proper authorization, documentation, and change management processes should security be reduced. I addition, the reduction in security should be as controlled as possible to affect the least number of systems if not just the systems requiring the adjustments.

In the next chapter, we'll dive deep into storage in VMware vSphere, a critical component of your vSphere environment.

The Bottom Line

Identify the components of virtual networking.   Virtual networking is a blend of virtual switches, physical switches, VLANs, physical network adapters, VMkernel adapters, uplinks NIC teaming, virtual machines, and port groups.

> **Master It**   What factors contribute to the design of a virtual network and the components involved?

Create virtual switches and distributed virtual switches.   vSphere supports both vSphere Standard Switches and vSphere Distributed Switches. vSphere Distributed Switches bring new functionality to the vSphere networking environment, including private VLANs and a centralized point of management for ESXi clusters.

> **Master It**   You've asked a fellow vSphere administrator to create a vSphere Distributed Switch for you, but the administrator can't complete the task because he can't find out how to do this with an ESXi host selected in the vSphere Client. What should you tell this administrator?

Create and manage NIC teaming, VLANs, and private VLANs.   NIC teaming allows virtua switches to have redundant network connections to the rest of the network. Virtual switches also provide support for VLANs, which provide logical segmentation of the network, and private VLANs, which provide added security to existing VLANs while allowing systems to share the same IP subnet.

Master It   You'd like to use NIC teaming to make the best use of physical uplinks for both greater redundancy and improved throughput, even under network contention. Which load-balancing policy on the distributed switch should you use?

Master It   How do you configure both a vSphere Standard Switch and a vSphere Distributed Switch to pass VLAN tags all the way up to a guest OS?

Configure virtual switch security policies.   Virtual switches support security policies for allowing or rejecting Promiscuous mode, allowing or rejecting MAC address changes, and allowing or rejecting forged transmits. All of the security options can help increase Layer 2 security.

Master It   You have a networking application that needs to see traffic on the virtual network that is intended for other production systems on the same VLAN. The networking application accomplishes this by using Promiscuous mode. How can you accommodate the needs of this networking application without sacrificing the security of the entire virtual switch?

Master It   Another vSphere administrator on your team is trying to configure the security policies on a distributed switch but is having some difficulty. What could be the problem?

Chapter 6

Creating and Configuring Storage Devices

Storage has always been a critical element for any environment, and the storage infrastructure supporting vSphere is no different. Storage is one of the most important parts of your virtual infrastructure to get right. This chapter will help you with all the elements required for a proper storage subsystem design, starting with vSphere storage fundamentals at the datastore and virtual machine (VM)–level and extending to best practices for configuring a storage array. Good storage design is critical for anyone building a virtual infrastructure.

IN THIS CHAPTER, YOU WILL LEARN TO

◆ Differentiate and understand the fundamentals of shared storage

◆ Understand vSphere storage options

◆ Configure storage at the vSphere layer

◆ Configure storage at the VM layer

◆ Leverage best practices for shared storage with vSphere

Reviewing the Importance of Storage Design

Storage design has always been important, but it becomes more so for virtualized infrastructure, for mission-critical applications, and for offerings based on Infrastructure as a Service (IaaS). You can probably imagine why this is the case:

Advanced Capabilities   Many of vSphere's advanced features depend on shared storage; vSphere High Availability (HA), vSphere Distributed Resource Scheduler (DRS), vSphere Fault Tolerance (FT), and some parts of VMware Site Recovery Manager all have critical dependencies on shared storage.

Performance   People understand the benefits that virtualization brings—consolidation, higher utilization, more flexibility, and higher efficiency. But often, people have initial questions about how vSphere can deliver performance for individual applications when it is inherently consolidated and oversubscribed. Likewise, the overall performance of the VMs and the entire vSphere cluster both depend on shared storage, which can also be highly consolidated and oversubscribed.

Availability The overall availability of your virtualized infrastructure, and by extension, the VMs running on that infrastructure, depend on the shared storage infrastructure. Designing high availability into this infrastructure element is paramount. If the storage is not available, vSphere HA will not be able to recover, and the VMs will be affected. (We discuss vSphere HA in detail in Chapter 7, "Ensuring High Availability and Business Continuity.")

Although design choices at the server layer can make the vSphere environment relatively more or less optimal, design choices for shared resources such as networking and storage can sometimes make the difference between virtualization success and failure. This is especially true for storage because of its critical role. Storage design choices remain important regardless of whether you are using storage area networks (SANs), which present shared storage as disks or logical units (LUNs); network attached storage (NAS), which presents shared storage as remotely accessed file systems; or a converged storage infrastructure using local server disks such as vSAN. You can create a shared storage design that lowers the cost and increases the efficiency, performance, availability, and flexibility of your vSphere environment.

 Real World Scenario

THE IMPORTANCE OF PROPERLY DESIGNED STORAGE

Before we get too far into this topic, we want to *re*-emphasize the importance of storage design. We have seen a large number of vSphere environments over the years, and in my experience nearly all of the most common performance-related problems could be traced back to storage. Although it is a common industry joke to "blame the network" when things go wrong, we believe that getting a solid understanding of the underlying storage systems in your environment will save you *many* headaches down the road.

This chapter breaks down these topics into the following main sections:

◆ "Examining Shared Storage Fundamentals" covers broad topics of shared storage that are critical with vSphere, including hardware architectures, protocol choices, and key terminology. Although these topics apply to any environment that uses shared storage, understanding these core technologies is a prerequisite to understanding how to apply storage technology in a vSphere implementation.

◆ "Implementing vSphere Storage Fundamentals" covers how storage technologies covered in the previous main section are applied and used in vSphere environments. This main section is broken down into a section on VMFS datastores ("Working with VMFS Datastores"), raw device mappings ("Working with Raw Device Mappings"), NFS datastores ("Working with NFS Datastores"), vSAN ("Working with vSAN "), and virtual machine–level storage configurations ("Working with Virtual Machine–Level Storage Configuration").

◆ "Leveraging SAN and NAS Best Practices" covers how to pull together all the topics discussed to move forward with a design that will support a broad set of vSphere environments.

Examining Shared Storage Fundamentals

vSphere 6.7 offers numerous storage choices and configuration options relative to previous versions of vSphere or to nonvirtualized environments. These choices and configuration options apply at two fundamental levels: the virtualization layer and the VM layer. The storage requirements for a vSphere environment and the VMs it supports are unique, making broad generalizations impossible. The requirements for any given vSphere environment span use cases include virtual servers, containers, desktops, templates, and virtual CD/DVD (ISO) images. The virtual server use cases vary from light-utility VMs with few storage performance considerations to the largest workloads possible, with incredibly important storage layout considerations.

Let's start by examining this at a fundamental level. Figure 6.1 shows a simple three-host vSphere environment attached to shared storage.

FIGURE 6.1
When ESXi hosts are connected to that same shared storage, they share its capabilities.

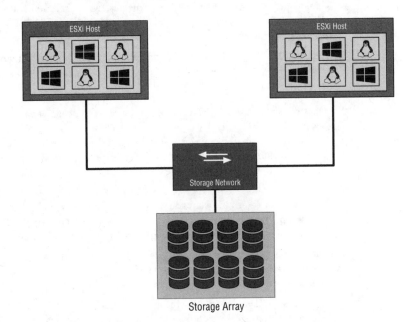

It's immediately apparent that the ESXi hosts and the VMs will be contending for the shared storage asset. In a way similar to how ESXi can consolidate many VMs onto a single ESXi host, the shared storage consolidates the storage needs of all the VMs.

When sizing or designing the storage solution, you focus on attributes like capacity (gigabytes, terabytes, or petabytes) and performance, which is measured in bandwidth (megabytes per second, or MBps), throughput (KB/s, MB/s, GB/s), and latency (in milliseconds). Because of drive density growth, the conversation focus has moved from capacity being the main focus to throughput and latency, especially as flash storage becomes more pervasive throughout the datacenter. It may go without saying, but designing for availability, redundancy, and fault tolerance is also of paramount importance.

DETERMINING PERFORMANCE REQUIREMENTS

How do you determine the storage performance requirements of an application that will be virtualized, a single ESXi host, or even a complete vSphere environment? There are many rules of thumb for key applications, and the best practices for every application could fill a book. Here are some quick considerations:

◆ Online transaction processing (OLTP) databases need low latency (as low as you can get, but a few milliseconds is a good target). They are also sensitive to input/output operations per second (IOPS), because their I/O size is small (4 KB to 8 KB). TPC-C and TPC-E benchmarks generate this kind of I/O pattern.

◆ Decision support system/business intelligence databases and SQL Server instances need high bandwidth, which can be hundreds of megabytes per second because their I/O size is large (64 KB to 1 MB). They are not particularly sensitive to latency; TPC-H benchmarks generate the kind of I/O pattern used by these use cases.

◆ Copying files, deploying from templates, using Storage vMotion, and backing up VMs (within the guest or via vSphere Storage APIs) without using array-based approaches generally all need high bandwidth. In fact, the more, the better.

So, what does vSphere need? The answer is basic—the needs of the vSphere environment are the aggregate sum of all the use cases across all the VMs, which can cover a broad set of requirements. If the VMs are all small-block workloads and you don't do backups inside guests (which generate large-block workloads), then it's all about IOPS. If the VMs are all large-block workloads, then it's all about MBps. More often than not, the virtual infrastructure has a mix, so the storage design should be flexible enough to deliver a broad range of capabilities and capacity but without overbuilding.

How can you best determine what you will need? With small workloads, too much planning can result in overbuilding. You can use simple tools—including VMware Capacity Planner, Windows Perfmon, and top in Linux—to determine the I/O pattern of the applications and OSs that will be virtualized.

Also, if you have many VMs, consider the aggregate performance requirements and don't just look at capacity requirements. After all, 1,000 VMs with 10 IOPS each need an aggregate of 10,000 IOPS, which is 50 to 80 fast spindles, regardless of the capacity (in gigabytes or terabytes) needed.

On the flip side, flash-based storage can easily manage 10,000 IOPS with a single drive, but the capacity to run 1,000 VMs is unlikely to fit on a single flash device.

Larger VM I/O and critical workloads (such as virtualized SQL or Oracle Server instances, SharePoint, Exchange, SAP, and other use cases) should be where you spend some time planning and thinking about layout. There are numerous VMware published best practices and a great deal of VMware partner reference architecture documentation that can help with virtualizing business-critical applications (BCAs). We have listed a few resources for you:

◆ Exchange

`www.vmware.com/solutions/business-critical-apps/exchange.html`

◆ SQL Server

`www.vmware.com/solutions/business-critical-apps/sql-virtualization.html`

◆ Oracle

`www.vmware.com/solutions/business-critical-apps/oracle-virtualization.html`

- ◆ SAP

  www.vmware.com/solutions/business-critical-apps/sap-virtualization.html

- ◆ Big Data

  www.vmware.com/solutions/big-data.html

As with performance, the overall availability of the vSphere environment and the VMs depends on the same shared storage infrastructure, so a robust design is paramount. If the storage is not available, vSphere HA will not be able to recover, and the consolidated community of VMs will be affected.

The phrase "consolidated community of virtual machines" underscores the need to put more care and focus on the availability of the configuration than on the performance or capacity requirements. In virtual configurations, the availability impact of storage is more pronounced, so you must use greater care in an availability design than in the physical world. It's not just one workload being affected, it's multiple workloads.

At the same time, advanced vSphere options such as Storage vMotion and advanced array techniques allow you to add, move, or change storage configurations nondisruptively, making it unlikely that you'll create a design where you can't nondisruptively fix performance issues.

Before going too much further, it's important to cover several basics of storage:

- ◆ Local storage versus shared storage

- ◆ Common storage array architectures

- ◆ RAID technologies

- ◆ Midrange and enterprise storage array design

- ◆ Protocol choices

We'll start with a brief discussion of local storage versus shared storage.

Comparing Local Storage with Shared Storage

An ESXi host can have one or more storage options actively configured, including the following:

- ◆ Local SAS/SATA/SCSI storage

- ◆ Fibre Channel

- ◆ Fibre Channel over Ethernet (FCoE)

- ◆ iSCSI using software and hardware initiators

- ◆ NAS (specifically, NFS)

- ◆ InfiniBand

Traditionally, local storage has been used in a limited fashion with vSphere because so many of vSphere's advanced features—such as vSphere HA, vSphere DRS, and vSphere FT—required shared external storage. With vSphere Auto Deploy and the ability to deploy ESXi images directly to RAM at boot time, coupled with Host Profiles to automate the configuration of the ESXi Host, in *some* environments local storage isn't necessary.

With vSphere 5.0, VMware introduced a way to use local storage by installing a virtual appliance called the vSphere Storage Appliance, or simply VSA. At a high level, the VSA took local storage and presented it back to ESXi hosts as a shared NFS mount. There were some limitations, however. It could be configured with only two or three hosts, there were strict rules around the hardware that could run the VSA, and on top of that, it was licensed as a separate product. Although it did utilize the underused local storage of servers, the use case for the VSA simply was not valid for many organizations. The VSA has since been discontinued.

vSphere 5.5, however, introduced two features that are significantly more relevant to organizations than the VSA. vSphere Flash Read Cache and vSAN both take advantage of local storage, in particular local *flash* storage. vSphere Flash Read Cache takes flash-based storage and allows administrators to allocate portions of it as a read cache for VM read I/O that usually needs to come from a traditional SAN or NAS array. vSAN extends on the idea behind the VSA and presents the local storage as a distributed datastore across many hosts. This concept is similar to the VSA, but the use of a virtual appliance is not required, nor are NFS mounts; it's entirely built into the ESXi hypervisor. Think of this as shared *internal* storage. Later in this chapter, you'll see how vSAN works. Because flash is a resource that you can manage, but it's not "typical" storage, you can find information on it in Chapter 11, "Managing Resource Allocation."

vSphere 6.7 introduced a feature, Persistent Memory (PMEM), which resides between DRAM and disk storage in the data storage hierarchy. PMEM enables byte addressable updates and does not lose data if power is lost. Instead of having nonvolatile storage at the bottom with the largest capacity but the slowest performance, nonvolatile storage is now very close to DRAM in terms of performance.

So, how carefully do you need to design your *local* storage? The answer is simple: generally speaking, unless you are using local flash for caching or vSAN, careful planning is not necessary for storage local to the ESXi installation. ESXi stores very little locally, and by using host profiles and distributed virtual switches, you'll find it easy and fast to replace a failed ESXi host. During this time, vSphere HA will make sure the VMs are running on the other ESXi hosts in the cluster. However, taking advantage of features such as vSAN will certainly require careful consideration. Storage underpins your entire vSphere environment. Make the effort to ensure that your shared storage design is robust, taking into consideration internal- and external-based shared storage choices.

 Real World Scenario

No Local Storage? No Problem!

What if you don't *have* local storage? (Perhaps you have a diskless blade system, for example.) There are many options for diskless systems, including booting from Fibre Channel/iSCSI SAN and network-based boot methods like vSphere Auto Deploy (discussed in Chapter 2, "Planning and Installing VMware ESXi"). There is also the option of using USB or SD Card boot, a technique that we've employed on numerous occasions. Both Auto Deploy and USB boot give you some flexibility in quickly reprovisioning hardware or deploying updated versions of vSphere. Refer to Chapter 2 for more details on selecting the configuration of your ESXi hosts.

Shared storage is the basis for most vSphere environments because it supports the VMs themselves and because it is a requirement for many of vSphere's features. Shared *external* storage in SAN configurations (which encompasses Fibre Channel, FCoE, and iSCSI) and NAS (NFS) is always highly consolidated. This makes it efficient. Similar to the benefits of physical-to-virtual consolidation with regard to CPU and memory, SAN/NAS or vSAN can take the direct attached storage in physical servers that are 10% utilized and consolidate them to eighty 80% utilization.

As you can see, shared storage is a key design point. Whether it's shared external storage or you're planning to share the local storage system, it's important to understand some of the array architectures that vendors use to provide shared storage to vSphere environments. The high-level overview in the following section is neutral on specific storage array vendors because the internal architectures vary tremendously.

Defining Common Storage Array Architectures

This section is remedial for anyone with basic storage experience, but it's needed for vSphere administrators with no storage knowledge. For people unfamiliar with storage, the topic can be a bit disorienting at first. Server hardware across vendors tends to be relatively similar, but the same logic can't be applied to the storage layer because core architectural differences between storage vendor architectures are vast. In spite of that, storage arrays have several core architectural elements that are consistent across vendors, across implementations, and even across protocols. In addition, many storage vendors have developed vSphere integrations specific to their storage hardware and software platforms.

The elements that make up a shared storage array consist of external connectivity, storage processors, array software, cache memory, disks, and bandwidth:

External Connectivity   The external (physical) connectivity between the traditional storage array and the hosts (in this case, the ESXi hosts) is generally Fibre Channel or Ethernet, though InfiniBand and other rare protocols exist. The characteristics of this connectivity define the maximum bandwidth (given no other constraints, and there usually *are* other constraints) of the communication between the ESXi host and the shared storage array. External connectivity is typically referred to as front-end or FE connectivity and most often tied to a fabric for distributed sharing and scalability purposes.

Storage Processors   Different vendors have different names for storage processors, which are considered the brains of the array. They handle the I/O and run the array software. In most modern arrays, the storage processors are not purpose-built application-specific integrated circuits (ASICs) but instead are general-purpose x86 CPUs. Some arrays use PowerPC, some use specific ASICs, and some use custom ASICs for specific purposes. But in general, if you cracked open an array, you would most likely find an Intel or AMD CPU.

Array Software   Although hardware specifications are important and can define the scaling limits of the array, just as important are the functional capabilities the array software provides. The capabilities of modern storage arrays are vast, similar in scope to vSphere itself, and vary wildly among vendors. At a high level, the following list includes some examples of these array capabilities and key functions:

◆ Remote storage replication for disaster recovery. These technologies come in many flavor with features that deliver varying capabilities. These include varying recovery point objectives (RPOs), which reflect how current the remote replica is at any time, ranging from synchronous to asynchronous and continuous. Asynchronous RPOs can range from less than minutes to more than hours, and continuous is a constant remote journal that ca recover to varying RPOs. Other examples of remote replication technologies are technolo gies that drive synchronicity across storage objects (or "consistency technology"), com- pression, and many other attributes, such as integration with VMware Site Recovery Manager.

◆ Snapshot and clone capabilities for instant point-in-time local copies for test and develop ment and local recovery. These also share some of the ideas of the remote replication technologies like "consistency technology," and some variations of point-in-time protec- tion and replicas also have DVR-like continuous journaling locally and remotely where you can recover/copy any point in time.

◆ Capacity-reduction techniques such as archiving, compression, and deduplication

◆ Automated data movement between performance/cost storage tiers at varying levels of granularity

◆ LUN/file system expansion and mobility, which means reconfiguring storage properties dynamically and nondisruptively to add capacity or performance as needed

◆ Thin provisioning, which typically involves allocating storage on demand as applications and workloads require it

◆ Storage quality of service (QoS), which means prioritizing I/O to deliver a given MBps, IOPS, or latency

◆ Encryption of data on the fly or at rest by using self-encrypting drives or other means

Traditionally, array software defines the "persona" of the array, which in turn impacts core concepts and behavior. Arrays generally have a "file server" persona (sometimes with the ability to do some block storage by presenting a file as a LUN) or a "block" persona (generally with no ability to act as a file server). These days, most arrays are usually a combination of file servers and block devices.

Cache Memory   Every array differs as to how cache memory is implemented, but all have some degree of nonvolatile memory used for various caching functions, delivering lower latency and higher IOPS throughput by buffering I/O using write caches and storing com- monly read data to deliver a faster response time using read caches. Nonvolatility (meaning the ability to survive a power loss) is critical for write caches because the data is not yet committed to disk, but it's not critical for read caches. Cached performance is often used when describing shared storage array performance maximums (in IOPS, MBps, or latency) in specification sheets. These results generally do not reflect real-world scenarios. In most real-world scenarios, performance tends to be dominated by the disk performance (the type and number of disks) and is helped by write caches in most cases, but only marginally by read caches (with the exception of large relational database management systems, which depend heavily on read-ahead cache algorithms). One vSphere use case helped by read caches is a situation where many boot images are stored only once (through the use of vSphere or storage array technology), but this is also a small subset of the overall VM I/O pattern.

Disks   Arrays differ as to which type of disks (often called *spindles*) they support and how many they can scale to support. Drive capabilities are defined by a number of attributes. First, drives are often separated by the drive interface they use: Fibre Channel, serial-attached SCSI (SAS), and serial ATA (SATA). With the exception of enterprise flash drives (EFDs), drives are typically described by their rotational speed, noted in revolutions per minute (RPM). Fibre Channel drives typically come in 15K RPM and 10K RPM variants, SATA drives are usually found in 5400 RPM and 7200 RPM variants, and SAS drives are usually 15K RPM or 10K RPM variants. Second, EFDs, which are now mainstream, are solid state and have no moving parts; therefore, rotational speed does not apply (nor does the name *spindle*). The type and number of disks are very important. Coupled with how they are configured, this determines how a storage object (either a LUN for a block device or a file system for a NAS device) performs. Shared storage vendors generally use disks from the same disk vendors, so this is an area of commonality across shared storage vendors. The following list is a quick reference on what to expect under a random read/write workload from a given disk drive:

- 7,200 RPM SATA: 80 IOPS

- 10K RPM SATA/SAS/Fibre Channel: 120 IOPS

- 15K RPM SAS/Fibre Channel: 180 IOPS

- Commercial solid-state drives (SSD) based on Multi-Level Cell (MLC) technology: 1,000–100,000s IOPS

- Enterprise flash drives (EFD) based on Single-Level Cell (SLC) technology and much deeper, very high-speed memory buffers: 6,000–100,000s IOPS

FLASH STORAGE: MLC VS. SLC

There are two common types of memory inside enterprise flash drives. Multi-Level Cell (MLC)–based drives are generally more affordable and better suited for read-intensive workloads. These have a shorter wear cycle for writes. Single-Level Cell (SLC)–based drives are generally more expensive and better suited for write-intensive workloads.

Bandwidth (Megabytes per Second)   Performance tends to be more consistent across drive types when large-block, sequential workloads are used (such as single-purpose workloads like archiving or backup to disk), so in these cases, large SATA drives deliver strong performance at a low cost.

Explaining RAID

Redundant Array of Inexpensive (sometimes "Independent") Disks (RAID) is a fundamental and critical method of storing the same data several times. RAID is used to increase data availability (by protecting against the failure of a drive) and to scale performance beyond that of a single drive. Every array implements various RAID schemes (even if it is largely invisible in file server persona arrays where RAID is done below the file system, which is the primary management element).

Think of it this way: disks are mechanical, spinning, rust-colored surfaces. The read/write heads fly microns above the surface while reading minute magnetic field variations and writing data by affecting surface areas also only microns in size.

THE "MAGIC" OF SPINNING DISK DRIVE TECHNOLOGY

It really is a technological miracle that magnetic disks work at all. What a disk does all day long is analogous to a pilot flying a 747 at 600 miles per hour 6 inches off the ground and reading pages in a book while doing it!

In spite of the technological wonder of hard disks, they have unbelievable reliability statistics. But they do fail, and fail predictably, unlike other elements of a system. RAID schemes address this by leveraging multiple disks together and using copies of data to support I/O until the drive can be replaced, and the RAID protection can be rebuilt. Each RAID configuration tends to have different performance characteristics and different capacity overhead impact.

We recommend that you view RAID choices as a significant factor in your design. Most arrays layer additional constructs on top of the basic RAID protection. (These constructs have many different names, but common ones are *metas, virtual pools, aggregates,* and *volumes.*)

Remember, all the RAID protection in the world won't protect you from an outage if the connectivity to your host is lost, if you don't monitor and replace failed drives and allocate drives as hot spares to automatically replace failed drives, or if the entire array is lost. It's for these reasons that it's important to design the storage network properly, to configure hot spares as advised by the storage vendor, and to monitor for and replace failed elements. Always consider a disaster-recovery plan and remote replication to protect from complete array failure.

Let's examine the RAID choices:

RAID 0 This RAID level offers no redundancy and no protection against drive failure (see Figure 6.2). In fact, it has a *higher* aggregate risk than a single disk because any single disk failing affects the whole RAID group. Data is spread across all the disks in the RAID group, which is often called a *stripe.* This level delivers fast performance, but it is the only RAID type that is usually not appropriate for any production vSphere use because of the availability profile.

FIGURE 6.2
In a RAID 0 configuration, the data is striped across all the disks in the RAID set, providing very good performance but very poor availability.

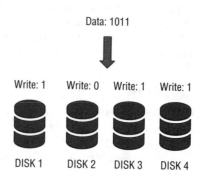

RAID 1, 1+0, 0+1 These mirrored RAID levels offer high degrees of protection but at the cost of 50% loss of usable capacity (see Figure 6.3). This is versus the raw aggregate capacity of the sum of the capacity of the drives. RAID 1 simply writes every I/O to two (or more) drives and can balance reads across all drives (because there are multiple copies). This can be coupled with RAID 0 to form RAID 1+0 (or RAID 10), which mirrors a stripe set, or to form RAID 0+1, which stripes data across pairs of mirrors. This has the benefit of being able to withstand multiple drives failing, but only if the drives fail on different elements of a stripe on different mirrors, thus making RAID 1+0 more fault tolerant than RAID 0+1. The other benefit of a mirrored RAID configuration is that, in the case of a failed drive, rebuild times can be very rapid, which shortens periods of exposure.

FIGURE 6.3

This RAID 10 2+2 configuration provides good performance and good availability, but at the cost of 50% of the usable capacity.

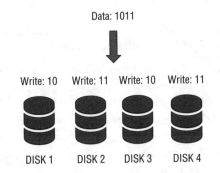

Parity RAID (RAID 5, RAID 6) These RAID levels use a mathematical calculation (an XOR parity calculation) to represent the data across several drives. This tends to be a good compromise between the availability of RAID 1 and the capacity efficiency of RAID 0. RAID 5 calculates the parity across the drives in the set and writes the parity to another drive. This parity block calculation with RAID 5 is rotated among the disks in the RAID 5 set.

Parity RAID schemes can deliver very good performance, but there is always some degree of write penalty. For a full-stripe write, the only penalty is the parity calculation and the parity write, but in a partial-stripe write, the old block contents must be read, a new parity calculation must be made, and all the blocks must be updated. However, generally modern arrays have various methods to minimize this effect.

Read performance, on the other hand, is generally excellent because a larger number of drives can be read from than with mirrored RAID schemes. RAID 5 nomenclature refers to the number of drives in the RAID group, so Figure 6.4 would be referred to as a RAID 5 4+1 set. In the figure, the storage efficiency (in terms of usable to raw capacity) is 80%, which is much better than RAID 1 or 10.

RAID 5 can be coupled with stripes, so RAID 50 is a pair of RAID 5 sets with data striped across them.

When a drive fails in a RAID 5 set, I/O can be fulfilled using the remaining drives and the parity drive, and when the failed drive is replaced, the data can be reconstructed using the remaining data and parity.

FIGURE 6.4
A RAID 5 4+1 configuration offers a balance between performance and efficiency.

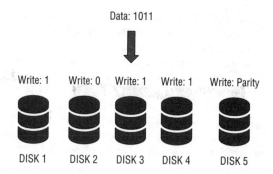

A KEY RAID 5 CONSIDERATION

One downside to RAID 5 is that only one drive can fail in the RAID set. If another drive fails before the failed drive is replaced and rebuilt using the parity data, data loss occurs. The period of exposure to data loss because of the second drive failing should be mitigated.

The period of time that a RAID 5 set is rebuilding should be as short as possible to minimize the risk. The following designs aggravate this situation by creating longer rebuild periods:

◆ Very large RAID groups (think 8+1 and larger), which require more reads to reconstruct the failed drive.

◆ Very large drives (think 2, 4, or 8 TB drives), which cause more data to be rebuilt.

◆ Slower drives that struggle heavily during the period when they are providing the data to rebuild the replaced drive and simultaneously support production I/O (think SATA drives, which tend to be slower during the random I/O that characterizes a RAID rebuild). The period of a RAID rebuild is actually one of the most stressful parts of a disk's life. Not only must it service the production I/O workload, but it must also provide data to support the rebuild.

The following technologies all mitigate the risk of a dual drive failure (and most arrays do various degrees of each of these items):

◆ Using proactive hot sparing, which shortens the rebuild period substantially by automatically starting the hot spare before the drive fails. The failure of a disk is generally preceded with read errors (which are recoverable; they are detected and corrected using on-disk parity information) or write errors, both of which are noncatastrophic. When a threshold of these errors occurs before the disk itself fails, the failing drive is replaced by a hot spare by the array. This is much faster than the rebuild after the failure, because the bulk of the failing drive can be used for the copy and because only the portions of the drive that are failing need to use parity information from other disks.

◆ Using smaller RAID 5 sets (for faster rebuild) and striping the data across them using a higher-level construct.

◆ Using a second parity calculation and storing it on another disk.

As described in the sidebar "A Key RAID 5 Consideration," one way to protect against data loss in the event of a single drive failure in a RAID 5 set is to use another parity calculation. This type of RAID is called RAID 6 (RAID-DP is a RAID 6 variant that uses two dedicated parity drives, analogous to RAID 4). This is a good choice when large RAID groups and SATA are used.

Figure 6.5 shows an example of a RAID 6 4+2 configuration. The data is striped across four disks, and a parity calculation is stored on the fifth disk. A second parity calculation is stored on another disk. RAID 6 rotates the parity location with I/O, and RAID-DP uses a pair of dedicated parity disks. This provides good performance and good availability but a loss in capacity efficiency. The purpose of the second parity bit is to withstand a second drive failure during RAID rebuild periods. It is important to use RAID 6 in place of RAID 5 if you meet the conditions noted in the previous sidebar and are unable to otherwise use the mitigation methods noted.

FIGURE 6.5

A RAID 6 4+2 configuration offers protection against double drive failures.

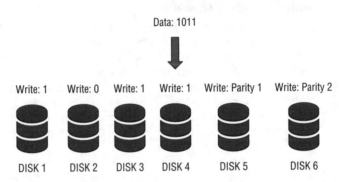

Although this is a reasonably detailed discussion of RAID levels, what you should take from it is that you shouldn't worry about it too much. Just don't use RAID 0 unless you have a proper use case for it. Use hot spare drives and follow the vendor best practices on hot spare density. EMC, for example, generally recommends one hot spare for every thirty drives in its arrays, whereas Dell Compellent recommends one hot spare per drive type and per drive shelf. Just be sure to check with your storage vendor for their specific recommendations.

For most vSphere implementations, RAID 5 is a good balance of capacity efficiency, performance, and availability. Use RAID 6 if you have to use large SATA RAID groups or don't have proactive hot spares. RAID 10 schemes still make sense when you need significant write performance. Remember that for your vSphere environment, it doesn't all have to be one RAID type; in fact, mixing different RAID types can be useful to deliver various tiers of performance/availability.

For example, you can use most datastores with a RAID 5 of spinning disks as the default LUN configuration, sparingly use RAID 10 schemes where needed, and use storage policy-based management, discussed later in this chapter, to ensure that the VMs are located on the storage that suits their requirements.

You should definitely make sure that you have enough spindles in the RAID group to meet the aggregate workload of the LUNs you create in that RAID group. The RAID type will affect the ability of the RAID group to support the workload, so keep RAID overhead (like the RAID 5 write penalty) in mind. Fortunately, some storage arrays can nondisruptively add spindles to a RAID group to add performance as needed, so if you find that you need more performance, you can correct it. Storage vMotion can also help you manually balance workloads.

If your storage systems use flash storage, either for caching or data at rest, these RAID considerations may change a little. Some storage arrays dynamically move data around based c the frequency of access to ensure the minimum average latency for all data. Other arrays have dedicated flash storage that the storage admin can allocate to read or write caching as required. may be a general cache for the entire array and all data, or the cache may be configured just to cover a smaller number of LUNs or NFS exports. Flash is changing the fundamentals of enter-prise storage, and there is no single right way to configure everything. Base your configuration on your storage array capabilities and storage vendor recommendations.

Now let's take a closer look at some specific storage array design architectures that will impact your vSphere storage environment.

Understanding vSAN

vSphere 5.5 introduced a brand-new storage feature, Virtual SAN, or simply vSAN. At a high level, vSAN pools the locally attached storage from members of a vSAN–enabled cluster and presents the aggregated pool back to all hosts within the cluster. This could be considered an "array" of sorts because just like a normal SAN, it has multiple disks presented to multiple host

As we mentioned earlier, in the section "Comparing Local Storage with Shared Storage," vSAN does not require any additional software installations. It is built directly into ESXi itself. Managed from vCenter Server, vSAN is compatible with all the other cluster features that vSphere offers, such as vMotion, HA, and DRS. You can even use Storage vMotion to migrate VMs on or off a vSAN datastore.

vSAN uses the disks directly attached to the ESXi hosts and is simple to set up, but there are few specific requirements. Listed here is what you'll need to get VSAN up and running:

◆ ESXi 5.5 or newer hosts

◆ vCenter Server 5.5 or newer

◆ One or more SSDs per host

◆ One or more HDDs per host for hybrid mode

◆ Storage controllers must be on the vSAN HCL

◆ Minimum of three hosts per vSAN cluster

◆ Maximum of 64 hosts per vSAN cluster

◆ 1 Gbps network between hosts (10 Gbps highly recommended and required for all-flash vSAN)

There are two types of vSAN configurations. The first is an all flash-based configuration that provides vSAN clusters with the highest performance available for both data in cache as well as data at rest. The original configuration that was introduced with vSphere 5.5 is a "hybrid" approach. It uses both flash-based and magnetic hard disks.

As you can see from the list, vSAN requires at least one flash-based device in each host. Wha may not be apparent from the requirements list is that in the hybrid configuration, capacity of th SSD is not actually added to the overall usable space of the vSAN datastore. Hybrid vSAN uses the flash tier as a read and write cache just as some external SANs do. When blocks are written t the underlying datastore, they are written to the flash tier first, and later the data can be relocate to the HDDs (capacity tier) if it's not considered to be frequently accessed. vSAN's read/write cache ratio is 70% read, 30% write.

vSAN doesn't use the traditional RAID concepts explained in the previous section; it uses what VMware is calling RAIN, or reliable array of independent nodes. So, if there's no RAID, how do you achieve the expected reliability when using vSAN? vSAN uses a combination of vSphere APIs for Storage Awareness (VASA) and storage policies to ensure that VMs are located on more than one disk and/or host to achieve their performance and availability requirements. This is why VMware recommends 10 Gbps networking between ESXi hosts when using vSAN. A VM virtual disk could be located on one physical host but could be running on another host's CPU and memory. The storage system is fully abstracted from the compute resources, as you can see in Figure 6.6. In all likelihood the VMs virtual disk files could be located on multiple hosts in the cluster to ensure a level of redundancy.

FIGURE 6.6
vSAN abstracts the ESXi host's local disks and presents them to the entire vSAN cluster to consume.

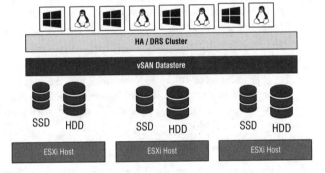

Storage policies are the key to vSAN and Virtual Volumes (VVOLs). They allow VMware administrators to define requirements for a policy and attach that policy to a VM or VMDK. Once vSAN (or VVOL) sees that policy, it will make placement decisions for the underlying VM files to ensure it gets placed in the correct location. Like VVOL, vSAN exposes these capabilities through VASA providers. The following are the capabilities that can be defined through the VASA provider policy options for vSAN:

Primary Level of Failures to Tolerate (PFTT)   Defines the number of host and device failures that a VM object can tolerate. For n failures tolerated, each piece of data written is stored in $n+1$ places, including parity copies if you're using RAID 5 or RAID 6.

When provisioning a VM, if you do not choose a storage policy, vSAN assigns this policy as the default VM storage policy.

If fault domains are configured, $2n+1$ fault domains with hosts contributing capacity are required. A host that is not part of any fault domain is considered its own single-host fault domain.

Default value: 1

Maximum value: 3

Secondary Level of Failures to Tolerate (SFTT)   In a stretched cluster, this rule defines the number of additional host failures that the object can tolerate after the number of site failures defined by PFTT is reached. If PFTT = 1 and SFTT = 2, and one site is unavailable, then the cluster can tolerate two additional host failures.

Default value: 1

Maximum value: 3

Number of Disk Stripes per Object   The minimum number of capacity devices across which each replica of a VM object is striped. A value higher than 1 might result in better performance, but also results in higher use of system resources.

Default value: 1

Maximum value: 12

In a hybrid environment, the disk stripes are spread across magnetic disks. In the case of an all-flash configuration, the striping is across flash devices that make up the capacity layer. Make sure that your vSAN environment has sufficient capacity devices present to accommodate the request.

Force Provisioning   If the option is set to Yes, the object is provisioned even if the Primary Level of Failures to Tolerate, Number of Disk Stripes per Object, and Flash Read Cache Reservation policies specified in the storage policy cannot be satisfied by the datastore. Use this parameter in bootstrapping scenarios and during an outage when standard provisioning is no longer possible.

Default value: No

The default is acceptable for most production environments. vSAN fails to provision a VM when the policy requirements are not met.

Object Space Reservation (%)   Percentage of the logical size of the VM disk (vmdk) object that must be reserved, or thick provisioned when deploying VMs.

Default value:: 0%

Maximum value: 100%

Flash Read Cache Reservation (%)   Flash capacity reserved as read cache for the VM object specified as a percentage of the logical size of the VM disk (vmdk) object. Reserved flash capacity cannot be used by other objects. Unreserved flash is shared fairly among all objects. Use this option only to address specific performance issues.

You do not have to set a reservation to get cache. Setting read cache reservations might cause a problem when you move the VM object, because the cache reservation settings are always included with the object.

The Flash Read Cache Reservation storage policy attribute is supported only for hybrid configurations. You must not use this attribute when defining a VM storage policy for an all-flash cluster.

Default value: 0%

Maximum value: 100%

Affinity In a stretched cluster, this rule is available only if the PFTT is set to 0. You can set the Affinity rule to None, Preferred, or Secondary. This rule enables you to limit VM objects to a selected site in the stretched cluster.

Default value: None

Disable Object Checksum If the option is set to No, the object calculates checksum information to ensure the integrity of its data. If this option is set to Yes, the object does not calculate checksum information.

vSAN uses end-to-end checksum to ensure the integrity of data by confirming that each copy of a file is exactly the same as the source file. The system checks the validity of the data during read/write operations, and if an error is detected, vSAN repairs the data or reports the error.

If a checksum mismatch is detected, vSAN automatically repairs the data by overwriting the incorrect data with the correct data. Checksum calculation and error-correction are performed as background operations.

The default setting for all objects in the cluster is No, which means that checksum is enabled.

Failure Tolerance Method Specifies whether the data replication method optimizes for Performance or Capacity. If you select RAID-1 (Mirroring) - Performance, vSAN uses more disk space to place the components of objects but provides better performance for accessing the objects. If you select RAID-5/6 (Erasure Coding) - Capacity, vSAN uses less disk space, but the performance is reduced. You can use RAID 5 by applying the RAID-5/6 (Erasure Coding) - Capacity attribute to clusters with four or more fault domains and set the Primary Level Of failures To Tolerate to 1. You can use RAID 6 by applying the RAID-5/6 (Erasure Coding) - Capacity attribute to clusters with six or more fault domains and set the Primary Level Of Failures To Tolerate to 2.

In stretched clusters with SFTT configured, this rule applies only to the current SFTT setting.

IOPS Limit for Object Defines the IOPS limit for an object, such as a VMDK. IOPS is calculated as the number of I/O operations, using a weighted size. If the system uses the default base size of 32 KB, a 64-KB I/O represents two I/O operations.

When calculating IOPS, read and write are considered equivalent, but the cache hit ratio and sequentiality are not considered. If a disk's IOPS exceeds the limit, I/O operations are throttled. If the IOPS limit for object is set to 0, IOPS limits are not enforced.

vSAN allows the object to double the rate of the IOPS limit during the first second of operation or after a period of inactivity.

vSAN provides a new way to use and scale out local storage devices. Not only that, but it also uses storage policy–based management (SPBM) to make operating these clusters with locally attached disks simple and hassle free. Let's now move on to more traditional storage systems in the form of SAN and NAS arrays.

Understanding Midrange and External Enterprise Storage Array Design

Some major differences exist in physical array design that can be pertinent in a vSphere design

Traditional external midrange storage arrays are generally arrays with dual-storage process cache designs where the cache is localized to one storage processor or another but commonly mirrored between them. (Remember that all vendors call storage processors something slightly different; sometimes they are called *controllers, heads, engines, or nodes*.) In cases where one of the storage processors fails, the array remains available, but in general, performance is degraded (unless you drive the storage processors to only 50% storage processor utilization during norm operation).

External enterprise storage arrays are generally those that scale to many more controllers an a much larger global cache (memory can be accessed through some common shared model). In these cases, multiple elements can fail while the array is being used at a very high degree of utilization, without any significant performance degradation.

Hybrid designs exist as well, such as scale-out designs where they can scale out to more than two storage processors but without the features otherwise associated with enterprise storage arrays. Often these are iSCSI-only arrays and leverage iSCSI redirection techniques (which are not options of the Fibre Channel or NAS protocol stacks) as a core part of their scale-out design

Design can be confusing, however, because VMware and storage vendors use the same word to express different things. To most storage vendors, an *active-active* storage array is an array tha can service I/O on all storage processor units at once, and an active-passive design is a system where one storage processor is idle until it takes over for the failed unit. VMware has specific nomenclature for these terms that is focused on the model for a *specific LUN*. VMware defines active-active and active-passive arrays in the following way (this information is taken from the *vSphere Storage Guide*):

Active-Active Storage System An active-active storage system provides access to LUNs simultaneously through all available storage ports without significant performance degrada tion. Barring a path failure, all paths are active at all times.

Active-Passive Storage System In an active-passive storage system, one storage processor actively providing access to a given LUN. Other processors act as backup for the LUN and ca be actively servicing I/O to other LUNs. In the event of the failure of an active storage port, one of the passive storage processors can be activated to handle I/O.

Asymmetrical Storage System An asymmetrical storage system supports asymmetric logical unit access (ALUA), which allows storage systems to provide different levels of acces per port. This permits the hosts to determine the states of target ports and establish priority for paths. (See the sidebar "The Fine Line Between Active-Active and Active-Passive" for more details on ALUA.)

Virtual Port Storage System Access to all LUNs is provided through a single virtual port. These are active-active devices where the multiple connections are disguised behind the sing virtual port. Virtual port storage systems handle failover and connection balancing transpar ently, which is often referred to as "transparent failover."

This distinction between array types is important because VMware's definition is based on th multipathing mechanics, not whether you can use both storage processors at once. The active-

active and active-passive definitions apply equally to Fibre Channel (and FCoE) and iSCSI arrays, and the virtual port definition applies to only iSCSI (because it uses an iSCSI redirection mechanism that is not possible on Fibre Channel/FCoE).

THE FINE LINE BETWEEN ACTIVE-ACTIVE AND ACTIVE-PASSIVE

Wondering why VMware specifies "without significant performance degradation" in the active-active definition? The reason is found within ALUA, a standard supported by many midrange arrays. vSphere supports ALUA with arrays that implement ALUA compliant with the SCSI Primary Commands (SPC-3) standard.

Midrange arrays usually have an internal interconnect between the two storage processors used for write cache mirroring and other management purposes. ALUA was an addition to the SCSI standard that enables a LUN to be presented on its primary path and on an asymmetrical (significantly slower) path via the secondary storage processor, transferring the data over this internal interconnect.

The key is that the "non-optimized path" generally comes with a significant performance degradation. The midrange arrays don't have the internal interconnection bandwidth to deliver the same response on both storage processors because a relatively small, or higher-latency, internal interconnect is used for cache mirroring for ALUA versus enterprise arrays with a very-high-bandwidth internal model.

Without ALUA, on an array with an active-passive LUN ownership model, paths to a LUN are shown as active, standby (designates that the port is reachable but is on a processor that does not have the LUN), and dead. When the failover mode is set to ALUA, a new state is possible: active non-optimized. This is not shown distinctly in the vSphere Web Client GUI, but it looks instead like a normal active path. The difference is that it is not used for any I/O.

So, should you configure your midrange array to use ALUA? Follow your storage vendor's best practice. For some arrays this is more important than others. Remember, however, that the non-optimized paths will not be used (by default) even if you select the Round Robin policy. An active-passive array using ALUA is not functionally equivalent to an active-passive array where all paths are used. This behavior can be different if using a third-party multipathing module—see the section "Reviewing Multipathing," later in this chapter.

By definition, all enterprise arrays are active-active arrays (by VMware's definition), but not all midrange arrays are active-passive. To make things even more confusing, not all active-active arrays (again, by VMware's definition) are enterprise arrays!

So, what do you do? What kind of array architecture is the right one for VMware? The answer is simple: all of them on VMware's Compatibility Guide work. You just need to understand how the one *you* have works.

Most customers' needs are well met by midrange arrays, regardless of whether they have an active-active, active-passive, or virtual port (iSCSI-only) design or whether they are NAS devices. Generally, only the most mission-critical virtual workloads at the highest scale require the characteristics of enterprise-class storage arrays. In these cases, *scale* refers to VMs that number in the thousands, datastores that number in the hundreds, local and remote replicas that number in the hundreds, and the highest possible workloads—all that perform consistently even after component failures.

The most important considerations are as follows:

◆ If you have a midrange array, recognize that it is possible to oversubscribe the storage processors significantly. In such a situation, if a storage processor fails, performance will be degraded. For some customers, that is acceptable because storage processor failure is rare. For others, it is not, in which case you should limit the workload on either storage processor to less than 50% or consider an enterprise array.

◆ Understand the failover behavior of your array. Active-active arrays use the fixed-path selection policy by default, and active-passive arrays use the most recently used (MRU) policy by default. (See the section "Reviewing Multipathing" for more information.)

◆ Do you need specific advanced features? For example, if you want disaster recovery, make sure your array has integration support on the VMware Site Recovery Manager Compatibility Guide. Or do you need array-integrated VMware snapshots? Do they have integrated management tools? More generally, do they support the vSphere Storage APIs? Ask your array vendor to illustrate its VMware integration and the use cases it supports.

We're now left with the last major area of storage fundamentals before we move on to discussing storage in a vSphere-specific context. The last remaining area deals with choosing a storage protocol.

Choosing a Storage Protocol

vSphere offers several choices for shared storage protocol, including Fibre Channel, Fibre Channel over Ethernet/FCoE/, iSCSI, and Network File System (NFS), which is a form of NAS. A little understanding of each goes a long way in designing the storage for your vSphere environment.

OVERVIEW OF FIBRE CHANNEL

SANs are most commonly associated with Fibre Channel storage because Fibre Channel was the first widely adopted protocol used with SANs. However, *SAN* refers to a network topology, not connection protocol. In fact, SAN refers to the ability to create block storage access through the use of a network, and although people often use the acronym *SAN* to refer to a Fibre Channel SAN, you can create a SAN topology using different types of protocols, including iSCSI, FCoE, and InfiniBand.

SANs were initially deployed to aggregate storage inside a datacenter while maintaining some of the characteristics of local or direct attached SCSI devices. A SAN is a network where storage devices (logical units, or LUNs, just as on a SCSI or SAS controller) are presented from a storage target (one or more ports on an array) to one or more initiators.

An initiator can come in both hardware and software forms. Hardware adapters, such as host bus adapters (HBA) for Fibre Channel and iSCSI, or converged network adapters (CNA), for iSCSI and FCoE are common, though software-based initiators are available for iSCSI and FCoE as well. See Figure 6.7.

Today, Fibre Channel HBAs have roughly the same cost as high-end multiport Ethernet interfaces or local SAS controllers, and (depending on the type) the per-port cost of a Fibre Channel switch is about twice that of a high-end managed Ethernet switch.

FIGURE 6.7

Both Fibre Channel and iSCSI SANs present LUNs from a target array to a series of initiators (in this case, the VMware iSCSI Software Adapter).

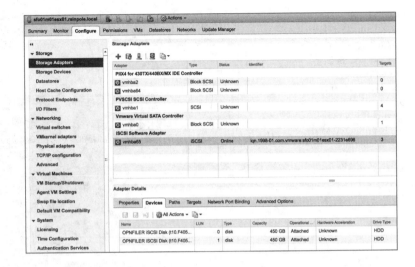

Fibre Channel typically uses an optical interconnect (though there are copper variants) because the Fibre Channel protocol assumes a very high-bandwidth, low-latency, and lossless physical layer. Standard Fibre Channel HBAs today support very-high-throughput, 4 Gbps, 8 Gbps, 16 Gbps, and 32 Gbps connectivity in single-, dual-, or quad-port options. A large number of HBAs are supported on vSphere; you can find the authoritative list at `www.vmware.com/resources/compatibility/search.php`. For end-to-end compatibility (in other words, from host to HBA to switch to array), every storage vendor maintains a similar compatibility matrix. When in doubt, the storage vendor's compatibility matrix should be the definitive source, as the level of detail for those configurations are more fine-grained.

From a connectivity standpoint, almost all cases use a common OM2 (orange-colored cables) multimode duplex LC/LC cable. The newer OM3 and OM4 (aqua-colored cables) are used for longer distances and are generally used for 10 Gbps Ethernet and 8/16 Gbps Fibre Channel (which otherwise have shorter distances using OM2). They all plug into standard optical interfaces, which can often be misleading. Different optical transceivers have different distance tolerances and using the wrong transceiver with the inappropriate cable can result in unpredictable storage networking performance.

The Fibre Channel protocol can operate in three modes: point-to-point (FC-P2P), arbitrated loop (FC-AL), and switched (FC-SW). Point-to-point and arbitrated loop are rarely used today, though they may have specific use cases. FC-AL is commonly used by some array architectures to connect their backend spindle enclosures (vendors give different hardware names to them, but they're the hardware elements that contain and support the physical disks), but the protocol is more generally used to connect to tape-based backup devices. Most modern arrays use switched fabric designs, which have higher bandwidth per disk enclosure and greater deployment flexibility.

Best practice for block-based storage systems is to have equal and redundant systems for purposes of high availability (HA). "SAN A/B" design is common and often expected in storage environments. As Figure 6.8 shows, each ESXi host has a minimum of two HBA ports, and each is physically connected to two Fibre Channel switches. Each switch has a minimum of two connections to two redundant front-end array ports (across storage processors).

FIGURE 6.8
The most common Fibre
Channel configura-
tion—a switched
Fibre Channel
(FC-SW) SAN. This
enables the Fibre
Channel LUN to be
easily presented to all
the hosts while
creating a redundant
network design.

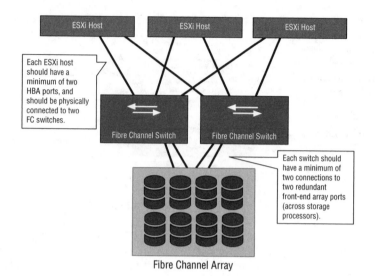

Fibre Channel Array

THE FABRIC: WHAT MAKES FIBRE CHANNEL "FIBRE CHANNEL"

Fibre Channel switched networks rely on the concept of a "fabric," which is a fundamental
concept in how the network works. In a fabric architecture, every switching device understands
the nature of every other switching device. Devices "log in" to the fabric, and depending on how
many switches participate in the system, that information is shared across all participating
switches. Routing information, login information, and zoning information are all included.
Unlike a typical Ethernet network topology, Fibre Channel networks are *deterministic*, that is, the
fabric understands and expects the relationships between end devices *before* they are added to
the network.

All the objects (initiators, targets, and LUNs) on a Fibre Channel SAN are identified by a
unique 64-bit identifier called a *worldwide name (WWN)*. WWNs can be worldwide node names
(for example, a device, such as an adapter, switch, or storage node) or port names (for example,
the ports on an adapter, switch, or array). For anyone unfamiliar with Fibre Channel, this concept
is simple. It's the same technique as Media Access Control (MAC) addresses on Ethernet.

Like Ethernet MAC addresses, WWNs have a structure. The most significant two bytes are
used by the vendor (the four hexadecimal characters starting on the left) and are unique to the
vendor, so there is a pattern for QLogic or Emulex HBAs, switches, or array vendors.

When an initiator (host device) attempts to connect to a Fibre Channel fabric, it must first
perform a *fabric login (FLOGI)*. The fabric processes the login and identifies the device's location
(that is, the switch port) and registers the device in the name server. Once that is complete, the
device attempts to log into the array port (PLOGI) using the worldwide port name (WWPN) of
the target array.

Obviously, it's important that devices do not log into other devices that they're not supposed
to. For that reason, Fibre Channel (and FCoE) fabrics also have the critical concept of zoning.
Zoning is used for the following two purposes:

♦ To ensure that a LUN that is required to be visible to multiple hosts in a cluster (for
example, in a vSphere cluster, a Microsoft Failover cluster, or an Oracle RAC cluster) has

common visibility to the underlying LUN while ensuring that hosts that should *not* have visibility to that LUN do not. For example, it's used to ensure that VMFS volumes aren't visible to Windows servers (with the exception of backup proxy servers using software that leverages the vSphere storage APIs for data protection).

◆ To create fault and error domains on the SAN fabric, where noise, chatter, and errors are not transmitted to all the initiators/targets attached to the switch. Again, it's somewhat analogous to one of the uses of VLANs to partition very dense Ethernet switches into broadcast domains.

Zoning is configured on the Fibre Channel switches via simple GUIs or CLI tools and can be configured by port or by WWN:

◆ Using port-based or "hard" zoning, you would zone by configuring your Fibre Channel switch to "put port 5 and port 10 into a zone that I'll call zone_5_10." Any device (and therefore any WWN) you physically plug into port 5 could communicate only to a device (or WWN) physically plugged into port 10. In this case, if you moved the cables, the zones would have to be modified.

◆ Using WWN-based or "soft" zoning, you would zone by configuring your Fibre Channel switch to "put WWN from this HBA and these array port WWNs into a zone I'll call ESXi_host1_CX_SPA_0." In this case, if you moved the cables, the zones would move to the ports with the matching WWNs.

The ESXi configuration shown in Figure 6.9 shows the LUN by its runtime, or "shorthand," name. Masked behind this name is an unbelievably long name that combines the initiator WWN, the Fibre Channel switch ports, and the Network Address Authority (NAA) identifier. This provides an explicit name that uniquely identifies not only the storage device but also the full end-to-end path.

FIGURE 6.9
The Edit Multipathing Policies dialog box shows the storage runtime (shorthand) name.

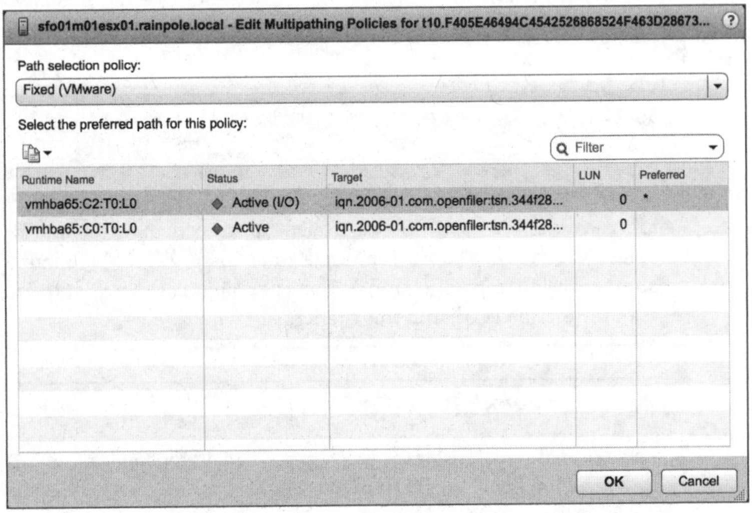

More details on storage object naming will be provided later in this chapter, in the sidebar "What Is All the Stuff in the Storage Device Details List?"

Zoning should not be confused with LUN masking. *Masking* is the ability of a host or an arr to intentionally ignore WWNs that it *can* actively see (in other words, that are zoned to it). Masking is used to further limit what LUNs are presented to a host (commonly used with test and development replicas of LUNs).

You can put many initiators and targets into a zone and group zones together, as illustrated Figure 6.10. For features like vSphere HA and vSphere DRS, ESXi hosts must have shared stora to which all applicable hosts have access. Generally, this means that every ESXi host in a vSphe environment must be zoned such that it can see each LUN. Also, every initiator (HBA or CNA) needs to be zoned to all the front-end array ports that *could* present the LUN. So, what's the bes configuration practice? The answer is single initiator/single target zoning. This creates smaller zones, creates less crosstalk, and makes it more difficult to administratively make an error that removes a LUN from all paths to a host or many hosts at once with a switch configuration erro

Remember that the goal is to ensure that every LUN is visible to all the nodes in the vSphere cluster. The left side of the figure is how most people who are not familiar with Fibre Channel start—multi-initiator zoning, with all array ports and all the ESXi Fibre Channel initiators in on massive zone. The middle is better—with two zones, one for each side of the dual-fabric Fibre Channel SAN design, and each zone includes all possible storage processors' front-end ports (critically, at least one from each storage processor!). The right one is the best and recommende zoning configuration—single-initiator/single-target zoning—however, this method requires more administrative overhead to create and manage all the zones.

When you're using single-initiator/single-target zoning as shown in the figure, each zone consists of a single initiator and a single target array port. This means you'll end up with multiple zones for each ESXi host, so that each ESXi host can see all applicable target array port (again, at least one from each storage processor/controller!). This reduces the risk of administra tive error and eliminates HBA issues affecting adjacent zones, but it takes a little more time to configure and results in a larger number of zones overall. It is always critical to ensure that eacl HBA is zoned to at least one front-end port on each storage processor.

Is There a Fibre Channel Equivalent to VLANs?

Actually, yes, there is. Virtual storage area networks (VSANs) were adopted as a standard in 2004. Like VLANs, VSANs provide isolation between multiple logical SANs that exist on a common physical platform. VSANs are the equivalent of individual SANs, and just as SANs can have multiple zones, VSANs can also have multiple zones. This gives SAN administrators greater flexibility and another layer of separation in addition to zoning. These are not to be confused with VMware's vSAN feature described earlier in this chapter.

How Different Is FCoE?

Aside from discussions of the physical media and topologies, the concepts for FCoE are identical to those of Fibre Channel. This is because FCoE was designed to be seamlessly interoperable with existing Fibre Channel–based SANs.

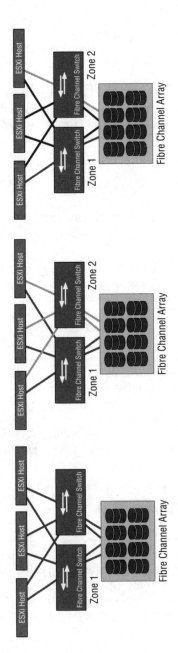

FIGURE 6.10

There are many ways to configure zoning. From left to right: multi-initiator/multi-target zoning, single-initiator/multi-target zoning, and single-initiator/single-target zoning.

The FCoE standard is maintained by the same T11 body as Fibre Channel and was standard ized in 2009 with the release of FC-BB-5, which included details for both "single-hop" and "multi-hop" FCoE. In 2013, T11 finalized FC-BB-6, which added additional support for point-to point and VN2VN (the FCoE analogy to FC-AL) as well as new topological fabrics. Nevertheless at the upper layers of the protocol stacks, Fibre Channel and FCoE are completely identical.

Ultimately, Fibre Channel over Ethernet is exactly what it sounds like: the Fibre Channel frame "sits on top of" an Ethernet Layer 2 frame.

It's important to note that an FCoE frame is completely encapsulated inside an Ethernet frame, and since the maximum size of an FC frame is 2112 bytes, FCoE requires "baby jumbo" frames to be enabled on the switches.

Because of this encapsulation, the WWNs of Fibre Channel addressing are still used for logging into the fabric and the end devices. Figure 6.8 (earlier in this chapter) shows an ESXi ho with FCoE CNAs, where the highlighted CNA has the following worldwide node name: world wide port name (WWNN: WWPN) in the identifier column:

```
20:00:00:25:b5:10:00:2c 20:00:00:25:b5:a0:01:2f
```

In this example, these are Cisco CNAs connected to an EMC VNX storage array.

OVERVIEW OF FIBRE CHANNEL OVER ETHERNET

We mentioned in the sidebar "How Different Is FCoE?" that FCoE was designed to be interoper able and compatible with Fibre Channel.

It's at the lower levels of the stack that the protocols diverge. Fibre Channel, as a protocol, is organized into different parts so that it is decoupled from the lower-level physical layer. To that end, the Fibre Channel standard makes provisions to run the protocol over different transporta tion types, including Layer 3/4 TCP/IP, Layer 2 Ethernet, pseudowire, and other transportation mechanisms. These backbone changes all fall under the purview of the FC-BB standards.

Fibre Channel is designed to guarantee in-order delivery and, as implemented in datacenter today, requires a lossless, low-jitter, high-bandwidth physical layer connection. To ensure that th same type of performance can be achieved using Ethernet, which is traditionally a lossy mediu and more forgiving of errors on the wire, additional considerations were required on the Ethernet side.

To address this need, the IEEE created a series of standards that enhance traffic delivery, the result of which makes a perfect combination for running lossless FCoE traffic simultaneously with lossy LAN traffic. Three key standards, all part of the Datacenter Bridging (DCB) effort, make this possible:

- ♦ Priority Flow Control (PFC, also called Per-Priority Pause)

- ♦ Enhanced Transmission Selection (ETS)

- ♦ Datacenter Bridging Exchange (DCBX)

There is an additional standard in Ethernet called IEEE 802.1pp that allows a link between devices to be separated into eight classes of service (CoS) values, called priorities. The term *priority* is somewhat of a misnomer as the term does not refer to the importance of the traffic, bu rather the class that the traffic belongs to. This becomes the foundation for multiprotocol traffic because it permits users to place traffic on specific priorities, each having its own specific behavioral characteristics.

Priority Flow Control (IEEE 802.1Qbb) is the standard that creates the lossless behavior on a specific priority without affecting other traffic on other CoSs (priorities). When using a lossless no drop priority, it is possible to isolate FCoE traffic and maintain in-order delivery through the use of judicious PAUSE frames, which pause the traffic until such time that it can be delivered with the frames in order.

ETS and DCBX are part of the same standard document (IEEE 802.1Qaz) and refer to two specific capabilities. First, ETS provides *minimum* bandwidth requirements for traffic groups. In the most common deployment of multiprotocol traffic, FCoE is given 50% of bandwidth and the remaining LAN traffic is given the other 50%. However, these are minimum guarantees, which means that each type of traffic is guaranteed to have at least 50% of the available bandwidth. If, on the other hand, FCoE traffic is not currently using all of its available bandwidth, the LAN traffic can use whatever additional capacity is available. But when FCoE needs its bandwidth back, it gets it, at least to the 50% setting.

The second part, DCBX, is simply an extension of the Link Layer Discovery Protocol (LLDP), which permits settings to be exchanged between devices. For example, when a CNA comes online, it can receive its settings (including ETS, FCoE settings, and so forth) from the switch using the DCBX protocol.

Used together, these three protocols allow Fibre Channel frames to be transported in a lossless fashion, independent of lossy traffic being transported along the same wire at the same time. Figure 6:11 illustrates Fibre channel encapsulation in an Ethernet frame.

FIGURE 6.11

FCoE encapsulates Fibre Channel frames into Ethernet frames for transmission over a lossless Ethernet transport.

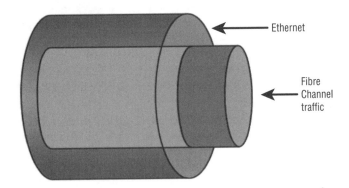

Ethernet

Fibre Channel traffic

UNDERSTANDING THE PHYSICAL LAYER

FCoE uses whatever physical cable plant that 10 Gb Ethernet uses. Today, 10 GbE connectivity varies between optical (same cables as Fibre Channel), Twinax (which is a pair of coaxial copper cables), InfiniBand-like CX cables, and 10 Gb shielded twisted pair (UTP) use cases via the 10GBase-T standard. Each has its specific distance-based use cases and varying interface cost, size, and power consumption.

Be careful not to let cost be the deciding factor in choosing appropriate physical layer connectivity. It is all too easy to mismatch transceivers and cabling simply because they "fit" together. Because FCoE has more stringent requirements for bit error rates (BERs), the use of 10GBase-T is particularly tricky. For example, datasheets for 10GBase-T Ethernet switches will easily qualify distances of 100 meters (or possibly more) for 10 Gb throughput, knowing that inherent errors in the wire will be compensated by upper-layer protocols to retransmit. FCoE, on the other hand, requires tighter controls, and so it's important to note that only Cat 6a (not just Cat 6) and Cat 7 are supported for FCoE traffic. Not only that, but because of the higher resistance of copper (compared to optical cabling) the supported distance winds up being around 30 meters.

In short, it's important to make sure that the physical layer is given appropriate consideration when planning datacenter architectures.

CHOOSING BETWEEN FCOE AND OTHER PROTOCOLS

Because FCoE uses Ethernet, why use FCoE instead of NFS or iSCSI over 10 Gb Ethernet? The answer is usually driven by the following two factors:

♦ There are existing infrastructure, processes, and tools in large enterprises that are designed for Fibre Channel. Because of the nature of the storage systems in place, it may be preferable to preserve their lifespan in the datacenter. In fact, storage systems are the most persistent in the datacenter, and new servers that are refreshed more frequently can use converged adapters to reduce capital expenditures while still accessing existing storage systems without the need of stateful gateways. In other words, you can grow in existing environments without a "rip and replace" model. The largest cost savings, power savings, cable and port reduction, and impact on management simplification are on this layer from the ESXi host to the first switch.

♦ Certain applications require a lossless, extremely low-latency transport network model, something that cannot be achieved using a transport where dropped frames are normal and long-window TCP retransmit mechanisms are the protection mechanism. Now, this is a very high-end set of applications, and those historically were not virtualized. This, however, is no longer the case, so I/O models that can deliver those performance envelopes while still supporting a converged network become more important.

In practice, the debate of iSCSI versus FCoE versus NFS on 10 Gb Ethernet infrastructure is not material. All FCoE adapters are converged adapters, referred to as converged network adapters (CNAs). They support native 10 GbE (and therefore also NFS and iSCSI) as well as FCoE simultaneously, and they are presented by the ESXi host as both Ethernet and Fibre Channel adapters. If you have FCoE support, in effect you have it all. All protocol options are yours.

A list of FCoE CNAs supported by vSphere can be found in the I/O section of the VMware Compatibility Guide.

UNDERSTANDING iSCSI

iSCSI brings the idea of a block storage SAN to customers with no Fibre Channel infrastructure. iSCSI is an Internet Engineering Task Force (IETF) standard for encapsulating SCSI control and data in TCP/IP packets, which in turn are encapsulated in Ethernet frames. Figure 6.12 shows how iSCSI is encapsulated in TCP/IP and Ethernet frames. TCP retransmission is used to handle dropped Ethernet frames or significant transmission errors. Storage traffic can be intense relative to most LAN traffic. This makes it important that you minimize retransmits, minimize dropped frames, and ensure that you have a bet-the-business Ethernet infrastructure when using iSCSI.

FIGURE 6.12
Using iSCSI, SCSI control and data are encapsulated in both TCP/IP and Ethernet frames.

Although Fibre Channel is often viewed as having higher performance than iSCSI, in many cases iSCSI can more than meet the requirements for many customers, and a carefully planned and scaled-up iSCSI infrastructure can, for the most part, match the performance of a moderate Fibre Channel SAN.

Also, iSCSI and Fibre Channel SANs are roughly comparable in complexity and share many of the same core concepts. Arguably, getting the first iSCSI LUN visible to an ESXi host is simpler than getting the first Fibre Channel LUN visible for people with expertise with Ethernet but not Fibre Channel because understanding worldwide names and zoning is not needed. In practice, designing a scalable, robust iSCSI network requires the same degree of diligence that is applied to Fibre Channel. You should use VLAN (or physical) isolation techniques similarly to Fibre Channel zoning, and you need to scale up connections to achieve comparable bandwidth. Look at Figure 6.13 and compare it to the switched Fibre Channel network diagram in Figure 6.8.

FIGURE 6.13
Notice how the topology of an iSCSI SAN is the same as a switched Fibre Channel SAN.

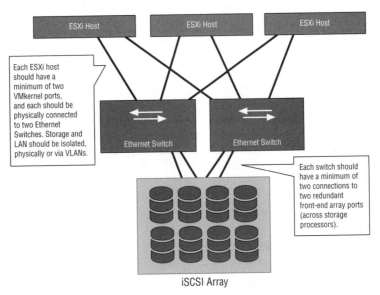

In this example, each ESXi host has a minimum of two VMkernel adapters, and each is physically connected to two Ethernet switches. (Recall from Chapter 5, "Creating and Configuring a vSphere Network," that VMkernel adapters are used by the hypervisor for network traffic such as IP-based storage traffic, like iSCSI or NFS.) Storage and LAN are isolated, physically or via VLANs. Each switch has a minimum of two connections to two redundant front-end array network interfaces (across storage processors).

The one additional concept to focus on with iSCSI is the concept of *fan-in ratio*. This applies to all shared storage networks, including Fibre Channel, but the effect is often most pronounced with Gigabit Ethernet (GbE) networks. Across all shared networks, there is almost always a higher amount of bandwidth available across all the host nodes than there is on the egress of the switches and front-end connectivity of the array. It's important to remember that the host bandwidth is gated by congestion wherever it occurs. Don't minimize the array port-to-switch configuration. If you connect only four GbE interfaces on your array and you have 100 hosts with two GbE interfaces each, then expect contention, because your fan-in ratio is too large.

Also, when iSCSI and iSCSI SANs are examined, many core ideas are similar to Fibre Channel and Fibre Channel SANs, but in some cases, there are material differences. Let's look at the terminology:

iSCSI Initiator   An iSCSI initiator is a logical host-side device that serves the same function as a physical host bus adapter in Fibre Channel/FCoE or SCSI/SAS. iSCSI initiators can be software initiators (which use host CPU cycles to load/unload SCSI payloads into standard TCP/IP packets and perform error checking) or hardware initiators (the iSCSI equivalent of a Fibre Channel HBA or FCoE CNA). Examples of software initiators that are pertinent to vSphere administrators are the native ESXi software initiator and the guest software. Examples of iSCSI hardware initiators are add-in cards like the QLogic QLA 405x and QLE 406x host bus adapters. These cards perform all the iSCSI functions in hardware. An iSCSI initiator is identified by an iSCSI qualified name (referred to as an IQN). An iSCSI initiator uses an iSCSI network portal that consists of one or more IP addresses. An iSCSI initiator "logs in" to an iSCSI target.

iSCSI Target   An iSCSI target is a logical target-side device that serves the same function as a target in Fibre Channel SANs. It is the device that hosts iSCSI LUNs and masks to specific iSCSI initiators. Different arrays use iSCSI targets differently; some use hardware while others use software implementations, but largely this is unimportant. More important is that an iSCSI target doesn't necessarily map to a physical port as is the case with Fibre Channel; each array does this differently. Some have one iSCSI target per physical Ethernet port; some have one iSCSI target per iSCSI LUN, which is visible across multiple physical ports; and some have logical iSCSI targets that map to physical ports and LUNs in any relationship the administrator configures within the array. An iSCSI target is identified by an iSCSI qualified name (an IQN). An iSCSI target uses an iSCSI network portal that consists of one or more IP addresses.

iSCSI Logical Unit   An iSCSI LUN is a logical device hosted by an iSCSI target. There can be one or more LUNs behind a single iSCSI target.

iSCSI Network Portal   An iSCSI network portal is one or more IP addresses that are used by an iSCSI initiator or iSCSI target.

iSCSI Qualified Name   An iSCSI qualified name (IQN) serves the purpose of the WWN in Fibre Channel SANs; it is the unique identifier for an iSCSI initiator, target, or LUN. The format of the IQN is based on the iSCSI IETF standard.

Challenge Authentication Protocol   CHAP is a widely used basic authentication protocol, where a password exchange is used to authenticate the source or target of communication. Unidirectional CHAP is one-way; the source authenticates to the destination, or, in the case of iSCSI, the iSCSI initiator authenticates to the iSCSI target. Bidirectional CHAP is two-way; the iSCSI initiator authenticates to the iSCSI target, and vice versa, before communication is established. Although Fibre Channel SANs are viewed as intrinsically secure because they are physically isolated from the Ethernet network, and although initiators not zoned to targets cannot communicate, this is not by definition true of iSCSI. With iSCSI, it is possible (but not recommended) to use the same Ethernet segment as general LAN traffic, and there is no intrinsic zoning model. Because the storage and general networking traffic could share networking infrastructure, CHAP is an optional mechanism to authenticate the source and destination of iSCSI traffic for some additional security. In practice, Fibre Channel and iSCSI SANs have the same security and same degree of isolation (logical or physical).

IP Security   IPsec is an IETF standard that uses public-key encryption techniques to secure the iSCSI payloads so that they are not susceptible to man-in-the-middle security attacks. Like CHAP for authentication, this higher level of optional security is part of the iSCSI standards because it is possible (but not recommended) to use a general-purpose IP network for iSCSI transport, and in these cases, not encrypting data exposes a security risk (for example, a man-in-the-middle attack could determine data on a host it can't authenticate to by simply reconstructing the data from the iSCSI packets). IPsec is used relatively rarely because it has a heavy CPU impact on the initiator and the target.

Static/Dynamic Discovery   iSCSI uses a method of discovery where the iSCSI initiator can query an iSCSI target for the available LUNs. Static discovery involves a manual configuration, whereas dynamic discovery issues an iSCSI-standard SendTargets command to one of the iSCSI targets on the array. This target then reports all the available targets and LUNs to that particular initiator.

iSCSI Naming Service   The iSCSI Naming Service (iSNS) is analogous to the Domain Name System (DNS); it's where an iSNS server stores all the available iSCSI targets for a very large iSCSI deployment. iSNS is rarely used.

Figure 6.14 shows the key iSCSI elements in an example logical diagram. This diagram shows iSCSI in the broadest sense.

In general, the iSCSI session can be multiple TCP connections, called *Multiple Connections Per Session*. Note that this cannot be done in vSphere. An iSCSI initiator and iSCSI target can communicate on an iSCSI network portal that can consist of one or more IP addresses. The concept of network portals is done differently on each array; some arrays always have one IP address per target port, whereas some arrays use network portals extensively. The iSCSI initiator logs into the iSCSI target, creating an iSCSI session. You can have many iSCSI sessions for a single target, and each session can have multiple TCP connections (Multiple Connections Per Session, which isn't currently supported by vSphere). There can be varied numbers of iSCSI LUNs behind an iSCSI target, many or just one. Every array does this differently. We'll talk more about the particulars of the vSphere software iSCSI initiator implementation in the section "Adding a LUN via iSCSI," later in this chapter.

What about the debate regarding hardware iSCSI initiators (iSCSI HBAs) versus software iSCSI initiators? Figure 6.15 shows the differences among software iSCSI on generic network interfaces, network interfaces that do TCP/IP offload, and full iSCSI HBAs. Clearly there are more things the ESXi host needs to process with software iSCSI initiators, but the additional CPU is relatively light. Fully saturating several GbE links will use less than one core of a modern CPU, and the cost of iSCSI HBAs is usually less than the cost of slightly more CPU. Keep the CPU overhead in mind as you craft your storage design, but don't let it be your sole benchmark.

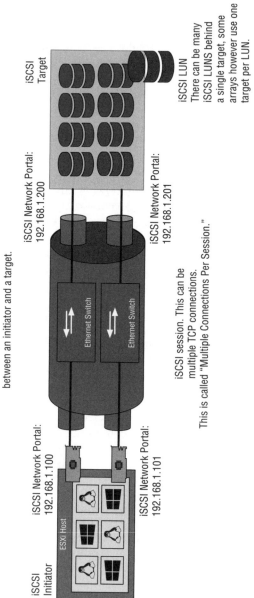

FIGURE 6.14
The iSCSI IETF standard has several different elements.

FIGURE 6.15

Some parts of the stack are handled by the adapter card versus the ESXi host CPU in various implementations.

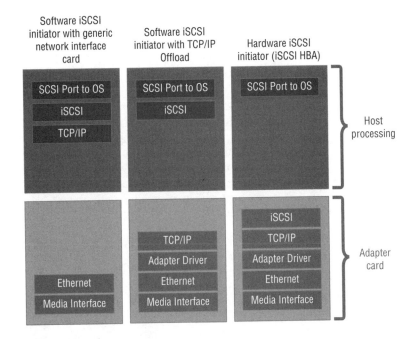

Also note the difference between a dependent hardware iSCSI adapter and an independent hardware iSCSI adapter. As the name suggests, the former depends on vSphere networking and iSCSI configuration, whereas the latter uses its own networking and iSCSI configuration.

Prior to vSphere 5.0, one thing that remained the exclusive domain of the iSCSI HBAs was booting from an iSCSI SAN. vSphere 5.0 and later includes support for iSCSI Boot Firmware Table (iBFT), a mechanism that enables booting from iSCSI SAN with a software iSCSI initiator. You must have appropriate support for iBFT in the hardware. We might argue that using Auto Deploy would provide much of the same benefit as booting from an iSCSI SAN, but each approach has its advantages and disadvantages.

iSCSI is the last of the block-based shared storage options available in vSphere; now let's move on to the Network File System (NFS), the only NAS protocol that vSphere supports.

JUMBO FRAMES ARE SUPPORTED

VMware ESXi does support jumbo frames for all VMkernel traffic, including both iSCSI and NFS, and they should be used for IP based storage. However, it is then critical to configure a consistent, larger maximum transfer unit (MTU) size on *all* devices in all the possible networking paths; otherwise, Ethernet frame fragmentation will cause communication problems.

UNDERSTANDING THE NETWORK FILE SYSTEM

NFS protocol is a standard originally developed by Sun Microsystems to enable remote systems to access a file system on another host as if it were locally attached. vSphere 6.0 and later implements a client compliant with both NFSv3 and NFS v4.1 using TCP.

When NFS datastores are used by vSphere, no local file system (such as VMFS) is used. The file system is on the remote NFS server. This means that NFS datastores need to handle the same access control and file-locking requirements that vSphere delivers on block storage using the vSphere Virtual Machine File System, or VMFS (described in more detail later in the section "Examining the vSphere Virtual Machine File System"). NFS servers accomplish this through NFS file locks.

The movement of the file system from the ESXi host to the NFS server also means that you don't need to handle zoning or masking tasks. This makes an NFS datastore one of the easiest storage options to simply get up and running. On the other hand, it also means that all of the high availability and multipathing functionality that is normally part of a Fibre Channel, FCoE, or iSCSI storage stack is replaced by the networking stack. The implications of this are discussed later, in the section "Creating a Highly Available NFS Design."

Figure 6.16 shows the topology of an NFS configuration. Note the similarities to the topologies in Figure 6.8 and Figure 6.13.

FIGURE 6.16

The topology of an NFS configuration is similar to iSCSI from a connectivity standpoint but very different from a configuration standpoint.

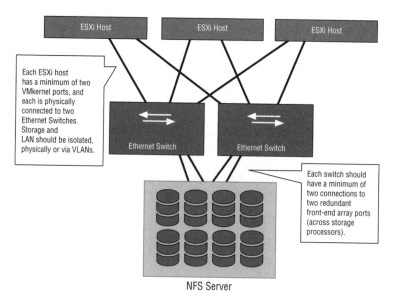

Technically, any NFS server that complies with NFSv3 or v4.1 over TCP will work with vSphere (vSphere does not support NFS over UDP), but similar to the considerations for Fibre Channel and iSCSI, the infrastructure needs to support your entire vSphere environment. Therefore, we recommend you use only NFS servers that are explicitly on the VMware HCL.

Using NFS datastores moves the elements of storage design associated with LUNs from the ESXi hosts to the NFS server. Instead of exposing block storage, which uses the RAID techniques described earlier for data protection, and allowing the ESXi hosts to create a file system (VMFS) on those block devices, the NFS server uses its block storage, protected using RAID, and creates its own file systems on that block storage. These file systems are then exported via NFS and mounted on your ESXi hosts.

In the early days of using NFS with VMware, NFS was categorized as being a lower-performance option; as such, it was used with ISOs and templates but not production VMs. If production VMs were used on NFS datastores, the historical recommendation would have been to relocate the VM swap to block storage. Although it is true that NAS and block architectures are different and, likewise, their scaling models and bottlenecks are generally different, this perception is mostly rooted in how people have used NAS historically.

The reality is that it's absolutely possible to build an enterprise-class NAS infrastructure, and many organizations choose to do so. NFS datastores can support a broad range of virtualized workloads and do not require you to relocate the VM swap. However, in cases where NFS will be supporting a broad set of production VM workloads, you will need to pay attention to the NFS server backend design and network infrastructure. You need to apply the same degree of care to bet-the-business NAS as you would if you were using block storage via Fibre Channel, FCoE, or iSCSI. With vSphere, your NFS server isn't being used as a traditional file server, where performance and availability requirements may be relatively low. Rather, it's being used as an NFS server supporting a mission-critical application, in this case, the vSphere environment and all the VMs on those NFS datastores.

NFS v3 vs. NFS v4.1

We mentioned previously that vSphere implements both NFS v3 and NFS v4.1 clients using TCP. This is important to note because it directly impacts your connectivity options. Let's first cover characteristics of NFS v3.

Each datastore that is connected via the NFS v3 protocol uses two TCP sessions to the NFS server: one for NFS control traffic and the other for NFS data traffic. In effect, this means that the vast majority of the NFS v3 traffic for a single datastore will use a single TCP session. Consequently, this means that link aggregation (which works on a per-flow basis from one source to one target) will use only one Ethernet link per datastore, regardless of how many links are included in the link aggregation group. To use the aggregate throughput of multiple Ethernet interfaces, you need multiple datastores, and no single datastore will be able to use more than one link's worth of bandwidth. The approach available to iSCSI (multiple iSCSI sessions per iSCSI target) is not available in the NFS use case. We'll discuss techniques for designing high-performance NFS datastores in the section "Creating a Highly Available NFS Design," later in this chapter.

As in the previous sections on common storage array architectures, the protocol choices available to the vSphere administrator are broad. You can make most vSphere deployments work well on all protocols, and each has advantages and disadvantages. The key is to understand and determine what will work best for you. Always remember, regardless of the protocol, storage design is important to ensure adequate performance in your virtual environment.

In the following section, we'll summarize how to make these basic storage choices.

Making Basic Storage Choices

Most vSphere workloads can be met by midrange array architectures (regardless of active-active, active-passive, asymmetrical, or virtual port design). Use enterprise array designs when mission-critical and very large-scale virtual datacenter workloads demand uncompromising availability and performance linearity.

As shown in Table 6.1, each storage choice can support most use cases. It's not about one versus the other but rather about understanding and leveraging their differences and applying them to deliver maximum flexibility.

TABLE 6.1: Shared storage choices

FEATURE	FIBRE CHANNEL SAN	ISCSI SAN	NFS	VSAN
ESXi boot (boot from shared storage)	Yes	Hardware initiator or software initiator with iBFT support	No	No
VM boot	Yes	Yes	Yes	Yes
Raw device mapping	Yes	Yes	No	No
Dynamic extension	Yes	Yes	Yes	Yes
Availability and scaling model	Storage stack (PSA), ESXi LUN queues, array configuration	Storage stack (PSA), ESXi LUN queues, array configuration	Network Stage (NIC teaming and routing), network and NFS server configuration	Storage stack (local), Network Stage (NIC teaming and routing)
VMware feature support (vSphere HA, vMotion, Storage vMotion, vSphere FT)	Yes	Yes	Yes	Yes

Picking a protocol type has historically been focused on the following criteria:

vSphere Feature Support   Although major VMware features such as vSphere HA and vMotion initially required VMFS, they are now supported on all storage types, including raw device mappings (RDMs) and NFS datastores. vSphere feature support is generally not a protocol-selection criterion, and there are only a few features that lag on RDMs and NFS, such as native vSphere snapshots on physical compatibility mode RDMs or the ability to create RDMs on NFS.

Storage Capacity Efficiency   Thin provisioning behavior at the vSphere layer, universally and properly applied, drives a very high efficiency, regardless of protocol choice. Applying thin provisioning at the storage array (on both block and NFS objects) delivers a higher overall efficiency than applying it only at the virtualization layer. Emerging techniques for gaining more efficiency from array capacity (such as detecting and reducing storage consumed when there is information in common, using compression, and data deduplication) are currently most effectively used on NFS datastores but are expanding to include block use cases. One common error is to look at storage capacity (GB) as the sole vector of efficiency; in many cases, the performance envelope requires a fixed number of spindles even with advanced caching techniques. Often in these cases, efficiency is measured in spindle density, not in GB. For most vSphere customers, efficiency tends to be a function of operational process rather than protocol or platform choice.

Performance   Many vSphere customers see similar performance regardless of a given protocol choice. Properly designed iSCSI and NFS over 10 Gigabit Ethernet can support very large VMware deployments.

Fibre Channel (and by extension, FCoE) generally delivers a better performance envelope with very large-block I/O (VMs supporting DSS database workloads or SharePoint), which tends to demand a high degree of throughput. Less important generally but still important for some workloads, Fibre Channel delivers a lower-latency model and also tends to have a faster failover behavior because iSCSI and NFS always depend on some degree of TCP retransmission for loss and, in some iSCSI cases, ARP, all of which drive failover handling into tens of seconds versus seconds with Fibre Channel or FCoE. Load balancing and scale-out with IP storage using multiple Ethernet links with IP storage can work for iSCSI to drive up throughput. Link aggregation techniques may help, but they work only when you have many TCP sessions. Because the NFS v3 client in vSphere uses a single TCP session for data transmission, link aggregation won't improve the throughput of individual NFS datastores. Broad availability of 10 Gb Ethernet brings higher-throughput options to NFS datastores.

You can make every protocol configuration work in almost all use cases; the key is in the details (covered in this chapter). In practice, the most important thing is what you know and feel comfortable with.

The most flexible vSphere configurations tend to use a combination of both VMFS (which requires block storage) and NFS datastores (which require NAS), as well as RDMs on a selective basis (block storage).

The choice of which block protocol should be used to support the VMFS and RDM use cases depends on the enterprise more than the technologies and tends to follow this pattern:

◆   iSCSI for customers who have never used and have no existing Fibre Channel SAN infrastructure

◆   Fibre Channel for those with existing Fibre Channel SAN infrastructure that meets their needs

◆   FCoE for those upgrading existing Fibre Channel SAN infrastructure

vSphere can be applied to a very broad set of use cases, from the desktop/laptop to the server and on the server workloads, ranging from test and development to heavy workloads and mission-critical applications. A one-size-fits-all model can work, but only for the simplest deployments. The advantage of vSphere is that all protocols and all models are supported. Becoming fixated on one model means that not everything is virtualized that can be, and the enterprise isn't as flexible and efficient as it can be.

Now that you've learned about the basic principles of shared storage and determined how to make the basic storage choices for your environment, it's time to see how these are applied in vSphere.

Implementing vSphere Storage Fundamentals

This part of the chapter examines how the shared storage technologies covered previously are applied in vSphere. We will cover these elements in a logical sequence, starting with core vSphere storage concepts. Next, we'll cover the storage options in vSphere for datastores to contain groups of VMs (VMFS datastores and NFS datastores). We'll follow that discussion with options for presenting disk devices directly into VMs (raw device mappings). Finally, we'll examine VM–level storage configuration details.

Reviewing Core vSphere Storage Concepts

One of the core concepts of virtualization is encapsulation. What used to be a physical system is encapsulated by vSphere, resulting in VMs that are represented by a set of files. Chapter 9, "Creating and Managing Virtual Machines," provides more detail on the specific files that compose a VM and their purpose. For reasons described already, these VM files reside on the shared storage infrastructure (with the exception of a raw device mapping, or RDM, which will be discussed shortly).

In general, vSphere uses a shared-everything storage model. All ESXi hosts in a vSphere environment use commonly accessed storage objects using block storage protocols (Fibre Channel, FCoE, or iSCSI, in which case the storage objects are LUNs), network attached storage protocols (NFS, in which case the storage objects are NFS exports), or VMware's vSAN protocol built into vSphere. Depending on the environment, these storage objects will be exposed to the majority of your ESXi hosts, although not necessarily to all ESXi hosts in the environment. In Chapter 7, we will again review the concept of a cluster, which is a key part of features like vSphere HA and vSphere DRS. Within a cluster, you'll want to ensure that all ESXi hosts have visibility and access to the same set of storage objects.

Before we get into the details of how to configure the various storage objects in vSphere, we need to first review some core vSphere storage technologies, concepts, and terminology. This information will provide a foundation on which we will build later in the chapter. Let's start with a look at the vSphere Virtual Machine File System, a key technology found in practically every vSphere deployment.

EXAMINING THE VSPHERE VIRTUAL MACHINE FILE SYSTEM

The vSphere Virtual Machine File System (VMFS) is a common configuration option for many vSphere deployments. It's similar to NTFS for Windows Server and ext3 for Linux. Like these file systems, it is native; it's included with vSphere and operates on top of block storage objects. If you're leveraging any form of block storage and you're not using an RDM LUN, you're using VMFS.

The purpose of VMFS is to simplify the storage environment. It would clearly be difficult to scale a virtual environment if each VM directly accessed its own storage rather than storing the set of files on a shared volume. VMFS creates a shared storage pool that is used for one or more VMs.

Though similar to NTFS and ext3, VMFS differs from these common file systems in several important ways:

◆ It was designed to be a clustered file system from its inception; neither NTFS nor ext3 is a clustered file system. Unlike many clustered file systems, it is simple and easy to use.

◆ VMFS's simplicity is derived from its transparent distributed locking mechanism. This is generally much simpler than traditional clustered file systems with network cluster lock managers.

◆ VMFS enables simple direct-to-disk, steady-state I/O that results in high throughput at a low CPU overhead for the ESXi hosts.

◆ Locking is handled using metadata in a hidden section of the file system, as illustrated in Figure 6.17. The metadata portion of the file system contains critical information in the form of on-disk lock structures (files), such as which ESXi host is the current owner of a given VM, ensuring that there is no contention or corruption of the VM.

FIGURE 6.17
VMFS stores metadata in a hidden area of the first extent.

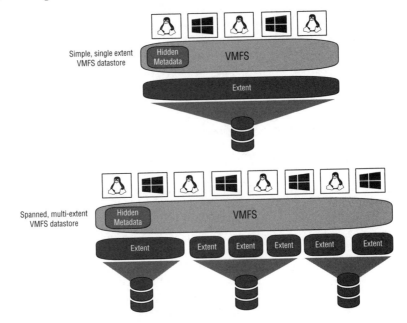

◆ Depending on the storage array's support for VAAI (explained later in this chapter), when these on-disk lock structures are updated, the ESXi host performing the update momentarily locks the LUN using a nonpersistent SCSI lock (SCSI Reserve/Reset commands). This operation is completely transparent to the vSphere administrator.

◆ These metadata updates do *not* occur during normal read/write I/O operations and do not represent a fundamental scaling limit when compared with more traditional file systems.

◆ During the metadata updates, there is minimal impact to the production I/O (covered in a VMware white paper at `www.vmware.com/resources/techresources/1059`). This impact is negligible to the ESXi host holding the SCSI lock but more pronounced on the other hosts accessing the same VMFS datastore.

◆ These metadata updates include, but are not limited to the following

   ◆ The creation or deletion of a file in the VMFS datastore (powering on a VM, creating/deleting a VM, or taking a snapshot, for example)

   ◆ Actions that change the ESXi host that owns a VM (vMotion and vSphere HA)

   ◆ Changes to the VMFS file system itself (extending the file system or adding a file system extent)

vSphere 6.7 and SCSI-3 Dependency

In vSphere 6.7, like previous vSphere versions, only SCSI-3–compliant block storage objects are supported. Most major storage arrays have, or can be upgraded via their array software, to full SCSI-3 support, but check with your storage vendor before upgrading. If your storage array doesn't support SCSI-3, the storage details shown on the Configuration tab for the vSphere host will not display correctly.

In spite of this requirement, vSphere still uses SCSI-2 reservations for general ESXi-level SCSI reservations (not to be confused with guest-level reservations). This is important for asymmetric logical unit access (ALUA) support, covered in the section "Reviewing Multipathing," later in this chapter.

Earlier versions of vSphere exclusively used VMFS version 3 (VMFS-3), and vSphere 5.0, 5.1, 5.5, and 6.0 continue to provide support for VMFS-3. In addition to supporting VMFS-3, vSphere 5.0 introduced VMFS version 5 (VMFS-5), with further enhancements in vSphere 5.5 and 6.0. Only hosts running ESXi 5.0 or later support VMFS-5; hosts running ESX/ESXi 4.x will not be able to see or access VMFS-5 datastores; and the ability to create VMFS-3 datastores was removed from ESXi 6. ESXi 6.5 introduced VMFS version 6 (VMFS-6). VMFS-6 is only supported on hosts running ESXi 6.5 or later.

In ESXi 6.7, VMFS-3 is considered End of Life (EOL). When an ESXi 6.7 host mounts a VMFS-3 datastore, it will automatically upgrade it to VMFS-5. Upgrades from VMFS-3 datastores to VMFS-5 happen in place and online, without any disruption to the VMs running on that datastore, provided all of your ESXi hosts with access to the datastore are running vSphere 5.x or 6.x.

Later in this chapter, the section "Working with VMFS Datastores," provides more details on how to create, expand, delete, and upgrade VMFS datastores.

Closely related to VMFS is the idea of multipathing, a topic that we will discuss in the next section.

Reviewing Multipathing

Multipathing is the term used to describe how a host, such as an ESXi host, manages storage devices that have multiple ways (or paths) to access them. Multipathing is extremely common in Fibre Channel and FCoE environments and is also found in iSCSI environments. We won't go so far as to say that multipathing is strictly for block-based storage environments, but we will say that multipathing for NFS is generally handled much differently than for block storage.

In vSphere 4, VMware and VMware technology partners spent considerable effort overhauling how the elements of the vSphere storage stack that deal with multipathing work. This architecture, known as the Pluggable Storage Architecture (PSA), is still present in vSphere 6.7 as well. Figure 6.18 shows an overview of the PSA.

One of the key goals in the development of the PSA was to make vSphere multipathing much more flexible. Pre–vSphere 4 versions of VMware ESX/ESXi had a rigid set of lists that determined failover and multipathing policies, and this architecture was updated only with major VMware releases. With the PSA's modular architecture, vSphere administrators have a much more flexible approach.

Four different modules compose the PSA:

◆ Native multipathing plug-in (NMP)

◆ Storage array type plug-in (SATP)

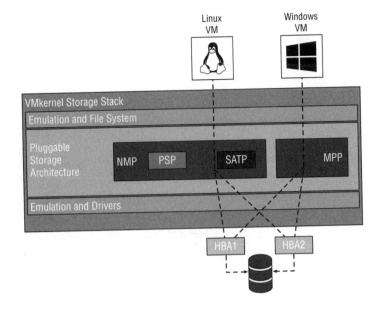

FIGURE 6.18
vSphere's Pluggable Storage Architecture is highly modular and extensible.

- ◆ Path selection plug-in (PSP)

- ◆ Multipathing plug-in (MPP)

Any given ESXi host can have multiple modules in use at any point and can be connected to multiple arrays, and you can configure the combination of modules used (an NMP/SATP/PSP combination or an MPP) on a LUN-by-LUN basis.

Let's see how they work together.

Understanding the NMP Module

The NMP module handles overall MPIO (multipath I/O) behavior and array identification. The NMP leverages the SATP and PSP modules and isn't generally configured in any way.

Understanding SATP Modules

SATP modules handle path failover for a given storage array and determine the failover type for a LUN.

vSphere ships with SATPs for a broad set of supported storage arrays, with generic SATPs for nonspecified arrays and a local SATP for local storage. The SATP modules contain the rules on how to handle array-specific actions or behavior as well as any specific operations needed to manage array paths. This is part of what makes the NMP modular (unlike the NMP in prior versions); it doesn't need to contain the array-specific logic, and additional modules for new arrays can be added without changing the NMP. Using the SCSI Array ID reported by the array via a SCSI query, the NMP selects the appropriate SATP to use. After that, the SATP monitors, deactivates, and activates paths (and when a manual rescan occurs, detects new paths), providing information up to the NMP. The SATP also performs array-specific tasks such as activating passive paths on active-passive arrays.

To see what array SATP modules exist, enter the following command from an ESXi host CLI:

```
esxcli storage nmp satp list
```

Figure 6.19 shows the results this command returns (note that the default PSP for a given SATP is also shown).

FIGURE 6.19
Only the SATPs for the arrays to which an ESXi host is connected are loaded.

Understanding PSP Modules

The PSP module handles the actual path used for every given I/O.

The NMP assigns a default PSP, which can be overridden manually for every LUN based on the SATP associated with that device. This command (and the output captured in Figure 6.20) shows you the three PSPs vSphere includes by default:

```
esxcli storage nmp psp list
```

FIGURE 6.20
vSphere ships with three default PSPs.

Each of these PSPs performs path selection slightly differently:

◆ **Most Recently Used** (noted as VMW_PSP_MRU) selects the path it used most recently. If this path becomes unavailable, the ESXi host switches to an alternative available path and continues to use the new path while it is available. This is the default for active-passive array types.

◆ **Fixed** (noted as VMW_PSP_FIXED) uses the designated preferred path if it has been configured. Otherwise, it uses the first working path discovered at system boot time. If the ESXi host cannot use the preferred path, it selects a random alternative available path. The ESXi host automatically reverts to the preferred path as soon as the path becomes available. This is the default for active-active array types (or active-passive arrays that use ALUA with SCSI-2 reservation mechanisms—in these cases, they appear as active-active).

◆ **Round Robin** (noted as VMW_PSP_RR) rotates the path selection among all available optimized paths and enables basic load balancing across the paths and fabrics. This is not a weighted algorithm, nor is it responsive to queue depth, but it is a significant improvement. In prior ESXi versions, there was no way to load balance a LUN, and customers needed to statically distribute LUNs across paths, which was a poor proxy for true load balancing.

WHICH PSP IS RIGHT IF YOU'RE USING ALUA?

What do you do if your array can be configured to use ALUA, and therefore could use the Fixed, MRU, or Round Robin policy? See the earlier section "Understanding Midrange and External Enterprise Storage Array Design" for information on ALUA.

The Fixed and MRU path failover policies deliver failover only and work fine with active-active and active-passive designs, regardless of whether ALUA is used. Of course, they both drive workloads down a single path. Ensure that you manually select active I/O paths that are the "good" ports, which are the ones where the port is on the storage processor owning the LUN. You don't want to select the "bad" ports, which are the higher-latency, lower-throughput ones that transit the internal interconnect to get to the LUN.

The out-of-the-box load-balancing policy in vSphere (Round Robin) doesn't use the non-optimized paths (though they are noted as active in the vSphere Web Client). Third-party multipathing plug-ins that are aware of the difference between the asymmetrical path choices can optimize an ALUA configuration.

Perform the following steps to see what SATP (and PSP) is being used for a given LUN in the vSphere Web Client:

1. In the vSphere Web Client, navigate to the Hosts and Clusters view.

2. Select a host from the list on the left; then select the Configure tab on the right.

3. Under the Storage subsection, click Storage Devices.

This opens the Storage Devices area. When a LUN or disk is selected from the list, an SATP will be listed near the bottom, as shown in Figure 6.21.

In this example, the array is an OpenFiler and the generic VMW_SATP_DEFAULT_AA is selected. The default PSP is Fixed (VMware). A change in the PSP takes place *immediately* when you change it. There is no confirmation. Note that the PSP is configurable on a LUN-by-LUN basis.

WHAT IS ALL THE STUFF IN THE STORAGE DEVICE DETAILS LIST?

In the runtime name, the C is the channel identifier, the Y is the target identifier, and the L is the LUN.

And that long text string starting with *naa*? That is the Network Address Authority ID, which is a unique identifier for the target and a LUN. This ID is guaranteed to be persistent through reboots and is used throughout vSphere.

FIGURE 6.21

The SATP for this datastore is VMW_SATP_DEFAULT_AA.

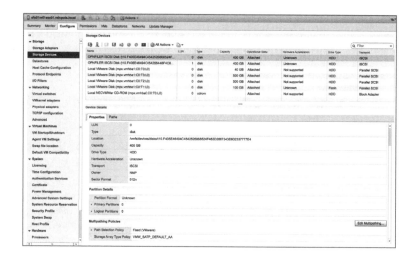

Understanding MPP Modules

The MPP module can add significantly enhanced multipathing to vSphere, and for the given LUNs it supports, it replaces the NMP, SATP, and PSP. The MPP claim policy (the LUNs that it manages) is defined on a LUN-by-LUN and array-by-array basis, and MPPs can coexist with NMP.

Because it replaces the NMP, SATP, and PSP, the MPP can change the path selection normally handled by the PSP. This allows the MPP to provide more sophisticated path selection than the VMware-supplied PSPs can, including selecting by host queue depth and, in some cases, the array target port state. As a result of this more sophisticated path selection, an MPP could offer notable performance increases or other new functionality not present in vSphere by default.

The PSA was written not only to be modular but also to support third-party extensibility; third-party SATPs, PSPs, and MPPs are technically possible. As of this writing, only a few MPPs were generally available, though other vendors are likely to create third-party SATPs, PSPs, and potentially full MPPs. Once the MPP is loaded on an ESXi host via the vSphere Web Client's host update tools, all multipathing for LUNs managed by that MPP become fully automated.

An Example of a Third-Party MPP

EMC PowerPath/VE is a third-party multipathing plug-in that supports a broad set of EMC and non-EMC array types. PowerPath/VE enhances load balancing, availability, and performance using the following techniques.

Load Balancing:

♦ Adjusts I/O paths constantly to leverage all available data paths for best performance

♦ Monitors and rebalances the environment

Availability:

◆ Through active management of intermittent path behavior

◆ Through more rapid path state detection

◆ Through automated path discovery behavior without manual rescan

Performance:

◆ Through better path selection using weighted algorithms, which is critical in cases where the paths are unequal (ALUA).

◆ Through monitoring and adjusting the ESXi host queue depth to select the path for a given I/O, shifting the workload from heavily used paths to lightly used paths.

◆ With some arrays by predictive optimization based on the array port queues. (The array port queues are generally the first point of contention and tend to affect all the ESXi hosts simultaneously; without predictive advance handling, they tend to cause simultaneous path choice across the ESXi cluster.)

In this section, you've seen how a third-party MPP might make multipathing decisions based on host or target queues. We'll review the importance of queuing in the next section.

THE IMPORTANCE OF LUN QUEUES

Queues are an important construct in block storage environments (across all protocols, including Fibre Channel, FCoE, and iSCSI). Think of a queue as a line at the supermarket checkout. Queues exist on the server (in this case the ESXi host), generally at both the HBA and LUN levels. They also exist on the storage array. Every array does this differently, but they all have the same concept. Block-centric storage arrays generally have these queues at the target ports, array-wide, at the array LUN levels, and finally at the spindles themselves. File-centric storage arrays generally have queues at the target ports and array-wide but abstract the array LUN queues because the LUNs actually exist as files in the file system. However, file-centric designs have internal LUN queues underneath the file systems themselves and then ultimately at the spindle level—in other words, it's internal to how the file server accesses its own storage.

The queue depth is a function of how fast things are being loaded into the queue and how fast the queue is being drained. How fast the queue is being drained is a function of the amount of time needed for the array to service the I/O requests. This is called the *service time*, and in the supermarket checkout it is the speed of the person behind the checkout counter (that is, the array service time).

VIEWING THE QUEUE

To determine how many outstanding items are in the queue, use esxtop, press U to get to the storage screen, and look at the QUED column. You can find more information about how to use this tool in Chapter 13, "Monitoring VMware vSphere Performance."

The array service time itself is a function of many things, predominantly the workload, then the spindle configuration, then the write cache (for writes only), then the storage processors, and finally, with certain rare workloads, the read caches.

For most customers, this issue will never come up, and all queuing will be happening behind the scenes. However, for some customers, LUN queues determine whether your VMs are happy or not from a storage performance perspective.

When a queue overflows (either because the storage configuration cannot handle the steady-state workload or because the storage configuration cannot absorb a burst), it causes many upstream effects to slow down the I/O. For IP-focused people, this effect is analogous to TCP windowing, which should be avoided for storage just as queue overflow should be avoided.

You can change the default queue depths for your HBAs and for each LUN/device. (See www.vmware.com for HBA-specific steps.) After changing the queue depths on the HBAs, you need to perform a second step at the VMkernel layer. You must change the amount of outstanding disk requests from the VMs to VMFS to match the HBA setting. You can do this in the ESXi advanced settings, as shown in Figure 6.22, or by using ESXCLI. In general, the default settings for queues and Disk.* are the best. We don't recommend changing these values unless instructed to do so by VMware or your storage vendor.

FIGURE 6.22

It is possible to adjust the advanced properties for advanced use cases, increasing the number of consecutive requests allowed to match adjusted queues.

If the queue overflow is not a case of dealing with short bursts but rather that you are underconfigured for the steady state workload, making the queues deeper can have a downside: higher latency. Then it overflows anyway. This is the predominant case, so before increasing your LUN queues, check the array service time. If it's taking more than 10 milliseconds to service I/O requests, you need to improve the service time, usually by adding more spindles to the LUN or by moving the LUN to a faster-performing tier.

The last topic we'll cover before moving on to more hands-on topics is the vSphere Storage APIs.

UNCOVERING THE vSPHERE STORAGE APIs

Formerly known as the vStorage APIs, the vSphere Storage APIs aren't necessarily application programming interfaces (APIs) in the truest sense of the word. In some cases, they are, but in other cases, they're simply storage commands that vSphere leverages.

vSphere offers several broad families of storage APIs:

◆ vSphere Storage APIs for Array Integration

◆ vSphere APIs for Storage Awareness

◆ vSphere Storage APIs for Site Recovery

◆ vSphere Storage APIs for Multipathing

◆ vSphere Storage APIs for Data Protection

Because of the previous naming conventions (vStorage APIs), some of these technologies are more popularly known by their acronyms. Table 6.2 maps the well-known acronyms to their official names.

TABLE 6.2:   vSphere Storage API acronyms

WELL-KNOWN ACRONYM	OFFICIAL NAME
VAAI	vSphere Storage APIs for Array Integration
VASA	vSphere APIs for Storage Awareness
VADP	vSphere Storage APIs for Data Protection

In this book, for consistency with the community and the marketplace, we'll use the well-known acronyms to refer to these technologies.

As we mentioned previously, some of these technologies are truly APIs. The Storage APIs for Multipathing are the APIs that VMware partners can use to create third-party MPPs, SATPs, and PSPs for use in the PSA. Similarly, the Storage APIs for Site Recovery encompass the actual programming interfaces that enable array vendors to make their storage arrays work with VMware's Site Recovery Manager product, and the Storage APIs for Data Protection (VADP) are the APIs that third-party companies can use to build virtualization-aware and virtualization-friendly backup solutions.

There are two sets remaining that we haven't yet mentioned, and that's because we'd like to delve into those a bit more deeply. Let's start with the Storage APIs for Array Integration.

Exploring the vSphere Storage APIs for Array Integration

The vSphere Storage APIs for Array Integration (more popularly known as VAAI) were first introduced in vSphere 4.1 as a means of offloading storage-related operations from the ESXi hosts to the storage array. Although VAAI is largely based on SCSI commands ratified by the T10 committee in charge of the SCSI standards, it does require appropriate support from storage vendors, so you'll want to check with your storage vendor to see what is required in order to support VAAI. In addition to the VAAI features introduced in vSphere 4.1, 5.0, and 5.5, vSphere 6.0 introduces even more storage offloads, while vSphere 6.5 and 6.7 improved upon them. Here's a quick rundown of the storage offloads available in vSphere 6.x:

Hardware-Assisted Locking Also called atomic test and set (ATS), this feature supports discrete VM locking without the use of LUN-level SCSI reservations. In the earlier section "Examining the vSphere Virtual Machine File System," we briefly described how vSphere uses SCSI reservations when VMFS metadata needs to be updated. Hardware-assisted locking allows for disk locking per sector on the storage array instead of the ESXi host locking the entire LUN, which temporarily isolates VMs on other hosts from accessing the locked LUN. Although all this happens in fractions of a second, it dramatically assists performance when lots of metadata updates are necessary (in large-scale environments or when powering on many VMs at the same time).

Hardware-Accelerated Full Copy Support for hardware-accelerated full copy allows storage arrays to make full copies of data completely internal to the array instead of requiring the ESXi host to read and write the data. This significantly reduces the storage traffic between the host and the array (and therefore the entire storage fabric) and can reduce the time required to perform operations like cloning VMs or deploying new VMs from templates. The source and destination datastore must be on the same array for this offload to function.

Hardware-Accelerated Block Zeroing Sometimes called write same, this functionality allows storage arrays to zero out large numbers of blocks to provide newly allocated storage without any previously written data. This can speed up operations like creating VMs and formatting virtual disks.

Thin Provisioning vSphere 5.0 added an additional set of hardware offloads around thin provisioning. First, vSphere is thin-provisioning aware, meaning that it will recognize when a LUN presented by an array is thin provisioned. In addition, vSphere 5.0 added, and vSphere 6.5 improved on the ability to reclaim dead space (space no longer used) via the T10 UNMAP command; this will help keep space utilization in thin-provisioned environments in check. Finally, vSphere also has support for providing advance warning of thin-provisioned out-of-space conditions and provides better handling for true out-of-space conditions.

STANDARDS-BASED OR PROPRIETARY?

So, is the functionality of VAAI standards-based or proprietary? Well, the answer is a little of both. In vSphere 4.1, the hardware-accelerated block zeroing was fully T10 compliant, but the hardware-assisted locking and hardware-accelerated full copy were not fully T10 compliant and required specific support from the array vendors. In vSphere 6.0, all three of these features are fully T10 compliant, as is the thin-provisioning support, and will work with any array that is also T10 compliant.

The NAS offloads, however, are not standards-based, and will require specific plug-ins from the NAS vendors to take advantage of these offloads.

Like previous versions, vSphere 6.7 includes hardware offloads for NAS:

Reserve Space This functionality lets you create thick-provisioned VMDKs on NFS datastores, much like what is possible on VMFS datastores.

Full File Clone The Full File Clone functionality allows offline VMDKs to be cloned (copied) by the NAS device.

Lazy File Clone This feature allows NAS devices to create native snapshots for the purpose of space-conservative VMDKs for virtual desktop infrastructure (VDI) environments. It's specifically targeted at emulating the Linked Clone functionality vSphere offers on VMFS datastores.

Extended Statistics When you're leveraging the Lazy File Clone feature, this feature allows more accurate space reporting.

In all cases, support for VAAI requires that the storage vendor's array be fully T10 compliant (for block-level VAAI commands) or support VMware's file-level NAS offloads via a vendor-supplied plug-in. Check with your storage vendor to determine what firmware revisions, software levels, or other requirements are necessary to support VAAI/VAAIv2 with vSphere 6.7.

The vSphere Web Client reports VAAI support, so it's easy to determine if your array has been recognized as VAAI capable by vSphere. Figure 6.23 shows a series of storage devices. Note the status of the Hardware Acceleration column—you can see that some datastores report Unknown in that column, which indicates that some, but not all, VAAI primitives are supported.

FIGURE 6.23
If some, but not all, of the hardware offload features are supported, the Hardware Acceleration status is listed as Unknown.

Storage Devices

Name	LUN	Type	Capacity	Operational State	Hardware Acceleration	Drive Type	Transport
OPNFILER iSCSI Disk (t10.F405E46494C4542526868524F...	0	disk	400 GB	Attached	Unknown	HDD	iSCSI
OPNFILER iSCSI Disk (t10.F405E46494C454256446F4C6...	1	disk	400 GB	Attached	Unknown	HDD	iSCSI
Local VMware Disk (mpx.vmhba1:C0:T0:L0)	0	disk	40 GB	Attached	Not supported	HDD	Parallel SCSI
Local VMware Disk (mpx.vmhba1:C0:T3:L0)	0	disk	500 GB	Attached	Not supported	HDD	Parallel SCSI
Local VMware Disk (mpx.vmhba1:C0:T2:L0)	0	disk	500 GB	Attached	Not supported	HDD	Parallel SCSI
Local VMware Disk (mpx.vmhba1:C0:T1:L0)	0	disk	100 GB	Attached	Unknown	Flash	Parallel SCSI
Local NECVMWar CD-ROM (mpx.vmhba0:C0:T0:L0)	0	cdrom		Attached	Not supported	HDD	Block Adapter

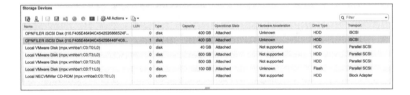

vSphere determines the hardware acceleration status for VMFS datastores and NFS datastores differently. For VMFS datastores, if all the SCSI commands are supported, the Hardware Acceleration status will list Supported. If all the commands are unsupported, it will list Not Supported. If at least one of the various SCSI commands is unsupported but others are supported, the status will be listed as Unknown. You can gather a bit more detail about which commands are supported or not supported by using the `esxcli` command-line. Run this command:

```
esxcli storage core device vaai status get
```

You'll get output that looks something like Figure 6.24. Note that on some LUNS, the commands are listed as unsupported. When there is at least one supported and one unsupported hardware offload feature per LUN, vSphere reports the status as Unknown.

FIGURE 6.24
The VAAI support detail is more granular when using ESXCLI compared with the Web Client.

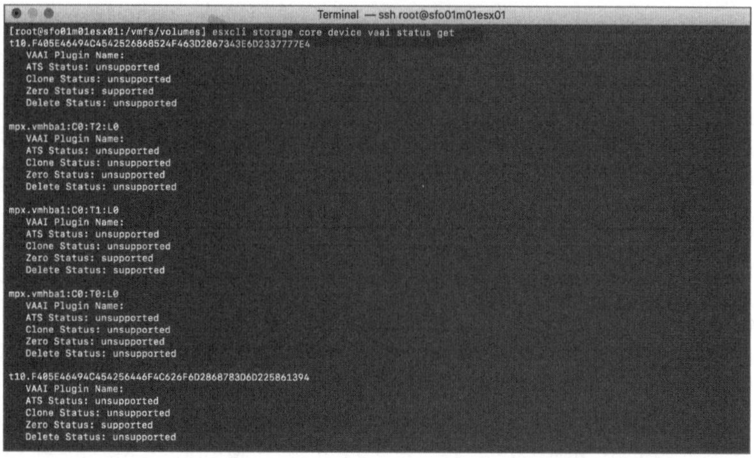

For the inquisitive types who are interested in just a bit more detail on how VAAI works and fits into the vSphere PSA, try running this command:

```
esxcli storage core claimrule list -c all
```

The output will look something like Figure 6.25.

FIGURE 6.25
VAAI works hand in hand with claim rules that are used by the PSA for assigning an SATP and PSP for detected storage devices.

This output shows you that VAAI works in conjunction with the claim rules that the PSA uses when determining the SATP and PSP for a given storage device.

VAAI is not the only mechanism for advanced storage integration with vSphere; with vSphere 5, VMware also introduced the Storage APIs for Storage Awareness, described in the next section.

DISABLING VAAI

There might be situations where disabling VAAI is required. Some advanced SAN fabric features, for example, aren't currently compatible with VAAI. To disable VAAI, set the values of the following advanced settings to 0 (zero):

◆ VMFS3.HardwareAcceleratedLocking

◆ DataMover.HardwareAcceleratedMove

◆ DataMover.HardwareAcceleratedInit

No reboot is necessary for this change to take effect. To re-enable VAAI, change the value for these advanced settings back to 1.

Exploring the vSphere Storage APIs for Storage Awareness

The vSphere APIs for Storage Awareness, more commonly known as VASA (from its previous name, the vStorage APIs for Storage Awareness), enables more advanced out-of-band communication between storage arrays and the virtualization layer. At a high level, VASA operates in the following manner:

◆ The storage array communicates its capabilities to the VASA provider. These capabilities could be just about anything: replication status, snapshot capabilities, storage tier, drive type, or IOPS capacity. Exactly which capabilities are communicated to the VASA provider are strictly determined by the storage vendor.

◆ The VASA provider communicates these capabilities to vCenter Server. This allows vSphere administrators to, for the very first time, see storage capabilities within vCenter Server.

To enable this communication, you must have a VASA provider supplied by your storage vendor. This VASA provider might be a separate VM supplied by the storage vendor, or it might be an additional service provided by the software on the array. The one restriction that VMware does place on the VASA provider is that it can't run on the same operating system as vCenter Server. Once you have this VASA provider, you'll add it to vCenter Server using the Storage Providers area found under vCenter Server Storage Providers, shown in Figure 6.26.

FIGURE 6.26
The Storage Providers area is where you go to enable communication between the VASA provider and vCenter Server.

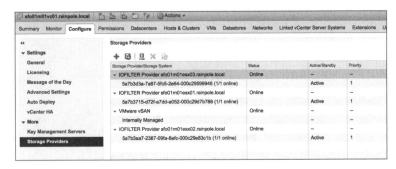

Once the storage provider has been added to vCenter Server, it will communicate storage capabilities up to vCenter Server.

However, the presence of these storage capabilities is only half the picture. The other half of the picture is what the vSphere administrator does with these capabilities: build policy-based VM storage policies, as described in the next section.

EXAMINING STORAGE POLICY–BASED MANAGEMENT

Working in conjunction with VASA, the principle behind storage policy–based management is simple: allow vSphere administrators to build VM storage policies that describe the specific storage attributes that a VM requires. Then, allow vSphere administrators to place VMs on datastores that are compliant with that storage policy, thus ensuring that the needs of the VM are properly serviced by the underlying storage. Once a VM is up and running, vCenter Server monitors will send an alert if a VM happens to be in breach of the assigned storage policy.

Working with storage policy–based management involves the following three steps:

1. Use VASA to populate system storage capabilities and/or create user-defined storage capabilities. System capabilities are automatically propagated to datastores; user-defined capabilities must be manually assigned.

2. Enable storage policies and create VM storage policies that define the specific features a VM requires from the underlying storage.

3. Assign a VM storage policy to a VM and then check its compliance (or noncompliance) with the assigned VM storage policy.

We'll provide the details on how to accomplish steps 2 and 3 later in the section "Assigning Virtual Machine Storage Policies." In the section "Assigning a Storage Capability to a Datastore," we'll show you how to assign a user-defined storage capability to a datastore.

In the section "Assigning Virtual Machine Storage Policies," you'll see how to create a VM storage policy and then determine the compliance or noncompliance of a VM with that storage policy.

For now, let's see how to create a user-defined storage capability. Keep in mind that the bulk of the power of storage policy–based management comes from the interaction with VASA to automatically gather storage capabilities from the underlying array. However, you might find it necessary or useful to define one or more additional storage capabilities that you can use in building your VM storage policies.

Before you can create a custom storage policy, you must have a tag to associate with it. Tags are explained in more detail in Chapter 3, "Installing and Configuring vCenter Server." The following steps outline how to create tags:

1. In the vSphere Web Client, navigate to the Home screen and select Tags and Custom Attributes.

2. Once in the Tags area, click the New Tag icon.

3. Name the tag **Gold Storage** and select New Category from the drop-down list.

4. The New Tag dialog box will expand so you can also create a category. Name this category **Storage Types**.

5. Change Cardinality to Many Tags Per Object.

6. Select the check boxes next to Datastore and Datastore Cluster, as shown in Figure 6.27.

7. Click OK.

8. Repeat steps 2 and 3 but select the Storage Types category you just created for additional silver and bronze tags.

Now that the preparation work is complete, you can perform the following steps to create a user-defined storage capability:

1. In the vSphere Web Client, select Policies And Profiles from the navigator and then click VM Storage Policies, shown in Figure 6.28.

2. On the VM Storage Policies screen, click the Create A New VM Storage Policy icon.

FIGURE 6.27
The New Tag dialog box can be expanded to also create a tag category.

FIGURE 6.28
The VM Storage Policies area in the vSphere Web Client is one place to create user-defined storage capabilities. You can also create them from the Datastores And Datastore Clusters view.

This will bring up the Create A New VM Storage Policy Wizard.

3. Provide a name and description for the new VM storage policy and click Next.

4. The Rule-Sets explanation is displayed. Click Next.

5. On the Common Rules page, click Next.

6. Select Tag Based Placement from the Storage Type drop-down list, and choose the tag category and the tag associated with the datastores; then click OK.

Multiple tags can be added to a single rule-set and multiple rule-sets can be added to a storage policy.

7. Click Next to finish the rule-set creation and verify the matching compatible datastore(s) on the following page.

8. Click Next and then Finish to exit the Create New VM Storage Policy dialog box.

Figure 6.29 shows a number of user-defined storage policies.

FIGURE 6.29
VM storage policies can match user-defined tags or vendor-specific capabilities.

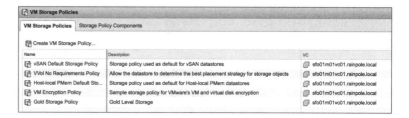

Any system-provided storage capabilities supplied by VASA providers will also show up in the Rule-Set page on the Create New VM Storage Policy dialog box. These can be substituted or used in conjunction with user-created tags as needed.

We'll come back to the VM Storage Policies area of the vSphere Web Client later in this chapter when we show you how to assign them to a VM. Before we get to that, there is a feature that debuted in vSphere 6 that you need to know. It's related to storage policies as well as the Storage APIs.

Understanding Virtual Volumes

In the previous sections, you saw that vSphere has a number of rich APIs that help facilitate vSphere to storage communication and automation. Let's look at how these APIs and policies are used in a feature called Virtual Volumes, or simply VVOLs. This technology attempts to change the way administrators manage their traditional storage arrays.

The VVOLs feature allows administrators to build feature and placement policies and then have the storage array place files (VMDKs) according to those policy requirements. These requirements could range from redundancy, IOPS, or latency to provisioning type, replication, or encryption. Usually storage administrators assign these capabilities to a LUN or an NFS mount, but with VVOLs, they can be applied to individual files.

Under the hood are a number of components that make up VVOLs, so before we get too far into the use cases, let's go over them.

VASA Provider

The VVOLs feature is not the first to introduce the concept of VASA providers, as you saw in the earlier section, "Exploring the vSphere Storage APIs for Storage Awareness." VASA providers help with communications between vSphere and the backend storage array. The type and protocol of the storage communication do not matter; the VASA 2.0 provider is the bridge between the two and helps enable the advanced storage features presented through VVOLs.

A number of storage arrays support and include a VASA provider today, but to support the additional features required for VVOLs an array firmware and VASA provider upgrade will likely be needed.

Once you have compatible array firmware and an associated Vasa Provider registered in vCenter Server, vSphere can then expose array functionality directly for use with storage policies. How is this different from storage-based policy management? It's not! The difference comes with *how*, or more accurately *where*, those policies are applied. As we mentioned, the key to understanding VVOLs is knowing that the array no longer ties capabilities to a single SAN, LUN, or NAS Export; it can attach those capabilities to a single file (usually a `.vmdk`).

Vasa Providers Can Manage Multiple Arrays

If you have multiple arrays within your environment of the same type, you may be able to use a single VASA provider to cover multiple arrays. Your storage vendor can advise you, but this is a possible configuration for some array types. Vasa Providers can be virtual appliances with special software loaded that communicate with the array; some have the Vasa Provider software running right in array firmware itself.

Protocol Endpoints (PEs)

Protocol Endpoints are a new component in the vSphere storage picture and they are used when using VVOLs. In a traditional FC, iSCSI, or NFS storage system, access control and all other "meta" storage communication happened over the same channel as the data transfer communication path. These two different types of communication have been separated through the use of Protocol Endpoints. While the physical storage fabric between your ESXi hosts and your storage array will not change when using VVOLs, the way in which you present your storage will.

Since VVOLs work with FC, FCoE, iSCSI, and NFS, you no longer have to worry about which protocol to use to allow for certain features to be enabled. Provided the array is VVOL enabled, the protocol is abstracted from this decision. All existing zoning and path policies get applied to the PE. You can simply decide which PE gets exposed to each host within your storage arrays management interface.

ESXi scans the storage fabric every few minutes for new PEs. The discovered PEs are maintained in the vCenter Server database, and once registered, can be used to expose Storage Containers.

Storage Container (SC)

When using VVOLs, instead of managing traditional LUNs, you manage storage containers (SCs). VVOLs are stored in SCs and VMs files are located inside these VVOLs. Although it may seem a complex hierarchy at first, it is necessary to enable the flexibility of VVOLs. Figure 6.30 shows how the structure logically fits together.

As with traditional storage LUNs, SCs are created by the storage administrator. SCs have no explicit restrictions and therefore capacity is based on what is available on the array. A single SC cannot stretch between arrays, but if a VM has multiple VMDKs, these files can reside between different SCs.

As mentioned in the previous section, "Protocol Endpoints (PEs)" ESXi hosts run a Discovery Process to scan for new protocol endpoints every 300 seconds. The end-to-end high-level process for getting VVOLs up and running looks like this:

FIGURE 6.30
The layout of VVOLs differs greatly from traditional LUNs.

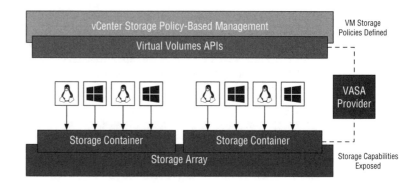

- The protocol endpoint and associated storage container is created on a backend storage array.

- Array capabilities are applied to each SC.

- The VASA provider discovers each SC and reports them to vCenter Server.

- VMs can then be provisioned in SC (shown as a datastore) with an associated storage policy.

SCs vs. LUNs

Table 6.3 outlines the scale differences between a LUN-based storage system and one that is enabled with VVOLs. It's easy to see that there are advantages, especially if you run up against the current vSphere LUN storage maximum limits.

TABLE 6.3:   VVOL storage containers vs. LUNs

	STORAGE CONTAINERS	**LUNS**
Maximum size	Unlimited (limited based on array capacity)	64TB
Number	1000s, based on array capability	256
Capabilities	VMDK based	LUN based
Commands	API	In-band file system

Do you still need to create datastores? In a word, yes. A datastore *is* a storage container. Although it's not formatted with VMFS like traditional datastores, you must still create one to ensure that all features are linked to the datastore construct (FT, HA, DRS, and so on). The real power of VVOLs comes when you apply a storage policy not to a datastore, but to a VM VMDK

Storage Policies

As noted earlier in this section, storage policies are built on capabilities presented by the array. Some arrays will only have a subset of capabilities, and others will have a fuller set. At times, th will depend on the array itself; other times, some features will be based on the licensing applied to the array (that is, what you've paid for). The storage capabilities are advertised to ESXi hosts through VASA APIs (VASA 2.0). Here are some of the possible capabilities:

◆ Disk Type

◆ Encryption

◆ Deduplication

◆ Replication

◆ Snapshots

◆ QOS

◆ IOPS

◆ Read and/or Write Latency

◆ Backup

◆ High Availability

These capabilities depend on what the particular array offers and will vary from array to array and vendor to vendor.

Virtual Volumes

Finally, we make it to what an *actual* Virtual Volume is: an object that represents a container for part of a VM. As explained in Chapter 9, a number of files make up VMs. VVOLs are effectively a container for each of these same files:

◆ Config-VVOL – Metadata

◆ `.lck`

◆ `.vmsd`

◆ `.hlog`

◆ `.nvram`

◆ `.vmx`

◆ `.log`

◆ Data-VVOL – VMDKs

◆ Mem-VVOL – Snapshots

◆ Swap-VVOL – Swap files

◆ Other-VVOL – Vendor specific

When an ESXi host is communicating with a storage array with VVOLs enabled, an I/O path is established through a VASA bind request. The VASA provider returns the protocol endpoint (PE) ID, to which the VVOL is bound, and a unique ID to be used for I/O between the bound VVOL and PE. In the case of Fibre Channel or iSCSI, this is a secondary LUN ID; for NAS storage, it's an actual file path.

The benefits of VVOLs are obvious: no more LUN limits, granular policy allocation, and a way to ensure all storage capabilities can be used by VMware administrators. Now that I've covered some old and new vSphere-specific storage theory, let's move on to working with these technologies. First, we'll look at datastores.

Working with VMFS Datastores

It's time to shift the focus away from concepts and into practice. Next, let's take a look at working with VMFS datastores. As you have learned, VMFS is the file system that vSphere uses for all block-based storage, so it's common. Working with VMFS datastores will be a daily task that you, as a vSphere administrator, will be responsible for accomplishing.

Let's start with adding a VMFS datastore. Every VMFS datastore is backed by a LUN, so first we'll need to review the process for adding a LUN to your ESXi hosts. The process for adding a LUN will vary based on the block storage protocol, so the next three sections will describe adding a LUN via Fibre Channel, adding a LUN via FCoE (these are essentially the same), and adding a LUN via iSCSI.

Adding a LUN via Fibre Channel

Adding a LUN to vSphere via Fibre Channel is really more of a task for the storage administrato (who might also be the vSphere administrator in some environments). As we mentioned earlier, in the section "Overview of Fibre Channel," making a LUN visible over a Fibre Channel SAN involves a few steps, only one of which is done in the vSphere environment:

1. Zone the Fibre Channel SAN so that the ESXi host(s) can see the target port(s) on the storage array.

2. On the storage array, present the LUN to the ESXi host(s). This procedure varies from vendor to vendor. In a NetApp environment, this involves adding the host's WWNs to ar initiator group (or *igroup*). Depending on your storage vendor, this process will be different, so refer to your storage vendor's instructions.

3. Rescan for new storage devices on the ESXi host.

That last step is the only one that involves the vSphere environment. There are two ways to rescan for new storage devices: you can rescan a specific storage adapter, or you can rescan all storage adapters.

Perform the following steps to rescan only a specific storage adapter:

1. In the vSphere Web Client, navigate to the Configure tab for a specific ESXi host in the Hosts And Clusters view.

2. In the Storage subsection, select Storage Adapters from the left.

   This will display the storage adapters recognized in the selected ESXi host.

3. Click the Rescan All Storage Adapters icon.

4. If you want to scan only for new LUNs that have been zoned or presented to the ESXi host, select Scan For New Storage Devices and deselect Scan For New VMFS Volumes.

5. If you want to scan only for new VMFS datastores, deselect Scan For New Storage Device and select Scan For New VMFS Volumes.

6. If you want to do both, simply click OK (both are selected by default). You'll see the appropriate tasks appear in the Tasks pane of the vSphere Web Client.

You'll note that two tasks appear in the Recent Tasks pane of the vSphere Web Client: a task for rescanning all the HBAs and a task for rescanning VMFS.

The task for rescanning the HBAs is pretty straightforward; this is a query to the host HBAs to see if new storage is available. If new storage is available to an adapter, it will appear in the details pane of the Storage Adapters area in the vSphere Web Client.

The second task is a bit different. The VMFS rescan is triggered automatically, and it scans available storage devices for an existing VMFS datastore. If it finds an existing VMFS datastore, it will attempt to mount the VMFS datastore and make it available to the ESXi host. Automatically triggering the VMFS rescan simplifies the process of making new VMFS datastores available to ESXi hosts.

In addition to rescanning just all HBAs or CNAs, you can rescan a single storage adapter. To do so, follow these steps:

1. In the vSphere Web Client, navigate to the Configure tab for a specific ESXi host in the Hosts And Clusters view.

2. From the Storage subsection, select Storage Adapters on the left.

3. Select one of the adapters in the list and then click the Rescan icon above the list.

RESCANNING AN ENTIRE CLUSTER

If you right-click a cluster object in the Hosts And Clusters view, you can also rescan an entire cluster for new storage objects by clicking Storage Rescan Storage.

Assuming that the zoning of your Fibre Channel SAN is correct, and that the storage has been presented to the ESXi host properly, your new LUN should appear in the details pane.

Once the LUN is visible, you're ready to create a new VMFS datastore on it, but before we get to that, let's explore the processes for adding a LUN via FCoE and via iSCSI.

ADDING A LUN VIA FCOE

The process for adding a LUN via FCoE depends on whether you are using a CNA where the FCoE is handled in hardware or you are using vSphere's software-based FCoE initiator.

In versions of vSphere prior to vSphere 5.0, FCoE was supported strictly in hardware, meaning that you could use FCoE only if you had an FCoE CNA installed in your ESXi host. In this configuration, the CNA drivers presented the CNAs to the ESXi host as if they were Fibre Channel HBAs. Therefore, the process of adding a LUN to an ESXi host using hardware-based FCoE was virtually identical to the process described in the previous section. Because it's so similar, we won't repeat those steps here.

However, vSphere 5.0 added the ability to perform FCoE in software via an FCoE software initiator. There is still an element of hardware support required, though; only certain network interface cards that support partial FCoE offload are supported. Refer to the *vSphere Compatibility Guide*.

Assuming you have a supported NIC, the process for configuring the software FCoE initiator is twofold: configure the FCoE networking and then activate the software FCoE adapter. In Chapter 5, we explained in much greater detail the networking components—including virtual switches and VMkernel adapters—that will be used in the next few sections.

Perform the following steps to configure the networking for software FCoE:

1. Log into the vSphere Web Client and connect to an ESXi host or to a vCenter Server instance.

2. Navigate to the Hosts And Clusters view.

3. Select a host from the Navigator panel and then click the Configure tab.

4. Click the VMkernal Adapters link.

5. Click the Add Host Networking icon to create a new vSphere Standard Switch with a VMkernel adapter.

   When you're selecting uplinks for the new vSwitch, be sure to select the NIC that supports partial FCoE offload. You can add multiple NICs to a single vSwitch, or you can add each FCoE offload-capable NIC to a separate vSwitch. However, once you add the NICs to a vSwitch, don't remove them or you'll disrupt the FCoE traffic.

   For more information on creating a vSphere Standard Switch, creating a VMkernel adapter, or selecting uplinks for a vSwitch, refer to Chapter 5.

6. Once you've configured the network, select the Storage Adapters subsection in the ESXi host Configure tab. (You should still be on this tab after completing the network configuration.)

7. Click the Add New Storage Adapter icon, select Software FCoE Adapter, and click OK.

8. In the Add Software FCoE Adapter dialog box, select the appropriate NIC (one that supports partial FCoE offload and that was used as an uplink for the vSwitch you created previously) from the drop-down list of physical adapters.

9. Click OK.

OTHER NETWORKING LIMITATIONS FOR SOFTWARE FCoE

Don't move a network adapter port from one vSwitch to another when FCoE traffic is active or you'll run into problems. If you made this change, moving the network adapter port back to the original vSwitch will correct the problem. Reboot your ESXi host if you need to move the network adapter port permanently.

Also, be sure to use a VLAN for FCoE that is not used for any other form of networking on your ESXi host.

Double-check that you've disabled Spanning Tree Protocol (STP) on the ports that will support software FCoE from your ESXi host. Otherwise, the FCoE Initialization Protocol (FIP) exchange might be delayed and cause the software adapter not to function properly.

vSphere will create a new adapter in the list of storage adapters. Once the adapter is created, you can select it to view its properties, such as getting the WWN assigned to the software adapter. You'll use that WWN in the zoning and LUN presentation as described in the section "Adding a LUN via Fibre Channel." After you've completed the zoning and LUN presentation, you can rescan the adapter to see the new LUN appear.

Next, we'll review the procedure for adding a LUN via iSCSI.

ADDING A LUN VIA iSCSI

As with FCoE, the procedure for adding a LUN via iSCSI depends on whether you are using hardware-based iSCSI (using an iSCSI HBA) or leveraging vSphere's software iSCSI initiator.

With a hardware iSCSI solution, the configuration takes place in the iSCSI HBA itself. The instructions for configuring your iSCSI HBA will vary from vendor to vendor; so refer to your vendor's documentation on how to configure it to properly connect to your iSCSI SAN. After the iSCSI HBA is configured, the process for adding a LUN via hardware-based iSCSI is much like the process for Fibre Channel, so we won't repeat the steps here.

If you instead choose to use vSphere's software iSCSI initiator, you can take advantage of iSCSI connectivity without the need for iSCSI hardware installed in your server.

As with the software FCoE adapter, there are a couple of different steps involved in setting up the software iSCSI initiator:

1. Configure networking for the software iSCSI initiator.

2. Activate and configure the software iSCSI initiator.

The following sections describe these steps in more detail.

Configuring Networking for the Software iSCSI Initiator

With iSCSI, although the Ethernet stack can technically be used to perform some multipathing and load balancing, this is not how iSCSI is generally designed. iSCSI uses the same multipath I/O (MPIO) storage framework as Fibre Channel and FCoE SANs. As a result, a specific networking configuration is required to support this framework. In particular, you'll need to configure the networking so that each path through the network uses only a single physical NIC. The MPIO framework can then use each NIC as a path and perform the appropriate multipathing functions. This configuration also allows iSCSI connections to scale across multiple NICs; using Ethernet-based techniques like link aggregation will increase overall throughput but will not increase throughput for any single iSCSI target.

Perform the following steps to configure the virtual networking properly for the software iSCSI initiator:

1. In the vSphere Web Client, navigate to the Hosts And Clusters view and select an ESXi host from the inventory panel.

2. Select the Configure tab and then click Virtual Switches.

3. Create a new vSwitch with at least two uplinks. Make sure all uplinks are listed as active NICs in the vSwitch's failover order.

   You can also use a vSphere Distributed Switch, but for simplicity, we'll use a vSwitch in this procedure.

USING SHARED UPLINKS VS. DEDICATED UPLINKS

Generally, a bet-the-business iSCSI configuration will use dedicated uplinks. However, if you are using 10 Gigabit Ethernet, you may have only two uplinks. In this case, you will have to use shared uplinks. If at all possible, we recommend configuring Quality of Service on the vSwitch, either by using a vSphere Distributed Switch with Network I/O Control or DSCP/QoS. This will help ensure that iSCSI traffic is granted the appropriate network bandwidth so that your storage performance doesn't suffer.

4. Create a VMkernel adapter for use by iSCSI. Configure the VMkernel adapter to use only one of the available uplinks on the vSwitch.

5. Repeat step 4 for each uplink on the vSwitch. Ensure that each VMkernel adapter is assigned only one active uplink and that no uplinks are shared between VMkernel adapters.

Figure 6.31 shows the NIC Teaming tab for an iSCSI VMkernel adapter; note that only one uplink is listed as an active NIC. All other uplinks must be set to unused in this configuration.

FIGURE 6.31

For proper iSCSI multipathing and scalability, only one uplink can be active for each iSCSI VMkernel adapter. All others must be set to unused.

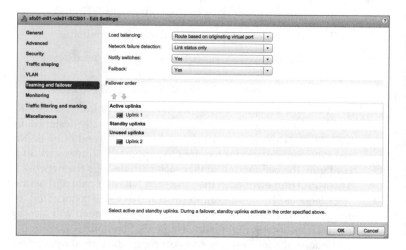

WHAT'S THE MAXIMUM NUMBER OF LINKS THAT YOU CAN USE FOR ISCSI?

You can use the method shown previously to drive I/O down eight separate vmnics.

Within the vSphere Web Client, you create both switches and VMkernel adapters. For more information on how to create a vSwitch, assign uplinks, create VMkernel adapters, and modify the NIC failover order for a vSwitch or VMkernel adapter, refer to Chapter 5.

When you finish with the networking configuration, you're ready for the next step.

Activating and Configuring the Software iSCSI Initiator

After configuring the network appropriately for iSCSI, perform these steps to activate and configure the software iSCSI initiator:

1. In the vSphere Web Client, navigate to the Hosts And Clusters view and select an ESXi host from the inventory panel.

2. Click the Configure tab and select the Storage Adapters subsection.

3. Click the Add New Storage Adapter (+) icon. From the Add Storage Adapter drop-down list, select Software iSCSI Adapter and click OK.

4. A dialog box will appear, informing you that a software iSCSI will be added to the list of storage adapters. Click OK.

   After a few moments, a new storage adapter under iSCSI Software Adapter will appear, as shown in Figure 6.32.

FIGURE 6.32

This storage adapter is where you will perform the configuration for the software iSCSI initiator.

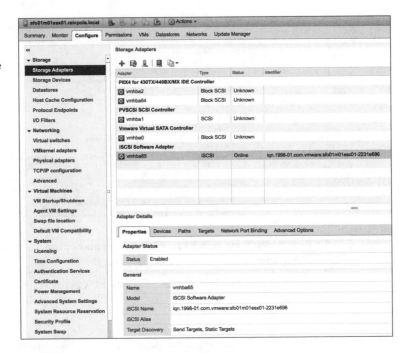

5. Select the new iSCSI adapter.

6. Click the Network Port Binding tab.

7. Click the Add button to add a VMkernel adapter binding.

   This will create the link between a VMkernel adapter used for iSCSI traffic and a physical NIC.

8. From the Bind With VMkernel Network Adapter dialog box, select a compliant port group.

   A compliant port group is a port group with a VMkernel adapter configured with only a single physical uplink. Figure 6.33 shows an example of two compliant port groups you could select to bind to the VMkernel network adapter.

   Click OK after selecting a compliant port group.

FIGURE 6.33
Only compliant port groups will be listed as available to bind with the VMkernel adapter.

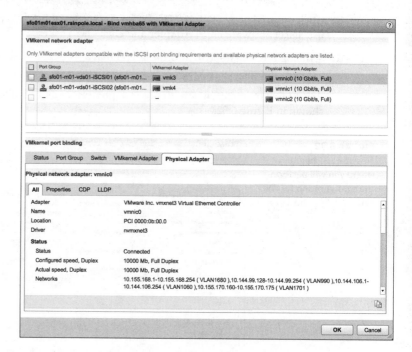

9. Repeat step 8 for each VMkernel adapter and uplink you created previously when configuring the network for iSCSI.

   When you've finished, the iSCSI initiator Properties dialog box will look something like Figure 6.34.

FIGURE 6.34
These settings allow for robust multipathing and greater bandwidth for iSCSI storage configurations.

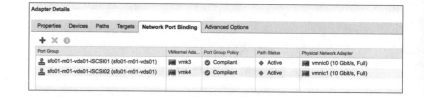

10. Select the Targets tab, and under Dynamic Discovery, click Add.

11. In the Add Send Target Server dialog box, enter the IP address(es) of the iSCSI target. Click OK when you've finished.

Configuring discovery tells the iSCSI initiator the iSCSI target it should communicate with to get details about available storage. The iSCSI initiator logs in to the target, which makes it known to the iSCSI target. This also populates all the other known iSCSI targets and populates the Static Discovery entries.

12. Finally, click the Rescan Adapter icon to discover any new storage devices.

If you've already performed the necessary masking/presentation tasks on the iSCSI array to make LUNs available, the LUN should now show up in the list of devices on the software iSCSI adapter, and you can use that LUN to create a VMFS datastore. If you haven't already presented the LUN to the ESXi host, you'll need to do so according to your vendor's instructions (every array vendor is different). After you present storage to the host, rescan the iSCSI adapter (using the procedure outlined in the section "Adding a LUN via Fibre Channel," earlier in this chapter), and this should cause the device to show up.

TROUBLESHOOTING iSCSI LUNs

If you're having a problem getting the iSCSI LUN to show up on your ESXi host, check the following troubleshooting list:

◆ Can you ping the iSCSI target from the initiator? (Use the Direct Console User Interface [DCUI] to test connectivity from the ESXi host or enable the ESXi shell and use the vmkping command.)

◆ Is MTU configured correctly on the VMkernel adapters? In other words, is the jumbo frames setting enabled, and if so, is it configured correctly end to end?

◆ Is the physical cabling correct? Are the link lights showing a connected state on the physical interfaces on the ESXi host, the Ethernet switches, and the iSCSI arrays?

◆ Are your VLANs configured correctly? If you've configured VLANs, have you properly configured the same VLAN on the host, the switch, and the interface(s) that will be used on the array for the iSCSI target?

◆ Is your IP routing correct and functional? Have you properly configured the IP addresses of the VMkernel adapter and the interface(s) that will be used on the array for the iSCSI target?

◆ Is iSCSI traffic being allowed through any firewalls? If the ping succeeds but subsequently the iSCSI initiator can't log into the iSCSI target, check whether TCP port 3620 is being blocked by a firewall somewhere in the path. Again, the general recommendation is to avoid firewalls in the midst of the iSCSI data path wherever possible to avoid introducing additional latency.

◆ Is your CHAP configuration correct? Have you correctly configured authentication on both the iSCSI initiator and the iSCSI target?

Now that you have a LUN presented and visible to the ESXi hosts, you can add (or create) a VMFS datastore on that LUN. We'll cover this process in the next section.

CREATING A VMFS DATASTORE

When you have a LUN available to the ESXi hosts, you can create a VMFS datastore.

Before starting this process, you'll want to double-check that the LUN for the new VMFS datastore is shown under the configuration's Storage Adapters list. (LUNs appear in the bottom of the vSphere Web Client properties pane associated with a storage adapter.) If you've provisioned a LUN that doesn't appear, rescan for new devices.

Perform the following steps to configure a VMFS datastore on an available LUN:

1. Launch the vSphere Web Client if it isn't already running and connect to a vCenter Server instance.

2. Navigate to the Hosts And Clusters view.

3. Select an ESXi host, click the Configure tab and then select the Datastores section.

4. Click the New Datastore icon to launch the New Datastore Wizard.

ANOTHER WAY TO OPEN THE NEW DATASTORE WIZARD

You can also access the New Datastore Wizard by right-clicking a datacenter or ESXi host object in the navigator and selecting Storage New Datastore from the menu.

---

5. On the first screen of the New Datastore Wizard, you are prompted for the storage type. Select VMFS, and click Next.

    We'll show you how to use the Add Storage Wizard to create an NFS and VVOL datastore in later sections.

6. Create a name for the new datastore, and then if prompted, select a host that can access the LUN.

    We recommend that you use as descriptive a name as possible. You might also consider using a naming scheme that includes an array identifier, a LUN identifier, a protection detail (RAID type and whether it is replicated remotely for disaster recovery purposes), or other key configuration data. Clear datastore naming can help the vSphere administrator later in determining VM placement and can help streamline troubleshooting if a problem arises.

7. Select the LUN on which you want to create the new VMFS datastore.

    For each visible LUN, you will see the LUN name and identifier information, along with the LUN. Figure 6.35 shows two available LUNs on which to create a VMFS datastore.

    After you've selected the LUN you want to use, click Next.

8. The next screen lets you choose the VMFS version. You should choose VMFS version 6 unless this is a mixed cluster with ESXi 6 or earlier hosts.

9. The next screen, shown in Figure 6.36, summarizes the details of the LUN selected and the action that will be taken. If it's a new LUN (no preexisting VMFS partition), the wizard will note that a VMFS partition will be created.

FIGURE 6.35
You'll choose from a list of available LUNs when creating a new VMFS datastore.

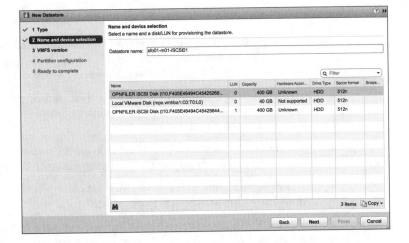

FIGURE 6.36
The Partition Layout screen provides information on the partitioning action that will be taken to create a VMFS datastore on the selected LUN.

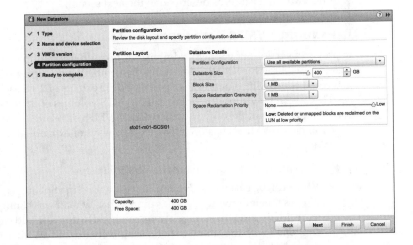

Click Next to continue. If the selected LUN has an existing VMFS partition, some different options will appear; see the section "Expanding a VMFS Datastore," later in this chapter, for more information.

Generally speaking, you will select Use All Available Partitions to use all the space available on the LUN. If you can't or don't want to use all of the space available on the LUN, change the datastore size and specify the size of the VMFS datastore you are creating. Click Next when you are ready to proceed.

10. At the Ready To Complete screen, double-check all the information. If everything is correct, click Finish; otherwise, use the Back button to go back and make any changes.

When you click Finish and finish creating the datastore, vSphere will trigger the remaining hosts in the same cluster to rescan for new devices. This ensures that the other hosts in the cluster will also see the LUN and the VMFS datastore on that LUN. You will still need to rescan for devices (using the process in the sections on adding a LUN) for ESXi hosts that are not in the same cluster.

After you've created a VMFS datastore, you may need to complete a few extra tasks. Althoug these tasks are storage-related, they appear in other areas of the book. Here's a quick reference to some of the other tasks you might need to perform on a VMFS datastore:

◆ To enable Storage I/O Control, a mechanism for enforcing prioritized access to storage I/O resources, refer to the section "Controlling Storage I/O Utilization" in Chapter 11, "Managing Resource Allocation."

◆ To create a datastore cluster to enable Storage DRS, refer to "Creating and Working with Datastore Clusters" in Chapter 12, "Balancing Resource Utilization."

◆ To create some alarms on this new VMFS datastore, refer to "Using Alarms" in Chapter 13 "Monitoring VMware vSphere Performance."

Creating new VMFS datastores is not the only way to make additional space available to vSphere for use by VMs. Depending on your configuration, you might be able to expand an existing VMFS datastore, as described in the next section.

EXPANDING A VMFS DATASTORE

In previous versions of vSphere, administrators could use multiple extents as a way of getting past the 2 TB limit for VMFS-3 datastores. By combining multiple extents, vSphere administrators could take VMFS-3 datastores up to 64 TB (32 extents of 2 TB each). VMFS-5 eliminates this need because it now supports single-extent VMFS volumes of up to 64 TB in size. However, adding extents is not the only way to expand a VMFS datastore.

If you have a VMFS datastore, there are two ways of expanding it to make more space available:

◆ You can dynamically expand the VMFS datastore.

VMFS can be easily and dynamically expanded in vSphere without adding extents, as long as the underlying LUN has more capacity than was configured in the VMFS datastore. Many modern storage arrays can nondisruptively add capacity to a LUN; when combined with the ability to nondisruptively expand a VMFS volume, this gives you a great deal of flexibility as a vSphere administrator.

◆ You can add an extent.

You can also expand a VMFS datastore by adding an extent. You need to add an extent if the underlying LUN on which the datastore resides does not have any additional free space available.

These procedures are extremely similar; many of the steps in both procedures are exactly the same.

Perform these steps to expand a VMFS datastore (either by nondisruptively expanding the datastore on the same LUN or by adding an extent):

1. In the vSphere Web Client, navigate to Hosts And Clusters.

2. Select a host on the left, and then click the Configure tab.

3. From the Datastores subsection, select the datastore you wish to expand.

4. Click the green Increase Datastore Capacity icon, shown in Figure 6.37. This will open the Increase Datastore Capacity Wizard.

FIGURE 6.37

From the Datastores subsection of the Configure tab, you can increase the size of the datastore.

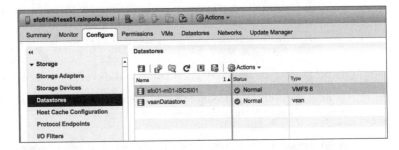

You'll note that this wizard looks similar to the Add Storage Wizard you saw previously when creating a new VMFS datastore.

5. If the underlying LUN has free space available, the Expandable column will report Yes, as shown in Figure 6.38. Select this LUN to nondisruptively expand the VMFS datastore using the free space on the same LUN.

FIGURE 6.38

If the Expandable column reports Yes, the VMFS volume can be expanded into the available free space.

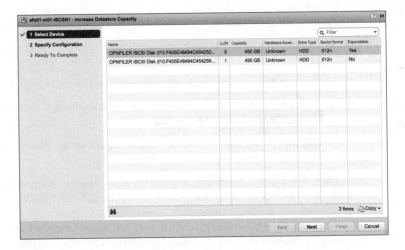

If the underlying LUN has no additional free space available, the Expandable column will report No, and you must expand the VMFS datastore by adding an extent. Select an available LUN.

Click Next when you are ready to proceed.

6. If you are expanding the VMFS datastore using free space on the LUN, the Specify Configuration screen will report that the free space will be used to expand the volume.

If you are adding an extent to the VMFS datastore, the Specify Configuration screen will indicate that a new partition will be created.

Click Next to proceed.

7. If you didn't want to use or couldn't use all of the free space on the underlying LUN, you could change the capacity from Maximize Available Space to Custom Space Setting and specify the amount. Generally, you will leave the default of Maximize Available Space selected. Click Next.

8. Review the summary information, and if everything is correct, click Finish.

Regardless of the procedure used to expand the datastore, it is nondisruptive—there is no need to evacuate VMs or incur downtime.

ASSIGNING A STORAGE CAPABILITY TO A DATASTORE

As we explained earlier in "Examining Storage Policy–Based Management," you can define your own set of storage capabilities. These user-defined storage capabilities will be used with system-provided storage capabilities (supplied by VASA) in determining the compliance or noncompliance of a VM with its assigned VM storage policy. We'll discuss the creation of VM storage policies and compliance later in this chapter, in the section "Assigning Virtual Machine Storage Policies." In this section, we'll show you how to assign a user-defined storage capability to a datastore.

Perform these steps to assign a user-defined storage capability to a datastore:

1. Launch the vSphere Web Client if it's not already running and connect to a vCenter Server instance.

Storage policy–based management requires a vCenter Server.

2. From the vSphere Web Client Storage view, right-click a datastore and select Tags & Custom Attributes ➤ Assign Tag.

vCenter Server will assign the selected capability to the datastore, and it will show up in the datastore details view.

Prior to vSphere 5.5, storage capabilities were directly assigned to a datastore. As you can see from the steps just outlined, the process is slightly different and uses tags to create a link between a datastore and a storage policy.

There are other datastore properties that you might also need to edit or change, such as renaming a datastore. That process is described in the next section.

RENAMING A VMFS DATASTORE

You can rename a VMFS datastore in two ways:

◆ Right-click a datastore object and select Rename.

◆ When a datastore is selected in the navigator, the Actions drop-down menu next to its name in the content area also has the Rename command.

Both methods will produce the same result; the datastore will be renamed. You can use whichever method better suits you.

Modifying the multipathing policy for a VMFS datastore is another important function you should be familiar with.

Modifying the Multipathing Policy for a VMFS Datastore

In the earlier section "Reviewing Multipathing," we described vSphere's Pluggable Storage Architecture (PSA) and how it manages multipathing for block-based storage devices. VMFS datastores are built on block-based storage devices, so viewing or changing the multipathing configuration for a VMFS datastore is an integral part of working with VMFS datastores.

Changing the multipathing policy for a VMFS datastore is done using the Manage Paths button on the Datastore Manage tab in the Settings subsection. The Edit Multipathing button is shown in Figure 6.39.

FIGURE 6.39

You'll use the Edit Multipathing button in the Datastore Manage Settings area to modify the multipathing policy.

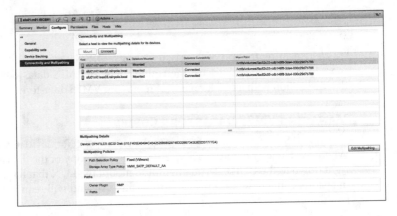

When you select Edit Multipathing, the Edit Multipathing Policies dialog box opens. From Figure 6.40 and from the information in this chapter, you should be able to deduce a few key facts:

◆ This VMFS datastore is hosted on an active-active storage array; the currently assigned policy is Fixed (VMware), which is the default for an active-active array.

◆ This VMFS datastore resides on the first LUN. This is noted by the LUN column and also the L0 in the runtime name.

To change the multipathing policy, simply select a new policy from the Path Selection Policy drop-down list and click OK. One word of caution: Choosing the wrong path selection policy for your specific storage array can cause problems, so be sure to choose a path selection policy recommended by your storage vendor. In this particular case, the Round Robin policy is also supported by active-active arrays such as the array hosting this LUN, so we'll change the path selection to Round Robin (VMware). Changes to the path selection are immediate and do not require a reboot.

FIGURE 6.40

This datastore resides on an active-active array. You can tell this by the currently assigned path selection policy and the storage array type information.

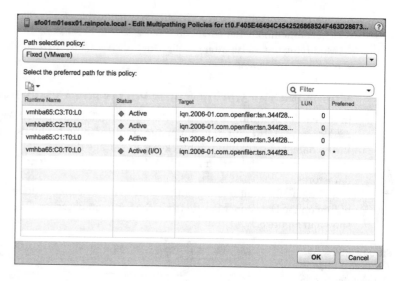

We're nearing the end of the discussion of VMFS datastores, but we do need to cover two more topics. First, we'll discuss managing copies of VMFS datastores, and then we'll wrap up this discussion with a quick review of removing VMFS datastores.

MANAGING VMFS DATASTORE COPIES

Every VMFS datastore has a universally unique identifier (UUID) embedded in the file system. When you clone or replicate a VMFS datastore, the copy of the datastore is a byte-for-byte copy, right down to the UUID. If you attempt to mount the LUN that has the copy of the VMFS datastore, vSphere will see this as a duplicate copy and will require that you do one of two things:

- Unmount the original and mount the copy with the same UUID.

- Keep the original mounted and write a new signature to the copy.

Other storage operations might also cause this behavior. If you change the LUN ID after creating a VMFS datastore, vSphere will recognize that the UUID is now associated with a new device (vSphere uses the NAA ID to track the devices) and will follow this behavior.

In either case, vSphere provides a GUI in the Add Storage Wizard where you can clearly choose which option you'd like to use in these situations:

- Choose Keep Existing Signature if you want to mount the datastore copy without writing a new signature. vSphere won't allow UUID collisions, so you can mount without resignaturing only if the original datastore has been unmounted or no longer exists (this is the case if you change the LUN ID, for example). If you mount a datastore copy without resignaturing and then later want to mount the original, you'll need to unmount the copy first.

- Choose Assign A New Signature if you want to write a new signature onto the VMFS datastore. You can then have both the copy and the original mount as separate and distinct datastores. Keep in mind that this process is irreversible—you can't undo the resignaturing operation. If the resignatured datastore contains any VMs, you will likely need to reregister those VMs in vCenter Server because the paths to the VM's configuration files will have changed. The section "Adding or Registering Existing VMs" in Chapter 9 describes how to reregister a VM. For VMFS datastores with large numbers of VMs to register to inventory, this can be accomplished quickly, easily, and dynamically with a PowerCLI script. Chapter 14, "Automating VMware vSphere," has more information about how to save time and automate administration tasks with PowerCLI.

Let's take a look at removing a VMFS datastore.

Removing a VMFS Datastore

Removing a VMFS datastore is, fortunately, as straightforward as it seems. To remove a VMFS datastore, simply right-click the datastore object and select Delete Datastore. The vSphere Web Client will prompt for confirmation, reminding you that you will lose all the files associated with all VMs on this datastore, before deleting the datastore. It is good practice to unmount any datastores prior to deleting them. This will ensure that all hosts are aware that the files on the datastore are going away. Remember that with clustered file systems like VMFS, every action you take on the datastore affects all connected hosts. For more information about correctly removing datastores from a host, check out the VMware KB here: `http://kb.vmware.com/kb/2004605.`

As with many of the other datastore-related tasks you've seen, the vSphere Web Client will trigger a VMFS rescan for other ESXi hosts so that all hosts are aware that the VMFS datastore has been deleted.

Like resignaturing a datastore, deleting a datastore is irreversible. Once you delete a datastore, you can't recover the datastore or any of the files that were stored in it. Be sure to double-check that you're deleting the right datastore before you proceed!

Let's now shift from working with VMFS datastores to working with another form of block-based storage, albeit one that is far less frequently used: raw device mappings (RDMs).

Working with Raw Device Mappings

Although the concept of shared pool mechanisms (like VMFS or NFS datastores) for VMs works well for many use cases, there are certain use cases where a storage device must be presented directly to the guest operating system inside a VM.

vSphere provides this functionality via an RDM. RDMs are presented to your ESXi hosts and then via vCenter Server directly to a VM. Subsequent data I/O bypasses the VMFS and Volume Manager completely, though management is handled via a mapping file that is stored on a VMFS volume.

In-Guest iSCSI as an Alternative to RDMs

In addition to using RDMs to present storage devices directly to the guest OS inside a VM, you can use in-guest iSCSI software initiators. We'll provide more information on that scenario in the section "Using In-Guest iSCSI Initiators," later in this chapter.

RDMs should be viewed as a tactical tool in the vSphere administrators' toolkit rather than as a common use case. A misconception is that RDMs perform better than VMFS. In reality, the performance delta between the storage types is within the margin of error of tests. Although it is possible to oversubscribe a VMFS or NFS datastore (because they are shared resources) and not an RDM (because it is presented to specific virtual machines only), this is better handled through design and monitoring rather than through the extensive use of RDMs. In other words, if your concerns about oversubscription of a storage resource are driving the choice of an RDM over a shared datastore model, simply avoid putting multiple VMs in the pooled datastore.

You can configure RDMs in two different modes.

Physical Compatibility Mode (pRDM)   In this mode, all I/O passes directly through to the underlying LUN device, and the mapping file is used solely for locking and vSphere management tasks. Generally, when a storage vendor says "RDM" without specifying further, it implies physical compatibility mode RDM. You might also see this referred to as a pass-through disk.

Virtual Compatibility Mode (vRDM)   In this mode, there is still a mapping file, but it enables more (not all) features that are supported with normal VMDKs. Generally, when VMware says "RDM" without specifying further, it implies a virtual mode RDM.

Contrary to common misconception, both modes support almost all vSphere advanced functions such as vSphere HA and vMotion, but there is one important difference: virtual mode RDMs can be included in a vSphere snapshot, whereas physical mode RDMs cannot. This inability to take a native vSphere snapshot of a pRDM also means that features that depend on snapshots don't work with pRDMs. In addition, a virtual mode RDM can go from virtual mode RDM to a virtual disk via Storage vMotion, but a physical mode RDM cannot.

PHYSICAL OR VIRTUAL? BE SURE TO ASK!

When a feature specifies RDM as an option, make sure to check the type: physical compatibility mode or virtual mode. Physical compatibility mode may have once been assumed because of legacy application or OS requirements, but as virtualization has become more commonplace, ensure you understand the true requirement. If possible, avoid all types of RDMs. They can be painful to manage when dealing with large and complex storage environments.

The most common use case for RDMs are VMs configured as Windows clusters. In recent Windows Server releases, this is called Windows Failover Clusters (WFC), and in Windows Server 2003, this is called Microsoft Cluster Services (MSCS). In Chapter 7, the section "Introducing Windows Server Failover Clustering" provides full details on how to use RDMs with Windows Server–based clusters.

Another important use case of pRDMs is that they can be presented from a VM to a physical host interchangeably. This gives pRDMs a flexibility that isn't found with virtual mode RDMs or virtual disks. This flexibility is especially useful in cases where an independent software vendor (ISV) hasn't yet embraced virtualization and indicates that virtual configurations are not supported. In this instance, the RDMs can easily be moved to a physical host to reproduce the issue on a physical machine.

In a small set of use cases, storage vendor features and functions depend on the guest directly accessing the LUN and therefore need pRDMs. For example, certain arrays, use in-band communication for management to isolate management from the IP network. This means the management traffic is communicated via the block protocol (most commonly Fibre Channel). In these cases, if they are used in a VM, they require pRDMs.

Finally, another example of storage features associated with RDMs are features such as application-integrated snapshot tools. These are applications that integrate with Microsoft Exchange, SQL Server, SharePoint, Oracle, and other applications to handle recovery modes and actions. Examples include EMC's Replication Manager, NetApp's SnapManager family, and Dell EqualLogic's Auto Volume Replicator tools. Previous generations of these tools required the use of RDMs, but most of the vendors now integrate with vCenter Server APIs. Check with your array vendor for the latest details.

In Chapter 7, we show you how to create an RDM, and we briefly discuss RDMs in Chapter 9.

We're now ready to shift away from block-based storage in a vSphere environment and move into a discussion of working with NAS/NFS datastores.

Working with NFS Datastores

NFS datastores are used in much the same way as VMFS datastores: as shared pools of storage for VMs. Although VMFS and NFS are both shared pools of storage for VMs, they are different in other ways. The two most important differences between VMFS and NFS datastores are as follows:

◆ With NFS datastores, the file system itself, including arbitration operations, is not managed or controlled by the ESXi host; rather, ESXi is using the NFS protocol via an NFS client to access a remote file system managed by the NFS server.

◆ With NFS datastores, all the vSphere elements of high availability and performance scaling design are not part of the storage stack but are part of the networking stack of the ESXi host.

These differences create some unique challenges in properly architecting an NFS-based solution. This is not to say that NFS is in any way inferior to block-based storage protocols; rather, the challenges that NFS presents are different challenges that many storage-savvy vSphere administrators have probably not encountered before. Networking-savvy vSphere administrators will be quite familiar with some of these behaviors.

Before going into detail on how to create or remove an NFS datastore, let's first address some of the networking-related considerations.

CRAFTING A HIGHLY AVAILABLE NFS DESIGN

High-availability design for NFS datastores is substantially different from that of block storage devices. Block storage devices use MPIO, which is an end-to-end path model. For Ethernet networking and NFS, the domain of link selection is from one Ethernet MAC to another Ethernet MAC, or one link hop. This is configured from the host to switch, from switch to host, and from NFS server to switch and switch to NFS server; Figure 6.41 shows the comparison. In the figure, "link aggregation" refers to NIC teaming where multiple connections are bonded together for greater aggregate throughput (with some caveats, explained in a moment).

FIGURE 6.41
NFS uses the network-
ing stack, not the
storage stack, for high
availability and load
balancing.

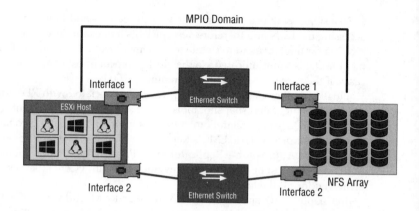

The mechanisms used to select one link, or another are fundamentally the following:

♦ A NIC teaming/link aggregation choice, which is set up per TCP connection and is either static (set up once and permanent for the duration of the TCP session) or dynamic (can be renegotiated while maintaining the TCP connection, but still always on only one link or the other).

♦ A TCP/IP routing choice, where an IP address (and the associated link) is selected based on Layer 3 routing.

How TCP is used in the NFS case is the key to understanding why NIC teaming and link aggregation techniques cannot be used to scale up the bandwidth of a single NFS datastore. MPIO-based multipathing options used for block storage and iSCSI are not options here, because NFS datastores use the networking stack, not the storage stack. The VMware NFS client uses two TCP sessions per datastore (as shown in Figure 6.42): one for control traffic and one for data flow. The TCP connection for the data flow is the vast majority of the bandwidth. With all NIC teaming/link aggregation technologies, Ethernet link choice is based on TCP connections. This happens either as a one-time operation when the connection is established with NIC teaming or dynamically, with 802.3ad. Regardless, there's always only one active link per TCP connection

FIGURE 6.42
Every NFS datastore has
two TCP connections to
the NFS server but
only one for data.

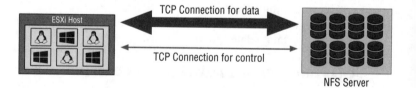

and therefore only one active link for all the data flow for a single NFS datastore.

This highlights that, as with VMFS, the "one big datastore" model is not a good design principle. However. NFS datastores are not gated by queue depths and can typically support many more VMs than a block datastore, so having fewer NFS datastores is likely. In the case of VMFS, it's not a good model because of the extremely large number of VMs and the implications on LUN queues (and to a far lesser extent, SCSI locking impact). In the case of NFS, it is not a good model because the bulk of the bandwidth would be on a single TCP session and therefore would use a single Ethernet link (regardless of network interface teaming, link aggregation, or routing). This has implications for supporting high-bandwidth workloads on NFS, as we'll explore later in this section.

Another consideration of highly available design with NFS datastores is that NAS device failover is generally longer than for a native block device. Block storage devices generally can fail over after a storage processor failure in seconds (or milliseconds). NAS devices, on the other hand, tend to fail over in tens of seconds and can take longer depending on the NAS device and the configuration specifics. Some NFS servers fail over faster, but these tend to be relatively rare in vSphere use cases. This long failover period should not be considered intrinsically negative but rather a configuration question that determines the fit for NFS datastores, based on the VM service-level agreement (SLA) expectation.

The key questions are these:

◆ How much time elapses before ESXi does something about a datastore being unreachable?

◆ How much time elapses before the guest OS does something about its virtual disk not responding?

FAILOVER IS NOT UNIQUE TO NFS

The concept of failover exists with Fibre Channel and iSCSI, though, as noted in the text, it is generally in shorter time intervals. This time period depends on specifics of the HBA configuration, but typically it is less than 30 seconds for Fibre Channel/FCoE and less than 60 seconds for iSCSI. Depending on your multipathing configuration within vSphere, path failure detection and switching to a different path might be much faster (nearly instantaneous).

The answer to both questions is a single word: time-outs. Time-outs exist at the vSphere layer to determine how much time should pass before a datastore is marked as unreachable, and time-outs exist within the guest OS to control the behavior of the guest OS. Let's look at each of these.

As of this writing, both EMC and NetApp recommend the same ESXi failover settings. Because these recommendations change, please be sure to refer to the latest recommendations from your storage vendor to be sure you have the right settings for your environment. Based on your storage vendor's recommendations, you can change the time-out value for NFS datastores by changing the values in the Edit Advanced System Settings dialog box, shown in Figure 6.43.

The current settings (as of this writing) that both EMC and NetApp recommend are as follows:

◆ NFS.HeartbeatDelta: 12

◆ NFS.HeartbeatTimeout: 5

◆ NFS.HeartbeatMaxFailures: 10

You should configure these settings across all ESXi hosts that will be connected to NFS datastores.

FIGURE 6.43

When you're configuring NFS datastores, it's important to extend the ESXi host time-outs to match the vendor best practices. This host is not configured with the recommended settings.

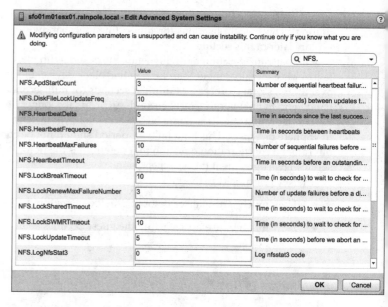

Here's how these settings work:

♦ Every NFS.HeartbeatDelta (or 12 seconds), the ESXi host checks to see that the NFS datastore is reachable.

♦ Those heartbeats expire after NFS.HeartbeatTimeout (or 5 seconds), after which another heartbeat is sent.

♦ If NFS.HeartbeatMaxFailures (or 10) heartbeats fail in a row, the datastore is marked as unavailable, and the VMs crash.

This means that the NFS datastore can be unavailable for a maximum of 125 seconds before being marked unavailable, which covers the large majority of failover events (including those fo both NetApp and EMC NAS devices serving NFS to a vSphere environment).

What does a guest OS see during this period? It sees a nonresponsive SCSI disk on the vSCSI adapter (similar to the failover behavior of a Fibre Channel or iSCSI device, though the interval i generally shorter). The disk time-out is how long the guest OS will wait while the disk is nonresponsive before throwing an I/O error. This error is a delayed write error, and for a boot volume it will result in the guest OS crashing. Windows Server, for example, has a disk time-out default of 60 seconds. A recommendation is to increase the guest OS disk time-out value to matc the NFS datastore time-out value. Otherwise, the VMs can time out their boot storage (which wi cause a crash) while ESXi is still waiting for the NFS datastore within the longer time-out value. Without extending the guest time-out, if vSphere HA is configured for VM monitoring, the VMs will reboot (when the NFS datastore returns), but obviously extending the time-out is preferable to avoid this extra step and the additional delay and extra I/O workload it generates.

Perform the following steps to set operating system time-out for Windows Server to match the 125-second maximum set for the datastore. You'll need to be logged into the Windows Server system as a user who has administrative credentials.

1. Back up your Windows Registry.

2. Select Start Run, type `regedit.exe`, and click OK.

3. In the left panel hierarchy view, double-click HKEY_LOCAL_MACHINE, then System, then CurrentControlSet, then Services, and then Disk.

4. Select the TimeOutValue value and set the data value to 125 (decimal).

There are two subcases of NFS that we want to examine briefly before we start showing you how to create and manage NFS datastores: large bandwidth workloads and large throughput workloads. Each of these cases deserves a bit of extra attention when planning your highly available design for NFS.

Supporting Large Throughput (MBps) Workloads on NFS

Throughput for large I/O sizes is generally gated by the transport link (in this case, the TCP session used by the NFS datastore is 1 Gbps or 10 Gbps) and overall network design. At larger scales, you should apply the same care and design as you would for iSCSI or Fibre Channel networks. In this case, it means carefully planning the physical network/VLAN, implementing end-to-end jumbo frames, and leveraging enterprise-class Ethernet switches with sufficient buffers to handle significant workload. At 10 GbE speeds, features such as TCP Segment Offload (TSO) and other offload mechanisms, as well as the processing power and I/O architecture of the NFS server, become important for NFS datastore and ESXi performance.

So, what is a reasonable performance expectation for bandwidth on an NFS datastore? From a bandwidth standpoint, where 1 Gbps Ethernet is used (which has 2 Gbps of bandwidth bidirectionally), the reasonable bandwidth limits are 80 MBps (unidirectional 100% read, or 100% write) to 160 MBps (bidirectional mixed read/write workloads) for a single NFS datastore. That limits scale accordingly with 10 Gigabit Ethernet. Because of how TCP connections are handled by the ESXi NFS client, and because of how networking handles link selection in link aggregation or Layer 3 routing decisions, almost all the bandwidth for a single NFS datastore will always use only one link. If you therefore need more bandwidth from an NFS datastore than a single Gigabit Ethernet link can provide, you have no other choice than to migrate to 10 Gigabit Ethernet, because link aggregation won't help (as explained earlier).

Supporting Large IOPS on NFS

High IOP workloads are usually gated by the backend configuration (as true of NAS devices as it is with block devices) and not the protocol or transport since they are also generally low throughput (MBps). By *backend*, we mean the array target. If the workload is cached, then it's determined by the cache response, which is almost always astronomical. However, in the real world most often the performance is not determined by cache response; the performance is determined by the spindle configuration that supports the storage object. In the case of NFS datastores, the storage object is the file system, so the considerations that apply at the ESXi host for VMFS (disk configuration and interface queues) apply within the NFS server.

Because the internal architecture of an NFS server varies so greatly from vendor to vendor, it's almost impossible to provide recommendations, but here are a few examples. On a NetApp FAS array, the IOPS achieved is primarily determined by the FlexVol/aggregate/RAID group configuration. On an EMC VNX array, it is likewise primarily determined by the Automated Volume Manager/dVol/RAID group configuration. Although there are other considerations (at a certain point, the scale of the interfaces on the array and the host's ability to generate I/Os become limited, but up to the limits that users commonly encounter), performance is far more often constrained by the backend disk configuration that supports the file system. Make sure your file system has sufficient backend spindles in the container to deliver performance for all the VMs that will be contained in the file system exported via NFS.

With these NFS storage design considerations in mind, let's move forward with creating and mounting an NFS datastore.

NFS MOUNTS WITH A DNS HOSTNAME

Thus far, we've been talking about how NFS always uses only a single link, and how you always need to use multiple VMkernel adapters and multiple NFS exports in order to use multiple links.

Normally, vSphere requires that you mount an NFS datastore using the same IP address or hostname and path on all hosts. vSphere 5.0 added the ability to use a DNS hostname that resolves to multiple IP addresses. However, each vSphere host will resolve the DNS name only once. This means that it will resolve to only a single IP address and will continue to use only a single link. In this case, there is no exception to the rule. However, this configuration can provide some rudimentary load balancing for multiple hosts accessing a datastore via NFS over multiple links.

CREATING AND MOUNTING AN NFS DATASTORE

In this section, we'll show you how to create and mount an NFS datastore in vSphere. The term *create* here is a bit of a misnomer; the file system is actually created on the NFS server and just exported. That process we can't really show you, because the steps vary so greatly from vendor to vendor. What works for one vendor is likely to be different for another vendor.

Before you start, ensure that you've completed the following steps:

1. You created at least one VMkernel adapter for NFS traffic. If you intend to use multiple VMkernel adapters for NFS traffic, ensure that you configure your vSwitches and physical switches appropriately, as described earlier in "Crafting a Highly Available NFS Design."

2. You configured your ESXi host for NFS storage according to the vendor's best practices, including time-out values and any other settings. As of this writing, many storage vendor recommend an important series of advanced ESXi parameter settings to maximize performance (including increasing memory assigned to the networking stack and changing other characteristics). Be sure to refer to your storage vendor's recommendations for using its product with vSphere.

3. You created a file system on your NAS device and exported it via NFS. A key part of this configuration is the specifics of the NFS export itself; the ESXi NFS client must have full root access to the NFS export. If the NFS export was exported with root squash, the file system will not be able to mount on the ESXi host. (Root users are downgraded to unprivileged file system access. On a traditional Linux system, when `root squash` is configured on the export, the remote systems are mapped to the "nobody" account.) You have one of two options for NFS exports that are going to be used with ESXi hosts:

    ◆ Use the `no_root_squash` option and give the ESXi hosts explicit read/write access.

    ◆ Add the ESXi host's IP addresses as root-privileged hosts on the NFS server.

For more information on setting up the VMkernel networking for NFS traffic, refer to Chapter 5. For more information on setting up your NFS export, refer to your storage vendor's documentation.

After you complete the preceding steps, you're ready to mount an NFS datastore. To mount an NFS datastore on an ESXi host, follow these steps:

1. Make a note of the IP address on which the NFS export is hosted as well as the name (and full path) of the NFS export; you'll need this information later in this process.

2. Launch the vSphere Web Client and connect to an ESXi host or to a vCenter Server instance.

3. In the vSphere Web Client, navigate to the Storage view.

4. Right-click the datacenter object and select Storage New Datastore. This launches the New Datastore Wizard.

5. On the Storage Type screen, select Network File System. Click Next.

6. On the Name And Configuration screen, you'll need to supply three pieces of information:

   ◆ First, you'll need to supply a datastore name. As with VMFS datastores, we recommend a naming scheme that identifies the NFS server and other pertinent information for easier troubleshooting.

   ◆ Second, a protocol selection is required, NFS 3 or 4.1. Generally you will want to select 4.1 if your storage system supports it. As the warning on this screen says, never access the same NFS mount with both versions 3 and 4.1—this is likely to cause data corruption issues.

   ◆ You'll need to supply the IP address on which the NFS export is hosted. If you don't know this information, you'll need to go back to your storage array and determine what IP address it is using to host the NFS export. In general, identifying the NFS server by IP addresses is recommended, but we don't recommend that you use a hostname—it places an unnecessary dependency on DNS and generally it is being specified on a relatively small number of hosts. There are, of course, some cases where a hostname may be applicable—for example, where NAS virtualization techniques are used to provide transparent file mobility between NFS servers—but this is relatively rare. Also, refer to the sidebar "NFS Mounts with a DNS Hostname", which describes another configuration where you might want to use a hostname that resolves to multiple IP addresses.

   ◆ You'll need to supply the folder or path to the NFS export. Again, this is determined by the NFS server and the settings on the NFS export.

   Figure 6.44 shows an example of the Name And Configuration screen of the New Datastore Wizard, with the necessary information supplied.

7. If the NFS datastore should be read-only, select Mount NFS As Read Only.

   You might need to mount a read-only NFS datastore if the datastore contains only ISO images, for example.

   When you click Next to continue, your server IP and folder path will be validated.

FIGURE 6.44
Mounting an NFS datastore requires that you know the IP address and the export name from the NFS server.

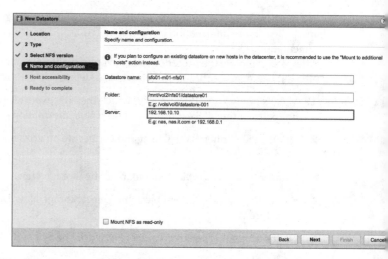

8. If you selected NFS 4.1, you will need to ensure each host is joined to AD and the NFS credentials are set. For more information, see the NFS 4.1 details in the "Understanding the Network File System" section.

9. On the following screen, select one or multiple hosts you want to connect to this datastore.

10. Review the information on the summary screen. If everything is correct, click Finish to continue; otherwise, go back and make the necessary changes.

When you click Finish, the vSphere Web Client will mount the NFS datastore on the selected ESXi host and the new NFS datastore will appear in the list of datastores, as you can see in Figure 6.45.

FIGURE 6.45
NFS datastores are listed among VMFS datastores, but the information provided for each is different.

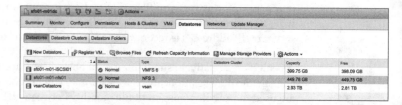

TROUBLESHOOTING NFS CONNECTIVITY

If you're having problems getting an NFS datastore to mount, the following list can help you troubleshoot the problem:

◆ Can you ping the IP address of the NFS export from the ESXi host? Use the Direct Console User Interface [DCUI] to test connectivity from the ESXi host or enable the ESXi shell and use the `vmkping` command.

◆ Is the physical cabling correct? Are the link lights showing a connected state on the physical interfaces on the ESXi host, the Ethernet switches, and the NFS server?

◆ Are your VLANs configured correctly? If you've configured VLANs, have you properly configured the same VLAN on the host, the switch, and the interface(s) that will be used on your NFS server?

◆ Is your IP routing correct and functional? Have you properly configured the IP addresses of the VMkernel adapter and the interface(s) that will be used on the NFS server?

◆ Is the NFS traffic being allowed through any firewalls? If the ping succeeds but you can't mount the NFS export, check to see if NFS is being blocked by a firewall somewhere in the path. Again, the general recommendation is to avoid firewalls in the midst of the data path wherever possible to avoid introducing additional latency.

◆ Are jumbo frames configured correctly? If you're using jumbo frames, have you configured jumbo frames on the VMkernel adapter, the vSwitch or distributed vSwitch, all physical switches along the data path, and the NFS server?

◆ Are you allowing the ESXi host root access to the NFS export?

Unlike VMFS datastores in vSphere, you need to add the NFS datastore on each host in the vSphere environment. Also, it's important to use consistent NFS properties (for example, a consistent IP/domain name) as well as common datastore names; this is not enforced. VMware provides a helpful reminder on the Name And Configuration screen, which you can see earlier in Figure 6.44. In the vSphere Web Client you can now add additional hosts to an existing NFS datastore without needing the NFS server IP and folder. Simply right-click an NFS datastore and select All vCenter Actions Mount Datastore To Additional Host.

After the NFS datastore is mounted, you can use it as you would any other datastore, you can select it as a Storage vMotion source or destination, you can create virtual disks on it, or you can map ISO images stored on an NFS datastore into a VM as a virtual CD/DVD drive.

As you can see, using NFS requires a simple series of steps, several fewer than using VMFS. And yet, with the same level of care, planning, and attention to detail, you can create robust NFS infrastructures that provide the same level of support as traditional block-based storage infrastructures.

Working with vSAN

Now that we've covered traditional storage, let's take a look at vSAN. As discussed previously, vSAN pools together server-attached storage to provide a highly resilient shared datastore suitable for any virtualized workload.

vSAN requires certified hardware, specifically disk controllers and the disks themselves. VMware has made it easy to purchase servers that are ready to run vSAN by working with hardware OEMs to create vSAN ReadyNodes. Though a ReadyNode is not required to utilize vSAN, you must ensure your hardware is on the compatibility list for the specific version of vSAN.

vSAN releases are not coupled with vSphere releases, and as such, capabilities can change quickly. VMware has created a site called Storage Hub (storagehub.vmware.com), which contains all the latest up-to-date information on vSAN.

vSAN uses disk groups on each ESXi host that contributes storage to the cluster. Disk groups can be either hybrid or all-flash. Mixing hybrid and all-flash disk groups in the same cluster is not supported.

Disk Group A disk group is a unit of physical storage capacity on a host and a group of physical devices that provide performance and capacity to the vSAN cluster. On each ESXi host that contributes its local devices to a vSAN cluster, devices are organized into disk groups.

Each disk group must have one flash cache device and one or multiple capacity devices. The devices used for caching cannot be shared across disk groups and cannot be used for other purposes. A single caching device must be dedicated to a single disk group. In hybrid clusters, flash devices are used for the cache layer and magnetic disks are used for the storage capacity layer. In an all-flash cluster, flash devices are used for both cache and capacity.

vSAN Datastore After vSAN is enabled on a cluster, a single vSAN datastore is created. It appears as another type of datastore in the list of datastores that might be available, such as VVOLs, VMFS, and NFS. A single vSAN datastore can provide different service levels for each VM or each virtual disk. In vCenter Server, storage characteristics of the vSAN datastore are presented as a set of capabilities. You can reference these capabilities, discussed earlier in this chapter, when defining a storage policy. You can then apply these storage policies to a VM or an individual VMDK depending on the workloads requirements.

NETWORK REQUIREMENTS

Like iSCSI and NFS, vSAN relies on the network. When you're running vSAN in hybrid mode, 1 Gb uplinks are required and 10 Gb uplinks are recommended. When you're running vSAN in all-flash mode, 10 Gb uplinks are required.

In vSAN versions prior to vSAN 6.6, multicast was required on the network, specifically IGMP. In vSAN 6.6 and later releases, vSAN utilizes unicast. This allows for a much simplier and flexible network topology, such as routing vSAN traffic without requiring multicast routing (PIM).

Generally speaking, NIC teaming, such as a LAG, can provide a marginal improvement in performance, but this is not guaranteed. The complexity and additional expense rarely justify the use of NIC teaming for the vSAN network.

vSAN requires its own VMkernel interface with the vSAN traffic type enabled. Refer to Chapter 5 for specifics on creating VMkernels.

CREATING A vSAN DATASTORE

Before you can create the vSAN datastore, you must create the vSAN VMkernel interfaces on each host. Enabling vSAN on the vSphere cluster uses a configuration wizard that automatically creates the vSAN datastore. Remember, vSAN datastores are only available to the hosts in the vSphere cluster where vSAN is enabled (see Figure 6.46 and Figure 6.47).

To enable vSAN, complete the following steps:

1. Launch the vSphere Web Client and connect to a vCenter Server instance.

2. In the Navigator, select Hosts And Clusters and select the cluster to enable vSAN on.

3. Click the Configure tab and select General under vSAN.

4. Click the Configure button.

FIGURE 6.46

vSAN is enabled on this cluster.

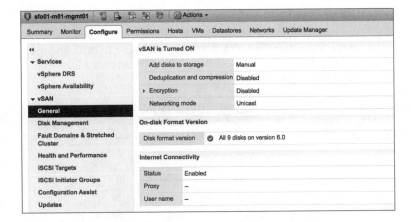

FIGURE 6.47

vSAN Disk Groups

5. Select the vSAN capabilities for the cluster (many of these capabilities require all-flash vSAN), and then click Next.

6. The Network Validation page ensures the settings for the vSAN VMkernels are configured correctly. Click Next if no configuration errors are found. If configuration errors are found, close the wizard and correct the errors displayed before continuing.

7. The Claim Disks page is where you create disk groups. For each ESXi host, select at least one flash disk for the cache tier and at least one capacity disk; then click Next.

8. On the Ready To Complete page, review the configuration, and then click Finish.

Working with Virtual Machine–Level Storage Configuration

Let's move from ESXi- and vSphere-level storage configuration to the storage configuration details for individual VMs.

First, we'll review virtual disks and the types of virtual disks supported in vSphere. Next, we'll review the virtual SCSI controllers. Then the discussion moves to VM storage policies and how to assign them to a VM, and we'll wrap up this discussion with a brief exploration of using an in-guest iSCSI initiator to access storage resources.

INVESTIGATING VIRTUAL DISKS

Virtual disks (referred to as VMDKs because of the filename extension used by vSphere) are how VMs encapsulate their disk devices (if not using RDMs), and they warrant further discussion. Figure 6.48 shows the properties of a VM. Hard disk 1 is a 50 GB thin-provisioned virtual disk on an NFS datastore.

FIGURE 6.48
This VM has a virtual disk on an NFS datastore.

Virtual disks come in three formats:

Thin-Provisioned Disk In this format, the size of the VDMK file on the datastore is only as much as is used (or was at some point used) within the VM itself. The top of Figure 6.49 illustrates this concept. For example, if you create a 500 GB virtual disk and place 100 GB of data in it, the VMDK file will be 100 GB in size. As I/O occurs in the guest, the VMkernel zeroes out the space needed right before the guest I/O is committed and grows the VMDK file similarly. Sometimes, this is referred to as a *sparse file*. Note that space deleted from the file system of the guest OS won't necessarily be released from the VMDK; if you added 50 GB of data but then turned around and deleted 50 GB of data, the space wouldn't necessarily be released to the hypervisor so that the VMDK can shrink in size. (Some guest OSs support the necessary T10 SCSI commands to address this situation.)

Thick-Provisioned Lazy Zeroed In this format (sometimes referred to as a flat disk), the size of the VDMK file on the datastore is the size of the virtual disk that you create, but within the

FIGURE 6.49
A thin-provisioned virtual disk uses only as much as the guest OS in the VM uses. A flat disk doesn't pre-zero unused space, so an array with thin provisioning would show only 100 GB used. A thickly provisioned (eager zeroed) virtual disk consumes 500 GB immediately because it is pre-zeroed.

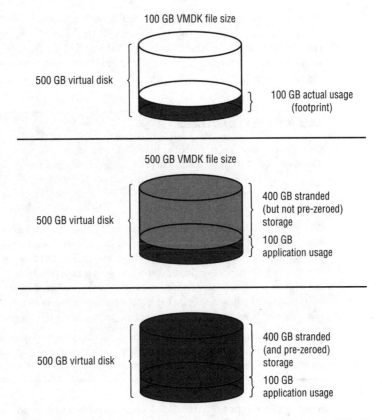

file, it is not pre-zeroed at the time of initial creation. For example, if you create a 500 GB virtual disk and place 100 GB of data in it, the VMDK will appear to be 500 GB at the datastore file system, but it contains only 100 GB of data on disk. This concept is shown in the center of Figure 6.49. As I/O occurs in the guest, the VMkernel zeroes out the space needed right before the guest I/O is committed, but the VDMK file size does not grow (since it was already 500 GB).

Thick-Provisioned Eager Zeroed Thick-provisioned eager zeroed virtual disks, also referred to as eagerly zeroed disks or eager zeroed thick disks, are truly thick. In this format, the size of the VDMK file on the datastore is the size of the virtual disk that you create, and within the file, it is pre-zeroed, as shown at the bottom of Figure 6.49. For example, if you create a 500 GB virtual disk and place 100 GB of data in it, the VMDK will appear to be 500 GB at the datastore file system, and it contains 100 GB of data and 400 GB of zeros on disk. As I/O occurs in the guest, the VMkernel does not need to zero the blocks prior to the I/O occurring. This results in slightly improved I/O latency and fewer backend storage I/O operations during initial I/O operations to new allocations in the guest OS, but it results in significantly more backend storage I/O operations up front during the creation of the VM. If the array supports VAAI, vSphere can offload the up-front task of zeroing all the blocks and reduce the initial I/O and time requirements.

This third type of virtual disk occupies more space initially than the first two, but it is required if you are going to use vSphere FT. (If they are thin-provisioned or flat virtual disks conversion occurs automatically when the vSphere FT feature is enabled.)

As you'll see in Chapter 12, you can convert between these virtual disk types using Storage vMotion.

ALIGNING VIRTUAL DISKS

Do you need to align the virtual disks? The answer is it depends on the guest operating system. Although not absolutely mandatory, we recommend that you follow VMware's best practices for aligning the volumes of guest OS's, across all vendor platforms and all storage types. These are the same as the very mature standard techniques for aligning the partitions in standard physical configurations from most storage vendors.

Why do this? Aligning a partition aligns the I/O along the underlying RAID stripes of the array, which is particularly important in Windows environments. (Windows Server from 2008 on automatically aligns partitions.) This alignment step minimizes the extra I/Os by aligning the I/Os with the array RAID stripe boundaries. Extra I/O work is generated when the I/Os cross the stripe boundary with all RAID schemes as opposed to a full stripe write. Aligning the partition provides a more efficient use of what is usually the most constrained storage array resource, IOPS. If you align a template and then deploy from a template, you maintain the correct alignment.

Why is it important to do this across vendors and across protocols? Changing the alignment of the guest OS partition is a difficult operation once data has been put in the partition, so it is best done up front when creating a VM or when creating a template.

Some of these types of virtual disks are supported in certain environments and others are no VMFS datastores support all three types of virtual disks (thin, flat, and thick), but NFS datastore support only thin unless the NFS server supports the VAAIv2 NAS extensions and vSphere has been configured with the vendor-supplied plug-in. Figure 6.50 shows the window for creating a new virtual disk for a VM (a procedure described in full detail in Chapter 9) on a VMFS data-

FIGURE 6.50
VMFS datastores support all three virtual disk types.

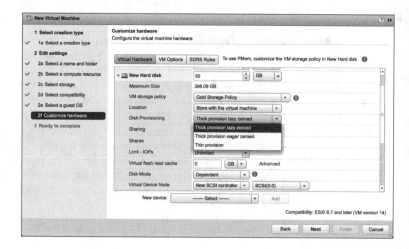

store; the two thick provisioning options are not available if you are provisioning to an NFS datastore that does not have VAAIv2 support.

Is there a way to tell which type of virtual disk a VM is using? Certainly. The free space indication within the guest OS is always going to indicate the maximum size of the virtual disk, so you won't be able to use that. Fortunately, VMware provides two other ways to determine the disk type:

◆ On the Summary tab of a VM, the vSphere Web Client provides statistics on currently provisioned space as well as used space. Figure 6.51 shows the statistics for a deployed VM running Ubuntu 16.

FIGURE 6.51
The Summary tab of a VM will report the total provisioned space as well as the used space.

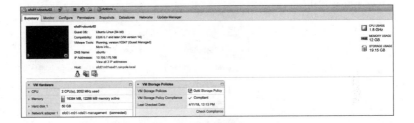

◆ The Edit Settings dialog box will also display the virtual disk type for a selected virtual disk in a VM. Using the same deployed instance of Ubuntu as an example, Figure 6.52 shows the information supplied in this dialog box. You can't determine current space usage, but you can at least determine what type of disk is configured.

Closely related to virtual disks are the virtual SCSI adapters that are present within every VM.

FIGURE 6.52
The Edit Settings dialog box tells you what kind of disk is configured, but it doesn't provide current space usage statistics.

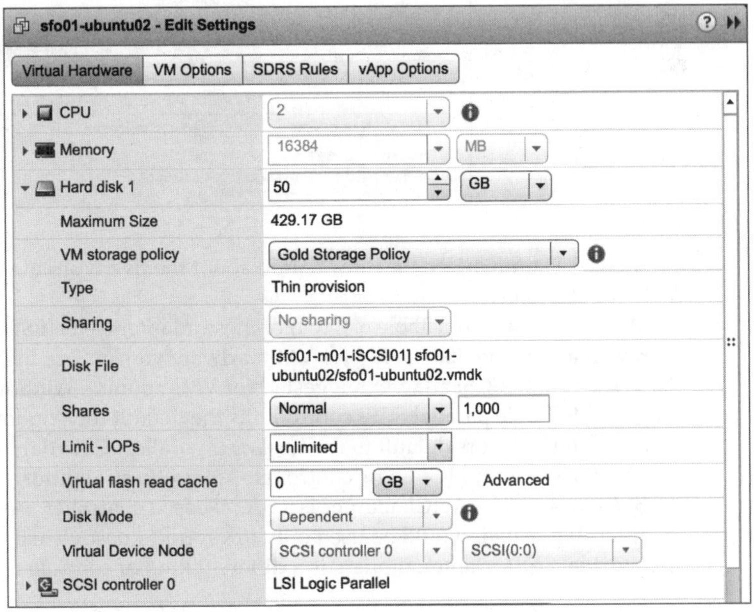

sfo01-ubuntu02 - Edit Settings				? ▸▸
Virtual Hardware	VM Options	SDRS Rules	vApp Options	

▸ 🖥 CPU	2 ▾	❶
▸ 🧠 Memory	16384 ▾	MB ▾
▾ 💾 Hard disk 1	50 ▲▼	GB ▾
Maximum Size	429.17 GB	
VM storage policy	Gold Storage Policy ▾	❶
Type	Thin provision	
Sharing	No sharing ▾	
Disk File	[sfo01-m01-iSCSI01] sfo01-ubuntu02/sfo01-ubuntu02.vmdk	
Shares	Normal ▾	1,000
Limit - IOPs	Unlimited ▾	
Virtual flash read cache	0	GB ▾ Advanced
Disk Mode	Dependent ▾	❶
Virtual Device Node	SCSI controller 0 ▾	SCSI(0:0) ▾
▸ 💾 SCSI controller 0	LSI Logic Parallel	

EXPLORING VIRTUAL STORAGE ADAPTERS

You configure virtual storage adapters in your VMs, and you will attach these adapters to virtu disks and RDMs, just as a physical server needs an adapter to connect physical hard disks to. I the guest OS, each virtual storage adapter has its own HBA queue, so for intense storage work-loads, configuring multiple virtual SCSI adapters within a single guest has its advantages.

There are a number of virtual storage adapters in ESXi, as shown in Figure 6.53.

FIGURE 6.53

A VM can use various virtual SCSI adapters. You can configure up to four virtual SCSI adapters for each VM.

Table 6.4 summarizes the information about the five types of virtual storage adapters avail-able for you to use.

As you can see from Table 6.4, two of these adapters—the LSI Logic SAS and VMware Paravirtual—are available only for VM hardware version 7 or higher. The LSI Logic SAS contro ler is the default SCSI adapter suggested for VMs running Windows Server 2008 and 2008 R2, and the LSI Logic parallel SCSI controller is the default for Windows Server 2003. Many of the various Linux flavors default to the BusLogic parallel SCSI adapters.

The BusLogic and LSI Logic controllers are pretty straightforward; they emulate a known SCSI controller. The AHCI adapter is a SATA-based controller used to replace the older IDE adapter. Typically it would be used only to support guest virtual CD-ROM drives. The VMware Paravirtual SCSI adapter, though, is a different kind of controller.

TABLE 6.4:   Virtual SCSi and SATA storage adapters in vSphere 6.7

VIRTUAL STORAGE ADAPTER	VM HARDWARE VERSIONS SUPPORTED	DESCRIPTION
AHCI (SATA)	10, 11, 12, 13, 14	The AHCI is the only non-SCSI storage adapter. Introduced in vSphere 5.5, this virtual SATA adapter is compatible with newer Windows and Linux OSs and supports all Mac OS X versions. It supports a maximum of four adapters per VM and 30 virtual drives per adapter. Typically, it's used for virtual CD-ROM devices.
BusLogic parallel	4, 7, 8, 9, 10, 11, 12, 13, 14	This virtual SCSI adapter emulates the BusLogic parallel SCSI adapter. The BusLogic adapter is well supported for older guest OSs but doesn't perform as well as some other virtual SCSI adapters.
LSI Logic parallel	4, 7, 8, 9, 10, 11, 12, 13, 14	The LSI Logic parallel SCSI virtual adapter is well suited for and well supported by newer guest OSs. Both LSI Logic controllers provide equivalent performance.
LSI Logic SAS	7, 8, 9, 10, 11, 12, 13, 14	The LSI Logic SAS controller is a better choice than LSI Logic parallel when the guest OS is phasing out support for parallel SCSI in favor of SAS. Performance between the two controllers is equivalent.
VMware Paravirtual	7, 8, 9, 10, 11, 12, 13, 14	The VMware Paravirtual SCSI adapter is a virtualization-optimized controller that provides higher throughput with lower CPU overhead but at the cost of guest OS compatibility.

In short, paravirtualized devices (and their corresponding drivers) are specifically optimized to communicate more directly with the underlying VM Monitor (VMM); they deliver higher throughput and lower latency, and they usually significantly lower the CPU impact of the I/O operations. This is the case with the VMware Paravirtual SCSI adapter in vSphere. We'll discuss paravirtualized drivers in greater detail in Chapter 9.

Compared to other virtual SCSI adapters, the paravirtualized SCSI adapter shows improvements in performance for virtual disks as well as improvements in the number of IOPS delivered at any given CPU utilization. The paravirtualized SCSI adapter also shows improvements (decreases) in storage latency as observed from the guest OS.

If the paravirtualized SCSI adapter works so well, why not use it for everything? One reason is that this is an adapter type that exists only in vSphere environments, so you won't find the drivers for the paravirtualized SCSI adapter on the install disk for most guest OSs. In general, we recommend using the virtual SCSI adapter suggested by vSphere for the boot disk and the

paravirtualized SCSI adapter for any other virtual disks, especially other virtual disks with acti
workloads.

As you can see, you have lots of options for configuring VM level storage. When you factor i
different datastores and different protocol options, how can you ensure that VMs are placed on
the right storage? This is where VM storage policies come into play.

Assigning Virtual Machine Storage Policies

Virtual machine storage policies are a key component of storage policy–based management. Tw
types of storage capabilities can be assigned to a VM storage policy:

◆   System-provided storage capabilities are presented to vCenter Server via the
     VASA provider.

◆   User-defined storage capabilities can also be assigned but must be built manually
     using tags.

Either way, VM storage policies help shape and control how VMs are allocated to storage.

Throughout this chapter, we have shown you how to configure the various components for
end-to-end storage policies, but let's recap the requirements before we move on to the final step
In the section "Examining Storage Policy–Based Management," we explained how to configure
tags and tag categories to assign to storage policy rule sets for datastores. We also described how
to create rule sets based on those tags and capabilities discovered by VASA, as shown in
Figure 6.54. The last component you need to configure is linking the VM to the storage policy itself.

FIGURE 6.54

This VM storage policy
requires a specific
user-defined storage
capability.

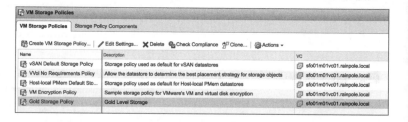

On the Summary tab for a VM is a widget that shows compliance or noncompliance with
the assigned VM storage policy. For a VM that does not have a storage policy assigned, the
box is empty, as shown in Figure 6.55. (You'll see how to assign a storage policy in the
next section.)

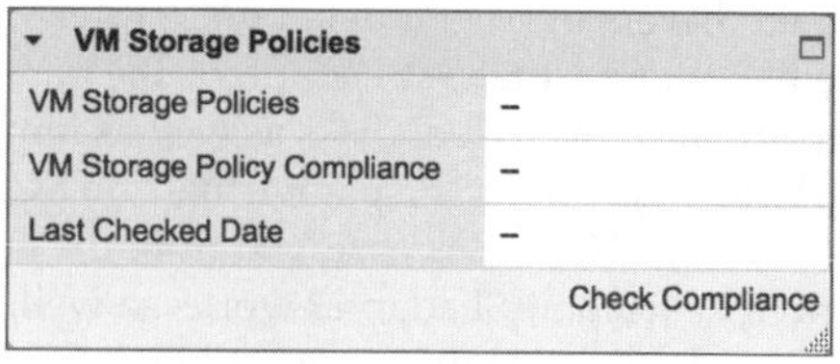

FIGURE 6.55

This VM does not have a
VM storage policy
assigned yet.

Perform these steps to assign a VM storage policy to a VM:

1. In the vSphere Web Client, navigate to either the Hosts And Clusters view or the VMs And Templates view.

2. Right-click a VM from the inventory panel and select Edit Settings.

3. In the Edit Settings dialog box, click the arrow next to the virtual hard disk(s).

4. From the drop-down list under VM Storage Policy, select the VM storage policy you want to assign to the VM's configuration and configuration-related files.

5. For each virtual disk listed, select the VM storage policy you want associated with it.

Figure 6.56 shows a VM with a VM storage policy assigned to virtual hard disk 1.

FIGURE 6.56
Each virtual disk can have its own VM storage policy, so you tailor VM storage capabilities on a per-virtual disk basis.

6. Click OK to save the changes to the VM and apply the storage policy.

After a VM storage policy is assigned, this area will show the compliance (or noncompliance) of the VM's current storage with the assigned storage policy, as shown in Figure 6.57 and Figure 6.58.

FIGURE 6.57

The storage capabilities specified in this VM storage policy don't match the capabilities of the VM's current storage location.

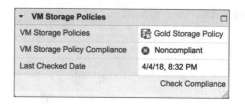

FIGURE 6.58

This VM's current storage is compliant with its assigned VM storage policy.

Figure 6.57 and Figure 6.58 also show the date and time of the last compliance check. Note that you can force a compliance check by clicking the Check Compliance link.

When we discuss creating VMs and adding virtual disks to a VM in Chapter 9, we'll revisit the concept of storage policy–based management and VM storage policies.

In addition to the various methods you've seen so far for accessing storage from a VM, there's still one method left: using an in-guest iSCSI initiator.

USING IN-GUEST iSCSI INITIATORS

As mentioned earlier in this chapter, in the section "Working with Raw Device Mappings," RDMs are not the only way to present storage devices directly to a VM. You can also use an in-guest iSCSI initiator to bypass the hypervisor and access storage directly.

The decision to use in-guest iSCSI initiators or not will depend on numerous factors, including, but not limited to, your storage configuration (e.g., whether your array supports iSCSI and/or your workload supports the vSAN iSCSI target), your networking configuration and policy (e.g., whether you have enough network bandwidth to support the additional iSCSI traffic on th VM facing networks), your application needs (e.g., whether you have applications that need or are specifically designed to work with in-guest iSCSI initiators, or applications that need RDMs that could work with in-guest iSCSI initiators instead), consolidation target (e.g., whether you afford the extra CPU and memory overhead in the VMs as a result of using an in-guest iSCSI initiator), and your guest OS (e.g., whether there's a software iSCSI initiator for your particular guest OS).

Should you decide to use an in-guest iSCSI initiator, keep in mind the following tips:

◆ The storage that you access via the in-guest initiator will be separate from the NFS and VMFS datastores you'll use for virtual disks. Keep this in mind so that you can plan your storage configuration accordingly—unless you use the vSAN iSCSI target, in which case the storage would be the same.

◆ You will be placing more load and more visibility on the VM networks because all iSCSI traffic will bypass the hypervisor. You'll also be responsible for configuring and supplying redundant connections and multipathing separately from the configuration you might have supplied for iSCSI at the hypervisor level. This could result in a need for more physical NICs in your server than you had planned.

◆ If you are using 10 Gigabit Ethernet, you might need to create a more complex QoS/ Network I/O Control configuration to ensure that the in-guest iSCSI traffic is appropriately prioritized.

◆ You'll lose Storage vMotion functionality for storage accessed via the in-guest iSCSI initiator because the hypervisor is not involved.

◆ For the same reason, vSphere snapshots would not be supported for in-guest iSCSI initiator–access storage.

As with many different areas in vSphere, there is no absolute wrong or right choice, only the correct choice for your environment. Review the impact of using iSCSI initiators in the guest OSs, and if it makes sense for your environment, proceed as needed.

THE vSAN iSCSI TARGET

vSAN now supports running an iSCSI target service to serve iSCSI LUNs to a specific set of workloads. In vSphere 6.5, these workloads were limited to physical servers, such as Oracle RAC servers. In vSphere 6.7, VMs can use an in-guest iSCSI initator, this includes support for Windows Server Failover Clustering. VMs using in-guest iSCSI initiators may reside on the vSAN datastore, or on other storage. See VMware KB `kb.vmware.com/s/article/2148216` for the latest information on the vSAN iSCSI Target Service and KB `kb.vmware.com/s/article/2147661` for guidelines on Windows Server Failover Clustering.

Also note that vSphere Replication, vSphere Data Protection APIs, Snapshots, and VMware Site Recovery Manager are not supported with guests leveraging the vSAN iSCSI service.

THIN PROVISIONING: SHOULD YOU DO IT IN THE ARRAY OR IN VMWARE?

The general answer is that *both* are right.

If your array supports thin provisioning, it's generally more efficient to use array-level thin provisioning in most operational models. If you thick-provision at the LUN or file system level, there will always be large amounts of unused space until you start to get it highly utilized, unless you start small and keep extending the datastore, which operationally is heavyweight.

Also, when you use thin-provisioning techniques at the array level using NFS or block storage, you always benefit. In vSphere, the common default virtual disk types, both thin and flat (with the exception of thick provisioned, which in vSphere is used far more rarely), are friendly to storage array–level thin provisioning since they don't pre-zero the files.

Thin provisioning also tends to be more efficient the larger the scale of the thin pool. On an array, this construct (often called a *pool*) tends to be larger than a single datastore and therefore more efficient because thin provisioning is more efficient at larger scales of thinly provisioned objects in the oversubscribed pool.

One other benefit of thin provisioning on the array, which is sometimes overlooked, is the extra capacity available for non-virtual storage. When you're thin provisioning within vSphere only, the VMFS datastore takes the entire datastore capacity on the array, even if the datastore itself has no VMs stored within it.

Is there a downside to thin on thin? Not really, if you are able and willing to carefully monitor usage at both the vSphere layer and the storage layer. Use vSphere or third-party usage reports in conjunction with array-level reports and set thresholds with notification and automated action on both the vSphere layer and the array level, if your array supports that. (See Chapter 13 for more information on creating alarms to monitor datastores.) Why? Even though vSphere 5.0 added thin-provisioning awareness and support, thin provisioning still needs to be carefully managed for out-of-space conditions because you are oversubscribing an asset that has no backdoor. Unlike the way VMware oversubscribes guest memory that can use VM swap if needed, if you run out of actual capacity for a datastore, the VMs on that datastore will be affected. When you use thin on thin, it can be marginally more efficient but can accelerate the transition to oversubscription and an outage.

An example here is instructive. If the total amount of provisioned space at the virtual disk layer in a datastore is 500 GB with thick virtual disks, the datastore needs to be at least 500 GB in size, and therefore the LUN or NFS exported file system would need to look as if it were at least 500 GB in size. Now, those thick virtual disks are not actually using 500 GB; imagine that they have 100 GB of used space, and the remainder is empty. If you use thin provisioning at the storage array level, you provision a LUN or file system that is 500 GB, but only 100 GB in the pool is used. The space used cannot exceed 500 GB, so monitoring is needed only at the storage layer.

Conversely, if you use thin virtual disks, technically the datastore needs to be only 100 GB in size. The exact same amount of storage is being used (100 GB), but clearly there is a possibility of quickly needing more than 100 GB since the virtual disks could grow up to 500 GB without any administrative action, with only the VMs writing more data in their guest OSs. Therefore, the datastore *and* the underlying storage LUN/file system must be monitored closely, and the administrator must be ready to respond with more storage on the array and grow the datastore if needed.

There are only two exceptions to the "always thin provision at the array level if you can" guideline. The first is in the most extreme performance use cases, because the thin-provisioning architectures generally have a performance impact (usually marginal, and this varies from array to array) compared to a traditional thick-storage configuration. The second is large, high-performance RDBMS storage objects when the amount of array cache is significantly smaller than the database; therefore, the actual backend spindles are tightly coupled to the host I/O. These database structures have internal logic that generally expects I/O locality, which is a fancy way of saying that they structure data expecting the on-disk structure to reflect their internal structure. With very large array caches, the host and the backend spindles with RDBMS-type workloads can be decoupled, and this consideration is irrelevant. These two cases are important but rare. "Always thin provision at the array level if you can" is a good general guiding principle.

In the last section of this chapter, we'll pull together everything you've learned in the previous sections and summarize with some recommended practices.

Leveraging SAN and NAS Best Practices

After all the discussion of configuring and managing storage in vSphere environments, here are the core principles:

◆ Pick a storage architecture for your immediate and midterm scaling goals. Don't design for extreme growth scenarios. You can always use Storage vMotion to migrate up to larger arrays.

◆ Consider using VMFS and NFS together; the combination provides a great deal of flexibility. Consider VVOLs if your storage array supports it.

◆ When sizing your initial array design for your entire vSphere environment, think about availability, performance (IOPS, MBps, latency), and then capacity—always together and *generally* in that order.

The last point in the previous list cannot be overstated. People who are new to storage tend to think primarily in the dimension of storage capacity (TB) and neglect availability and performance. Capacity is generally not the limit for a proper storage configuration. With modern large-capacity disks (hundreds of GB and TB+ per disk is common) and capacity reduction techniques such as thin provisioning, deduplication, and compression, you can fit a *lot* on a very small number of disks. Therefore, capacity is now not usually the driver of efficiency.

To make this clear, an example scenario will help. First, let's work through the capacity-centered planning dynamic:

◆ You determine you will have 150 VMs that are each 50 GB in size.

◆ This means that at a minimum, if you don't apply any special techniques, you will need 7.5 TB (150 × 50 GB). Because of extra space for vSphere snapshots and VM swap, you assume 25% overhead, so you plan 10 TB of storage for your vSphere environment.

◆ With 10 TB, you could fit that on approximately 13 large 1 TB SATA drives (assuming a 10+2 RAID 6 and one hot spare).

◆ Thinking about this further and trying to be more efficient, you determine that while the virtual disks will be configured to be 50 GB, on average they will need only 20 TB, and the rest will be empty, so you can use thin provisioning at the vSphere or storage array layer. Using this would reduce the requirement to 3 TB, and you decide that with good use of vSphere managed datastore objects and alerts, you can cut the extra space down from 25% to 20%. This reduces the requirement down to 3.6 TB.

◆ Also, depending on your array, you may be able to deduplicate the storage itself, which has a high degree of commonality. Assuming a conservative 2:1 deduplication ratio, you would then need only 1.5 TB of capacity—and with an additional 20% for various things, that's 1.8 TB.

◆ With only 1.8 TB needed, you could fit that on a very small 3+1 RAID 5 using 750 GB drives, which would net 2.25 TB.

This would be much cheaper, right? Much more efficient, right? After all, you've gone from thirteen 1 TB spindles to four 750 GB spindles.

It's not that simple. The reason will be clear as we go through planning a second time, but th time work through the same design with a performance-centered planning dynamic:

♦ You determine you will have 150 VMs (the same as before).

♦ You look at their workloads, and although they spike at 200 IOPS, they average at 50 IOPS, and the duty cycle across all the VMs doesn't seem to spike at the same time, so yo decide to use the average.

♦ You look at the throughput requirements and see that although they spike at 200 MBps during a backup, for the most part, they drive only 3 MBps. (For perspective, copying a file to a USB 2 memory stick can drive 12 MBps, so this is a small amount of bandwidth for a server.) The I/O size is generally small, in the 4 KB size.

♦ Among the 150 virtual purpose machines, though most are general-purpose servers, there are 10 that are close to "monster VMs" (for example, Exchange servers and some SharePoint backend SQL Server machines) that require specific planning, so you put them aside to design separately using the reference architecture approach. The remaining 140 VMs can be characterized as needing an average of 7,000 IOPS (140 × 50 IOPS) and 420 MBps of average throughput (140 × 3 MBps).

♦ Assuming no RAID losses or cache gains, 7,000 IOPS translates to the following:

  ♦ Thirty-nine 15K RPM Fibre Channel/SAS drives (7,000 IOPS/180 IOPS per drive)

  ♦ Fifty-nine 10K RPM Fibre Channel/SAS drives (7,000 IOPS/120 IOPS per drive)

  ♦ Eighty-seven 5,400 RPM SATA drives (7,000 IOPS/80 IOPS per drive)

  ♦ One enterprise flash drive (10,000+ IOPS per drive)

♦ Assuming no RAID losses or cache gains, 420 MBps translates into 3,360 Mbps. At the array and the ESXi hosts layers, this will require the following:

  ♦ Two 4 Gbps Fibre Channel array ports (although it could fit on one, you need two for high availability).

  ♦ Two 10 GbE ports (though it could fit on one, you need two for high availability).

  ♦ Four 1 GbE ports for iSCSI or NFS. NFS will require careful multidatastore planning t hit the throughput goal because of how it works in link aggregation configurations. iSCSI will require careful multipathing configuration to hit the throughput goal.

♦ If you're using block devices, you'll need to distribute VMs across datastores to design the datastores and backing LUNs themselves to ensure that they can support the IOPS of the VMs they contain so the queues don't overflow.

♦ It's immediately apparent that the SATA drives are not ideal in this case (they would require 87 spindles!). Using 300 GB 15K RPM drives (without using enterprise flash drives), at a minimum you will have 11.7 TB of raw capacity, assuming 10% RAID 6 capacity loss (10.6 TB usable). This is more than enough to store the thickly provisioned VMs, not to mention their thinly provisioned and then deduplicated variations.

◆ Will thin provisioning and deduplication techniques save capacity? Yes. Could you use that saved capacity? Maybe, but probably not. Remember, we've sized the configuration to meet the IOPS workload—unless the workload is lighter than we measured or the additional workloads you would like to load on those spindles generate no I/O during the periods the VMs need it. The spindles will all be busy servicing the existing VMs, and additional workloads will increase the I/O service time.

What's the moral of the story? That thin provisioning and data deduplication have no usefulness? That performance is all that matters?

No. The moral of the story is that to be efficient you need to think about efficiency in multiple dimensions: performance, capacity, power, operational simplicity, and flexibility. Here is a simple five-step sequence you can use to guide the process:

1. Look at your workload, and examine the IOPS, MBps, and latency requirements.

2. Put the outliers to one side, and plan for the average.

3. Use reference architectures and a focused plan to design a virtualized configuration for the outlier heavy workloads.

4. Plan first on the most efficient way to meet the aggregate performance workloads.

5. Then, by using the performance configuration developed in step 4, back into the most efficient capacity configuration to hit that mark. Some workloads are performance bound (step 4 is the constraint), and some are capacity bound (step 5 is the constraint).

Let's quantify all this learning into applicable best practices.

When thinking about performance:

◆ Do a little engineering by simple planning or estimation. Measure sample hosts or use VMware Capacity Planner to profile the IOPS and bandwidth workload of each host that will be virtualized onto the infrastructure. If you can't measure, at least estimate. For virtual desktops, estimate between 5 and 20 IOPS. For light servers, estimate 50 to 100 IOPS. Usually, most configurations are IOPS bound, not throughput bound, but if you can, measure the average I/O size of the hosts (or again, use Capacity Planner). Although estimation can work for light server use cases, for heavy servers, don't ever estimate, measure them. It's so easy to measure, it's absolutely a "measure twice, cut once" case, particularly for VMs you know will have a heavy workload.

◆ For large applications (Exchange, SQL Server, SharePoint, Oracle, MySQL, and so on), the sizing, layout, and best practices for storage for large database workloads are not dissimilar to physical deployments and can be a good choice for RDMs or VMFS volumes with no other virtual disks. Also, leverage joint-reference architectures available from VMware and the storage vendors.

◆ Remember that the datastore will need to have enough IOPS and capacity for the total of all the VMs. Just remember 80 to 180 IOPS per spindle, depending on spindle type (refer to the Disks item in the list of elements that make up a shared storage array in the section "Defining Common Storage Array Architectures" earlier in this chapter), to support the aggregate of all the VMs in it. If you just add up all the aggregate IOPS needed by the sum of the VMs that will be in a datastore, you have a good approximation of the total. Additional I/O is generated by the zeroing activity that occurs for thin and flat (not thick, which is pre-zeroed up front), but this tends to be negligible. You lose some IOPS because of the RAID protection, but you know you're in the ballpark if the number of spindles supporting the datastore (via a file system and NFS or a LUN and VMFS) times the number of IOPS per spindle is more than the total number of IOPS needed for the aggregate workload. Keep your storage vendor honest and you'll have a much more successful virtualization project!

◆ Cache benefits are difficult to predict; they vary a great deal. If you can't do a test, assume they will have a large effect in terms of improving VM boot times with RDBMS environments on VMware but almost no effect otherwise, so plan your spindle count cautiously.

When thinking about capacity:

◆ Consider not only the VM disks in the datastores but also their snapshots, their swap, and their suspended state and memory. A good rule of thumb is to assume 25% more than from the virtual disks alone. If you use thin provisioning at the array level, oversizing the datastore has no downside because only what is necessary is actually used.

◆ There is no exact best practice datastore-sizing model. Historically, people have recommended one fixed size or another. A simple model is to select a standard guideline for the number of VMs you feel comfortable with in a datastore, multiply that number by the average size of the virtual disks of each VM, add the overall 25% extra space, and use that as a standardized building block. Remember, VMFS and NFS datastores don't have an effective limit on the number of VMs—with VMFS, you need to consider disk queuing and, to a much lesser extent, SCSI reservations; with NFS, you need to consider the bandwidth to a single datastore.

◆ Be flexible and efficient. Use thin provisioning at the array level if possible, and if your array doesn't support it, use it at the vSphere layer. It never hurts (so long as you monitor), but don't count on it resulting in needing fewer spindles (because of performance requirements).

◆ If your array doesn't support thin provisioning but does support extending LUNs, use thin provisioning at the vSphere virtual disk layer, but start with smaller VMFS volumes to avoid oversizing and being inefficient.

◆ In general, don't oversize. Every modern array can add capacity dynamically, and you can use Storage vMotion to redistribute workloads. Use the managed datastore function to set thresholds and actions, and then extend LUNs and the VMFS datastores using the vSphere VMFS extension capability or grow NFS datastores.

When thinking about availability:

◆ Spend the bulk of your storage planning and configuration time to ensure that your design has high availability. Check that array configuration, storage fabric (whether Fibre Channel or Ethernet), and NMP/MPP multipathing configuration (or NIC teaming/link aggregation and routing for NFS) are properly configured. Spend the effort to stay up-to-date with the interoperability matrices of your vendors and the firmware update processes.

◆ Remember, you can deal with performance and capacity issues as they come up nondisruptively (VMFS expansion/extends, array tools to add performance, and Storage vMotion). Something that affects the overall storage availability will be an emergency.

When deciding on a VM datastore placement philosophy, there are two common models: the predictive scheme and the adaptive scheme.

The predictive scheme allows you to do the following:

◆ Create several datastores (VMFS or NFS) with different storage characteristics and label each datastore according to its characteristics.

◆ Locate each application in the appropriate RAID for its requirements by measuring the requirements in advance.

◆ Run the applications and see whether VM performance is acceptable (or monitor the HBA queues as they approach the queue-full threshold).

◆ Use RDMs sparingly as needed.

The adaptive scheme allows you to do the following:

◆ Create a standardized datastore building-block model (VMFS or NFS).

◆ Place virtual disks on the datastore. Remember, regardless of what you hear, there's no practical datastore maximum number. The question is the performance scaling of the datastore.

◆ Run the applications and see whether disk performance is acceptable (on a VMFS datastore, monitor the HBA queues as they approach the queue-full threshold).

◆ If performance is acceptable, you can place additional virtual disks on the datastore. If it isn't, create a new datastore and use Storage vMotion to distribute the workload.

◆ Use RDMs sparingly.

Our preference is a hybrid. Specifically, you can use the adaptive scheme coupled with (starting with) two wildly divergent datastore performance profiles (the idea from the predictive scheme): one for utility VMs and one for priority VMs.

Always read, follow, and leverage the key documentation:

◆ VMware's Fibre Channel, iSCSI SAN, and vSAN configuration guides

◆ VMware Compatibility Guide

◆ Your storage vendor's best practices/solutions guides

Sometimes the documents go out of date. Don't just ignore the guidance if you think it's incorrect; use the online community or reach out to VMware or your storage vendor to get the latest information.

Most important, have no fear!

Physical host and storage configurations have historically been extremely static, and the penalty of error in storage configuration from a performance or capacity standpoint was steep. The errors of misconfiguration would inevitably lead not only to application issues but to complex work and downtime to resolve. This pain of error has ingrained in administrators a tendency to overplan when it comes to performance and capacity.

Between the capabilities of modern arrays to modify many storage attributes dynamically and Storage vMotion (the ultimate "get out of jail free card," including complete array replacement o vSAN!), the penalty and risk are less about misconfiguration, and now the risk is more about oversizing or overbuying. You cannot be trapped with an underperforming configuration you can't change nondisruptively.

More important than any storage configuration or feature per se is to design a highly availabl configuration that meets your immediate needs and is as flexible to change as VMware makes the rest of the IT stack.

The Bottom Line

Differentiate and understand the fundamentals of shared storage. vSphere depends on shared storage for advanced functions, cluster-wide availability, and the aggregate performance of all the VMs in a cluster. Designing a high-performance and highly available shared storage infrastructure is possible on Fibre Channel, FCoE, and iSCSI SANs, and is possible using NAS; it's available from midrange to enterprise storage architectures. Always design the storage architecture to meet the performance requirements first, and then ensure that capacity requirements are met as a corollary.

> **Master It** Identify examples where each of the protocol choices would be ideal for different vSphere deployments.

> **Master It** Identify the three storage performance parameters and the primary determinant of storage performance and how to quickly estimate it for a given storage configuration.

Understand vSphere storage options. vSphere has four fundamental storage presentation models: vSAN, VMFS on block, RDM, and NFS. The most flexible configurations use all four, predominantly via a shared-container model and selective use of RDMs.

> **Master It** Characterize use cases for vSAN, VMFS datastores, NFS datastores, and RDMs.

> **Master It** If you're using VMFS and there's one performance metric to track, what woulc it be? Configure a monitor for that metric.

Configure storage at the vSphere layer. After a shared storage platform is selected, vSphere needs a storage network configured. The network (whether Fibre Channel or Ethernet based) must be designed to meet availability and throughput requirements, which are influenced by protocol choice and vSphere fundamental storage stack (and in the case of vSAN and NFS, the network stack) architecture. Proper network design involves physical redundancy and physical or logical isolation mechanisms (SAN zoning and network VLANs). With connectivity in place, configure LUNs and VMFS datastores and/or NFS exports/NFS datastores using the predictive or adaptive model (or a hybrid model). Use Storage vMotion to resolve hot spots and other non-optimal VM placement.

Master It What would best identify an oversubscribed VMFS datastore from a performance standpoint? How would you identify the issue? What is it most likely to be? What would be two possible corrective actions you could take?

Master It A VMFS volume is filling up. What are three possible nondisruptive corrective actions you could take?

Master It What would best identify an oversubscribed NFS volume from a performance standpoint? How would you identify the issue? What is it most likely to be? What are two possible corrective actions you could take?

Configure storage at the VM layer. With datastores in place, create VMs. During the creation of the VMs, place VMs in the appropriate datastores, and employ selective use of RDMs but only where required. Leverage in-guest iSCSI where it makes sense but understand the impact to your vSphere environment.

Master It Without turning the machine off, convert the virtual disks on a VMFS volume from thin to thick (eager zeroed thick) and back to thin.

Master It Identify where you would use a physical compatibility mode RDM and configure that use case.

Leverage best practices for shared storage with vSphere. Read, follow, and leverage key VMware and storage vendors' best practices and solutions guide documentation. Don't oversize up front, but instead learn to leverage VMware and storage array features to monitor performance, queues, and backend load, and then nondisruptively adapt. Plan for performance first and capacity second. (Usually capacity is a given for performance requirements to be met.) Spend design time on availability design and on the large, heavy I/O VMs, and use flexible pool design for the general-purpose VMFS and NFS datastores.

Master It Quickly estimate the minimum usable capacity needed for 200 VMs with an average VM size of 40 GB. Make some assumptions about vSphere snapshots. What would be the raw capacity needed in the array if you used RAID 10? RAID 5 (4+1)? RAID 6 (10+2)? What would you do to nondisruptively cope if you ran out of capacity?

Master It Using the configurations in the previous question, what would the minimum amount of raw capacity need to be if the VMs are actually only 20 GB of data in each VM, even though they are provisioning 40 GB and you used thick on an array that didn't support thin provisioning? What if the array did support thin provisioning? What if you used Storage vMotion to convert from thick to thin (both in the case where the array supports thin provisioning and, in the case where it doesn't)?

Master It Estimate the number of spindles needed for 100 VMs that drive 200 IOPS each and are 40 GB in size. Assume no RAID loss or cache gain. How many if you use 500 GB SATA 7200 RPM? 300 GB 10K Fibre Channel/SAS? 300 GB 15K Fibre Channel/SAS? 160 GB consumer-grade SSD? 200 GB enterprise flash?

Chapter 7

Ensuring High Availability and Business Continuity

Ensuring high availability and business continuity is a key part of virtualization that is often overlooked or considered after the fact. It is equally as important as configuring storage devices and setting up virtual networking. Virtualization and VMware vSphere in particular enable advanced ways to provide high availability and business continuity. There are multiple layers where vSphere administrators can help provide high availability in a variety of ways, depending on the needs of the business and the unique requirements of the organization or application. Additionally, business continuity needs also should be taken into consideration to ensure the organization can function in the event of an outage. This chapter discusses some of the tools and techniques available to you.

IN THIS CHAPTER, YOU WILL LEARN TO

◆ Understand Windows clustering and the different types of clusters

◆ Use vSphere's built-in high-availability functionality

◆ Recognize differences between high-availability solutions

◆ Understand additional components of business continuity

Understanding the Layers of High Availability

Even in non-virtualized environments, there are multiple ways to achieve high availability for Operating System (OS) instances and applications. When you introduce virtualization into the mix with vSphere, you gain additional methods of providing high availability. Figure 7.1 shows these various layers.

At each layer are tools and techniques for providing high availability and business continuity:

◆ At the Application layer, options include Oracle Real Application Clusters (RAC), or simply application resiliency through a micro-services architecture.

◆ At the OS layer, solutions include OS clustering functionality, such as Windows Server Failover Clustering (WSFC).

◆ The Virtualization layer offers a number of features for high availability, including vSphere High Availability (HA), vSphere Fault Tolerance (FT), and stretched (metro) storage clusters.

♦ At the Physical layer, high availability is achieved through redundant hardware—multiple network interface cards (NICs) or host bus adapters (HBAs), multiple storage area network (SAN) switches and fabrics, multiple paths to storage, multiple controllers in storage arrays, redundant power supplies, and so forth.

FIGURE 7.1
Each layer has its own forms of high availability.

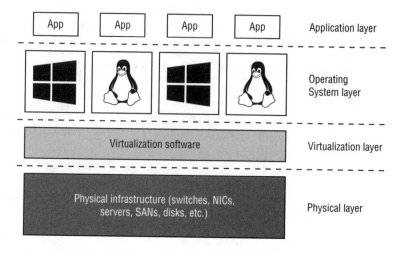

Each of these technologies or techniques has its own strengths and weaknesses. For example, providing redundancy at the Physical layer is great, but it doesn't help with failures at the Application layer. Conversely, protecting against application failures won't help much if the underlying hardware isn't redundant. As you set forth to establish high availability for your virtualized workloads, keep in mind that there is no "one size fits all" solution. Use the right tool for the job based on your specific requirements.

Given that this is a book on vSphere, we can cover only some of the possibilities for ensuring high availability, so let's focus our efforts on four key technologies or techniques that help provide high availability:

♦ OS clustering in Microsoft Windows

♦ ESXi host clustering using vSphere HA

♦ Virtual machine (VM) mirroring using vSphere FT

♦ vSAN stretched storage clustering

After a discussion of these four broad areas, this chapter explores areas relating to business continuity. You can find details relating to high availability at the Physical layer in other chapters of this book, such as Chapter 5, "Creating and Configuring a vSphere Network," and Chapter 6, "Creating and Configuring Storage Devices."

First, though, let's start with a well-known technique for achieving high availability at the OS level: OS clustering, specifically clustering Microsoft Windows Server instances.

Clustering VMs

Because Windows Server is widely used in corporate and enterprise datacenters today, it's quite likely that you've been asked to create or support a Windows-based cluster. There are two primary ways to use clustering to provide high availability for Windows Server:

◆ Network Load Balancing (NLB) clustering

◆ Windows Server Failover Clustering (WSFC)

Although both of these methods are described as clustering, they each target very different purposes. NLB typically provides scalable performance, whereas WSFC usually focuses on providing redundancy and high availability in the form of active/passive workload clustering.

Some experts say that vSphere HA eliminates the need for WSFC because—as you'll see later in this chapter in the section "Implementing vSphere High Availability"—vSphere HA can provide failover in the event of a physical host failure. That's true, but it's important to understand that these high-availability mechanisms operate at different layers (refer back to Figure 7.1). WSFC operates at the OS layer, providing redundancy in the event that one of the OS instances in the cluster fails. That OS failure could be the result of hardware failure. vSphere HA (and vSphere FT) operates at a layer beneath the OS and doesn't operate in exactly the same way. As you'll see throughout this chapter, each of the high-availability mechanisms described in this chapter has advantages and disadvantages. You'll want to understand these fully to choose the right approach for your specific environment.

Let's start with a quick review of NLB clustering and how you can use it in your vSphere environment.

Introducing Network Load Balancing Clustering

The Network Load Balancing configuration involves an aggregation of stateless servers that balances the requests for applications or services. In a typical NLB cluster, all nodes are active participants in the cluster and are consistently responding to requests for services. If one of the nodes in the NLB cluster goes down, client connections are simply redirected to another available node in the NLB cluster. NLB clusters are most commonly deployed to enhance performance and availability. Because client connections could be directed to any available node within the cluster, NLB clusters are best suited for scenarios involving stateless connections and protocols, such as environments using Microsoft Internet Information Services (IIS), virtual private networking, or Apache, to name a few. Figure 7.2 summarizes the architecture of an NLB cluster made up of Windows-based VMs (the architecture is the same for physical systems).

NETWORK LOAD-BALANCING SUPPORT FROM VMware

As of this writing, VMware supports NLB, but you must run NLB in Multicast mode to support vMotion and VMs on different physical hosts. If NLB is running in Unicast mode, then the VMs must all be running on the same host, which is generally not a good idea if you want high availability! Another option to consider would be VMware NSX or third-party load balancers to achieve the same results. For more information about using NLB and Unicast, see https://kb.vmware.com/kb/1556 in the VMware Knowledge Base.

FIGURE 7.2

An NLB cluster can contain up to 32 active nodes (only 5 are shown here), and traffic is distributed equally across each available node. The NLB software allows the nodes to share a common name and IP address that is referenced by clients.

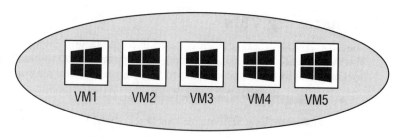

Load balanced identity: www.rainpole.local (10.1.1.10)

NLB clusters aren't the right fit for every application or workload. For applications and workloads that aren't a good fit for NLB, Microsoft offers Windows Server Failover Clustering.

Introducing Windows Server Failover Clustering

Unlike NLB clusters, Windows Server Failover Clustering (WSFC) clusters (which we'll refer to as server clusters, failover clusters, or simply WSFC from here on) are used solely for the sake of availability. Server clusters do not enhance performance outside of high availability. In a typical server cluster, multiple stateful nodes are configured to be able to own a service or application resource, but only one node owns the resource at a given time. Server clusters are most often used for applications like Microsoft SQL Server and DHCP services, in which each shares the need for a common datastore. The common datastore houses the information accessible by the node that is online and currently owns the resource as well as the other possible owners that could assume ownership in the event of failure. Each node requires at least two network connections: one for the production network and one for the cluster service heartbeat between nodes. Figure 7.3 details the structure of a server cluster built using physical systems. (We'll illustrate several ways server clusters are built with VMs later in the next section, "Reviewing VM Clustering Configurations.")

FIGURE 7.3

Server clusters are best suited for applications and services like SQL Server, DHCP, and so on, which use a common dataset.

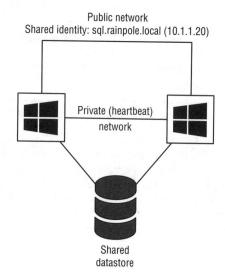

Public network
Shared identity: sql.rainpole.local (10.1.1.20)

Private (heartbeat) network

Shared datastore

Server clusters, when constructed properly, provide automatic failover of services and applications hosted across multiple cluster nodes. When multiple nodes are configured as a cluster for a service or application resource, only one node owns the resource at any given time. When the current resource owner experiences failure, causing a loss in the heartbeat between the cluster nodes, another node assumes ownership of the resource to allow continued access with minimal data loss. Windows Server has several ways of configuring Windows Server Failover Clustering, or Microsoft Cluster Server (MSCS). Because this is a VMware book and not a Windows Server book, we'll limit examples to the most recent Windows Server version, 2016. To configure multiple Windows Server 2016 nodes into a Microsoft cluster, you must ensure the following requirements are met:

◆ Nodes must be running either the Standard Edition or the Datacenter Edition of Windows Server 2016.

◆ All nodes should have access to the same storage device(s). The specific details of the storage device(s) and how they are shared will depend on how the cluster is built.

◆ All nodes should have two similarly connected and configured network adapters: one for the production (or public) network and one for the heartbeat (or private) network.

◆ All nodes should have Microsoft Cluster Services for the version of Windows that you are using.

Earlier versions of Microsoft Exchange aligned to the shared storage based on the cluster model that was just explained. However, Exchange 2010 introduced a new concept: the database availability groups (DAGs). Although you can still install Exchange with an application-based cluster configuration, it no longer requires shared storage; it uses local storage on each node instead. Because of the I/O profile that Exchange can require, local storage is considered a better fit for this application. Before we describe how to build a server cluster running Microsoft Windows Server 2016 on vSphere, let's discuss the various scenarios of how server clusters can be built.

REVIEWING VM CLUSTERING CONFIGURATIONS

Building a server cluster with Windows Server 2016 VMs can be achieved with one of three different configurations:

Cluster in a Box   The clustering of VMs on the same ESXi host is also known as a *cluster in a box*. This is the easiest of the three configurations to set up. Minimal configuration needs to be applied to make this work.

Cluster Across Boxes   The clustering of VMs that are running on different ESXi hosts is known as a *cluster across boxes*. In much earlier versions, VMware had restrictions in place for this configuration in earlier versions: the cluster node's C: drive must be stored on the host's local storage or local VMFS datastore, the cluster shared storage must be stored on Fibre Channel external disks, and you must use raw device mappings on the storage. In vSphere 4 and later, this was changed and updated to allow VMDK files on the SAN and to allow the cluster VM boot drive or C: drive on the SAN. Subsequently, prior to vSphere 6, vMotion and vSphere Distributed Resource Scheduler (DRS) were not supported using Microsoft-clustered VMs. However, apart from a few less restrictive requirements, WSFC is now supported without too many limits.

Physical-to-Virtual Clustering The clustering of a physical server and a VM together is often referred to as a *physical-to-virtual cluster*. This configuration of using physical and virtual servers together gives you the best of both worlds; the only restriction is that you cannot use Virtual Compatibility mode with the RDMs.

The sections that follow examine all three configurations in more detail.

Building Windows-based server clusters has long been considered an advanced technology practiced only by those with high technical skills in implementing and managing high-availability environments. Although this might be more rumor than truth, server clusters are certainly a complex solution to set up and maintain, and running on top of a hypervisor can increase this complexity.

Although you might succeed in setting up clustered VMs, you may not receive support for your clustered solution if you violate any of the clustering restrictions put forth by VMware. The following list summarizes and reviews the dos and don'ts of clustering VMs as published by VMware:

◆ Even though 32-bit and 64-bit Microsoft operating systems can be configured as nodes in server cluster, Microsoft is no longer supporting 32-bit operating systems, so they will not be discussed.

◆ Majority node set clusters with application-level replication (for example, Microsoft Exchange cluster continuous replication or database availability groups) are supported.

◆ Up to five-node clustering is allowed for Windows Server 2008 SP2 and above.

◆ Clustering does not support in-guest NIC teaming within the VMs.

◆ VMs configured as cluster nodes must use the LSI Logic SAS adapter.

◆ VMs in a clustered configuration are not valid candidates for vSphere FT or Storage DRS They can be part of a cluster that has these features enabled, but the features must be disabled for the VMs participating in the server cluster.

◆ VMs in a server cluster cannot use N_Port ID Virtualization.

◆ All the ESXi systems hosting VMs that are part of a server cluster must be running the same version of ESXi.

◆ VMs in a clustered configuration should all be the same hardware version (version 11 or later).

There is something else that you need to do. You must set the I/O timeout to 60 seconds or more by modifying `HKLM\System\CurrentControlSet\Services\Disk\TimeOutValue`, and if you re-create a cluster, you'll need to reset the value again. Additionally, it's a good idea to check this value on each node when VMware Tools is installed or upgraded.

So, let's delve into some more details on clustering and look at the specific clustering options available in the virtual environment. We'll start with the most basic design configuration: the cluster in a box.

Examining Cluster-in-a-Box Scenarios

The cluster-in-a-box scenario involves configuring two VMs hosted by the same ESXi host as nodes in a server cluster. The shared disks of the server cluster can exist as VMDK files stored on local Virtual Machine File System (VMFS) volumes or on a shared VMFS volume. Figure 7.4 details the configuration of a cluster in a box.

Figure 7.4

A cluster-in-a-box configuration does not provide protection against a single point of failure. Therefore, it is not a common or suggested form of deploying Microsoft server clusters in VMs.

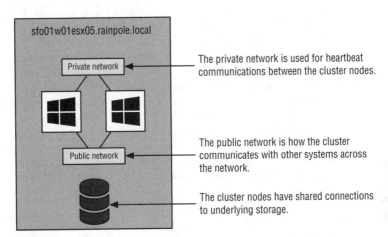

sfo01w01esx05.rainpole.local

Private network

Public network

The private network is used for heartbeat communications between the cluster nodes.

The public network is how the cluster communicates with other systems across the network.

The cluster nodes have shared connections to underlying storage.

After reviewing the diagram of a cluster-in-a-box configuration, you might wonder why you would want to deploy such a thing. With both VMs running on the same host, if that host fails, both VMs fail. This architecture contradicts the very reason for creating failover clusters. A cluster-in-a-box configuration still contains a single point of failure that can result in downtime of the clustered application. If the ESXi host hosting the two-node cluster-in-a-box configuration fails, then both nodes are lost and a failover does not occur. It's a relatively simple setup to configure and is probably best suited for learning or testing the cluster service configurations. You may also find yourself in a situation where it's needed for planned downtime or patching.

CONFIGURATION OPTIONS FOR VIRTUAL CLUSTERING

As suggested in the first part of this chapter, you deploy server clusters for high availability. In a vSphere-based outage, high availability is not achieved by using a cluster-in-a-box configuration, and therefore you should avoid this configuration for any type of critical production applications and services.

Examining Cluster-Across-Boxes Configurations

Although the cluster-in-a-box scenario is more of an experimental or educational tool for clustering, the cluster-across-boxes configuration provides a solid solution for critical VMs with stringent uptime requirements—for example, the enterprise-level servers and services like SQL

Server and Exchange Server that are heavily relied on by the bulk of end users. The cluster-across-boxes scenario, as the name applies, draws its high availability from the fact that the two nodes in the cluster are managed on different ESXi hosts. In the event that one of the hosts fails, the second node of the cluster will assume ownership of the cluster group and its resources, and the service or application will continue responding to client requests.

The cluster-across-boxes configuration requires that VMs have access to the same shared storage, which must reside on a Fibre Channel, FCoE, or iSCSI storage device to the ESXi hosts where the VMs run. Typically these are external storage protocols; however, with the release of vSAN 6.7, the iSCSI target that is built into vSAN can now support WSFC. The virtual hard drives that make up the operating system volume of the cluster nodes can be a standard VMDK implementation; however, the drives used as the shared storage must be set up as a special kind of drive called a *raw device mapping* (RDM). An RDM is a feature that allows a VM to establish direct access to a LUN on a SAN device. For more information about vSAN iSCSI targets and also about RDMs refer to Chapter 6.

A cluster-across-boxes configuration requires a more complex setup than a cluster-in-a-box configuration. When clustering across boxes, all communication between VMs and all communication from VMs and storage devices must be configured properly. Figure 7.5 provides details on the setup of a two-node VM cluster-across-box configuration using Windows Server 2016 as the guest OS.

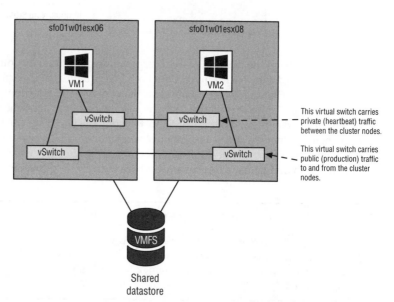

FIGURE 7.5
A Microsoft cluster built on VMs residing on separate ESXi hosts requires shared storage access from each VM using an RDM.

USING RAW DEVICE MAPPINGS IN YOUR VIRTUAL CLUSTERS

An RDM is not a direct access to a LUN, and it is not a normal virtual hard disk file. An RDM is a blend of the two. When you're adding a new disk to a VM, as you'll soon see, the Add Hardware Wizard presents the RDMs as an option on the Select A Disk page. This page defines the RDM as having the ability to give a VM direct access to the SAN, thereby allowing SAN management. This may seem like a contradiction to the opening statement of this sidebar; however, oddly enough, there is something that makes both statements true.

By selecting an RDM for a new disk, you're forced to select a compatibility mode for the RDM. An RDM can be configured in either Physical Compatibility mode or Virtual Compatibility mode. The Physical Compatibility mode option allows the VM to have direct raw LUN access. The Virtual Compatibility mode, however, is the hybrid configuration that allows raw LUN access but only through a VMDK file acting as a proxy. The following image details the architecture of using an RDM in Virtual Compatibility mode.

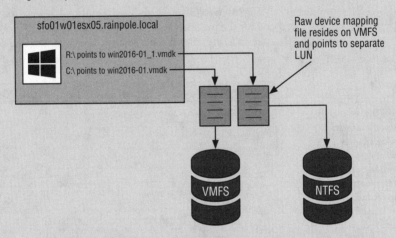

So, why choose one over the other if both are ultimately providing raw LUN access? Because the RDM in the Virtual Compatibility mode file allows you to take snapshots. By using the Virtual Compatibility mode, you can use snapshots on top of the raw LUN access in addition to any SAN-level snapshot or mirroring software. Or, of course, in the absence of SAN-level software, the VMware snapshot feature can certainly be a valuable tool. The decision to use Physical Compatibility or Virtual Compatibility is predicated solely on the need to use VMware snapshot technology or when using physical-to-virtual clustering.

Make sure you document things well when you start using RDMs. Any storage that is presented to ESXi that is not formatted with VMFS and has not already been allocated as an RDM will show up as available storage. If all the administrators are not on the same page, it used to be very easy to take a LUN used for an RDM and re-provision that LUN as a VMFS datastore, effectively blowing away the RDM data in the process. RDMs are now hidden by default when they are allocated, but we've seen this mistake happen firsthand, and it is a very quick process to erase any data that is there. You can go so far as to create a separate column in vCenter Server to list any configured RDM LUNs to make sure everyone has a reference point; similarly, you might want to use a tag or more restrictive permissions (explained in Chapter 3, "Installing and Configuring vCenter Server").

Let's keep moving and perform the steps to configure Microsoft Cluster Services on Windows Server 2016 across VMs on separate ESXi hosts.

Creating the First Cluster Node in Windows Server 2016

Perform these steps to create the first cluster node:

1. Using the vSphere Web Client, create a new VM, and install Windows Server 2016 (or clone an existing VM or template with Windows Server 2016 already installed).

   Refer to Chapter 9, "Creating and Managing Virtual Machines," for more details on creating VMs; see Chapter 10, "Using Templates and vApps," for more information on cloning VMs.

2. Configure the VM with two NICs, as shown in Figure 7.6—one for the public (production) network and one for the private (heartbeat) network. Assign IP addresses within Windows Server 2012 as needed. Shut down the VM after you complete the networking configuration.

FIGURE 7.6

A node in a Microsoft Windows Server cluster requires at least two NICs. One adapter must be able to communicate on the production network, and the second adapter is configured for internal cluster heartbeat communication.

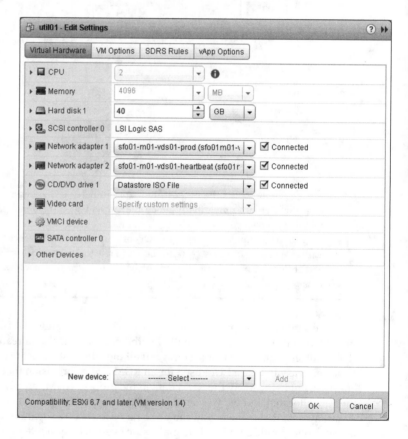

3. Right-click the new VM and select Edit Settings.

4. Click the New Device drop-down, select RDM Disk, and click Add, as shown in Figure 7.7.

FIGURE 7.7
Add a new device of type RDM Disk for the first node in a cluster and Existing Hard Disk for additional nodes.

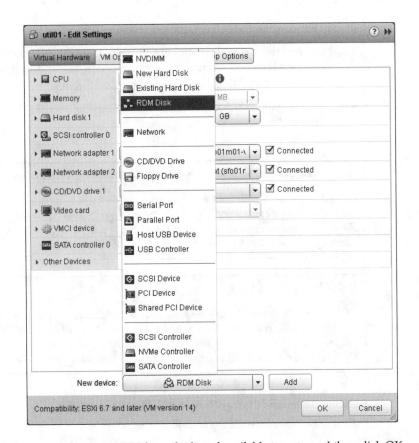

5. Select the appropriate target LUN from the list of available targets, and then click OK.

   Reminder: make sure you have the correct LUN or you could overwrite important data!

6. Click the arrow next to the New Hard Disk item, and next to Location, choose "Store with the virtual machine to keep the VMDK proxy file on the same datastore as the VM." Note that if your virtual machine is on NFS storage, you will need to choose a VMFS datastore to place this disk onto.

7. Select either Physical or Virtual for the RDM compatibility mode.

   Older, unsupported versions of Windows have different requirements. In this case, select Physical and then click Next.

8. Select the virtual device node to which the RDM should be connected.

   Note that you must select a different SCSI node; you can't put the RDM on SCSI 0.0.

9. Repeat steps 2 through 8 to configure additional RDMs for shared storage locations needed by nodes of a Microsoft server cluster.

In this case, you're going to present a single RDM.

10. Power on the first node of the cluster. Verify that you've assigned valid IP addresses to the network adapters configured for the production and heartbeat networks. Then format the new drive representing the RDM and assign drive letters.

11. Proceed to the next section to configure the second cluster node and the respective ESXi host.

RDM REQUIREMENTS FOR EARLIER VERSIONS OF WINDOWS SERVER

Originally, when building a cluster across multiple ESXi hosts using Windows Server 2003, you could use Virtual mode RDMs. Since Windows Server 2003 is no longer supported by Microsoft, it's best that you move to a more modern OS. Using Windows Server 2008 or later to build the cluster across ESXi hosts, you must use Physical Compatibility mode.

SCSI NODES FOR RDMs

RDMs used for shared storage in a Microsoft server cluster must be configured on a SCSI node that is different from the SCSI to which the hard disk is connected and that holds the operating system. For example, if the operating system's virtual hard drive is configured to use the SCSI0 node, the RDM should use the SCSI1 node. This rule applies to both virtual and physical clustering.

Creating the Second Cluster Node in Windows Server 2016

Follow these steps to create the second cluster node:

1. Using the vSphere Web Client, create a second VM running Windows Server 2016 that is a member of the same Active Directory domain as the first cluster node. Ensure that the VM has two NICs and that the NICs have appropriate IP addresses assigned for the production (public) and heartbeat (private) networks.

2. Shut down the second VM.

3. Add the same RDMs to the second cluster node.

This time around, you can't select Raw Device Mappings, because the LUN you selected when setting up the first node won't be listed (it's already been used). Instead, select Existing Hard Disk, as listed earlier in Figure 7.7, and then navigate to the location of the VMDK proxy file. (If you selected Store With The Virtual Machine in step 6 for setting up the first node, you'll find a VMDK file there with the same size as the backing LUN.)

Be sure to use the same SCSI node values on the second VM. For example, if the first node used SCSI 1:0 for the first RDM, configure the second node to use the same configuration. Don't forget to edit the SCSI bus sharing configuration for the new SCSI adapter (Physical SCSI bus sharing).

4. Power on the second VM.

5. Verify that the hard drives corresponding to the RDMs can be seen in Disk Manager. At this point, the drives will show a status of Healthy, but drive letters will not be assigned.

Creating the Failover Cluster in Windows Server 2016

Perform the following steps to create the management cluster:

1. Log into the first node as an administrative user.

2. Launch Server Manager if it doesn't launch automatically.

3. Navigate to the Add Roles And Features Wizard, and click through until you get to the list of features.

4. From the list of features, select Failover Clustering and click Next.

5. In the pop-up box that appears, accept the additional features that need to be installed by clicking Add Features.

6. Check the box to restart if required, and click Install.

7. Repeat this process on the second node.

With failover clustering installed on both nodes, you can validate the cluster configuration to ensure that everything is configured properly:

1. Log into the first node as an administrative user.

2. From the Start menu, launch Administrative Tools and then open the Failover Cluster Manager.

3. Click Validate A Configuration. This launches the Validate A Configuration Wizard. Click Next to start the wizard.

4. Enter the names of both the first and second cluster nodes, clicking Add after each server name to add it to the list. Click Next.

5. Leave the default selection (Run All Tests) and click Next.

6. Click Next at the Confirmation step.

7. Review the report. If any errors are reported, follow the guidance to address the errors. Click Finish when you are done.

Now you're ready to create the cluster. Follow these steps:

1. You should still be logged into the first node as an administrative user and have the Failover Cluster Manager console open. Click Create A Cluster.

2. At the first screen of the Create Cluster Wizard, click Next.

3. Enter the names of both nodes, and click Add after each server to add it to the list. Click Next to continue.

4. On the Confirmation screen, validate both the node names and the cluster name. Check the box to add all eligible storage to the cluster and click Next.

5. The Create Cluster Wizard will perform the necessary steps to create the cluster and brin the resources online. When it has completed, review the report and click Finish.

After the cluster is up and running, you can use the Failover Cluster Manager to add resources, applications, and services. Some applications, such as Microsoft SQL Server and Microsoft Exchange Server, not only are cluster-aware applications but also allow you to create server cluster as part of the standard installation wizard. Other cluster-aware applications and services can be configured into a cluster using the cluster administrator. Refer to the document tion for Microsoft Windows Server and/or the specific application you want to cluster for more details.

EXAMINING PHYSICAL-TO-VIRTUAL CLUSTERING

The last type of clustering scenario to discuss is physical-to-virtual clustering. As you might ha guessed, this involves building a cluster with two nodes where one node is a physical machine and the other node is a VM. Figure 7.8 details the setup of a two-node physical-to-virtual cluste

FIGURE 7.8
Clustering physical machines with VM counterparts can be a cost-effective way of providing high availability.

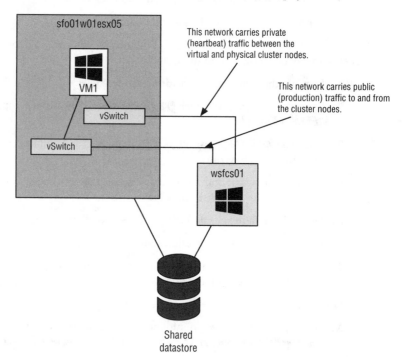

The constraints surrounding the construction of a physical-to-virtual cluster are identical to those noted in the previous configuration. Likewise, the steps to configure the VM acting as a

node in the physical-to-virtual cluster are identical to the steps outlined in the previous section, remembering that you must set up the RDMs in Physical Compatibility mode, regardless of the version of Windows Server you're using. The VM must have access to all the same storage locations as the physical machine. The VM must also have access to the same pair of networks used by the physical machine for production and heartbeat communication, respectively.

The advantage to implementing a physical-to-virtual cluster is the resulting high availability with lower cost. As you would expect, having appropriately sized virtual machines and hosts with no overcommitment will allow for multiple physical host cluster node failures. Figure 7.9 shows an example of many-to-one physical-to-virtual clustering.

FIGURE 7.9
Using a single powerful ESXi system to host multiple failover clusters is one use case for physical-to-virtual clustering.

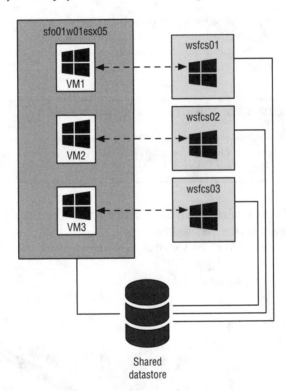

Shared datastore

OS CLUSTERING IS NOT LIMITED TO WINDOWS

Although we've discussed only Windows Server–based OS clustering methods in this section, you are not limited to Windows to use OS clustering. Other supported OSs also offer ways to provide high availability within the OS itself.

Now that I've covered OS clustering in Windows Server, let's take a look at VMware's version of high availability. VMware has a built-in option called vSphere High Availability. As you'll see, vSphere HA uses a very different method than OS clustering to provide high availability.

Implementing vSphere High Availability

You've already seen how you can use OS clustering to provide high availability for OSs and applications. vSphere provides a feature intended to provide high availability at the virtualization layer, vSphere Availability, a component that provides for automatic failover of VMs. Because the term *high availability* can mean different things to different people, VMware renamed the previously named "vSphere High Availability" and "vSphere Availability Clusters" to just "vSphere Availability." However, since "vSphere HA" is the more widely used term throughout the VMware ecosystem and within the vSphere Web Client UI, that's the name we'll use throughout this book.

It's important to understand the behavior of vSphere HA to ensure you are using the right availability mechanism to meet the requirements of your organization. Depending on your requirements, one of the other availability mechanisms described in this chapter might be more appropriate.

A COMPLETE REWRITE FROM OLDER VERSIONS

The underpinnings of vSphere HA (now called vSphere Availability) underwent a complete rewrite in vSphere 5.0 and has been incrementally improved since then. If you are familiar with older versions of vSphere, keep this in mind as you look at how vSphere Availability behaves in this version.

Understanding vSphere High Availability Clusters

The vSphere High Availability feature, or more simply, vSphere HA, is designed to provide an automatic restart of the VMs that were running on an ESXi host at the time it became unavailable, as shown in Figure 7.10.

FIGURE 7.10
vSphere Availability provides an automatic restart of VMs that were running on an ESXi host when it failed.

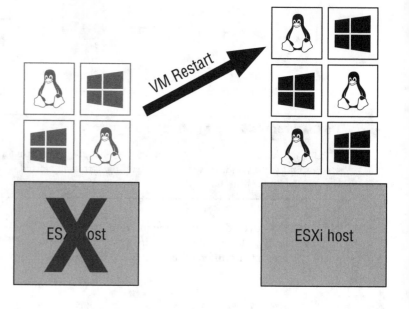

vSphere HA primarily targets ESXi host failures, but it can also protect against VM failures and respond to storage connectivity issues. In all cases, vSphere HA uses a restart of the VM as the mechanism for addressing the detected failure. This means there is a period of downtime when a failure occurs. Unfortunately, you can't calculate the exact duration of the downtime because it is unknown ahead of time how long it will take to boot a VM or a series of VMs. From this, you can gather that vSphere HA might not provide the same level of high availability found in other high-availability solutions. Further, when a failover occurs between ESXi hosts as a result of the vSphere HA feature, there is a slight potential for data loss and/or filesystem corruption because the VM was immediately powered off when the server failed and then brought back up minutes later on another server. However, given the journaling filesystems in use by Windows and many distributions of Linux, this possibility is relatively slim.

---

vSphere HA Experience in the Field

As recounted by Nick

I want to mention my own personal experience with vSphere HA and the results I encountered. Your mileage might vary, but this should give you a reasonable idea of what to expect. I had a VMware ESXi host that was a member of a five-host cluster. This host crashed some time during the night, and when the host went down, it took anywhere from 15 to 20 VMs with it. vSphere HA kicked in and restarted all the VMs as expected.

What made this an interesting experience is that the crash must have happened right after the polling of the monitoring and alerting server. All the VMs that were on the general alerting schedule were restarted without triggering any alerts. Some of the VMs with more aggressive monitoring that tripped off alerts were recovered before anyone was able to log into the system and investigate. I tried to argue the point that if an alert never fired, did the downtime really happen? I did not get too far with that argument, but I was pleased with the results. vSphere Proactive HA might have been able to detect that this failure was happening and performed a vMotion to evacuate the host prior to that failure, but this feature was not part of vSphere at the time.

In another case, during testing I had a VM running on a two-host cluster. I pulled the power cords on the host that the VM was running to create the failure. My time to recovery from pull to ping was between 5 and 6 minutes and most of that time was the application starting back up on the rebooted VM. That's not too bad for general use but not good enough for all cases. vSphere Fault Tolerance can now fill that gap for even the most important and critical servers in your environment.

We'll talk more about vSphere FT and Proactive HA in a bit.

Understanding vSphere High Availability's Core Components

On the surface, the functionality of vSphere HA is similar to the functionality provided in previous versions of vSphere. Under the covers, though, from vSphere 5.0 on, HA uses a VMware-developed tool known as Fault Domain Manager (FDM). FDM was developed from the ground up to replace Automated Availability Manager (AAM), which powered vSphere HA in earlier versions of vSphere. AAM had a number of notable limitations, including a strong dependence on name resolution and scalability limits. FDM was developed to address these limitations while still providing all the same functionality from earlier versions of vSphere. FDM also offers a few significant improvements over AAM:

◆ FDM uses a master/slave architecture that does not rely on primary/secondary host designations.

◆ FDM uses both the management network and storage devices for communication.

◆ FDM supports IPv6.

◆ FDM addresses the issues of both network partition and network isolation.

FDM uses the concept of an agent that runs on each ESXi host. This agent is separate and decoupled from the vCenter management agents that vCenter uses to communicate with ESXi hosts (the management agent is known as vpxa). This agent gets installed into the ESXi hosts at opt/vmware/fdm and stores its configuration files at /etc/opt/vmware/fdm (note that you must enable SSH and the ESXi shell in order to view these directories).

Although FDM is markedly different from AAM, as an end user you will notice very little difference in how vSphere HA operates. Therefore, we generally won't refer to FDM directly, but instead to vSphere HA. But you should be aware of the underlying differences.

When vSphere HA is enabled, the vSphere HA agents participate in an election to pick a vSphere HA master. The vSphere HA master is responsible for the following key tasks within a vSphere HA–enabled cluster:

◆ Monitors slave hosts and will restart VMs in the event of a slave host failure.

◆ Monitors the power state of all protected VMs. If a protected VM fails, the vSphere HA master will restart the VM.

◆ Manages the list of hosts that are members of the cluster and manages the process of adding and removing hosts from the cluster.

◆ Manages the list of protected VMs. It updates this list after each user-initiated power-on power-off operation. These updates are at the request of vCenter Server, which requests the master to protect or unprotect VMs.

◆ Caches the cluster configuration. The master notifies and informs slave hosts of changes the cluster configuration.

◆ The vSphere HA master host sends heartbeat messages to the slave hosts so that the slave hosts know the master is alive.

◆ Reports state information to vCenter Server. vCenter Server typically communicates only with the master.

As you can see, the role of the vSphere HA master is quite important. For this reason, if the existing master fails a new vSphere HA master is automatically elected. The new master will then take over the responsibilities listed here, including communication with vCenter Server.

DOES VCENTER SERVER TALK TO VSPHERE HA SLAVE HOSTS?

There are a few instances in which vCenter Server will talk to vSphere HA agents on slave hosts: when it is scanning for a vSphere HA master, when a host is reported as isolated or partitioned, or if the existing master informs vCenter that it cannot reach a slave agent.

Once an ESXi host in a vSphere HA–enabled cluster elects a vSphere HA master, all other hosts become slaves connected to that master. The slave hosts have the following responsibilities:

◆ A slave host watches the runtime state of the VMs running locally on that host. Significant changes in the runtime state of these VMs are forwarded to the vSphere HA master.

◆ vSphere HA slaves monitor the health of the master. If the master fails, slaves will participate in a new master election.

◆ vSphere HA slave hosts implement vSphere HA features that don't require central coordination by the master. This includes VM health monitoring.

The role of any given ESXi host within a vSphere HA–enabled cluster is noted on the Summary tab of the ESXi host within the vSphere Web Client. The composite screenshot in Figure 7.11 shows how the vSphere Web Client presents this information.

FIGURE 7.11
The status of an ESXi host as either master or slave is provided on the host's Summary tab. Here you can see both a master host and a slave host.

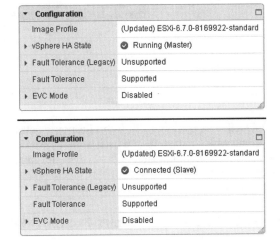

We mentioned that vSphere HA uses the management network as well as storage devices to communicate. In the event that the master cannot communicate with a slave across the management network, the master can check its *heartbeat datastores*—selected datastores used by vSphere HA for communication—to see if the slave host is still alive. This functionality is what helps vSphere HA deal with network partition as well as network isolation.

Network partition is the term that describes the situation in which one or more slave hosts cannot communicate with the master even though they still have network connectivity with each other. In this case, vSphere HA can use the heartbeat datastores to detect whether the partitioned hosts are still live and whether action needs to be taken to protect VMs on those hosts or initiate an election for a new master within the network partition.

Network isolation is the situation in which one or more slave hosts have lost all management network connectivity. Isolated hosts can neither communicate with the vSphere HA master nor communicate with other ESXi hosts. In this case, the slave host uses heartbeat datastores to notify the master that it is isolated. The slave host uses a special binary file, the host-X-poweron file, to notify the master. The vSphere HA master can then take the appropriate action to ensure that the

VMs are protected. We'll discuss network isolation and how an ESXi host reacts to network isolation later in this chapter, in the section "Response for Host Network Isolation."

Figure 7.12 shows the files on a VMFS datastore that vSphere HA uses for storage heartbeating between the vSphere HA master and slave hosts.

FIGURE 7.12
vSphere HA uses the host-*X*-poweron files for a slave host to notify the master that it has become isolated from the network.

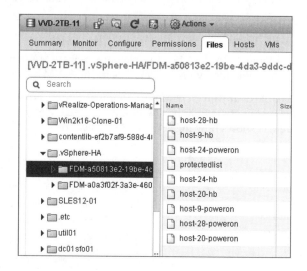

In the section "Detailing Failure and Response Settings," later in this chapter, you'll learn how to determine which datastores are used as heartbeat datastores as well as how to tell vSphere HA which datastores should or should not be used for heartbeating.

Before moving on to enabling vSphere HA to protect your VMs, let's take a moment to look at Virtual Machine Component Protection.

VIRTUAL MACHINE COMPONENT PROTECTION

The previous section discussed the behavior of HA under various scenarios. Primarily, these are focused on either a total outage of the host, or the loss of network connectivity. Although this is great capability, scenarios such as loss of storage due to an all paths down (APD) or permanent device loss (PDL) event cannot be addressed without additional functionality. Enter Virtual Machine Component Protection (VMCP).

VMCP was introduced as part of vSphere HA in vSphere 6.0. Its purpose is to detect storage access failures and allows for a user-configurable automated response for affected virtual machines, including alerts and HA initiated restarts.

It stands to reason that if you are relying on HA to restart affected VMs there will be different outcomes based on the configuration settings. Table 7.1 shows the different responses from VMCP that can be configured in an APD or PDL event.

Although these settings are enabled at the cluster level, you can override them for particular VMs in the same manner as your HA responses.

TABLE 7.1: VMCP failure responses

FAILURE CONDITION	RESPONSE SETTING
Datastore With PDL	Disabled—No action will be taken.
	Issue Events—Only events will be logged and displayed in the UI.
	Power Off And Restart VMs—This will find a host in the cluster that still has connectivity to the datastore and restart the VM on this host.
Datastore With APD	Disabled—No action will be taken.
	Issue Events—Only events will be logged and displayed in the UI.
	Power Off And Restart VMs (Conservative)—The VM will only be shut down if it knows another host can restart it.
	Power Off And Restart VMs (Aggressive)—The VM will always be shut down and will then try to find another host to restart it.

Let's walk through a PDL scenario and see how the process works. Failure detection occurs at the storage layer, with the Pluggable Storage Architecture (PSA) detecting the PDL error code as issued by the storage array. This event is then passed through to hostd, which tags it for VMCP to capture. VMCP monitors the datastore properties, `vim.host.mountInfo.accessible` and `vim.host.mountInfo.inaccessibleReason`. If it's inaccessible, VMCP will assess the impact to the VM (such as having one or more files on the affected datastore) using the property `vim.virtualmachine.storage.perDatastoreUsage`, and then take the action as configured in the cluster settings.

When there is an APD event, there is no way to get any communications from the array to gather status or sense codes. The host will simply continue to retry the I/O operation until either the storage device comes back online, or the APD timeout value is reached. By default this is 140 seconds. Once an APD even has been declared, VMCP kicks in and instructs vSphere HA to take the appropriate action.

Let's move on and look at enabling vSphere Availability, which will include configuring VMCP for PDL and APD events.

Enabling vSphere HA

To implement vSphere HA, you must ensure all of these requirements are met:

- All hosts in a vSphere HA–enabled cluster must have access to the same shared storage locations used by all VMs on the cluster. This could be any Fibre Channel, FCoE, iSCSI, NFS, or vSAN datastores used by VMs.

- All hosts in a vSphere HA cluster should have an identical virtual networking configuration. If a new switch is added to one host, the same new switch should be added to all hosts in the cluster. If you are using a vSphere Distributed Switch (vDS), all hosts should be participating in the same vDS.

A TEST FOR vSPHERE HA

An easy and simple test for identifying vSphere HA capability for a VM is to perform a vMotion. The requirements of vMotion are actually more stringent than those for performing a vSphere HA failover, though most of the requirements are identical. In short, if a VM can successfully perform a vMotion across the hosts in a cluster, without changing the datastore, then it is safe to assume that vSphere HA will be able to power on that VM from any of the hosts. To perform a full test of a VM on a cluster with four ESXi hosts, perform a vMotion from host 1 to host 2, host 2 to host 3, host 3 to host 4, and finally host 4 back to host 1. If it works, then the VM, and therefore the cluster, has passed the test!

As with earlier versions, vSphere HA is a cluster-level configuration. To use vSphere HA to protect VMs, you must first place your ESXi hosts into a cluster. Remember, a vSphere cluster represents a logical aggregation of CPU and memory resources. With vSphere HA, a cluster also represents a logical protection boundary. VMs can be protected by vSphere HA only if they are running on an ESXi host in a vSphere HA–enabled cluster.

If you don't already have a cluster created that you want to enable vSphere HA on, perform the following steps:

1. If the vSphere Web Client is not already running, launch it and connect to a vCenter Server instance. vSphere HA is available only when you're using vCenter Server.

2. Within the Hosts And Clusters view, right-click the datacenter object and select New Cluster as shown in Figure 7.13. The New Cluster dialog box will appear.

3. Type a name for your cluster, such as **sfo01-m01-mgmt**. You now have the option of enabling vSphere HA, along with some other features. Leave the boxes unticked for now and just click OK.

Now that you have a brand new empty cluster, you have two tasks to complete before testing vSphere HA. First, you need to enable vSphere HA on the newly created cluster. Second, you need to drag hosts that are currently registered in vCenter Server to this new cluster. Both steps are required, and it doesn't matter which order you perform them in. Once you have a cluster created in the vSphere Web Client, with ESXi hosts allocated to the cluster, it should look like Figure 7.14. In this example, sfo01m01vc01 is the name of the vCenter Server, sfo01-m01dc is the datacenter name, and sfo01-m01-mgmt01 is the cluster name.

Let's go through enabling vSphere HA on a cluster to see what changes in the vSphere UI.

1. If the vSphere Web Client is not already running, launch it and connect to a vCenter Server instance. vSphere HA is available only when you're using vCenter Server.

2. Right-click a cluster object and select Settings. This takes you to the Configure tab for the cluster.

3. Select vSphere Availability in the list of Services, and on the right side of the content area click the Edit button to enter the cluster settings.

4. Click the Turn ON vSphere HA check box, as shown in Figure 7.15, and then click OK.

FIGURE 7.13
Clusters need to be
created in Datacenter
objects within vCenter.

FIGURE 7.14
Once a cluster is created,
hosts can be allocated
to the cluster to pool
their resources.

When vSphere HA is enabled for a cluster, it will elect a master, and the other hosts in the cluster will become slave hosts connected to that master host. You can observe this process by watching the All Tasks pane of the vSphere Web Client when you enable vSphere HA. Figure 7.16 shows an example of the tasks that are generated when you enable vSphere HA for a cluster.

FIGURE 7.15
Enabling vSphere HA for a cluster is a simple check box.

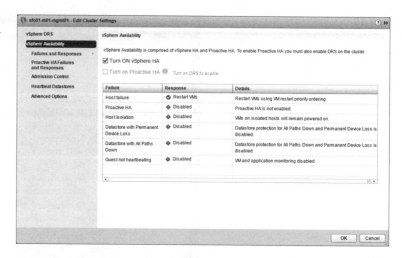

FIGURE 7.16
As you can see in the All Tasks pane, vSphere HA elects a master host when it is enabled on a cluster of ESXi hosts.

After vSphere HA is enabled, you may occasionally need to temporarily halt it, such as during a maintenance window. Previously, we discussed the behavior of vSphere HA when a network partition or network isolation occurs. Note that the Enable Host Monitoring check box shown in Figure 7.17 is not checked; this is how you can temporarily disable the host-monitoring function of vSphere HA during network maintenance so as not to trigger network partition or network isolation behaviors.

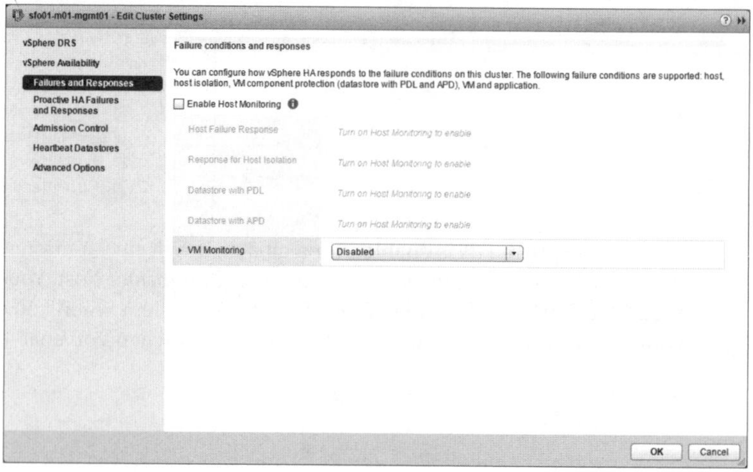

FIGURE 7.17
Deselecting the Enable Host Monitoring option when you're performing network maintenance will prevent vSphere HA from unnecessarily triggering network isolation or network partition responses.

Now that you have vSphere HA enabled, there are many settings that you can configure to customize the type of behavior and response that you would like vSphere HA to perform.

Configuring vSphere High Availability

After vSphere HA is enabled, there are a number of ways to configure the different components of vSphere HA. Grouped within the UI, these configuration items revolve around several key areas:

- Failures and Responses

- Proactive HA Failure and Responses

- Admission Control

- Heartbeat Datastore

- Advanced Options

Each of these configuration areas is described in detail in the following sections. We'll outline these settings in the same order that you find them within the Edit Cluster Settings dialog box.

DETAILING FAILURE AND RESPONSE SETTINGS

When vSphere HA is first enabled, only the most basic settings are turned on by default. The vSphere HA FDM agent is installed on each host, and Host Monitoring is turned on, as shown in Figure 7.18. The default response for a host failure is to restart the affected VMs on other available hosts in the cluster, but all other options are disabled. In this section, we'll go through each setting and explain the changes that happen when it's enabled.

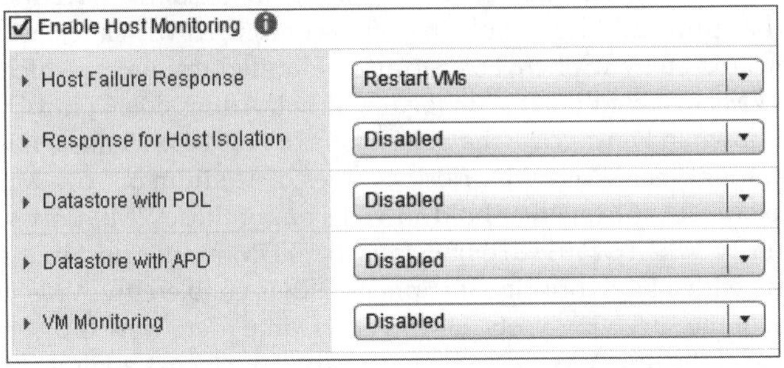

FIGURE 7.18
vSphere HA only turns on the basic host failure monitoring capabilities initially.

☑ Enable Host Monitoring ⓘ	
▸ Host Failure Response	Restart VMs ▾
▸ Response for Host Isolation	Disabled ▾
▸ Datastore with PDL	Disabled ▾
▸ Datastore with APD	Disabled ▾
▸ VM Monitoring	Disabled ▾

Host Failure Response

Within the Failure Conditions And Responses section of the vSphere HA Cluster Settings, there are a number of configuration options. By default, when you enable vSphere HA on a cluster, the Failure Response is set to Restart VMs. As stated within the UI, this will happen only when a host has failed, and it will do so in the order determined by the importance of each VM, or more specifically, their restart priority.

Not all VMs are equal. Some VMs are more important or more critical and require higher priority when ensuring availability. When an ESXi host experiences failure and the remaining cluster hosts are tasked by vSphere HA with bringing VMs back online, they have a finite amount of resources before there are no more resources to allocate to VMs that need to be powered on. This is especially true when Admission Control is set to Disabled, allowing more VMs to be powered on than the cluster could support given a failure. Rather than leave important VMs to chance, a vSphere HA–enabled cluster allows you to prioritize VMs through VM Restart Priority.

For VMs that should be brought up first, the restart priority should be set to Highest, or maybe High if they are important but not critical. For VMs that should be brought up if resources are available, the restart priority can be set to Medium, Low, or Lowest. For VMs that will not be missed for a period of time and should not be brought online when available resources are low, the restart priority should be set to Disabled. You can define a default restart priority for the entire cluster, as shown in Figure 7.19, but what if there is a VM that is more (or less) important? The VM Overrides section allows you to define a per-VM restart priority. We'll cover VM overrides later in the chapter.

FIGURE 7.19
All VMs in the cluster are given the same restart priority unless a VM is given a specific VM Override.

The restart priority is put into place only for the VMs running on the ESXi hosts that experience an unexpected failure. VMs running on hosts that have not failed are not affected by the restart priority. It is possible that VMs configured with a restart priority of High might not be powered on by vSphere HA because of limited resources, which is in part because of lower-priority VMs that continue to run (again, only if Admission Control was set to Disabled). For example, as shown in Figure 7.20, the ESXi host sfo01w01esx05 hosts four VMs with a priority of High and four other VMs with priority values of Medium or Low. Meanwhile, sfo01w01esx06 and sfo01w01esx07 together hold 13 VMs, but of those VMs, only two are considered of High priority. When sfo01w01esx05 fails, the FDM master host in the cluster will begin powering the VMs with a High priority. If vSphere DRS is enabled, the VMs will be automatically placed on one of the surviving hosts. However, assume there were only enough resources to power on three of the four VMs with High priority. That leaves a High-priority VM powered off while all other VMs of Medium and Low priorities continue to run on the remaining hosts.

At this point, you can still manually remedy this imbalance. Any business continuity plan in a virtual environment built on vSphere should include a contingency plan that identifies VMs to be powered off to make resources available for those VMs with higher priority because of the network services they provide. If the budget allows, construct the vSphere HA cluster to ensure that there are ample resources to cover the needs of the critical VMs, even in times of reduced computing capacity. You can enforce guaranteed resource availability for restarting VMs by setting Admission Control to Enabled, as described in the section "Configuring vSphere HA Admission Control," later in this chapter.

FIGURE 7.20

High-priority VMs from a failed ESXi host might not be powered on because of a lack of resources—resources consumed by VMs with a lower priority that are running on the other hosts in a vSphere HA– enabled cluster.

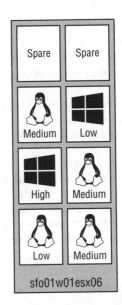

The ability to control the way VMs restart when there has been a host failure can also be tweaked further by changing the VM Dependency Restart Condition. Again, this is a cluster-wide setting and can be changed on a per-VM basis using the VM Overrides section. This setting allows you to create a delay between VMs, or groups of VMs being powered on.

Let's say you have three VMs that make up an application. VM1 is the database server, VM2 is the application server, and VM3 is the web front-end server. The ESXi host that is running these VMs fails, and vSphere HA kicks in and begins to restart the VMs on other hosts in the cluster. If you leave the VM Dependency Restart Condition at the default setting of Resources Allocated, each VM will start almost simultaneously. Depending on your situation, this may or may not be what you desire, especially if the VMs host an application that needs to be started in the correct order. There can be a slight delay between when a host reserves the resources and when the VM actually powers on.

The other alternatives are that you can set the dependency to Guest Heartbeats or even Application Heartbeats detected. This will lengthen the vSphere HA restart duration considerably. Guest Heartbeats are only sent to the ESXi host once VM Tools has started within the guest OS of the VM. Application Heartbeats are only sent to the ESXi host once VM Tools has started along with the application that talks to the Application Monitoring API within VM Tools. This is dependent on the application being capable of doing this and is not commonplace today. You can find out more information about VM and Application heartbeats in the section VM Monitoring. Subsequent to these restart conditions, you can also add custom additional delays and a timeout. The timeout is set to 10 minutes by default, which you may want to reduce if you are using one of the heartbeat dependencies. Ten minutes is a long time between a lot of VMs if the heartbeats are not being received but the VMs are working correctly behind the scenes.

Finally, vSphere HA now has the ability to orchestrate the restart order, in addition to the priority and dependencies. We'll discuss that in the section Configuring vSphere HA Groups, Rules, Overrides, and Orchestrated VM Restart. However, before we get there, you need to understand what happens when a host does not fail but is isolated in some way.

Response for Host Network Isolation

Previously, we introduced FDM as the underpinning for vSphere HA and how it uses the ESXi management network to communicate between the master host and all connected slave hosts. When the vSphere HA master is no longer receiving status updates from a slave host, the master assumes that host has failed and instructs the other connected slave hosts to spring into action to power on all the VMs that the missing host was running.

But what if the host with the missing heartbeat was not really missing? What if the heartbeat was missing but the host was still running? This is the scenario described in the section "Understanding vSphere High Availability's Core Components," which discussed the idea of *network isolation*. When an ESXi host in a vSphere HA–enabled cluster is isolated—that is, it cannot communicate with the master host nor can it communicate with any other ESXi hosts or any other network devices—then the ESXi host triggers the isolation response configured in the dialog box shown in Figure 7.21. As you can see, the default isolation response for the entire cluster is Leave Powered On. Although it's generally not recommended, you can change this setting for the entire cluster here or for one or more specific VMs in the VM Overrides section.

FIGURE 7.21

Hosts can be set to gracefully shut down or simply power off their VMs when they become isolated from the rest of the cluster.

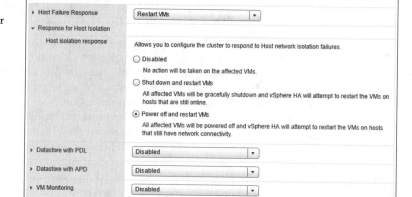

Because vSphere HA uses the ESXi management network as well as connected datastores (via datastore heartbeating) to communicate, network isolation is handled a bit differently than in versions of vSphere 4.1 and prior. In previous versions, when a host was isolated, it would automatically trigger the configured isolation response. A host considered itself isolated when it was not receiving heartbeats from any other hosts and when it could not reach the *isolation address* (by default, the default gateway on the management network).

From vSphere 5.0 on, the process for determining if a host is isolated is slightly different. A host that is the master is looking for communication from its slave hosts; a host that is running as a slave is looking for updates from the master host. In either case, if the master or slave is not receiving any vSphere HA network heartbeat information, it will then attempt to contact the isolation address (by default, the default gateway on the management network). If it can reach the default gateway or an additional configured isolation address (or addresses), then the ESXi host considers itself to be in a network partition state and reacts as described in the section

"Understanding vSphere High Availability Clusters." If the host can't reach the isolation address, it considers itself isolated. Here is where this behavior diverges from the behavior of previous versions.

At this point, an ESXi host that has determined that it is network-isolated will modify a special bit in the binary host-X-poweron file on all datastores that are configured for datastore heartbeating (more on that in the section "Heartbeat Datastores"). The master sees that this bit, used to denote isolation, has been set and is therefore notified that this slave host has been isolated. When a master sees that a slave has been isolated, the master locks another file used by vSphere HA on the heartbeat datastore. When the isolated host sees that this file has been locked by a master, it knows that the master is assuming responsibility for restarting the VMs—remember that only a master can restart VMs—and the isolated host is then free to execute the configured isolation response. Therefore, even if the isolation response is set to Shut Down or Power Off, that action won't take place until the isolated slave has confirmed, via the datastore heartbeating structures, that a master has assumed responsibility for restarting the VMs.

The question still remains, though: should you change the Host Isolation Response setting? The answer to this question is highly dependent on the virtual and physical network infrastructures in place. Let's look at a couple of examples.

Let's say you have a host in which both the ESXi management network and the VM networks are connected to the same virtual switch bound to a single network adapter (clearly not a generally recommended configuration). In this case, when the cable for the uplink on this vSwitch is unplugged, communication to the ESXi management network and every VM on that computer is lost. The solution, then, should be to shut down the VMs. When an ESXi host determines it is isolated and has confirmed that a master host has assumed responsibility for restarting the VMs, it can execute the isolation response so that the VMs can be restarted on another host with full network connectivity.

A more realistic example might be a situation in which a single vSwitch has two uplinks but both uplinks go to the same physical switch. If this vSwitch hosts both the ESXi management and VM networks, the loss of that physical switch means that both management traffic and VM traffic have been interrupted. Setting Host Isolation Response to Shut Down would allow vSphere HA to restart those VMs on another ESXi host and restore connectivity to the VMs.

However, a network configuration that employs multiple uplinks, multiple vSwitches, and multiple physical switches, as shown in Figure 7.22, should probably leave Host Isolation Response set to Leave Powered On. In this scenario it's unlikely that a network isolation event would also leave the VMs on that host inaccessible.

CONFIGURING THE ISOLATION RESPONSE ADDRESS

In some highly secure virtual environments, management access is limited to a single, non-routed management network. In these cases, the security plan calls for the elimination of the default gateway on the ESXi management network. The idea is to lock the ESXi management network onto the local subnet, thus preventing any type of remote network access to the management interfaces. The disadvantage, as you might have guessed, is that without a default gateway IP address configured for the management network, there is no isolation address to ping as a determination of network isolation status.

It is possible, however, to customize the isolation response address for scenarios just like this. The IP address can be any IP address but should be one that is not going to be unavailable or taken from the network at any time.

Perform the following steps to define a custom isolation response address:

1. Use the vSphere Web Client to connect to a vCenter Server instance.

2. Open the Hosts And Clusters View, right-click an existing cluster, and select the Configure option.

3. Ensure that vSphere Availability is selected in the left column and click the Edit button.

4. Click on the Advanced Options section and click the Add button.

5. Enter **das.isolationaddress** in the Option column in the Advanced Options (HA) dialog box.

6. Enter the IP address to be used as the isolation response address for ESXi hosts that cannot communicate with the FDM master host.

7. Click OK.

This interface can also be configured with the following options:

◆ `das.isolationaddress1` to specify the first address to try

◆ `das.isolationaddress2` to specify the second address to try

◆ `das.AllowNetwork` to specify a different port group to use for HA heartbeat

FIGURE 7.22
The option to leave VMs running when a host is isolated should be set only when the virtual and the physical networking infrastructures support high availability.

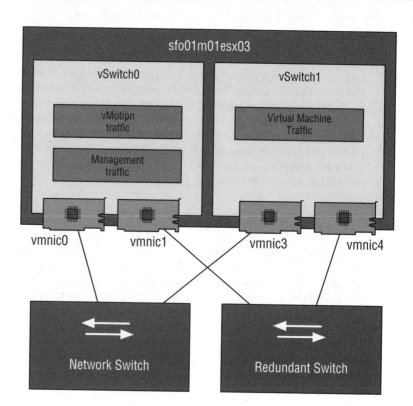

While it's great to have options for when a host is isolated or segmented from a network perspective, how can you ensure that the correct response happens if there's a storage-related issue? Next, we'll talk about how you can configure Virtual Machine Component Protection (VMCP) to ensure this scenario is covered too.

Datastore with PDL and APD

When storage outages occur, vSphere HA can ensure that VMs are restarted in a relatively timely manner on an alternate host, depending on the outage type. As outlined earlier in the chapter, in the section "Virtual Machine Component Protection," a permanent device loss (PDL) is a datastore failure when a host can still communicate with the array to get status, but the datastore is unavailable. This might be because of a configuration issue, or a problem with the storage array. The storage device has been unexpectedly unpresented from the host without an unmount command. An all paths down (APD) event is a little more significant because it occurs when there is no way to communicate with the storage array at all. The ESXi host has no way of knowing if and when the storage device might become available; therefore, after 140 seconds, it declares an APD event.

Generally speaking, if there's a storage outage for one host, it will often affect multiple hosts. If the storage is down for an entire cluster, there isn't much vSphere HA can do to get you out of that predicament, but if one or more ESXi hosts can still access the storage that a VM resides on, VMCP can help vSphere HA detect and respond. But how should it respond? Alerting an administrator to the fact that this has occurred in the UI and event log is a good start, but most administrators would probably want something a little more proactive than that.

SHUTDOWN VS. POWER OFF

Remember that with PDL and APD storage outages, there is no way to gracefully shut down the VM guest OS. Since there is no way for the VM to read or write from its virtual hard disk VMDKs, it is simply powered off. In this case, there is a small chance you may lose data, or get data corruption. With a bit of luck, modern journaled file systems used by Windows and Linux should be able to handle an unexpected storage loss without too many problems. Your application or database may not be so lucky, which is why even when using vSphere HA, you should always have a backup of your VMs on a separate storage device. There's more information on backups in the section "Providing Data Protection."

For the PDL failure response, the only other option is to power off all VMs on the affected host(s) and then start them on VMs that can still access the datastore that holds the VM. APD failure responses can be a little more flexible. Not only can you simply restart the affected VMs on another host provided they have access to the datastore, you can also ensure the affected VMs are powered off even if vSphere HA can't guarantee that another host will be able to power them on. This might be handy if you don't want VMs to remain online—and potentially hung—if there's a storage outage. Remember, these VMs may still be responding to network I/O, so your end users or the applications themselves may not be aware that the VM has no access to storage. Finally, as part of the APD response, vSphere HA has the ability to delay the failure response a little longer, as shown in Figure 7.23. This is to make sure that the storage doesn't come back online suddenly while vSphere is already busily recovering VMs on other hosts. The Response

Delay is configurable to allow vSphere HA to simply reset the VMs on the original host if the APD event is cleared before the delay timeout occurs. If your VMs have had no access to storage for 320 seconds (140 seconds for APD timeout + 3 minutes for the response delay), it's a good idea to reset them and let the OS ensure that all hard disks are checked for consistency before resuming normal operations.

FIGURE 7.23

vSphere HA can be set to respond to PDL and APD storage outages differently.

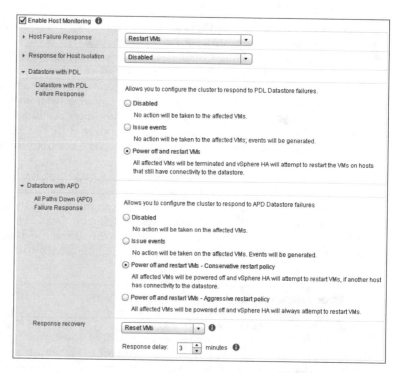

So far, you've only seen how vSphere HA handles ESXi host failures. In the next section, you'll learn how to use vSphere HA to help protect against guest OS and application failures as well.

VM Monitoring

In addition to monitoring for ESXi host, network, and storage failures and then reacting accordingly, vSphere HA can also look for guest OS and application failures. When a failure is detected, vSphere HA can restart the VM. Figure 7.24 shows the area of the Edit Cluster Settings dialog box where you configure this behavior.

FIGURE 7.24

You can configure vSphere HA to monitor for guest OS and application heartbeats and restart a VM when a failure occurs.

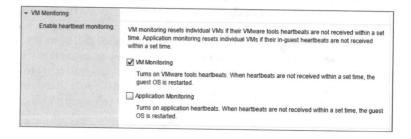

The foundation for this functionality is built into VMware Tools, which Chapter 9 describes in greater detail. VMware Tools provides a series of heartbeats from the guest OS up to the ESXi host on which that VM is running. By monitoring these heartbeats in conjunction with disk and network I/O activity, vSphere HA can attempt to determine if the guest OS has failed. If there are no VMware Tools heartbeats, no disk I/O, and no network I/O for a period of time, then vSphere HA—if VM Monitoring is enabled—will restart the VM under the assumption that the guest OS has failed. To help with troubleshooting, vSphere also takes a screen shot of the VM's console right before vSphere HA restarts the VM. This might help capture any sort of diagnostic information, such as a kernel dump for Linux-based systems, or blue-screen STOP error (BSOD) for Windows-based systems.

vSphere HA also has application monitoring. This functionality requires third-party software to take advantage of APIs built into VMware Tools to provide application-specific heartbeats to vSphere HA. By leveraging these APIs, third-party software developers can further extend the functionality of vSphere HA to protect against the failure of specific applications. To enable VM or application monitoring, simply select the desired level of protection from the VM Monitoring Status check boxes (shown earlier in Figure 7.24).

If you have enabled VM or application monitoring, you can then adjust the monitoring sensitivity. This slider bar controls how often vSphere HA will restart a VM based on a loss of VMware Tools heartbeats and a lack of disk and network I/O traffic. The slider bar also controls the failure window before which vSphere HA will restart a VM again after a maximum number of failures. Table 7.2 shows the values set by each position on the slider.

TABLE 7.2:   VM monitoring sensitivity settings

MONITORING SENSITIVITY SETTING	FAILURE INTERVAL	MINIMUM UPTIME	MAXIMUM FAILURES	FAILURE WINDOW
Low	2 minutes	8 minutes	3	7 days
Medium	1 minute	4 minutes	3	24 hours
High	30 seconds	2 minutes	3	1 hour

Here's how to read this information:

Failure Interval   If vSphere HA doesn't detect any VMware Tools heartbeats, disk I/O, or network I/O within this time frame, it will consider the VM failed and will restart the VM.

Minimum Uptime   vSphere will wait for a set amount of time after the VM has been powered on before starting to monitor VMware Tools heartbeats. This is to ensure that the OS has time to boot and heartbeats have time to stabilize.

Maximum Failures   This is the maximum number of times vSphere HA will restart a VM within the specified failure window. If Maximum Failures is set at 3 and a VM is marked as failed a fourth time within the specified failure window, it will not be automatically restarted. This prevents vSphere HA from endlessly restarting problematic VMs.

Failure Window   vSphere will restart the VM only a maximum number of times (Maximum Failures) within this time frame. If more failures occur within this period of time, the VM is not restarted.

If these predefined options aren't sufficient, you can select Custom and specify your own values for Failure Interval, Minimum Uptime, Maximum Per-VM Resets (Maximum Failures), and Maximum Resets Time Window (Failure Window). Figure 7.25 shows a custom VM Monitoring sensitivity configuration.

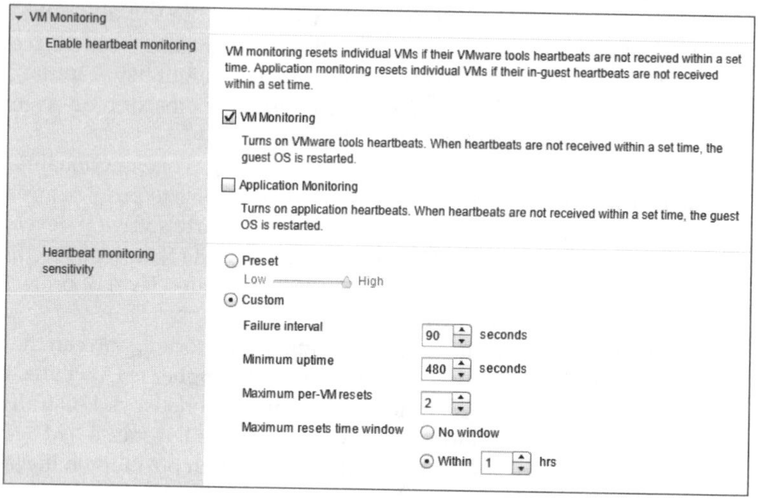

FIGURE 7.25

The Custom option provides specific control over how vSphere HA monitors VMs for guest OS failure.

GETTING STARTED WITH PROACTIVE HA FAILURE AND RESPONSES

Proactive HA is a feature that was introduced in vSphere 6.5, but the name is a little misleading because it's not actually a vSphere HA feature. It is, however. a vSphere Availability feature, which is why it is under the cluster settings within the vSphere Client. Proactive HA is actually more akin to DRS than it is to vSphere HA.

When a server is functioning normally—that is, without some kind of significant failure—vSphere HA assumes that everything is fine, and nothing needs to be done to ensure the availability of the VMs in the cluster. But what if everything is not fine? Shouldn't vSphere HA know if one of the servers has a failed fan or power supply? This could lead to an outage if not addressed soon. In most servers, things like fans, power supplies, and even network cards are redundant—the server can still function if one (or sometimes more) is lost. Proactive HA takes advantage of this redundancy and will proactively migrate VMs off degraded hosts to ensure the VMs can continue to operate even if the host's health continues to deteriorate.

When you first try to enable Proactive HA, the UI will tell you that DRS needs to be enabled, which is a simple check box in the Edit Cluster Settings dialog box, just above vSphere Availability. DRS is extensively covered in Chapter 12, "Balancing Resource Utilization." Once vSphere DRS is enabled, the check box to turn on Proactive HA becomes available. To use Proactive HA, you will need to have a Proactive HA Provider registered with vCenter Server. This provider is simply a vCenter plug-in that, once registered, will talk back to some central system that has the hardware status for each of the ESXi hosts. The implementation of this plug-in will vary for each hardware vendor. Contact your server vendor to find out if they support a vCenter plug-in for Proactive HA monitoring.

Assuming you have a registered plug-in and DRS is enabled on the cluster, what configuration settings can be used to proactively avoid downtime within a vSphere cluster? That too will vary depending on what the vendor monitors and implements within the plug-in. The items that hardware vendors can choose to monitor include the following:

◆ Power supplies

◆ Fans

◆ Local storage devices (such as local SD cards)

◆ Memory modules

◆ Network cards

After looking at this list, you can see that some items are more important than others. For example, if a single fan shuts down, the chances are that the other fans within the server would simply throttle up and compensate for the lost airflow of the failed fan. However, if a memory module fails, things start to get more serious. Each Proactive HA Provider will come with different status defaults for each failure type, but these can be changed within the Proactive HA Provider's upstream monitoring software. This provider will assign a severity to the individual event, and then Proactive HA will respond to these accordingly. The events can have a gray state and a green state that represent Unknown and Healthy, respectively. If an event is unhealthy, it could have a severity level such as a yellow state for Moderate and a red state for Critical. These last two will trigger a response, which we'll look at next.

The two configuration settings that need to be explained are the Automation Level and the Remediation actions that can be seen in Figure 7.26. As with most vSphere HA settings, you can simply set this feature to notify you of a possible problem. In the case of Proactive HA, that is Manual mode. The vCenter Web Client will suggest migration recommendations within the DRS recommendations UI but will not take action on your behalf. When set to automated, Proactive HA will take actions without needing your approval. Proactive HA sends the recommendations through to DRS, and DRS will act on them on your behalf. This will happen regardless of the automation level that DRS is set to. Proactive HA and DRS are two separate features, they just use the same functionality for different use cases.

FIGURE 7.26

Proactive HA Failures And Responses are configured within the Edit Cluster dialog box under vSphere Availability, even though Proactive HA integrates with vSphere DRS too.

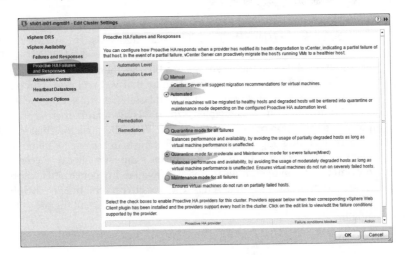

Proactive HA can be set to one of three Remediation modes:

♦ Quarantine mode for all failures

♦ Quarantine mode for moderate and Maintenance mode for severe failure (Mixed)

♦ Maintenance mode for all failures

Just as when you put a host into Maintenance mode manually when DRS is enabled on a cluster, all VMs are evacuated from the host. Once a host is in Maintenance mode, it is not able to have VMs running until it is set to exit Maintenance mode. Quarantine mode is slightly different—it too will evacuate the running VMs; however, it will not do so if there are constraints on the cluster. These constraints might be because of VM or host anti-affinity rules, or if the cluster becomes over-committed with no more resources available, among other potential constraints.

This leads to another good question you might be asking: "How do I ensure that my cluster is not over committed, and I don't run out of resources during an outage?" That is exactly what Admission Control can help you with.

CONFIGURING vSPHERE HA ADMISSION CONTROL

vSphere HA Admission Control settings control the behavior of the vSphere HA–enabled cluster with regard to cluster capacity. Specifically, should vSphere HA allow the user to power on more VMs than it has capacity to support in the event of a failure? Or should the cluster prevent more VMs from being powered on than it can actually protect? That is the basis for Admission Control.

Admission Control is enabled by default when vSphere HA is turned on and has four main settings:

♦ Disabled: Allow VM power-on operations that violate availability constraints

♦ Slot Policy (powered-on VMs)

♦ Cluster resource percentage

♦ Dedicated failover hosts

Consider for a moment that you have a cluster of four identical ESXi hosts. Running on these four ESXi hosts are several identically configured VMs. These VMs consume a total of 75% of the resources in the cluster. This cluster is configured for a single ESXi host failure to tolerate (we'll go into more detail on these settings in a bit). Further, let's say you now want to power on one more VM, and the resource consumption by that VM will push you past the 75 percent resource usage mark. It is at this point that the Admission Control settings will come into play.

If Admission Control is Enabled, which it is by default, then vSphere HA would block the power-on operation of this additional VM. Why? Because the cluster is already at the limit of the capacity it could support if one of the ESXi hosts in the cluster failed (one host out of our four identical hosts is equal to 25% of the cluster's capacity). Because you've told vSphere HA to prevent power-on operations that violate availability constraints, vSphere HA will prevent you from starting more VMs than it has resources to protect. In effect, vSphere HA is guaranteeing you that you'll always have enough resources to restart all the protected VMs in the event of a failure.

If Admission Control is set to Disabled, vSphere HA will let you power on VMs until all of the cluster's resources are allocated. If there is an ESXi host failure at that point, it's possible that some of the VMs would not be able to be restarted because there are not sufficient resources to power on all the VMs. vSphere HA allowed you to exceed the availability constraints of the cluster.

OVERCOMMITMENT IN A vSPHERE HA–ENABLED CLUSTER

When the Admission Control setting is set to allow VMs to be powered on even if they violate availability constraints, you could find yourself in a position where more resources are allocated to VMs than actually exists.

This situation, called *overcommitment*, can lead to poor performance on VMs that become forced to page information from fast RAM out to the slower disk-based swap file. Yes, your VMs will start, but after the host gets maxed out, the whole system and all VMs will slow down dramatically. This will increase the amount of time that HA will need to recover the VMs. What should have been a 20- to 30-minute recovery could end up being an hour or even more. Refer to Chapter 11, "Managing Resource Allocation," for more details on resource allocation and how vSphere handles memory overcommitment.

You should be able to see now how integral the Admission Control settings are. When Admission Control is enabled, the settings control its behavior by determining how many resources need to be reserved and the limit that the cluster can handle and still be able to tolerate failure.

The Admission Control settings are illustrated in Figure 7.27.

FIGURE 7.27
The Admission Control settings will determine how a vSphere HA–enabled cluster determines availability constraints.

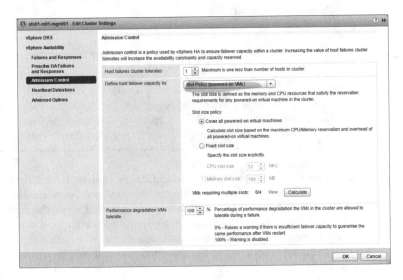

Let's dive into the detail of the different ways Admission Control can be configured:

Host Failures Cluster Tolerates   This is the number of hosts that vSphere HA will try to account for when it reserves capacity within the cluster. The question is: how many host failures do you want to be able to protect against at any one time. The higher this is set to, the fewer resources will be available to power on VMs within the cluster. One is usually enough in most circumstances, especially for smaller cluster sizes. The next three options all use this number in their calculations; they just do it in slightly different ways.

Slot Policy (Powered-on VMs)   Allows you to specify how many host failures the cluster should be configured to withstand. Because the ESXi hosts may have different amounts of RAM and/or CPU capacity, and because the VMs in the cluster may have different levels of resource allocation, vSphere HA uses the idea of a slot to calculate the capacity of the cluster. This option also gives you the flexibility to specify the slot size of the cluster. We'll discuss slots in more detail in just a moment.

Cluster Resource Percentage   Allows you to simply specify how many host failures vSphere HA should reserve capacity for. vSphere HA will calculate a percentage of the cluster's total resources that will be reserved for spare capacity in the event of a failure. You can override this and specify different percentages for CPU and memory if you wish. The availability constraints are established by simply calculating the specified percentage of the cluster's total available resources. This is by far the simplest Admission Control setting to grasp, and the one we would recommend in most cases. The percentage is calculated whenever hosts are moved in and out of the cluster, so there will always be enough reserved based on the Host Failures Cluster Tolerates setting.

Use Dedicated Failover Hosts   Allows you to specify one or more ESXi hosts as failover hosts. These hosts are used as spare capacity, and in the event of a failure, vSphere HA will use these hosts to restart VMs.

BE CAREFUL ABOUT USING FAILOVER HOSTS

When you select a specific ESXi host as a vSphere HA failover host, it's almost like putting that host into Maintenance mode. vSphere DRS (which you'll learn about in Chapter 12) won't place VMs here at startup and won't consider these hosts in its load-balancing calculations. You can't manually power on VMs on the failover host(s) either. These hosts are truly set aside as spare capacity.

Below each of the three available configuration options for Admission Control is a new warning mechanism that is used to alert administrators if performance will be impacted after a failure. The Performance Degradation VMs Tolerate setting can be configured anywhere from 0% to 100%, with 100% being the default resulting in no warnings. If you have some kind of Service Level Agreement (SLA) stating that in the event of a failure, a performance reduction of 25% is acceptable before breaching the agreement, this setting will be invaluable. Changing this setting will result in a warning within the vSphere Web Client if you power on too many VMs within the cluster. It will alert you to the fact that you have breached your tolerance for VM degradation in the event of a host failure, but it will not stop you from powering on additional VMs like Admission Control itself will.

For the most part, the Admission Control settings are pretty easy to understand. One area that can be confusing, however, involves slots and slot sizes, which are used by vSphere HA when Admission Control is set to failover capacity by a Slot Policy (Powered-on VMs).

Why slots and slot sizes? vSphere HA has always used slots and slot sizes for calculating reserved failover capacity. Up until vSphere 6.5, this was the only way that it was calculated (short of reserving a specific host). Slot sizes were used because the ESXi hosts in the cluster might have different configurations: one host might have 8 CPU cores and 96 GB of RAM, whereas another host might have 12 CPU cores and 256 GB of RAM. Similarly, the VMs in the cluster are likely to have different resource configurations. One VM might need 4 GB of RAM, but another VM might require 8 GB of RAM. Some VMs will have one vCPU, and other VMs will have 2, 4, or more vCPUs. Because vSphere doesn't know in advance which host will fail and which VMs will be affected by that failure (naturally), vSphere HA needed a way to establish a "least common denominator" to express the overall capacity of the cluster. Once that overall capacity of the cluster can be expressed, vSphere HA can set aside the appropriate amount of resources to protect against the configured number of host failures.

Here's how slots and slot sizes work. First, vSphere HA examines all the VMs in the cluster to determine the largest values for reserved memory and reserved CPU. For example, if one of the VMs in the cluster has a 2 GB memory reservation but all others do not have a memory reservation, vSphere HA will use 2 GB as the value for calculating slots based on memory. In the same fashion, if one VM has a reservation for 2 GHz of CPU capacity but all other VMs don't have any reservation value, it will use 2 GHz as the value. Basically, vSphere HA constructs the least common denominator as a VM with the largest memory reservation and the largest CPU reservation.

WHAT IF THERE ARE NO RESERVATIONS?

vSphere HA uses reservations (described in Chapter 11) to calculate the slot size. If no VMs have reservations for CPU or memory, vSphere will use the default value of 32 MHz for CPU to calculate slot size. For memory, vSphere HA will use the largest memory overhead value when calculating the slot size.

After it has constructed the least common denominator, vSphere HA calculates the total number of slots that each ESXi host in the cluster could support. Then it determines how many slots the cluster could support if the host with the largest number of slots were to fail (a worst-case scenario). vSphere HA performs these calculations and comparisons for both CPU and memory and then uses the most restrictive result. If vSphere HA calculated 50 slots for memory and 100 slots for CPU, then 50 is the number vSphere HA uses. VMs are then assigned to the slots to determine how many slots are used and how many slots are free, and Admission Control uses this to determine whether additional VMs can be powered on (enough slots remain) or cannot be powered on (not enough slots are available).

The slot-size calculation algorithm just described can result in unexpected settings when you have an unbalanced cluster. An *unbalanced cluster* is a cluster with dramatically different ESXi hosts, such as a host with 64 GB of RAM, along with an ESXi host with 256 GB of RAM in the same cluster. You might also have an unbalanced cluster if you have dramatically different resource reservations assigned to VMs in the cluster (for example, one VM with an 8 GB memory reservation while all the other VMs use much less than that). Although you can fine-tune the behavior of the vSphere HA slot-calculation mechanism using advanced settings, it's generally not recommended. For these situations, you have a couple of options:

◆ You could place similarly sized VMs (or similarly sized hosts) in their own cluster.

◆ You could use percentage-based availability constraints (via the Cluster Resource Percentage setting) instead of host failures or failover hosts.

Using reservations on resource pools might be another way to help alleviate the impact to slot size calculations, if the reservations are absolutely necessary. Refer to Chapter 11 for more detail on both reservations and resource pools. In the end, we would highly encourage you to use the Admission Control setting.

Before we wrap up the discussion about vSphere HA configuration settings and talk about how to manage vSphere HA and ensure VM interdependencies are met, let's briefly touch on the final setting within the Edit Cluster Settings dialog box: Heartbeat Datastores.

HEARTBEAT DATASTORES

Datastore heartbeating originated in vSphere HA in vSphere 5.0. By communicating through shared datastores when the ESXi management network is not available, vSphere HA provides greater protection against outages due to network partition or network isolation.

This part of the vSphere HA configuration allows you to specify which datastores should be used by vSphere HA for heartbeating. Figure 7.28 shows the Datastore Heartbeating section of the Edit Cluster dialog box.

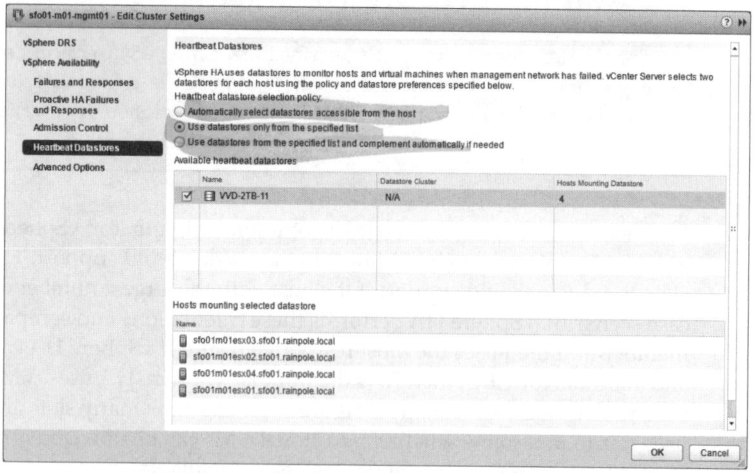

FIGURE 7.28

Select the shared datastores that vSphere HA should use for datastore heartbeating.

vSphere HA provides three different settings for how the administrator can influence the selection of datastores for heartbeating:

Automatically Select Datastores Accessible From The Host   This option disables the manual selection of datastores from the list. With this option enabled, any cluster datastore could be used by vSphere HA for heartbeating.

Use Datastores Only From The Specified List   This option constrains vSphere HA to using only those datastores selected from the list of datastores. If one of those datastores becomes unavailable for whatever reason, vSphere HA will not perform heartbeating through a different datastore.

Use Datastores From The Specified List And Complement Automatically If Needed   This is a blend of the previous two options. With this option, you select the preferred datastores that vSphere HA should use. vSphere HA chooses from among the datastores in that list. If one of the datastores becomes unavailable, vSphere HA will choose a different datastore, until none of the preferred datastores are available. At that point it will choose any available cluster datastore.

The last option is probably the most flexible, but how would you know which datastores were being used by vSphere HA? In the next section, we'll show you how to tell which datastores vSphere HA is actually using for datastore heartbeating as well as how to determine the slot size, see any cluster configuration issues, and gather information on the total number of protected and unprotected VMs.

As you have seen by now, there are many different areas and settings to configure with vSphere HA. There is, however, one more really useful area you should know. vSphere HA has the option of configuring per-VM monitoring settings in the VM Overrides section of the Cluster settings. This allows you, on a per-VM basis, to enable or disable VM monitoring and application monitoring sensitivity levels. Thus, if you need VM monitoring for only a few VMs, you can define a default cluster setting and then configure the exceptions accordingly. Also in this section you have the ability to group VMs and hosts together for applying these different settings.

Configuring vSphere HA Groups, Rules, Overrides, and Orchestrated VM Restart

When you have a system that is as highly automated as vSphere HA, there will always be times when you need to change what would normally be acceptable for a particular VM or groups of VMs. Thankfully, vSphere clusters have settings that can change the way it responds for particular VMs. In this section, we'll discuss the following settings:

◆   VM/Host Groups

◆   VM/Host Rules

◆   VM Overrides

First, let's talk about why you would want to group VMs or Hosts together using VM/Host Groups. Typically, if you are configuring a rule, you may want to apply that rule to more than one VM or host. Grouping like VMs or hosts together allows you to link the rule to a single group, instead of to each member of the group as shown in Figure 7.29. After you have a group of VMs or hosts together, what can you do with it? That is where the VM/Host Rules come in.

FIGURE 7.29
Grouping hosts and VMs allows you to add rules to a group instead of each item.

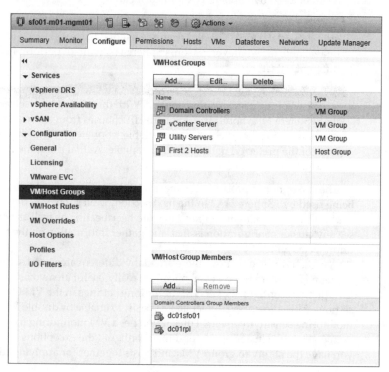

Applying a rule to a group is a simple affair. Give the rule a name, decide the Rule Type, and add the rule members. The different Rule Types are

- Keep Virtual Machines Together
- Separate Virtual Machines
- Virtual Machines to Hosts
- Virtual Machines to Virtual Machines

To give you an overview of what you might want to use these different Rule Types for, here i a scenario that uses each type of rule in the same cluster. Keep in mind that both DRS and vSphere HA use these rules to respond to their respective events. More information about DRS can be found in Chapter 11.

In this example (shown in Figure 7.29), we will configure rules against a cluster that includes the following VMs:

- Dc01rpl

- Dc01sfo01

- Sfo01m01vc01

- Util01

- Util02

The first rule is a VM-to-VM rule, or Run VMs Based On Group Dependency. This rule has two groups of VMs: a domain controllers VM group and a vCenter Server VM group. This rule will ensure that vCenter will not try to start before a domain controller is online, as you can see in Figure 7.30. In this example, we authenticate to Active Directory, and use it for DNS and as a time-sync server. vCenter will not function correctly without our Active Directory functioning first.

FIGURE 7.30
This VM/Host rule will ensure that the Domain Controller VMs are always running before it tries to restart vCenter Server.

The second rule is another VM-to-VM rule: Run VMs Based On Group Dependency. This rule says that the utility servers shouldn't start until vCenter has started. As you can see, our domain controllers start first, then vCenter, and finally our utility servers.

The third rule is a VM-to-Hosts rule, or Run VMs On Hosts. We create a rule that applies to both a group of VMs and a group of hosts. In this case, we are creating a "Should" rule that say vCenter should run on the first two hosts in the cluster. This is a best-effort rule, but it won't st any VMs from starting if it cannot be met. Therefore, this rule can be broken if needed. There a also Should Not, Must, and Must Not rules. The latter two rules are fixed and cannot be broker This could potentially be bad because if the first two hosts were unavailable for some reason, these VMs would not power on. We create this Should rule so that, in the event of an outage an vCenter is down, we only need to try looking directly on two hosts instead of each host throug out the cluster. Remember, if vCenter is down, then the only UI you can look at is the host clien for each ESXi host. These rules are also called VM-Host Affinity/Anti-Affinity rules.

The fourth rule is a Separate VMs rule. This rule states that any VMs that are members of thi rule must not be running on the same ESXi server. In this case, we want to keep our domain controllers on different ESXi hosts within the vSphere Cluster to ensure that access to Active Directory does not depend on a single ESXi host.

The fifth and final rule is a Keep VMs together rule. It is exactly the opposite of the Separate VMs rule. For this example, we chose to keep the utility servers on the same ESXi host.

All of these rules can be seen together in Figure 7.31.

FIGURE 7.31
Rules can be enabled or disabled individually and will show any conflicts within the UI.

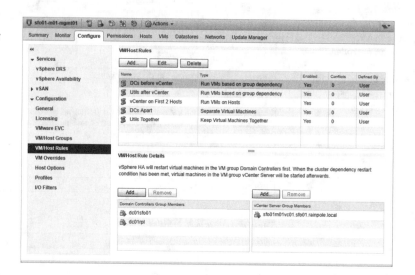

As we previously discussed, vSphere HA can restart VMs very quickly, without waiting to se if the previous power on was successful. Unless you configure the vSphere HA VM dependency restart condition to wait for the guest OS for each VM, each VM will effectively be booting at the same time, regardless of the restart priority set. However, we don't want to wait for each VM in the VM Restart Priority order VMs to boot sequentially. How do we ensure that the VMs we car about most come up in the right order while the rest of the VMs in our cluster start as soon as they can in an outage? That is where VM Overrides come in.

VM Overrides allow you to configure modified vSphere HA (and DRS) settings to a specific VM or group of VMs as an exception to the normal cluster wide settings. This allows you to configure a group of VMs to restart as a highest priority but have all the other VMs in the cluster restart with a normal priority, as shown in Figure 7.32. Or you could have a group of VMs for which vSphere HA always waits until their guest heartbeats are detected before moving on. When you couple the VM Override functionality with the VM/Host Rules, you can get very granular in how your VMs respond after an outage.

FIGURE 7.32
VM Overrides allow you to change cluster-wide settings for each VM with different needs.

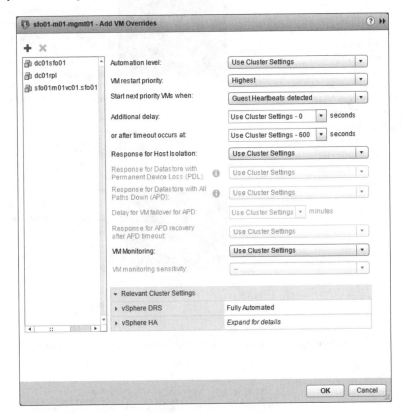

Managing vSphere High Availability

Many vSphere HA functions are calculated automatically, such as slot size, total number of slots, selection of hosts for datastore heartbeating, and the selection of the master/slave roles by FDM. Without proper exposure of these values, it would be difficult to properly manage vSphere HA and its operation. Fortunately, VMware included information about vSphere HA in the vSphere web client to make it easier to manage vSphere HA.

Some of the information is pretty easy to find. For example, the Summary tab of an ESXi host in a vSphere HA–enabled cluster will display the master/slave status, as shown earlier in Figure 7.11.

Similarly, the protected/unprotected status of a VM—indicating that the vSphere HA master has recognized that the VM has been powered on and has taken responsibility for restarting it in the event of a failure—is also noted on the Summary tab of a VM. You can see this in Figure 7.33.

FIGURE 7.33
This blended figure shows the difference between a VM currently listed as Unprotected by vSphere HA and one that is listed as Protected by vSphere HA; note the icon with the arrow next to the Windows logo. VMs may be unprotected because the master has not yet been notified by vCenter Server that the VM has been powered on and needs to be protected.

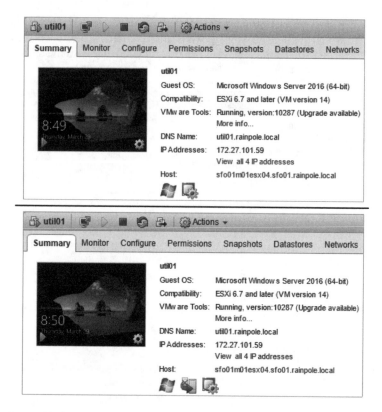

However, other pieces of information are found under Cluster Monitor vSphere HA, as shown in Figure 7.34.

FIGURE 7.34
The vSphere HA Summary tab holds a wealth of information about vSphere HA and its operation. The current vSphere HA master, the number of protected and unprotected VMs, and the datastores used for heartbeating are all found here.

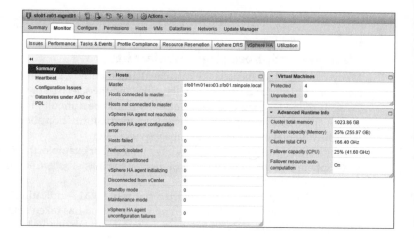

THE SUMMARY AREA

The Summary area outlines all the relevant details for vSphere HA-enabled clusters. Divided into three sections, this area gives you the following information:

◆ Hosts lists the current vSphere HA master and the number of slave hosts connected to the master host. Although the vSphere HA master status is also displayed on the Summary tab for an ESXi host, using this dialog box might be easier and faster for clusters with a large number of hosts.

◆ Virtual Machines shows the current number of protected and unprotected VMs. This gives you a quick "at a glance" protection summary and is a fast way to determine how many, if any, VMs are unprotected by vSphere HA.

◆ Advanced Runtime Info exposes the vSphere HA calculations for slot size, total slots in cluster, used slots, available slots, and failover slots. This is very useful information to have. If you have Admission Control set to Enabled and aren't able to power on VMs that you think you should be able to power on, checking this dialog box for the slot size might reveal that the slot size is different than what you were expecting.

HEARTBEAT AREA

The Heartbeat area shows which datastores are currently being used by vSphere HA for heartbeating. If you haven't explicitly defined which datastore can or should be used, this is where you can tell which datastores were selected by vSphere HA for heartbeating.

CONFIGURATION ISSUES AREA

In the Configuration Issues area, vSphere HA will display any configuration issues—for example, if the cluster has exceeded the configured failover capacity. You might also see warnings about management network redundancy (if the ESXi management network isn't redundant and protected against single points of failure). Based on the issues displayed here, you can take the appropriate action to correct the problem or potential problem.

DATASTORES UNDER APD OR PDL

The Datastores Under APD Or PDL area will list any hosts and datastores that are currently affected by either an All Paths Down or a Permanent Device Loss event. Typically, you will also get an alarm, but these types of events will be collated here if this alarm is not visible.

vSphere HA is a powerful feature, and we highly recommend its use in every vSphere implementation. However, vSphere HA does rely on restarting VMs in order to provide that level of high availability. What if there are applications for which you need a higher level of availability? vSphere offers that functionality with vSphere Fault Tolerance (FT). vSphere FT provides zero downtime, zero data loss, and continuous availability for your applications.

That may sound pretty impressive. But how does it work? That's the focus of the next section.

Introducing vSphere SMP Fault Tolerance

Since the introduction of vSphere Fault Tolerance (FT) in vSphere 4, you have been limited to protecting workloads only with a single vCPU. vSphere 6.0 introduced SMP-FT, a complete re-write of vSphere Fault Tolerance that allows you to protect VMs with up to four vCPUs. So, even if you have a machine that you want to protect that has only a single vCPU, under vSphe 6.0 it will be delivered using the new SMP-FT technology. The only time you will see FT on a vSphere 6.0 cluster is for virtual machines that were enabled for FT on a version of vSphere cluster prior to 6.0, which was then upgraded to vSphere 6.0.

Previous versions of vSphere FT used a technology called vLockstep, but it was limited to a single vCPU per FT-enabled VM. vSphere SMP-FT uses a new technology called FastCheckpointing to scale beyond a single vCPU. Whereas vLockstep would take an input ar execute it simultaneously on both the primary and secondary VMs, FastCheckpointing instea executes on the primary VM only and then sends the result to the secondary VM. This approa bypasses issues such as knowing on which vCPU an instruction should be executed, as well a situations where vCPUs are sharing memory with each other. To ensure that machine states a kept consistent, outgoing network packets from the primary VM are held until the secondary is up-to-date.

So, what else has changed between the new and old technologies used to implement Fault Tolerance? Let's start by looking at some key differences between the two, as shown in Table '

TABLE 7.3:   Comparing FT and SMP-FT

	FAULT TOLERANCE	SMP FAULT TOLERANCE
# CPUs supported	1	≤8
Memory virtualization hardware assist	Not supported	Supported
Disk format	Eager zero thick	Thin provisioning
VMDK redundancy	Not supported	Mandatory
VADP backups	Not supported	Supported
Required network bandwidth	1 GB	10 GB
DRS	Partially supported	Partially supported
Protected VMs per host	≤4	≤4
Paravirtualized Devices	Not supported	Supported

Before we show you how to enable vSphere SMP-FT, let's take a look at how it behaves. you enable SMP-FT, a vMotion is initiated that takes a copy of both the memory and virtua disks, registering the virtual machine's VMX file against the secondary host, while the virtua machine disk files are copied to a secondary datastore that you define during the configura- tion process.

SECONDARY DATASTORE REQUIREMENTS

Technically, you can place a FT VM's disk files on the same datastore as the original VM; however, that is not supported. The reason for this is to avoid a single point of failure relating to the underlying storage system.

This means two distinct copies of each virtual machine disk must be kept in sync, protecting you from the loss of a datastore. As you can imagine, these two copies are partially responsible for the increase in the network bandwidth requirement to support SMP-FT.

Let's take a look at the rest of the requirements for SMP-FT. Because vSphere SMP-FT is matching instruction for instruction and memory for memory to create two identical VMs running on two different ESXi hosts, there are some very stringent requirements for vSphere SMP-FT. These requirements exist at three levels: the cluster level, host level, and VM level.

vSphere SMP-FT has the following requirements at a cluster level:

◆ Host certificate checking must be enabled. This is the default for vCenter Server 4.1 and later.

◆ The cluster must have at least two ESXi hosts running the same SMP-FT version or build number. The FT version is displayed in the Fault Tolerance section of the ESXi host's Summary tab.

◆ vSphere HA must be enabled on the cluster. vSphere HA must be enabled before you can power on vSphere SMP-FT enabled VMs.

In addition, vSphere SMP-FT has the following requirements on each ESXi host:

◆ SMP-FT is supported only on vSphere 6 and later.

◆ The ESXi hosts must have access to the same datastores and networks where the VM is attached.

◆ The ESXi hosts must have a Fault Tolerance logging network connection configured. This vSphere SMP-FT logging network requires at least 10 Gigabit Ethernet (GbE) connectivity; 40 and 100 GbE are also supported. Multiple links can be bonded together, but this only benefits multiple VMs enabled for FT on the same host.

◆ The hosts must have CPUs that are vSphere SMP-FT compatible.

◆ Hosts must be licensed for vSphere SMP-FT.

◆ Hardware Virtualization (HV) must be enabled in the ESXi host's BIOS in order to enable CPU support for vSphere SMP-FT.

Finally, vSphere SMP-FT has the following requirements on any VM that is to be protected:

◆ Only VMs with up to four vCPUs are supported with vSphere SMP-FT. VMs with more than four vCPUs are not compatible with vSphere SMP-FT.

◆ VMs must be running a supported guest OS.

◆ VM files must be stored on shared storage that is accessible to all applicable ESXi hosts.

◆ Physical mode RDMs are not supported, although Virtual Mode RDMs are. The Eager Zero Thick requirement has been removed, which means that the disk format can be Thin Provisioned, Lazy Zero Thick, or Eager Zero Thick.

◆ The VM must not have any snapshots. You must remove or commit snapshots before you can enable vSphere SMP-FT for a VM. Note that snapshots initiated via vStorage APIs for Data Protection (VADP) are supported.

◆ The VM must not be a linked clone.

◆ The VM cannot have any USB devices, sound devices, serial ports, or parallel ports in its configuration. Remove these items from the VM configuration before attempting to enable vSphere SMP-FT.

◆ The VM cannot use N_Port ID Virtualization (NPIV).

◆ Nested page tables/extended page tables (NPT/EPT) are not supported. vSphere SMP-FT will disable NPTs/EPTs on VMs for which vSphere SMP-FT is enabled.

◆ The VM cannot use NIC passthrough or the older vlance network drivers. Turn off NIC passthrough and update the networking drivers to vmxnet2, vmxnet3, or E1000.

◆ The VM cannot have CD-ROM or floppy devices backed by a physical or remote device. You'll need to disconnect these devices or configure them to point to an ISO or FLP image on a shared datastore.

As you can see, vSphere SMP-FT has very specific requirements in order to be properly supported.

vSphere SMP-FT also introduces some operational changes that must be taken into account as well:

◆ It is recommended that power management (also known as *power capping*) be turned off in the BIOS of any ESXi host that will participate in vSphere SMP-FT. This helps ensure uniformity in the CPU speeds of the ESXi hosts in the cluster.

◆ Although you can use vMotion with a vSphere SMP-FT protected VM, you cannot use Storage vMotion. By extension, this means that vSphere SMP-FT–protected VMs cannot take advantage of Storage DRS. To use Storage vMotion, you must first turn off vSphere SMP-FT.

◆ Hot-plugging devices is not supported, so you cannot make any virtual hardware changes when a vSphere SMP-FT–protected VM is powered on.

NO HARDWARE CHANGES INCLUDES NO NETWORK CHANGES

Changing the settings of a virtual network card while a VM is running requires that the network card be unplugged and then plugged back in. As a result, you can't make changes to virtual network cards while vSphere SMP-FT is running.

Be sure to keep these technical constraints in mind when deciding where and how to use vSphere SMP-FT in your environment.

Now you're ready to enable vSphere SMP-FT on a VM. Perform the following steps:

1. If the vSphere Web Client is not already running, launch it and connect to a vCenter Server instance. vSphere SMP-FT is available only when using vCenter Server.

2. Navigate to the Hosts And Clusters or VMs And Templates view. Right-click a running VM and then select Fault Tolerance ➪ Turn On Fault Tolerance.

3. Next, you will need to select a datastore for the configuration file (vmx), the tie breaker file, and each of the virtual disks (vmdk) for the protected virtual machine.

4. On the next screen, select a host on which the secondary VM will run. After you have reviewed your settings on the final screen, the creation task begins, as shown in Figure 7.35.

FIGURE 7.35
vSphere SMP-FT uses vMotion to create the virtual machine runtime and files as it is powered on for the first time.

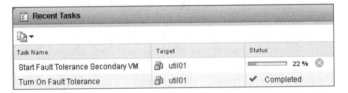

5. When the process is complete, the VM's icon in the Navigator tree will turn a darker color. Figure 7.36 shows a VM that has been enabled for vSphere SMP-FT.

LIMITATIONS TO SMP's UTILIZATION OF DRS?

Unlike FT, SMP-FT's utilization of DRS is limited to providing initial placement of your virtual machines. This means that when you enable SMP-FT on a DRS-enabled cluster, VM Overrides will be configured to disable DRS on the protected VM.

And that's it. It is that simple—at least on the surface.

FIGURE 7.36
The circled darker VM icon indicates that vSphere SMP-FT is enabled for this VM.

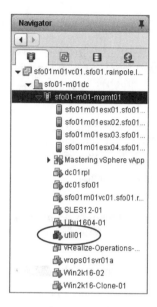

Behind the scenes, after vSphere SMP-FT is turned on, vCenter Server will initiate the creatic of the secondary VM using vMotion. Both the primary and secondary VMs will have their own disk(s), and using VMware FastCheckpoint, SMP-FT will then be able to keep the VMs in sync. SMP-FT uses a network connection between the ESXi hosts to keep the primary and secondary VMs in sync (recall from our earlier discussion of requirements that the ESXi hosts must have a Fault Tolerance logging connection established; Chapter 5 provides more detail on how to configure this network connection). Only the primary VM will respond to other systems across the network, which leaves the secondary VM a silent partner. You can almost compare this to active/passive cluster configuration in that only one node owns the shared network at a time. When the ESXi host supporting the primary VM fails, the secondary VM takes over immediatel with no break in network connection. A reverse ARP is sent to the physical switch to notify the network of the new location of the VM. Does that sound familiar? It is exactly what vMotion does when the VM switches to a new host. After the secondary VM becomes the primary, the creation of the new secondary VM is repeated until the sync is locked (see Figure 7.37).

FIGURE 7.37
The vSphere Web Client shows vSphere SMP-FT status information in the Fault Tolerance area on the Summary tab of a VM.

After you have met the requirements, you can enable vSphere SMP-FT. There is no additiona configuration to be performed once it has been enabled.

Before wrapping up this discussion of vSphere SMP-FT, we'll discuss using vSphere SMP-FT in conjunction with vSphere HA.

Using vSphere SMP Fault Tolerance with vSphere High Availability

vSphere SMP-FT works in conjunction with vSphere HA. Recall that vSphere HA must be enabled on both the cluster and the VM in order to enable SMP-FT. As mentioned previously, if the ESXi host where the primary VM is running fails, the secondary VM takes over and a new secondary VM is created automatically to ensure protection. But what happens if multiple host failures occur? In that case, vSphere HA will restart the primary VM. SMP-FT will then re-create the secondary VM on another host to ensure protection.

In the event of a guest OS failure, vSphere SMP-FT will take no action because, as far as SMP-FT is concerned, the VMs are in sync. Both VMs will fail at the same time and place. vSphere HA VM monitoring—if enabled—can detect the failure in the primary and restart it, and the secondary creation process will start again. Have you noticed a pattern about the secondary VMs? After the sync has failed, the secondary machine is always re-created. It is worth noting at this point that if a secondary is re-created after an event, the vMotion process is initiated again to copy the virtual machine disks. This means that re-enabling SMP-FT may be a time-consuming process because it requires a full re-creation of the files, not just a differential copy.

ONE OS IMAGE VS. TWO OS IMAGES

Many people misunderstand vSphere SMP-FT's behavior when it comes to guest OS failure. If the guest OS in the primary VM crashes, the guest OS in the secondary VM is also going to crash. Although these appear to be two separate guest OS instances, they are really one synchronized guest OS instance running on two different ESXi hosts. A failure in one will mean a failure in both.

This is markedly different from traditional guest OS clustering solutions, which rely on two separate and distinct guest OS instances. If one of the guest OS instances fails, the other instance is still up and running and can take over for the failed instance. Windows Server Failover Clustering (WSFC) is one example of this sort of configuration.

Understanding these differences between guest OS clustering and vSphere SMP-FT will help you choose the right high-availability mechanism for your application and needs.

Examining vSphere Fault Tolerance Use Cases

vSphere SMP-FT is not designed or meant to be run on all of your VMs. You should use this service sparingly and take this form of fault tolerance only for your most important VMs. If you think about the requirements, it's not too hard to understand the resource-overhead placed on hosts. SMP-FT does not simply add a VM to another host. The amount of bandwidth and processing required for the disk, network, memory, and CPU is considerable. The documentation for VMware's configuration maximums states that there should be no more than four vSphere SMP-FT protected VMs (primary or secondary) on any single ESXi host. There are advanced settings within vSphere that allow you to override these maximums, but having the hardware to support such a configuration is important. If there's a problem, VMware Global Support Service (GSS) would likely get you to revert the changes to help fix any issues you may run into. The most important thing to remember is that once you have primary and secondary VMs locked and in sync, you will be using double the resources for each protected VM, plus the additional bandwidth to transfer every bit of changed disk, memory, and CPU instructions to the secondary VM.

Now that you're familiar with some high-availability options, let's move on to planning and designing for disaster recovery.

Planning for Business Continuity

High availability is only part of the solution; it's one component in the bigger picture of business continuity. Business continuity is about ensuring that the business can continue operating in the face of a significant event. High availability deals with business continuity from a fairly narrow perspective: ensuring that the business can continue operating in the event of a physical server failure, an OS or application failure, or a network component failure. There are many types of failures that you must account for and protect against; we'll discuss the following two primary types here:

- ◆ Protecting against the loss of data due to equipment failure, software malfunction, or simple user error (such as deleting something by mistake, which most of us have done at one time or another)

- ◆ Planning for disaster recovery in the event your entire datacenter is rendered unusable or unavailable

Most organizations have a policy or a set of policies that define the processes, procedures, tools, and technologies that help address these failure scenarios. As you review the information provided in the following sections, you'll want to be sure that any solution you are considering complies with and in some cases complements, your company's policy for business continuity. If your company doesn't yet have a policy for business continuity, now is a great time to create one.

In the next two sections, we'll look at both of these failure scenarios, along with some of the products and technologies that are applicable. Let's start with data protection.

Providing Data Protection

Backups are an essential part of every IT department's responsibilities, yet they're often the source of the greatest conflict and frustration. Many organizations hoped that virtualizing would make backups easier, and in some ways, it has. In other ways, it has made backups more difficult. We'll examine the basic methods for backing up VMs, but because there are many different products that can be used for backups, we'll concentrate on general functionality enabled by the common backup solutions such as Avamar, Commvault, NetBackup, and Veeam. All of these backup products use a combination of agents and the vSphere Storage APIs for Data Protection, or VADP. You can read more about these APIs in Chapter 6.

EXAMINING VM BACKUP METHODS

There are three high-level methods of backing up VMs in a VMware vSphere environment:

◆ Running a backup agent of some sort in the guest OS

◆ Leveraging vSphere snapshots and VADP

◆ Using array-based snapshot integration

Various backup applications might have slight variations, but the basic methods remain the same. Each of these methods has its own advantages and disadvantages, and no one solution will be the right fit for all customers.

Figure 7.38 illustrates the flow of information when using backup agents inside the guest OS.

FIGURE 7.38
Running backup agents inside the guest OS can provide application- and OS-level integration, but not without some drawbacks.

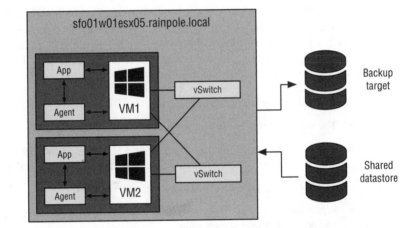

As you can see from Figure 7.38, running a backup agent within the guest OS affords you OS-level and application-level awareness and integration. The backup agent can leverage the APIs of the guest OS to integrate with the OS and applications running in the OS (for example, by leveraging the Volume Shadow Copy Service in Windows). This allows the backup agent to perform granular backups, such as specific tables within a SQL database, particular mailboxes in Microsoft Exchange, or a subset of files within a Linux filesystem.

However, running backup agents within the guest OS has its drawbacks:

◆ The network traffic typically runs across the network, which can create bottlenecks. This is especially true if the backup traffic runs across the same network as end user–facing traffic.

◆ To avoid bottlenecks with end user–facing traffic, organizations introduced dedicated backup networks. This means more NICs in the ESXi hosts, separate vSwitches, separate physical switches, additional vNICs in the VMs, and additional complexity in the guest

OS and the solution as a whole. Separate backup networks can also complicate trouble-shooting and operations.

♦ The backup agents are individually running in each guest OS instance, so as more and more VMs (and guest OS instances) are consolidated onto physical servers, this creates additional overhead. This can, in some circumstances, translate to longer backup windows.

♦ Some backup vendors charged a separate license for every installation of the backup agent, which has decreased the financial benefits of virtualization and consolidation.

Despite these drawbacks, the tight OS- and application-level integration that backup agents offer makes them the preferred choice in areas where granularity and application integration are paramount.

The second significant way that you perform backups in the vSphere environment is to operate outside the guest OS. Instead, leverage the snapshot functionality of VMware vSphere to unlock the VM's virtual disks and then back up the virtual disks directly. When the backup of the virtual disk is complete, commit the snapshot and you're finished. The framework for driving this process in an automated fashion—so that backup vendors can make it easier to use—is VADP.

The overall process looks something like this:

1. The backup software requests a snapshot of the virtual disks for the VM to be backed up.

2. VMware vSphere creates a snapshot, and all writes to the virtual disks for that VM now start flowing into the delta disks. The base VMDK files are unlocked.

3. The backup application backs up the base VMDK files.

4. When the backup of the base VMDK files is complete, the backup software requests vSphere to commit the snapshot.

5. The writes in the delta disk are committed to the base VMDK, and the snapshot is removed.

6. The process repeats itself for the next VM.

VADP helps provide a standard interface for backup vendors to interact with vSphere for backing up VMs, and it introduces a few other useful features. Changed Block Tracking (CBT), for example, allows vSphere and backup applications to track which blocks in a VMDK have changed and back up only those changed blocks. You can consider CBT the VMDK block equivalent to the archive flag in DOS and NTFS.

SNAPSHOTS ARE NOT BACKUPS

While backup software that utilizes VADP actually does take snapshots as part of its process, taking VM snapshots manually for backups is a really bad idea. It's not uncommon to see this done within many IT organizations, but there are numerous pitfalls you may come across. For example:

♦ No auto committing back to the base VMDK files means you can accidentally have multiple levels of snapshots without knowing (unless you specifically go looking).

- Snapshots can inadvertently be rolled back.

- Snapshots are not stored on secondary storage by default.

- A snapshot is a change log of the original virtual disk.

- VMware recommends a maximum age for a single snapshot be no more than 72 hours.

Like in-guest backups, VADP-based backups also have advantages and disadvantages:

- There is generally less processor and memory overhead because there's no need to run a backup agent inside every guest OS instance. Depending on the environment, this might allow you to achieve a higher consolidation ratio or provide better performance for your workloads.

- Because there is generally little to no coordination with applications running in the guest OS instances, VADP-based backups typically cannot provide the same level of backup/restore granularity as in-guest backups. There may also be issues ensuring application consistency.

- Depending on how you implement the VADP-based backup solution, file-level restores may be difficult. Some of these solutions require that you restore the entire VM and then manually pull out the individual file or files that need to be restored. Be sure to consider this operational issue in your evaluation.

USING YOUR STORAGE ARRAY TO PROTECT DATA

Many storage vendors have started adding the ability to do point-in-time snapshots of data on the array. The specifics of how the snapshots work will vary from vendor to vendor, and—as with so many other aspects of IT—each approach has its advantages and disadvantages. The result of this functionality is the ability to hold point-in-time views of your company's information for a predetermined amount of time. This time frame could be hours, days, weeks, or months depending on the amount of disk space you have allocated. These snapshots can serve as a "first line of defense" in data protection.

Here's an example. Let's say a VM was deleted by accident. With point-in-time restore, you can dial back in time to right before the VM was deleted. Mount the LUN from that specific moment in time, and restore your VM. Though not traditionally thought of as a suitable replacement for other backup solutions, array-based snapshots and even array replication are starting to make a lot more sense. As data footprints continue to grow and businesses demand more aggressive recovery point objectives (RPOs) and recovery time objectives (RTOs), traditional backup solutions can struggle to meet business needs. Array capabilities have continued to mature and now offer a number of different business continuity and disaster recovery options such as offsite replication and offloading to lower storage tiers.

Recovering from Disasters

High availability makes up only half of the ability to keep your application/systems up in day-to-day operation. The other half is disaster recovery, which is the ability to recover from a catastrophic failure. The risks posed by hurricanes, earthquakes, and other natural and man-made disasters underscore how important it is to establish a thoughtfully designed plan that you can execute with certainty. Entire datacenters can be destroyed by one of these events, and even the datacenters that survive and keep functioning do not stay operational for long when generators run out of gas. When real events like Hurricane Katrina or Harvey occur, the aftermath drives the point home that businesses need to be prepared.

Before virtualization, the disaster recovery (DR) team showed up, and the remote recovery site was slated with the task of recovering the enterprise in a timely manner. A timely manner back then was at least a few days to build and install the recovery servers and then restore the enterprise from the backup media.

Sounds simple, right? Well, in theory, it is supposed to be, but problems always occur during the process. First, during the recovery process, you can rarely restore your environment at the remote datacenter location to the same make and model that you run in your current environment. Thus, after you restore your data from your backup media, you are greeted with the pretty blue screen that announces that the drivers are different. For the most part, after the restore completes, you can rerun the installation of the drivers for the recovery servers, but Murphy tends to show up and lay down his law.

Second, the restore process itself is another form of literal contention. If your backup strategy does not consider which servers you want to recover first, then during a disaster, when you try to restore and bring up systems based on importance, you waste a lot of time waiting for tape machines to become available. This contention becomes even worse if your backups span more than one tape. Speaking of tapes, it is not uncommon for tapes to become corrupt and unreadable. Backups are completed and the tapes are sent off site but not tested until they are needed. If all goes well, you might finish your restore in a few days, but success can be elusive.

Today, a majority of data is kept on the SAN, and the data is replicated to another SAN at your remote disaster recovery co-location site. So, your data is waiting for you when you need to perform a recovery, which speeds up the process. At first this remote replication was an expensive undertaking because only the high-dollar enterprise SANs had this capability. Over the years, though, this approach has become the standard, and software solutions have started enabling similar functionality without the need for matching hardware at each endpoint.

To set up SAN replication, a company purchases two SANs to be set up at different locations, and the data is replicated between the two sites. Many vendors offer replication solutions, and the particulars of these replication solutions vary. Some replication solutions use Fibre Channel (or Fibre Channel over IP [FCIP]); others use standard TCP/IP connections. Some replication solutions support only that vendor's storage arrays (like EMC SRDF or NetApp SnapMirror), and other replication solutions support heterogeneous storage environments. Some replication solutions allow for replicated data to be "split off" for other purposes (it might be good for backups); others don't have that functionality.

In spite of these differences, all replication solutions fall into one of two very broad areas:

♦ Synchronous replication solutions

♦ Asynchronous replication solutions

In synchronous replication solutions, the primary array waits until the secondary array has acknowledged each write before sending a write acknowledgment back to the host, ensuring that the replicated copy of the data is always as current as the primary. In this situation latency comes into play, and it increases significantly with distance. Therefore, you must limit the distance between synchronous replication solutions to keep latency to a minimum.

Asynchronous replication solutions transfer data to the secondary array in chunks and do not wait for a write acknowledgment from the remote array before acknowledging the write to the host. Using this method, the remote copy of the data will never be as current as the primary copy, but this method can replicate data over very long distances and with reduced bandwidth requirements.

In a vSphere environment, you can combine SAN- and/or host-based replication—synchronous or asynchronous—with VMware Site Recovery Manager (SRM), a workflow automation tool that helps administrators with the task of orchestrating the startup of all the VMs in a datacenter. SRM is a great product but well outside the scope of this book. However, you can refer to the VMware SRM website at `www.vmware.com/products/site-recovery-manager/` for more information.

---

vSphere High Availability Failover with Synchronous Replication

Earlier in this chapter, we told you that you could not perform HA failover to another site. As a general rule, this is true—even with synchronous SAN replication. However, in recent times, a number of storage vendors (including VMware's vSAN) have developed vSphere Metro Storage Cluster solutions that make combining synchronous replication and HA a possibility.

SAN-based replication is great, but there may be times when it's just not feasible. For smaller businesses or remote offices, the size and cost of the infrastructure cannot be justified. Inevitably, DR is still a requirement, and for this reason, VMware has an IP-based replication engine simply called vSphere Replication.

Using vSphere Replication

The ability to make a copy of your important data and workloads at a remote location is often one of the top priorities for business management. They realize that recovering important workloads and data is crucial to keeping the business operating, and the quicker they can be up and running, the less productivity they potentially lose. As discussed in the previous section, "Recovering from Disasters," replicating data from your primary location to a secondary location can be performed using SAN-based replication, but this can be a costly solution. The other option available to VMware administrators is the built-in vSphere Replication.

vSphere Replication was introduced in SRM 5.0 and decoupled as a separate new feature in vSphere version 5.1; it has been continually improved since then. It provides VM-based replication and recovery at the hypervisor level. This means that there are no external requirements to provide the replication, apart from network connectivity between two locations. Available for every license level above Essentials Plus, vSphere Replication can copy VMs within the same cluster or to a different cluster, which means your target and source could be either the same vCenter or a completely different vCenter on the other side of the country! Before we show you how to configure vSphere Replication, we'll explain the architecture and limitations of this feature.

As mentioned earlier, vSphere Replication can be configured regardless of the underlying storage system or protocol. It will work with locally attached SATA, SAS, vSAN, Fibre Channel SANs, or IP-based NASs. vSphere Replication has no preference of type and is even flexible enough for the source and destination to differ in storage configuration, as shown in Figure 7.39.

FIGURE 7.39
vSphere Replication can work between datacenters, as long as there is a network joining them.

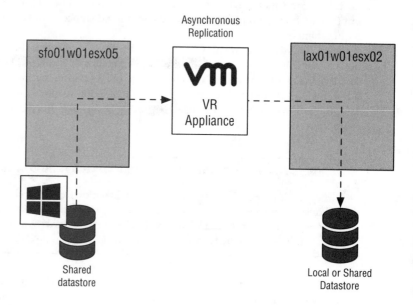

The following constraints affect how vSphere Replication can be configured:

◆ Maximum replication time (RPO): 24 hours

◆ Minimum replication time (RPO): 15 minutes (or 5 minutes if vSAN is used for the source and destination datastores)

◆ Maximum protected VMs: 2000/instance

◆ Maximum instances: 10/vCenter Server

vSphere Replication is installed by deploying a virtual appliance to extend the feature set within vSphere. The installation is much like that of vCenter Operations Manager for example. Let's step through the installation process, and then we'll show you how to configure a VM to replicate to a different cluster under a single vCenter Server instance. Follow these steps to install vSphere Replication:

1. If the vSphere Web Client is not already running, launch it and connect to a vCenter Server instance.

2. Right-click a cluster or datacenter object and select Deploy OVF Template.

3. Browse to the local file where you downloaded the vSphere Replication appliance OVF file. Click Next to proceed to the next screen.

4. Choose a name and datacenter location for the appliance, then click Next.

5. Select a host, cluster or resource pool to host the appliance, and then click Next.

6. Review the details to ensure that they are correct. Click Next to proceed to the EULA screen.

7. Click the Accept button, and then click Next to continue.

8. Choose 2 or 4 vCPUs for the Virtual Appliance. This is based on how large your ESXi host CPUs are. If you have 4 or more cores per NUMA node, select 4 vCPUs; otherwise, select 2 vCPUs. Then click Next.

9. Decide on the storage format and datastore, keeping in mind that the appliance doesn't hold any of the replication data itself.

10. Choose the appropriate network configuration and click Next. If using a static IP, it can only be entered after clicking Next.

11. Configure the appliance password and other template values, (including the Static IP if you selected this on the previous step). The settings can be seen in Figure 7.40. Click Next to continue.

FIGURE 7.40
The network configuration for the vSphere Replication appliance happens before it is deployed.

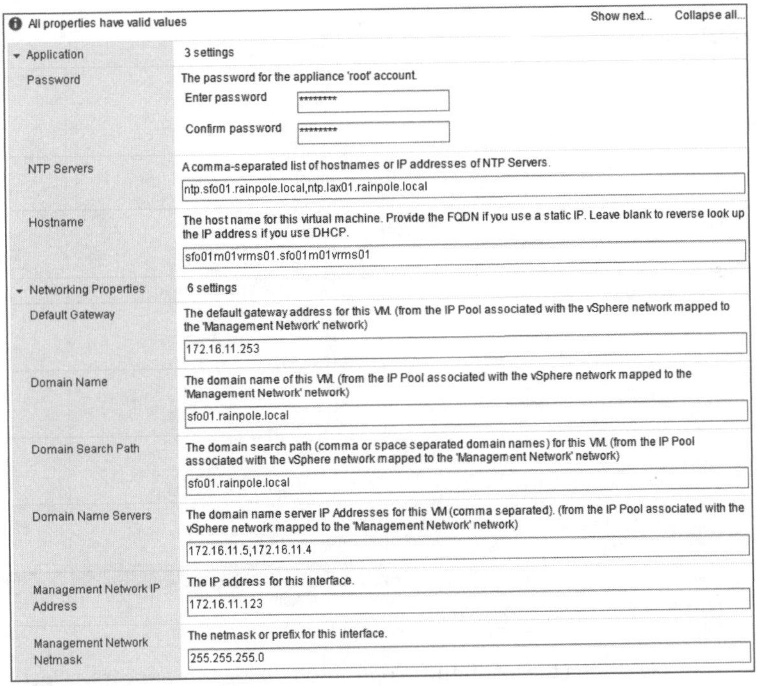

12. On the second-to-last screen, you will be asked to choose a vCenter service for the vSphere Replication appliance. In this case, we have only one. Click Next to continue.

13. Review the selections, and then click the Finish button to begin the deployment.

14. Once the vSphere Replication appliance has finished deploying, power it on as you would any VM.

On the main vSphere Web Client home page, a new icon has been created labeled vSphere Replication. Within this section, you can monitor existing replication jobs and configure target sites. Most of the actual configuration happens when you want to set up a VM for replication. Adding additional sites is as simple as deploying another vSphere Replication Virtual Appliance and then adding it to Target Sites. For simplicity, let's assume you have only a single site and you want to configure a local replication of a VM. Follow these steps:

1. If the vSphere Web Client is not already running, launch it and connect to a vCenter Server instance.

2. Open the Hosts And Clusters or VMs And Templates view.

3. When you right-click a VM, there is now an additional menu at the bottom labeled vSphere Replication. Within this menu, select Configure Replication as shown in Figure 7.41.

FIGURE 7.41

New menus are often added in the vSphere Web Client when virtual appliances that add functionality are deployed.

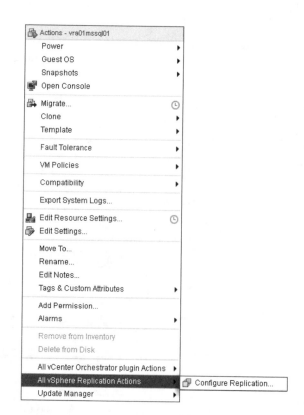

4. When the Configure Replication dialog box appears, select the target site. In this case, the only site is the local one.

5. The next screen allows you to choose a replication server appliance. Select Auto-Assign and click Next.

6. On the Target Location screen, you can pick the datastore you wish the replica to reside on. Choose this wisely because you could fill this datastore with replication data, depending on your RPO schedule. Click Next to continue.

7. The Replication options let you pick a guest OS quiescing method, with Microsoft Shadow Copy Services (VSS) as the only available option. Quiescing will ensure that the VSS-aware applications running on the VM have flushed all their cached data to disk before taking a copy.

8. The Recovery Settings page is the most important settings page because this is where you set the frequency of replication and how many copies to keep. Set your RPO to 8 hours and the point-in-time instances to 3 per day for 5 days, as shown in Figure 7.42.

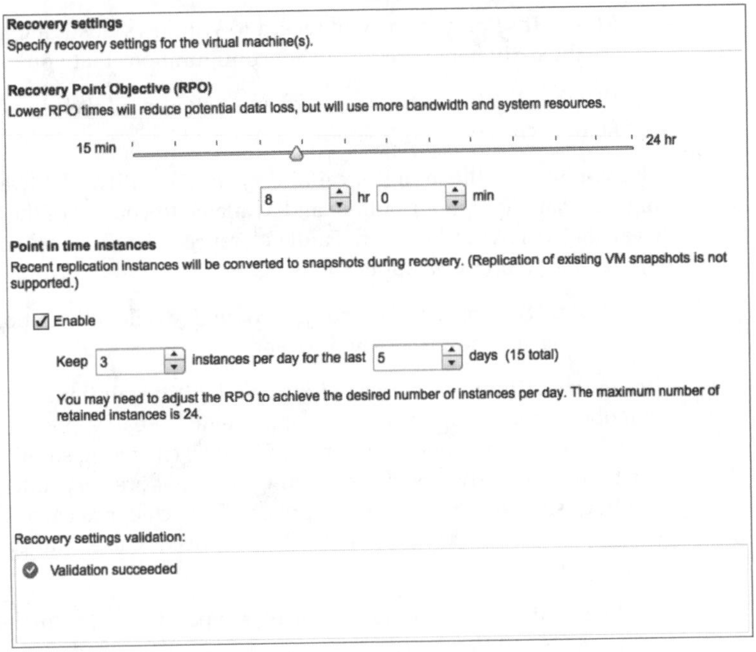

FIGURE 7.42
Always configure the recovery settings within vSphere Replication to match (or exceed) your application's RPO requirements.

9. On the final page, review all the settings and click Finish.

Your VM will now be replicated to the site and datastore as per the replication settings. If at some stage you need to recover the VM, simply click the vSphere Replication icon on the vCenter home screen, find the VM in the Replications lists, and select Recover. You will then be asked for a destination to recover to. Keep in mind that when recovering VMs, initially they are powered on without being connected to any port groups. This ensures that if they are recovered while another copy exists on the network, there will not be any conflicts.

In this chapter, we explained that high availability is for increasing uptime while business continuity is about ensuring that a business can continue in the event of a significant adverse event. The bottom line, to be blunt, is that you'd better have both in place in your environment.

High availability is an important part of any IT shop, and you should design and create a solution with proper care. However, you cannot stop there; you absolutely must test, test, and test again any solution to make sure that your solution works as designed and, most important, that it will work when you need it.

The Bottom Line

Understand Windows clustering and the different types of clusters. Windows clustering plays a central role in the design of any high-availability solution for both virtual and physical servers. Windows clustering gives us the ability to have application failover to the secondary server when the primary server fails.

> **Master It**   Specifically with regard to Windows clustering in a virtual environment, what are three different types of cluster configurations that you can have?

> **Master It**   What is the key difference between NLB clusters and Windows failover clusters?

Use vSphere's built-in high-availability functionality. VMware Virtual Infrastructure has high-availability options built in and available to you out of the box: vSphere High Availability (HA) and vSphere Fault Tolerance (FT). These options help you provide better uptime for your critical applications.

> **Master It**   What are the two types of high-availability options that VMware provides in vSphere, and how are they different?

Recognize differences between high-availability solutions. A high-availability solution that operates at the application layer, like Oracle Real Application Cluster (RAC), is different in architecture and operation from an OS-level clustering solution like Windows failover clustering. Similarly, OS-level clustering solutions are very different from hypervisor-based solutions such as vSphere HA or vSphere FT. Each approach has advantages and disadvantages, and today's administrators will likely need to use multiple approaches in their datacenter.

> **Master It**   Name one advantage of a hypervisor-based high-availability solution over an OS-level solution.

Understand additional components of business continuity. There are other components of ensuring business continuity for your organization. Data protection (backups) and replication of your data to a secondary location are two areas that can help ensure that business continuity needs are satisfied, even in the event of a disaster.

> **Master It**   What are three methods to replicate your data to a secondary location, and what is the golden rule for any continuity plan?

Chapter 8

Securing VMware vSphere

On a scale of 1 to 10 in importance, security always rates close to a 10 in setting up and managing a vSphere environment. Well, maybe not—but it should. Even though VMware has increased the capabilities and features that come with its products, these same products and features must fit within the security policies applied to other servers. Most of the time, ESXi and vCenter Server fit easily within those security policies, but occasionally the process is a bit of a challenge. This chapter examines the tools and techniques that will help you ensure that your vSphere environment appropriately follows the security policies of your organization.

IN THIS CHAPTER, YOU WILL LEARN TO

- ◆ Configure and control authentication to vSphere

- ◆ Manage roles and access controls

- ◆ Control network access to services on ESXi hosts

- ◆ Integrate ESXi and vCenter Server with Active Directory

Overview of vSphere Security

As with most other areas of security within information technology, securing a vSphere environment means securing all the various components of vSphere. Specifically, securing vSphere involves securing the following components:

- ◆ The ESXi hosts

- ◆ vCenter Server

- ◆ The virtual machines (VMs), including the guest operating systems (guest OSs) running inside the VMs

- ◆ The applications running in the VMs

In this chapter, we'll discuss the security considerations for the vSphere components: the ESXi hosts, Platform Services Controller, vCenter Server, and the VM data along with the guest OSs running in your VMs. Each of these components has its own unique set of security challenges, and each has specific ways of addressing those security challenges. For example, ESXi has a different set of security challenges than the Windows-based vCenter Server or the Linux-based vCenter Server virtual appliance. We won't address how to secure the applications *within* your VMs, because that task falls well outside the scope of this book, though we will address how to secure the VM itself. However, we encourage you to keep application-level security in mind as you work toward securing your vSphere environment. When you're considering how to secure the various components involved in a vSphere environment, take into account the following three aspects:

- Authentication

- Authorization

- Accounting

This model—often referred to as the AAA model—describes the way in which users must be authenticated (properly identified as who they claim to be), authorized (enabled or permitted to perform a task, which also includes network access controls), and accounted for (all actions are tracked and logged for future reference). In using this AAA model, you can ensure that you've covered the key aspects of securing the various components of a vSphere environment. We'll use the AAA model as a rough guideline to structure the discussion of securing vSphere in this chapter.

As you work your way through this chapter, keep in mind that some of the recommendations we make here have absolutely nothing to do with virtualization. Because virtualizing with vSphere affects many areas of the datacenter, you must also consider those areas when you look at security. Further, some of the recommendations we make are made elsewhere in the book, so you might see some duplicate information. Security should be woven into every aspect of your vSphere design and implementation, so it's completely natural that you'll see some of the same tips during this focused discussion on security, and apply them across each of your infrastructure's layers.

The first components we'll discuss securing are the ESXi hosts.

Securing ESXi Hosts

VMware ESXi sits at the heart of vSphere, so any discussion of how to secure vSphere includes information on how to secure ESXi. In the following sections, we'll explore securing your ESXi hosts using the AAA model as a guiding framework, starting with the concept of authentication.

Working with ESXi Authentication

The majority of what you need to do as a vSphere administrator involves working with vCenter Server. Even so, it's still necessary to examine how ESXi handles user authentication, because the mechanism vCenter Server uses to manage ESXi hosts also relies on ESXi authentication. Additionally, you may occasionally need to connect directly to an ESXi host. Although using vCenter Server eliminates the largest part of the need to connect directly to an ESXi host, the need does not go away entirely. There are instances when a task cannot be accomplished through vCenter Server, such as in the following situations:

- vCenter Server is not available or is down.

- You are troubleshooting ESXi boot and configuration problems.

Because the need to authenticate to ESXi still exists (even if you are authenticating indirectly through vCenter Server), you should know the options for managing users on ESXi hosts. You have two basic options: managing users locally on each host or integrating with Active Directory. We'll cover each of these options in the following sections.

Managing Users Locally

In most cases, the number and frequency of local user accounts on an ESXi host have both diminished considerably. Usually, you need only two or three accounts for access to an ESXi host. Why two or three and not just one? You need at least two accounts in case one account is unavailable, such as when a user is on vacation or is sick or an accident occurs. As you already know, users on ESXi hosts are, by default, managed independently per ESXi host. Because you need fewer local accounts, many organizations find that the administrative overhead of managing only a few accounts across multiple ESXi hosts is an acceptable burden.

If this is the case in your environment, you have two ways of managing users locally: using command-line tools or using the embedded VMware Host Client. The method that is right for you will largely depend on your experience and preferences. For example, we feel comfortable using the command line, so using the command-line interface (CLI) would be our first choice. However, if you are more comfortable within a graphical user interface (UI), the VMware Host Client is the better option for you. We'll describe both methods so you can choose the method that works best for you.

Perform the following steps to view local users with the vSphere Client:

1. Launch a web browser if one is not already running and connect to an ESXi host's IP address or fully qualified domain name. This will automatically redirect you to the Host Client. Use **root** to authenticate.

   Remember, the vSphere Web Clients (Flash-based or HTML5-based) cannot directly manage ESXi hosts and you cannot manage ESXi local users and groups in either client while connected to a vCenter Server instance.

2. Select Manage from the Navigator pane on the left.

3. Click the Security & Users tab in the content pane on the right; then click the Users button in the lower pane.

In the Users area, you can create new users, edit existing users (including changing the password), and delete users. We'll walk through each of these tasks shortly.

You can also use the CLI to manage local users. Although ESXi offers a local shell (covered in a bit more detail in the section "Controlling Local CLI Access," later in this chapter), the preferred way of using the CLI to work with ESXi is via the vSphere CLI (also referred to as the vCLI). We find that using PowerCLI locally is the best way of working with the vSphere CLI. To describe the process for creating, editing, and deleting local users or groups in the next few sections, we'll be using PowerCLI. You'll learn more about PowerCLI in Chapter 14, "Automating VMware vSphere," but for now, we'll cover some very simple cmdlets that will enable you to accelerate some of these repetitions operations.

Let's take a look at creating, editing, and deleting a user or group.

Creating a Local User

Perform the following steps to create a local user using the VMware Host Client. These steps assume you're already viewing the Security & Users tab in the VMware Host Client.

1. Click the Users button, and then click Add user icon.

   This opens the Add A User dialog box.

2. Supply a username and (optionally) a description for your user.

3. Enter and confirm the password for the new user account.

4. Click OK to create the user with the specified values.

   The new user appears in the list of users.

In the section "Managing ESXi Host Permissions," you'll see how to assign a role to this user to control what actions the user is allowed to perform.

GROUP FUNCTIONS ON ESXi HOSTS

Creating, modifying, and deleting local groups directly on a vSphere host was a supported function up to and including version 5.0. In subsequent releases, the function has been deprecated, and attempts to perform group-related functions will fail, regardless of whether the action is attempted through the client or CLI. If you need to use groups for permissions, consider adding your hosts to an Active Directory domain, which allows local permissions to be enforced at a group level.

You can also use the PowerCLI to create users, but as mentioned earlier, not groups. To use the CLI to create a new user, you can execute the following single line of code:

```
New-VMHostAccount -Id <Local User> -UserAccount
```

Figure 8.1 shows the PowerCLI cmdlet New-VMHostAccount prompting for a password to perform the command as well as the password for the new user account.

FIGURE 8.1
The New-
VMHostAccount
command prompts for a
password to execute the
command and then
prompts for a password
for the new user you
are creating.

As mentioned previously, creating a new user is only part of the process; in order to use that account with the Host Client, you also need to assign a role. We'll cover roles and permissions in the section "Managing ESXi Host Permissions," later in this chapter.

Now let's take a look at editing a user both from the vSphere Client and from the CLI.

Editing a Local User

Perform the following steps to edit a local user or group using the vSphere Client:

1. Launch a web browser and connect to an ESXi host's Client. Select Manage from the Navigator pane on the left, and then click the Security & Users tab.

2. Click the user you want to modify and select Edit User.

   This opens the Edit User dialog box.

3. In the Edit User dialog box, make any necessary changes to the user account.

   As you can see in Figure 8.2, the User Name field cannot be changed.

FIGURE 8.2
For a user, you can change the description or password, but you can't change the User Name field.

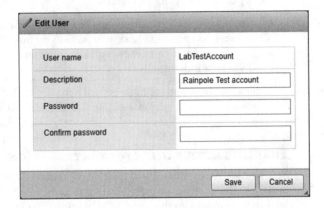

4. Click OK to make the changes to the selected user account.

To use the CLI to update a user's password, you can execute the following single line of code:

```
Set-VMHostAccount -UserAccount <Local User> -Password <Password>
```

Let's wrap up this discussion of managing local users with a review of how to delete local users from an ESXi host.

Deleting a Local User

Perform the following steps to delete a local user from a specific ESXi host using the vSphere Client:

1. Launch a web browser and connect to an ESXi host's Client. Select Manage from the Navigator pane on the left, and then click the Security & Users tab.

2. Click the user you want to remove and select Remove User from the context menu. When prompted for confirmation, select Yes.

To use the PowerCLI to delete a local user or group, you can execute the following single line of code:

```
Get-VMHostAccount -ID <Local User> | Remove-VMHostAccount -Confirm
```

TO VCENTER OR NOT TO VCENTER

The best way to administer a vSphere environment consisting of multiple hosts or a cluster is to connect the vSphere Web Client to a vCenter Server instance. Although you can connect via the Host Client to an ESXi host, you lose a great deal of functionality. If you didn't purchase vCenter Server, you may have no choice other than to connect to the ESXi hosts. In such instances, you'd have to create user accounts locally on the ESXi hosts for VM administration as outlined in this section.

Now that you have an idea of the specific steps used to manage users locally on each ESXi host, what are the security challenges involved in doing so? And how can those security challenges be addressed? Here are two examples:

◆ You must manually manage users separately on each and every ESXi host. If you forget delete a user account for a departing employee on a specific ESXi host, you've just create a potential security problem.

◆ There is no way to centrally enforce password policies. Although you can set password policies on each ESXi host, you have to do this separately on every ESXi host in your environment. If you ever need to change the password policy, you must do so on each ESXi host individually.

You can address both of these security challenges by leveraging functionality provided by VMware with ESXi to integrate authentication into Active Directory, as you'll see in the next section.

ENABLING ACTIVE DIRECTORY INTEGRATION

You've already seen how, by default, ESXi uses local users to assign permissions to directories and files. The presence of these local users is the key to the ESXi security model, as you'll see later in this chapter, in the section "Managing ESXi Host Permissions." Although these local users form the foundation of the ESXi security model, managing them locally on every ESXi host in the enterprise can create a great deal of administrative overhead and has some security challenges, as we've already described.

What if you were able to continue to accommodate the need for local access to an ESXi host but in a way that avoided some of the security challenges of managing users locally?

One answer to these security challenges is to use a centralized security authority. In vSphere you can use Active Directory, a widely deployed directory service, as the centralized security authority for ESXi hosts. As you'll see later in this chapter, in the section "Authenticating Users with Single Sign-On," vCenter Server can already leverage Active Directory, so allowing your ESXi hosts to leverage the same security authority makes sense.

Before you can join your ESXi hosts into Active Directory, you need to satisfy four prerequisites:

◆ The time on your ESXi hosts must be synchronized with the time on the Active Directory domain controllers. ESXi supports NTP, and in Chapter 2, "Planning and Installing VMware ESXi," you learned how to configure NTP on your ESXi hosts.

◆ Your ESXi hosts must be able to resolve the Active Directory domain name and locate the domain controllers via DNS. Typically, this means configuring the ESXi hosts to use the same DNS servers as the Active Directory domain controllers, and just like NTP, this is covered in Chapter 2.

◆ The fully qualified domain name (FQDN) of the ESXi host must use the same domain suffix as the Active Directory domain.

◆ You must create an ESX Admins group in Active Directory. Place the user accounts that should be permitted to authenticate with an ESXi host in this group. You can't use any other group name; it must be named ESX Admins.

After you have satisfied these prerequisites, you can configure your ESXi host to authenticate to Active Directory.

Perform these steps to configure your ESXi host to use Active Directory as its centralized security authority:

1. Launch a web browser if one is not already running, and connect to an ESXi host's IP address or fully qualified domain name. This will automatically redirect you to the Host Client. Use **root** to authenticate.

2. Select Manage from the Navigator pane on the left.

3. Click the Security & Users tab in the content pane on the right, then click the Authentication button in the lower pane.

4. Click Join Domain in the upper-left corner.

5. In the Join Domain dialog box, supply the FQDN of the Active Directory domain that this ESXi host will use for authentication.

6. Specify a username and password that has permission to allow the host to join the domain.

7. Click the Join Domain button.

When the ESXi host is joined to Active Directory, users will be able to authenticate to an ESXi host using their Active Directory credentials. With the Host Client or the PowerCLI, users can use either the domain\username or the username@domain syntax. From PowerCLI, users will be prompted to supply the username and to supply the password in another prompt if the password is excluded, as in this example:

```
Get-VMHostAuthentication -VMHost sfo01m01esx01.rainpole.local | Set-
VMHostAuthentication -JoinDomain -Domain Rainpole.local -User Administrator
```

Although managing how users authenticate is important, it's also important to control how users access ESXi hosts. In the next section, we'll examine how you can control access to your ESXi hosts.

Controlling Access to ESXi Hosts

The second part of the AAA model is authorization, which encompasses access control mechanisms that affect local access or network access. In the following sections, we'll describe the mechanisms available to you to control access to your ESXi hosts.

CONTROLLING LOCAL ACCESS

ESXi offers direct access via the server console through the Direct Console User Interface (DCUI). We've shown you screen shots of the DCUI in other parts of this book, such as in Chapter 2.

Access to the DCUI on an ESXi host is limited to users who have the Administrator role on that host. We haven't discussed the concept of roles yet (see "Managing ESXi Host Permissions," later in this chapter, for more details), but this limitation on the DCUI allows you to control who is permitted to access the DCUI. As with other forms of security, it's important to secure access to the host via the physical server console, and limiting DCUI access to users with the Administrator role helps accomplish that goal.

Controlling Local CLI Access

ESXi has a CLI environment that is accessible from the server's physical console. However, by default, this CLI environment—known as the ESXi Shell—is disabled. If you need CLI access to ESXi, you must first enable the ESXi Shell. You can enable the ESXi Shell via the DCUI or via the vSphere Client.

Perform these steps to enable the ESXi Shell via the DCUI:

1. Access the console of the ESXi host using the physical server console or some KVM mechanism (many server vendors provide remote console functionality).

2. Press F2 to log into the DCUI. When prompted for username and password, supply a username and password with permission to access the DCUI (this user must have the Administrator role for this ESXi host).

3. Navigate down to Troubleshooting Options and press Enter.

4. Select Enable ESXi Shell.

   This enables the CLI environment on the ESXi host.

5. Press Esc until you return to the main DCUI screen.

6. Press Alt+F1 to access the CLI environment on that ESXi host, or alternatively launch a remote SSH session and run **dcui** at the command prompt.

If your host is using local authentication, you can authenticate using a user account defined locally on that host. If your host is using Active Directory authentication as described in the previous section, you can log in using Active Directory credentials (using either the domain\ username or the username@domain syntax).

Perform the following steps to enable the ESXi Shell via the vSphere Client:

1. Launch a web browser if one is not already running and connect to an ESXi host's IP address or fully qualified domain name. This will automatically redirect you to the Host Client. Use **root** to authenticate.

2. Select Manage from the Navigator pane on the left.

3. Click the Services tab in the content pane on the right.

   This displays all the Services available on the ESXi host and their current running state.

4. Select ESXi Shell from the list of services and then click Actions.

5. Click Start.

   A banner should appear indicating that the ESXi Shell started successfully and the service should now be listed as Running.

   The ESXi Shell is now available.

You can now use the local CLI at the ESXi host's console. It's important to note, though, that VMware doesn't recommend regular, routine use of the ESXi Shell as your primary means of managing and maintaining ESXi. Instead, you should use the Host Client and/or the PowerCLI and resort to the ESXi Shell only when absolutely necessary.

Although following these steps gets you local CLI access, it doesn't get you remote CLI access. For remote CLI access, another step is required, as you'll see in the next section.

CONTROLLING REMOTE CLI ACCESS VIA SSH

Secure Shell, often referred to as just SSH, is a widely known and widely used encrypted remote console protocol. SSH was originally developed in 1995 to replace other protocols—such as `telnet`, `rsh`, and `rlogin`—that did not provide strong authentication and did not protect against password-sniffing attacks on the network. SSH gained rapid adoption, and the SSH-2 protocol is now a proposed Internet standard with the Internet Engineering Task Force (IETF).

ESXi includes SSH as a method of remote console access. This allows vSphere administrators to use an SSH client—such as `PuTTY.exe` on Windows or OpenSSH on Linux or Mac OS X—to remotely access the CLI of an ESXi host in order to perform management tasks. However, as with the ESXi Shell, SSH access to an ESXi host is disabled by default. To gain remote CLI access to an ESXi host via SSH, you must first enable the ESXi Shell and enable SSH. You've already seen how to enable the ESXi Shell; now we'll show you how to enable SSH, both via the DCUI and via the Host Client.

Perform the following steps to enable SSH via the DCUI:

1. Access the console of the ESXi host using the physical server console or some KVM mechanism (many server vendors provide remote console functionality).

2. Press F2 to log into the DCUI. When prompted for username and password, supply a username and password with permission to access the DCUI (this user must have the Administrator role for this ESXi host).

3. Navigate down to Troubleshooting Options and press Enter.

4. Select Enable SSH. This enables the SSH server (or daemon) on the ESXi host.

5. Press Esc until you return to the main DCUI screen.

Follow these steps to enable SSH via the Host Client:

1. Launch a web browser if one is not already running and connect to an ESXi host's IP address or fully qualified domain name. This will automatically redirect you to the Host Client. Use **root** to authenticate.

2. Select Manage from the Navigator pane on the left.

3. Click the Services tab in the content pane on the right.

4. Select SSH from the list of services and then click Actions.

5. Click Start.

   A banner should appear indicating that the SSH started successfully and the services should now be listed as Running.

6. You can now use `PuTTY.exe` (Windows) or OpenSSH (Mac OS X, Linux, and other Unix variants) to establish an SSH session to the ESXi host.

As with local CLI access, VMware recommends against using SSH as a means of routinely managing your ESXi hosts. In fact, in earlier versions of vSphere, SSH access to ESXi was unsupported. It is supported in this version of vSphere, but VMware still recommends against regular use. If you want to use a CLI environment, we recommend getting familiar with the PowerCLI or vCLI as your primary CLI environment.

ROOT LOGIN IS ENABLED BY DEFAULT VIA SSH

Generally speaking, allowing the root user to log into a host via SSH is considered a violation of security best practices. However, in vSphere 5.0 and later, when SSH and the ESXi Shell are enabled, the root user is allowed to log in via SSH. This is yet one more reason to keep SSH and the ESXi Shell disabled during the normal course of operation. Lucky for you, SSH and ESXi Shell are, in fact, disabled by default.

Although VMware provides SSH as a means of accessing the CLI environment on an ESXi host, this version of SSH does not provide all the same flexibility as a "full" SSH installation. This further underscores the need to use SSH on an as-needed basis as well as the need for additional access controls for your ESXi hosts, such as a network firewall.

CONTROLLING NETWORK ACCESS VIA THE ESXI FIREWALL

ESXi ships with a firewall that controls network traffic into or out of the host. This firewall gives the vSphere administrator an additional level of control over what types of network traffic are allowed to enter or leave the ESXi hosts.

By default, the ESXi firewall allows only incoming and outgoing connections necessary for managing the VMs and the ESXi host. The following default ports are among those that are open:

- TCP 443 and 902: Host Client, vCenter Agent
- UDP 53: Domain Name System (DNS) client
- TCP and UDP 427: Common Information Model (CIM) Service Location Protocol (SLP)
- TCP 8000: vMotion
- TCP 22: SSH

To see the full list of ports that are open on an ESXi host, you can use the Host Client connected directly to an ESXi host, as illustrated in Figure 8.3, or use the vSphere Web Client connected to a vCenter server, select a host, and navigate to Configure ➢ System ➢ Security Profile.

From this same area of the Host Client, you can also enable additional ports through the firewall or disable ports that are currently open. A number of predefined ports and related services that can be configured are listed here.

FIGURE 8.3
The Firewall Rules tab located under the Networking area in the Host Client shows the current ESXi firewall configuration.

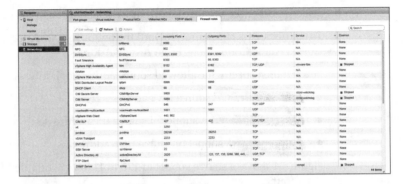

Perform the following steps to enable or disable traffic through the ESXi firewall:

1. Launch a web browser if one is not already running and connect to an ESXi host's IP address or fully qualified domain name. This will automatically redirect you to the Host Client. Use **root** to authenticate.

2. Select Networking from the Navigator pane on the left.

3. Click the Firewall Rules tab in the content pane on the right.

   This displays all the firewall rules available on the ESXi host, their current running state and what daemon the rule is associated with.

4. To enable a particular type of traffic through the ESXi firewall, select the service and click Actions ➤ Enable. To disable a type of traffic, repeat this workflow of clicking Actions ➤ Disable.

The ESXi firewall also allows you to configure more fine-grained controls over network access by specifying source addresses from which traffic should be allowed. This gives you the ability to enable certain types of traffic through the ESXi firewall but restrict access to specific IP addresses or groups of IP addresses.

Perform these steps to limit access to a network service to a specific source:

1. Launch the Web Client and connect to a vCenter Server instance.

2. Select an ESXi host from the inventory view and select the Configure tab.

   You might need to navigate to the Hosts And Clusters view first if you are connected to a vCenter Server instance.

3. From the Systems section, select Security Profile.

4. Click the Edit button to the right of the content area.

   This opens the Edit Security Profile dialog box.

5. Select a port or service that is currently enabled through the firewall.

6. To restrict access to a source, toward the bottom of the dialog box, deselect the check box labeled Allow Connections From Any IP Address.

You can then specify the allowed source address or addresses in three different formats:

◆ 192.168.1.24: A source IPv4 address

◆ 192.168.1.0/24: A subnet of source IPv4 addresses

◆ 2001::1/64: A subnet of source IPv6 addresses

Figure 8.4 shows a source subnet of 172.16.11.0/24 configured for the selected network traffic.

FIGURE 8.4
Traffic to the selected network traffic on this ESXi host will be limited to addresses from the specified subnet.

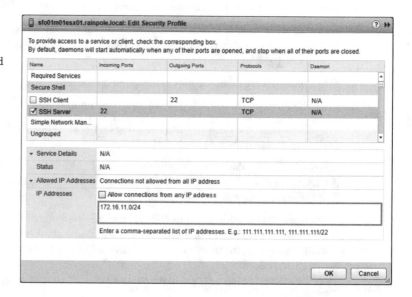

7. Click OK to close the Edit Security Profile dialog box and return to the Security Profile page.

This feature of the ESXi firewall gives you much more flexibility in not only defining what services are allowed into or out of your ESXi hosts but also in defining the source of the traffic into or out of the host. The two previous examples illustrate how to perform firewall tasks with both the Host Client and the vSphere Web Client. There may be the odd occasion when you need to configure your own ports and services through the firewall, and this needs to be performed through the ESXi Shell or via SSH.

The following steps will guide you through creating your own custom firewall rules; however, it should be noted that these do not persist through a reboot of the host.

1. Log on to the ESXi shell via SSH.

2. To display the current firewall rules, run the following command:

```
esxcli network firewall ruleset list
```

3. Make a backup of the firewall configuration file:

```
cp /etc/vmware/firewall/service.xml /etc/vmware/firewall/service.xml.bak
```

4. Allow the firewall configuration file to be changed with the following:

```
chmod 644 /etc/vmware/firewall/service.xml
```

5. Toggle the sticky bit flag using the following command:

```
chmod +t /etc/vmware/firewall/service.xml
```

6. Open the firewall configuration file with a text editor; in this example Vi is used:

```
vi /etc/vmware/firewall/service.xml
```

7. As shown in Figure 8.5, add a service following the same syntax as those that already exist in the file:

```
<service id='0101'>
  <id>customservice</id>
  <rule id='0000'>
    <direction>inbound</direction>
    <protocol>tcp</protocol>
    <porttype>dst</porttype>
    <port>
      <begin>1337</begin>
      <end>13377</end>
    </port>
  </rule>
  <rule id='0001'>
    <direction>outbound</direction>
    <protocol>tcp</protocol>
    <porttype>srv</porttype>
    <port>
      <begin>1337</begin>
      <end>13377</end>
    </port>
  </rule>
  <enabled>true</enabled>
  <required>false</required>
</service>
```

8. Change the firewall configuration permissions back to their original value:

```
chmod 444 /etc/vmware/firewall/service.xml
```

9. Update the firewall configuration by running the following command:

```
esxcli network firewall refresh
```

10. List the firewall rules again to ensure that the changes are active:

```
esxcli network firewall ruleset list
```

FIGURE 8.5

Adding the correct XML to the services .xml file allows you to customize the ESXi host firewall ports.

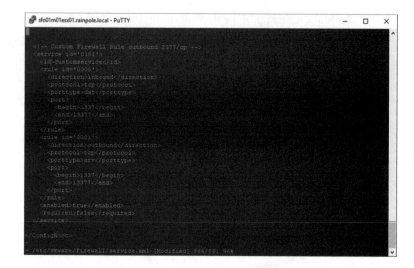

Maintaining the ESXi firewall configuration is an important part of ESXi host security.

Another recommended security practice is to isolate the ESXi management network to control network access to the management interfaces of your ESXi hosts. You can accomplish this using a network firewall, a technique that's described in the next section.

CONTROLLING NETWORK ACCESS TO THE ESXI MANAGEMENT INTERFACES

The ESXi firewall allows you to control access to specific TCP/IP ports on an ESXi host, but an additional step to consider is a network firewall to control access to the management interfaces of the ESXi host. Using a network firewall to enforce access control lists (ACLs) that govern which systems can connect to the management interfaces of ESXi hosts is a complementary step to using the ESXi firewall. It follows the well-known recommended practice of using "defense in depth."

Should you choose to isolate the management interfaces of your ESXi hosts on a separate network segment, keep in mind the following two important considerations:

◆ Be sure to allow proper access from vCenter Server to the ESXi hosts. You can handle this by allowing the appropriate ports through the firewall or by adding an extra network interface on the isolated management segment to the vCenter Server system. We prefer the latter approach, but both approaches are perfectly valid.

◆ Don't forget to allow access from systems on which you will run vCLI or PowerCLI scripts if you'll be accessing the ESXi hosts directly. If the vCLI or the PowerCLI scripts will be connecting to vCenter Server, you just need to allow access to vCenter Server.

 **Real World Scenario**

USING A JUMP BOX

One technique that we've seen, and used, in a fair number of installations is a *jump box*. This is a system—typically a Windows Server–based system—that has network interfaces to the isolated management network as well as to the rest of your network segments. You'll connect to the jump box and then connect from there to your vSphere environment using the Host Client, vSphere Web Client, PowerCLI, vCLI, or other tools. This neatly sidesteps the issue of having to create firewall rules to allow traffic into or out of the isolated management network but still provides access to manage the environment. If you are thinking about isolating the management interfaces of your ESXi hosts, a jump box might be an approach to consider for your environment. By design, a jump box bridges connectivity between two isolated subnets. Although this does satisfy management needs, it may be in contention with your organization's security policy. Check with your security team before implementing this type of solution.

Controlling network access to your ESXi hosts is an important part of your overall security strategy, but it's also important to keep your ESXi hosts patched against security vulnerabilities.

Keeping ESXi Hosts Patched

Another key component in maintaining the security of your vSphere environment is keeping your ESXi hosts fully patched and up-to-date. On an as-needed basis, VMware releases security patches for ESXi. Failing to apply these security patches could expose your vSphere environment to potential security risks.

vSphere Update Manager (VUM) is the tool VMware supplies with vSphere to address this need. We discussed the VUM extensively in Chapter 4, "Maintaining VMware vSphere." To keep your vSphere environment as secure as possible, you should strongly consider using VUM in your environment to keep your ESXi hosts patched.

In the next section, we'll move on to another aspect of authorization: access controls to manage what a user is allowed to do on an ESXi host after being authenticated.

Managing ESXi Host Permissions

We've shown you how to manage users, both locally and through Active Directory integration. Another key aspect of ESXi host security is the concept of *roles*.

Both vCenter Server and ESXi hosts use the same structured security model to allow users to manage portions of the virtual infrastructure. This model consists of users, groups, roles, privileges, and permissions, as shown in Figure 8.6.

FIGURE 8.6
vCenter Server and ESXi share a common security model for assigning access control.

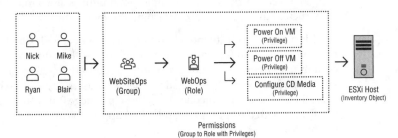

Permissions
(Group to Role with Privileges)

From a security standpoint, the items that differ between the non–vCenter Server environment and the vCenter Server environment are predominantly in the following two areas:

- The location of the user objects created

- The level of granularity of the roles and privileges available in each environment

You've already seen how ESXi can define users locally on each ESXi host or leverage Active Directory as a centralized security authority. As you'll see later in this chapter, in the section "Authenticating Users with Single Sign-On," and as we covered in Chapter 3, "Installing and Configuring vCenter Server," vCenter can also leverage a directory such as Active Directory as centralized security authority. Prior to vSphere 5.1, the Windows-based vCenter Server was a member of Active Directory, and permissions were leveraged through this connection. From vSphere 5.1 on, the architecture has significantly changed with the introduction of vCenter Sing Sign-On (SSO). We'll explain more about SSO later in this chapter. This is the first key differenc in managing permissions for environments that don't use vCenter Server versus environments that do.

The second key difference is the level of granularity of the roles and privileges available in each environment. To explain this difference, we must first discuss and define roles and privileges.

For environments that don't have vCenter Server, or where the administrator chooses to hav users authenticate directly to the ESXi hosts to perform management tasks, it is important to st with a discussion of the security model.

In the vCenter Server/ESXi security model's most basic format, users or groups are assigne to a role that has privileges. The user-role-privilege combination is then associated with an obje in the inventory as a permission. This means there are four basic components to the vCenter Server/ESXi security model:

User or Group A user is an authentication mechanism; a group is a way of collecting users In earlier sections of this chapter, you saw how to manage users and how ESXi can leverage local users from Active Directory. Users and groups form a basic building block of the security model.

Privilege A privilege is an action that you can perform on an inventory object. This would include allocating space in a datastore, powering on a VM, configuring the network, or attaching a virtual CD/DVD to a VM.

Role A role is a collection of privileges. Both vCenter and ESXi ship with built-in roles, as you'll see shortly, and you can also create your own custom roles.

Permission A permission allows a user to perform the activities specified by a role assigne to an inventory object. For example, you might assign a role that has all privileges to a particular inventory object. Attaching the role to the inventory object creates a permission.

This modular security model provides a great deal of flexibility. You can either use the built-roles provided with ESXi or create custom roles with custom sets of privileges and assign those custom roles to inventory objects in order to properly re-create the correct set of abilities in the virtual infrastructure. By associating roles with users or groups, you need to define the role onl once; then, whenever someone needs those privileges, all you have to do is associate the appro-priate user with the appropriate role. This approach can help simplify the management of permissions.

An ESXi host has the following three default roles:

No Access The No Access role works as the name suggests. This role prevents access to an object or objects in the inventory. The No Access role can be used if a user was granted acces higher up in the inventory. The No Access role can also be used at lower-level objects to prevent object access. For example, if a user is granted permissions on the ESXi host but should be prevented from accessing a specific VM, you could use the No Access role on that specific VM.

Read-Only   Read-Only allows a user to see the objects within the vSphere Client inventory. It does not allow the user to interact with any of the visible objects in any way. For example, a user with the Read-Only permission would be able to see a list of VMs in the inventory but could not act on any of them, such as performing a power operation.

Administrator   The Administrator role has the utmost authority, but it is only a role, and it needs to be assigned using a combination of a user or a group object and an inventory object such as a VM.

With only three built-in roles on ESXi hosts, the defaults don't leave room for much flexibility. In addition, the default roles just described can't be modified, so you can't customize them. However, don't let that slow you down. Any limits created by the default roles are easily overcome by creating custom roles. You can create custom roles that will better suit your needs, or you can clone existing roles to make additional roles to modify for your own purposes.

Let's take a closer look at how to create a custom role.

CREATING CUSTOM ROLES

If you find that the default roles provided with ESXi don't suit your organization's needs with regard to permissions and management, you should create custom roles to better map to your business needs. For example, assume that a set of users needs to interact with the console of a VM and also needs to change the CD and floppy media of those VMs. These needs aren't properly reflected in any of the default roles, so a custom role is necessary.

Perform the following steps to create a custom role named Operator:

1. Launch a web browser if one is not already running, and connect to an ESXi host's IP address or fully qualified domain name. This will automatically redirect you to the Host Client. Use **root** to authenticate.

2. Select Manage from the Navigator pane on the left.

3. Click the Security & Users tab in the content pane on the right, then click the Roles button in the lower pane.

4. Click the Add Role button.

5. Type the name of the new role in the Name text box (in this example, **Operator**), and then select the privileges that will be required by members of the role, as shown in Figure 8.7.

   The privileges shown in Figure 8.7 allow users or groups assigned to the Operator role to interact with the console of a VM, change the CD and floppy media, and change the power state of a VM.

6. Click OK to complete the custom role creation.

FIGURE 8.7
Custom roles strengthen management capabilities and add flexibility to permission delegations.

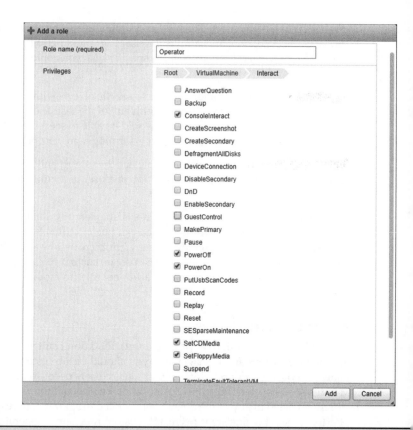

The new Operator role is now defined, but it's not operational yet. You must still assign user or groups to the role and apply the role to the ESXi host and/or individual VM(s).

GRANTING PERMISSIONS

As simple and useful as roles are, they are not functional until a user is assigned to the role and the role is then assigned to an inventory object as a permission. Assume that a group of users exists that needs to interact with all VMs that are web servers. If access control is managed through the ESXi host, you have to create a user account on that host (or leverage an Active Directory user or group account). Once these users exist, you can execute the security model.

Perform the following steps to grant VM access control to a user or Active Directory group:

1. Launch a web browser if one is not already running, and connect to an ESXi host's IP address or fully qualified domain name. This will automatically redirect you to the Host Client. Use **root** to authenticate.

2. Right-click the Host object in the navigator pane on the left to bring up the context menu, and select Permissions.

3. Click the Add User button in the Manage Permissions dialog box.

4. In the Add User For Host area, select the appropriate user or group from the Select A User drop-down list (for example, WinESXOps).

   Use the Domain drop-down box to show users from Active Directory if you've configured your ESXi host to integrate with Active Directory.

   Once you've found the user you want, click the Add button, and then click OK. This returns you to the Assign Permissions dialog box, where the user is listed on the left side.

5. From the Select A Role drop-down list, choose the role to which the selected users should be assigned. In this case, select Operator—the role you defined earlier—from the drop-down list to assign that role to the selected user or group.

What if you have an ESXi host that will host 30 VMs and only 10 of those are the web server VMs? If you assign the permission at the ESXi host level, as we just demonstrated, you'll assign that role to all 30 VMs, not just the 10 web server VMs. This is because when you assign a permission, an option named Propagate To All Children is enabled by default. Figure 8.8 shows the Add User For Host section; note the option to propagate permissions in the upper-left area of the dialog box.

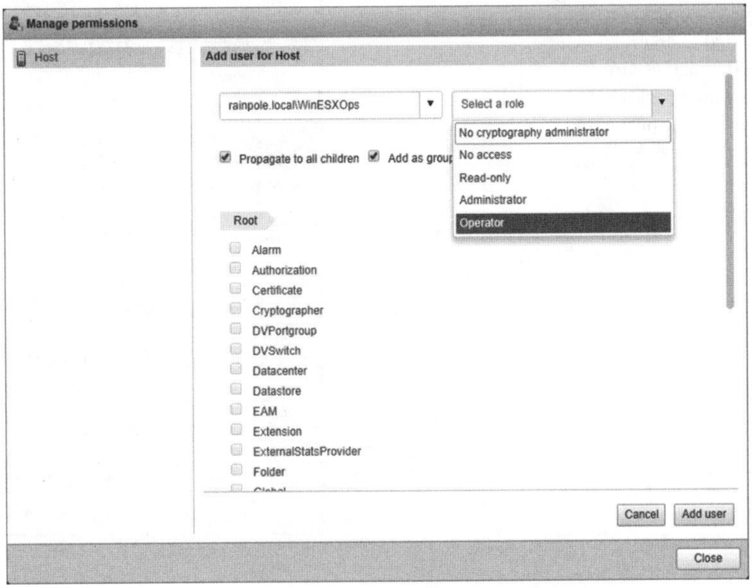

FIGURE 8.8
By default, assigning a permission to an object will propagate that permission to all child objects.

This option works like the security inheritance settings in a Windows filesystem. It allows the privileges assigned in this role to be applied to objects beneath the selected object. For example, the Operator role is applied as a permission on the ESXi host in the inventory panel and the Propagate To All Children option is enabled, all members of the Operator role will be able to interact with *all* the VMs hosted on the ESXi host. Although this certainly simplifies access control implementation, it adds another problem: the permissions of the Operator role have been overextended and now apply to all VMs and not just the web servers. With access control granted at the host level, members of the Operator role will be able to change floppy and CD media and use the console of the web server VMs, but they will also be able to do that on any other VM in the inventory.

To make this work as you would expect, you would have to assign permissions on each of the 10 web server VMs individually. Clearly, this is not an efficient process. Further growth resulting in more web server VMs would require additional administrative effort to ensure access control.

Alternatively, you could use the No Access role on the non–web server VMs to prevent access but this method also does not scale well and requires administrative overhead.

This issue presents one of the drawbacks of managing access control on an individual ESXi host. Keep in mind as well that all the steps we have discussed so far would have to be performed on each ESXi host in the virtual infrastructure. What if there were a way to organize the inventory of VMs? In other words, what if you could create a "container object" for the web server VMs, such as a folder, and put all the web server VMs into it? Then you could assign the group to the role at the parent object level and let inheritance take over. As shown in Figure 8.9, the problem is that folder objects are not possible on a single ESXi host. Unfortunately, as of the writing of this book, the creation of resource pools or something of this nature for a higher-tier form of organization and permissions management hasn't yet been implemented in the Host Client.

FIGURE 8.9
Folder objects cannot be added to an individual ESXi host, leaving resource pools as the only viable option to group VMs.

Now that you know how to assign permissions, you should know how to remove them as well. Let's look at that next.

REMOVING PERMISSIONS

When your management needs change or if you've made some improper permissions assignments, you can remove permissions. In the section "Granting Permissions," we walked you through the process of assigning the Operator role permission on the ESXi host. Now that you have a resource group in place to give you more granular control over permissions, you should remove the permissions you previously applied to the host.

Follow these steps to remove permissions on an object in the inventory:

1. Launch a web browser if one is not already running, and connect to an ESXi host's IP address or fully qualified domain name. This will automatically redirect you to the Host Client. Use **root** to authenticate.

2. Right-click the Host object in the navigator pane on the left to bring up the context menu, and select Permissions.

3. Click the user or group to be removed in the Manage Permissions dialog box, and then click the Remove User option.

Though no warning appears, you should be cognizant that users may retain their permissions because of assignments on parent objects higher in the hierarchy. In this case, you want to remove the objects on the parent object (the ESXi host) because those permissions have been applied to the child object (the virtual machines). In other cases, though, it might be necessary to keep permissions on the parent object.

After you assign permissions throughout the inventory, it is easy to lose track of what you have previously done. Of course, if your company mandates documentation, there might already be a solid audit trail. However, it is easy to see existing role usage from PowerCLI. While it's a bit jarring to hear this, at the moment the Host Client doesn't have a means of quickly identifying where all users and their associated roles are situated.

IDENTIFYING PERMISSION USAGE

As the inventory of VMs grows larger and more complex, it's likely that the permissions granted to these various objects will also become complex. In addition, as company needs and management strategies change over time, these permissions must change as well. Combined, these factors can create an environment where the permissions usage is quite complex and hard to decipher.

To help combat this issue, you can use a simple PowerCLI cmdlet Get-VIPermission to help you identify where roles have been assigned and what permissions have been granted in the inventory.

To identify what roles have been assigned as a permission, execute the following code:

```
Get-VIPermission | Select Role, Principal, IsGroup, Entity, Propagate |
Sort-Object -Property Role |ft -AutoSize | more
```

You can use the following code to narrow the scope down to look for users and groups that are mapped to a specific role and their locations. This may be quite useful when you're updatin the permissions used in a role to ensure that you don't inadvertently provide a user or group with elevated access to resources or capabilities they normally should not have.

```
Get-VIPermission | Select Role, Principal, IsGroup, Entity, Propagate | Sort-
    Object –Propert Role | Where-Object {$_.Role -eq 'Operator'} |ft -AutoSize | mor
```

The combined outputs from the preceding two code examples help identify where in the inventory hierarchy the role is used, as you can see in Figure 8.10.

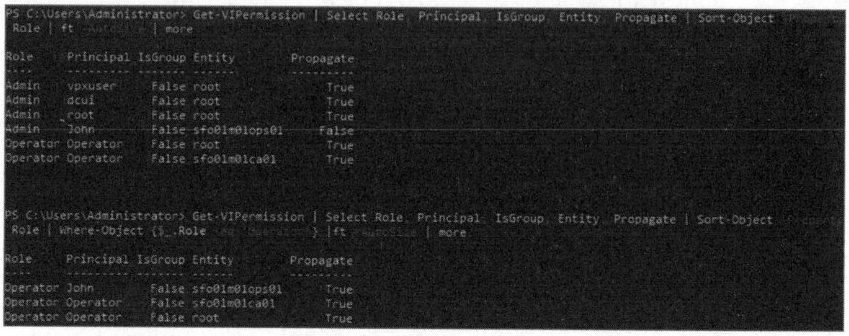

FIGURE 8.10

The Get-VIPermission cmdlet provides a breakdown of where roles are currently in use.

PowerCLI has a wide variety of uses, and the Get-VIPermission cmdlet is just one that allows you to track down where permissions have been assigned so that you can edit or remove them when necessary. But it's not only permissions that need to be removed—sometimes roles need to be removed too.

EDITING AND REMOVING ROLES

Over time, it is almost inevitable that management needs will change. At times, you might have to create new roles, edit an existing role, or even delete a role. If the privileges assigned to a role are no longer applicable in your environment, you should edit the role to add or remove the necessary privileges.

Perform the following steps to edit a role:

1. Launch a web browser if one is not already running, and connect to an ESXi host's IP address or fully qualified domain name. This will automatically redirect you to the Host Client. Use **root** to authenticate.

2. Right-click the Host object in the navigator pane on the left to bring up the context menu, and select Permissions.

3. Click the user or group to be edited in the Manage Permissions dialog box, and select Assign Role.

4. Make the desired changes by adding or removing privileges in the Set Permissions dialog box. Click Assign Role when you finish.

As we mentioned earlier in this chapter, ESXi won't allow you to edit the default roles.

If a role is no longer used, it should be removed to minimize the number of objects to be viewed and managed. Perform the following steps to delete a role:

1. Launch a web browser if one is not already running, and connect to an ESXi host's IP address or fully qualified domain name. This will automatically redirect you to the Host Client. Use **root** to authenticate.

2. Select Manage from the Navigator pane on the left.

3. Click the Security & Users tab in the content pane on the right, and then click the role to be deleted in the lower pane.

4. Click the Remove Role button, and when prompted with the removal warning, click Yes to finish.

   Fortunately, the warning will prevent you from accidentally deleting any roles that are still associated with a user or group within the ESXi host. Considering how tedious it is to audit a host in order to identify what permissions are assigned where, leaving the Remove Only If Unused option when cleaning up roles means you won't have to make your users suffer through unnecessary outages.

When a role is in use and is selected for removal, the ESXi host offers the opportunity to only delete the role once all existing role members have been disassociated or to simply drop all members from the role during deletion. This eliminates the chance of accidentally deleting roles that are being used in the inventory.

Now that you understand how to work with local users, groups, roles, and permissions on an individual ESXi host, be aware that you are unlikely to do much of this. Managing local user accounts is administratively more cumbersome because of the lack of centralized management and authentication. Active Directory integration addresses a great deal of this, allowing you to collapse your user and group management into one centralized directory. However, you will still find that you perform most, if not all, of your access control work within vCenter Server. As you'll see in the section "Managing vCenter Server Permissions," later in this chapter, vCenter Server offers greater flexibility than managing individual ESXi hosts.

The last area of ESXi host security we'll discuss pertains to the third A in the AAA model: accounting—in other words, logging. Let's take a close look at how to handle logs for your ESXi hosts.

Configuring ESXi Host Logging

Capturing information in the system logs is an important aspect of computer and network security. The system logs provide a record, or an accounting, of the actions performed, the events encountered, the errors experienced, and the state of the ESXi host and the VMs on that host.

Every ESXi host runs a syslog daemon (service) that captures events and logs them for future reference. Assuming that you've installed ESXi onto some local disks, the default location for the logs is a 4 GB scratch partition that the ESXi installer creates. Although this provides long-term storage for the ESXi host logs, there is no centralized location for them, making analysis of the logs more difficult than it should be. You would have to connect to each host individually to review the logs for that host.

Further, if you are booting from SAN or if you are using vSphere Auto Deploy, there is no local scratch partition, and logs are stored in memory on the ESXi host—which means they disappear when the ESXi host is restarted. Clearly, this is not an ideal configuration. Not only does it lack centralized access to the logs, but it also lacks long-term storage for the logs.

The typical solution to both of these issues is a vSphere integrated or third-party syslog server, a server that runs a syslog daemon and is prepared to accept the log entries from the various ESXi hosts. Though the Syslog Collector service in vCenter Server is not long available in vSphere 6.7, to make things easier, VMware introduced Log Insight for vCenter Server, which entitles you to 25 syslog clients (OSIs).

Securing the ESXi Boot Process

Secure Boot and Trusted Platform Module (TPM) 2.0 are two additional key security components that ensure the ESXi hosts in your environment are, in fact, *your* hosts. This is done by validating and securing each of the hosts' boot processes. Though it's an abstract way of thinking of the Triple As of Security, rather than using the lens of users interacting with the environment, Secure Boot and TPM 2.0 shift the lens to the ESXi host's perspective. Through stored digital certificates in the Unified Extensible Firmware Interface (UEFI), the host can secure its state.

Let's take a closer look at Secure Boot and TPM 2.0, and their harmonious relationship.

SECURE BOOT

Secure Boot is a protocol of the UEFI firmware and is designed to validate the digital signatures of the bootloaders against a known list of stored whitelisted and blacklisted certificates maintained in the firmware. This ensures that the generalized end-to-end bootloader process is not compromised by the likes of malware that has been injected into the system, such as a root kit, which would inherently change the bootloader's signature. We explained this in more detail back in Chapter 2, but basically, ESXi builds on UEFI and Secure Boot by ensuring that the Boot Loader, VMkernel, and the vSphere Installation Bundle (VIBs) are all signed by either the Microsoft UEFI Public Certificate Authority or a VMware Public key.

With Secure Boot and UEFI now in the mix with ESXi, the boot process now performs like this:

1. You power on the ESXi Host.

2. The ESXi Boot Loader is validated against the Microsoft public key in the UEFI store.

3. The ESXi Boot Loader then validates the VM Kernel against the VMware public key.

4. The VM Kernel runs a Secure Boot verification process (Secure Boot Verifier) on each VIB to validate them against the VMware public key.

5. After all of the preceding steps have been performed, the Management Services (hostd, vpxa, dcui, Yup! Etc.) are allowed to run.

As you can see, this process forms a root or chain of trusts beginning with the firmware installed within your host and extends out to the individual VIBs contained within the kernel. If a single link in the chain has been "bent" by a malicious process, the entire boot process fails. This new method of security has a few consequences: by nature of the root of trusts, the VMkernel verification process does not need to waste cycles (time) in unpacking each of the VIBs to validate the contents, thus speeding up the process. Unfortunately, for those home lab users or even administrators that rely on Community Supported VIBs, Secure Boot cannot be used, because these VIBs do not contain the appropriate digital signatures either from VMware or partners.

Perform these steps to verify your Profile Acceptance Level of your ESXi host:

1. Launch the vSphere Web Client if it is not already running, and connect to an instance of vCenter Server.

2. Navigate to the Hosts And Clusters view by selecting Home ➤ Hosts And Clusters. You can also use the Navigator pane or the Ctrl+Alt+2 keyboard shortcut.

3. Navigate down from your datacenter object to your cluster, and select one of your ESXi hosts.

4. Click the Configure tab in the content area, and under the Systems section, click Security Profile.

5. In the content area to the left, scroll down until you find Host Image Profile Acceptance Level, and then click Edit.

6. You can use the Acceptance Level drop-down menu in the Host Image Profile Acceptance Level dialog box to toggle between Community, Partner Supported, VMware Accepted, and VMware Certified. Partner Supported is the minimum acceptance level required for Secure Boot to function, which is also the default Acceptance Level.

7. Click OK.

Perform these steps to verify that your host supports Secure Boot:

1. Establish an SSH session to one of the ESXi 6.7 hosts.

2. Navigate to `/usr/lib/vmware/secureboot/bin/`.

3. Run the following command to create a store:

```
./secureBoot.py -c
```

If all is successful, you should see an output indicating that you can enable Secure Boot on the ESXi host, as shown in Figure 8.11. However, due to the variety of different implementations that vendors use for their UEFI, enabling Secure Boot is outside the scope of this book, though it should be covered in your vendor's documentation.

FIGURE 8.11

The Secure Boot verification script (secureBoot.py) can help identify any installed VIBs that are not properly signed.

TRUSTED PLATFORM MODULE 2.0

A Trusted Platform Module (TPM) is a specialized microcontroller (cryptoprocessor) designed to securely create and store assets. And while the full extent of what TPM can do is outside the scope of this book, the most important takeaway is that it functions as a means to retain platform identifying artifacts, such as encryption keys and platform measurements, in a trustworthy fashion. To give you a basic understanding of how TPM works, we will focus on TPM 2.0 and its use within ESXi. TPM 1.2 and TPM 2.0 cover many of the same use cases and features, but they have two entirely different implementations, with no backwards compatibility between them. Though you may have a TPM 1.2 microcontroller in your ESXi host, the new features of vSphere 6.7 will only take advantage of a TPM 2.0 microcontroller.

Again, ESXi leverages its local TPM 2.0 microcontroller to store measurements of a known good boot of ESXi, creating what is called an *attestation*. An attestation can be thought of as a declarative process where the evidence presented is trustworthy. Under the context of ESXi, this requires the use of Secure Boot. By building not only on top of Secure Boot's principle of Root of Trust but on the actual process of booting with Secure Boot enabled, TPM captures and securely stores the boot process measurements and creates a hash—an Attestation Key. This stored key can then, on subsequent (re)boots of the ESXi hosts, be requested by the vCenter Server in the form of an Attestation Report, which will compare its stored key from the host and perform an attestation assessment. Essentially, if the key presented from TPM on the host matches what is stored in vCenter, then vCenter Server can assert the host's authenticity. That is, by the nature of Secure Boot, the host is booted using only digitally signed VIBs. This indicates the host is untampered and secure from the last time it rebooted. If the key presented from the ESXi host does not match what vCenter Server has stored, then the assessment will fail, and vCenter Server will report this to the administrator.

Follow these steps to see a report of your ESXi hosts and their attestation status via the vSphere Client (HTML5):

1. Launch the vSphere Client (`https://<vcenter.domain.name>/ui`), if it is not already running, and connect to a vCenter Server instance.

2. Navigate to the Hosts And Clusters view by selecting Home ➤ Hosts And Clusters.

3. Navigate down from your datacenter object to your cluster, and then click Monitor in the content area on the right.

4. Click Security in the lower content area.

As shown in Figure 8.12, the Security area displays all of your ESXi hosts in the cluster, their status of attestation, the last time the host was verified, what version of TPM the host is using, and any messages that the host may have generated during the attestation assessment. As you can see, in our current lab, the ESXi hosts do not currently have any TPM microcontrollers installed, indicated by the N/A status across all columns. The Security area can also be observed at the Datacenter and vCenter Server levels within the vSphere Client, but we found that as you go further up the tree, the number of hosts that you are exposed to, and the lack of context, may be overwhelming.

FIGURE 8.12
Hosts can have two states of attestation after sending their report to vCenter Server: Green or Red. The former indicates the host is fully trusted, while the latter means that the host is not trusted.

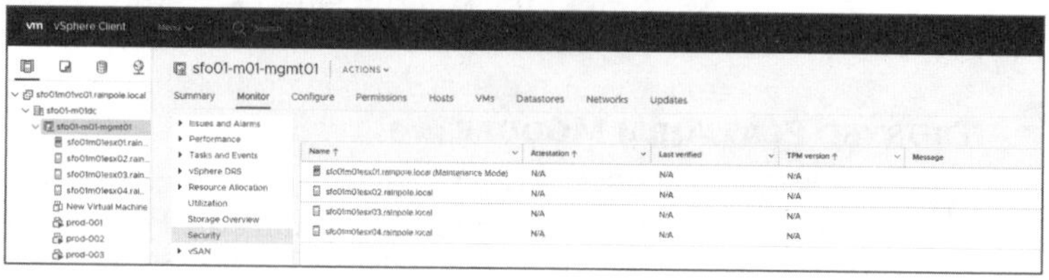

Reviewing Other ESXi Security Recommendations

In addition to all the security recommendations we've made so far with regard to ESXi hosts, other recommended practices you should follow include these:

◆ Set a root password for the ESXi host. You can set the root password, if it has not already been set, via the server's console by pressing F2. More information on working with the ESXi console is available in Chapter 2.

◆ Use host profiles in vCenter Server. Host profiles can help ensure that the configuration of the ESXi hosts does not drift or change from the settings specified in the host profile. We discussed host profiles in Chapter 3.

◆ Enable lockdown mode for your ESXi hosts. Enabling lockdown mode disables console-based user access and direct access via the vSphere Client. Root access via the vMA is also restricted.

Now that we've looked at the various ways to secure your ESXi hosts, it's time to move on to securing vCenter Server, the second major component in your vSphere environment.

Securing vCenter Server

For the most part, knowing how to secure vCenter Server involves knowing how to secure the underlying OS. For environments that have deployed the Windows Server–based version of vCenter Server, this means securing Windows Server. For environments using the Linux-based vCenter Server virtual appliance, it means securing Photon OS Linux. Because it's a virtual appliance, though, there isn't a lot you can do to secure the preinstalled Photon OS Linux instance.

For those environments running the Windows Server–based version of vCenter Server, securing Windows Server is a topic that has been discussed many, many times, so we won't go into great detail here. The following security recommendations are among the more common ones:

◆ Stay current on all Windows Server patches and updates. This helps protect you against potential security exploits.

◆ Harden the Windows Server installation using published best practices and guidelines from Microsoft.

In addition to these standard security recommendations, we can offer a few other security recommendations that are specific to vCenter Server and the Platform Services Controller:

◆ Be sure to stay current on vCenter Server patches and updates.

◆ Place the vCenter Server backend database on a separate system (physical or VM), if possible, and follow recommended practices to secure the separate system.

◆ If you are using Windows authentication with SQL Server, use a dedicated service account for vCenter Server—don't allow vCenter Server to share a Windows account with other services or applications.

- ◆ Be sure to secure the separate database server and backend database using published security practices from the appropriate vendor. This includes securing the database serve itself (Microsoft SQL Server or Oracle) as well as the underlying OS for that database server (Windows Server, Linux, or other).

- ◆ Replace the default self-signed SSL certificates with a valid SSL certificate from a trusted root authority for vCenter Server and all of its components.

SSL CERTIFICATE REPLACEMENT

With the separation of vCenter components for vSphere version 5.1 and later, the complexity for replacing the default SSL certificates has increased. VMware has addressed this complexity in vSphere 6 by adding the Certificate Manager.

In addition to these recommendations, there are other steps you should take to ensure that vCenter Server—and the infrastructure being managed by vCenter Server—is appropriately secured and protected.

The first thing that we will address is certificate replacement for your vSphere environment.

Managing vSphere Certificates

Certificate management has always been an onerous task for vSphere administrators. This is largely due to the fact that each component in the architecture needs a valid certificate, and that each certificate needed to be in a specific format. vSphere 6.x introduces some significant advances, through the introduction of the VMware Endpoint Certificate Store (VECS) and the VMware Certificate Authority (VMCA).

The following sections will show how VECS and VMCA work together to improve certificate management in vSphere 6.x. It should be noted that though most of this book has covered interacting with a vSphere environment via the Flash-based vSphere Web Client, we'll deviate slightly in the next couple of sections as certificate management now has its own UI within the HTML5-based vSphere Client.

Working with Certificate Stores

VECS is a client-side certificate and secret store that is deployed on each PSC and VC, and allows services to use any certificate authority (CA) that you choose.

There are three system-wide stores in VECS:

MACHINE_SSL_CERT This store contains both the SSL private key and the certificate. It can only be read and modified by the root account.

TRUSTED_ROOTS This store contains all trusted root certificates that VECS is aware of. It is readable by any account and modifiable by root only.

TRUSTED_ROOT_CRLS This store is where the all Trusted Root CRLs are stored. Like the TRUSTED_ROOTS store, it is readable by any account and modifiable by root only.

Interaction with VECS and its stores can be achieved through the use of a comprehensive API set as well as the HTML5-based vSphere Client. Dealing with the API is outside the scope of this book, however, let's look at some examples of how to use the command-line tool `vecs-cli` to perform some common tasks. If you are using the Linux variant of the PSC (or VCSA), you will need to enable the BASH shell using the `shell` command.

To launch the shell, you will need to type **shell** at the prompt.

CREATING A CERTIFICATE STORE

Perform these steps to create a certificate store using the CLI:

1. Establish an SSH session to the VCSA.

2. Navigate to `/usr/lib/vmware-vmafd/bin`.

3. Run the following command to create a store:

```
./vecs-cli store create --name <store_name>
```

DELETING A CERTIFICATE STORE

Perform these steps to delete a certificate store using the CLI:

1. Establish an SSH session to the VCSA.

2. Navigate to `/usr/lib/vmware-vmafd/bin`.

3. Run the following command to delete a store:

```
./vecs-cli store delete --name <store_name>
```

LISTING CERTIFICATE STORES

Perform these steps to list all of the certificate stores:

1. Establish an SSH session to the VCSA.

2. Navigate to `/usr/lib/vmware-vmafd/bin`.

3. Run the following command to list all stores:

```
./vecs-cli store list
```

MANAGING CERTIFICATE REVOCATION LISTS

VECS communicates with Certificate Revocation List (CRL) endpoints. If you upload a trusted Root Certificate that has a CRL Distribution Point, the CRL will be automatically downloaded and added to the TRUSTED_ROOT_CRLS store. However, it should be noted that revocation does not happen at the application level, but rather at the browser. That is to say, if you revoke the certificates from an authority, this won't bring the vCenter or PSC to a screeching halt, but it will prevent access through the vSphere Clients.

LISTING ENTRIES IN A CERTIFICATE STORE

1. Establish an SSH session to the VCSA.

2. Navigate to `/usr/lib/vmware-vmafd/bin.`

3. Run the following command to list entries in the MACHINE_SSL_CERT store:

   ```
   ./vecs-cli entry list --store MACHINE_SSL_CERT --text
   ```

For a comprehensive list of commands for working with certificate stores, please check the official VMware documentation.

Let's switch gears and look at some examples of how to interact with the different VECS stores within the vSphere Client and perform some common tasks.

ACCESSING THE CERTIFICATE STORES

Perform these steps to access the certificate stores using the vSphere Client:

1. Launch the vSphere Client (`https://<vcenter.domain.name>/ui`), if it is not already running, and connect to a vCenter Server instance.

2. Navigate to Administration ➤ Certificate ➤ Certificate Management.

3. In the Server IP/FQDN field, supply the name of either your Platform Services Controller or vCenter Server that you set up in Chapter 3, supply your administrator account and password, and then click Login and Manage Certificates.

As shown in Figure 8.13, the Certificate Management area is divided into the different stores previously covered, starting with the Machine SSL Certificate store, followed by the different Solution User Certificate Stores and the Trusted Root store.

FIGURE 8.13
The Certificate Management UI provides the ability to log into any nodes in your vSphere 6.7 environment, along with a number of operations for managing.

VIEWING A CERTIFICATE STORE

Perform these steps to view the certificate within a certificate store using the vSphere Client:

1. Launch the vSphere Client (`https://<vcenter.domain.name>/ui`), if it is not already running, and connect to a vCenter Server instance.

2. Navigate to Administration ➤ Certificate ➤ Certificate Management.

3. In the Server IP/FQDN field, supply the name of either your Platform Services Controller or vCenter Server that you set up in Chapter 3, supply your administrator account and password, and then click Login and Manage Certificates.

4. Under the Machine SSL Certificate area, specifically the __Machine_Cert tile, click View Details to bring up the certificates within the store. This same operation can be used for other stores.

Having a certificate store is great, but the complex part of certificate management with vSphere is the process of generating CSRs, fulfilling requests, changing certificate formats, and then committing them to the store. Let's take a look at how that has been simplified with the new Certificate Manager.

Getting Started with Certificate Management

Certificate management in vSphere 6.7 is accomplished by either a command-line tool called the Certificate Management Utility (CMU) or via the HTML5-based vSphere Client, which are both provided by VMware to make it easier for you to interact with VMCA and VECS when replacing certificates in your environment. Typically, certificates are replaced based on one of two approaches—regenerating self-signed certificates or using an external certificate authority (CA). Certificate Manager supports all of these approaches, either by generating certificates using VMCA as the root CA, importing a certificate from your own CA, or by importing a signed CA certificate to replace the VMCA root certificate. The last approach means that VMCA is acting as an intermediate CA, and any certificates generated would have a full chain back to the root CA. Conversely, the vSphere Client supports only regenerating certificates using the VMCA as a root CA or importing a certificate from your own CA.

Let's take a look at Certificate Manager, and run through the process for regenerating the certificates in your environment.

1. Connect to your PSC with SSH.

2. Run **shell** to switch to the BASH shell, and then launch the shell using the shell command.

3. Launch the Certificate Manager by running **/usr/lib/vmware-vmca/bin/ certificate-manager**.

4. You will see all of the available options for certificate management, as shown in Figure 8.14. Select option 4: "Regenerate a New VMCA Root Certificate and replace all certificates."

5. If this is your first time performing certificate operations, you will be prompted to enter values for `certool.cfg`; on all subsequent operations, you will be asked if you wish to update the details.

6. You'll be prompted to provide the account administrator@vsphere.local and its password to access the PSC, be it embedded or external.

7. Supply the information in the following list; press the Enter key after completing each field:

   ◆ Provide your two-letter country code.

   ◆ Provide a name. We suggested using the PSC's fully qualified domain name.

◆ Include a value for Organization.

◆ Type a value for Organization Unit.

◆ Provide your state code.

◆ Type in your locality.

FIGURE 8.14
Certificate Manager provides a number of operations for managing certificates in your vSphere 6.x environment.

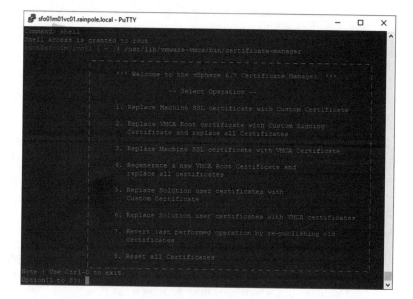

8. If you want to include the IP Address of your PSC, add it now and press Enter. Note that this is an optional field and does not need to be included.

9. Supply the information in the following list; press the Enter key after completing each field:

◆ A valid email address

◆ The FQDN of your PSC

10. You will be prompted with a warning that you are going to regenerate Root Certificate and all other certificates using VMCA, and asked if you wish to continue. Type **Y** and press Enter.

At this point, your interaction with Certificate Manager is complete, but what is happening in the background?

1. A new certificate store BACKUP_STORE is created in VECS by running `vecs-cli store create --name BACKUP_STORE`.

2. The new Root certificate is generated by the VMCA by running `certool --selfca`.

3. The machine SSL certificate will be regenerated and pushed to VECS store using `vecs-cli entry delete` and `vecs-cli-entry create`. Further, the certificate will be pushed into the Lookup Service of the PSC, ensuring that future solutions that query the vCenter or Platform Services Controller will retrieve the proper certificate.

4. All solution user certificates will be regenerated and pushed to VECS store using `vecs-cli entry delete` and `vecs-cli entry create`.

5. PSC is updated for all solution users using `dir-cli service update`.

6. All services are restarted.

After this process is complete, your certificates have all been successfully implemented and can be viewed in the vSphere Web Client by taking the following steps, or using the steps previously covered for the vSphere Client in Viewing a Certificate Store:

1. Go to the Administration menu.

2. Select System Configuration.

3. Select Nodes.

4. Select your PSC.

5. Click the Manage tab.

6. Select the Certificate Authority subtab.

7. Click the Verify Password link, enter your password, and click OK.

From here, you can view your certificates, the issuer, and their expiry dates. Now that you understand certificate management in vSphere 6.7, let's review vCenter Server authentication.

BACKING UP YOUR CERTIFICATES

A backup of your certificates is done whenever an operation is performed with the Certificate Manager. If an operation fails, make sure to use the Revert Last Operation option to get back to your known good configuration. Only one level of rollback can be performed, so be careful.

Authenticating Users with Single Sign-On

As with ESXi, users will need to authenticate to get access to vCenter Server in order to perform any tasks. The process for how this authentication works changed significantly starting with vSphere 5.1 with the introduction of vCenter Single Sign-On. How you handle that authentication depends on your environment. Both the Windows Server–based version of vCenter Server and the Linux-based vCenter Server virtual appliance offer the same authentication mechanisms. Generally you will probably authenticate against Active Directory, although you could manage users locally within Single Sign-On itself or even connect it to OpenLDAP. Because using Active Directory and using local SSO users are the most common methods of authentication, we'll focus on them for this discussion.

In the following sections, we'll cover these three topics:

◆ Configuring Single Sign-On for authentication against Active Directory

◆ Configuring Single Sign-On for authentication against local users

◆ Understanding how vCenter Server authenticates against ESXi with vpxuser

CONFIGURING SSO ON THE vCENTER SERVER APPLIANCE FOR ACTIVE DIRECTORY

In older versions of vSphere, when vCenter was installed on a Windows Server computer, leveraging Active Directory was pretty simple: join the computer to an Active Directory domain before installing vCenter, and vCenter would—by virtue of how Windows integrates with Active Directory—automatically be able to take advantage of users stored within Active Directory. If you chose not to join Active Directory, the Windows-based version of vCenter would need to be configured for use with an external directory service. With VMware's strong push to the vCenter Server Appliance, later versions of vSphere followed a similar mechanism to leverage Active Directory: join the appliance to an Active Directory domain after it's been deployed within the environment, and through the use of Likewise, you could then take advantage of all users and groups stored within Active Directory.

vSphere 5.1 introduced SSO for the first time, and VMware made some additional changes in vSphere 5.5. The key to SSO and Active Directory integration is the SSO administrator, or "master" account. This account can be used to configure all additional directory services post-installation.

When installing vCenter, you will be asked which user or group should be added as a vCenter administrator. By default, the built-in SSO administrator@vsphere.local user account will be used. These default settings in SSO do not by default extend permissions to users within Active Directory. This is a good thing; you don't want to add users who aren't necessarily involved in the administration of the vSphere environment. Generally speaking, you want to assign a permission to only those users who actually need it; this is part of the *principle of least privilege*, a key concept in computer security.

The issue is this: prior to vSphere 5.5, by default the domain Administrators group—this is the Active Directory Administrators group—was given the Administrator role in vCenter Server (we'll discuss vCenter Server roles in more detail in the section "Managing vCenter Server Permissions," later in this chapter). This permission assignment happened at the vCenter Server object and was propagated down to all child objects. Although using the role in this way makes some sense within small to medium environments, our experience shows that in many organizations some members of the Administrators group have nothing to do with the virtualization infrastructure. Granting those users privileges inside vCenter Server is a violation of security best practices; not having the domain group Administrators in SSO Server is, therefore, a good idea.

Perform the following steps to add the vCenter Server Appliance to Active Directory:

1. Log on to the vCenter Web Client as the SSO administrator. Unless you have created another account, the username is administrator@vsphere.local.

2. On the Home screen, select System Configuration.

3. In the Navigator pane, under System Configuration, select Nodes, and let the pane load your Platform Services Controller and vCenter Server.

4. Click the Platform Services Controller node, or if you are using an Embedded PSC on your vCenter Server, click the Manage tab.

5. Click Active Directory under the Manage content area, and then click the Join button in the top-right corner.

6. In the Join Active Directory dialog box, supply the name of the Active Directory domain and the username and password of an account that has permission to join the virtual appliance to the domain. Note that you should enter only the username and not `domain\ username` or `username@domain`.

7. Click Save Settings.

   An onscreen message tells you that any change to the Active Directory configuration will require a restart of the virtual appliance, so the next step is to reboot the virtual appliance.

8. Select the Actions tab.

9. Click the Reboot button. When prompted for a reason, enter a meaningful description and click OK.

   The virtual appliance will reboot.

Next, perform the following steps to add Active Directory to be used as a source for vCenter Server users:

1. Log on to the vCenter Web Client as the SSO administrator. Unless you have created another account, the username is `administrator@vsphere.local`.

2. Click Administration in the Navigator pane.

3. Under the Single Sign-On section, click Configuration.

4. Select the second tab, labeled Identity Sources.

5. Click the green plus icon to add a new identity source.

6. In the Add Identity Source dialog box, you have four options:

   ◆ Active Directory (Integrated Windows Authentication)

   ◆ Active Directory As An LDAP Server

   ◆ Open LDAP

   ◆ Local OS

The first two options relate to Active Directory, but their connection method is slightly different. Using Windows authentication requires a user or computer account with the relevant rights to traverse the entire directory, and Kerberos is used to authenticate.

The second Active Directory option uses LDAP to connect instead of Kerberos.

The third option, Open LDAP, is quite simply a way to integrate with OpenLDAP. This could be a connection to a Windows- or Linux-based OpenLDAP system.

The final option is Local OS. This relates to the operating system on which SSO is installed—in our case, a Photon OS system. This integrates SSO with the local users that are configured within the operating system itself.

In this example, we'll connect to Active Directory using Windows authentication and a machine account. This is the simplest way to get SSO to integrate with Active Directory it prepopulates the Active Directory domain name that the SSO server belongs to and car therefore use the machine account for authentication.

7. With these options selected, click Finish to close the dialog box.

vCenter Server, and more specifically Single Sign-On, is linked with Active Directory. You ca now add users from your domain to specific roles within your vSphere environment. We will explain this in detail later in the chapter.

If you are connected directly to a host at this time, you can monitor the progress of the reboo using the VM console within the vSphere Client. Once the virtual appliance has rebooted successfully, you can test the Active Directory integration by logging into the virtual appliance' web interface using Active Directory credentials. You can use either the domain\username or th username@domain syntax to log in.

If the login is successful, you're ready to proceed to the next step. If not, you'll need to troubleshoot the Active Directory integration. The vCenter Server virtual appliance supports SS logins, so you can log in via SSH and review the logs to see what errors were logged during the configuration.

If you're having problems with Active Directory integration, refer to the following list:

◆ Verify that the time on the virtual appliance is synchronized with the time on the Active Directory domain controllers.

◆ Ensure that the virtual appliance is able, via DNS, to resolve the domain name and locate the Active Directory domain controllers. This typically means using the same DNS serve that Active Directory uses.

◆ Verify that there is no firewall between the virtual appliance and the Active Directory domain controllers or that all necessary traffic is permitted through any firewalls that are present.

Once you've verified that the Active Directory integration is working, you're ready to procee with the second step in configuring the vCenter Server virtual appliance for Active Directory.

ADDING PERMISSIONS FOR ACTIVE DIRECTORY USERS OR GROUPS

Although you've successfully configured the Active Directory integration for the vCenter Server virtual appliance, you still can't use any Active Directory credentials to log in using the vSphere Client. To log in via the vSphere Web Client, you must first grant access to one or more Active Directory users or groups within the vCenter Server hierarchy.

Perform these steps to grant permissions to an Active Directory user or group in order to log into the vCenter Server virtual appliance via the vSphere Web Client:

1. If the vSphere Web Client isn't already running, launch it and connect to a vCenter Server instance.

2. Log in using the administrator@vsphere.local account and the password you config- ured, and click Login.

3. Select the Hosts and Clusters Inventory object from the Home page, and select your vCenter Server.

4. Click the Permissions tab on the horizontal menu and then click the Add Permission button (the green plus symbol).

5. Click the Add button; then from the Domain drop-down box, select the Active Directory domain.

6. Find the user or group to add, click the Add button, and then click OK.

We do not recommend using a specific user account here; instead, leverage a security group within Active Directory. Recall that ESXi integration into Active Directory requires a security group called ESX Admins; you might want to leverage that group here as well.

7. In the Assign Role drop-down box, select Administrator, and ensure that the Propagate To Child Objects check box is selected.

This ensures that the selected Active Directory users and/or groups have the Administrator role within the vCenter Server virtual appliance. By default, only the predefined administrator@vsphere.local account has this role.

8. Click OK to return to the vSphere Web Client.

After completing this process, you'll be able to log into the vSphere Web Client using an Active Directory username and password. You're all set—the vCenter Server virtual appliance is configured to use Active Directory.

Before we move on to the topic of managing permissions within vCenter Server, one quick item we'd like to discuss pertains to how vCenter Server interacts with ESXi hosts. It's important to understand how vCenter Server uses a special user account as a proxy account for managing your ESXi hosts.

Understanding the vpxuser Account

At the beginning of this chapter, we showed you how the ESXi security model employs users, groups, roles, privileges, and permissions. We also showed you how to manage local users and to integrate your ESXi hosts with Active Directory.

As you'll see in the section "Managing vCenter Server Permissions," later in this chapter, vCenter Server uses the same user/group-role-privilege-permission security model. When vCenter Server is present, all activities are funneled through vCenter Server using SSO accounts that have been assigned a role that has, in turn, been assigned to one or more inventory objects as a permission. This combination of SSO account, role, and inventory object creates a permission that allows (or disallows) the user to perform certain functions. The user accounts exist in Active Directory or OpenLDAP or on the SSO Server computer itself, not on the ESXi hosts, and the permissions and roles are defined within vCenter Server, not on the ESXi hosts. Because the user doesn't log into the ESXi host directly, this minimizes the need for many local user accounts on the ESXi host and thus provides better security. Alas, there still is a need, however small or infrequent, for local accounts on an ESXi host used primarily for administration, which is why we talked earlier about managing local users and integrating ESXi authentication into Active Directory.

Because the user accounts exist outside the ESXi hosts, and because the roles, privileges, and permissions are defined outside the ESXi hosts, when you use vCenter Server to manage your virtual infrastructure, you are only creating a task and not directly interacting with the ESXi hosts or the VMs. This is true for any user using vCenter Server to manage hosts or VMs. For instance, let's say Shane, an administrator, wants to log into vCenter Server and create a new VM. Shane first needs the proper role—perhaps a custom role you created specifically for the purpose of creating new VMs—assigned to the proper inventory object or objects within vCenter Server.

Assuming the correct role has been assigned to the correct inventory objects—let's say it's a resource pool—Shane has what he needs to create, modify, and monitor VMs. But Shane's user account does not have direct access to the ESXi hosts when he's logged into vCenter Server. In fact, a proxy account is used to communicate Shane's tasks to the appropriate ESXi host or VM. This account, vpxuser, is the only account that vCenter Server stores and tracks in its back-end database.

VPXUSER SECURITY

The vpxuser account and password are stored in the vCenter Server database and on the ESXi hosts; this account is used to communicate from a vCenter Server computer to an ESXi host. The vpxuser password consists of 32 (randomly selected) characters, which is rotated every 30 days, is encrypted using SHA1 on an ESXi host, and is obfuscated on vCenter Server. Each vpxuser password is unique to the ESXi host being managed by vCenter Server.

No direct administrator intervention is warranted or advised for this account because that would break vCenter Server functions needing this account. The account and password are never used by humans, and they do not have shell access on any ESXi hosts. Thus, it isn't necessary to manage this account or include it with normal administrative and regular user account security policies.

Any time vCenter Server polls an ESXi host or an administrator creates a task that needs to be communicated to an ESXi host, the vpxuser account is used. On the ESXi hosts that are managed by vCenter Server, the vpxuser account exists (it's created automatically by vCenter Server; this is why vCenter Server asks you for the root password when adding a host to the inventory) and is assigned the Administrator role. This gives the vpxuser account the ability to perform whatever tasks are necessary on the individual ESXi hosts managed by vCenter Server. When a user logs into vCenter Server, vCenter Server applies its security model (roles, privileges, and permissions) to that user, ensuring that the user is permitted to perform only the tasks for which they are authorized. On the backend, though, all these tasks are proxied onto the individual ESXi hosts as vpxuser.

You should now have a good idea of what's involved in vCenter Server authentication. We'd like to focus now on vCenter Server permissions, which control what users are allowed to do after they've authenticated to vCenter Server.

Managing vCenter Server Permissions

The security model for vCenter Server is identical to that explained in the previous section for an ESXi host: take a user or group and assign them to a role (which has one or more privileges assigned) for a specific inventory object. The key difference is that vCenter Server enables new objects in the inventory hierarchy that aren't possible with individual ESXi hosts. This would include objects like clusters and folders (both discussed in Chapter 3). vCenter Server also supports resource pools (introduced earlier in the section "Using Resource Pools to Assign

Permissions" and which we'll discuss in greater detail in Chapter 11). vCenter Server also allows you to assign permissions in different ways; for example, an ESXi host has only one inventory view, whereas vCenter Server has the Hosts And Clusters view, VMs And Templates view, Storage view, and Networking view. Permissions—the assignment of a role to one or more inventory objects—can occur in any of these views.

As you can see, this means that vCenter Server allows you to create much more complex permissions hierarchies than you could create using only ESXi hosts.

Recall that a key part of the security model is the role—the grouping of privileges that you assign to a user or group in a permission. Let's take a close look at the predefined roles that come with vCenter Server.

REVIEWING VCENTER SERVER'S ROLES

Whereas the ESXi host is quite limited in its default roles, vCenter Server provides many more, thereby offering a much greater degree of flexibility in constructing access control. Although both security models offer the flexibility of creating custom roles, ESXi includes only three default roles, and although vCenter Server 5.5 provided nine roles (including the same three offered in ESXi), vCenter 6.7 now provides a total of fourteen roles. Figure 8.15 details all of the default vCenter Server roles. These roles are visible from within the vSphere Web Client by selecting Home ➤ Roles.

FIGURE 8.15
The vCenter Server default roles offer much more flexibility than an individual ESXi host offers.

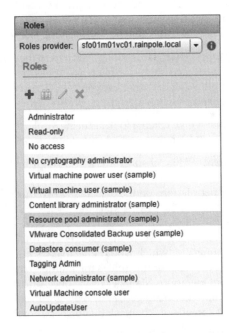

As you can see, VMware provides a large number of default roles in a vCenter Server installation, though the roles themselves can be selectively added or removed during the vCenter installation process. Remember, just as with the default ESXi roles, vCenter Server will prevent you from modifying the No Access, Read-Only, and Administrator roles—you must clone them in order to customize them. Once you clone one of the built-in roles, you can customize the privileges assigned to that role to meet your specific needs.

The key to using these roles effectively is to understand the functions of each. First, let's get acquainted with the new roles added in vSphere 6.x:

No Cryptography Administrator With the introduction of VM Encryption in vSphere 6.5, new level of administration was added that, if in the hands of a compromised administrator could bring a datacenter down. With the No Crypto Administrator role, you can now assign users this role to allow them to access all capabilities of an administrator with the exception manipulating cryptographic operations such as encrypting VMs, decrypting VMs, or changing vCenter's Key Management Server. This is practical for lower-level or newer administrators that may be well-versed in vSphere, but you may want to limit their ability to interact with encryption policies.

Tagging Admin In vSphere 5.5, the only role with the ability to create, manipulate, or interact with tags was the Administrator. With vSphere 6.0 and later, you can now assign users this role to allow them to create, edit, and delete tags—not to mention assign or unassign tags for objects. This is practical for solutions that may want to tag a VM such as an antivirus solution or provisioning engine.

Content Library Administrator This role has all of the required permissions to administer the Content Library and the associated contents throughout their respective life cycles. This includes creating a Content Library, adding files and synchronizing across multiple Content Libraries, removing content, and deleting Content Libraries when they are no longer required

AutoUpdateUser This role is mapped to the AutoUpdate@vsphere.local user, which is automatically created in vSphere 6.7. It has an extremely limited amount of permissions, simply allowing the service account to log events, and is primarily used for lifecycle management purposes when integrating with VMware Cloud on AWS.

Now that we've taken a look at the new roles included with vSphere 6.x, here's a refresher on the roles retained in the product from vSphere 5.5:

No Access This role prevents a user or group from gaining access. The idea behind the role is to prevent a user or group with permissions at some point higher in the hierarchy from having permissions on the object to which this role is assigned. For instance, you may have granted Eileen the Virtual Machine User role at the datacenter level, which would allow her administer all the VMs in the datacenter, but a security concern exists if she has access to one of the accounting VMs in that datacenter. You could assign Eileen to the No Access role on the Accounting VM, which would effectively supersede her Virtual Machine User privileges.

The other use for this role is for solutions that pull inventory data from vSphere (such as vCenter Operations Manager or vCloud Automation Center). You may not want all objects to be monitored or managed, and so by specifically denying access to the associated service account you effectively mask that object from the solution in question.

Read-Only Read-Only allows users to see the vCenter Server inventory. It does not allow them to interact with any of the VMs in any way through the vSphere Client or the web client except to see the power status of each VM in the inventory where they have the Read-Only role applied.

Administrator A user assigned to an object with the Administrator role will have full administrative capabilities over that object in vCenter Server. Note that this does *not* grant *any* privileges within the guest OSs installed inside the VMs, aside from the ability to install or upgrade VMware Tools and initiate a graceful guest OS shutdown. For instance, a user assigned the Administrator role for a VM may be able to change the RAM assigned to the VM and alter its performance parameters (Shares, Reservations, and Limits) but may not even have the permissions to log into that VM unless they have been granted that right from within the guest OS.

The Administrator role can be granted at any object level in the hierarchy, and the user or group that is assigned the role at that level will have vCenter Server administrative privileges over that object and (if the inheritance box is selected) any child objects in the hierarchy. The remaining roles are sample roles, and they are intended to provide vSphere administrators with an idea of how to organize roles and permissions to model the appropriate administrative structure:

Virtual Machine Power User (Sample) The Virtual Machine Power User sample role assigns permissions to allow a user to perform most functions on VMs. This includes tasks such as configuring CD and floppy media, changing the power state, taking and deleting snapshots, and modifying the configuration. These permissions apply only to VMs. The idea here is, for example, if users are granted this role at a datacenter level, they would be able to manage only VMs in that datacenter and would not be able to change settings on objects such as resource pools in that datacenter.

Virtual Machine User (Sample) The Virtual Machine User sample role grants the user the ability to interact with a VM but not the ability to change its configuration. Users can operate the VM's power controls and change the media in the virtual CD-ROM drive or floppy drive as long as they also have access to the media they want to change. For instance, a user who is assigned this role for a VM will be able to change the CD media from an ISO image on a shared storage volume to their own client system's physical CD-ROM drive. If you want them to be able to change from one ISO file to another (both stored on a Virtual Machine File System [VMFS] volume or Network File System [NFS] volume), they will also need to be granted the Browse Datastore permission at the parent of the datastore object in the vCenter Server hierarchy—usually the datacenter in which the ESX/ESXi host is located.

Resource Pool Administrator (Sample) The Resource Pool Administrator sample role grants the user the ability to manage and configure resources with a resource pool, including VMs, child pools, scheduled tasks, and alarms.

VMware Consolidated Backup User (Sample) As the role name suggests, the VMware Consolidated Backup User sample role grants the user the privileges required for performing a backup of a VM using VCB.

Datastore Consumer (Sample) The Datastore Consumer sample role is targeted at users who need only a single permission: the permission to allocate space from a datastore. Clearly, this role is very limited.

Network Administrator (Sample) Similar to the Datastore Consumer role, the Network Administrator sample role has only a single permission, and that is the permission to assign networks.

These default roles provide a good starting point, but they won't meet every company's needs. If you need something more than what is provided by default, you'll need to create a custom role. We describe this process in the next section.

WORKING WITH vCENTER SERVER ROLES

What if the default roles supplied with vCenter Server don't provide you with the necessary functionality for a particular grouping of users? Well, it depends on what the problem is. Let's take the most basic problem. You've chosen a best-fit role to assign a user privileges, but the role you've selected lacks a key permission, or it grants a few permissions that you don't want included. To get the exact fit you need, you can clone the role and then customize it.

Perform the following steps to clone a role in vCenter Server:

1. Launch the vSphere Web Client if it is not already running, and connect to a vCenter Server instance.

2. Navigate to the Roles area from the Home screen.

3. Right-click the role that you want to clone, and select Clone from the context menu or select the role and click the clone icon above the list.

After you've cloned the role, you can add or remove privileges as needed. We described the process of editing a role earlier in the section "Editing and Removing Roles."

LEAVE THE BUILT-IN SAMPLE ROLES INTACT

We recommend leaving all of the built-in sample roles intact and unmodified. vCenter Server prevents you from modifying the No Access, Read-Only, and Administrator roles but does not prevent you from modifying the rest of the roles. To help avoid confusion among multiple administrators, we recommend leaving the built-in sample roles intact and cloning them to a new custom role instead.

To assign a permission to an object within vCenter, you use the same principles as with ESXi hosts. Assign a user to a role and then the role to an object within the vCenter Web Client. Before we delve into what privileges will be assigned to a role, let's run through an example of how to assign a permission to an object within the vSphere Web Client:

1. Log on to the vCenter Web Client as a vCenter administrator. Unless you have created another account, the account is `administrator@vsphere.local.`

2. Navigate to the object for which you want to change the permissions. In this example, locate the vCenter Server object.

3. Click the Permissions tab, then click the green plus arrow to bring up the Add Permission dialog box.

4. In the left column, click the Add button.

5. The Select Users/Groups dialog box allows you to select from a Domain drop-down list. This list is populated with your identity sources previously configured within SSO. Select your Active Directory identity source.

6. Find the Active Directory user from the list. Click the Add button and then click OK.

7. With the user now specified in the list, it's time to assign a role. Select Administrator from the Assigned Role drop-down list and then click OK.

    The Active Directory user can now log in using the vSphere Web Client and manage vCenter.

By default, just as with the Host Client, the Propagate To Children check box is selected. All objects that are children of the currently selected object will also receive the permission you are granting. By assigning permissions at a vCenter object and leaving Propagate To Children selected, you are giving this user permissions over every object this vCenter Server instance manages. This includes ESXi hosts, VMs, networks, and datastores, to name a few. Keep this in mind when assigning permissions and only ever give the minimum required access.

UNDERSTANDING vCENTER SERVER PRIVILEGES

Roles are very useful, but now that you've started to peek into the properties of the roles and how to edit them, you also need to understand each of the privileges and what they do for you in terms of customizing roles. Remember that privileges are individual tasks assigned to roles. Without privileges assigned, roles are useless, so it's important to understand the privileges available within vCenter Server.

The list of privileges is rather long, but it's broken down into some general categories, so let's look at what each of the categories means in general terms:

Alarms Controls the ability to create, modify, delete, disable, and acknowledge vCenter Server alarms.

Auto Deploy Controls the ability to use vSphere Auto Deploy for dynamically provisioning ESXi hosts at boot time.

Certificates Controls the ability to manage certificates for vSphere and its services.

Content Library Controls the ability to create, delete, and modify the Content Library and its contents.

Cryptographic Operations Controls the ability to create, delete, and modify cryptographic elements.

Datacenter Controls the ability to create, delete, move, and rename datacenters inside vCenter Server. The privilege for working with an IP pool is also found in the Datacenter category.

Datastore Controls who can access files stored on an ESXi attached volume. These privileges need to be assigned at the parent object of the ESXi host itself—for instance, a datacenter, an ESXi cluster, or a folder that contains ESXi hosts.

Datastore Cluster Controls who is permitted to configure a datastore cluster (used with profile-based storage and Storage DRS).

Distributed Switch Controls who can create, delete, or modify distributed virtual switche

ESX Agent Manager Controls the ability to view, configure, or modify ESX host agents.

Extension Controls the ability to register, update, or unregister extensions in vCenter Serv An example of an extension is vSphere Update Manager (VUM).

External Stats Provider Controls the ability to register, update, or unregister solutions tha integrate with vCenter Server for Proactive Distributed Resource Scheduler (DRS).

Folder Controls the creation, deletion, and general manipulation of folders in the vCenter Server hierarchy.

Global Includes the ability to manage vCenter Server license settings and server settings such as SNMP and SMTP.

Health Update Provider Controls the ability to register, update, or unregister solutions tha integrate with vCenter Server for Proactive HA.

Host Controls what users can do with ESXi hosts in the inventory. This includes tasks such as adding and removing ESXi hosts from the inventory, changing the host's memory configu ration, and changing the firewall settings.

Host Profile Controls creating, editing, deleting, and viewing host profiles.

Image Builder Controls who can access, create, edit, and delete depots and images within Auto Deploy.

Network Controls the configuration or removal of networks from the vCenter Server inventory.

Performance Controls the ability of users to modify the intervals at which the performance chart information is displayed on the Performance tab of an object.

Permissions Controls who has the ability to modify the permissions assigned to a role and who can manipulate a role/user combination for a particular object.

Profile-Driven Storage Controls who can view and update profile-driven storage.

Resource Controls resource pool manipulation, including creating, deleting, or renaming t pool; also controls migration by using vMotion and applying DRS recommendations.

Scheduled Task Controls the configuration of tasks and the ability to run a task that is scheduled inside vCenter Server.

Sessions Controls the ability to view and disconnect vSphere Client sessions connected to vCenter Server and to send a global message to connected vSphere Client users.

Storage Views Controls changing the server configuration and looking at storage views.

Tasks Controls the ability to create or update tasks.

Transfer Service Controls the ability to monitor and manage the transfer service componer of Content Library.

VMware VSAN Controls the ability to monitor and manage VSAN.

VMware vSphere Update Manager Controls who can access, configure, create, edit, and perform remediations with vSphere Update Manager.

Virtual Machine Controls the manipulation of VMs in the vCenter Server inventory, including the ability to create, delete, or connect to the remote console of a VM. Controls the power state of a VM, the ability to change floppy and CD media, and the ability to manipulate templates, among other privileges.

Distributed Virtual Port (dvPort) Group Controls who can create, delete, and modify distributed virtual port groups on distributed virtual switches.

vApp Controls the configuration and management of vApps, such as the ability to add VMs to a vApp; clone, create, delete, export, or import a vApp; power on or power off the vApp; and view the Open Virtualization Format (OVF) environment.

vService Controls the ability to create, remove, and modify vService dependencies with vApps.

vSphere Tagging Controls who can create, edit, assign, and delete tags and categories.

What really matters is how these various privileges are assigned to roles. As you saw earlier, vCenter Server ships with some default roles already defined. Some of these—the No Access, Read-Only, and Administrator roles—are fairly well understood and cannot be modified. The other predefined roles are listed in Table 8.1 along with the privileges that are assigned to each role by default.

TABLE 8.1: Privileges for sample roles

PREDEFINED ROLE	ASSIGNED PRIVILEGES
Content Library Administrator	Content Library ➤ Add Library Item, Create Local Library, Create Subscribed Library, Delete Library Item, Delete Subscribed Library, Download Files, Evict Library Item, Evict Subscribed Library, Probe Subscription Information, Read Storage, Sync Library Item, Sync Subscribed Library, Type Introspection, Update Configuration Settings, Update Files, Update Library, Update Library Item, Update Local Library, Update Subscribed Library, View Configuration Settings
Tagging Admin	vSphere Tagging ➤ Assign Or Unassign vSphere Tag, Create vSphere Tag, Create vSphere Tag Category, Delete vSphere Tag, Delete vSphere Tag Category, Edit vSphere Tag, Edit vSphere Tag Category, Modify UsedBy Field For Category, Modify UsedBy Field For Tag
No Cryptographic Administrator	Alarm, AutoDeploy, Certificates, Content Library, Datacenter, Datastore, Datastore Cluster, Distributed Switch, ESX Agent Manager, Extension, External Stats Provider, Folder, Global (with the exception of Diagnostics), Health Update Provider, Host (with the exceptions Add Host to Cluster, Add Standalone Host, and Manage User Groups), Host Profile, ImageBuilder, Network, Performance, Profile-driven Storage, Resource, Schedule Task, Sessions, Storage Views, Tasks, Transfer Service, VMware vSAN, VMware vSphere Update Manager, Virtual Machine, dvPort Group, vApp, vService, vSphere Tagging

(con'

TABLE 8.1 Privileges for sample roles *(CONTINUED)*

PREDEFINED ROLE	ASSIGNED PRIVILEGES
Virtual Machine Power User	Datastore ➤ Browse Datastore Global ➤ Cancel Task Scheduled Task ➤ Create Tasks, Modify Task, Remove Task, Run Task Virtual Machine Configuration ➤ Add Existing Disk, Add New Disk, Add Or Remove Device, Advanced, Change CPU Count, Change Resource, Disk Lease, Memory, Modify Device Settings, Remove Disk, Rename, Reset Guest Information Settings, Upgrade Virtual Hardware Virtual Machine ➤ Interaction ➤ Acquire Guest Control Ticket, Answer Question, Configure CD Media, Configure Floppy Media, Console Interaction, Device Connection, Power Off, Power On, Reset, Suspend, VMware Tools Install Virtual Machine ➤ State ➤ Create Snapshot, Remove Snapshot, Rename Snapshot Revert To Snapshot
Virtual Machine User	Global ➤ Cancel Task Scheduled Task ➤ Create Tasks, Modify Task, Remove Task, Run Task Virtual Machine ➤ Interaction ➤ Answer Question, Configure CD Media, Configure Floppy Media, Console Interaction, Device Connection, Power Off, Power On, Reset, Suspend, VMware Tools Install
Resource Pool Administrator	Alarms ➤ Create Alarm, Modify Alarm, Remove Alarm Datastore ➤ Browse Datastore Folder ➤ Create Folder, Delete Folder, Move Folder, Rename Folder Global ➤ Cancel Task, Log Event, Set Custom Attribute Permissions ➤ Modify Permissions Resource ➤ Assign Virtual Machine To Resource Pool, Create Resource Pool, Migrate, Modify Resource Pool, Move Resource Pool, Query vMotion, Relocate, Remove Resource Pool, Rename Resource Pool Scheduled Task Virtual Machine ➤ Configuration Add Existing Disk, Add New Disk, Add Or Remove Device, Advanced, Change CPU Count, Change Resource, Disk Lease, Memory, Modify Device Settings, Raw Device, Remove Disk, Rename, Reset Guest Information, Settings, Upgrade Virtual Hardware Virtual Machine ➤ Interaction ➤ Answer Question, Configure CD Media, Configure Floppy Media, Console Interaction, Device Connection, Power Off, Power On, Reset, Suspend, VMware Tools Install Virtual Machine ➤ Inventory Create From Existing, Create New, Move, Register, Remove, Unregister Virtual Machine ➤ Provisioning ➤ Allow Disk Access, Allow Read-Only Disk Access Allow Virtual Machine Download, Allow Virtual Machine Files Upload, Clone Template, Clone Virtual Machine, Create Template From Virtual Machine, Customize, Deploy Template, Mark As Template, Mark As Virtual Machine, Modify Customization Specification, Read Customization Specifications Virtual Machine ➤ State ➤ Create Snapshot, Remove Snapshot, Rename Snapshot, Revert To Snapshot

PREDEFINED ROLE	ASSIGNED PRIVILEGES
VMware Consolidated Backup User	Virtual Machine ➤ Configuration Disk Lease Virtual Machine ➤ Provisioning ➤ Allow Read-Only Disk Access, Allow Virtual Machine Download Virtual Machine ➤ State Create Snapshot, Remove Snapshot
Datastore Consumer	Datastore ➤ Allocate Space
Network Administrator	Network ➤ Assign Network

As you can see, vCenter Server is very specific about the privileges you can assign to roles. The fact that these privileges are specific can sometimes complicate the process of granting users the ability to perform seemingly simple tasks within vCenter Server. Let's review a couple of examples of how privileges, roles, and permissions combine in vCenter Server.

DELEGATING THE ABILITY TO CREATE VMS AND INSTALL A GUEST OS

One common access control delegation in a virtual infrastructure is to give a group of users (for example, a provisioning or deployment team) the rights to create VMs. After just browsing through the list of available privileges, it might seem simple to accomplish this. It is, however, more complex than meets the eye. Providing a user with the ability to create a VM involves assigning a combination of privileges at multiple levels throughout the vCenter Server inventory.

COMBINING PRIVILEGES, ROLES, AND PERMISSIONS IN vCENTER SERVER

So far, we've shown you all the pieces you need to know in order to structure vCenter Server to support your company's management and operational requirements. How these pieces fit together, though, can sometimes be more complex than you might expect. In the next few paragraphs, we'll walk you through an example.

Here's the scenario: within your IT department, one group handles building all Windows servers. Once the servers are built, operational control of the servers is handed off to a separate group. Now that you have virtualized your datacenter, this same separation of duties needs to be re-created within vCenter Server. Sounds simple, right? You just need to configure vCenter Server so that this group has the ability to create VMs. This group is represented within Active Directory with a group object (this Active Directory group is named IT-Provisioning), and you'd like to leverage the Active Directory group membership to control who is granted these permissions within vCenter Server.

In the following steps, we've deliberately kept some of the items at a high level. For example, we don't go into how to create a role or how to assign that role to an inventory object as a permission, because those tasks are covered elsewhere in this chapter.

Perform the following steps to allow a Windows-based group to create VMs:

1. Use the vSphere Web Client to connect to a vCenter Server instance. Log in with a user account that has been assigned the Administrator role within vCenter Server.

2. On the Home screen, click the Roles icon.

3. Create a new role called **VMCreator**.

4. Assign the following privileges to the **VMCreator** role:

   - Datastore ➤ Allocate Space
   - Virtual Machine ➤ Inventory ➤ Create New
   - Virtual Machine ➤ Configuration ➤ Add New Disk
   - Virtual Machine ➤ Configuration ➤ Add Existing Disk
   - Virtual Machine ➤ Configuration ➤ Raw Device
   - Resource ➤ Assign Virtual Machine To Resource Pool

   These permissions allow the VMCreator role to only create new VMs, not clone existing VMs or deploy from templates. Those actions would require additional privileges. For example, to allow this role to create new VMs from existing VMs, you would add the following privileges to the VMCreator role:

   - Virtual Machine ➤ Inventory ➤ Create From Existing
   - Virtual Machine ➤ Provisioning ➤ Clone Virtual Machine
   - Virtual Machine ➤ Provisioning ➤ Customize

5. Add a permission on a folder, datacenter, cluster, or host for the Windows-based group (IT-Provisioning in our example) with the VMCreator role.

   If you don't assign the role to a datacenter object, then you'll need to assign it separately to a folder in the VMs And Templates view. Otherwise, you'll run into an error when trying to create the VM.

   Similarly, if you don't assign the role to the datacenter object, the group won't have permission on any datastore objects. Datastore objects are children of the datacenter object, so permissions applied to a datacenter object will, by default, propagate to the datastores. Without permissions on at least one datastore object (either via propagation or via direct assignment), you'll end up unable to create a new VM because you can't choose a datastore in which to store the VM.

6. If you want or need the Windows-based group to see other objects within the vCenter Server hierarchy, assign the group the Read-Only role on the applicable objects.

   For example, if the group should see all objects within the datacenter, add the Read-Only role on the datacenter object.

At this point, the privileges for creating a VM are complete; however, the IT-Provisioning group does not have the rights to mount a CD/DVD image and therefore cannot install a guest OS. Consequently, more permissions are required to allow the IT-Provisioning group to not only create the VMs and put them in the right place within vCenter Server but also to install the guest OS within those VMs.

Perform the following steps to allow the Windows-based IT-Provisioning group to install a guest OS from a CD/DVD image file:

1. Use the vSphere Web Client to connect to a vCenter Server instance. Log in with a user account that has been assigned the Administrator role within vCenter Server.

2. On the Home screen, click the Roles icon.

3. Create a new role named **GOS-Installers**.

4. Assign the following privileges to the GOS-Installers role:

   ◆ Datastore ➤ Browse Datastore

   ◆ Virtual Machine ➤ Configuration

   ◆ Virtual Machine ➤ Interaction

5. Assign the desired Windows-based group (IT-Provisioning in our example) the GOS-Installers role on the datacenter, folder, cluster, or host, as applicable.

   Keep in mind that you can't have the same user or group with two different roles on the same object.

As you can see, the seemingly simple task of creating a VM involves a couple of different roles and a number of permissions. This is only a single example; there are obviously an almost infinite number of other configurations where you can create roles and assign permissions to the various objects within ESXi and vCenter Server.

 Real World Scenario

vCenter Server Permissions Interaction

In organizations both large and small, users often belong to multiple groups, and those groups are assigned different levels of permissions on different objects. Let's look at the effects of multiple group memberships and permission assignments in the virtual infrastructure.

In one scenario, let's look at the effective permissions when a user belongs to multiple groups with different permissions on objects at different levels in the inventory. In this example, a user named Rick Avsom is a member of the Res_Pool_Admins and VM_Auditors Windows groups. The Res_Pool_Admins group is assigned membership in the Resource Pool Admins vCenter Server role, and the permission is set at the Production resource pool. The VM_Auditors group is assigned membership in the Read-Only vCenter Server role, and the permission is set at the Win2016-02 VM. The Win2016-02 VM resides within the Production resource pool.

When the user is logged on to the vCenter Server computer as Rick Avsom, the inventory reflects only the objects available to him through his permissions. Based on the permission assignment described, Rick Avsom will be able to manage the Production resource pool and will have full privileges over the Win2016-01 VM to which the Resource Pool Admin privileges are propagating. However, Rick Avsom cannot manage the Win2016-02 VM, for which he is limited to Read-Only privileges. Thus, users in multiple groups with conflicting permissions on objects lower in the inventory are granted only the permissions configured directly on the object.

Another common scenario involves the effective permissions when a user belongs to multiple groups with different permissions on the same objects. In this example, a user named Sue Rindlee is a member of the VM_Admins and VM_Auditors Windows groups. The VM_Admins group has been assigned membership in the Virtual Machine Power User vCenter Server role, and the VM_Auditors group is assigned membership in the Read-Only vCenter Server role. Both of these roles have been assigned permissions on the Production resource pool.

When the user is logged on to the vCenter Server computer as Sue Rindlee, the inventory reflects only the objects available to her through her permissions. Based on the permission assignment described, Sue Rindlee will be able to modify all of the VMs in the Production resource pool. This validates that Sue's Virtual Machine Power User status through membership in the VM_Admins group prevails over the Read-Only status obtained through her membership in the VM_Auditors group.

In this scenario, the effective permission is a cumulative permission when a user belongs to multiple groups with different permissions on the same object. Even if Sue Rindlee belonged to a group assigned to the No Access vCenter Server role, her Virtual Machine Power User role would prevail. However, if Sue Rindlee's user account was added directly to a vCenter Server object and assigned the No Access role, she would not have access to any of the objects to which that permission has propagated.

Even with a good understanding of permission propagation, you should always proceed with caution and maintain the principle of least privilege to ensure that no user has been extended privileges beyond those necessary as part of a job role. You should also conduct regular audits to ensure that there has been no drift of assigned permissions.

When delegating authority, always err on the side of caution. Do not provide more permissions than are necessary for the job at hand. Just as in any other information systems environment, your access-control implementation is a living object that will consistently require consideration and revision. Manage your permissions carefully, be flexible, and expect that use and administrators alike are going to be curious and will push their access levels to the limits. Stay a step ahead, and always remember the principle of least privilege.

We'll conclude our discussion of vCenter Server security with a quick look at vCenter Server logging.

Configuring vCenter Server Appliance Logging

As mentioned earlier, in the section "Configuring ESXi Host Logging," logging is an important part of security as well as an extremely useful tool in troubleshooting. You've seen how to hand logging for ESXi; now let's take a quick look at vCenter Server Appliance syslog streaming.

vCenter Server Appliance can forward its logs via syslog—and in 6.7, it can send logs out to three different destinations!—using its VAMI and Appliance Management APIs. The syslog clie can be configured to use TLS, TCP, RELP (Reliable Event Logging Protocol), or UDP; however, due to limitations with UDP, only the first three protocols will provide you with a proper connection status report in the UI. Figure 8.16 shows this section of the vSphere Appliance Management Interface.

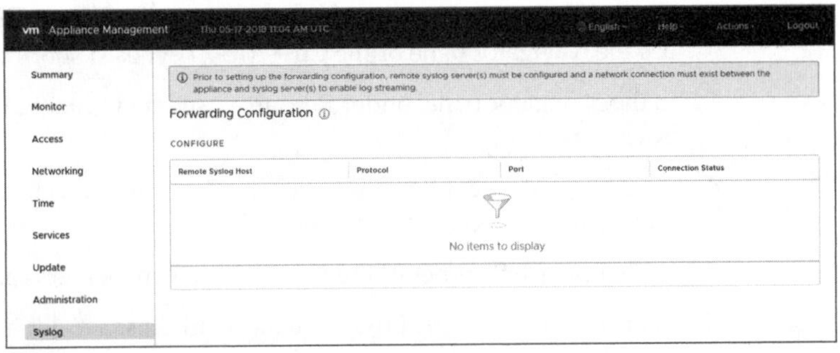

FIGURE 8.16
vCenter Server and Platform Services Controllers can forward their logs to a syslog server via the Syslog section of the vSphere Appliance Management Interface.

Again, as discussed in the "Configuring ESXi Host Logging" section, you can leverage the same centralized VMware-based vRealize Log Insight instance. However, that is a separate product and outside the scope of this book. That said, due to the nature of syslog, you can use any syslog server within your environment to collect and archive the vCenter logs.

In the next section of this chapter, we'll shift the focus to securing the third and final component of your vSphere environment: the VMs.

Securing Virtual Machines

As with vCenter Server, any discussion of how to secure a VM is really a discussion of how to secure the guest OS within that VM. Entire books have been and are being written about how to secure Windows, Linux, Solaris, and the other guest OSs vSphere supports, so we won't attempt to cover that sort of material here. However, we will provide three recommendations for securing VMs such that, if your datacenter does ever get compromised, the attack vector of your workloads is very limited. Three of these are specific to the vSphere virtualized environment, whereas the other is broader and more general.

First, we want to call your attention to the vSphere encryption policies.

Configuring a Key Management Server for VM and VSAN Encryption

vSphere provides some outstanding data encryption functionality by integrating with an External Key Management Server (KMS) running version 1.1 of the Key Management Interoperability Protocol (KMIP). KMIP is an extensibility protocol that permits interactions with cryptographic keys. Under the context of vCenter Server, the system lets you dynamically create and pull keys into your vSphere environment for the purpose of performing encryption. After trust is established between vCenter Server and your KMS infrastructure, you can set several different security-related policies to help maintain the security of your VMs and datastores.

ESTABLISHING TRUST FROM VCENTER SERVER TO YOUR KMS

Since Key Management Servers are separate products and outside the scope of this book, we won't be covering how to design and configure your KMS infrastructure. That said, as long as you have a KMIP 1.1–compliant KMS in your environment, you can use the following steps to integrate vCenter Server with it to establish VM and VSAN encryption:

1. Launch the vSphere Web Client if it is not already running, and connect to an instance of vCenter Server.

2. Navigate to VMs And Templates by selecting Home ➤ Global Inventory Lists. You can al
   use the Navigator pane or the Ctrl+Alt+7 keyboard shortcut.

3. In the Navigator pane, under Resources, select vCenter Server, and then select your
   vCenter Server.

4. From the middle content area, click the Configuration tab, and then click on the Key
   Management Servers section under More.

5. In the upper-left corner of the Key Management Servers content area, click Add KMS.

6. In the Add KMS dialog box, leave the KMS Cluster field set to Create New Cluster.
   Provide a name and alias in the Cluster Name and Server Alias fields, along with the full
   qualified domain, server port of your KMS as well as the service account and password
   the vendor supports this), as shown in Figure 8.17.

FIGURE 8.17
You can integrate
vCenter Server with
multiple Key
Management Servers.

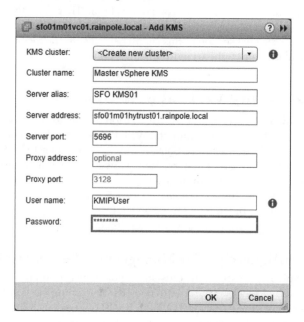

7. Click OK, and then click Yes to establish this KMS as the vCenter Server's default.

8. Next, the vCenter Server will pull the certificate from your KMS, as shown in Figure 8.18
   and prompt you to establish the final trust. If the certificate presented from the KMS
   matches what you have on record, click Trust.

9. Depending on your KMS vendor, additional steps may be needed in order to fully
   establish a trust between vCenter Server and the KMS. You can upload additional
   certificates from the KMS by clicking on your new KMS in the middle content area, and
   then clicking Establish Trust With KMS in the context menu.

10. In the Establish Trust With KMS dialog box, shown in Figure 8.19, you can select from a medley of additional options that may be specific to your KMS vendor's setup guidance. If one of these options is needed, go ahead and select the appropriate radio button, and then click OK.

    Additional configuration that is specific to a particular KMS vendor is outside the scope of this book, so check with your security team or vendor if additional steps are required. This may include:

    ◆ Uploading all Root Certificate Authority certificates in the environment

    ◆ Uploading the vCenter Server certificate itself to the KMS

    ◆ Using a Certificate Signing Request that can be signed by the KMS then transferred back to the vCenter Server

    ◆ Uploading additional certificates and private keys from the KMS

FIGURE 8.19

Depending on your KMS vendor, additional steps may be required to fully establish a trust between your KMS and your vCenter Server.

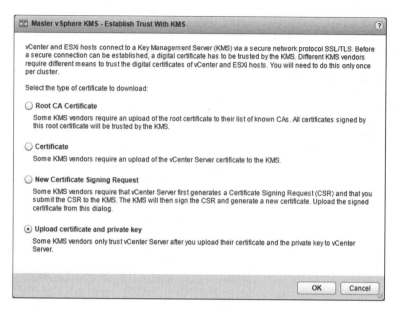

Now that we've integrated a KMS with vCenter Server, as shown in Figure 8.20, this opens the door to additional methods of encryption via storage-based policies and the use of a virtual Trusted Platform Module (vTPM). However, before we can begin applying policies (covered in-depth in Chapter 6), we need to ensure that the ESXi hosts in the environment have had their Security Profiles enabled for encryption.

FIGURE 8.20

It is best practice to have two replicating Key Management Servers presented to each vCenter Server KMS Cluster for redundancy purposes.

ENABLING HOST ENCRYPTION

Perform these steps to change the Host Encryption Mode of your ESXi hosts:

1. Launch the vSphere Web Client if it is not already running, and connect to an instance of vCenter Server.

2. Navigate to the Hosts And Clusters screen by selecting Home ➤ Hosts And Clusters. You can also use the Navigator pane or the Ctrl+Alt+2 keyboard shortcut.

3. Navigate down from your datacenter object to your cluster, and select one of your ESXi hosts.

4. Click the Configure tab in the content area, and under the Systems section, click Security Profile.

5. In the content area to the left, scroll down until you find Host Encryption Mode, and then click Edit.

6. From the Set Encryption Mode dialog box, use the drop-down for Encryption Mode and switch the setting to Enabled; then click OK. This setting will be automatically configured on all ESXi hosts in the cluster.

With all of the prerequisites for encryption within your vSphere environment met, we can apply encryption to our virtual machines. With the KMS integration, a few items are automatically handled for you; the one that's most important for this section is the VM Storage Policy called VM Encryption Policy, which can now consume the services from the default KMS.

ENABLING VM ENCRYPTION

Perform the following steps to apply the VM Encryption Policy and enable encryption of an existing virtual machine:

1. Assuming you are still logged into the vSphere Web Client, navigate to the VMs And Templates screen by selecting Home ➤ VMs And Templates. You can also use the Navigator pane or the Ctrl+Alt+3 keyboard shortcut.

2. Right-click on one of your powered-off virtual machines, and from the context menu, select VM Policies ➤ Edit VM Storage Policies.

3. In the Edit VM Storage Policies dialog box, you can either globally apply the storage policy to all components that compose the Virtual Machine, which includes the VM home folder and Virtual Disks, or you can apply the storage policy to just the VM home folder. You cannot apply the storage policy to just the hard disks, leaving the virtual machine components unencrypted. Since we want to ensure that all components are enabled for encryption on the virtual machine, use the global application method: from the VM Storage Policy drop-down list, select the VM Encryption Policy as shown in Figure 8.21, and then click Apply to All.

4. Click OK to apply the policy. It may take a while to apply depending on the size of the virtual machine's disks.

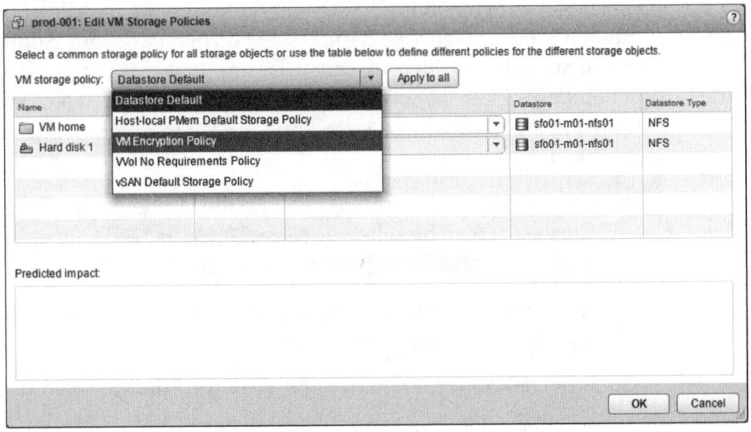

FIGURE 8.21
You have the option to encrypt only the home directory of a virtual machine or all components of the virtual machine including the disks.

After the policy is applied, the virtual machine's virtual disks and building blocks, such as the vmx and nvram files, are all encrypted. You can confirm this by reviewing the Summary page of the virtual machines. Within the VM Hardware and the VM Storage Policies portlets, you should now see an Encryption section covering the files being encrypted along with the VM Encryption Policy's compliance state, respectively, as shown in Figure 8.22. To decrypt the virtual machines you just need to power the virtual machine off and change the storage policy to one that does not contain the Common Rule of Encryption, such as Datastore Default. It's really as simple as that, just as long as you have the permissions to handle cryptography within vCenter Server!

FIGURE 8.22
Depending on the objects you apply the policy to, the Summary screen portlets will change context for easy tracking.

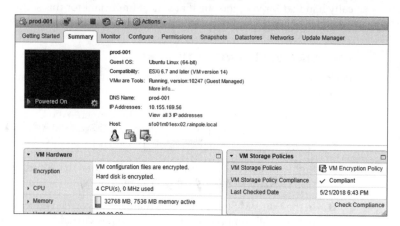

Finally, we'll take a look at vSAN encryption, if you just so happen to be running this in your environment.

ENABLING vSAN ENCRYPTION

If you are using vSAN in your environment, then your VSAN clusters will automatically populate after you set up KMS as your default; however, you still need to enable VSAN encryption on the clusters. Keep in mind that this operation is very I/O-intensive. It's also destructive because each of the disks and diskgroups need to be reformatted to achieve encryption at the datastore level. So enabling VSAN encryption in the middle of the workweek is ill-advised. Further, it is best practice to deploy your KMS on a separate datastore from the vSAN datastore that you are going to encrypt, thus ensuring that if anything happens to the KMS services, you don't end up locking down your vSAN datastore. This avoids creating a circular dependency.

Perform the following steps to apply vSAN Encryption and enable encryption of your vSAN cluster:

1. Assuming you are still logged into the vSphere Web Client, navigate to the Hosts And Clusters screen by selecting Home ➢ Hosts And Clusters. You can also use the Navigator pane or the Ctrl+Alt+3 keyboard shortcut.

2. Right-click on the cluster that's running VSAN, and select Settings. In the middle content area, under VSAN, click General.

3. From the middle content pane, click the Edit button in the top-right corner across from the vSAN enablement state, which should be On.

4. In the Edit vSAN Settings dialog box, click the check box next to Encryption. Notice that the KMS Cluster has automatically been set to the default KMS established at the beginning of this section, as shown in Figure 8.23. For the sake of this workflow, you do not need to use the Erase Disks Before Use, but in a production environment, this usage will wipe existing data from the storage devices as they are encrypted at the expense of an increased completion time.

FIGURE 8.23

Using the Erase Disks Before Use option enables a customer running VSAN in a secure environment to purge the disks of all data during the reformatting process.

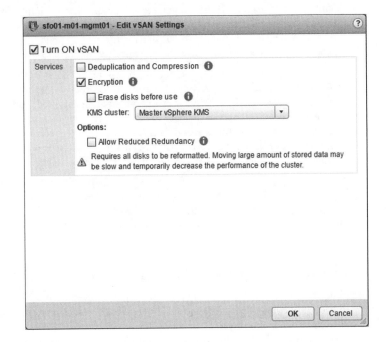

5. Click OK. Allow the reconfiguration process to complete—this may take a while depending on the size of your environment.

When the process is complete, all files on the vSAN datastore are encrypted, all virtual machines and their corresponding data are protected, and only administrators with the cryptographic permissions discussed earlier can decrypt the infrastructure.

Next, we want to call your attention to the virtual Trusted Platform Module (vTPM) and virtualization-based security.

 Real World Scenario

CHOOSING BETWEEN VM ENCRYPTION AND vSAN ENCRYPTION

This question often comes up: which encryption option should you choose for your environment? Obviously, using traditional, IP-based storage in your infrastructure would preclude you from using vSAN encryption. But in the scenario where you have moved to hyperconverged infrastructure and decided to leverage vSAN, which of these options is the best?

There are advantages and disadvantages to both solutions. VM encryption is implemented via VAIO (vSphere APIs for IO Filters), which is, from a high level, a framework that allows interception and manipulation with I/O that a virtual machine sends down to the storage device. By placing the encryption 'filter' high in the I/O path via VAIO, all data sent across the wire can be encrypted, which is great as far as security is concerned because it protects data-in-flight *and* data-at-rest. However, it acts as a double-edged sword: When data is encrypted so high in the I/O path and it finally comes to rest on the storage device, it becomes nearly impossible to apply, say, deduplication and compression to save on space, because encrypted blocks cannot be deduped or compressed. This is not that big a deal if you are only applying the storage policy to a small set of VMs within a larger populace, but when applied broadly, this can have an impact across storage operations.

vSAN encryption, on the other hand, sits much further down in the I/O path. As the data travels to the vSAN destination, it arrives un-encrypted before passing through the cache tier and destaging in the storage tier. There it must be encrypted and decrypted, and then re-encrypted at each tier. The benefits of this approach include the ability to apply deduplication and compression to the virtual machines before the at-rest data is encrypted, but this comes at the cost of having every virtual machine residing on the vSAN datastore encrypted. There is no fine-tuning or specificity with the application of encryption—it's either on or it's off for all of the residences of the datastore.

As we've mentioned throughout the book, what you decide to use in your vSphere environment comes down to the requirements. So ensure you have a long talk with your security team about which option best suits your datacenter's needs.

Virtual Trusted Platform Module 2.0

Similar to the physical TPM microcontroller discussed earlier in this chapter, and its application to ESXi, a virtual TPM (vTPM) device specializes in securely creating and storing assets. Rather than leveraging the physical, on-host TPM microcontroller to store all of the virtual machine attestation keys, which has quite a few drawbacks (namely a lack of storage capacity and slow performance of the hardware microcontroller), a vTPM device is presented to the supporting guest OS (which is limited to only Windows 10 or Windows Server 2016 in this release). The vTPM then stores the data in the VM's nvram file (explained in more detail in Chapter 9, "Creating and Managing Virtual Machines"). The keys are not exposed to the guest OS, just the device for creation and storage purposes, thus the keys are kept out of the reach of nefarious attackers. Further, storing the keys in the nvram file allows for the virtual machine and all of its components to be transported around on multiple hosts via vMotion rather than being appended to a host indefinitely due to its dependency on a physical hardware device.

In order to ensure that the vTPM data is secure, as covered in the preceding section, you must have VM encryption configured on the vCenter Server. This not only ensures that the encryption storage policy can be applied to the virtual machine and its disks in order to secure the essential TPM data, but VM encryption also must be there to even expose the virtual device to the virtual machine.

We'll cover the deployment of virtual machines in more detail in Chapter 9, but for now, follow these steps to add a vTPM to a Windows virtual machine via the vSphere Client (HTML5

1. Launch the vSphere Client (`https://<vcenter.domain.name>/ui`), if it is not already running, and connect to a vCenter Server instance.

2. Navigate to the VMs And Templates screen by selecting Home ➤ VMs And Templates.

3. Right-click on a powered-off Windows 10 or Windows Server 2016 virtual machine, and select Edit Settings from the context menu.

4. In the Edit Settings dialog box, click New Device, and then select Trusted Platform Module. After the TPM has been added, click OK.

Once this virtual device has been added to the VM, you can identify its use either inside or outside of the system. Inside the system, you can run `tpm.msc` to verify that the vTPM2.0 device has been picked up successfully in Windows, as shown in Figure 8.24. Outside the system, within the vSphere Client, you can navigate to the VMs tab on the folder, cluster, or datacenter containing your virtual machine, and add the TPM column, as shown in Figure 8.25. From there, now that a TPM device has been presented to the guest OS, you can now enable some of the features within Windows, such as BitLocker or UEFI Secure Boot.

FIGURE 8.24
The vTPM device will show up under the manufacturer name VMW (for VMware), with a specification version of 2.0.

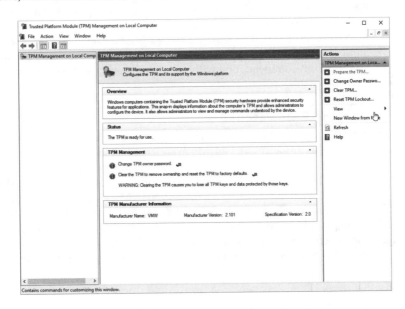

FIGURE 8.25
You can use the columns and filters to track down any and all virtual machines running a vTPM device in your environment.

Configuring Network Security Policies

vSphere provides some outstanding virtual networking functionality, particularly with the addition of the vSphere Distributed Switch and third-party distributed virtual switches. These virtual switches provide several security-related policies that you can set to help ensure that the security of your VMs is maintained. We discussed all these settings in Chapter 5, "Creating and Configuring a vSphere Network."

The key security-related network security policies you can set in the vSphere virtual networking environment are as follows:

- Promiscuous mode

- MAC address changes

- Forged transmits

VMware recommends keeping all of these policies set to Reject. If there is a valid business need for one of these features to be allowed, you can use per-port group settings to enable the appropriate feature only for the specific VM or machines that require such functionality. One example we've used before is a network-based intrusion detection/intrusion prevention system (IDS/IPS). Rather than allowing promiscuous mode—required for most IDS/IPS to work—on the entire vSwitch, create a separate port group just for that VM and allow promiscuous mode on that port group only.

When considering the security of your VMs, be sure to keep these network security policies in mind, and be sure that they are configured for the correct balance of functionality versus security.

Our next recommendation with regard to securing VMs is much more general but a valid recommendation nevertheless.

Keeping VMs Patched

As with your ESXi hosts and your vCenter Server computer, it's imperative to keep the guest OS in your VMs properly patched. My experience has shown that many security problems could have been avoided with a proactive patching strategy for the guest OSs in the VMs.

In vSphere 4.x, you could use vSphere Update Manager (then called vCenter Update Manager) to patch the guest OSs inside your VMs. From vSphere 5.0 and later, this functionality has been removed, and vSphere Update Manager—covered in detail in Chapter 4—focuses on keeping your ESXi hosts patched and up-to-date. It's important, therefore, to deploy some sort of guest OS patching solution that will help you ensure that your guest OSs remain patched and current with all vendor-supplied security fixes and updates. In Chapter 9, we'll delve into the process of creating and managing VMs.

The Bottom Line

Configure and control authentication to vSphere.　Both ESXi and vCenter Server have authentication mechanisms, and both products can utilize local users or users defined in external directories. Authentication is a basic tenet of security; it's important to verify that users are who they claim to be. You can manage local users on your ESXi hosts using either the traditional vSphere Client or the command-line interface (such as the vSphere Management Assistant). Both the Windows-based and the Linux-based virtual appliance versions of vCenter Server can leverage Active Directory, OpenLDAP, or local SSO accounts for authentication as well.

Master It　You've asked an administrator on your team to create some accounts on an ESXi host. The administrator is uncomfortable with the command line and is having a problem figuring out how to create the users. Is there another way for this administrator to perform this task?

Manage roles and access controls. Both ESXi and vCenter Server possess a role-based access control system that combines users, groups, privileges, roles, and permissions. vSphere administrators can use this role-based access control system to define very granular permissions that define what users are allowed to do with the vSphere Client against an ESXi host or the vSphere Client against a vCenter Server instance. For example, vSphere administrators can limit users to specific actions on specific types of objects within the vSphere Client. vCenter Server ships with some sample roles that help provide an example of how you can use the role-based access control system.

> **Master It** Describe the differences between a role, a privilege, and a permission in the ESXi/vCenter Server security model.

Control network access to services on ESXi hosts. ESXi provides a network firewall that you can use to control network access to services on your ESXi hosts. This firewall can control both inbound and outbound traffic, and you have the ability to further limit traffic to specific source IP addresses or subnets.

> **Master It** Describe how you can use the ESXi firewall to limit traffic to a specific source IP address.

Integrate with Active Directory. All the major components of vSphere—the ESXi hosts and vCenter Server (both the Windows Server–based version and the Linux-based virtual appliance) as well as the vSphere Management Assistant—support integration with Active Directory. This gives vSphere administrators the option of using Active Directory as their centralized directory service for all major components of vSphere 5.5.

> **Master It** You've just installed a new ESXi host into your vSphere environment and you are trying to configure the host to enable integration with your Active Directory environment. For some reason, though, it doesn't seem to work. What could be the problem?

Get familiar with KMS in your vSphere environment. Having a KMS infrastructure in your environment enables a multitude of features within vSphere, including VSAN and VM encryption, as well as vTPM2.0 devices for virtual machines. This gives you, the administrator, multiple tools at your disposal to secure your environment based on the available technologies presented and requirements given.

> **Master It** You've been tasked by your boss with deploying vTPM2.0 devices to all of your Windows 10 workloads for the upcoming updates being pushed from Microsoft. What prerequisites do you need to have in place before you can start adding these devices to your workloads?

Chapter 9

Creating and Managing Virtual Machines

The VMware ESXi hosts are installed, vCenter Server is running, the networks are blinking, the storage is carved, and the VMFS volumes are formatted. Let the virtualization begin! With the virtual infrastructure in place, you as the administrator must shift your attention to deploying the virtual machines.

IN THIS CHAPTER, YOU WILL LEARN TO

- ◆ Create a virtual machine
- ◆ Install a guest operating system
- ◆ Install VMware Tools
- ◆ Manage virtual machines
- ◆ Modify virtual machines

Understanding Virtual Machines

It is common for IT professionals to refer to a Windows or Linux system running on an ESXi host as a *virtual machine* (VM). Strictly speaking, this term is not 100% accurate. Just as a physical machine is bare-metal hardware before the installation of an operating system, a VM is an empty shell before the installation of a guest operating system (the term "guest operating system" is used to denote an operating system instance installed into a VM). From an everyday usage perspective, though, you can go on calling the Windows or Linux system a VM. Any references you see to "guest operating system" (or "guest OS") are references to instances of Windows, Linux, or Solaris—or any other supported operating system—installed in a VM.

If a VM is not an instance of a guest OS running on a hypervisor, then what is a VM? The answer to that question depends on your perspective. Are you "inside" the VM, looking out? Or are you "outside" the VM, looking in?

Examining Virtual Machines from the Inside

From the perspective of software running inside a VM, a VM is really just a collection of virtual hardware resources selected for the purpose of running a guest OS instance.

So, what kind of virtual hardware makes up a VM? By default, VMware ESXi presents the following fairly generic hardware to the VM:

◆ Phoenix BIOS

◆ Intel 440BX motherboard

◆ Intel PCI AHCI controller

◆ IDE CD-ROM drive

◆ BusLogic parallel SCSI, LSI Logic parallel SCSI, or LSI Logic SAS controller

◆ AMD or Intel CPU, depending on the physical hardware

◆ Intel E1000, Intel E1000e

◆ Standard VGA video adapter

VMware selected this generic hardware to provide the broadest level of compatibility across the entire supported guest OSs. As a result, it's possible to use commercial off-the-shelf drivers when installing a guest OS into a VM. Figure 9.1 shows a few examples of VMware vSphere providing virtual hardware that looks like standard physical hardware. Both the network adapter and the storage adapter—identified as an Intel(R) 82574L Gigabit Network Connection and an LSI SAS 3000 series adapter, respectively—have corresponding physical counterparts, and drivers for these devices are available in many modern guest OSs.

FIGURE 9.1
VMware ESXi provides both generic and virtualization-optimized hardware for VMs.

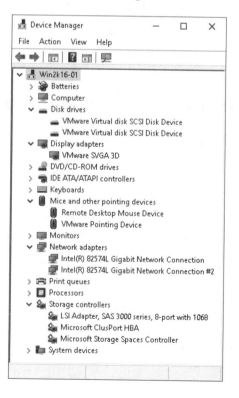

However, VMware vSphere may also present virtual hardware that is unique to the virtualized environment. Look back at the display adapter in Figure 9.1. There is no such physical card as a VMware SVGA 3D display adapter; this is a device that is unique to the virtualized environment. These virtualization-optimized devices, also known as paravirtualized devices, are designed to operate efficiently within the virtualized environment created by the vSphere hypervisor. Because these devices have no corresponding physical counterpart, guest OS–specific drivers should optimally be provided. VMware Tools, described later in this chapter in the section "Installing VMware Tools," satisfies this function and provides virtualization-optimized drivers to run these devices.

A physical machine might have a certain amount of memory installed, a certain number of network adapters, or a particular number of disk devices, and the same goes for a VM. A VM can include the following types and numbers of virtual hardware devices:

◆ Processors: between 1 and 128 processors with vSphere Virtual SMP (the number of processors depends on your vSphere licenses)

◆ Memory: maximum of 6 TB of RAM

◆ SCSI controller: maximum of 4 SCSI controllers

◆ SATA controller: maximum of 4 SATA controllers

◆ Network adapter: maximum of 10 network adapters

◆ Parallel port: maximum of 3 parallel ports

◆ Serial port: maximum of 32 serial ports

◆ Floppy drive: maximum of 2 floppy disk drives on a single floppy disk controller

◆ A single USB controller with up to 20 USB devices connected

◆ Keyboard, video card, and mouse

Hard drives are not included in this list, because VM hard drives are generally added as SCSI or AHCI devices. With up to 4 SCSI controllers and 15 devices per controller for a total of 60 SCSI / 256 PVSCSI devices per VM; it's possible to boot only from 1 of the first 8. Each VM can have a maximum of 4 SATA controllers with 30 devices per controller for a total of 120 possible virtual hard drives or CD/DVD drives. If you are using IDE hard drives, then the VM is subject to the limit of 4 IDE devices per VM, as mentioned previously.

SIZE LIMITS FOR VIRTUAL HARD DRIVES

The maximum size for any non-RDM virtual hard drive presented to a VM is 62 TB, up from just shy of 2 TB in earlier vSphere versions. That's a lot of storage for just one VM and a welcome change for organizations looking to virtualize large-scale business-critical applications. Raw device maps (RDMs) have a 2 TB size limitation, but they also have other considerations to keep in mind. You can find all this explained with further detail in Chapter 6, "Creating and Configuring Storage Devices."

There's another perspective on VMs besides what the guest OS instance sees. There's also the external perspective—what does the hypervisor see?

Examining Virtual Machines from the Outside

To better understand what a VM is, you must consider more than just how a VM appears from the perspective of the guest OS instance (for example, from the "inside"), as we've just done. You must also consider how a VM appears from the "outside." In other words, you must consider how the VM appears to the ESXi host running the VM.

From the perspective of an ESXi host, a VM consists of several types of files stored on a supported storage device. The two most common files that compose a VM are the configuration file and the virtual hard disk file. The configuration file—hereafter referred to as the VMX file—is a plain-text file identified by a .vmx filename extension, and it functions as the virtual resource recipe of the VM. The VMX file defines the virtual hardware that resides in the VM. The number of processors, the amount of RAM, the number of network adapters, the associated MAC addresses, the networks to which the network adapters connect, and the number, names, and locations of all virtual hard drives are stored in the configuration file.

Listing 9.1 shows a sample VMX file for a VM named Win2k16-01.

LISTING 9.1:   Example virtual machine configuration (VMX) file

```
.encoding = "UTF-8"
config.version = "8"
virtualHW.version = "14"
nvram = "Win2k16-01.nvram"
pciBridge0.present = "TRUE"
svga.present = "TRUE"
pciBridge4.present = "TRUE"
pciBridge4.virtualDev = "pcieRootPort"
pciBridge4.functions = "8"
pciBridge5.present = "TRUE"
pciBridge5.virtualDev = "pcieRootPort"
pciBridge5.functions = "8"
pciBridge6.present = "TRUE"
pciBridge6.virtualDev = "pcieRootPort"
pciBridge6.functions = "8"
pciBridge7.present = "TRUE"
pciBridge7.virtualDev = "pcieRootPort"
pciBridge7.functions = "8"
vmci0.present = "TRUE"
hpet0.present = "TRUE"
svga.vramSize = "8388608"
numvcpus = "2"
memSize = "8192"
firmware = "efi"
powerType.powerOff = "default"
powerType.suspend = "default"
powerType.reset = "default"
sched.cpu.units = "mhz"
sched.cpu.affinity = "all"
```

```
sched.mem.affinity = "all"
vm.createDate = "1522466316920854"
scsi0.virtualDev = "lsisas1068"
scsi0.present = "TRUE"
sata0.present = "TRUE"
usb_xhci.present = "TRUE"
scsi0:0.deviceType = "scsi-hardDisk"
scsi0:0.fileName = "Win2k16-01.vmdk"
sched.scsi0:0.shares = "normal"
sched.scsi0:0.throughputCap = "off"
scsi0:0.present = "TRUE"
ethernet0.virtualDev = "e1000e"
ethernet0.dvs.switchId = "50 31 c1 44 80 43 3a e4-0f f9 af fc 51 70 31 bd"
ethernet0.dvs.portId = "25"
ethernet0.dvs.portgroupId = "dvportgroup-37"
ethernet0.dvs.connectionId = "1342651053"
ethernet0.shares = "normal"
ethernet0.addressType = "vpx"
ethernet0.generatedAddress = "00:50:56:b1:17:84"
ethernet0.present = "TRUE"
sata0:0.deviceType = "cdrom-image"
sata0:0.fileName = "/vmfs/volumes/f1d1c1d7-c1f5832d/ISO/en_windows_server_2016_
updated_feb_2018_x64_dvd_11636692.iso"
sata0:0.present = "TRUE"
floppy0.startConnected = "FALSE"
floppy0.clientDevice = "TRUE"
floppy0.fileName = "vmware-null-remote-floppy"
displayName = "Win2k16-01"
guestOS = "windows9srv-64"
uefi.secureBoot.enabled = "TRUE"
disk.EnableUUID = "TRUE"
toolScripts.afterPowerOn = "TRUE"
toolScripts.afterResume = "TRUE"
toolScripts.beforeSuspend = "TRUE"
toolScripts.beforePowerOff = "TRUE"
uuid.bios = "42 31 4a 79 76 61 3d a7-b2 1c 85 c1 4c 39 74 de"
vc.uuid = "50 31 ae 0b 94 66 7d 30-09 45 46 7c 4e a7 65 8a"
migrate.hostLog = "Win2k16-01-379a765e.hlog"
sched.cpu.min = "0"
sched.cpu.shares = "normal"
sched.mem.min = "0"
sched.mem.minSize = "0"
sched.mem.shares = "normal"
numa.autosize.cookie = "20001"
numa.autosize.vcpu.maxPerVirtualNode = "2"
sched.swap.derivedName = "/vmfs/volumes/f1d1c1d7-c1f5832d/Win2k16-01/Win2k16-01-
69d1c780.vswp"
uuid.location = "56 4d ee 39 55 03 32 69-e7 b6 f5 c5 18 22 5e 87"
```

```
scsi0:0.redo = ""
pciBridge0.pciSlotNumber = "17"
pciBridge4.pciSlotNumber = "21"
pciBridge5.pciSlotNumber = "22"
pciBridge6.pciSlotNumber = "23"
pciBridge7.pciSlotNumber = "24"
scsi0.pciSlotNumber = "160"
ethernet0.pciSlotNumber = "192"
usb_xhci.pciSlotNumber = "224"
vmci0.pciSlotNumber = "32"
sata0.pciSlotNumber = "33"
scsi0.sasWWID = "50 05 05 69 76 61 3d a0"
vmci0.id = "1278833886"
vm.genid = "-7568173620057645264"
vm.genidX = "-3723198889589970316"
monitor.phys_bits_used = "43"
vmotion.checkpointFBSize = "8388608"
vmotion.checkpointSVGAPrimarySize = "8388608"
cleanShutdown = "FALSE"
softPowerOff = "FALSE"
usb_xhci:4.present = "TRUE"
usb_xhci:4.deviceType = "hid"
usb_xhci:4.port = "4"
usb_xhci:4.parent = "-1"
```

Reading through the Win2k16-01.vmx file, you can determine the following facts about this VM:

- From the guestOS line, you can see that the VM is configured for a guest OS referred to as "windows9srv-64"; this corresponds to Windows Server 2016 64-bit.

- Based on the memsize line, you know the VM is configured for 8 GB of RAM.

- The scsi0:0.fileName line tells you the VM's hard drive is located in the file Win2k16-01.vmdk.

- The VM has a floppy drive configured, based on the presence of the floppy0 lines, but it does not start connected (see floppy0.startConnected).

- The VM has a single network adapter configured to the Distributed Virtual Switch "dvportgroup-37" port group, based on the ethernet0 lines.

- Based on the ethernet0.generatedAddress line, the VM's single network adapter has an automatically generated MAC address of 00:50:56:b1:17:84.

Although the VMX file is important, it is only the structural definition of the virtual hardware that composes the VM. It does not store any actual data from the guest OS instance running inside the VM. A separate type of file, the virtual hard disk file, performs that role.

The virtual hard disk file, identified by a .vmdk filename extension and hereafter referred to as the VMDK file, holds the actual data stored by a VM. Each VMDK file represents a disk device.

For a VM running Windows, the first VMDK file would typically be the storage location for the C: drive. For a Linux system, it would typically be the storage location for the root, boot, and a few other partitions. Additional VMDK files can be added to provide additional storage locations for the VM, and each VMDK file will appear as a physical hard drive to the VM.

IN-GUEST STORAGE

Although virtual disks and RDMs are the responsibility of vSphere's storage stack and as such will be listed in the VM hardware inventory, they will be visible to vSphere. Any in-guest iSCSI or NFS mounts may also tie in additional storage for the guest OS but will not be represented in any VMX or VMDK file. In fact, using storage in this way is totally invisible to vSphere; it will just appear as network traffic to and from the particular VM. Depending on how you manage your environment, your operations monitoring tools may not function as you might expect when using in-guest storage options.

Although we refer to a virtual hard disk file as a VMDK file, in reality there are two different files that compose a virtual hard disk. Both of them use the `.vmdk` filename extension, but each performs a very different role: one is the VMDK descriptor file, and the other is the VMDK flat file. There's a good reason why we—and others in the virtualization space—refer to a virtual hard disk file as a VMDK file, though, and Figure 9.2 helps illustrate why.

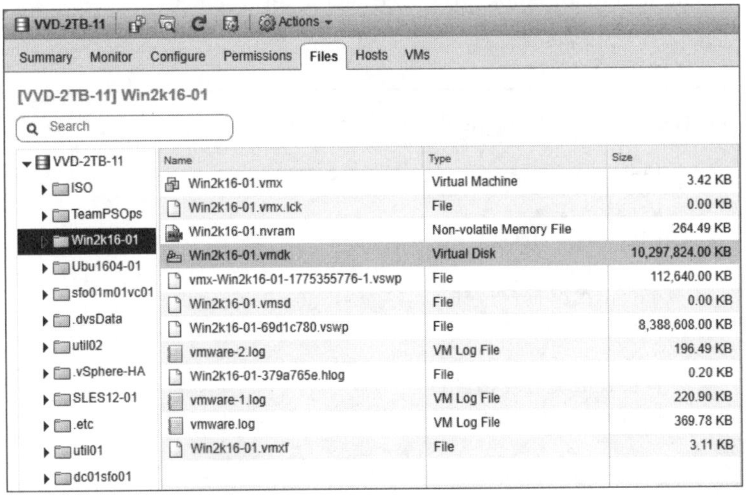

FIGURE 9.2
The file browser in the vSphere Web Client shows only a single VMDK file.

Looking closely at Figure 9.2, you'll see only a single VMDK file listed. In actuality, though, there are two files, but to see them you must go to a command-line interface. From there, as shown in Figure 9.3, you'll see the two different VMDK files: the VMDK descriptor (the smaller of the two) and the VMDK flat file (the larger of the two and the one that has `-flat` in the filename).

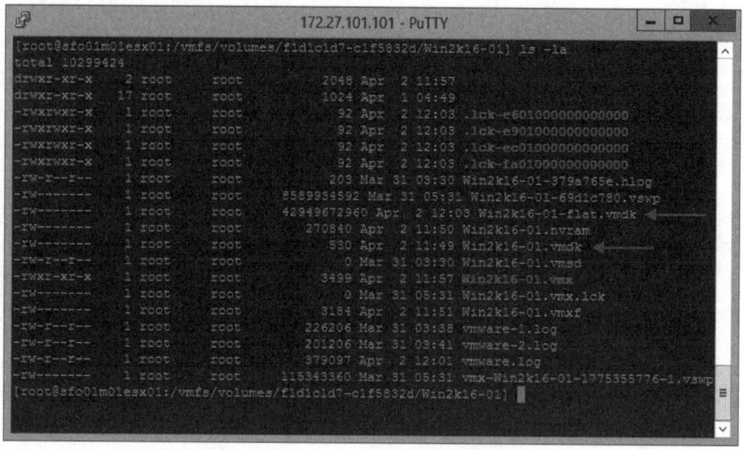

FIGURE 9.3

There are actually two VMDK files for every virtual hard disk in a VM, even though the vSphere Web Client shows only a single file.

Of these two files, the VMDK descriptor file is a plain-text file and is human-readable; the VMDK flat file is a binary file and is not human-readable. The VMDK descriptor file contains only configuration information and pointers to the flat file; the VMDK flat file contains the actual data for the virtual hard disk. Naturally, this means that the VMDK descriptor file is typically very small, whereas the VMDK flat file could be as large as the configured virtual hard disk in the VMX. So, a 40 GB virtual hard disk could mean a 40 GB VMDK flat file, depending on other configuration settings you'll see later in this chapter.

Listing 9.2 shows the contents of a sample VMDK descriptor file.

LISTING 9.2: Example VMDK descriptor file

```
# Disk DescriptorFile
version=1
encoding="UTF-8"
CID=48e9936b
parentCID=ffffffff
createType="vmfs"

# Extent description
RW 83886080 VMFS "Win2k16-01-flat.vmdk"

# The Disk Data Base
#DDB

ddb.adapterType = "lsilogic"
ddb.geometry.cylinders = "5221"
ddb.geometry.heads = "255"
ddb.geometry.sectors = "63"
ddb.longContentID = "aee33d712f7493abea5f879648e9936b"
ddb.thinProvisioned = "1"
```

```
ddb.toolsInstallType = "1"
ddb.toolsVersion = "10304"
ddb.uuid = "60 00 C2 9b 2f 41 49 0b-44 03 0b 21 29 32 18 0b"
ddb.virtualHWVersion = "14"
```

There are several other types of files that make up a VM. For example, when the VM is running there will most likely be a VSWP file, which is a VMkernel swap file. You'll learn more about VMkernel swap files in Chapter 11, "Managing Resource Allocation." There will also be an NVRAM file, which stores the VM's BIOS settings.

Now that you have a feel for what makes up a VM, let's get started creating some VMs.

Creating a Virtual Machine

Creating VMs is a core part of using VMware vSphere, and VMware has made the process as easy and straightforward as possible. Let's walk through the process, and we'll explain the steps along the way.

vSphere WEB CLIENT VS. vSphere DESKTOP CLIENT VS. vSphere HOST CLIENT

VMware has moved away from the old "thick" or "C#" Windows-based vSphere Desktop Client in favor of the multiplatform-compatible Web-based clients. You can no longer use the installable vSphere Desktop Client to connect to vSphere. To create virtual machines and other basic admin tasks, the procedure is mostly the same regardless of the client used. When using vCenter Server, we recommend that you use the vSphere Web Client until the HTML-based "vSphere Client" is declared feature parity. When connecting to individual ESXi hosts use the IP or hostname of the host browse to the vSphere Host Client directly from there. You can read more about this in Chapter 2, "Planning and Installing VMware ESXi."

Perform the following steps to create a VM from scratch:

1. If it's not already running, launch the vSphere Web Client, and connect to a vCenter Server instance. If a vCenter Server instance is not available, launch the vSphere Host Client and connect directly to an ESXi host.

2. In the inventory tree, right-click the name of a datacenter, a cluster, a resource pool, or an individual ESXi host, and select the New Virtual Machine option, as shown in Figure 9.4.

3. When the New Virtual Machine Wizard opens, select Create A New Virtual Machine, shown in Figure 9.5, and then click Next.

4. Type a name for the VM, select a location in the inventory list where the VM should reside, and click Next.

5. If you selected a cluster without vSphere DRS enabled or you are running vSphere DRS in manual mode, you'll need to select a specific host within the cluster on which to create the VM. Select an ESXi host or cluster from the list and then click Next, as shown in Figure 9.6.

FIGURE 9.4
You can launch the New Virtual Machine Wizard from the context menu of a vCenter datacenter, virtual datacenter, an ESXi cluster, or an individual ESXi host.

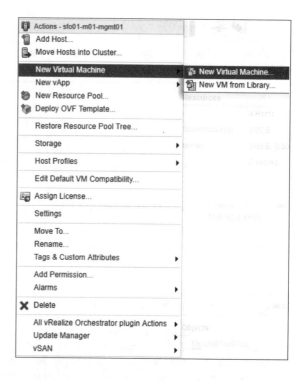

FIGURE 9.5
Options for creating a new virtual machine when using the vSphere Web Client

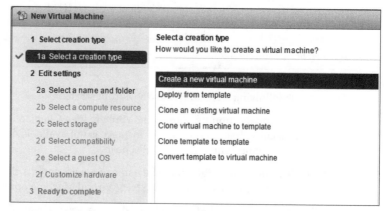

LOGICAL INVENTORY AND PHYSICAL INVENTORY

The inventory location you select when you create a new VM in vCenter, as shown in Figure 9.6, is a logical location. This inventory location does not correspond to the server on which that VM will run or the datastore on which that VM will be stored. This logical inventory displays in the vSphere Web Client when you select VMs And Templates as the inventory view.

FIGURE 9.6

The compute resource selected here is a DRS enabled cluster. When the VM is powered on DRS will select the best ESXi host to run the VM.

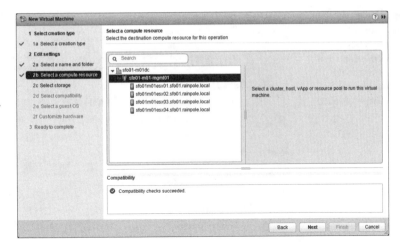

6. Select a datastore where the VM files will be located and click Next.

   As you can see in Figure 9.7, the vSphere Web Client shows a fair amount of information about the datastores (size, provisioned space, free space, type of datastore). However, the vSphere Web Client doesn't show information such as IOPS capacity or other performance statistics. In Chapter 6, we discussed storage service levels, which allow you to create VM storage policies based on storage attributes provided to vCenter Server by the storage vendor (as well as user-defined storage attributes created and assigned by the vSphere administrator). In Figure 9.7, you can see the VM Storage Policy drop-down list, which lists the currently defined storage service levels.

FIGURE 9.7

You can use storage service levels to help automate VM storage placement decisions when you create a new VM.

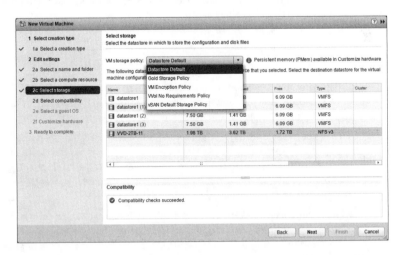

When you select a storage service level, the datastore listing will separate into two groups: compatible and incompatible. Compatible datastores are datastores whose attributes or capabilities satisfy the storage service level as defined in the VM Storage Policies;

FIGURE 9.8
When using VM storage policies, select a compatible datastore to ensure that the VM's storage needs are properly satisfied.

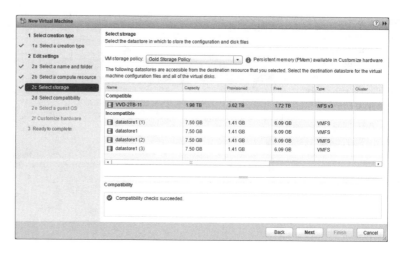

incompatible datastores are datastores whose attributes do not meet the criteria specified in the storage service level. Figure 9.8 shows a storage service level selected and a compatible datastore selected for this VM's storage.

For more information on VM storage policies, refer to Chapter 6.

7. Select a VMware VM version. vSphere 6.7 introduces a new VM hardware version, version 14. As with earlier versions of vSphere, previous VM hardware versions are also supported. If the VM you are creating will be shared with ESXi hosts running on earlier versions, then choose the appropriate version to match the lowest version host. For example, if the VM will be used only with vSphere 6.0, then choose ESXi 6.0 and later (VM version 11). Click Next.

RUNNING VMS FROM PREVIOUS VERSIONS OF ESXI

Unlike older major versions of ESX/ESXi, version 6 allows you to run VMs created in earlier versions of ESXi without any sort of upgrade process. Some readers may recall that the upgrade from ESX 2.*x* to ESX 3.*x*, for example, required a "DMotion" upgrade process or significant downtime for the VMs.

This is not to say that there won't be any downtime for VMs when upgrading from earlier versions to vSphere 6, just that the downtime isn't required to occur during the upgrade of the hosts themselves. You can even upgrade VMware Tools in each VM without rebooting them. However, one task that does require VM downtime—upgrading the virtual hardware to version 14—can be scheduled and performed at a later date (upon the next reboot).

vSphere supports a Default VM Compatibility level that can be configured at either the datacenter, cluster, or host level. With the Default VM Compatibility setting, you define a default value for the virtual machine version for newly created virtual machines. By setting Default VM Compatibility at a high level within your hierarchy, such as at the cluster level or datacenter, you can be sure that newly deployed virtual machines will have the correct VM version.

Only the newest VM version, version 14, supports the latest features found in vSphere. If your environment is running only ESXi 6.7, you should consider setting Default VM Compatibility to ESXi 5.5 or later in order to take advantage of all of the new virtual machine features found in vSphere 6.7.

Follow these steps to set the Default VM Compatibility on an object:

1. Right-click on a Datacenter, Cluster, or Host object within the vSphere Hierarchy in the vSphere Web Client.

2. Select Edit Default VM Compatibility.

3. Using the drop-down menu, select the default VM version that the UI should display when creating new VMs and click OK.

8. Select the drop-down box that corresponds to the operating system family, select the correct operating system version, and then click Next. As you'll see later in this chapter, this helps the vSphere Web Client provide recommendations for certain values later in the wizard.

9. At this point, you are taken to the Customize Hardware screen where you can customize the virtual hardware that will be presented to your virtual machine. To start, you'll choose how many virtual CPUs will be presented to your virtual machine. Select the number of virtual CPUs by using the drop-down box next to CPU. When you finish configuring virtual CPUs, click Next to continue.

   You can select between 1 and 128 virtual CPU sockets, depending on your vSphere license. Additionally, you can choose the number of cores per virtual CPU socket. The total number of cores supported per VM with VM hardware version 14 is 128. The number of cores available per virtual CPU socket will change based on the number of virtual CPU sockets selected. For specific information about how many virtual cores are available per virtual CPU socket, refer to `docs.vmware.com`.

   Keep in mind that the operating system you will install into this VM must support the selected number of virtual CPUs. Also keep in mind that more virtual CPUs doesn't necessarily translate into better performance, and in some cases larger values may negatively impact performance.

10. Configure the VM with the determined amount of RAM by typing in the desired memory value, as shown in Figure 9.9. The default memory sizing is listed in megabytes (MB), so it may be easier to change it to gigabytes (GB) so that you do not need to know the precise number of megabytes. When you've selected the amount of RAM you want allocated to the VM, click Next.

    As shown in Figure 9.9, the vSphere Web Client displays recommendations about the minimum and recommended amounts of RAM based on the earlier selection of operating system and version. This is one of the reasons the selection of the correct guest OS is important when creating a VM.

    The amount of RAM configured on this page is the amount of RAM the guest OS reflects in its system properties, and it is the maximum amount that a guest OS will ever be able to use. Think of it as the virtual equivalent of the amount of physical RAM installed in a system. Just as a physical machine cannot use more memory than is physically installed in it, a VM cannot access more memory than it is configured to use.

FIGURE 9.9

Based on guest OS selection, the vSphere Web Client provides some basic guidelines on the amount of memory you should configure for the VM.

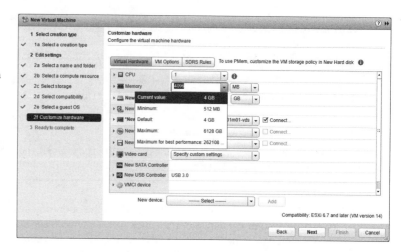

DO YOU KNOW WHERE YOUR MEMORY IS?

The setting on the Customize Hardware page is not a guarantee that physical memory will be used to achieve the configured value. As we discuss in Chapter 11, memory for a VM might be physical RAM, VMkernel swap file space, or some combination of the two, depending on how your VM memory reservations and overcommitments are configured.

11. Select the number of network adapters, the type of each network adapter, and the network to which each adapter will connect. Figure 9.10 shows a screen shot of configuring virtual NICs.

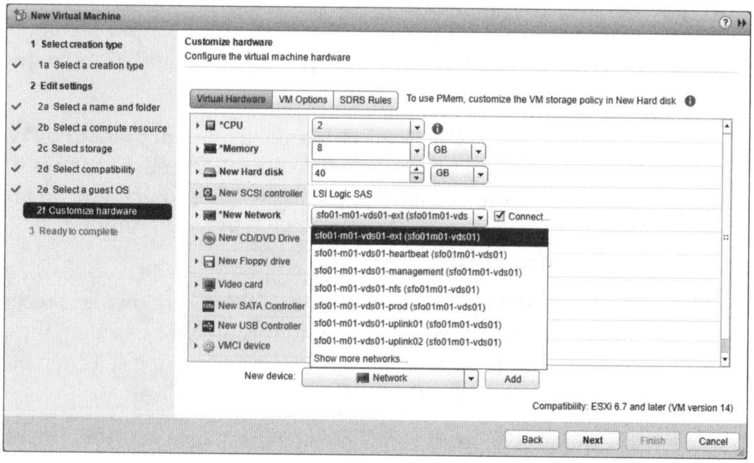

FIGURE 9.10

You can configure a VM with up to 10 network adapters, of the same or different types, that reside on the same or different networks as needed.

> ### MORE INFORMATION ON VIRTUAL NIC ADAPTERS
>
> VMware has detailed descriptions of the virtual NIC adapter types and the support requirements for each on its website at `http://kb.vmware.com/kb/1001805`.

12. Select New SCSI Controller to expand the selection area, and then click the drop-down box to choose the appropriate SCSI adapter for the operating system selected on the Select A Guest OS page of the Create New Virtual Machine Wizard.

The correct default driver should already be selected based on the previously selected operating system. For example, the LSI Logic parallel adapter is selected automatically when Windows Server 2003 is selected as the guest OS, but the LSI Logic SAS adapter is selected when Windows Server 2008, 2012, or 2016 is chosen as the guest OS. We provided some additional details on the different virtual SCSI adapters in Chapter 6.

> ### VIRTUAL MACHINE SCSI CONTROLLERS
>
> Windows 2000 has built-in support for the BusLogic parallel SCSI controller, whereas Windows Server 2003 and later operating systems have built-in support for the LSI Logic parallel SCSI controller. Additionally, Windows Server 2008, 2012, and 2016 have support for the LSI Logic SAS controller. Windows XP doesn't have built-in support for any of these, requiring a driver disk during installation. Choosing the wrong controller will result in an error during the operating system installation. The error states that hard drives cannot be found. Choosing the wrong SCSI controller during a physical-to-virtual (P2V) operation will result in a "blue screen error" for a Windows guest OS inside the VM, and the Windows installation will fail to boot. When selecting your Guest OS and Family in the New Virtual Machine Wizard, the hardware automatically generated will always be compatible.

13. A virtual hard disk is configured automatically when you create a new virtual machine. If you need to add a new virtual hard disk, select the New Device drop-down box at the bottom of the screen, as shown in Figure 9.11.

You are presented with the following options for adding a virtual disk to your VM.

◆ The New Hard Disk option allows the user to create a new virtual disk (a VMDK file) that will house the guest OS's files and data. Since a virtual hard disk is already added by default when a new virtual machine is created, using this option is useful if the virtual machine needs two disks (such as when an operating system drive and a data drive are required).

◆ The Existing Hard Disk option allows a VM to be created using a virtual disk that is already configured with a guest OS or other data and that resides in an available datastore.

◆ The RDM Disk option allows a VM to have raw SAN LUN access. Raw device mappings (RDMs) are discussed in a bit more detail in Chapter 6.

FIGURE 9.11

A virtual disk is configured automatically when you create a new virtual machine. You can also add additional virtual disks by using the New device option.

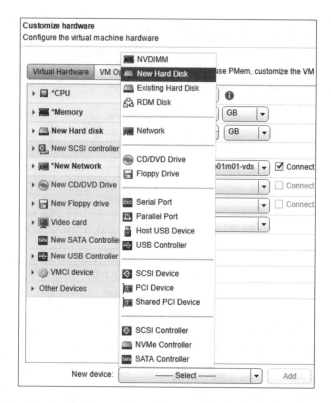

Since a virtual hard disk is already configured by default, we'll use it to install our guest OS and we won't need to add another virtual disk.

ADDING EXISTING DISKS

The existing virtual disk doesn't have to contain an instance of the guest OS; it can contain data that perhaps will serve as a secondary drive inside the VM. The ability to add existing disks with data makes virtual hard drives extremely portable, generally allowing users to move them from VM to VM or even share them for clustering, without repercussions. You will obviously need to address any guest OS–specific issues such as partitions, filesystem type, or permissions.

---

14. When you're either adding a new virtual hard disk or using the one provided by default, options are available for the creation of the new virtual disk. Select New Hard Disk to expand the selection area and access these options, as shown in Figure 9.12. First, configure the desired disk size for the VM hard drive. The maximum size will be determined b the format of the datastore on which the virtual disk is stored. Next, select the appropria Disk Provisioning option:

◆ To create a virtual disk with all space allocated at creation but not pre-zeroed, select Thick Provision Lazy Zeroed. In this case, the VMDK flat file will be the same size as the specified virtual disk size. A 40 GB virtual disk means a 40 GB VMDK flat file.

◆ To create a virtual disk with all space allocated at creation and pre-zeroed, select Thick Provision Eager Zeroed. This option is required in order to support vSphere Fault Tolerance. This option also means a "full-size" VMDK flat file that is the same size as the size of the virtual hard disk.

◆ To create a virtual disk with space allocated on demand, select the Thin Provision option. In this case, the VMDK flat file will grow depending on the amount of data actually stored in it, up to the maximum size specified for the virtual hard disk.

Depending on your storage platform, storage type, and storage vendor's support for vSphere's storage integration technologies like VAAI or VASA, some of these options might be grayed out. For example, an NFS datastore that does not support the VAAIv2 extensions will have these options grayed out, as only thin-provisioned VMDKs are supported. (VAAI and VASA are discussed in greater detail in Chapter 6.)

There are two options for the location of the new virtual disk. These options are available by selecting the drop-down box next to the Location field. Keep in mind that these options control physical location, not logical location; they will directly affect the datastore and/or directory where files are stored for use by the hypervisor.

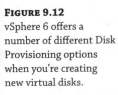

◆ The option Store With The Virtual Machine will place the file in the same subdirectory as the configuration file and the rest of the VM files. This is the most commonly selected option and makes managing the VM files easier.

◆ The Browse option allows you to browse the available datastores and store the VM file separately from the rest of the files. You'd typically select this option when adding new virtual hard disks to a VM or when you need to separate the operating system virtual disk from a data virtual disk.

You can configure other options, such as shares, limits, or Virtual Flash sizing (discussed in greater detail in Chapter 6) for the virtual machine you are creating, if required.

FIGURE 9.12
vSphere 6 offers a number of different Disk Provisioning options when you're creating new virtual disks.

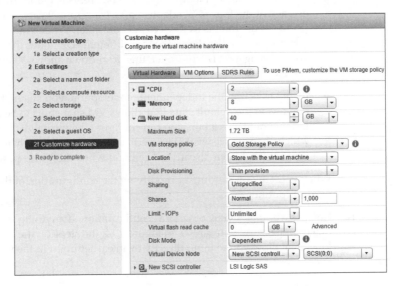

15. The Virtual Device Node option lets you specify the SCSI node, IDE controller, or SATA controller to which the virtual disk is connected. The Disk Mode option allows you to configure a virtual disk in Independent mode, as shown in Figure 9.13. The disk mode is not normally altered, so you can typically accept the default values provided, as shown Figure 9.13.

FIGURE 9.13
You can configure the virtual disk on a number of different SCSI adapters and SCSI IDs, and you can configure it as an independent disk.

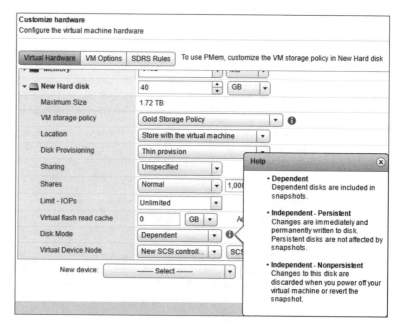

◆ The Virtual Device Node drop-down box reflects the 15 different SCSI nodes availab on each of the four SCSI adapters a VM supports. When using Para-virtualized SCS (PVSCSI) the limit is 64 devices per controller. When you're using an IDE controller, this drop-down list shows the four different IDE nodes that are available. When you're using a SATA controller, this drop-down shows 30 different SATA nodes that are available.

◆ By not selecting the Independent mode option, you ensure that the virtual disk remains in the default state that allows VM snapshots to be created. If you select the Independent check box, you can configure the virtual disk as a persistent disk, in which changes are written immediately and permanently to the disk, or as a nonper sistent disk, which discards all changes when the VM is powered off.

When you are done adding or modifying the configuration of the virtual machine, select Next to continue.

16. Complete a final review of the VM configuration. If anything is incorrect, go back and make changes. As you can see in Figure 9.14, the steps on the left side of the wizard are links that allow you to jump directly to an earlier point in the wizard and make changes.

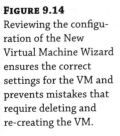

FIGURE 9.14
Reviewing the configuration of the New Virtual Machine Wizard ensures the correct settings for the VM and prevents mistakes that require deleting and re-creating the VM.

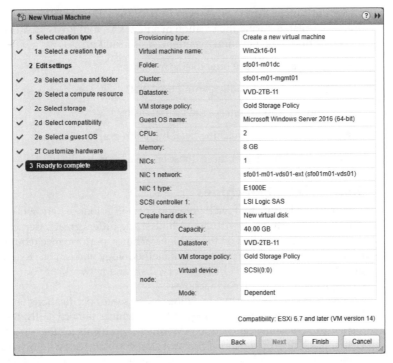

As you can see, the process for creating a VM is pretty straightforward. What's not so straightforward, though, are some of the values that should be used when creating new VMs. What are the best values to use?

Choosing Values for Your New Virtual Machine

Choosing the right values to use for the number of virtual CPUs, the amount of memory, or the number or types of virtual NICs when creating your new VM can be difficult. Fortunately, there's lots of documentation out there on CPU and RAM sizing as well as networking for VMs, so our only recommendation is to right-size the VMs based on your needs (see the sidebar "Provisioning Virtual Machines Is Not the Same as Provisioning Physical Machines," later in this chapter).

VIRTUAL MACHINE SIZING

Determining the right size for your VMs is a crucial part of your overall vSphere design, and it can impact a number of areas. For more information on how right-sizing VMs affects other areas of your vSphere design, refer to *VMware vSphere Design* by Forbes Guthrie and Scott Lowe (Sybex, 2013).

For areas other than the ones we just described, the guidance isn't quite so clear. Out of all t options available during the creation of a new VM, four areas tend to consistently generate questions from both new and experienced users alike:

◆ How can I find out how to size my VMs?

◆ How should I handle naming my VMs?

◆ How big should I make the virtual disks?

◆ Does my virtual machine need high-end graphics?

Let's talk about each of these questions in a bit more detail.

Sizing Virtual Machines

You might be hoping that we'll give you specific guidance here about how to size your virtual machines. Unfortunately virtual machine sizing differs greatly depending on the environment, the applications installed on the virtual machines, performance requirements, and many other factors. Instead, it's better to discuss a methodology you can use to understand the resource utilization requirements (CPU, memory, disk, and network) of your physical servers before redeploying them as virtual machines.

Simply sizing your virtual machines to the same specifications used for physical servers can lead to oversizing (or undersizing) virtual machines unnecessarily. Both oversizing and undersizing a virtual machine can lead to performance problems for that virtual machine and for other virtual machines on the same ESXi host. Not correctly sizing your virtual machines can negatively impact consolidation ratios, too, ultimately requiring your cluster(s) to scale up or scale out.

Instead, a process called capacity planning can help you understand how to size your virtual machines. With capacity planning you learn over time how your current physical servers are utilized and then use that information to size your virtual machines. A typical capacity planning exercise takes place over a two-to-four-week period and uses tools to automatically monitor and report on the performance of physical servers. By monitoring your servers over time, such as over a 30-day period, you can capture normal business cycles such as end-of-month processing that you might otherwise miss if you monitor for only a short time.

Two of the most common tools used for capacity planning are free, though as you'll see, one of them is not available to everyone. Perhaps the most well-known is a product by VMware called Capacity Planner. The other product, Microsoft Assessment and Planning Toolkit, may n be as well known, but it's still a useful tool.

FREE, BUT NOT FOR EVERYONE

VMware Capacity Planner is a free product, but it is not available for everyone to use. Capacity Planner is available only to VMware or VMware's certified partners. If you're an end user of VMware's products, you cannot access Capacity Planner yourself. You can find out more details on Capacity Planner here:

www.vmware.com/products/capacity-planner.html

Not already working with VMware or a partner? Luckily, you can usually work with your VMware representative to get access to Capacity Planner for servers in your environment.

Alternatively, the Microsoft Assessment and Planning Toolkit is a free download on Microsoft's website and is available to everyone. You can download it here:

`www.microsoft.com/en-us/download/details.aspx?id=7826`

Both tools produce similar results, such as average and maximum utilization values for CPU, memory, disk, network, and other more specific performance counters. Capacity Planner is customizable and allows you to add custom performance counters to monitor beyond the standard Windows or application counters. Microsoft Assessment and Planning Toolkit is less customizable, but it includes advanced reporting for Microsoft applications (like SQL Server or SharePoint Server) that are useful if you're looking to virtualize these applications.

The process for using these tools is also similar for both. After running the capacity planning analysis over time, you review the results to understand the actual utilization of your servers. These tools also allow you to produce reports that tell you how many ESXi hosts (or in the case of Microsoft Assessment and Planning Toolkit, Hyper-V hosts, though the results are applicable to ESXi as well) you'll need to support the environment. For example, if you monitor 70 total physical servers, the tools may tell you that, based on the actual utilization of each server, you need only 7 total ESXi hosts to support those servers as virtual machines. Your results will vary depending on the actual utilization in your environment.

Capacity planning is such a useful exercise because it tells you the true utilization of your servers before you convert them to virtual machines. Let's say you have a physical server with two CPUs, each with eight cores and 64 GB of RAM, and that server runs Microsoft SQL Server. You might think that because SQL Server is typically an important application, the server must be fully utilized. In reality, a capacity planning exercise may reveal that the server uses only two CPU cores and 8 GB of RAM. When you virtualize that server, you can reduce the resources down to what the server actually uses and save resources for other virtual machines.

VIRTUAL MACHINE RIGHTSIZING

It's always much easier to add resources to an undersized VM than it is to pull back resources that are already provisioned to a VM and its guest OS. Not only do some programs set configuration details upon installation to match the resources they think they always have, but more often than not, application owners will not want you to take resources away from them.

Whether you're just starting out on your virtualization journey or you're moving on to virtualizing more critical applications, capacity planning will provide valuable information for properly sizing your virtual machines. Without performing a capacity planning exercise, you are mostly just guessing at how many ESXi hosts you'll need to support the environment or how to properly size your virtual machines.

Naming Virtual Machines

Choosing the display name for a VM might seem like a trivial assignment, but you must ensure that an appropriate naming strategy is in place. We recommend making the display names of VMs match the hostnames configured in the guest OS being installed. For example, if you inter to use the name Server1 in the guest OS, the VM display name should match Server1.

It's important to note that if you use spaces in the virtual display name—which is allowed— then using command-line tools to manage VMs becomes a bit tricky because you must quote or the spaces on the command line. In addition, because DNS hostnames cannot include spaces, using spaces in the VM name would create a disparity between the VM name and the guest OS hostname. Ultimately, this means you should avoid using spaces and special characters that are not allowed in standard DNS naming strategies to ensure similar names both inside and outside the VM. Aside from whatever policies might be in place from your organization, this is usually matter of personal preference.

The display name assigned to a VM also becomes the name of the folder in the VMFS volume where the VM files will live. At the file level, the associated configuration (VMX) and virtual hard drive (VMDK) files will assume the name supplied in the display name text box during V. creation. Refer to Figure 9.15, where you can see that the user-supplied name of `Win2k16-01` is reused for both the folder name and the filenames for the VM. If a VM happens to be renamed any stage, all the associated files will retain the original name until a Storage vMotion occurs on the VM. Once the vMotion is complete, the majority of the files associated with that VM adhere to the new VM name. Note that file and VM names are case specific. You will learn more detail about Storage vMotion in Chapter 12, "Balancing Resource Utilization."

FIGURE 9.15

The display name assigned to a VM is used in a variety of places.

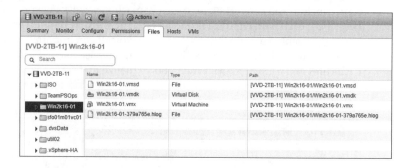

Sizing Virtual Machine Hard Disks

The answer to the third question—how big to make the hard disks in your VM—is a bit more complicated. There are many different approaches, but some best practices facilitate the management, scalability, and backup of VMs. First, you should create VMs with multiple virtual disk files to separate the operating system from the custom user/application data. Separating the system files and the user/application data will make it easy to increase the number of data driv in the future and allow a more practical backup strategy. A system drive of 30 GB to 40 GB, for example, usually provides ample room for installation and continued growth of the operating system. The data drives across different VMs will vary in size because of underlying storage system capacity and functionality, the installed applications, the function of the system, and the number of users who connect to the computer. However, because the extra hard drives are not operating system data, it will be easier to adjust those drives when needed.

Keep in mind that additional virtual hard drives will pick up on the same naming scheme as the original virtual hard drive. For example, a VM named Server1 that has an original virtual hard disk file named `Win2k16-01.vmdk` will name the new virtual hard disk file `Win2k16-01_1.vmdk`. For each additional file, the last number will be incremented, making it easy to identify all virtual disk files related to a particular VM. Figure 9.16 shows a VM with two virtual hard disks so that you can see how vSphere handles the naming for additional virtual hard disks.

FIGURE 9.16
vSphere automatically appends a number to the VMDK filename for additional virtual hard disks.

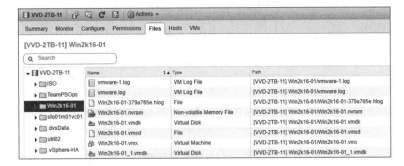

In Chapter 10, "Using Templates and vApps," we'll revisit the process of creating VMs to see how to use templates to implement and maintain an optimal VM configuration that separates the system data from the user/application data. At this point, though, now that you've created a VM, you're ready to install the guest OS into the VM.

PROVISIONING VIRTUAL MACHINES IS NOT THE SAME AS PROVISIONING PHYSICAL MACHINES

You need to approach provisioning VMs differently from the way you provisioned physical machines in the past. After all, didn't underutilized and overprovisioned servers lead you to use virtualization to consolidate your workloads?

In the physical world, you provision servers based on the maximum you think that server might ever need throughout its lifetime. Because the intended workload for a server might shift over that lifetime, you probably provision the physical server with more CPU resources and more RAM than it really needs.

In the virtual environment, though, VMs should be provisioned only with the resources they really need. Additional resources can be added later should the workload need them, sometimes with no downtime required.

In the event that you don't make this shift in thinking, you'll end up much like our client who had the same problem. During the early phases of the client's consolidation project, they provisioned VMs with the same level of resources given to physical machines. It wasn't until they ran out of resources in the virtual environment and had a far lower consolidation ratio than anticipated that they could be convinced to change their provisioning practices. After they changed their provisioning practices, the client improved their consolidation ratio without negatively impacting the level of service they could provide. Right-sizing your VMs is a good thing!

Virtual Machine Graphics

Depending on what kind of virtual machines you're deploying in your environment, you may need to think about graphics performance. For backend systems, such as database systems or email platforms, the graphics performance of the virtual machine is not important and is not something you typically have to worry about. If you're deploying a virtual desktop infrastructure (VDI), however, the graphics performance and capabilities of the virtual machine are likely to be a key consideration.

For VDI solutions like VMware Horizon View, end users no longer run a full desktop or laptop but instead connect to their virtual desktop (running on vSphere) from a variety of endpoint devices. These devices could be laptops, desktops, thin or zero clients, or even tablets and smartphones. The virtual desktop often acts as a complete desktop replacement for end users, so the desktop needs to perform as well as (or better than) the physical hardware that is being replaced.

In order to provide high-end graphics capabilities to virtual machines, vSphere 6 introduced Virtual Shared Graphics Acceleration (vSGA) and in vSphere 6.5 vGPUs were introduced in partnership with Nvidia. This technology allows you to install physical graphics cards of a specific type into your ESXi host and then offload the processing of 3D rendering to the physical graphics cards instead of the host CPUs. This offloading helps to reduce overall CPU utilization by allowing hardware that is purpose-built for rendering graphics to perform the processing. Additional functionality in vSphere 6.7 has been introduced for users of vGPUs with regard to VM mobility. Provided the latest hardware and driver VIBs are loaded in each ESXi host, VMs can now be vMotioned between hosts without needing to be powered off.

Although the 3D rendering settings are configured in the settings of a virtual machine, they are intended only for use with VMware Horizon. If you are using a VDI solution other than VMware Horizon, speak to the vendor to learn if 3D rendering on vSphere is supported.

Installing a Guest Operating System

A new VM is analogous to a physical computer with an empty hard drive. All the components are there but without an operating system. After creating the VM, you're ready to install a supported guest OS. The following OSs are some of the more commonly installed guest OSs supported by ESXi (this is not a comprehensive list as there are over 200 supported OSs listed on the vSphere 6.7 Guest OS Compatibility Guide):

- Windows XP, Vista, 7/8/10

- Windows Server 2000/2003/2008/2012/2016/2019

- Red Hat Enterprise Linux 3/4/5/6/7

- CentOS 4/5/6/7

- SUSE Linux Enterprise Server 8/9/10/11/12

- Debian Linux 6/7/8/9

- Oracle Linux 4/5/6/7

- Sun Solaris 10/11

- FreeBSD 7/8/9/10
- Ubuntu Linux
- CoreOS
- Apple OS X/macOS

VIRTUAL MAC SERVERS

VMware vSphere has support for many different guest OSs. Notably, vSphere 5 added support for Apple Macintosh OS X Server 10.5 and 10.6. vSphere 6.7 continues this and allows you to run Mac OS X, and macOS VMs on your VMware ESXi hosts. However, it's critically important to note that this is supported only when running ESXi on specific models of the Apple computers. VMware has restricted the installation of OS X and macOS to only Apple hardware to ensure the EULA is met. Check the VMware Compatibility Guide for details.

Also, keep in mind that just because a particular operating system is *supported* to run as a VM, the vendor may no longer support the operating system itself. This is particularly important when running VMs connected to the Internet. Sometimes it may be better to build a new VM running a modern OS that has security updates written for it on an ongoing basis.

Installing any of these supported guest OSs follows the same common order of steps for installation on a physical server, but the nuances and information provided during the install of each guest OS might vary greatly. Because of the differences involved in installing different guest OSs or different versions of a guest OS, we won't go into any detail on the actual guest OS installation process. We'll leave that to the guest OS vendor. Instead, we'll focus on guest OS installation tasks that are specific to a virtualized environment.

Working with Installation Media

In the physical world, administrators typically put the OS installation media in the physical server's optical drive, install the OS, and then are done with it. Well, in a virtual world, the process is similar, but here's the issue—where do you put the CD when the server is virtual? There are a couple of ways to handle it. One way is quick and easy, and the other takes a bit longer but pays off later.

VMs have a few ways to access data stored on optical disks. VMs can access optical disks in one of three ways (Figure 9.17 shows the Datastore ISO File option selected):

Client Device This option allows an optical drive local to the computer running the vSphere Web Client to be mapped into the VM. For example, if you are using the vSphere Web Client on your corporate-issued laptop, you can simply insert a CD/DVD into your local optical drive and map that into the VM with this option. This is the quick-and-easy method referenced earlier.

Host Device This option maps the ESXi host's optical drive into the VM. VMware administrators would have to insert the CD/DVD into the server's optical drive in order for the VM to have access to the disk. This option is only available from the Hardware Portlet in the VM's Summary tab as shown in Figure 9.18.

Datastore or Library ISO File These last two options map an ISO image (see the sidebar "ISO Image Basics") to the VM. Although using an ISO image typically requires an additional step—creating the ISO image from the physical disk—nearly all server software is being distributed as an ISO image that can be leveraged directly from within your vSphere environment.

FIGURE 9.17
VMs can access optical disks physically located on the vSphere Web Client system, located on the ESXi host, or stored as an ISO image.

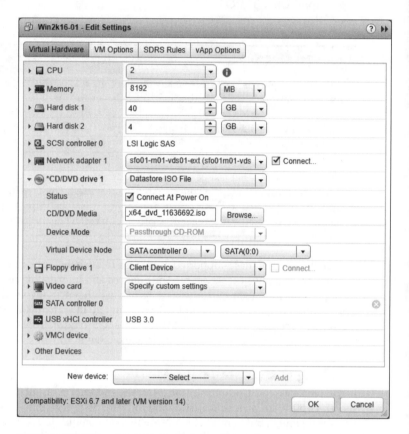

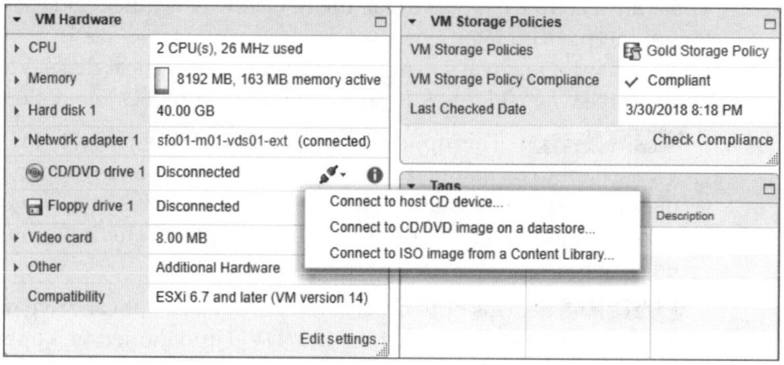

FIGURE 9.18
The Summary tab of a VM allows the connection of a VMs virtual CD/DVD drive to the physical CD/DVD drive in the ESXi host that is running the VM.

ISO IMAGE BASICS

An ISO image is an archive file of an optical disk. The name is derived from the International Organization for Standardization (ISO) 9660 file system standard used with CD-ROM media, and the ISO format is widely supported by many different software vendors. A variety of software applications can work with ISO images. In fact, most CD-burning software applications for Windows, Linux, and OS X can create ISO images from existing physical disks or burn ISO images to a physical disk.

ISO images are the recommended way to install a guest OS because they are faster than using an actual optical drive and can be quickly mounted or dismounted with little effort.

Before you can use an ISO image to install the guest OS, though, you must first put it in a location that ESXi can access. Generally, this means uploading it directly into a datastore accessible to your ESXi hosts or into a feature introduced in vSphere 6.0, the Content Library.

Perform these steps to upload an ISO image into a datastore:

1. Use the vSphere Web Client to connect to a vCenter Server instance or browse to the vSphere Host Client to connect to an individual ESXi host.

2. From the vSphere Web Client menu bar, select Storage.

3. Right-click the datastore to which you want to upload the ISO image and select Browse Files from the context menu.

4. Select the destination folder in the datastore where you want to store the ISO image. Use the Create A New Folder button (it looks like a folder with a green plus symbol) if you need to create a new folder in which to store the ISO image.

5. From the toolbar in the Files screen, click the Upload button (it looks like a disk with a green arrow pointing into the disk). From the dialog box that appears, select the ISO image as shown in Figure 9.19 and click Open.

The vSphere Web Client uploads the file into the selected folder in that datastore.

You can find out how to perform a similar action with Content Libraries in Chapter 10. After the ISO image is uploaded to an available datastore or into a Content Library, you're ready to install a guest OS using that ISO image.

Using the Installation Media

Once you have the installation media in place—by using the local CD/DVD-ROM drive on the computer where you are running the vSphere Web Client or by creating and uploading an ISO image into a datastore—you're ready to use that installation media to install a guest OS into the VM.

Perform the following steps to install a guest OS using an ISO file on a shared datastore:

1. Use the vSphere Web Client to connect to a vCenter Server instance or use the vSphere Host Client to connect to an individual ESXi host where a VM has been created.

2. If you're not already in the Inventory Trees or VMs And Templates view, use the menu bar to select Home ➤ Inventory Trees ➤ VMs And Templates (the second of four icons above the inventory tree).

FIGURE 9.19
Use the Upload button to upload ISO images for use when installing guest OSs.

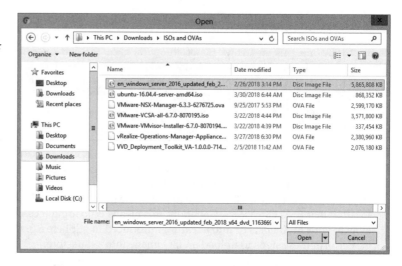

3. In the inventory tree, expand out the tree to display and right-click the new VM. Select the Edit Settings menu option. The Virtual Machine Properties window opens.

4. Expand the CD/DVD Drive 1 hardware option to expose the additional properties.

5. Change the drop-down box to Datastore ISO File, and select the Connect At Power On check box. If you fail to select that check box, the VM will not boot from the selected ISO image.

6. Click the Browse button to browse a datastore for the ISO file of the guest OS.

7. Navigate through the available datastores until you find the ISO file of the guest OS to be installed. After you select the ISO file, the properties page is configured similar to the one shown previously in Figure 9.17. Click OK to close the VM's Edit Settings dialog box.

8. Right-click the virtual machine and select Power On from the menu. Alternatively, you can use the Actions drop-down option on the properties page of the virtual machine or simply click the Power On green arrow on the content area title bar. Since there is no existing OS on the VM's virtual hard disk, the VM boots from the mounted ISO image and begins the installation of the guest OS.

9. Click the VM's console to open a remote session. Alternatively, you can use the Open Console option from the Properties page of the virtual machine as shown in Figure 9.20.

10. Follow the onscreen instructions to complete the guest OS installation. These will vary depending on the specific guest OS you are installing; refer to the documentation for that guest OS for specific details regarding installation.

VIRTUAL MACHINE GUEST OSS

For a complete list of guest OSs and all respective information regarding installation notes and known issues, refer to the list available on the VMware website at `http://partnerweb.vmware.com/GOSIG/home.html`.

FIGURE 9.20

Opening the console to a VM can be done in various different ways, through the Summary screen, the content area tool bar, or the Actions menu.

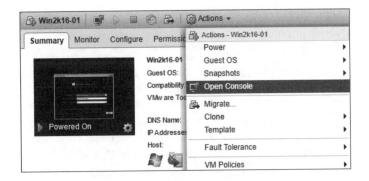

Working in the Virtual Machine Console

Working within the VM console is like working at the console of a physical system. From here, you can do anything you need to do to the VM: you can access the VM's BIOS and modify settings, you can turn the power to the VM off (and back on again), and you can interact with the guest OS you are installing or have already installed into the VM. We'll describe most of these functions later in this chapter in the sections "Managing Virtual Machines" and "Modifying Virtual Machines," but there is one thing that we want to point out now.

The vSphere Web Client must have a way to know if the keystrokes and mouse clicks you're generating go to the VM or if they should be processed by the vSphere Web Client itself. To do this, it uses the concept of *focus*. When you click within a VM console, that VM will have the focus: all of the keystrokes and the mouse clicks will be directed to that VM. Until you have VMware Tools installed—a process we'll describe in the next section, you usually have to manually tell the vSphere Web Client when you want to shift focus out of the VM. To do this, you use the vSphere Web Client's special keystroke: Ctrl+Alt. When you press Ctrl+Alt, the VM relinquishes control of the mouse and keyboard and returns it to the vSphere Web Client. Keep that in mind when you are trying to use your mouse and it won't travel beyond the confines of the VM console window. Just press Ctrl+Alt, and the VM will release control. Some of the more modern Guest OS installations will relinquish control when you move the mouse edge of the console window, but it is handy to know the keystrokes in case this is not automatic.

Once you've installed the guest OS, you should then install and configure VMware Tools. We discuss VMware Tools installation and configuration in the next section.

MICROSOFT LICENSING AND WINDOWS ACTIVATION FOR VIRTUAL MACHINES

As the virtualization market has matured, Microsoft has adjusted its licensing practices to reflect that market. In spite of those adjustments—or perhaps because of them—there is often confusion about the virtualization licensing available for the Windows Server operating system. Microsoft has reduced the number of versions of the operating system you need to license compared with prior versions of Windows Server. The following list of licensing data is a combination of information from both Microsoft and VMware:

◆ Microsoft Windows Server licenses are attached to the physical machine, not to the VM. Specifically, the Windows Server 2016 license is attached to the CPUs of the physical server. Microsoft calls this "Core-bases licensing."

♦ A licensed copy of Windows Server 2016 Datacenter Edition entitles a user to install and run an unlimited number of virtual Windows instances (VMs) on the physical server to which that license is assigned.

♦ A licensed copy of Windows Server 2016 Standard Edition grants the user the right to install and run up to two Windows instances (VMs) on the physical server when all physical cores in the server is licensed.

♦ Downgrade rights exist so that a physical server licensed with Windows Server 2012 Datacenter Edition can run unlimited VMs running either Datacenter Edition or Standard Edition. This also applies to running previous versions of Windows Server.

♦ vMotion, which moves a running VM to a new host, does not violate a Microsoft licensing agreement as long as the target ESXi host is licensed for the post-vMotion number of VMs and you maintain active Software Assurance on your Windows licenses.

Because Microsoft requires Windows Server licenses to be attached to physical hardware, many organizations are choosing to license their physical hardware with the Windows Server 2016 Datacenter Edition. This gives the organization the ability to run an unlimited number of Windows Server instances on that hardware, and downgrade or previous version rights allow the organization to use the Standard, Enterprise, or Datacenter Edition of Windows Server 2008 or Standard or Datacenter Edition of Windows Server 2012.

Activation is another area requiring a bit of planning. If your licensing structure for a Windows Server guest OS does not fall under the umbrella of a volume licensing agreement, you will be required to activate the operating system with Microsoft within 60 days of installation. Activation can be done automatically over the Internet or by calling the provided regional phone number. With Windows Server operating systems specifically, the activation algorithm takes into account the hardware specifications of the server. In light of this, when enough hardware changes have been made to significantly change the operating system, Windows requires reactivation. To facilitate the activation process and especially to reduce the possibility of reactivation, you should make adjustments to memory and processors and install VMware Tools prior to performing the activation.

Installing VMware Tools

Although VMware Tools is not installed by default, the package is an important part of a VM. VMware Tools offers several great benefits without any detriments. Recall from the beginning of this chapter that VMware vSphere offers certain virtualization-optimized (or *paravirtualized*) devices to VMs in order to improve performance. In many cases, these paravirtualized devices do not have device drivers present in a standard installation of a guest OS. The device drivers for these devices are provided by VMware Tools, which is just one more reason why VMware Tools is an essential part of every VM and guest OS installation.

In other words, installing VMware Tools should be standard practice and not an optional step in the deployment of a VM. The VMware Tools package provides the following benefits:

♦ Optimized NIC drivers.

♦ Optimized SCSI drivers.

♦ Enhanced video and mouse drivers.

♦ VM heartbeat.

◆ VSS support to enable guest quiescing for snapshots and backups. Many VMware and third-party applications and tools rely on the VMware Tools VSS integration.

◆ Enhanced memory management.

◆ API access for VMware utilities (such as PowerCLI) to reach into the guest OS.

VMware Tools also helps streamline and automate the management of VM focus so you can move into and out of VM consoles easily and seamlessly without the Ctrl+Alt keyboard command.

The VMware Tools package is available for Windows, Linux, NetWare, Solaris, OSX, and FreeBSD; however, the installation methods vary because of the differences in the guest OSs. In all cases, the installation of VMware Tools can start when you select the option to install VMware Tools from the vSphere Web Client. Do you recall our discussion earlier about ISO images and how ESXi uses them to present CDs/DVDs to VMs? That's exactly the functionality being leveraged in this case. When you select to install VMware Tools, vSphere will mount an ISO as a CD/DVD for the VM, and the guest OS will reflect a mounted CD-ROM that has the installation files for VMware Tools.

WHERE TO FIND THE VMware TOOLS ISOs

In case you're curious, you'll find the VMware Tools ISO images located in the /vmimages/tools-isoimages directory on an ESXi host. This directory is visible only if you enable the ESX Shell on your ESXi hosts and then open an SSH connection to the host; it is not visible from the vSphere Web Client. The ISO images are placed there automatically during installation; you do not have to download them or obtain them from the installation CD-ROM, and you do not need to do anything to manage or maintain them.

As we mentioned previously, the exact process for installing VMware Tools will depend on the guest OS. Because Windows and Linux make up the largest portion of VMs deployed on VMware vSphere in most cases, those are the two examples we'll discuss. First, we'll walk you through installing VMware Tools into a Windows-based guest OS.

Installing VMware Tools in Windows

Perform these steps to install VMware Tools into Windows Server 2012 running as a guest OS in a VM (the steps for other versions of Windows are similar):

1. Use the vSphere Web Client to connect to a vCenter Server instance or use the vSphere Host Client to connect to an individual ESXi host.

2. If you aren't already in the Inventory Trees or VMs And Templates inventory view, use Home ➤ Inventory Trees or Home ➤ VMs And Templates to navigate to one of these views.

3. Right-click the VM in the inventory tree and select Open Console. You can also use the Open Console option on the properties page of the virtual machine.

4. If you aren't already logged into the guest OS in the VM, select Send Ctrl+Alt+Delete and log into the guest OS.

5. Right-click the virtual machine and select Guest OS ➤ Install VMware Tools. A dialog box providing additional information appears. Click Mount to mount the VMware Tools ISO and dismiss the dialog box.

6. An AutoPlay dialog box appears, prompting the user for action. Select the option Run Setup64.exe.

   If the AutoPlay dialog box does not appear, open Windows Explorer and double-click the CD/DVD drive icon. The AutoPlay dialog box should then appear.

7. Click Next on the Welcome To The Installation Wizard For VMware Tools page.

8. Select the appropriate setup type for the VMware Tools installation, and click Next.

   For most situations, you will choose the Typical radio button. The Complete installation option installs all available features, whereas the Custom installation option allows for the greatest level of feature customization.

9. Click Install.

   During the installation, you may be prompted one or more times to confirm the installation of third-party device drivers; select Install for each of these prompts.

   If the AutoRun dialog box appears again, simply close the dialog box and continue with the installation.

10. After the installation is complete, click Finish.

11. Click Yes to restart the VM immediately, or click No to manually restart the VM at a later time.

HOW TO JUMP OUT OF A CONCOLE

Remember that before VMware Tools is installed into a guest OS, the ability to seamlessly move into and out of the guest OS in the console doesn't exist. Instead, you must click into the VM console in order to interact with the guest OS. When you are finished, you must press Ctrl+Alt (Windows / Linux) or Ctrl + Command (macOS) to release the mouse and keyboard. After VMware Tools is installed, this happens automatically when you move the mouse outside the VM console area.

To install the enhanced VMware video driver and improve the graphical console performance on older Windows VMs, perform the following steps:

1. From the Start menu, select Run. In the Run dialog box, type `devmgmt.msc` and click OK. This will launch the Device Manager console.

2. Expand the Display Adapters entry.

3. Right-click the Standard VGA Graphics Adapter or VMware SVGA II item, and select Update Driver Software.

4. Click Browse My Computer For Driver Software.

5. Using the Browse button, navigate to the following directory:

```
C:\Program Files\Common Files\VMware\Drivers\wddm_video
```

Then click Next.

6. After a moment, Windows will report that it has successfully installed the driver for the VMware SVGA 3D (Microsoft Corporation – WDDM) device. Click Close.

7. Restart the VM when prompted.

After Windows restarts in the VM, you should notice improved performance when using the graphical console. Note that this procedure is no longer required in Windows Server 2012 and newer. The VMware SVGA 3D driver is automatically installed along with VMware Tools.

For older versions of Windows, such as Windows Server 2003, you can further improve the responsiveness of the VM console by configuring the hardware acceleration setting. It is, by default, set to None; setting it to Maximum provides a much smoother console session experience. The VMware Tools installation routine reminds you to set this value at the end of the installation, but if you choose not to set hardware acceleration at that time, it can easily be set later. We highly recommended that you optimize the graphical performance of the VM's console. (Note that Windows XP has this value set to Maximum by default.)

Perform the following steps to adjust the hardware acceleration in a VM running Windows Server 2003 (or Windows XP, in case the value has been changed from the default):

1. Right-click an empty area of the Windows Desktop, and select the Properties option.

2. Select the Settings tab, and click the Advanced button.

3. Select the Troubleshooting tab.

4. Move the Hardware Acceleration slider to the Full setting on the right, as shown in Figure 9.21.

FIGURE 9.21
Changing the hardware acceleration feature of an older Windows guest OS is a common and helpful adjustment for improving mouse performance.

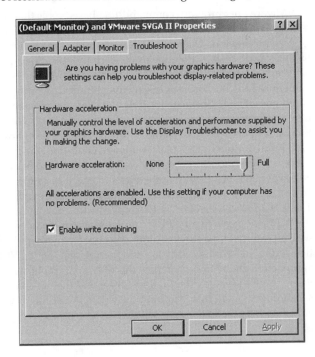

Now that the VMware Tools installation is complete and the VM is rebooted, the system tray displays the VMware Tools icon, the letters *VM* in a small gray box (Windows Taskbar settings might hide the icon). The icon in the system tray indicates that VMware Tools is installed and operational.

In previous versions of vSphere, double-clicking the VMware Tools icon in the system tray would bring up a set of configurable options. As of vSphere 5.1, that interface has been removed and replaced with the informational screen shown in Figure 9.22. Previously you could configure time synchronization, show or hide VMware Tools from the Taskbar, and select scripts to suspend, resume, shut down, or turn on a VM.

FIGURE 9.22
As of vSphere 5.1, you can no longer configure properties in VMware Tools by interacting with the icon in the system tray.

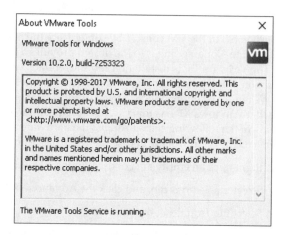

VMware now provides command-line-based tools that will allow you to configure these settings. You can access these by browsing to the installation directory of VMware Tools.

As with previous versions of VMware Tools, time synchronization between the guest OS and the host is disabled by default. You'll want to use caution when enabling time synchronization between the guest OS and the ESXi host because Windows domain members rely on Kerberos for authentication and Kerberos is sensitive to time differences between computers. A Windows-based guest OS that belongs to an Active Directory domain is already configured with a native time synchronization process against the domain controller in its domain that holds the PDC Emulator operations master role. If the time on the ESXi host is different from the time on the PDC Emulator operations master domain controller, the guest OS could end up moving outside the 5-minute window allowed by Kerberos. When the 5-minute window is exceeded, Kerberos will experience errors with authentication and replication.

You can take a few approaches to managing time synchronizations in a virtual environment. The first approach involves not using VMware Tools time synchronization and relying instead on the W32Time service and a PDC Emulator with a Registry edit that configures synchronization with an external time server. Another approach involves disabling the native time synchronization across the Windows domain and then relying on the VMware Tools feature. A third approach might be to synchronize the VMware ESXi hosts and the PDC Emulator operations master with the same external time server and then to enable the VMware Tools option for synchronization. In this case, both the native W32Time service and VMware Tools should be adjusting the time to the same value.

VMware has a few Knowledge Base articles that contain the latest recommendations for timekeeping. For Windows-based guest OS installations, refer to `http://kb.vmware.com/kb/1318` or refer to the older, but still relevant document "Timekeeping in VMware Virtual Machines" at the following location:

`http://www.vmware.com/files/pdf/Timekeeping-In-VirtualMachines.pdf`

CONFIGURING NTP ON ESXi

If you do choose to synchronize the guest OS to the ESXi host using VMware Tools, be sure to synchronize the ESXi host to an authoritative time source using NTP. Refer to Chapter 2 for more information on configuring ESXi to synchronize with an NTP-based time server. We recommend that the NTP settings for guest OSs are set to the same external time source instead of host synchronization.

We've shown you how to install VMware Tools into a Windows-based guest operation system, so now we'd like to walk through the process for a Linux-based guest OS.

Installing VMware Tools in Linux

A number of versions (or distributions) of Linux are available and supported by VMware vSphere. While they are all called "Linux," they do have subtle differences from one distribution to another that make it difficult to provide a single set of steps that would apply to all Linux distributions. In this section, we'll describe two different methods for installing VMware Tools. First, we'll show you a simple installation process, using Open VM Tools and a package manager. For this example, we will use Ubuntu 16.04 LTS. After that, we'll use SuSE Linux Enterprise Server (SLES) version 11 to show you how to install VMware Tools using an ISO mounted from the ESXi host. SuSE is a popular enterprise-focused distribution of Linux, and version 11 doesn't include Open VM Tools.

INSTALLING VMWARE TOOLS USING OPEN VM TOOLS

Open VM Tools (OVT) is nearly the same as the normal VMware Tools, but it's packaged and updated slightly differently. Like the normal VMware Tools that ships with ESXi and can be installed from an ISO, OVT is a set of services, modules, and drivers that allow you to more seamlessly manage your Linux based VMs. OVT has one distinct difference: the method in which you install and update it. By including Open VM Tools as an open source project that's available to anyone, installing and updating can be customized depending on the Linux distribution. There are a number of Linux distributions that include Open-VM-Tools:

◆ Fedora

◆ Devian

◆ OpenSUSE

◆ Ubuntu

◆ Red Hat Enterprise Linux

◆ SUSE Linux

◆ CentOS

◆ Oracle Linux

To install Open VM Tools into a VM running Ubuntu 16.04 LTS, perform the following steps:

1. Use the vSphere Web Client to connect to a vCenter Server instance or use the vSphere Host Client to connect to an individual ESXi host.

2. You will need access to the console of the VM onto which you're installing VMware Tools. Right-click the VM and select Open Console.

UPDATE REPOSITORY

You need to ensure your VM has access to its update repository to install Open VM Tools. This could be internal or Internet-based, depending on how your environment is configured.

---

3. Log into the Linux guest OS using an account with appropriate permissions or the ability to escalate permissions (**sudo <command>**) to install OVT.

4. To ensure you are getting the most up to date version, run **sudo apt-get-update**.

5. Once your package manager is updated, install Open VM Tools by running **sudo apt-get install open-vm-tools**.

6. If this is the first time the OVT is being installed on this VM, you will need to reboot for it to start up correctly. Future updates should not require a reboot.

INSTALLING VMWARE TOOLS IN LINUX USING AN ISO

Perform the following steps to install VMware Tools into a VM running the 64-bit version of SLES 11 as the guest OS:

1. Use the vSphere Web Client to connect to a vCenter Server instance or use the vSphere Host Client to connect to an individual ESXi host.

2. You will need access to the console of the VM onto which you're installing VMware Tools. Right-click the VM and select Open Console.

3. Log into the Linux guest OS using an account with appropriate permissions. This will typically be the root account or an equivalent (some Linux distributions, including Ubuntu, disable the root account but provide an administrative account you can use).

4. Right-click the virtual machine and choose Guest OS ➢ Install VMware Tools. Click Mount in the dialog box that pops up.

5. Assuming that you have a graphical user environment running in the Linux VM, a file system browser window will open to display the contents of the VMware Tools ISO that was automatically mounted behind the scenes.

6. Open a Linux terminal window. In many distributions, you can right-click a blank area of the file system browser window and select Open In Terminal.

7. If you are not already in the same directory as the VMware Tools mount point, change directories to the location of the VMware Tools mount point using the following command (the exact path may vary from distribution to distribution and from version to version; this is the path for SLES 11):

   `cd /media/VMware\ Tools`

8. Extract the compressed TAR file (with the `.tar.gz` filename extension) to a temporary directory, and then change to that temporary directory using the following commands:

   `tar -zxf VMwareTools-x.y.z-xxxxxxx.tar.gz -C /tmpcd /tmp/vmware-tools-distrib`

9. In the `/tmp/vmware-tools-distrib` directory, use the **sudo** command to run the `vmware-install.pl` Perl script with the following command:

   `sudo ./vmware-install.pl`

   Enter the current account's password when prompted.

10. The installer will provide a series of prompts for information such as where to place the binary files, where the init scripts are located, and where to place the library files. Default answers are provided in brackets; you can just press Enter unless you need to specify a different value that is appropriate for this Linux system.

11. After the installation is complete, the VMware Tools ISO will be unmounted automatically. You can remove the temporary installation directory using these commands:

    `cdrm -rf /tmp/vmware-tools-distrib`

12. Reboot the Linux VM for the installation of VMware Tools to take full effect.

The steps described here were performed on a VM running SLES 12 64-bit. Because of variations within different versions and distributions of Linux, the commands you may need to install VMware Tools within another distribution may not exactly match what we've listed here. However, these steps do provide a general guideline of what the procedure looks like.

VMware Tools for Linux

When installing VMware Tools to a Linux guest OS, you'll note that the path to the TAR file and the numbers in the TAR filename will vary. Depending on your Linux distribution, the VMware Tools installer may also provide instructions for replacing the Ethernet driver with an updated VMXNET driver. Typically, these instructions involve unloading the older drivers, scanning for new devices, loading the new VMXNET driver, and then bringing the network interfaces back up.

After VMware Tools is installed, the Summary tab of a VM object identifies the status of VMware Tools as well as other information such as operating system, CPU, memory, DNS (host) name, IP address, and current ESXi host. Figure 9.23 shows a screen shot of this information for the Windows Server 2016 VM into which we installed VMware Tools earlier.

If you are upgrading to vSphere 6.7 from a previous version of VMware vSphere, you will have outdated versions of VMware Tools running in your guest OSs. You'll want to upgrade

FIGURE 9.23
You can view details about VMware Tools, DNS name, IP address, and so forth from the Summary tab of a VM object.

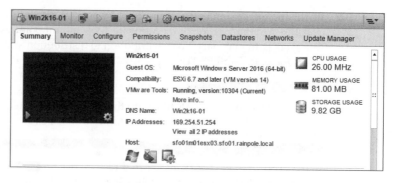

these in order to get the latest drivers. In Chapter 4, "Maintaining VMware vSphere," we discuss the use of vSphere Update Manager to assist in this process, but you can also do it manually.

For Windows-based guest OSs, the process of upgrading VMware Tools is as simple as right-clicking a VM and selecting Guest OS ➤ Upgrade VMware Tools. Select the option labeled Automatic Tools Upgrade and click OK. vCenter Server will install the updated VMware Tools and automatically reboot the VM, if necessary.

For other guest OSs, upgrading VMware Tools typically means running through the install process again, or running through an update in the Linux package manager. For more information, refer to the instructions for installing VMware Tools on SLES and Ubuntu.

Creating VMs is just one aspect of managing VMs. In the next sections, we look at some additional VM management tasks.

Managing Virtual Machines

In addition to creating VMs, vSphere administrators must perform a range of other tasks. Although most of these tasks are relatively easy to figure out, we include them here for completeness.

Adding or Registering Existing VMs

Creating VMs from scratch, as described earlier, is only one way of getting VMs into the environment. It's entirely possible that you, as a vSphere administrator, might receive pre-created VMs from another source. Suppose you receive the files that compose a VM—notably, the VMX and VMDK files—from another administrator and you need to put that VM to use in your environment. You've already seen how to use the vSphere Web Client–based file browser to upload files into a datastore, but what needs to happen once it's in the datastore? In this case, you need to register the VM. The process of registering the VM adds it to the vCenter Server (or ESXi host) inventory and allows you to then manage the VM.

Perform the following steps to add (or register) an existing VM into the inventory:

1. Use the vSphere Web Client to connect to a vCenter Server instance or use the vSphere Host Client to connect to an individual ESXi host.

2. A VM can be registered from a number of different views within the vSphere Web Client. The Storage inventory view, though, is probably the most logical place to do it. Navigate to the Storage inventory view by using the menu bar or the navigation bar.

3. Right-click the datastore containing the VM you want to register. From the context menu, select Register VM as shown in Figure 9.24.

4. Use the file browser to navigate to the folder where the VMX file for the VM resides. Select the correct VMX file and click OK.

FIGURE 9.24
You invoke the Register
Virtual Machine
Wizard by right-click-
ing the datastore and
selecting Register VM.

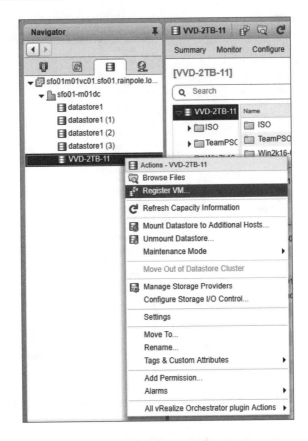

5. The Register Virtual Machine Wizard prepopulates the name of the VM. It does this by reading the contents of the VMX file. Accept the name or type a new one; then select a logical location within the inventory and click Next.

6. Choose the cluster on which you'd like to run this VM and click Next.

7. If you selected a cluster for which VMware DRS is not enabled or is set to Manual, you must also select the specific host on which the VM will run. Choose a specific host and click Next.

8. Review the settings. If everything is correct, click Finish; otherwise, use the hyperlinks on the left side of the wizard or the Back button to go back and make any necessary changes.

When the Register Virtual Machine Wizard is finished, the VM will be added to the vSphere Web Client inventory. From here, you're ready to manipulate the VM in whatever fashion you need, such as powering it on.

Changing VM Power States

There are six different commands involved in changing the runlevel and power state of a VM. Figure 9.25 shows these six commands on the context menu displayed when you right-click a VM and select Power.

FIGURE 9.25

The Power submenu allows you to power on, power off, suspend, or reset a VM as well as interact with the guest OS if VMware Tools is installed.

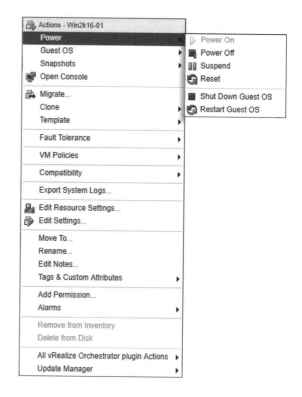

By and large, these commands are self-explanatory, but there are a few subtle differences in some of them:

Power On and Power Off These function exactly as their names suggest. They are equivalent to toggling the virtual power button on the VM without any interaction with the guest O' (if one is installed).

BE CAREFUL WITH POWER OFF

Although the behavior of the Power Off option can be configured in the Virtual Machine Properties dialog box—see the VM Options tab under the settings for each virtual machine—testing showed that the default value of Power Off (which is Shut Down Guest) still did not behave in the same manner as the actual Shut Down Guest command. Instead, the Power Off command simply turned off power and did not invoke an orderly shutdown of the guest OS.

Suspend This command suspends the VM. When you resume the VM, it will start back right where it was when you suspended it.

Reset This command will reset the VM, which is not the same as rebooting the guest OS. This is the virtual equivalent of pressing the Reset button on the front of the computer.

Shut Down Guest OS This command works only if VMware Tools is installed, and it works through VMware Tools to invoke an orderly shutdown of the guest OS. To avoid file system or data corruption in the guest OS instance, you should use this command whenever possible.

Restart Guest OS Like the Shut Down Guest command, this command requires VMware Tools and initiates a reboot of the guest OS in a graceful fashion.

Removing VMs

If you have a VM that you need to keep but that doesn't have to be listed in the VM inventory, you can remove the VM from the inventory. This keeps the VM files intact, and the VM can be re-added to the inventory (that is, registered) at any time later on using the procedure described earlier in this chapter, in the section "Adding or Registering Existing VMs."

To remove a VM, right-click a powered-off VM and, from the context menu, select Remove From Inventory. Select Yes in the Confirm Remove dialog box, and the VM will be removed from the inventory. You can use the vSphere Web Client file browser to verify that the files for the VM are still intact in the same location on the datastore.

REMOVING A VM FROM THE INVENTORY

Removing a VM from the inventory means it's out of sight and out of mind. If the intent is to preserve the data for later use, make sure the datastore or VM is backed up or has an array-based backup because the datastore will appear empty from a VM inventory perspective. This could lead to a premature or unintended deletion of the underlying LUN or datastore, thereby also deleting the stateful VM data.

Deleting VMs

If you have a VM that you no longer need at all—meaning you don't need it listed in the inventory and you don't need the files maintained on the datastore—you can completely remove the VM. Be careful, though; this is not something that you can undo!

To delete a VM entirely, right-click a powered-off VM and select Delete from Disk from the context menu. The vSphere Web Client will prompt you for confirmation, reminding you that you are deleting the VM and its associated base disks (VMDK files). Click Yes to continue removing the files from both inventory and the datastore. Once the process is done, you can once again use the vSphere Web Client file browser to verify that the VM's files are gone.

Adding existing VMs, removing VMs from inventory, and deleting VMs are all relatively simple tasks. The task of modifying VMs, though, is significant enough to warrant its own section.

Modifying Virtual Machines

Just as physical machines require hardware upgrades or changes, a VM might require virtual hardware upgrades or changes to meet changing performance demands. Perhaps a new memory-intensive client-server application requires an increase in memory, or a new data-mining application requires a second processor or additional network adapters for bandwidth-heavy FTP traffic. In each of these cases, the VM requires a modification of the virtual hardware configured for the guest OS to use. Of course, this is only one task that an administrator charged with managing VM could be responsible for completing. Other tasks might include leveraging vSphere's snapshot functionality to protect against a potential issue with the guest OS inside a VM. We describe both of these tasks in the following sections, starting with how to change the hardware of a VM.

Changing Virtual Machine Hardware

In most cases, modifying a VM requires that the VM be powered off. There are exceptions to this rule, as shown in Figure 9.26. You can hot-add a USB controller, a SATA controller, an Ethernet adapter, a hard disk, or a SCSI device. Later in this chapter, you'll see that some guest OSs also support the addition (and subtraction) of virtual CPUs or RAM while they are powered on as well. Not all guest OS versions will see the new hardware configuration right away—you may need to reboot for the changes to take effect.

FIGURE 9.26
Users can add some types of hardware while the VM is powered on. If virtual hardware cannot be added while the VM is powered on, the operation will fail.

When you're adding new virtual hardware to a VM using the vSphere Web Client, the options are similar to those used while creating a VM. For example, to add a new virtual hard disk to an existing VM, you would use the New Device drop-down box at the bottom of the Virtual Machine Edit Settings dialog box. In Figure 9.26, you see that you can add a virtual hard disk to a VM while it is powered on. From there, the vSphere Web Client uses the same steps shown earlier in this chapter in Figure 9.11, Figure 9.12, and Figure 9.13. The only difference is that now you're adding a new virtual hard disk to an existing VM. As an example, we'll go through the steps to add an Ethernet adapter to a VM (the steps are the same regardless of whether the VM is actually running).

Perform these steps to add an Ethernet adapter to a VM:

1. Launch the vSphere Web Client and connect to a vCenter Server instance or use the vSphere Host Client to connect to an individual ESXi host.

2. If you aren't already in an inventory view that displays VMs, switch to the Inventory Trees or VMs And Templates view using the Home Inventories menu.

3. Right-click the VM to which you want to add the Ethernet adapter, and select Edit Settings.

4. Select the New Device drop-down box at the bottom of the screen and select Network. Click the Add button next to the New Device drop-down box to add the Ethernet adapter to the virtual machine.

5. Expand the New Network option to gain access to additional properties.

6. Select the network adapter type, the network to which it should be connected, and whether the network adapter should be connected at power-on, as shown in Figure 9.27.

7. Review the settings and click OK.

Besides adding new virtual hardware, users can make other changes while a VM is powered on. For example, you can mount and unmount CD/DVD drives, ISO images, and floppy disk images while a VM is turned on. We described the process for mounting an ISO image as a virtual CD/DVD drive earlier in this chapter, in the section "Installing a Guest Operating System." You can also assign and reassign adapters to virtual networks while a VM is running. All of these tasks are performed in the VM Properties dialog box, which you access by selecting Edit Settings from the context menu for a VM.

DOES ANYONE STILL USE FLOPPY DRIVES?

New VMs created in a vSphere environment automatically come with a floppy drive, although in our experience it is rarely used. In fact, about the only time that it does get used is when a custom storage driver needs to be added during installation of a Windows-based guest OS. Unless you know you will need to use a floppy drive, it's generally safe to remove it from the hardware list.

If you are running Windows Server 2008 or above, or any modern Linux distribution, you also gain the ability to add virtual CPUs or RAM to a VM while it is running. To use this functionality,

FIGURE 9.27

To add a new network adapter, you must select the adapter type, the network, and whether it should be connected at power-on.

you must first enable it. In a somewhat ironic twist, the VM for which you want to enable hot-add must be powered off.

To enable hot-add of virtual CPUs or RAM, perform these steps:

1. Launch the vSphere Web Client, if it is not already running, and connect to a vCenter Server instance.

2. Navigate to either the Inventory Trees or VMs And Templates inventory view.

3. If the VM for which you want to enable hot-add is currently running, right-click the VM and select Power ➤ Shut Down Guest. The VM must be shut down in order to enable hot-add functionality.

4. Right-click the VM and select Edit Settings.

5. On the Virtual Hardware tab, select CPU to expand the available options. Select the Enable CPU Hot Add check box in the CPU Hot Plug option.

6. To enable memory hot-add, select Memory to expand the available options. Select the Enable check box in the Memory Hot Plug option to enable hot-plug memory.

7. Click OK to save the changes to the VM.

Once this setting has been configured, you can add RAM or virtual CPUs to the VM when it is powered on. Figure 9.28 shows a powered-on VM that has memory hot-add enabled. Figure 9.29 shows a powered-on VM that has CPU hot-plug enabled; you can change the number of virtual CPU sockets, but you can't change the number of cores per virtual CPU socket.

FIGURE 9.28
The ability to add memory to a VM that is already powered on is restricted to VMs with memory hot-add enabled.

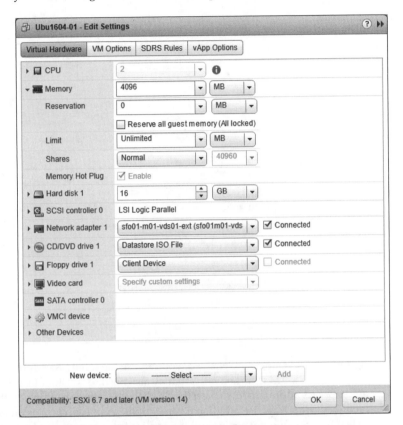

POWERING OFF THE VM VS. SHUTTING DOWN THE GUEST

Recall from earlier in this chapter that the context menu of a VM contains two items that appear to perform the same function:

◆ The Power ➤ Power Off command does exactly that: it powers off the VM. It's like pulling out the power cord unexpectedly. The guest OS has no time to prepare for a shutdown.

◆ The Power ➤ Shut Down Guest OS command issues a shutdown command to the guest OS so that the guest OS can shut down in an orderly fashion. This command requires that VMware Tools be already installed, and it ensures that the guest OS won't be corrupted or damaged by an unexpected shutdown.

In day-to-day operation, use the Shut Down Guest OS option. Use the Power Off option only when doing so is absolutely necessary.

FIGURE 9.29
With CPU hot-plug enabled, more virtual CPU sockets can be configured, but the number of cores per CPU cannot be altered.

Once these features are enabled, you can use the same procedure to add hardware as you would when a VM is turned off. You may also need to consider (and test) that just because the OS supports adding hardware on the fly, the applications running on the OS may not. That is, you may not always see additional benefit if the application maps out the potential resources when first run, but not again until the application is stopped and restarted.

Aside from the changes described so far, configuration changes to a VM can take place only when the VM is in a powered-off state. When a VM is powered off, all of the various configuration options are available to change: RAM, virtual CPUs, or adding or removing other hardware components such as CD/DVD drives or floppy drives.

ALIGNING VIRTUAL MACHINE FILE SYSTEMS

In Chapter 6, we introduced the concept of aligning VMFS, and we suggested that the VM's file system should also be aligned. If you construct VMs with separate virtual hard drives for the operating system and data, then you are most concerned with the alignment of the file system for the data drive because the greatest amount of I/O occurs on that drive. For example, a VM with Disk 0 (that holds the operating system) and a blank disk called Disk 1 (that holds data that will incur significant I/O) should have Disk 1 aligned. The need to align the guest file system applies to older distributions of Linux and older versions of Windows. For example, Windows 7, Windows Server 2008, and later align themselves properly during installation, but earlier versions do not.

Perform the following steps to align Disk 1 of a VM running a version of Windows earlier than Windows Server 2008:

1. Log into the VM using an account with administrative credentials.

2. Open a command prompt, and type **Diskpart**.

3. Type **list disk**, and press Enter.

4. Type **select disk 1**, and press Enter.

5. Type **create partition primary align = 64**, and press Enter.

6. Type **assign letter =X**, where X is an open letter that can be assigned.

7. Type **list part** to verify the 64 KB offset for the new partition.

8. Format the partition.

This may seem like a tedious task to perform for all your VMs. It *is* a tedious task; however, you realize the benefits when you have a significant I/O requirement. One way to get around this issue is to use templates that have already had their disks aligned. You can read more about templates in Chapter 10. In the end, the storage array will have more IOPS available because the overall demand from each virtual machine is lower. Finally, also note that this is not necessary for virtual machines on VSAN or using in-guest iSCSI.

As you can see, running your operating system in a VM offers advantages when it comes time to reconfigure hardware, even enabling such innovative features as CPU hot-plug. There are other advantages to using VMs too; one of these advantages is a vSphere feature called snapshots.

Using Virtual Machine Snapshots

VM snapshots allow administrators to create point-in-time checkpoints of a VM. The snapshot captures the state of the VM at a specific point in time. VMware administrators can then revert to their pre-snapshot state in the event the changes made since the snapshot should be discarded. Or, if the changes should be preserved, the administrator can commit the changes and delete the snapshot.

This functionality can be used in a variety of ways. Suppose you'd like to install the latest vendor-supplied patch for the guest OS instance running in a VM but you want to be able to recover in case the patch installation runs amok. By taking a snapshot *before* installing the patch, you can revert to the snapshot in the event the patch installation doesn't go well. You've just created a safety net for yourself. Keep in mind that snapshots do not affect RDM virtual hard disks or in-guest mounted iSCSI or NFS file systems. Also remember snapshots are made on a per-VM basis. If you have an application with multiple tiers and that is spread between multiple virtual machines, you may encounter application inconsistencies when reverting snapshots.

OTHER FEATURES THAT LEVERAGE SNAPSHOTS

Snapshots are leveraged by vSphere Update Manager and are also used by various VM backup frameworks.

Earlier versions of vSphere did not allow Storage vMotions to occur when a snapshot was present, but this limitation was removed in vSphere 5.

Perform the following steps to create a snapshot of a VM:

1. Use the vSphere Web Client to connect to a vCenter Server instance or use the vSphere Host Client to connect to an individual ESXi host.

2. Navigate to either the Inventory Trees or VMs And Templates inventory view.

3. Right-click the VM in the inventory tree and select Snapshots ➤ Take Snapshot.

4. Provide a name and description for the snapshot, as shown in Figure 9.30, and then click OK.

FIGURE 9.30
Providing names and descriptions for snapshots is an easy way to manage multiple historical snapshots.

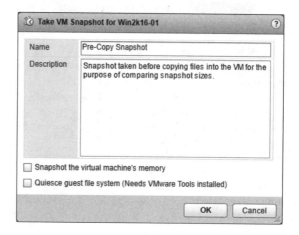

As shown in Figure 9.30, there are two options when taking snapshots:

♦ The option Snapshot The Virtual Machine's Memory specifies whether the RAM of the VM should also be included in the snapshot. When this option is selected, the current contents of the VM's RAM are written to a file ending in a `.vmsn` filename extension.

♦ The option Quiesce Guest File System (Needs VMware Tools Installed) controls whether the guest file system will be quiesced—or quieted—so that it is considered consistent. A special command is sent to the OS to flush all buffers and commit them to disk instead of holding them in memory. This can help ensure that the OS and application data within the guest file system is intact in the snapshot.

When a snapshot is taken, depending on the previous options, some additional files are created on the datastore, as shown in Figure 9.31.

It is a common misconception for administrators to think of snapshots as full copies of VM files. As you can clearly see in Figure 9.31, a snapshot is not a full copy of a VM. VMware's snapshot technology consumes minimal space while still reverting to a previous snapshot by allocating only enough space to store the changes rather than making a full copy.

FIGURE 9.31

When a snapshot is taken, some additional files are created on the VM's datastore.

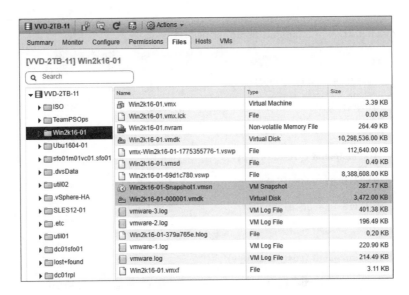

To demonstrate snapshot technology and illustrate its behavior (for practice only), we performed the following steps:

1. We created a VM with a default installation of Windows Server 2016 with a single hard drive (recognized by the guest OS as drive C:). The virtual hard drive was thin provisioned on a VMFS volume with a maximum size of 40 GB.

2. We took a snapshot named FirstSnap.

3. We added approximately 3 GB of data to drive C:, represented as WIN2K16-01.vmdk.

4. We took a second snapshot named SecondSnap.

5. Once again, we added approximately 3 GB of data to drive C:, represented as WIN2K16-01.vmdk.

Review Table 9.1 for the results we recorded after each step. Note that these results were recorded as part of our example and may differ from your results if you perform a similar test.

As you can see in Table 9.1, the underlying guest OS is unaware of the presence of the snapshot and the extra VMDK files that are created. ESXi, however, knows to write changes to the VM's virtual disk to the snapshot VMDK, properly known as a *delta disk* (or a *differencing disk*). These delta disks start small and over time grow to accommodate the changes stored within them.

Despite the storage efficiency that snapshots attempt to maintain, over time they can eat up a considerable amount of disk space. Therefore, use them as needed, but be sure to remove older snapshots on a regular basis. Also be aware that there are performance ramifications to using snapshots. Because disk space must be allocated to the delta disks on demand, ESXi hosts must update the metadata files (files with the .sf filename extension) every time the differencing disk grows. To update the metadata files, LUNs must be locked, and this might adversely affect the performance of other VMs and hosts using the same LUN. It is a generally recommended practice to reserve around 20% of capacity on your datastores for snapshots, VM swap files, and other metadata.

TABLE 9.1: Snapshot demonstration results

	VMDK SIZE	NTFS SIZE	NTFS FREE SPACE
Start (pre-first snapshot)			
WIN2K16-01.vmdk (C:)	8.6 GB	40 GB	31 GB
First snapshot (pre-data copy)			
WIN2K16-01.vmdk (C:)	10.3 GB	40 GB	29.7 GB
WIN2K16-01-000001.vmdk	17.4 MB		
First snapshot (post-data copy)			
WIN2K16-01.vmdk (C:)	10.3 GB	40 GB	26.5 GB
WIN2K16-01-000001.vmdk	3.1 GB		
Second snapshot (pre-data copy)			
WIN2K16-01.vmdk (C:)	10.3 GB	40 GB	26.5 GB
WIN2K16-01-000001.vmdk	3.1 GB		
WIN2K16-01-000002.vmdk	17.4 MB		
Second snapshot (post-data copy)			
WIN2K16-01.vmdk (C:)	10.3 GB	40 GB	23.3 GB
WIN2K16-01-000001.vmdk	3.1 GB		
WIN2K16-01-000002.vmdk	3.1 GB		

To view or delete a snapshot or revert to an earlier snapshot, you use the Snapshot Manager. Follow these steps to access the Snapshot Manager:

1. Use the vSphere Web Client to connect to a vCenter Server instance or use the vSphere Host Client to connect to an individual ESXi host.

2. In the inventory tree, right-click the name of the VM, and from the context menu, select Snapshots ➤ Manage Snapshots.

3. Select the appropriate snapshot to fall back to, as shown in Figure 9.32, and then click the Revert To button.

FIGURE 9.32

The Snapshot Manager can revert to a previous snapshot, but all data written since that snapshot was taken and that hasn't been backed up elsewhere will be lost.

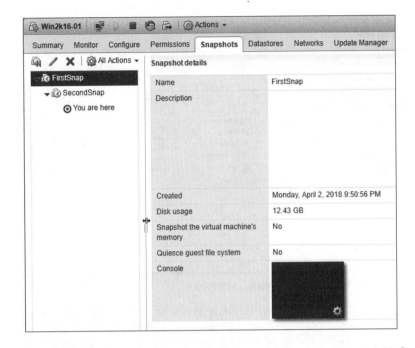

To further illustrate the nature of snapshots, see Figure 9.33 and Figure 9.34. Figure 9.33 shows the file system of a VM running Windows Server 2016 after data has been written into two new folders named temp1 and temp2. Figure 9.34 shows the same VM but after reverting to a snapshot taken before that data was written. As you can see, it's as if the new folders never even existed. Test this out for yourself to see what kind of damage you can do, and undo (using a test VM of course).

FIGURE 9.33

This VM running Windows Server 2012 has had some data placed into two temporary folders.

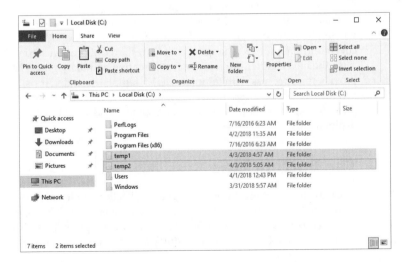

FIGURE 9.34

The same VM, after reverting to a snapshot taken before the temporary folders were created, no longer has any record of the data.

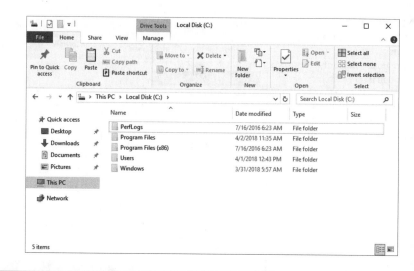

REVERTING TO A SNAPSHOT

Reverting to a snapshot incurs a loss of data. Any data that was written since the snapshot has occurred will no longer be available, along with any applications that were installed since the snapshot was taken. Therefore, revert to snapshots only if you have determined that the loss of data is acceptable or if the data is backed up elsewhere.

As you can see, snapshots are a great way to protect yourself from unwanted changes to the *data* stored in a VM. Snapshots aren't backups and should not be used in place of backups. However, they can protect you from misbehaving application installations or other processes that might result in data loss or corruption.

There are additional VM management tasks that we'll discuss in other chapters. For example, you might want to migrate a VM from one ESXi host to another ESXi host using vMotion; this is covered in Chapter 12. Changing a VM's resource allocation settings is covered in Chapter 11.

In the next chapter, we'll move from creating and managing VMs to streamlining the VM provisioning process with templates, OVF templates, and vApps. Although VMware makes the VM provisioning process pretty easy, we'll show you how using templates can simplify server provisioning even more while bringing some consistency to your VM and guest OS deployments.

The Bottom Line

Create a virtual machine.   A VM is a collection of virtual hardware pieces, like a physical system—one or more virtual CPUs, RAM, video card, SCSI devices, IDE devices, floppy drives, parallel and serial ports, and network adapters. This virtual hardware is virtualized and abstracted from the underlying physical hardware, providing portability to the VM.

Master It   Create two VMs, one intended to run Windows Server 2012 and a second intended to run SLES 11 (64-bit). Make a list of the differences in the configuration that are suggested by the Create New Virtual Machine Wizard.

Install a guest operating system.   Just as a physical machine needs an operating system, a VM also needs an operating system. vSphere supports a broad range of 32-bit and 64-bit operating systems, including all major versions of Windows Server, Windows 10, Windows 7, XP, and Windows 2000 as well as various flavors of Linux, macOS, FreeBSD, Novell NetWare, and Solaris.

Master It   What are the three ways in which a guest OS can access data on a CD/DVD, and what are the advantages of each approach?

Install VMware Tools.   For maximum performance of the guest OS, it needs to have virtualization-optimized drivers that are specially written for and designed to work with the ESXi hypervisor. VMware Tools provides these optimized drivers as well as other utilities focused on better operation in virtual environments.

Master It   A fellow administrator contacts you and is having a problem installing VMware Tools. This administrator has selected the Install/Upgrade VMware Tools command, but nothing seems to be happening inside the VM. What could be the cause of the problem?

Manage virtual machines.   Once a VM has been created, the vSphere Client makes it easy to manage. Virtual floppy images and CD/DVD drives can be mounted or unmounted as necessary. vSphere provides support for initiating an orderly shutdown of the guest OS in a VM, although this requires that VMware Tools be installed. VM snapshots allow you to take a point-in-time "picture" of a VM so that administrators can roll back changes if needed.

Master It   What is the difference between the Shut Down Guest command and the Power Off command?

Modify virtual machines.   vSphere offers a number of features to make it easy to modify VMs after they have been created. Administrators can hot-add certain types of hardware, like virtual hard disks and network adapters, and some guest OSs also support hot-adding virtual CPUs or memory, although this feature must be enabled first.

Master It   Which method is preferred for modifying the configuration of a VM: editing the VMX file or using the vSphere Client?

Master It   Name the types of hardware that cannot be added while a VM is running.

Chapter 10

Using Templates and vApps

Creating VMs manually and installing guest operating systems (guest OSs) into those VMs is fine on a small scale, but what if you need to deploy lots of VMs? What if you need to ensure that your VMs are consistent and standardized? Through vCenter Server, VMware vSphere offers a solution: VM cloning and templates. In this chapter, we'll show you how to use cloning, templates, and vApps to help streamline the deployment of VMs in your environment.

IN THIS CHAPTER, YOU WILL LEARN TO

- ◆ Clone VMs

- ◆ Create a VM template

- ◆ Deploy new VMs from a template

- ◆ Deploy a VM from an Open Virtualization Format (OVF) template

- ◆ Export a VM as an OVF template

- ◆ Organize templates and media

- ◆ Work with vApps

Cloning VMs

If you've ever wished for a faster way to provision a new server into your environment, you'll be glad to know VMware vSphere fulfills that wish in a big way. When you are using vCenter Server in your environment, you have the ability to clone a VM—that is, you can make a copy of the VM, including the VM's virtual disks. How does this help provision new VMs faster? Think about it: what takes the most time when creating a new VM? It's not creating the VM itself, because that takes only minutes. It's installing the guest OS—whether it is Windows Server, Linux, or some other supported guest OS—that takes up the bulk of the time needed to create a new VM. Once the OS is installed, it can also take a significant amount of time to configure settings and install applications. Using vCenter Server to clone a VM—which means also cloning the VM's virtual disks—keeps you from having to install the guest OS into the cloned VM. By cloning VMs, you eliminate the need to perform a guest OS installation into every new VM. At a bare minimum after the OS installation, VMware Tools should be installed on all VMs, especially those that are destined to become templates.

THE FIRST GUEST OS INSTALLATION IS STILL NEEDED

We mentioned in the previous paragraph that cloning a VM eliminates the need to perform a guest OS installation into every new VM. That's true—assuming you actually installed the guest OS into the VM that you're cloning. As you consider using VM cloning to help provision new VMs, recognize that you still need to install the guest OS into your source VM. Some things just can't be eliminated!

As you may have already guessed, when cloning VMs, there's a potential problem. If you are making a clone of a guest OS installation, that means you'll now have two VMs with the same IP address, same computer name, same MAC address, and so forth. Not to worry, though: VMware built the ability to customize the guest OS installation into the cloned VM so that you preserve the guest OS installation but create a new identity in the cloned VM. For Linux-based guest OSs, VMware leverages open source tools to customize the installation; for Windows-based guest OSs vCenter Server will leverage Microsoft's well-known Sysprep tool. Using the vCenter, you can create any number of customization specifications to tailor your cloned VMs and give them individual personalities. What exactly is a customization specification? Let's dive in and take a look.

Creating a Customization Specification

vCenter Server's customization specification works hand in hand with the tools for customizing VM clones (Sysprep for VMs with a Windows-based guest OS; open source tools for a VM with a Linux-based guest OS). As you'll see later in the chapter, in the section "Cloning a Virtual Machine," you have to provide vCenter Server with the information necessary to give the cloned VM its own unique identity. This includes the IP address, passwords, computer name, and licensing information. With customization specification, you provide all the information only once and then apply it as needed when cloning a VM.

OUTDATED WINDOWS CUSTOMIZATIONS NOT AVAILABLE

Prior to vSphere 6.7, vCenter was capable of customizing VMs using Sysprep for nearly every version of Windows, dating all the way back to Windows 2000. The process required manually uploading the different OS-specific versions of Sysprep to the vCenter Server. With the release of vSphere 6.7, only Windows Vista or later and Windows Server 2008 or later OSs are supported for customization. These versions of Windows have Sysprep built in; therefore, uploading the Sysprep files to the vCenter server is not required.

You can still manually build and clone VMs using earlier Windows OSs, but you won't be able to customize the OS using a customization specification.

You can create a customization specification in the following two ways:

◆ By creating it during the process of cloning a VM

◆ By using the Customization Specification Manager in vCenter Server

We'll show you how to create a customization specification while cloning a VM in the section "Cloning a Virtual Machine." For now, let's look at how to use the Customization Specification Manager.

To access the Customization Specification Manager, from the vSphere Web Client Home screen, select Customization Specification Manager, as shown in Figure 10.1. You can also access it from selecting Policies And Profiles from the Home drop-down menu anywhere within the vCenter Web Client.

FIGURE 10.1

The Customization Specification Manager is readily accessible from the home page of the vSphere Web Client in the Management tab.

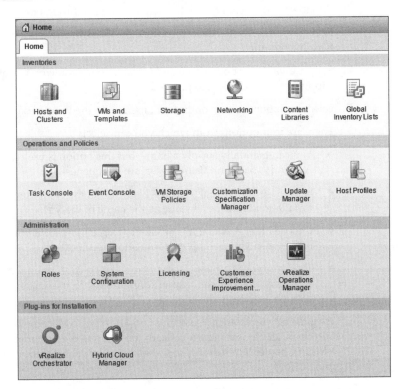

Once you're in the Customization Specification Manager area of vCenter Server, you can create a new customization specification or edit an existing customization specification. The process is almost identical, and in both cases it involves the New VM Guest Customization Wizard. VM Guest Customizations can be created for both Windows and Linux, but Linux customizations are limited to VM name, Time Zone, and Network settings.

As an example, perform the following steps to create a new customization specification for Windows:

1. If the vSphere Web Client isn't already running, launch it and connect to a vCenter Server instance. (This functionality is available only when connecting to vSphere Web Client, not the vSphere Host Client.)

2. Navigate to the Customization Specification Manager by selecting Home ➢ Customization Specification Manager.

Alternatively, you can also find the Customization Specification Manager by selecting Policies And Profiles from the Home drop-down menu anywhere within the vSphere Web Client.

3. Click the first icon to create a new customization specification. This opens the vSphere Web Client Guest Customization Wizard.

4. From the Target Virtual Machine OS drop-down box, select either Windows or Linux. Windows is the default, which is what we'll step through here.

5. Provide a name for the customization specification and, optionally, a description. Click Next to continue.

6. Supply a value for both Name and Organization (you won't be able to proceed until you supply both). Click Next to proceed.

7. Select an option for the computer name within the Windows guest OS installation.

There are four options from which you can select:

◆ You can manually supply a name, but this option is useless without also selecting Append A Numeric Value To Ensure Uniqueness.

◆ Select Use The Virtual Machine Name to set the computer name within the guest OS installation to the same value as the name of the VM.

◆ Choose Enter A Name In The Clone/Deploy Wizard if you want to be prompted for a name when you use this customization specification.

◆ The fourth option uses a custom application configured with vCenter Server. Because there is no custom application configured with this instance of vCenter Server, this option is currently disabled (grayed out).

We generally recommend selecting Use The Virtual Machine Name. This keeps the guest OS computer name matched up with the VM name, as recommended when creating new VMs in Chapter 9, "Creating and Managing Virtual Machines." Figure 10.2 shows the four options.

FIGURE 10.2
The Guest Customization Wizard offers four options for naming a cloned VM.

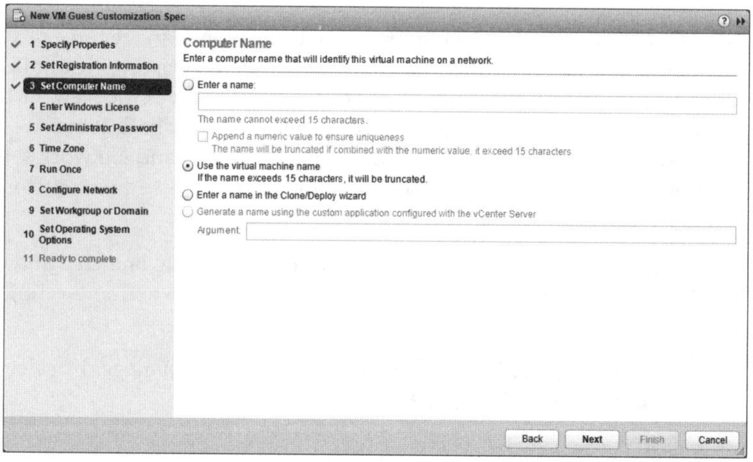

After you select the option you want to use in this customization specification, click Next.

8. Provide a Windows product key and select the appropriate server licensing mode (Per Seat or Per Server) if you are configuring a Windows Server OS. Click Next.

9. Enter the password for the local Windows Administrator account and then confirm the password.

   If you'd like to log on automatically as Administrator (perhaps to help with any automated configuration scripts), select Automatically Log On As The Administrator and specify how many times you want to log on automatically. Click Next to continue.

10. Select the correct time zone and click Next.

11. If you have any commands you want to run the first time a user logs on, supply those commands at the Run Once screen of the vSphere Web Client Windows Guest Customization Wizard. Click Next if you have no commands to run or when you have finished entering commands to run.

12. Choose the settings you'd like to apply to the network configuration:

    ◆ If you want to use DHCP to assign an IP address to the VM's network interfaces, select Typical Settings.

    ◆ If you want to assign a static IP address to any of the network interfaces, you'll need to select Custom Settings, and the wizard will prompt you to input that information.

    Some administrators don't want to use DHCP but still want to ensure that each VM has a unique IP address. To see how this can be done in the customization specification, select Manually Select Custom Settings as shown in Figure 10.3

FIGURE 10.3
Click the pencil icon to customize the network interface settings.

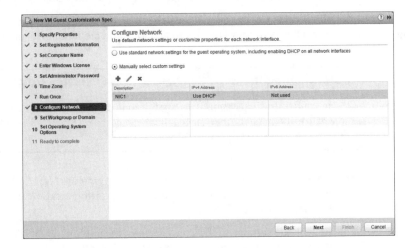

13. On the Configure Network screen, click the small pencil above the description field of the NIC1 line. This will open the Edit Network dialog box shown in Figure 10.4.

FIGURE 10.4

The Edit Network dialog box has an option to prompt the user for an address.

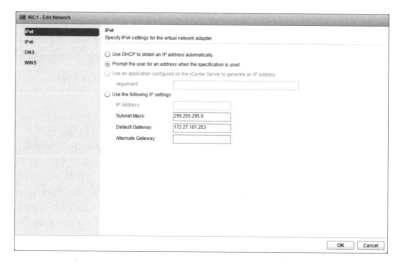

To assign a static IP address to cloned VMs without having to modify the customization specification every time, you must choose Prompt The User For An Address When The Specification Is Used. When you select this option, vCenter Server will prompt the user to supply a unique static IP address every time the specification is used when cloning a VM.

14. Select Prompt The User For An Address When The Specification Is Used. You must then supply a subnet mask, default gateway, and preferred and alternate DNS servers. Fill in these values, click OK, and then click Next.

15. Select whether you want the Windows-based guest OS to join a workgroup or a domain.

If the guest OS should join a workgroup, supply the workgroup name. If the guest should join a domain, supply the domain name and credentials to join the domain. Click Next.

JOINING DOMAINS WITH CUSTOMIZATION SPECIFICATIONS

When configuring a customization specification to join a VM to a Windows domain, you must adhere to a number of formatting requirements. VMware KB 1012314 outlines the requirements at `http://kb.vmware.com/kb/1012314`.

---

16. Generally speaking, you will want to leave Generate New Security ID (SID) selected. This is used to ensure you don't run into strange authentication and identification issues with the cloned VM. Click Next.

17. Review the settings in the final screen of the vSphere Web Client Windows Guest Customization Wizard to ensure that you have the right values supplied.

If you need to change anything, use the hyperlinks on the left or the Back button to go back and change the values. Otherwise, click Finish to complete the creation of the customization specification.

Because a customization specification for Windows usually contains product keys, you'll probably need to create multiple specifications for different versions or editions of Windows. Repeat the previous steps to create additional specifications.

IMPORTING, EXPORTING, AND CLONING SPECIFICATIONS

A customer migrating to a new vSphere environment didn't wish to set up their large number of customization specifications from scratch. We used vSphere's ability to export, import, and clone to save all the additional effort.

The Customization Specification Manager gives you options for importing from a file, exporting to a file, and cloning the selected specification. Although you can transfer specifications between environments using these tools, you will lose some of the saved sensitive information such as product keys. You can add this information back to the specification after importing it.

Now that you have a customization specification in place, all you need is a source VM with a guest OS installed and you're ready to clone and customize a VM.

CUSTOMIZATION SPECIFICATIONS AREN'T REQUIRED

You aren't required to create customization specifications. However, you will be required to supply the information found in a customization specification when you clone a VM. Because you have to enter the information anyway, why not do it only once by creating a customization specification?

Cloning a Virtual Machine

If you've performed all the steps in the previous two sections, then cloning a VM is actually simple.

Perform the following steps to clone a VM:

1. If the vSphere Web Client isn't already running, launch it and connect to an instance of vCenter Server. Cloning isn't possible when connecting directly to an ESXi host.

2. Navigate to either the Hosts And Clusters or VMs And Templates inventory tree.

3. Right-click a VM and select Clone, Clone to Virtual Machine. This opens the Clone Existing Virtual Machine Wizard.

4. Supply a name for the VM and select a logical inventory location for the VM. Click Next.

5. Select the host or cluster on which the VM will run. Click Next.

6. If you selected a cluster for which DRS is not enabled or that is configured in Manual mode, you must select the specific host on which you want to run the VM. Click Next.

7. If prompted, select the resource pool in which the VM should be placed. Click Next.

8. Select the desired virtual disk format and select a target datastore or datastore cluster. Use the Advanced button if you want to place the VM's configuration files in a different location from the virtual hard disks. Click Next to continue.

9. At this point, the Clone Existing Virtual Machine Wizard is prompting you for guest customization options, as shown in Figure 10.5.

FIGURE 10.5
The Clone Existing Virtual Machine Wizard offers several options for customizing the guest OS.

If you want to use a customization specification that you already created, you would select Customize The Operating System. In this case, let's see how to create a specification while cloning the VM, so select Customize The Operating System and click Next.

10. Click the Create a Specification icon and the Guest Customization Spec Wizard opens.

This is the same wizard you used to create the customization specification in the earlier section "Creating a Customization Specification." Refer back to that section for the specific details to use as we walk through the sections of this wizard.

At the end of the Guest Customization Spec, shown in Figure 10.6, the specification is saved for later use.

You've now seen both ways to create a customization specification within the vSphere Web Client. Click Finish to complete the guest customization process and return to the Clone Existing Virtual Machine Wizard.

11. Select the newly created specification and then click Next.

12. Review the settings for cloning the VM. If any of the settings are incorrect, use the Back button or the links on the left to go back to the appropriate section and make any desired changes. Otherwise, click Finish to start the VM cloning process.

When the VM cloning process kicks off, the vSphere Web Client will show a new active task in the Recent Tasks area, as shown in Figure 10.7. Here, you can monitor the progress of the cloning operation.

FIGURE 10.6
Your guest OS customizations as a specification are saved for later use, even if created in the middle of the VM cloning wizard.

FIGURE 10.7
The cloning task in the vSphere Web Client provides feedback on the current status of the VM cloning operation.

Once the cloning is complete, you can power on the VM. Note that the guest OS customization won't begin until you power on the VM. After you power on the VM and the guest OS loads, the vSphere Web Client will kick in and start the guest customization process. Depending on the guest OS, it may take at least one reboot before the customization process is complete. Ensure you give the VM some time to finish the process before logging in—if you interrupt the process, it may result in an incomplete build.

CLONING RUNNING VMs

It's possible to clone even powered-on VMs! The context menu of a VM provides a Clone option that allows you to make a copy of the VM. The Clone To New Virtual Machine option from the Commands list on a VM summary page accomplishes the same task. These commands are available for VMs that are powered off as well as VMs that are powered on. Keep in mind that unless you customize the guest OS, an exact copy of the original VM will be made. This could be especially useful when you're looking to create a test environment that mirrors a live production environment to simulate an upgrade or change.

As you can see, cloning VMs—which may take only a few minutes, depending on the size of the VM and the speed of your infrastructure—is a much faster way of deploying new VMs than manually creating the VM and installing the guest OS. What if you needed to create tens or even hundreds of VMs in a matter of minutes? vSphere has a behind-the-scenes way of doing just that.

Introducing vSphere Instant Cloning

Creating a clone of a VM in a matter of minutes can be very helpful, but if you want to create a large number of identical VMs, the cloning process can take hours. Let's say your job involves administering a pool of virtual desktops in a virtual desktop infrastructure (VDI) farm, or maybe you are spinning up a large number of VMs for developers to work on an exact replica of the main production environment. VMware has enhanced the traditional cloning capabilities to increase the speed and reduce the resource overhead when there's a need to create multiple versions of a source VM at the same time.

It's easy to derive from its name that instant cloning is fast, but just how fast is it? That depends on a few things, such as the ESXi host speed, utilization, and the size of the source VM, but usually it is somewhere between one and a few seconds. Not only can it create VMs quickly, but it can do it in parallel too—up to eight VMs can be cloned simultaneously! So, in a best-case scenario, you could generate 100 brand new identical VMs in a 10- to 20-second time frame. Instant cloning is very, very fast.

The Instant Clone feature will create VMs that run in the exact state their source VM does by leveraging a few technologies: vMotion, Transparent Page Sharing, and delta disks. With traditional VM cloning, a complete set of the source VM's virtual hardware is created. You get a copy of the all virtual disk (.VMDK) files, a copy of the VMs configuration (.VMX) files, and even a copy of the in-guest memory (if the cloned VM is currently running). All this data copying takes time, and if you followed the examples in the previous section, you understand just how long it takes for each clone to be created. The way Instant Clone works is completely different. The result is more or less the same, in that you still get a new VM, but you don't get brand new copies of the virtual disks or in-guest memory for running VMs. Instant Clone uses a function known as copy-on-write to share both memory and disk data with the source VM, and only making a copy of the changes when the cloned VM needs to modify something. That way, it can keep a single copy of all data without needing to duplicate anything, and it can create new VMs based on the same original VM very quickly. This is very similar to the way that disk snapshots work, which you can read about in Chapter 9.

There are two different ways to instantly clone a virtual machine. The source VM can be in a powered-on and running state or it can be set to a special powered-on and "frozen" state. We'll explain the details behind the two options and why you would use one over the other.

INSTANT CLONING RUNNING VMs

Instantly cloning a powered-on VM requires no special prerequisites. Simply run the instant clone API against an existing parent VM and a new clone will be created. This may be advantageous if you need an exact copy of a VM at a point in time, but this is not always what you want if the source VM is constantly changing. To put that another way, let's say you want to create two instant clones of a source VM, but you initiate two separate clone operations 5 minutes apart. The two resulting VMs are clones of their source at the time of creation, but not necessarily clones of each other if the source VM changed within this 5-minute gap. This may or may not be a good thing, depending on what you want to use the clone for. There is also a limit of 256 instant clones that you can run off a single source VM. This limit is because of the way that the delta disks are created, which you can see in Figure 10.8. When a running VM is instantly cloned, there is a new additional delta disk created on the source VM and the cloned VM's delta disk is pointed at the new source delta disk in the disk hierarchy. You might recall that there is a limit of 256 snapshots for each VM, which is exactly the same reason there is a limit of 256 instant clones that can be created from a single powered-on VM.

FIGURE 10.8

The instant-clone process for powered-on VMs creates a new delta disk on the source VM each time a clone is created.

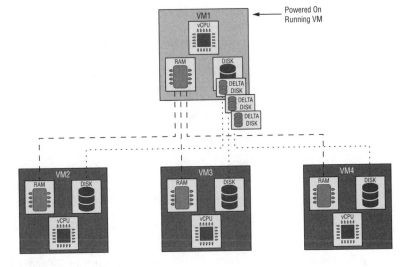

INSTANT CLONING FROZEN VMs

Instantly cloning a powered-on VM that is in a frozen state gets around the previously mentioned issues. Your resulting clone VM is the same as a clone made days or weeks later, provided the source VM has not been un-frozen between clone operations. You can effectively think of a frozen source VM as a template. This is ideal if you need a large number of identical VMs, as long as the source VM doesn't need to be available when the cloning operation takes place. Instant clones of frozen VMs are also more efficient in the way their delta disks are created, which is why there is no limit to the number of clones you can create from a frozen VM. As Figure 10.9 shows, a frozen VM only has a single delta disk no matter how many clones are created. Each clone VMs delta disk points back to the same original source VMs delta disk.

FIGURE 10.9

Frozen VMs will never have more than a single delta disk and can be cloned as many times as needed.

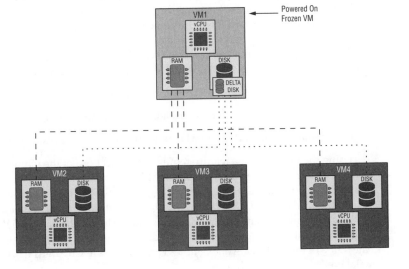

What exactly is a frozen VM? That's a good question because it's not a state that VMs have ever been in prior to the Instant Clone feature. A frozen VM is a VM that is powered on but has its CPU halted. It is no longer responding to any OS functions, hardware interrupts, network traffic, or anything else. The ability to freeze a VM requires that VMware Tools is installed in the guest OS and can only be enabled with a command from within the guest OS itself. The only way to unfreeze a frozen VM is to power off or reset the VM.

Before we run through an example of how to initiate an instant clone, let's walk through the process that's happening behind the scenes. This process happens almost instantaneously:

1. A source VM calls on the Instant Clone API.

2. The ESXi host creates a new shell, or destination VM, with the same hardware configuration as the source VM.

3. The ESXi host temporarily pauses the source VM, if it is not frozen already.

4. The *source* VM creates a delta disk, or snapshot, that points to the source VM's original (or previous delta) VMDK in the disk hierarchy.

5. The *destination* VM creates a delta disk that points to the *source* VM's latest delta disk, if it is not frozen. If it is frozen, that delta disk will point to the original `.VMDK` in the source VM's disk hierarchy. (The destination VM does not point to its own `.VMDK`.)

6. Transparent Page Sharing points the destination VM memory back to the source VM's memory.

7. The ESXi host un-pauses the source VM, if it is not frozen.

8. The destination VM is now available for use.

Any VM that has been instant-cloned is a regular VM. That means it can be protected with vSphere HA, and it can be moved around manually with vMotion or automatically with DRS. You can back it up, restore it, and use it as you would any other VM. However there is one small but important thing you will want to do with nearly every VM that is cloned: give it a custom identity. Each clone created has a brand new virtual network adapter when the shell is created, but the IP address allocated to that adapter is still the same as the source unless you change it. Also, the OS that's running on the clone will not know that the network adapter's hardware MAC address has changed. There are a few ways you could remediate this.

◆ Disable and re-enable each network adapter for Windows OS clones.

◆ Unbind and bind each network adapter for Linux OS clones.

◆ Set the destination clone VM's network adapter to be disabled within the API call.

Using the Instant Clone feature requires the direct use of the vSphere API or some extensive CLI that takes advantage of the vSphere API. There is no user interface for Instant Clone, so there is nothing to find in the vSphere Web Client, the ESXi Host Client, or even the new HTML5 client. Because Instant Clone is designed to be used as part of a bigger automated workflow, using an API makes sense. Other products like VMware Horizon and VMware on AWS will use this API for integration. While understanding this feature is important, using the API is outside the scope of this chapter. API examples can be found in Chapter 14, "Automating VMware vSphere."

NOTE   As you can probably guess, some vSphere features are not compatible with Instant Clone. You cannot use fault tolerance, encrypted VMs, raw device mappings, or pass-through devices on the VMs that you wish to clone. But aside from that, the clone VMs behave just as if you built them by hand.

Through VM cloning and instant cloning, administrators can create a library of "gold VM images," which are master copies of VMs that have certain settings and a particular guest OS installed. The only problem with this approach is that these VMs, which are intended to serve as master copies and not be changed, can still be powered on and modified. This potential short-coming is addressed through VM templates within vCenter Server. We'll show you how templates work in the next section.

Creating Templates and Deploying Virtual Machines

In a vSphere environment, what would traditionally take several hours to do is now reduced to a matter of minutes. In this chapter, you've already seen how you can quickly and easily spin up new VMs with VM cloning and customization specifications, complete with the guest OS already installed. The templates feature of vCenter Server builds on this functionality to help you roll out new VMs quickly and easily with limited administrative effort while protecting the master VMs from inadvertent changes.

Although VM templates have been around for a number of releases, vSphere 6.0 introduced a new concept, Content Libraries. Similar to some functionality found in VMware vCloud Director, these libraries store and organize not just VM templates, but also ISO images, floppy disk images, and scripts. First, we'll walk you through using templates, and then later in the chapter, we'll explain how to use Content Libraries.

YOU'LL NEED VCENTER SERVER FOR THESE FEATURES

Because templates leverage cloning to deploy new VMs, it's only possible to use templates when using vCenter Server to manage your ESXi hosts, which is why you have to use the vSphere Web Client.

---

vCenter Server offers four options for creating templates:

◆   Clone To Template

◆   Clone To Template In Library

◆   Convert To Template

◆   Export OVF Template

In all cases, you'll start with a VM that already has an instance of a guest OS installed. As the names suggests, the Clone To features copy this initial VM to a template format or another VM, leaving the original VM intact. Similarly, the Convert To Template feature takes the initial VM and changes it to template format, thereby removing the ability to perform power operations on the VM without converting back to VM format. Using either approach, once the VM is in template format, that template cannot be powered on or have its settings edited. It's now in a protected format that prevents administrators from inadvertently or unintentionally modifying the "gold image" from which other VMs are deployed.

When considering which VMs you should convert to templates, remember that the idea behind a template is to have a pristine system configuration that can be customized as needed for deployment to the target environment. Any information stored on a VM that becomes a template will become part of the new system deployed from that template. If you have VMs that are critical servers for production environments with applications installed, those are not good candidates for templates. The best VMs to use for templates are VMs with a new, clean installation of the guest OS and any other base components. At a minimum, you should always install VMware Tools.

In fact, we recommend creating a new VM specifically for use as a template or creating the template from a VM as soon after creation as possible. This ensures that the template is as pristine as possible and that all VMs cloned from that template will start out the same way.

You can convert a VM to a template using the context menu of the VM or the Convert To Template link in the Commands list. Figure 10.10 shows the ways an existing powered-on VM can be changed into a template format. Because templates cannot be modified, to make changes or perform updates to a template you must first convert the template back to a VM, then update it, and finally convert it back to a template. Note that the Convert To Template command is grayed out if the VM is currently powered on. To use the Convert To Template command, the VM must be powered off. We'll cover exporting to an OVF template in the section "Using OVF Templates," later in this chapter.

FIGURE 10.10

Users can either convert a powered off VM to a template or clone any VM to a template.

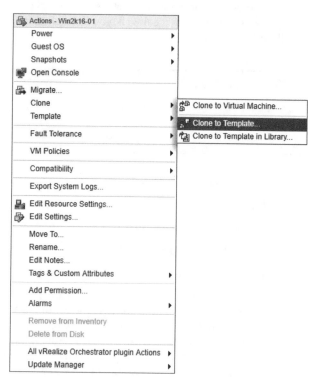

Cloning a Virtual Machine to a Template

The Clone To Template feature provides the same result as the conversion method; it creates a template you can deploy as a new VM. It differs from the conversion method in that the original VM remains intact. By leaving the original VM in a format that can be powered on, the Clone To Template feature facilitates making updates to the template. This means you don't have to store the template object definition in the same datastore from which the VM was built. Notice also that in addition to the standard Clone To Template command, another option is available: a destination Content Library. We'll explain Content Libraries as a destination later in this chapter.

Perform the following steps to clone a VM into a template format:

1. Use the vSphere Web Client to connect to a vCenter Server instance. Cloning and templates are not supported when using the vSphere Client to connect directly to an ESXi host because doing so requires vCenter.

2. Navigate to the Hosts And Clusters or VMs And Templates inventory tree.

   Either view lets you clone to a template, but you'll only be able to see the template in the VMs And Templates inventory tree.

3. Right-click the VM to be used as a template, and select Clone ➤ Clone To Template.

4. Type a name for the new template in the Template Name text box, select a logical location in the inventory to store the template, and then click Next.

5. Select the host or cluster where the template should be hosted, and click Next.

6. If you selected a cluster for which DRS is disabled or that is configured for Manual operation, you must select a specific host in the cluster. Click Next.

7. At the top of the next screen, shown in Figure 10.11, select the disk format for the template.

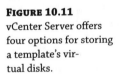

FIGURE 10.11
vCenter Server offers four options for storing a template's virtual disks.

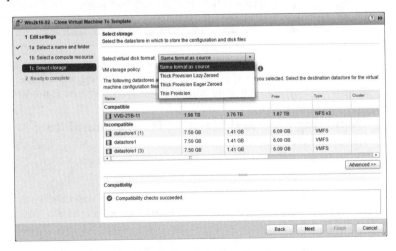

Four options are available for the template's disk format:

◆ The Same Format As Source option keeps the template's virtual disks in the same format as the VM that is being cloned.

- Thick Provision Lazy Zeroed means that the space is fully allocated when the virtual disk is created but the space is not zeroed out upon creation.

- Thick Provision Eager Zeroed allocates all space on creation and zeroes all the space out before it can be used. This format is required for use with vSphere FT and will generally take the longest time to complete. However, if the block zeroing VMware vSphere Storage APIs – Array Integration (VAAI) primitive is used, the time to complete will vary depending on the storage type. More information on VAAI and storage features can be found in Chapter 6, "Creating and Configuring Storage Devices."

- Thin Provision format commits space on demand, meaning that the virtual disks will occupy only as much space as is currently used by the guest OS. This is the default virtual disk type when creating VMs on NFS storage and should not be confused with thin provisioning performed by the storage array.

These options are the same as when performing a Storage vMotion, which is detailed in Chapter 6.

8. If you have defined any VM storage policies, choose the appropriate storage policy from the Storage Service Class drop-down list. If VM storage policies haven't been enabled or none are defined, this drop-down list is disabled (grayed out). Click Next to continue.

9. Review the template configuration information, and click Finish.

You Don't Customize Templates

You'll note that you didn't have an option to customize the template. The guest OS customization occurs when you deploy VMs from a template, not when you create the template itself. Remember that templates can't be powered on, and guest OS customization requires that the VM be powered on.

Templates have a different icon than the one used to identify a VM in the vCenter Server inventory. The template objects are available by clicking a datacenter object and then selecting the Virtual Machines tab or by adjusting the inventory tree to the VMs And Templates view.

Deploying a Virtual Machine from a Template

After you have created a library of templates, provisioning a new VM is as easy as right-clicking the template you'd like to use as the base system image.

Perform these steps to deploy a VM from a template:

1. Use the vSphere Web Client to connect to a vCenter Server instance. Cloning and templates are not supported when using the vSphere Host Client to connect directly to an ESXi host.

2. Locate the template object to be used as the VM baseline. You will find the template object in the VMs And Templates inventory tree, and it has a different icon than normal VMs.

3. Right-click the template object and select New VM From This Template. This launches the Deploy From Template Wizard.

4. Type a name for the new VM in the VM's Name text box, select a logical location in the inventory to store the VM, and then click Next.

5. Select the cluster or host on which the VM should run, and then click Next.

6. If you selected a cluster for which DRS is not enabled or that is configured to operate in Manual mode, you must select the specific host on which to run the VM. Click Next.

7. If prompted, select the resource pool in which the VM should be located and click Next.

8. Select the desired virtual disk format for the VM to be created from the template.

9. If you have defined any VM storage policies, choose the appropriate storage policy from the VM Storage Policy drop-down list, and then select the destination datastore or datastore cluster. Click the Advanced button (shown in Figure 10.12 but not selected) if you need to place VM configuration files and virtual disks in separate locations.

FIGURE 10.12
Select a datastore for a new VM based on the vMotion, DRS, HA, and other constraints of your organization.

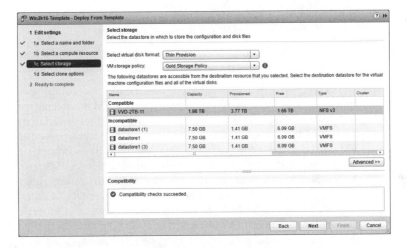

10. Select if you want to customize the guest OS (you almost certainly do) or hardware and if you want to power on the VM after it has been created. Then click Next.

11. You can use an existing customization specification by selecting Customize Using An Existing Customization Specification, or you can select Customize Using The Customization Wizard to supply the customization information interactively. We've shown you both options already. In this case, let's use the specification you created earlier, so select Customize Using An Existing Customization Specification and select the specification you created earlier. Click Next.

> **FEW EXCEPTIONS FOR CUSTOMIZING**
>
> We do not recommend you deploy from a template without customizing the VM unless you have a specific requirement to do so. This will result in a VM that has the same guest OS and network configuration as the original template. Although this might not cause any problems the first time you deploy from this template, it will almost assuredly cause problems for future deployments.
>
> The only instances in which you would choose not to customize the OS would be if you have already taken steps within the guest OS installation (such as running Sysprep in a VM with a Windows-based guest OS) before converting it to a template, or if you have ensured that deploying the template will not conflict with existing machines on the network.

12. Because the customization specification you created earlier was created with the option to prompt the user for the static IP address to be assigned to the guest OS, the Deploy From Template Wizard now prompts you for the IP address. Enter the IP address you want to assign to this VM and click Next. If the customization had been configured to use DHCP, the wizard would skip this step.

13. Review the template deployment information.

If you need to make changes, use the hyperlinks or the Back button to go back. Otherwise click Finish to start the VM deployment from the template.

vCenter Server will proceed to copy all the files that comprise the template into a new location on the selected datastore. The first time the new VM is powered on, vCenter Server will kick in and perform the customization according to the values stored in the customization specification or the values you entered in the Guest Customization Wizard. Aside from those changes, the new VM will be an exact copy of the original template. By incorporating the latest patches and updates in your templates, you can thus be sure that your cloned VMs are up to date and consistent.

Templates are a great way to help standardize the configuration of your VMs while also speeding up the deployment of new VMs. Unfortunately, vCenter Server doesn't make it possible for you to easily transport a template between vCenter Server instances or between different installations of VMware vSphere. To help address that limitation, VMware helped develop a new industry standard: the Open Virtualization Format (OVF) standard.

Using OVF Templates

Open Virtualization Format (formerly called Open Virtual Machine Format) is a Distributed Management Task Force (DMTF) standard format for describing the configuration of a VM. Although it was originally pioneered by VMware and other industry contributors, most virtualization vendors now support OVF as well. VMware vSphere 6.7 provides OVF support in three ways:

- Deploying new VMs from an OVF template (essentially, importing a VM in OVF format)
- Exporting a VM as an OVF template
- Storing OVF templates within a Content Library

Let's look first at deploying VMs from an OVF template.

Deploying a VM from an OVF Template

To deploy a VM from an OVF template, right-click a host, cluster, datacenter, or vCenter Server and select Deploy OVF Template. This initiates a wizard that walks you through deploying a new VM from the OVF template. Figure 10.13 shows that vCenter Server can deploy OVF templates stored locally or those stored remotely and accessible with a URL.

FIGURE 10.13

vCenter Server uses a wizard to deploy templates from OVF.

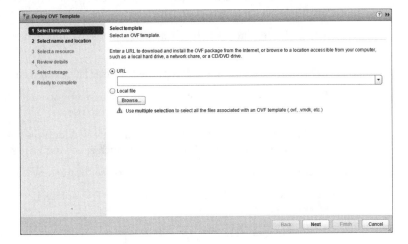

Aside from selecting the source location of the OVF template, you follow the same process to deploy a VM from an OVF template whether you import it from a local set of files or download it from the Internet. Remember that you can configure some OVF template options, so depending on the template you import you may have more or less information to enter on the deployment screens than the example here.

Perform the following steps to deploy a VM from an OVF template:

1. If it is not already running, launch the vSphere Web Client and connect to a vCenter Server instance or an ESXi host.

2. From within the vSphere Web Client Hosts And Clusters view, right-click a host and select Deploy OVF Template.

3. Select the source location of the OVF template—which must be provided in OVF or OVA format—and click Next.

OVF OR OVA?

Later in this chapter, in the section "Examining OVF Templates," we'll provide more information on the difference between OVF and OVA.

---

4. Supply a name for the new VM you're deploying from the OVF template, and select a location within the vCenter Server inventory.

This is a logical location, not a physical location; you'll select the physical location (where the new VM will run and where the virtual hard disk files will be stored) in the next step

5. Select a cluster, an ESXi host, or a resource pool where the new VM will run, and then click Next.

6. If you selected a cluster for which vSphere DRS is not enabled or that is set to Manual, yo must select a specific host on which to run the VM. Select an ESXi host and click Next.

7. The OVF Template Details screen summarizes the information about the template. Click Next to continue.

8. Click the Accept button to accept the end-user license agreement, and click Next.

9. Choose the datastore or datastore cluster where you want to store the new VM. Click Nex after you've selected the datastore you want to use.

   If you are unsure of how much space the new VM requires, the OVF Template Details screen, described in step 4, shows how much space the VM requires.

10. Select the virtual disk format you want to use for the new VM, and then click Next.

11. Map each source network defined in the OVF template to a destination network in vCenter Server.

   The destination networks are port groups or dvPort groups, as you can see in Figure 10.1- For more information about port groups, see Chapter 5, "Creating and Configuring a vSphere Network."

FIGURE 10.14
Source networks defined in the OVF template are mapped to port groups and dvPort groups in vCenter Server.

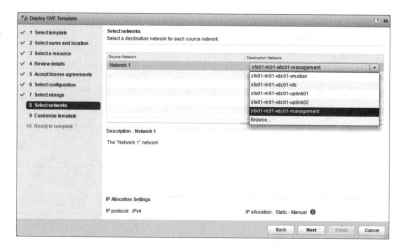

Some OVF templates will ask you to confirm how IP addresses should be assigned to the new VM, as you can see in Figure 10.15. Fill out the settings you prefer (Static – Manual or DHCP) along with the other required network settings and click Next.

FIGURE 10.15
vSphere administrators
have different options
for controlling how new
VMs are deployed
from OVF templates
and assigned an
IP address.

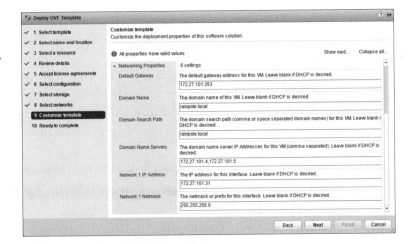

SELECTING THE CORRECT IP ALLOCATION POLICY

Generally, you will select either Static – Manual or DHCP from the IP Allocation drop-down list. The Transient option requires specific configurations to be enabled within vCenter Server (IP pools created and configured) as well as support within the guest OS inside the OVF template. This support usually takes the form of a script or an executable application that sets the IP address.

---

12. Some OVF templates will now prompt the user to input certain properties that will be used by the new VM.

For example, if you selected Static – Manual as the IP address allocation mechanism in step 11, you would be prompted to assign an IP address in this step. Supply the correct value, and then click Next to continue.

13. The Ready To Complete screen summarizes the actions to be taken while deploying the new VM from the OVF template. If everything is correct, click Finish; if anything is incorrect, use the Back button to go back and make the correct selection.

Once the deployment of the new VM from the OVF template is complete, the new VM is treated like any other VM in the inventory. You can power it on, power it off, clone it, or snapshot it—refer to Chapter 9 for more details on these tasks.

The other way vCenter Server allows you to work with OVF is to export a VM as an OVF template.

Exporting a VM as an OVF Template

vCenter Server lets you export an existing VM as an OVF template. This functionality could be used in a number of ways:

◆   Creating a template that could be transported between multiple vCenter Server instances

◆   Transporting a VM from one vSphere installation to another vSphere installation

♦ Transporting a VM to or from a different hypervisor that supports the OVF standard

♦ Allowing a software vendor to package its product as a VM and easily distribute it to customers

Whatever your reason for exporting a VM as an OVF template, the process is relatively straightforward.

Follow these steps to export a VM as an OVF template:

1. If it is not already running, launch the vSphere Web Client and connect to a vCenter Server instance.

2. From within the vSphere Web Client, locate the VM you wish to export.

3. Right-click the VM and select Template ➤ Export OVF Template. This opens the Export OVF Template dialog box.

4. Supply a name for the OVF template, and choose the format:

♦ The Folder Of Files (OVF) format puts the separate components of an OVF template—the manifest (MF) file, the structural definition (OVF) file, and the virtual hard disk (VMDK) file—as separate files in a folder.

♦ OVA template—a single file archive export—is no longer an option via the UI.

5. Supply an annotation for the OVF template if desired.

6. Choose to export the image files for floppy and optical devices if needed.

7. The advanced options like Include BIOS UUID and Include MAC Addresses, shown in Figure 10.16, will cause conflicts if you have more than one copy in the same environment so use these options with care.

FIGURE 10.16
There are a number of advanced options when exporting VMs as an OVF template, but they must be used carefully to avoid conflicts.

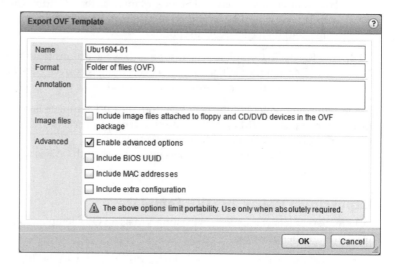

8. When you are ready to begin the export, click OK.

9. The selected VM is exported as a download from the web browser.

After you successfully export the VM as an OVF template, you can use the steps in the earlier section "Deploying a VM from an OVF Template" to import that VM back into a VMware vSphere implementation.

BE AWARE OF BROWSER POP-UP BLOCKERS

When exporting VMs as an OVF, your browser will try to download the exported files automatically. Depending on your browser's settings, these downloads will appear as pop-ups and may be blocked, as you can see in the following figure:

3e2-19be-4da3-9ddc-ddcd232252e0%253AVirtualMachine%253Avm-54...

Pop-ups blocked

The following pop-ups were blocked on this page:

- https://sfo01m01vc01.sfo01.rainpole.local...b13-48f4-ada4-f06cde6595f2/Ubu1604-01.ovf
- https://sfo01m01vc01.sfo01.rainpole.local...48f4-ada4-f06cde6595f2/Ubu1604-01-1.vmdk
- https://sfo01m01vc01.sfo01.rainpole.local/...3-48f4-ada4-f06cde6595f2/Ubu1604-01-2.iso

- ◉ Always allow pop-ups from https://sfo01m01vc01.sfo01.rainpole.local
- ○ Continue blocking pop-ups

Manage   Done

Before we move away from the topic of OVF templates, let's take a quick look at the structure and components that make up an OVF template.

Examining OVF Templates

Looking at the resulting files from the previous example, three files make up the OVF template you exported out of vCenter Server:

- ◆ The name of the manifest file ends in .mf, and the file contains SHA-1 digests of the other two files. This allows vCenter Server (and other applications that support the OVF specification) to verify the integrity of the OVF template by computing the SHA-1 digests of the other files in the package and comparing them against the SHA-1 digests in the manifest file. If the digests match, then the contents of the OVF template have not been modified.

PROTECTING THE MANIFEST

The manifest contains SHA-1 digests to help an application verify that the components of the OVF template have not been modified. But what protects the manifest? The OVF specification lets you use an optional X.509 digital certificate that can verify the integrity of the manifest file as well.

◆ The OVF descriptor is an XML document with a filename ending in .ovf and containing information about the OVF template such as product details, virtual hardware, requirements, licensing, a full list of file references, and a description of the contents of the OVF template. Listing 10.1 shows the partial contents of the OVF descriptor for the VM exported from vCenter Server in the previous section. (We added backslashes (\) where a line has been manually wrapped to help with the readability of the OVF descriptor.)

◆ The virtual hard disk file has a filename ending in .vmdk. The OVF specification supports multiple virtual hard disk formats, not just the VMDK files used by VMware vSphere, but obviously vCenter Server and VMware ESXi only natively support virtual hard disks in the VMDK format. Depending on the OVF template, it may contain multiple VMDK files, all of which would need to be referenced in the OVF descriptor file (refer to the <DiskSection> in the OVF descriptor file in Listing 10.1).

LISTING 10.1: Partial contents of a sample OVF descriptor file

```
<?xml version='1.0' encoding='UTF-8'?>
<Envelope xmlns="http://schemas.dmtf.org/ovf/envelope/1" xmlns:ovf="http://
    schemas.dmtf.org/ovf/envelope/1" xmlns:vmw="http://www.vmware.com/
    schema/ovf" xmlns:rasd="http://schemas.dmtf.org/wbem/wscim/1/cim- \
    schema/2/CIM_ResourceAllocationSettingData" xmlns:vssd="http://
    schemas.
    dmtf.org/wbem/wscim/1/cim- \ schema/2/CIM_VirtualSystemSettingData">
  <References>
    <File ovf:id="file1" ovf:href="Ubu1604-01-1.vmdk"/>
    <File ovf:id="file2" ovf:href="Ubu1604-01-2.iso" ovf:size="889192448"/>
    <File ovf:id="file3" ovf:href="Ubu1604-01-3.nvram" ovf:size="8684"/>
  </References>
  <DiskSection>
    <Info>List of the virtual disks</Info>
    <Disk ovf:capacityAllocationUnits="byte" ovf:format="http://www.vmware.
      com/interfaces/specifications/vmdk.html#streamOptimized"
      ovf:diskId="vmdisk1" ovf:capacity="17179869184" ovf:fileRef="file1"/>
  </DiskSection>
  <NetworkSection>
    <Info>The list of logical networks</Info>
    <Network ovf:name="sfo01-m01-vds01-ext">
      <Description>The sfo01-m01-vds01-ext network</Description>
    </Network>
  </NetworkSection>
  <VirtualSystem ovf:id="Ubu1604-01">
    <Info>A Virtual system</Info>
    <Name>Ubu1604-01</Name>
    ...
  </VirtualSystem>
</Envelope>
```

The OVF specification allows two different formats for OVF templates, which we've discussed briefly. OVF templates can be distributed as a set of files, like the one we exported from vCenter Server in the previous section. In this case, it's easy to see the different components of the OVF template, but it's a bit more complicated to distribute unless you are distributing the OVF template as a set of files on a web server (keep in mind that vCenter Server and VMware ESXi can deploy VMs from an OVF template stored at a remote URL).

OVF templates can also be distributed as a single file. This single file has a name that ends in .ova and is in TAR format, and the OVF specification has strict requirements about the placement and order of components within the OVA archive. All the components already described are still present, but because everything is stored in a single file, it's more difficult to view them independently of each other. However, using the OVA (single-file) format does make it easier to move the OVF template between locations because you work with only a single file.

WANT EVEN MORE DETAIL?

The full OVF specification as approved by the Desktop Management Task Force (DMTF) is available from the DMTF website at www.dmtf.org/standards/ovf. At the time this book was written, the latest version of the specification was version 2.1.1, published in August 2015.

The OVF specification also gives OVF templates another interesting ability: the ability to encapsulate multiple VMs inside a single OVF template. The OVF descriptor contains elements that specify whether the OVF template contains a single VM (noted by the VirtualSystem element, which you can see in Listing 10.1) or multiple VMs (noted by the VirtualSystemCollection element). An OVF template that contains multiple VMs would allow a vSphere administrator to deploy an entire collection of VMs from a single OVF template.

Managing a number of VM Templates, OVFs, and other media files (ISOs and FLPs) can take a considerable amount of time, especially if you have multiple sites in your environment that might need copies of these files throughout. Fortunately, VMware introduced Content Libraries with vSphere 6.0 that can help administrators manage these files.

Using Content Libraries

Content Libraries are a way of storing VMware templates, OVF templates, ISO/FLP media files, or any file that you may want cataloged separate from your deployed VMs. They can be synchronized between vCenter Servers to allow a "publish once, consume elsewhere" scenario. You can even subscribe to a Content Library that you might not own, such as a public Content Library from your favorite Linux distribution or maybe a private library from your virtual firewall vendor.

Setting up Content Libraries is relatively straightforward, but understanding how they work behind the scenes will make all the difference when using them for the first time. First we'll explain how Content Libraries work, and then we'll show you how to configure them.

Content Library Data and Storage

More useful in larger environments with multiple sites, Content Libraries can have any file type uploaded to them for storage and synchronization with other vCenter Servers.

When you configure your own Content Library, the storage backing can be either a standard vSphere datastore or it can be configured on a local disk mount point attached to the vCenter Server itself. Most people configure Content Libraries on a datastore for consistency. When you deploy large OVF files, a datastore-based Content Library will provide faster deployment times; however, if there are large rates of change within the Content Library, a vCenter file system backing might be a better choice. It comes down to how big and how much change you expect for your Content Library.

Uploading files to the Content Library will do one of two things. With a non-VM template such as an ISO or Floppy Disk media, the Content Library will simply store the file. When uploading VM templates that are not in OVF format, the Content Library will convert them upon upload. It does this for a number of reasons. First, OVF files contain a file checksum to ensure the contents are transferred correctly. Second, when synchronizing VM templates you may want only the descriptor and not the payload until deployment time (more on this shortly). Third, it allows the content changes to be tracked through a versioning mechanism.

Content Library Synchronization

The real power behind Content Libraries is the subscription and transfer services that it offers. Content Libraries can be configured in four configurations:

Local Content Library   Local Content Libraries are for individual use only. You cannot subscribe to them or synchronize content between them and other libraries.

Local Content Library – Published Externally   Published Content Libraries are the parent or source library that you can subscribe *to*. All changes to the content are made to the published library, and the subscribers get those changes based on their individual synchronization settings.

Subscribed Content Library – Automatic   Subscribed Content Libraries that are set to automatically download changes receive all content as soon as it is made available and downloaded from the Published parent library. The content includes all the metadata and the payload binary data.

Subscribed Content Library – On Demand   On Demand Content Libraries only download metadata without any actual payload binary data. When a VM template is requested from this library, synchronization is initiated for that item only.

When you configure Published Content Libraries, they can be password protected, but the credentials are not integrated with vCenter, SSO, or ESXi. This is because Content Libraries are designed to work without vCenter as a boundary. Integrating into a centralized identity system could be a security risk. The credentials are set on a per–Content Library basis with a non-configurable username of vcsp and a password set upon creation.

Now that you understand some of the inner workings of Content Libraries, we'll show you how to set one up for publishing and then subscribe to an existing one.

Creating and Publishing a Content Library

To set up a Content Library, you first determine the type you intend to create and the type of storage you plan to use. In this example, we're going to create a Local – Published Content Library backed by a vSphere datastore:

1. If it is not already running, launch the vSphere Web Client and connect to a vCenter Server instance.

2. From within the vSphere Web Client vCenter Home view, select Content Libraries from the navigation pane.

3. Select the Create New Library button.

4. Give the library a name and notes, select the desired vCenter Server if you have multiple, and then click Next.

5. On the Configure Content Library screen, select Local Content Library, and check the Publish Externally and Enable Authentication check boxes.

6. Supply a password and click Next. Remember, this password is not related to vCenter, SSO, or Active Directory.

7. Change the radio button to Select a datastore and specify where you would like the library to reside. Click Next to Continue.

8. Review the Content Library settings as shown in Figure 10.17, and click Finish to create the Content Library.

FIGURE 10.17
Content Libraries can be useful when managing templates and images for multiple site locations.

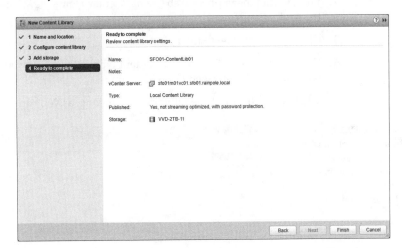

Once the library has been created, it will appear in the Content Libraries list. Editing it, as shown in Figure 10.18, will show the External Publication settings such as the subscription URL and password. There is also a button you can click to copy the URL to the clipboard.

Subscribing to a Content Library

After you have created a Content Library in a primary location, you are then able to subscribe to this library from multiple secondary locations. As explained earlier in this section, there are two options to configure for subscribed libraries, Automatic and On Demand. Depending on the deployment scenario, each option has a place. I would recommend the Automatic setting for high bandwidth sites with adequate storage. Low bandwidth or remote sites with limited storage

FIGURE 10.18
Editing the settings of a
Content Library will
expose the subscription
URL if it is set to
Published Externally.

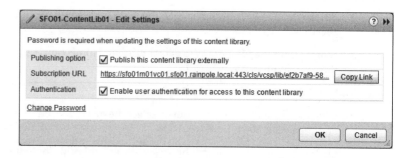

capacity might be better suited with the On Demand option. This option reduces both the transfer bandwidth and storage requirements, but you may have to wait for the first use of a particular file to download locally.

Now that you understand the options available, let's see how to configure a Subscribed Content Library.

1. If it is not already running, launch the vSphere Web Client and connect to a vCenter Server instance.

2. From within the vSphere Web Client vCenter Home view, select Content Libraries from the navigation pane.

3. Click the Create New Library button.

4. Change the type to Subscribed Content Library, and enter the Subscription URL that can be found in the published library's settings.

The URL for the published library is quite long, as you can see in Figure 10.19.

FIGURE 10.19
The Subscription URL is
used to locate the
JSON file that holds
the Content
Library details.

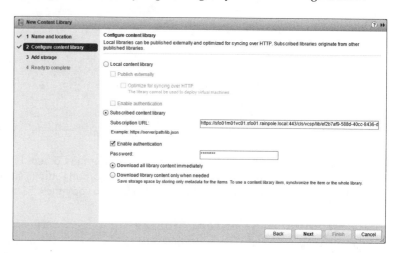

5. Select the Enable Authentication check box, and enter the password for the published library.

6. For the download setting, you can accept the default, Immediately Download All Library Content, and click Next to continue.

7. Most likely, you will be required to accept an SSL certificate thumbprint to subscribe to the published library. If this prompt comes up in your environment, click Yes.

8. Change the radio button selection to Datastore and specify where you would like the library to reside. Click Next to Continue.

9. Review the Content Library settings, and click Finish to create the Content Library.

As you can see, creating and subscribing to Content Libraries is relatively straightforward; however, this feature should make managing large numbers of templates, ISOs, and scripts a little easier. In the final section of this chapter, we will explain how vSphere leverages the ability of OVF templates to encapsulate multiple VMs in a key feature known as vApps.

Operating Content Libraries

Now that you have Content Libraries configured, it's time to start populating them and allowing the replication engine to copy files between your various libraries. For simplicity, let's walk through an example with one Local Content Library (SF001-ContentLib01) that is set to Published Externally, and one Subscribed Content Library (LAX01-ContentLib01) that is set to automatic synchronize new content.

IMPORTING FILES TO A CONTENT LIBRARY

Uploading, or importing, a file to a Content Library is relatively simple—just find the content library you want to put the file in and click the Import Item button. Remember, you can upload any file type you like, but only OVF and ISO files will be useable when trying to deploy VMs or load CD media from elsewhere within the vSphere UI. To upload files, follow these steps:

1. If it is not already running, launch the vSphere Web Client, and connect to a vCenter Server instance.

2. From within the vSphere Web Client vCenter Home view, select Content Libraries from the navigation pane.

3. Select the Local Content Library option from the list of available Content Libraries in vCenter Server.

4. Click the Import Item button. This will open the Import Library Item dialog box.

5. From the Import Library Item dialog box, select Local File and click Browse.

6. Find an ISO, or another file you want replicated between locations, and click Open.

7. Change the name of the file or item, and add any notes if required.

8. Click OK to import (upload) the file to the Content Library location.

IMPORTING VM TEMPLATES TO A CONTENT LIBRARY

As mentioned in the "Creating Templates and Deploying Virtual Machines" section, it is possible to clone VMs and templates to a Content Library. It's simply a matter of using the context menu and selecting Clone ➤ Clone To Template In Library for VMs, or simply Clone To Library for existing templates as shown in Figure 10.20.

FIGURE 10.20
Adding existing VMs and templates can be done from their right-click menu.

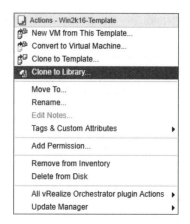

As mentioned in the "Content Library Data and Storage" section, when a VM or template is uploaded to a Content Library, it is converted to the OVF template. In Figure 10.21, you can see this process in the Recent Tasks section.

FIGURE 10.21
All VMs and templates are converted to the OVF template as they are being uploaded to a Content Library.

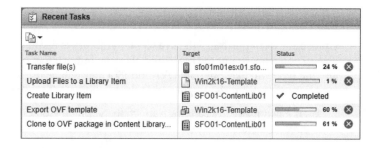

SYNCHRONIZING CONTENT LIBRARIES

Content Libraries that are set to subscribe will automatically synchronize this new file based on the Content Library service settings on the vCenter Server. You can read more about the vCenter Server Services settings in Chapter 3. There is also a way to force a library synchronization if you don't want to wait for the schedule to kick in:

1. If it is not already running, launch the vSphere Web Client and connect to a vCenter Server instance.

2. From within the vSphere Web Client vCenter Home view, select Content Libraries from the navigation pane.

3. Select the Subscribed Content Library option from the list of available Content Libraries in vCenter Server.

4. Click the Synchronize button to force synchronization between the local published library and the subscribed library.

Consuming Files from a Content Library

Once you have a Content Library filled with templates and ISOs, you can access the files from the following locations:

◆ From within the Content Library, you can click Create VM From Library on the Templates tab to start the New VM Wizard.

◆ You can use the context menu on a datacenter, cluster, or host object and select New VM From Library.

◆ Editing an existing VM gives you the option to specify a Content Library ISO file instead of selecting one from a datastore, as shown in Figure 10.22.

FIGURE 10.22
If ISO files are in a Content Library, they can be easier to find.

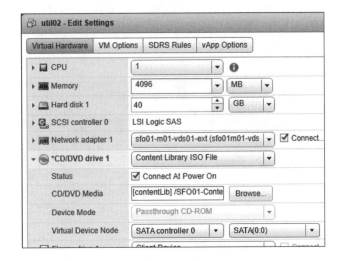

Now that you know how to organize templates and media, how do you organize running VMs that have a relationship? That is what we will cover next.

Working with vApps

With vApps, vSphere administrators can combine multiple VMs into a single unit. Why is this functionality useful? Increasingly, enterprise applications are no longer constrained to a single VM. Instead, they may have components spread across multiple VMs. For example, a typical multitier application might have one or more front-end web servers, an application server, and a backend database server. Although each of these servers is a discrete VM and could be managed as such, they are also part of a larger application that is servicing the organization. Combining these different VMs into a vApp allows the vSphere administrator to manage the different VMs as a single unit.

In the following sections, we'll show you how to work with vApps, including creating and editing vApps. Let's start with creating a vApp.

Creating a vApp

Creating a vApp is a two-step process. First, you create the vApp container and configure any settings. Second, you add one or more VMs to the vApp by cloning existing VMs, deploying from a template, or creating a new VM from scratch in the vApp. You repeat the process of adding VMs until you have all the necessary VMs contained in the vApp.

Perform these steps to create a vApp:

1. If it is not already running, launch the vSphere Web Client and connect to a vCenter Server instance, or launch the traditional vSphere Client and connect to a stand-alone ESXi host.

2. Ensure that you are in an inventory tree that will allow you to create a vApp by selecting Hosts And Clusters or VMs And Templates.

3. Right-click an existing host, resource pool, or cluster and select New vApp, New vApp. This launches the New vApp Wizard.

LIMITATIONS ON CREATING NEW VAPPS

Although you can create vApps inside other vApps, you can't create a vApp on a cluster that does not have vSphere DRS enabled. You can find more information on DRS in Chapter 12, "Balancing Resource Utilization."

---

4. If using the Web Client, you will be asked if you wish to create a new vApp or clone an existing vApp. In this example, we are creating a new vApp, so choose that option and click Next to continue.

5. Supply a name for the new vApp.

   If you are connected to vCenter Server, you must also select a location in the folder hierarchy in which you want to store the vApp. (This is a logical placement, not a physical one.)

6. Click Next. This advances the New vApp Wizard to the Resource Allocation step. If you need to adjust the resource allocation settings for the vApp, you may do so here.

   By default, as shown in Figure 10.23, a new vApp is given normal priority, no reservation and no limit on CPU or memory usage. It's important to note, however, that these default settings might not fit into your overall resource allocation strategy. Be sure to read Chapter 11, "Managing Resource Allocation," for more information on the impact of these settings on your vApp.

7. Click Next to proceed to the final step in the New vApp Wizard. Review the settings for the new vApp. If everything is correct, click Finish; otherwise, go back in the wizard to make adjustments.

After the vApp is created, you can add VMs to the vApp. There are a few ways to do this:

FIGURE 10.23
You will want to ensure that these default resource allocation settings are appropriate for your specific environment.

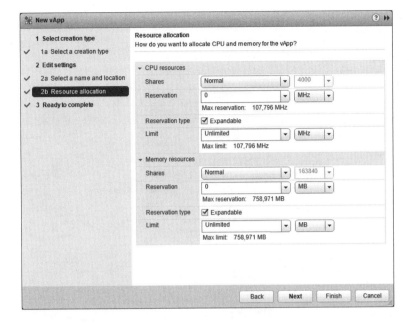

- You can clone an existing VM into a new VM inside the vApp. We described the process of cloning a VM earlier in this chapter, in the section "Cloning a Virtual Machine"; that same procedure applies here.

- You can deploy a new VM from a vCenter Server template and put the new VM into the vApp.

- You can create an entirely new VM from scratch inside the vApp. Because you are creating a new VM from scratch, you must install the guest OS into the VM; cloning an existing VM or deploying from a template typically eliminates this task.

- You can drag and drop an existing VM and add it to a vApp.

Once the vApp is created and you've added one or more VMs to it, you'll probably need to edit some of the vApp's settings.

Editing a vApp

A vApp is a container of sorts that has properties and settings just as the VMs within that vApp have properties and settings. To help avoid confusion about where a setting should be set or edited, VMware has tried to make the vApp container as lean and simple as possible. There are only a few settings that can be edited at the vApp level.

EDITING A VAPP'S RESOURCE ALLOCATION SETTINGS

To edit a vApp's resource allocation settings, right-click a vApp and select Edit Settings from the context menu. This will bring up the Edit vApp dialog box, shown in Figure 10.24.

FIGURE 10.24
The Edit vApp dialog box is where you can make any changes that need to be made to a vApp's configuration similar to an individual VM configuration.

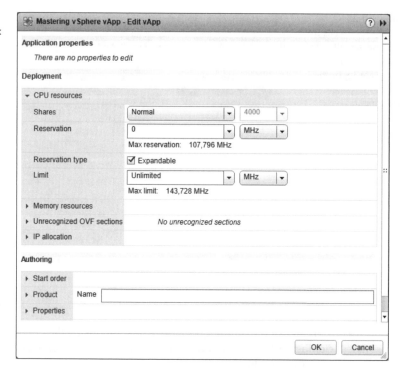

Within the Edit vApp dialog box, the vApp's resource allocation settings will be exposed. Here you can assign a higher or lower priority of access to resources, reserve resources for the vApp, or even limit the resources used by the vApp. If you don't understand what these settings mean or how they are used yet, don't worry—Chapter 11 provides complete details on using these settings in your VMware vSphere environment.

EDITING A vAPP'S IP ALLOCATION SCHEME

In the Edit vApp dialog box, the Authoring IP Allocation Scheme option allows you to modify how IP addresses will be allocated to VMs contained within the vApp, as shown in Figure 10.25.

The three possible IP allocation settings are Static – Manual, Transient, and DHCP:

♦ When you use the Static – Manual option, the IP addresses must be manually set in the guest OS instance inside the VM.

♦ The Transient option leverages vCenter Server's ability to create and manage IP pools to assign IP addresses to the VMs inside a vApp. When the VMs are powered off, the IP addresses are automatically released.

♦ The DHCP option leverages an external DHCP server to assign IP addresses to the VMs in a vApp.

FIGURE 10.25
There are different
options for assigning IP
addresses to VMs
inside a vApp. DHCP
or granular settings
via the OVF environ-
ment can be
configured.

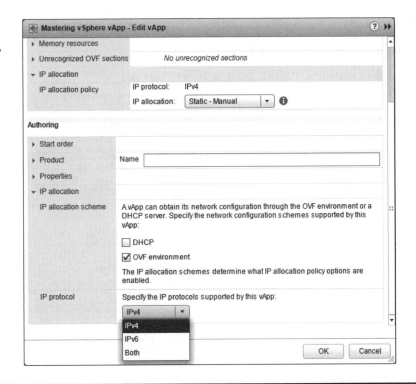

IP POOLS VS. DHCP

You might initially think that using Transient with IP pools means that vCenter Server uses a DHCP-like mechanism to assign IP addresses to VMs inside a vApp without any further interaction from the user. Unfortunately, this is not the case. Using Transient with IP pools requires the guest OSs in the VMs within the vApp to have some sort of support for this functionality. This support is typically in the form of a script, executable, or other mechanism whereby an IP address is obtained from the IP pool, and it is assigned to the guest OS inside the VM. It is not the same as DHCP, and it does not replace or supplant DHCP on a network segment.

When you first create a vApp, you will find that the only IP allocation policy that you can select here is Static – Manual. You must enable the other two options before you can select them. You enable the other IP allocation options by selecting the OVF Environment check box in the IP Allocation area. This activates the Advanced IP Allocation dialog box shown in Figure 10.26.

EDITING A VAPP'S AUTHORING SETTINGS

The Authoring area of the Edit vApp dialog box is where you can supply some additional metadata about the vApp, such as product name, product version, vendor name, and vendor URL. The values supplied here might be prepopulated if you have a vApp that you received from a vendor, or you might enter these values yourself. Either way, the values set here show up on the Details area of the Summary tab on the vApp. Figure 10.27 shows a vApp's metadata as it appears in the vSphere Web Client.

FIGURE 10.26
If you want to use the
Transient (also called
OVF Environment) or
DHCP options, you
must enable them in
this dialog box.

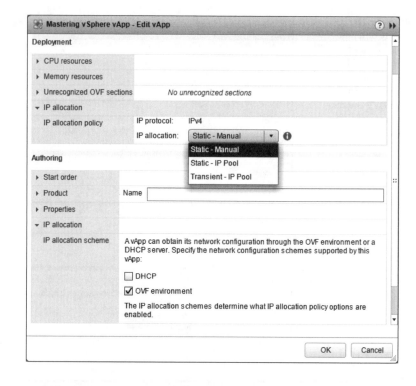

FIGURE 10.27
The vSphere Web Client
displays the metadata
in the Summary tab of
a vApp object.

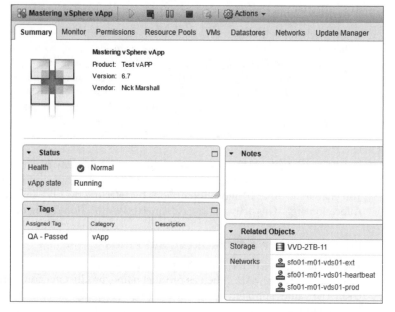

EDITING A vAPP'S POWER SETTINGS

One of the most useful advantages of a vApp is that you can power on or power off all the VMs in a vApp, in the correct order, in one step. We'll show you how that's done in just a moment—although you probably have already figured it out—but first, let's cover the vApp's power settings.

The Start Order section of the Edit vApp dialog box is where you can set the startup order of the VMs and specify how much time will elapse between VMs booting up. Also, this is where you can set the shutdown action and timing.

For the most part, the only thing you'll need to adjust here is the startup/shutdown order. Use the up and down arrows to move the order of the VMs so that the VMs boot up in the correct sequence. For example, you may want to ensure that the backend database VM comes up before the middle-tier application server, which should in turn come up before the front-end web server. You can control all this from the Start Order section. Generally speaking, most of the defaults here are fine.

Note that we said *most* of the defaults. There are two default settings that we recommend you change. Shutdown Action is, by default, set to Power Off. We recommend you change this to Guest Shutdown (which will require VMware Tools to be installed in the guest OS instance). You can set this on a per-VM basis, so if you have a VM that doesn't have the tools installed—not a recommended situation, by the way—then you can leave Shutdown Action set to Power Off. And since you'll likely have VMware Tools installed, we also recommend that you select the VMware Tools Are Ready check box. This will ensure that you don't have to wait two full minutes after the VM has booted for it to be ready, provided VMware Tools has started up correctly first.

Figure 10.28 shows the Shutdown Action option for the VM named `Win2k16-01` set to Guest Shutdown instead of Power Off.

FIGURE 10.28
Using Guest Shutdown instead of Power Off is recommended. Selecting VMware Tools Are Ready will ensure the next VM starts as quickly as possible.

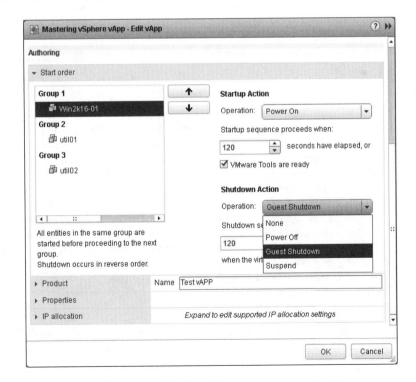

Changing a vApp's Power State

The process for powering on or powering off a vApp is the same as for a standard VM. You can select one of the following three methods to power on a vApp:

◆ The Power On command in the Actions Power menu, as shown in Figure 10.29

◆ The Power On button on the vSphere Web Client toolbar, also shown in Figure 10.29

◆ The Power On command from the vApp's context menu, accessible by right-clicking a vApp

FIGURE 10.29
The Actions menu for a vApp offers options to change the power state for all VMs within the vApp.

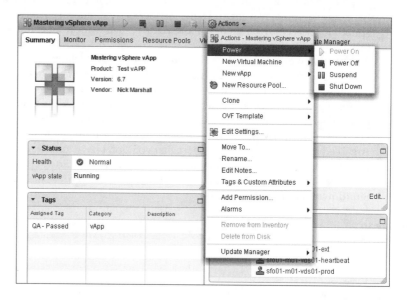

The Start Order section in the vApp's properties controls what happens when the user tells vCenter Server to power on the vApp; you can see this earlier in Figure 10.28. vCenter Server will power on all the VMs in a group, wait the specified period of time, then power on the VMs in the next group, wait the specified period of time, and so on. You can control the order in which VMs should be started as well as the waiting period between the groups by editing the settings shown in the Start Order section.

Once the vApp is up and running, you can suspend the vApp or power down the vApp just as you would suspend or power down a stand-alone VM. Depending on the settings on the Start Order section, the VMs within a vApp can be configured in different ways to respond to a Power Off request to the vApp itself. As recommended in the previous section, it's probably best to set Guest Shutdown as the action to take in response to a request to power off the vApp. Shutdown occurs in the reverse order from startup of the vApp.

Cloning a vApp

You can clone a vApp in much the same way you'd clone individual VMs.

Perform these steps to clone a vApp:

1. If the vSphere Web Client is not already running, launch it and connect to a vCenter Server instance. You must connect to vCenter Server in order to clone a vApp.

2. Navigate to either the Hosts And Clusters or VMs And Templates view; both of them show the vApp objects in the inventory.

3. Right-click the vApp and select Clone.

4. In the Clone vApp Wizard, select a host, cluster, or resource pool on which to run the new vApp. Because vApps require vSphere DRS, you cannot select a cluster on which vSphere DRS is not enabled. Click Next.

5. Supply a name for the new vApp, and select a logical inventory location for the vApp. Click Next to continue.

6. Select a target datastore or datastore cluster, and then click Next. Note that you do not have the option to select a VM storage policy. Although member VMs can have VM storage policies assigned, you can't assign a VM storage policy to the vApp itself.

7. Select the target virtual disk format. Click Next.

8. If the vApp has specific properties defined, you will next have the option to edit those properties for the cloned vApp. Click Next when you are ready to continue.

9. Review the settings for the new vApp, and use the Back button or the links on the left to go back and make changes if needed. If everything is correct, click Finish.

vCenter Server will clone the vApp container object and all VMs within the vApp. vCenter Server will not, however, customize the guest OS installations inside the VMs in the vApp; the administrator assumes the burden of ensuring that the VMs in the cloned vApp are customized appropriately.

So far in this chapter, you've seen how to clone VMs, customize cloned VMs, create templates, work with OVF templates, use Content Libraries, and work with vApps. In the last section of this chapter, we'll take a quick look at importing VMs from other environments into your VMware vSphere environment.

Importing Machines from Other Environments

VMware offers a stand-alone free product called vCenter Converter to help you take OS installations on physical hardware and migrate them—using a process called a physical-to-virtual (P2V) migration—into a virtualized environment running vSphere. Not only does vCenter Converter provide P2V functionality, but it also provides virtual-to-virtual (V2V) functionality. The V2V functionality allows VMs created on other virtualization platforms to be imported into VMware vSphere. You can also use VMware Converter's V2V functionality to export VMs out of VMware vSphere to other virtualization platforms. This V2V functionality is particularly helpful in moving VMs between VMware's enterprise-class virtualization platform, VMware vSphere, and VMware's hosted virtualization platforms, such as VMware Workstation for Windows or Linux or VMware Fusion for Mac OS X. Although VMware created all these products, slight differences in the architecture of the products require VMware Converter or a similar tool to move VMs between the products.

The Bottom Line

Clone a VM.   The ability to clone a VM is a powerful feature that dramatically reduces the amount of time to get a fully functional VM with a guest OS installed and running. vCenter Server provides the ability to clone VMs and to customize VMs, ensuring that each VM is unique. You can save the information to customize a VM as a customization specification and then reuse that information over and over again. vCenter Server can even clone running VMs.

Master It   Where and when can customization specifications be created in the vSphere Client?

Master It   A fellow administrator comes to you and wants you to help streamline the process of deploying Solaris x86 VMs in your VMware vSphere environment. What do you tell him?

Create a VM template.   vCenter Server's templates feature is an excellent complement to the cloning functionality. With options to clone or convert an existing VM to a template, vCenter Server makes it easy to create templates. By creating templates, you ensure that your VM master image doesn't get accidentally changed or modified. Then, once a template has been created, you can use vCenter Server to clone VMs from that template, customizing them in the process to ensure that each one is unique.

Master It   Of the following tasks, which are appropriate to be performed on a VM running Windows Server 2016 that will eventually be turned into a template?

a. Align the guest OS's file system to a 64 KB boundary.

b. Join the VM to Active Directory.

c. Perform some application-specific configurations and tweaks.

d. Install all patches from the operating system vendor.

Deploy new VMs from a template.   By combining templates and cloning, VMware vSphere administrators have a powerful way to standardize the configuration of VMs being deployed, protect the master images from accidental change, and reduce the amount of time it takes to provision new guest OS instances.

Master It   Another VMware vSphere administrator in your environment starts the wizard for deploying a new VM from a template. She has a customization specification she'd like to use, but there is one setting in the specification she wants to change. Does she have to create an all-new customization specification?

Deploy a VM from an Open Virtualization Format (OVF) template.   Open Virtualization Format (OVF) templates provide a mechanism for moving templates or VMs between different instances of vCenter Server or even entirely different and separate installations of VMware vSphere. OVF templates combine the structural definition of a VM along with the data in the VM's virtual hard disk and can exist either as a folder of files or as a single file. Because OVF templates include the VM's virtual hard disk, OVF templates can contain an installation of a guest OS and are often used by software developers as a way of delivering their software preinstalled into a guest OS inside a VM.

Master It A vendor has given you a zip file that contains a VM they are calling a *virtual appliance*. Upon looking inside the zip file, you see several VMDK files and a VMX file. Will you be able to use vCenter Server's Deploy OVF Template functionality to import this VM? If not, how can you get this VM into your infrastructure?

Export a VM as an OVF template. To assist in the transport of VMs between VMware vSphere installations, you can use vCenter Server to export a VM as an OVF template. The OVF template will include the configuration of the VM as well as the data found in the VM.

Master It You are preparing to export a VM to an OVF template. You want to ensure that the OVF template is easy to transport via a USB key or portable hard drive. Which format is most appropriate, OVF or OVA? Why?

Organize templates and media. Organizing and synchronizing templates and media around larger environments can be troublesome. Content Libraries (instead of SAN-based replication), scheduled copy scripts, and "sneaker net" can be used to ensure the right templates and files are in the right places.

Master It List the file types that cannot be added to Content Libraries for synchronization.

Work with vApps. vSphere vApps leverage OVF as a way to combine multiple VMs into a single administrative unit. When the vApp is powered on, all VMs in it are powered on, in a sequence specified by the administrator. The same goes for shutting down a vApp. vApps also act a bit like resource pools for the VMs contained within them.

Master It Name two ways to add VMs to a vApp.

Chapter 11

Managing Resource Allocation

The ability for a single physical server to host many virtual machines (VMs) has a massive value in today's modern datacenters. But let's face it: there are limits to how many VMs can run on a VMware ESXi host. To make the most of the platform, you need to understand how the four key resources—memory, processors, disks, and networks—are consumed by the VMs running on the host, and how the host consumes those resources. The methods used to arbitrate access to each of these resources on an ESXi host are a bit different. This chapter discusses how an ESXi host allocates these resources and how you can change the way these resources are consumed.

IN THIS CHAPTER, YOU WILL LEARN TO

- ◆ Manage memory allocation
- ◆ Manage CPU utilization
- ◆ Create and manage resource pools
- ◆ Control network I/O utilization
- ◆ Control storage I/O utilization
- ◆ Use local flash storage

Reviewing Virtual Machine Resource Allocation

A significant advantage of server virtualization is the ability to allocate resources to a virtual machine (VM) based on the actual performance requirements for the guest OS and application or services. In legacy physical server environments, a server was often provided more resources than the application or services required because it was purchased with a specific budget and the server specifications were maximized for the budget provided.

For example, consider a simple Dynamic Host Configuration Protocol (DHCP) server. Based on an average, entry-level rackmount server, would DHCP services really benefit from a server with dual socket, 10-core processors, 32 GB of memory, and mirrored 240 GB solid state drives? And does it really need to consume a minimum of 1U of rack space in the datacenter along with its own three- or five-year service contract? In most situations, the services will underutilize the server resources.

With server virtualization, you can create a VM that is ideally suited for the DHCP server role. For example, you could create a VM with a more-suitable 2 GB or 4 GB of memory (depending on the guest OS), a single CPU, and 20 GB to 40 GB of disk space, all of which are provided by the ESXi host on which the VM is running. With the remaining resources, you can create additional VMs with the resources they need to effectively operative without the overallocation of valuable memory, CPU, and storage.

Allocating resources based on the required or the anticipated need of the guest OS and the applications or services that will run inside a VM is the essence of *right-sizing* your workloads, which we discussed in Chapter 9, "Creating and Managing Virtual Machines." By right-sizing the VMs in your organization, it allows you to achieve greater efficiency and higher consolidation ratios—more VMs per physical server in your datacenter.

However, even when you right-size and add more and more VMs to the platform, each VM places additional demands on the ESXi host as the resources are consumed to support the workloads. At some point, a host will run out of one, or more, of these key resources. For example, consider the following resource management situations.

♦   What does an ESXi host do when it runs out of resources?

♦   How does an ESXi host manage VMs that are requesting more resources than the physical server can provide?

♦   How can you guarantee that a guest OS and its applications and services get the resources they need without being starved by VMs (e.g., a "noisy neighbor")?

VMware vSphere offers a set of controls designed to guarantee access to resources when necessary, control the use of resources, and prioritize access to resources when available resources are low. Specifically, VMware vSphere offers three methods for controlling or modifying resource allocation: reservations, limits, and shares.

The behavior of these mechanisms varies based on the resource, but the fundamental concepts of each mechanism are as follows:

Reservations   Reservations act as guarantees for a resource type. Reservations may be used when you want to ensure that, no matter what else is going on, a specific VM or set of VMs is assured access to a set amount of a resource from startup through shutdown.

Limits   Limits restrict the amount of a resource type that a VM can consume. By default, a VM has a limit applied based on how it's constructed. For example, a VM that is configured with a single virtual CPU (vCPU) is limited to using only that single vCPU. This vSphere feature offers you an even greater level of granularity over how the resources are used. Depending on the resource type for which the limit is being applied, the specific behavior of ESXi will change. We will discuss this in detail in this chapter under the sections for each resource type.

Shares   Shares establish priority during periods of contention. When VMs compete for limited resources, an ESXi host prioritizes which VMs move to the front of the queue to gain access to the resources. The feature determines the priority. The VMs with higher share value will be marked for higher priority and therefore will receive prioritized access to an ESXi host's resources.

Figure 11.1 shows these three mechanisms displayed in the properties of a VM.

FIGURE 11.1
Reservations, limits, and shares offer fine-grained control over resource allocation.

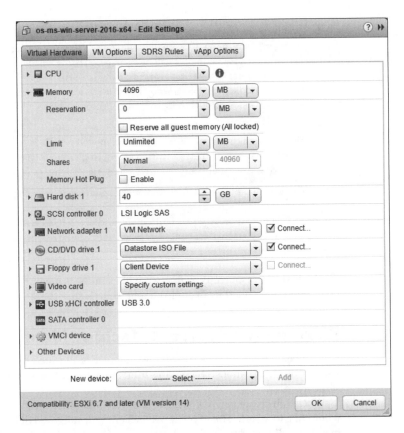

Throughout the chapter, we will discuss how one or more of these three methods—reservations, limits, and shares—are applied to control or modify resource allocation across all four key resources in a vSphere environment: memory, CPU, storage, and network.

THE GAME PLAN FOR GROWTH

Managing a datacenter can be challenging for businesses of all sizes. Organizations must learn to not only manage but also anticipate growth without jeopardizing the performance and reliability of their applications and services. Establishing and executing plans to manage workload and platform—VMs and vSphere—growth is an essential function of today's modern datacenter.

One approach is to construct standard practices that establish the following:

◆ Standard configurations—What is the standard, baseline configuration for a new business workload? Does your organization have a "virtualize by default" policy? Rationalize and define the standard operating systems, baseline resources allocations, in-guest tools, and so forth, as a starting point for new workloads. By establishing a set of standards for VMs, you will increase efficiency and ensure workloads are right-sized on day-one.

◆ Build and configuration—What is the standard creation and delivery model for new VMs to the business? Determine if VMs will be generated from standardized master templates and how the lifecycle of those templates will be managed. Define who will have the ability to create, update, patch, and version the templates. You may also wish to determine if automation will be required to create, update, patch, and then package standard configurations by defining and automating workload builds through code (e.g., manifested builds).

◆ Exception criteria—What decision points are established when requesting a VM with specifications beyond the standard configuration models? While standard configurations are great, they typically will not address all workload requirements for your organization. There will be exceptions, and you should document what criteria warrant an exception.

◆ Capacity planning—What percentage of resources may be consumed before availability and performance levels are in jeopardy? This both affects and is affected by other design points, like $n+1$ redundancy. At what point do you add hosts to a cluster? What is the maximum size of a cluster for your environment? And when does adding resources constitute building a new cluster?

The first VM resource-type that we will examine is memory. Memory is often the first resource to become constrained in an environment, so let's start there.

Working with Virtual Machine Memory

We will begin with a discussion of how memory is allocated to a VM. Later, we will discuss how you can use reservations, shares, and limits to help control or modify how your VMs consume memory.

When you create a new VM in the vSphere Web Client, you are asked how much memory you would like to assign. The vSphere Web Client will suggest a default value based on the recommended configuration for the selected guest OS (the selected guest OS in this case is Microsoft Windows Server 2016 64-bit), as shown in Figure 11.2.

The amount of memory you allocate is the amount the guest OS will see—in this example, 4,096 MB. This is the same as if you build a physical server and insert a set of four 1,024 MB DIMMs into the system board. When you install the Microsoft Windows Server 2016 guest OS onto this VM, the guest OS will report 4,096 MB of memory. Additionally, the memory that the VM has been allocated during the configuration is the maximum amount of memory the guest OS will be able to access—the default upper limit. Like a physical server with four 1,024 MB DIMMs installed, this VM will not be able to use more than 4,096 MB of memory provided by an ESXi host.

Assume for a moment that you have a single ESXi host with 32 GB of memory available to run VMs for your organization. For the sake of math, let's also assume that hypervisor is using some host memory and there's 32 GB available for the VMs to consume. In the case of the new VM, it will comfortably run, leaving approximately 28 GB of memory for other workloads. (There is some additional overhead that we will discuss later, but for now let's assume that the 28 GB is available to other workloads.)

What happens when you run seven more VMs, each configured with 4 GB? Each additional VM will request 4 GB of memory from the ESXi host. At this point, eight VMs will be accessing the physical memory, and you will have allocated all 32 GB of memory to the workloads. The ESXi hypervisor has now run out of a critical resource: memory.

FIGURE 11.2
The memory configuration settings for a VM indicate the amount of memory the VM "thinks" it has.

What happens when you create a ninth VM—will it power on? If this is a cluster and you have configured vSphere High Availability admission control to allow it, then the short answer is yes, and some of the key technologies that enable administrators to overcommit memory—that is, to allocate more memory to VMs than is physically installed on the ESXi host—are quite advanced. Because these technologies are integral to understanding how memory allocation works with VMware vSphere, let's examine these technology features and how they work.

Understanding ESXi Advanced Memory Technologies

VMware ESXi supports many technology features for advanced memory management. ESXi is capable of performing memory over commitment in a manner that is guest OS agnostic.

ESXi DOES NOT REQUIRE GUEST OS INVOLVEMENT

Other commercially available hypervisors may offer the ability to overcommit memory, but these products support the functionality for only a specific guest OS.

VMware ESXi uses five different memory-management technologies to ensure the host memory is used as efficiently as possible: idle memory tax, transparent page sharing, ballooning memory compression, and swapping.

If you are interested in more in-depth information on some of these memory management technologies, we recommend reading "Memory Resource Management in VMware ESX Server," by Carl A. Waldspurger, available online at `http://www.waldspurger.org/carl/papers/esx-mem-osdi02.pdf`.

IDLE MEMORY TAX

Before VMware ESXi actively starts making changes to relieve memory pressure, it ensures that VMs are not actively hording memory by charging more for the idle memory. Up to 75% of the memory allocated to each VM can be borrowed to service another through the Idle Memory Tax (IMT).

This setting is configurable on a per-VM basis within the Advanced Virtual Machine Settings (see Chapter 9). Under most circumstances, it is not necessary, nor recommended, to modify the IMT unless there is a specific requirement.

Inside each guest OS, VMware Tools should be installed and running where it will use the balloon driver to determine which memory blocks are allocated but idle and, therefore, available to be borrowed. The balloon driver is also used in a more active fashion, which we will discuss later in this chapter.

TRANSPARENT PAGE SHARING

The next memory-management technology ESXi uses is *transparent page sharing* (TPS), in which identical memory pages are shared among VMs to reduce the total number of memory pages consumed. The hypervisor computes hashes of the contents of memory pages to identify pages that contain identical memory. If it finds a match, TPS compares the matching memory pages to exclude any false positives. Once the pages are confirmed to be identical, the hypervisor will transparently remap the memory pages of the VMs to share the same physical memory page and thereby reduce overall host memory consumption. Advanced parameters are also available to fine-tune the behavior of the page-sharing techniques.

Normally, ESXi works on 4 KB memory pages and will use transparent page sharing on all memory pages. However, when the hypervisor is taking advantage of hardware offloads available in the CPUs—such as Intel Extended Page Tables (EPT) Hardware Assist or AMD Rapid Virtualization Indexing (RVI) Hardware Assist—then the hypervisor uses 2 MB memory pages, also known as large pages. In these cases, ESXi will not share these large pages, but it will compute hashes for the 4 KB pages inside the large pages. If the hypervisor needs to invoke swapping, the large pages are broken into small pages. Having these hashes already computed allows the hypervisor to invoke the page sharing before they are swapped out.

WHY IS TPS DISABLED BY DEFAULT?

On October 16, 2014, VMware released KB article 2080735 (which you can find at `https://kb.vmware.com/kb/2080735`) that indicated TPS will no longer be enabled by default. This was in response to a research paper that demonstrated using TPS to gain access to the AES encryption key of a machine sharing pages. Although the likelihood of this occurring in real-world scenarios is minimal, VMware made the decision to allow customers to evaluate the risk and the option to enable TPS in their environment, if desired. KB article 2097593 (`https://kb.vmware.com/kb/2097593`) provided an update with additional details on TPS memory-management capabilities and new default settings.

BALLOONING

As we previously discussed, ESXi memory-management technologies are guest OS agnostic—the choice of VM guest OS does not matter. While any supported guest OS can take advantage of all the ESXi memory management techniques, these technologies are not necessarily guest OS independent—meaning that they operate without interaction from the guest OS. While transparent page sharing operates independently of the guest OS, ballooning does not.

Ballooning involves the use of a driver—referred to as the balloon driver—installed into the guest OS. The balloon driver is included as part of VMware Tools and is subsequently deployed when the package is installed on a guest OS. The balloon driver responds to commands from the hypervisor to reclaim memory from the VM's guest OS. The balloon driver does this by requesting memory from the guest OS—a process called *inflating*—and then passing that memory back to the hypervisor for use by other VM workloads.

Because the guest OS can surrender the pages it is no longer using when the balloon driver requests memory, the hypervisor reclaims memory without any performance impact on the applications running inside that guest OS. If the guest OS is already under memory pressure such that the memory configured for the VM is insufficient for the guest OS and its applications, it is likely that inflating the balloon driver will invoke guest OS paging (swapping). This will impair the workload performance.

OPEN-VM-TOOLS

Open-VM-Tools (OVT) is an open-source version of VMware Tools for Linux led by VMware. By transitioning the VMware Tools for Linux into the Linux community, the project has moved upstream into the Linux kernel main line. Customers can now move away from managing the lifecycle of VMware tools for many Linux distributions because they are now included in the OS. This also allows the tools to be updated with newer versions, updates, or patches of each distribution. Learn more at `https://github.com/vmware/open-vm-tools`.

For information on guest OS compatibility for Open-VM-Tools, see the VMware Compatibility Guide at `http://www.vmware.com/resources/compatibility`.

THE BALLOON DRIVER

The balloon driver is part of VMware Tools described in detail in Chapter 9. The tools are specific to the guest OS, which means that VMs with the Linux guest OS would have a Linux-based balloon driver, and VMs with a Windows-based guest OS would have a Windows-based balloon driver.

Regardless of the guest OS, the balloon driver works in the same fashion. When an ESXi host is running low on physical memory and constrained, the hypervisor will signal the balloon driver to *inflate* by requesting memory from the VM's guest OS. The memory granted to the balloon driver during the inflation is passed back to the hypervisor so that it can use these memory pages and redistribute memory to other VMs. This technique reduces the need to swap and minimizes the performance impact of memory constraints. When the memory pressure on the host subsides, the balloon driver will *deflate*, returning memory to the original guest OS.

A key advantage that ESXi gains from using a guest OS-specific balloon driver is that it is the guest OS that makes the decision on which pages can be borrowed during the balloon driver process. In some cases, inflating the balloon driver can release memory back to the hypervisor without degrading the VM performance because the guest OS can release unused or idle pages.

MEMORY COMPRESSION

Memory compression is an additional memory-management technique that an ESXi host has at its disposal. When an ESXi host reaches the point where hypervisor swapping is necessary, the VMkernel will attempt to compress memory pages and keep them in memory in a compressed memory cache. Pages that can be successfully compressed by at least 50% are placed into the compressed memory cache instead of being written to disk and can then be recovered far faster i the guest OS needs to access the memory page. Memory compression can dramatically reduce the number of pages that must be swapped to disk and improves the performance of an ESXi host that is under strong memory pressure. By default, 10% of VM memory is used for the compression cache; however, this figure is configurable. The percentage initiates at zero and grows to the default or configured value when the VM memory starts to swap. Compression is only invoked when the ESXi host reaches the point that VMkernel swapping is required.

SWAPPING

Two forms of swapping are involved in managing memory in ESXi. The first is *guest OS swapping*, in which the guest OS inside the VM swaps pages out to its own virtual disk according to its memory management algorithms. Generally, this is due to memory requirements that are higher than available memory. In a virtualized environment, this translates to a VM being configured with less memory than the guest OS and its applications or services require, such as trying to run Windows Server 2016 with only 1 GB of memory and an application server. Guest OS swapping falls strictly under the control of the guest OS and *is not* controlled by the hypervisor.

The second type of swapping is *hypervisor swapping*. When none of the previously described technologies—transparent page sharing, ballooning, and memory compression—trim guest OS memory usage enough, the ESXi host will invoke hypervisor swapping. Hypervisor swapping means that ESXi will begin swapping memory pages to disk in an effort to reclaim memory that is required for workloads. This swapping takes place without regard to whether the pages are being actively used by the guest OS. Since disk response times are *significantly* slower than memory response times, virtual-machine guest OS performance will be severely impacted when hypervisor swapping is invoked. For this reason, ESXi will not invoke swapping unless it is necessary. Hypervisor swapping is the last-resort option after all previously discussed memory-management techniques have been exhausted.

A key takeaway is that you should avoid hypervisor swapping, if at all possible, because it can have a significant and noticeable impact on your workload performance. Even hypervisor swapping to a flash device is considerably slower than directly accessing memory.

Although these advanced memory management technologies allow ESXi to effectively allocate more memory to VMs than there is actual physical memory in the host, they do not guarantee memory or prioritize access to memory. Even with these advanced memory management technologies, at some point it becomes necessary to exercise some control over how VMs access and consume the memory allocated to them. This is where you, as the vSphere administrator, can use reservations, limits, and shares—the three mechanisms described previously—to modify or control how the resources are allocated. Next, we will discuss how these mechanisms are used to control memory allocation.

Controlling Memory Allocation

Like all physical resources, memory is finite. The advanced memory-management technologies in ESXi assist with the efficient use of this finite resource by making it "go further" than it normally would. For fine-grained control over how ESXi allocates memory, you must turn to the three resource allocation mechanisms mentioned previously—reservations, shares, and limits. Figure 11.3 shows these three settings in the Virtual Machine Properties dialog box.

FIGURE 11.3
vSphere supports the use of reservations, limits, and shares to control memory allocation.

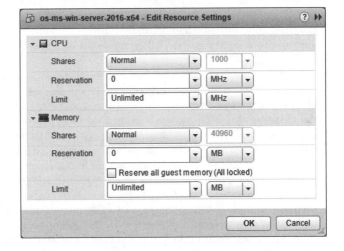

The steps for editing a Reservation, Limit, or Shares value for either memory or CPU are the same. Storage I/O and network I/O are handled a bit differently—we will discuss those in the appropriate sections later in this chapter. Storage I/O is covered in the section "Controlling Storage I/O Utilization," and network I/O is discussed in the section "Regulating Network I/O Utilization."

Perform the following steps to edit a VM's memory or CPU Reservation, Limit, or Shares value:

1. If vSphere Web Client is not already running, open a browser, connect to the vSphere Web Client on your vCenter Server instance, and log on.

2. Navigate to either the Hosts And Clusters view or the VMs And Templates view.

3. In the inventory, find the VM to edit.

4. Select the VM and select the Edit Resource Settings option from the Actions menu.

5. Adjust the Reservation, Limit, and/or Shares values as desired.

Now that you have seen how to adjust the Reservation, Limit, and Shares values, we will take a detailed look at the specific behaviors and how these mechanisms apply to memory usage and allocation.

USING MEMORY RESERVATIONS

Memory reservations are optional settings that may be applied on each VM. In the previous section, Figure 11.3 showed that the default memory reservation is 0 MB, which is the equivalent of no memory reservation. You can adjust the reservation value, but what does this value do?

When a memory reservation is specified in the virtual-machine resource settings, it is the amount of actual physical-server memory that the ESXi host *must* provide to this VM for it to power on. This memory reservation guarantees the designated amount of RAM configured in the Reservation setting. Recall that by default, the reservation is 0 MB, or no reservation. Using our previous example, where we configured a VM with 4 GB of RAM, a default reservation of 0 MB means the ESXi host is not required to provide the VM with any physical memory. If the host is not required to provide memory to the VM, then where will the VM get its memory? In the absence of a reservation, the VMkernel has the option to provide virtual-machine memory from the *VMkernel swap*.

VMkernel swap is the hypervisor swapping memory-management technique we previously discussed. VMkernel swap is implemented as an on-disk file with the .vswp extension and is automatically created when a VM is powered on. Note that the VMX swap files are unrelated to the VMkernel swap file and are overhead for VMX process running the VM on the ESXi host. By default, the per-VM VMkernel swap files reside on the same datastore and path as the VM configuration file and virtual disk files. However, you do have the option of relocating the VMkernel swap, which we will discuss later in this chapter, in a section titled "Configuring Swap to Host Cache." In the absence of a memory reservation (the default configuration), the size of the swap file will be equal in size to the amount of memory configured for the VM. Back to our previous example, a VM configured for 4 GB of memory will have a 4 GB VMkernel swap file that is stored, by default, in the same location as its configuration and virtual disk files.

In theory, this means that a VM could obtain its memory allocation entirely from VMkernel swap—or disk—resulting in a drastic performance degradation for the VM because disk access time is several orders of magnitude slower than RAM access time.

THE SPEED OF RAM

How slow is VMkernel swap compared to RAM? If you make some basic assumptions regarding RAM access times and disk seek times, you can see that both appear fast in terms of our human abilities but in relation to each other, RAM is far superior.

RAM access time = 10 nanoseconds (for example)

Rotational disk seek time = 8 milliseconds (for example)

SSD seek time = 500 microseconds (for example)

The difference between these is calculated as follows:

0.008 ÷ 0.00000001 = 800,000

or

0.0005 ÷ 0.00000001 = 50,000

RAM is accessed 800,000 times faster than traditional rotational disk or 50,000 times faster than SSD. To put it another way, if RAM took 1 second to access, then an average disk could take 800,000 seconds to access—or 9 1/4 days. Even with SSD swap cache, it would still take over half a day: ((800,000 × 60 seconds) × 60 minutes) × 24 hours = 9.259

((50,000 × 60 seconds) × 60 minutes) × 24 hours = 0.578

If VM performance is your goal, ensure that you size your hosts and cluster with enough physical memory to support your organization's VMs and workload. The difference in speed is also why adding memory compression to ESXi's arsenal of memory-management tools can make a big difference in performance, because it assists in avoiding swapping pages out to disk and keeps them in memory instead. Even compressed pages in RAM are significantly faster than pages swapped out to disk.

Just because a VM without a reservation could technically obtain all its memory from VMkernel swap does not mean all of its memory will come from swap when ESXi host memory is available. The ESXi hypervisor attempts to provide each VM with all of its requested memory, up to the maximum amount configured for that VM. Obviously, if a VM is configured with only 4 G or 4,096 MB of memory, it cannot request more. However, when an ESXi host does not have enough available memory to satisfy the VM's memory allocation, and when memory-management techniques—such as transparent page sharing, the balloon driver, and memory compression—are not enough, the VMkernel is forced to page some of each VM's memory out to its VMkernel swap file.

Reservations enable you to control how much of an individual VM's memory allocation must be provided by physical memory and may be provided by swap. Recall that a memory reservation specifies the amount of physical memory the ESXi host must provide a VM and that, by default, a VM has a memory reservation of 0 MB. This means that the ESXi host is not required to provide any real, physical memory. If necessary, all a VM's memory could be paged out to the VMkernel swap file.

What happens if you decide to set a memory reservation of 1,024 MB for the VM, as shown in Figure 11.4? How does this change the way this VM is allocated memory?

In this example, when the VM is powered on, the ESXi host must provide at least 1,024 MB of physical memory to support the VM's memory allocation. In fact, the VM is *guaranteed* 1,024 MB of physical memory. The host can provide the remaining 3,072 MB of memory from either physical memory or the VMkernel swap, as shown in Figure 11.5. Because a portion of the VM memory is guaranteed to be allocated directly from physical memory, ESXi reduces the size of the VMkernel swap file by the amount of the reservation. In this example, the VMkernel swap file is reduced in size by 1,024 MB to a total of 3,072 MB. This behavior is consistent with what you have seen so far: with a reservation of 0 MB, the VMkernel swap file is the same size as the amount of configured memory. As the reservation increases, the size of the VMkernel swap file subsequently decreases.

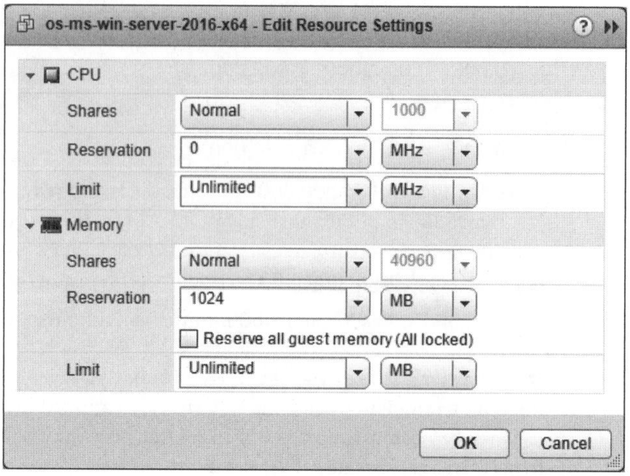

FIGURE 11.4

This memory reservation guarantees 1,024 MB of physical memory for the VM.

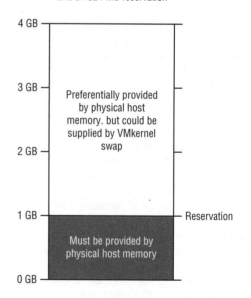

FIGURE 11.5

The memory reservation reduces the potential need for VMkernel swap space by the size of the reservation.

Virtual Machine with 4096 MB memory and a 1024 MB reservation

4 GB

3 GB

Preferentially provided by physical host memory. but could be supplied by VMkernel swap

2 GB

1 GB — Reservation

Must be provided by physical host memory

0 GB

The behavior ensures that a VM has at least some physical memory available to it even if the ESXi host is running more VMs than it has actual physical memory to support, but there is a downside. If you assume that each of the powered-on VMs on the host has a 1,024 MB reservation, and you have 8 GB of available physical memory in the host, then you will only be able to concurrently power-on eight VMs (8 × 1,024 MB = 8,192 MB). On a more positive note, if each VM is configured with an initial allocation of 4,096 MB, then you are now capable of running

VMs that would need 32 GB of memory on a host with only 8 GB. ESXi uses the technologies described previously—transparent page sharing, the balloon driver, memory compression, and VMkernel swap—to manage the allocation of more memory than is physically available on the host.

There is one additional side effect from using memory reservations. We previously discussed that using a memory reservation guarantees physical memory for the VM. This is true, but only as the guest OS in the VM requests memory. If you have a VM with a 1,024 MB reservation configured, then the ESXi host will allocate memory to the VM on an *as-needed basis* after the initial 1,024 MB of memory is allocated as part of the reservation. Memory is allocated on-demand; the presence of a reservation does not change this behavior. However, once the memory reservation is allocated, it is locked to the VM—it cannot be reclaimed via the balloon driver, and it will not be swapped out to disk or compressed.

On one hand, this is a good thing; it underscores the fact that the memory is guaranteed to this VM. On the other hand, it should be used carefully; once allocated to VM, reserved memory cannot be reclaimed for use by other VMs or the hypervisor.

RESERVED MEMORY AND TRANSPARENT PAGE SHARING

Reserved memory cannot be reclaimed by the hypervisor for other purposes—it is, after all, guaranteed to a VM. However, reserved memory can be shared via transparent page sharing. Transparent page sharing does not impact the availability of reserved memory, because the memory page is still accessible to the VM.

Like all the mechanisms described in this chapter, use memory reservations carefully and with a full understanding of the impact on the behavior and operations of an ESXi host.

USE MEMORY OVERCOMMITMENT WISELY

Although you can overcommit memory, do so wisely. ESXi advanced memory management technologies, such as transparent page sharing and idle page reclamation, help conserve memory; however, any workload that requires its memory allocation may incur a performance impact if the memory is not available.

Workloads running on VMs with a Windows guest OS often only use a portion of their configured memory. Generally, it is safe to overcommit memory by as much as 50% of the physical host memory without noticeable performance degradation. As an example, a physical server with 32 GB of memory could potentially host VMs configured with a cumulative allocation of 48 GB of memory. Larger overcommitment ratios are possible, particularly in virtual desktop environments where VMs in a desktop pool use the same base OS image, such as Windows 10. Wisely overcommit memory to maximize the value of your vSphere infrastructure by understanding the requirements of your VMs—including the guest OS, applications, and services—and how they consume resources.

USING MEMORY LIMITS

If you refer to Figure 11.3 (which was shown earlier in this chapter), you will also see a setting for a memory limit. By default, all new VMs are created without a limit, which means the memory assigned during a VM's creation is its effective limit. So, what is the purpose of the memory limit setting? It sets the actual limit on how much physical memory may be used by that VM.

To see this behavior in action, we will change the limit on this VM from the default setting of Unlimited to 2,048 MB.

The effective result of the configuration change is as follows:

♦ The VM is configured with 4,096 MB of memory and the guest OS inside the VM has 4,096 MB available to use.

♦ The VM has a reservation of 1,024 MB of memory, which means that the ESXi host *must* allocate and *guarantee* 1,024 MB of physical memory to the VM.

♦ Assuming the ESXi host has enough physical memory available the hypervisor will allocate memory to the VM, as needed, up to 2,048 MB (the limit). Upon reaching 2,048 MB, the balloon driver inflates to prevent the guest OS from using more memory beyond the limit. When the memory demand on the guest OS drops below 2,048 MB, the balloon driver deflates and returns memory to the guest. The effective result of this behavior is that the memory the guest OS uses remains below 2,048 MB (the limit).

♦ The "memory gap" of 1,024 MB between the reservation and the limit may be provided by either physical host memory or the VMkernel swap space. As always, the ESXi hypervisor will allocate physical memory if available.

The key concern with the use of memory limits is that they are enforced without guest OS awareness. When a VM is configured with 4 GB, the guest OS will think it has 4 GB of memory with which to operate, and it will behave accordingly. By placing a 2 GB limit on this VM, the VMkernel will enforce the VM to only use 2 GB of memory, and it will do so without the knowledge or cooperation of the guest OS. The guest OS will continue to behave as if it has 4 GB of memory, unaware that a limit has been placed on it by the hypervisor. If the working set size of the guest OS and its applications exceeds the memory limit, setting a limit will degrade the performance of the VM because the guest OS will be forced to swap pages to disk (guest OS swapping; not hypervisor swapping).

Generally, memory limits should be a temporary stop-gap measure when you need to reduce physical memory usage on an ESXi host and when a negative impact to performance is an acceptable implication. Ideally, you would not want to overprovision a VM and then constrain the memory usage with a limit on a long-term basis. In this scenario, the VM will typically perform poorly and would perform better if configured with less memory and no limit.

WHY USE MEMORY LIMITS?

Recall from our discussion that memory limits are enforced by the VMkernel without guest OS awareness. In many cases, memory limits can negatively impact the performance of a VM.

However, there are times when you might need to use memory limits as a temporary measure to reduce physical memory usage on your hosts—for example, when you need to perform maintenance on an ESXi host that is part of a vSphere cluster. In this scenario, you temporarily inhibit memory usage on lower-tier VMs, and vMotion these to other hosts in the cluster during a maintenance window to reduce any negative impact on workloads when resources are reduced.

By understanding that memory limits can have a negative impact on performance, you can be sure to use them only when that negative performance implication is understood and acceptable.

When used together, an initial memory allocation, a memory reservation, and a memory limit, can be powerful techniques in efficiently managing the available memory on an ESXi host.

Using Memory Shares

In Figure 11.3 (shown earlier in this chapter), there is a third setting labeled Shares that we have not yet discussed. The memory-reservation and memory-limit mechanisms help provide finer-grained controls over how ESXi should allocate memory to a VM. These mechanisms are always in use—that is, a Limit is enforced even if the ESXi host has plenty of physical memory available for a VM to use.

Memory shares perform quite differently. Shares are a proportional system that allows you to assign resource prioritization to VMs, but shares are used only when the ESXi host is experiencing physical memory contention—the VMs on a host are requesting more memory than the host can provide. If an ESXi host has plenty of memory available, shares do not play a role. However, when memory resources are scarce and the hypervisor needs to decide which VM should be given access to memory, shares establish a priority setting for a VM requesting memory that is greater than the reservation but less than the limit. Recall that memory under the reservation is guaranteed to the VM, and memory over the limit would not be allocated. Shares only affect the allocation of memory between the reservation and the limit.

In other words, if two VMs are requesting more memory than their reservation limit and more than the ESXi host can satisfy, share values can ensure that higher-priority access to the physical memory for one VM over the other.

While you could just increase the reservation for that VM, and it may be a valid technique, it may limit the total number of VMs that a host can run. Increasing the configured amount of memory may also require a reboot of the VM to become the effective allocation (unless the guest OS supports hot-add of memory and that feature has been enabled as described in Chapter 9), but shares can be dynamically adjusted while the VM is powered on.

Shares only come into play when an ESXi host cannot satisfy the requests for physical memory—contention. If an ESXi host has enough free physical memory to satisfy the allocation requests from the VMs, it does not need to prioritize those requests. It's only when an ESXi host does not have enough of a resource to go around that decisions are made on how the resource should be allocated.

For the sake of this discussion, assume you have two VMs—VM1 and VM2—each with a 1,024 MB reservation and a configured maximum of 4,096 MB, and both are running on an ESXi host with less than 2 GB of memory available to the VMs. If the VMs have an equal number of shares, such as 1,000 each (we will discuss values later), then as each VM requests memory above its reservation value, each will receive an equal quantity of memory from the ESXi host. Furthermore, because the host cannot supply all the memory to both VMs, each will swap equally to disk (VMkernel swap file). This assumes, of course, that ESXi cannot reclaim memory from other running VMs using the balloon driver or other memory-management technologies described earlier. If you change VM1's Shares setting to 2,000, then VM1 will have twice the shares VM2 has assigned to it. This means that when VM1 and VM2 are requesting the memory above their respective Reservation values, VM1 gets two memory pages for every one memory page that VM2 receives. If VM1 has more shares, VM1 has a higher-priority access to available memory in the host. Because VM1 has 2,000 out of 3,000 shares allocated, it will get 67%; VM2 has 1,000 out of 3,000 shares allocated and therefore gets only 33% percent. This creates the two-to-one behavior described previously. Each VM is allocated memory pages based on the proportion of the total number of shares allocated across all VMs. Figure 11.6 illustrates this behavior.

FIGURE 11.6
Shares establish relative priority based on the number of shares assigned out of the total shares allocated.

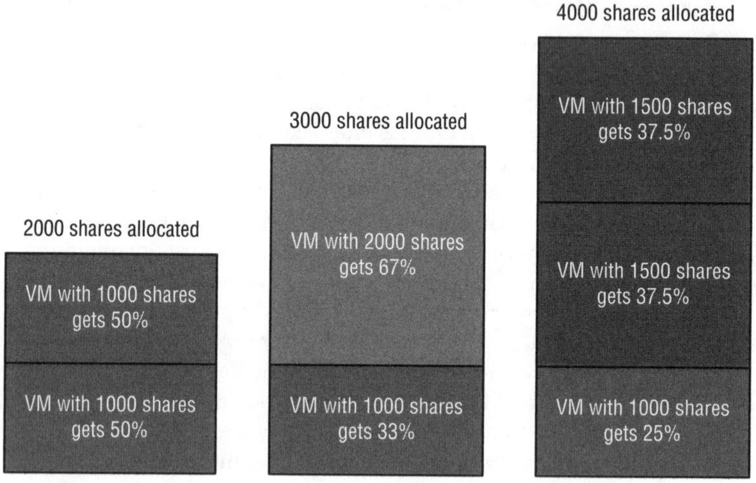

If you do not specifically assign shares to a VM, vSphere automatically assigns shares to a VM when it is created. Back in Figure 11.3, you can see the default Shares value is equal to 10 times the configured memory value when the memory allocation is expressed in terms of MB—more accurately, by default, 10 shares are granted to every MB assigned to a VM. The VM shown in Figure 11.3 has 4,096 MB of memory configured; therefore, its default memory Shares value is 40,960. This default allocation ensures that each VM is granted priority to memory on a measure that is directly proportional to the amount of memory configured for it.

As more and more VMs on an ESXi host are powered on, it gets more difficult to predict the actual memory utilization and the amount of access each VM gets. Later in this chapter, in the section "Using Resource Pools," we will discuss more sophisticated methods of assigning memory limits, reservations, and shares to a group of VMs using resource pools.

We have discussed how VMware ESXi uses advanced memory management technologies, but there is another aspect that you must also consider: overhead. The next section provides information on the memory overhead figures when using ESXi.

EXAMINING MEMORY OVERHEAD

As the saying goes, "nothing is free," and in the case of memory on an ESXi host, there is a cost. That cost is memory overhead. Several basic processes on an ESXi host will consume host memory. The VMkernel itself, various running hypervisor service daemons, and each powered on VM will result in the VMkernel allocating some memory to host each VM above the initial configured amount. The amount of physical memory allocated to power on each VM depends on the virtual CPU and memory configuration for each. VMware has improved the overhead requirements significantly over the last few vSphere releases. To give you an indication of what they are for version 6.7, see Table 11.1. The values have been rounded to the nearest whole number.

TABLE 11.1:   Virtual machine memory overhead

VIRTUAL MEMORY ASSIGNED (MB)	1 VCPU	2 VCPUs	4 VCPUs	8 VCPUs
256	20 MB	20 MB	32 MB	48 MB
1,024	26 MB	30 MB	38 MB	54 MB
4,096	49 MB	53 MB	61 MB	77 MB
16,384	140 MB	144 MB	152 MB	169 MB

Source: "Overhead Memory on Virtual Machines" - VMware vSphere 6.7 official documentation: `https://docs.vmware.com/`

As you plan the allocation of memory to your VMs, be sure to refer to these memory-overhead figures and include the overhead values in your calculations for how memory will be assigned and used. This is especially essential if you plan on using several VMs with large amounts of memory and virtual CPUs. As you can see in Table 11.1, in this situation, the memory overhead required could become a substantial factor.

SUMMARIZING HOW RESERVATIONS, LIMITS, AND SHARES WORK WITH MEMORY

The behavior of reservations, limits, and shares is slightly different for each of the four key resources. Here's a quick review of their behavior when used for controlling memory allocation:

◆ Reservations guarantee memory for a specific VM. Memory is not allocated until it's requested by the VM, but an ESXi host must have enough free memory to satisfy the entire reservation before the VM can power on. Therefore, you cannot reserve more memory than the server has physically available. Once allocated to a VM, reserved memory is not swapped, nor is it reclaimed by the ESXi host. It is locked for that VM.

◆ Limits enforce an upper boundary on the use of memory. Limits are enforced using the VMware Tools balloon driver and—depending on the VM's working set size—could have a negative impact on performance. As the VM approaches the limit—of which the guest OS is unaware—the balloon driver will inflate to keep memory usage under the limit. Th will result in the guest OS swapping to its disk, which will typically degrade performanc

♦ Shares apply only during periods of contention for the physical memory resources. They establish prioritized access to host memory. The VMs are prioritized based on a percentage of shares allocated versus total shares granted. During periods when the host is not experiencing memory contention, shares do not apply and will not affect memory allocation or usage.

A similar summary of the behavior of reservations, limits, and shares will be provided when they are used to control CPU usage, which is the topic of the next sections.

Managing Virtual Machine CPU Utilization

When creating a VM using the vSphere Web Client, you must configure two CPU-related fields. First, select how many virtual CPUs you want to allocate to the VM, and then assign the numbe of cores to those CPUs (see Figure 11.7). These CPU settings allow the VM's guest OS to use between 1 and 128 virtual CPUs from the ESXi host, depending on the guest OS and the vSpher edition license.

FIGURE 11.7
Both the number of sockets and number of cores per socket can be configured for VMs.

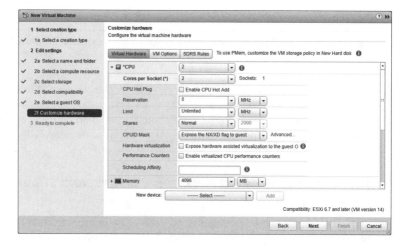

When VMware's engineers designed the hypervisor platform, they began with a real system board and used it to model the VM—in this case, it was based on the Intel 440BX chipset. The VM could emulate the PCI bus, which could be mapped to I/O devices through a standard interface, but how could a VM emulate a CPU?

The answer was "no emulation."

Think about a virtual system board that has a CPU socket "hole" where the CPU is added— and the guest OS simply looks through the socket and sees one of the cores in the host server. This allowed the engineers to avoid writing CPU emulation software that could change each time chipset vendors introduced a new instruction set. If there was an emulation layer, it would also add significant overhead, which would reduce the hypervisor-platform performance by adding more computational overhead.

How many CPUs should a VM have? Assume a VM is replacing a legacy, physical DHCP server that runs at less than 10% CPU utilization at its busiest point in the day. Most certainly, it does not need more than one virtual CPU. In fact, if you configure the VM with two virtual CPUs (vCPUs), then you may limit the scalability of the entire host.

The VMkernel simultaneously schedules CPU cycles for multi-vCPU VMs. When a dual-vCPU VM places a request for CPU cycles, the request goes into a queue for the host to process, and the host must wait until there are at least two physical cores or hyperthreads (if hyperthreading is enabled) with concurrent idle cycles to schedule that VM. A relaxed co-scheduling algorithm provides a bit of flexibility in allowing the cores to be scheduled on a slightly skewed basis, but even so, it can be more difficult for the hypervisor to find open time slots across two cores. This occurs even if the VM needs only a few clock cycles to do a task that can be scheduled with only a single processor.

On the other hand, if a VM needs two vCPUs because of the application or service design it will be processing on a constant basis, then it makes sense to assign two vCPUs to that VM—but only if the host has four or more total CPU cores. If your ESXi host is an older-generation dual-processor single-core system, then assigning a VM two vCPUs will mean that it owns all the CPU processing power on that host every time it gets CPU cycles. You will find that the overall performance of the host and any other VMs will be less than ideal. Of course, in today's market of multicore CPUs, this consideration is less significant than it was in previous hardware generations.

ONE (CPU) FOR ALL—AT LEAST TO BEGIN WITH

The base configuration for any VM should be a single vCPU to minimize creating unnecessary contention for physical processor time. Only when a VM's performance level and application architecture dictate the need for an additional CPU should one be allocated. Remember that a multi-CPU VM should be created only on ESXi hosts that have more cores than the number of vCPUs being assigned to that VM. Create a dual-vCPU VM only on a host with two or more cores, a quad-vCPU VM only on a host with four or more cores, an eight-vCPU VM only on a host with eight or more cores, and so forth.

Default CPU Allocation

Like the memory settings discussed previously, the Reservation, Limit, and Shares settings can be configured for CPU resources as well.

When a VM is created with a single vCPU, the total maximum CPU cycles for the VM are equal to the clock speed of the host system's core. In other words, if you create a new VM, it can see through the "hole in the system board," and it sees whatever the core is in terms of clock cycles per second—an ESXi host with a 2.2 GHz CPU's 10-core processer in it will allow the VM to see one 2.2 GHz core.

Figure 11.8 shows the default settings for CPU Reservation, Limits, and Shares.

FIGURE 11.8
By default, vSphere
provides no CPU
reservation, no CPU
limit, and 1,000
CPU shares.

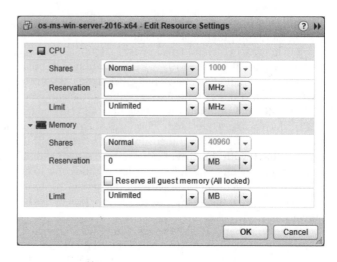

Setting CPU Affinity

In addition to reservations, limits, and shares, vSphere offers a fourth option for managing CPU usage: CPU affinity. CPU affinity allows you to statically associate a VM to a specific physical CPU core. CPU affinity is generally not recommended; it has a list of rather significant drawbacks:

- ◆ CPU affinity prevents vMotion.

- ◆ The hypervisor is unable to load-balance the VM across all the processing cores in the server. This prevents the hypervisor's CPU scheduler from making efficient use of the ho resources.

- ◆ Because vMotion is inhibited, you cannot use CPU affinities in a cluster where vSphere DRS isn't set to Manual operation.

Because of these limitations, most organizations avoid using CPU affinity. However, if, for example, you find that you need to use CPU affinity to adhere to licensing requirements or an extreme latency sensitive workload, you can configure your VM to use it.

Perform the following steps to configure CPU affinity:

1. If vSphere Web Client is not already running, open a browser, connect to the vSphere Web Client on your vCenter Server instance, and log on.

2. Navigate to either the Hosts And Clusters view or the VMs And Templates view.

3. In the inventory, find the VM to edit.

4. Select the VM and select the Edit Settings option from the Actions menu.

5. On the Virtual Hardware tab, click the triangle next to CPU.

6. In the Scheduling Affinity section, provide a list of the CPU cores this VM can access. For example, if you wanted the VM to run on cores 1 through 4, you could type **1–4**.

7. Click OK to save the changes.

Rather than using CPU affinity to guarantee CPU resources, consider using reservations.

CPU AFFINITY NOT AVAILABLE WITH FULLY AUTOMATED CLUSTERS

If you are using a vSphere Distributed Resource Scheduler–enabled cluster configured in fully auto-mated mode, CPU affinity cannot be set for VMs in that cluster. You must configure the cluster for manual/partially automated mode or set the VM automation mode to manual/partially automated to use CPU affinity.

Using CPU Reservations

As you saw in Figure 11.7, the default CPU reservation for a new VM is 0 MHz (no reservation). Recall that a reservation is a resource guarantee. By default, a VM is not guaranteed any CPU scheduling time by the VMkernel. When the VM has work to be done, it places its CPU request into the CPU queue, and the VMkernel schedules the request in sequence along with all of the other VM requests. On a lightly loaded ESXi host, it is unlikely the VM will wait long for CPU time; however, on a heavily loaded host, the time the VM may wait could be significant.

If you were to set a 1,024 MHz reservation, as shown in Figure 11.9, this would effectively ensure the amount of CPU available instantly to this VM when there is a need for CPU cycles.

FIGURE 11.9
A VM configured with a 1,024 MHz reserva-tion for CPU activity is guaranteed that amount of CPU capacity.

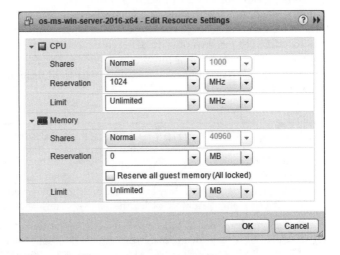

A CPU reservation has a notable impact on the behavior of the ESXi host and, as such, CPU reservations and memory reservations behave identically. The ESXi host must satisfy the reservation by providing enough resources to meet the reservations. If each VM you create has a 1,024 MHz reservation and your host has 12,000 MHz of CPU capacity, you can power on no more than 11 VMs (1,024 MHz × 11 = 11,264 MHz), even if each machine is idle. Notice the term "power on" instead of "create" was used; resources are allocated only when a VM is powered on, not created.

Although a CPU reservation behaves like a memory reservation, a CPU reservation is very different from a memory reservation when it comes to "sharing" reserved CPU cycles. Recall from the previous section that once reserved memory is allocated to the VM, it is never reclaimed, paged out to disk, or shared in any way. The same is not true for CPU reservations.

Suppose you have two VMs, VM1 and VM2, and VM1 has a CPU reservation of 1,024 MHz and VM2 has no reservation. If VM1 is idle and not using its reserved CPU cycles, those cycles can be given to VM2. If VM1 suddenly needs cycles, VM2 doesn't get them anymore, and they are assigned to VM1.The Reservation setting on a CPU is similar using the Reservation setting for memory, but it is also very different.

Earlier, we discussed how using a Limit setting with memory had some significant drawbacks, but what about CPU limits? We will cover that next.

Using CPU Limits

In addition to CPU reservations, you can set a limit on the amount of CPU allocated. This effectively limits the ability of a VM to use a maximum number of clock cycles per second, regardless of what the host has available. Keep in mind that a VM with a single-core vCPU hosted on a 2.2 GHz, dual-socket, 10-core processor host will see only a single 2.2 GHz core as its maximum, but as an administrator, you could alter the limit to prevent the VM from using the maximum core speed. For instance, you could set a 500 MHz limit on the DHCP server so that when it re-indexes the DHCP database, it will not attempt to take all the 2.2 GHz on the processor core that it can see. The CPU limit allows you to throttle the VM down to use less processing power than is available on the physical core. Not every VM needs to have access to the entire processing capability of the physical processor core.

The key drawback to using a CPU Limit setting is its performance impact on the guest OS and the applications or services running on the VM. The Limit setting is a true limit; the VM will not be scheduled to run on a physical CPU core more than the limit specifies, even if there are plenty of CPU cycles available. It is important, therefore, to understand the CPU processing needs of your workloads *before* arbitrarily setting any CPU limits in order to avoid significantly impacting their performance.

INCREASING CONTENTION IN THE FACE OF GROWTH

A common problem an administrator may encounter occurs when several VMs without limits are deployed on a new virtualized environment. The administrator and the consumer are accustomed to stellar performance levels early in the environment deployment; however, as more VMs are deployed that begin to compete for CPU cycles, the relative performance of the first VMs deployed will degrade.

One approach to combat this issue is to set a reservation of approximately 10 to 20% of a single core's clock rate and add approximately 20% to that value for a limit on the VM. For example, with 2.2 GHz CPUs in the host, each VM would start with a 220 MHz reservation and a 440 MHz limit. This would ensure that the VM performs similarly on both a lightly loaded ESXi host and a more heavily loaded ESXi host.

This is *only* an example starting point. It is possible to limit a VM that really does need more CPU capabilities, and you should always actively monitor the VMs to determine whether they are using all the CPU you are providing them. For example, you can use vRealize Operations to monitor the utilization for each VM over time to understand its workload requirements.

Using CPU Shares

The shares model in vSphere, which lets you prioritize access to resources when resource contention occurs, behaves similarly for both memory and CPU. Shares of CPU determine how much CPU is provided to a VM in the face of contention with other VMs needing CPU activity. By default, all VMs begin with an equal number of shares, which means that if VMs compete for CPU cycles on an ESXi host, each is serviced with equal priority. Keep in mind that the share value only affects those CPU cycles that are greater than the reservation set for the VM, and the share value applies only when the ESXi host has more requests for CPU cycles than it has CPU cycles to allocate.

In other words, the VM is granted access to its reservation cycles regardless of what else is happening on the host, but if the VM needs more CPU cycles—and there is competition—then the share values come into play. If there is no CPU contention on the host, and it has enough CPU cycles to go around for all VMs, the CPU Shares value will not impact CPU allocations.

Several conditions must be met for shares to be considered for allocating CPU cycles. The best way to determine this is to consider several scenarios. For the scenarios we will cover, assume the following details about the environment:

- The ESXi host includes dual, single-core, 3 GHz CPUs.

- The ESXi host has one or more VMs, each configured with a single vCPU.

Scenario 1   The ESXi host has a single VM powered on. The shares are set at the defaults for any running VMs. The Shares value will have no effect in this scenario because there is no competition between VMs for CPU time.

Scenario 2   The ESXi host has two idle VMs powered on. The shares are set at the defaults for the VMs. The Shares values have no effect in this scenario; there is no competition between VMs for CPU time, because both are idle.

Scenario 3   The ESXi host has two equally busy VMs powered on, and both are requesting maximum CPU capacity. The shares are set at the defaults for the VMs. Again, the Shares values have no effect in this scenario, because there is no competition between VMs for CPU time. In this scenario, each VM is serviced by a different core in the host.

Scenario 4   To force contention, both VMs are configured to use the same physical CPU by setting the CPU affinity. The ESXi host has two equally busy VMs powered on, and both are requesting maximum CPU capacity. This ensures contention between the VMs. The shares are set at the defaults for the VMs. Will the Shares values have any effect in this scenario? Yes! Because all VMs have equal Shares values, each VM has equal access to the host CPU queue, so you do not see any effects from the Shares values.

Scenario 5   The ESXi host has two equally busy VMs powered on, and both are requesting maximum CPU capacity with CPU affinity set to the same physical core. The shares are set as follows: VM1 is set to 2,000 CPU shares, and VM2 is set to the default 1,000 CPU shares. Will the Shares values have any effect in this scenario? Yes! VM1 has double the number of shares than what VM2 has. For every clock cycle that VM2 is assigned by the host, VM1 is assigned two clock cycles. Stated another way, out of every three clock cycles assigned to VMs by the ESXi host, two are assigned to VM1, and one is assigned to VM2. The diagram shown earlier in Figure 11.6 helps graphically reinforce how shares are allocated based on a percentage of the total number of shares assigned to all VMs.

Scenario 6 The ESXi host has three equally busy VMs powered on, and each is requesting maximum CPU capabilities with CPU affinity set to the same physical core. The shares are set as follows: VM1 is set to 2,000 CPU shares, and VM2 and VM3 are set to the default 1,000 CPU shares. Will the Shares values have any effect in this scenario? Yes! VM1 has double the number of shares that VM2 and VM3 have assigned. This means that for every two clock cycles that VM1 is assigned by the host, VM2 and VM3 are each assigned a single clock cycle. Stated another way, out of every four clock cycles assigned to VMs by the ESXi host, two cycles are assigned to VM1, one is assigned to VM2, and one is assigned to VM3. You can see that this has effectively watered down VM1's CPU capabilities.

Scenario 7 The ESXi host has three VMs powered on. VM1 is idle while VM2 and VM3 are equally busy, each VM is requesting maximum CPU capabilities, and all three VMs are set with the same CPU affinity. The shares are set as follows: VM1 is set to 2,000 CPU shares, and VM2 and VM3 are set to the default 1,000 CPU shares. The Shares values will still have an effect in this scenario. In this case, VM1 is idle, which means it is not requesting any CPU cycles; therefore, this means that VM1's Shares value is not considered when apportioning the host CPU to the active VMs. VM2 and VM3 would equally share the host CPU cycles because their shares are set to an equal value.

AVOID CPU AFFINITY SETTINGS

You should avoid the CPU affinity setting at all costs. Even if a VM is configured to use a single CPU (for example, CPU1), it does not guarantee that it will be the only VM accessing that CPU, unless every other VM is configured not to use that CPU.

vMotion capability will also be unavailable for every VM. Use shares, limits, and reservations as an alternative to retain the vMotion capability.

Given the preceding scenarios, if you were to extrapolate to a 10-core host with 30 or so VMs, it would be difficult to set Shares values on a VM-by-VM basis and to predict how the system will respond. The question then becomes, "Are shares a useful tool?"

The answer is yes, but in large enterprise environments, you must examine resource pools and the ability to set share parameters along with reservations and limits on collections of VMs. We will discuss resource pools in the upcoming "Using Resource Pools" section, after summarizing the behavior of reservations, limits, and shares when used to control CPU allocation and usage.

Summarizing How Reservations, Limits, and Shares Work with CPUs

The following list includes some key behaviors and facts surrounding the use of reservations, limits, and shares, when applied to controlling or modifying CPU usage:

◆ Reservations set on CPU cycles provide guaranteed processing power for VMs. Unlike memory, reserved CPU cycles can and will be used by ESXi to service other requests when needed. As with memory, the ESXi host must have enough real, physical CPU capacity to satisfy a reservation to power on a VM. Therefore, you cannot reserve more CPU cycles than the host can deliver.

◆ Limits on CPU usage simply prevent a VM from gaining access to additional CPU cycles even if CPU cycles are available to use. Even if the host has plenty of CPU processing power available to use, a VM with a CPU limit will not be permitted to use more CPU cycles than specified in the limit. Depending on the guest OS and the applications or services, this may or may not have an adverse effect on performance.

◆ Shares are used to determine CPU allocation when the ESXi host is experiencing CPU contention. Like memory, shares grant CPU access on a percentage basis calculated on the number of shares granted out of the total number of shares assigned. This means that the percentage of CPU cycles granted to a VM based on its Shares value is always relative to the number of other VMs and the total number of shares granted, and it is not an absolute value.

As you can see, there are some key differences as well as several similarities in how these mechanisms work for memory when compared to how they work for CPU.

We have discussed two of the four major resource types—memory and CPU. Before we can move on to the third resource type—networking—we need to discuss the concept of resource pools.

Using Resource Pools

The settings for VM resource allocation—memory and CPU reservations, limits, and shares—are methods that modify or control how resources are distributed to individual VMs or that modify the priority of VMs seeking access to resources.

In much the same logical way that you assign users to groups and then assign permissions to the groups, you can leverage resource pools to allocate resources to collections of VMs in a less tedious and more effective process. In other words, instead of configuring reservations, limits, or shares on a per-VM basis, you can use a resource pool to set those values on a group of VMs all at once.

A *resource pool* is a special type of container object, much like a folder, in the Hosts And Clusters view. You can create a resource pool on a standalone host or as a management object in a vSphere DRS-enabled cluster. Figure 11.10 shows the creation of a resource pool.

FIGURE 11.10

You can create resource pools on individual hosts and within clusters. A resource pool provides a management and performance configuration layer in the vCenter Server inventory.

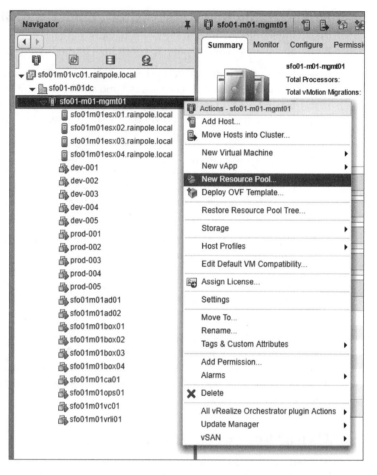

If you examine the properties of the resource pool, you will see two sections: one for CPU settings and one for Memory settings, expressed as Shares, Reservation, and Limit. When you apply resource settings to a resource pool, those settings affect all the VMs found within that resource pool container object. This provides a scalable method to adjust the resource settings for groups of VMs. Setting CPU and memory shares, reservations, and limits on a resource pool is similar to setting the same values on individual VMs. The behavior of these values, however, can be quite different on a resource pool than on an individual VM.

To illustrate how to set reservations, limits, and shares on a resource pool, as well as to explain how these values work when applied to a resource pool, we will use an example vSphere cluster with two resource pools. The resource pools are named Production and Development. Figure 11.11 and Figure 11.12 show the values that have been configured for the Production and Development resource pools, respectively.

Configuring Resource Pools

Before we discuss how resource pools behave with resource allocations, you must first create and configure the resource pools. Use the resource pools, shown earlier in Figure 11.11 and Figure 11.12, as examples for creating and configuring resource pools.

FIGURE 11.11
The Production resource pool is guaranteed CPU and memory resources and higher-priority access to resources in the face of contention.

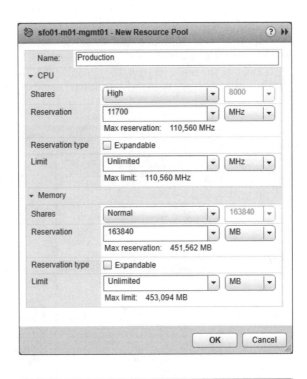

FIGURE 11.12
The Development resource pool is configured for lower-priority access to CPU and memory in the event of resource contention.

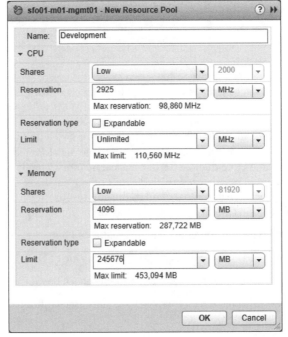

To create a resource pool, simply right-click either an individual ESXi host or a vSphere cluster, and select New Resource Pool. In the Create Resource Pool dialog box, you will need to supply a name for the new resource pool and set the CPU and Memory values as desired.

After creating the resource pool, simply move the VMs into it by clicking the VM in the inventory and dragging it onto the appropriate resource pool. The result is a hierarchy similar to the one that's shown in Figure 11.13.

FIGURE 11.13
VMs assigned to a resource pool consume resources allocated to the resource pool.

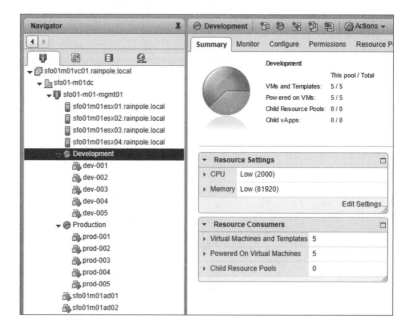

In this example, you have two classifications of servers—production and development—and you have created a resource pool for each classification. The goal is to ensure that if there is competition for a resource, the production VMs will be assigned higher-priority access to that resource. In addition to that goal, you need to ensure that the VMs in development cannot consume more than 24 GB of physical memory with their powered-on VMs. You do not care how many VMs run concurrently as part of the development group, only that they do not collectively consume more than 24 GB of physical memory. Finally, you need to guarantee that a minimum amount of resources is available for both groups.

To achieve your goal of guaranteeing resources for the production VMs, you will set the Production resource pool to use the following settings (refer to Figure 11.11):

♦ CPU resources area: Shares value of High.

♦ CPU resources area: Reservation value of 11,700 MHz.

♦ CPU resources area: Expandable check box Reservation Type is deselected.

♦ CPU resources area: No CPU limit (the Unlimited option in the Limit drop-down menu is selected).

◆ Memory resources area: Shares value of Normal.

◆ Memory resources area: Reservation value of 16,384 MB.

◆ Memory resources area: Expandable check box for Reservation Type is deselected.

◆ Memory resources area: No memory limit (the Unlimited option in the Limit drop-down menu is selected).

Similarly, you will apply the following settings to the development VMs in the Development resource pool (see Figure 11.12):

◆ CPU resources area: Shares value of Low.

◆ CPU resources area: Reservation value of 2,925 MHz.

◆ CPU resources area: Expandable check box for Reservation Type is deselected.

◆ CPU resources area: Limit value of 11,700 MHz.

◆ Memory resources area: Shares value of Low.

◆ Memory resources area: Reservation value of 4,096 MB.

◆ Memory resources area: Expandable check box for Reservation Type is deselected.

◆ Memory resources area: Limit value of 24,576 MB.

Setting these values on the resource pools involves right-clicking the resource pool, selecting Edit Settings, and then setting the required values.

Now that you have an example to work with, we will discuss what these settings will do to the VMs contained within each of the resource pools.

Understanding Resource Allocation with Resource Pools

In the previous section, you created two resource pools called Production and Development. The values for these resource pools are illustrated in Figure 11.11 and Figure 11.12. The goal behind creating these resource pools and setting the values on them was to ensure that a certain level of resources would always be available to production VMs—those found in the Production resource pool—and to limit the resources used by the development VMs—those found in the Development resource pool. In this example, you used all three values—Shares, Reservation, and Limit—to accomplish this goal. Next, we will review the behavior of each of these values when used on a resource pool.

MANAGING CPU USAGE WITH RESOURCE POOLS

First, we will examine the CPU Shares value assigned to the resource pools. As you saw in Figure 11.11, the CPU Shares value for the Production resource pool is set to High (8,000). Figure 11.12 shows that the Development CPU Shares value is set to Low (2,000). The impact of these two settings is similar to comparing the Shares values for CPU for two VMs—except in this case, if there is any competition for CPU resources between VMs in the Production and Development resource pools, the entire Production resource pool and all the VMs within the object have a higher priority. Figure 11.14 shows how this would break down with two VMs in each resource pool.

FIGURE 11.14
Two resource pools with different Shares values will be allocated resources proportional to their percentage of share ownership.

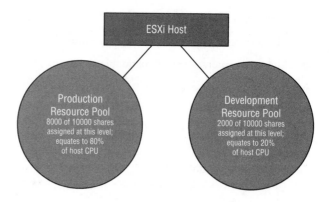

As you consider the details previously shown in Figure 11.13, keep in mind that the resource allocation occurs at each level. There are only two resource pools under the vSphere cluster, so the CPU is allocated 80/20 according to its Shares value. This means that the Production resource pool is allocated 80% of the CPU time, whereas, the Development resource pool receives only 20% of the CPU time.

Let's expand on Figure 11.13 and add the two VMs in each resource pool to get a more complete view of how Shares values work with a resource pool. In the resource pool, the CPU Shares values assigned to the VMs, if any, come into play. Figure 11.15 shows how this works.

FIGURE 11.15
The percentage of resources assigned to a resource pool via its Shares values is further subdivided according to the Shares values of the VMs within the pool.

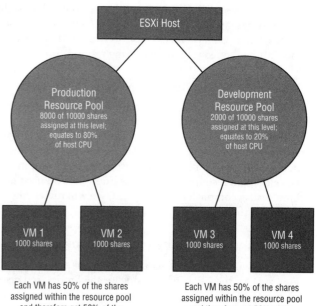

In Figure 11.15, there are no custom CPU shares assigned to the VMs. Recall that each VM will therefore use the default value of 1,000 CPU shares. With two VMs in the resource pool, this means each VM receives 50% of the available CPU resources for the resource pool in which it is located, therefore each has 50% of the total number of shares assigned within the resource pool. In this example, 40% of the host CPU capacity will be allocated to each of the two VMs in the Production resource pool. If there were three VMs in each resource pool, then the CPU allocated to the parent resource pool would be split three ways. Similarly, if there were four VMs, then the CPU would be split four ways. You can verify this breakdown of resource allocation using the Monitor tab on the selected cluster, ESXi host, or resource pool. Figure 11.16 shows the Resource Reservation section for a cluster with the Production and Development resource pools. The CPU button is selected, meaning that the vSphere Web Client is showing you the breakdown of CPU allocation for the selected cluster.

FIGURE 11.16

The Resource Reservation section of the Monitor tab can verify the allocation of resources to objects within the vCenter Server hierarchy.

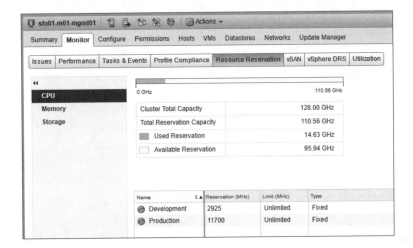

Note that in the Figure 11.16 screenshot, both the resource pools and VMs are directly in the root of the cluster, which, for all intents and purposes, is a resource pool itself. In this case, the sum of all the Shares values—for both resource pools as well as VMs—is used to calculate the percentage of CPU allocated.

SHARES APPLY ONLY DURING ACTUAL RESOURCE CONTENTION

Remember that share allocations come into play only when VMs are competing for a resource—in other words, when an ESXi host is unable to satisfy all the requests for a resource. If an ESXi host is running only eight single-vCPU VMs on top of two 10-core processors, there will not be contention to manage and Shares values will not apply. Be sure to keep this in mind when reviewing the results of Shares allocations like those displayed in Figure 11.16.

We now need to discuss an important consideration about the use of resource pools. It is possible to use resource pools as a form of inventory organization, as you would use VM folders.

Some organizations and administrators have taken to using resource pools in this way to help keep the inventory organized in a specific fashion. Although this is possible, this approach is not recommended.

We will review the Resource Allocation section as seen in the HTML5-based vSphere Web Client. Although the HTML5 client is not covered in this book, the Flash-based vSphere Web Client no longer provides a view that presents the share. The view in the HTML5-based vSphere Web Client helps to illustrate why using resources pools merely for organization is not recommended.

Look at Figure 11.17, which shows the Resource Allocation section for a cluster of ESXi hosts. In the root of this cluster are 12 VMs assigned a total of 22,000 shares. Because each of these VMs is using the default CPU Shares value (1,000 shares per vCPU), they each get equal access to the host CPU capacity—in this case, 4.5% per vCPU (the VM with 2,000 shares and 9% shares has two vCPUs, and the VMs with 4,000 shares and 18% have four vCPUs).

FIGURE 11.17

In the absence of custom CPU shares, CPU capacity is equally allocated to all VMs.

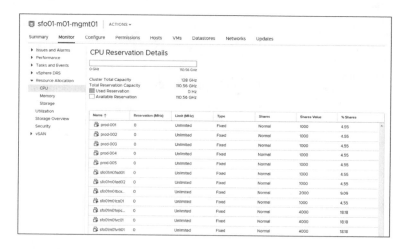

Now look at Figure 11.18. The only change here is that a "Production" resource pool has been added. No changes were made to any of the default values for the resource pool. The resource pool has a default CPU Shares value of 4,000. Note how the simple addition of this resource pool changes the default CPU allocation for the individual VMs by dropping it from 4.5% per vCPU to 3.8% per vCPU. The resource pool, on the other hand, now gets 15.3%. If you added a single VM with one vCPU to the resource pool, it would receive 15.3% of the CPU capacity, whereas other VMs would only receive 3.8% (or 7.6%percent for VMs with two vCPUs).

It is for this reason—the change on the resource allocation distribution—that it is *not recommended* to use resource pools merely for the purposes of organizing the VM inventory. However, if you insist on using resource pools in this way, be sure you understand the impact of configuring your environment in this manner. A better way to organize your inventory, and one that will not impact the performance, is to use VMs' folders or vSphere tags; for more information, see Chapter 3, "Installing and Configuring vCenter Server."

The next setting in the resource pool properties to evaluate is CPU Reservation for the CPU. Continuing with the examples shown earlier in Figure 11.11 and Figure 11.12, you can see a CPU Reservation value of 11,700 MHz has been set on the Production resource pool. The Development resource pool has a CPU Reservation value of 2,925 MHz.

FIGURE 11.18

By default, the addition of a resource pool will alter the resource allocation policy even if you do not set any custom values.

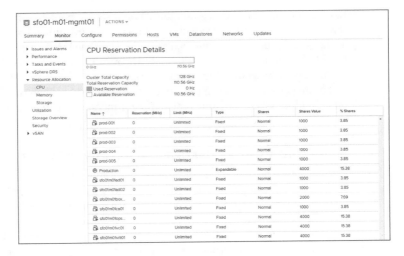

Note that the four ESXi hosts in the cluster hosting the resource pools have two eight-core 2.00 GHz Intel Xeon CPUs each, so this scenario essentially reserves six cores for the Production resource pool and two cores for the Development resource pool. This setting ensures that at least 11,700 MHz of CPU time is available for all the VMs located in the Production resource pool, or 2,925 MHz of CPU for VMs in the Development resource pool.

If the four ESXi hosts in the cluster have a total of 128,000 MHz CPU (4 hosts × 16 cores × 2,000 MHz = 128,000 MHz), this means 116,300 MHz of CPU time is available on the cluster for other reservations. If one more resource pool was created with a Reservation value of 116,300 MHz, then all available host CPU capacity would be reserved. This configuration means you will not be able to create any additional resource pools or any individual VMs with Reservation values set. Remember that the ESXi host or cluster must have enough resource capacity—CPU capacity, in this case—to satisfy all reservations. You cannot reserve more capacity than the host has.

The CPU Reservation setting has the option to make the reservation expandable. An expandable reservation—which can be enabled by selecting the Expandable check box next to Reservation Type—allows a resource pool to "borrow" resources from its parent host or parent resource pool to satisfy reservations set on individual VMs within the resource pool. Note however, that resource pools with an expandable reservation "borrow" from the parent only to satisfy reservations, not to satisfy requests for resources that exceed what was originally specified in the reservations. Neither of the resource pools has expandable reservations, so you can assign only 5,850 MHz of CPU capacity as reservations to individual VMs within each resource pool. Any attempt to reserve more than this amount will result in an error message explaining that you have exceeded the allowed limit.

Deselecting the Expandable check box does not limit the total amount of CPU capacity available to the resource pool; it limits only the total amount of CPU capacity that can be reserved within the resource pool. To set an upper limit on actual CPU usage, you must use a CPU Limit setting.

CPU Limit is the third setting on each resource pool. The behavior of the CPU limit on a resource pool is akin to its behavior on individual VMs except, in this case, the limit applies to all VMs placed in the resource pool object. All VMs combined are allowed to consume up to this

Limit value. In the example, the Production resource pool does not have a CPU limit assigned. In this case, the VMs in the Production resource pool are allowed to consume as many CPU cycles as the ESXi hosts in the cluster can provide. The Development resource pool, on the other hand, has a CPU Limit setting of 11,700 MHz. The result is that all the VMs in the Development resource pool are allowed to consume up to a maximum of 11,700 MHz of CPU capacity.

For the most part, CPU reservations, limits, and shares behave similarly on resource pools and on individual VMs. The same is also true for memory reservations, limits, and shares, as you will see in the next section.

MANAGING MEMORY USAGE WITH RESOURCE POOLS

In the memory portion of the resource pool settings, the first setting is the Shares value. This setting works in much the same way as memory shares works on individual VMs. It determines which group of VMs will be the first to release memory via the balloon driver—or if memory pressure is severe enough to activate memory compression or hypervisor swapping—in the face of contention. However, this setting specifies a priority value for all VMs in the resource pool when they compete for resources from other resource pools. Looking at the memory share settings in our example (Production = Normal and Development = Low), this means that if host memory is limited, VMs in the Development resource pool that need more memory than their reservation would have a lower priority than an equivalent VM in the Production resource pool. Figure 11.14, used earlier to help explain CPU shares on resource pool, applies here as well. As with CPU shares, you can also use the Resource Reservation section to view how memory resources are assigned to resource pools or VMs within resource pools.

The second setting is the resource pool's memory reservation. The memory Reservation value will reserve this amount of host memory for VMs in this resource pool, which effectively ensures that some physical memory is guaranteed to the VMs. As explained in the discussion on CPU reservations, the Expandable check box next to Reservation Type does not limit how much memory the resource pool can use, but rather how much memory you can reserve there.

With the memory Limit value, you set a limit on how much host memory a group of VMs can consume. If an administrative user has been added to a role with the Create VMs permission, the memory Limit value would prevent the administrator from powering on VMs that consume more than that amount of physical host memory. In our example, the memory Limit value on the Development resource pool is set to 24,576 MB. How many VMs can administrators in development create? As many as they wish.

Although this setting does nothing to limit the creation of VMs, it does place a limit on the powered-on VMs. So, how many can they run? The cap placed on memory use is not a per-VM setting but a cumulative setting. Administrators might be able to power on only one VM with all the memory or multiple VMs with lower memory configurations. If each VM is created without an individual memory Reservation value set, an administrator can operate as many concurrently powered-on VMs as they want. However, once the VMs consume 24,576 MB of host memory, the hypervisor will step in and prevent the VMs in the resource group from using any additional memory. Refer to our discussion of memory limits in the section "Using Memory Limits" for the techniques that the VMkernel uses to enforce the memory limit. If the administrator builds six VMs with 4,096 MB as the initial memory amount, then all four VMs will consume 24,576 MB (assuming no overhead, which we have already shown is not the case) and will run in physical memory. If an administrator tried to run 20 VMs configured for 2,048 MB of memory, then all 20 VMs will share the 24,576 MB of memory, even though their requirement is for 40,960 MB (20 × 2,048 MB)—the remaining amount of memory would most likely be provided by VMkernel swap. At this point, workload performance would be noticeably degraded.

If you want to clear a limit, select Unlimited from the Limit drop-down menu. This is true for both CPU limits as well as memory limits. By now, you should have a fair idea of how ESXi allocates resources to VMs as well as how you can tweak those settings to meet your specific demands and workloads.

As you can see, if you have groups of VMs with similar resource demands, using resource pools is a great way of ensuring consistent resource allocation. If you understand the hierarchical nature of resource pools—that resources are allocated first to the pool at its level in the hierarchy, and then the VMs in the resource pool—you should be able to effectively use resource pools.

As you have seen so far, you can control the use of CPU and memory; however, those are only two of the four core resources consumed by VM. In the next section, we will discuss how to control network traffic through network resource pools.

Regulating Network I/O Utilization

The resource pools we have discussed thus far only control CPU and memory usage. However, vSphere offers another type of resource pool, a *network resource pool*, which allows you to control and prioritize network utilization. Using network resource pools—to which you assign shares and limits—you can control incoming and outgoing network traffic. This feature is referred to as vSphere Network I/O Control or NIOC.

ONLY ON A DISTRIBUTED SWITCH

vSphere Network I/O Control applies only to vSphere Distributed Switches (vDS) version 4.1.0 or later and, prior to version 5.1.0, it was limited to outbound network traffic only. Refer to Chapter 5, "Creating and Configuring a vSphere Network," for more information on setting up or configuring a vDS.

When you enable NIOC on a vSphere Distributed Switch (vDS), vSphere activates the following nine predefined network resource pools:

◆ Fault Tolerance (FT) Traffic

◆ Management Traffic

◆ NFS Traffic

◆ Virtual Machine Traffic

◆ vSAN Traffic

◆ iSCSI Traffic

◆ vMotion Traffic

◆ vSphere Data Protection Backup Traffic

◆ vSphere Replication (VR) Traffic

Each of these network resource pools is visible on the Resource Reservation section of a vDS, as you can see in Figure 11.19.

FIGURE 11.19

Network resource pools on a vDS provide granular control of network traffic.

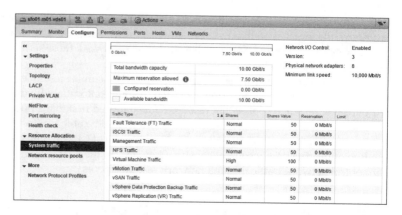

Two steps are involved in setting up and using NIOC. First, you must enable NIOC on a vDS, and second, you must create and configure the network resource pools as necessary. The first of these steps is already complete if you create a vDS with a version set to 6.0.0 or higher, since NIOC is enabled by default.

Perform the following steps to enable NIOC on an existing vDS:

1. If vSphere Web Client is not already running, open a browser, connect to the vSphere Web Client on your vCenter Server instance, and log on. Because NIOC relies on vDS, and vDS is available only with vCenter, NIOC cannot be used when connected directly to an ESXi host with the ESXi Host Client.

2. Navigate to the Networking view using the navigation bar or the Home screen.

3. Select the vDS for which you want to enable NIOC.

4. Right-click the vDS.

5. Click Edit and then Edit Settings.

6. Select Enabled in the Network I/O Control drop-down menu, and then click OK.

This enables NIOC on the distributed switch. The Resource Allocation section of the vDS object will note that NIOC is enabled, as shown in Figure 11.20.

In addition to enabling NIOC, you can modify the pre-defined network resource pools or create new resource pools, if you are using a vDS version 6.0.0 or above.

A network resource pool consists of three settings:

◆ The first value is Shares. Like the shares you used to prioritize access to CPU or memory when there was contention, physical adapter shares in a network resource pool establish priority for access to the physical network adapters when network contention exists. As with other types of shares, this value does not apply when no contention exists.

This value can be set to one of three predefined values, or you can set a custom value of up to 100. For the predefined values, Low translates to 25 shares, Normal equates to 50 shares, and High equals 100 shares.

FIGURE 11.20
vCenter Server provides
a clear indication that
NIOC is enabled
for a vDS.

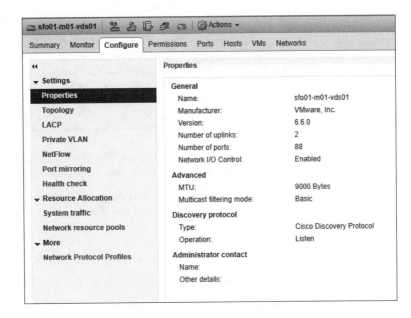

- The second value is Reservation. This value guarantees an amount of bandwidth (in Mbps) to the network resource pool.

- The final value is Limit. This value specifies an upper limit on the amount of network traffic (in Mbps) that the network resource pool may consume. Leaving Unlimited selected means that only the physical adapters can limit the network resource pool.

Figure 11.21 shows all three of the values for the predefined Fault Tolerance (FT) Traffic network resource pool.

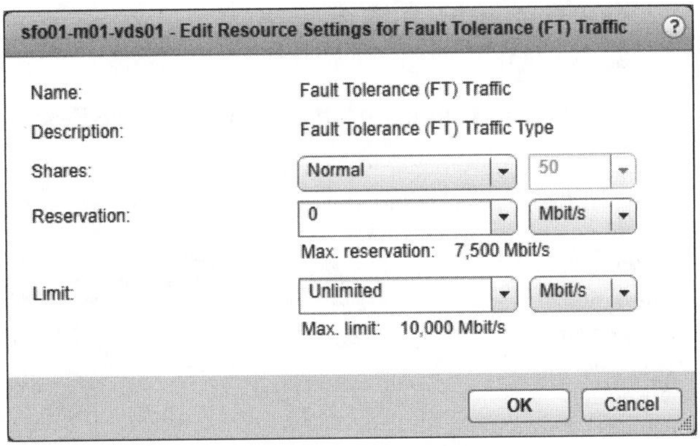

FIGURE 11.21
vSphere allows you to
modify the predefined
network
resource pools.

SYSTEM POOLS VS. USER-DEFINED POOLS

System-defined pools (as shown in Figure 11.21) use reservations, limits, and shares. User-defined pools only make use of reservations. This is because they are suballocations of the VM traffic network resource pool. The defined Reservation value of your VM network resource pool multiplied by the number of physical NICs in each host determines the amount of total bandwidth available to be reserved by user-defined pools.

You have the option of editing the predefined network resource pools or creating your own network resource pools. Perform the following steps to edit an existing network resource pool:

1. If vSphere Web Client is not already running, open a browser, connect to vSphere Web Client on your vCenter Server instance, and then log on.

2. Navigate to the Networking view.

3. Select the vDS that contains the network resource pool you want to modify.

4. Click the Resource Allocation section and ensure that you are on the System Traffic page.

5. Select the network resource pool you want to edit and click the Edit (pencil) icon.

6. In the Network Resource Pool Settings dialog box, modify the Shares, Reservation, and Limits settings as desired.

7. Click OK to save the changes to the network resource pool.

You might prefer to leave the predefined network resource pools intact and create your own. Follow these steps to create a new network resource pool:

1. If vSphere Web Client is not already running, open a browser, connect to vSphere Web Client on your vCenter Server instance, and log on.

2. Navigate to the Networking view.

3. Select the vDS on which you want to create the new network resource pool.

4. Click the Configure tab, and then click the Resource Allocation section.

5. Select Network Resource Pools; then click the Create a Network Resource Pool plus icon. The New Network Resource Pool dialog box appears (Figure 11.22).

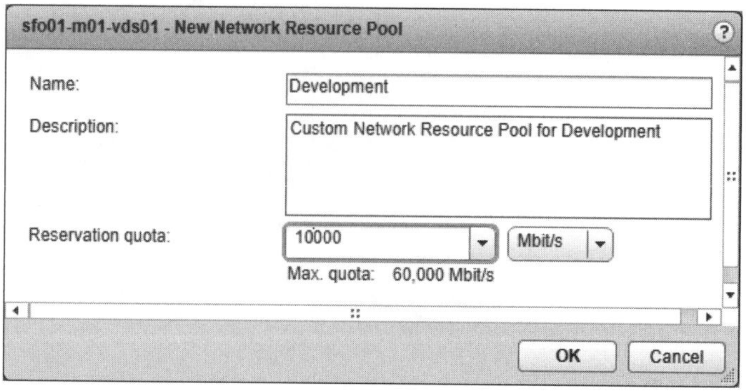

FIGURE 11.22
You have the option of creating new network resource pools for custom network traffic control.

sfo01-m01-vds01 - New Network Resource Pool

Name: Development

Description: Custom Network Resource Pool for Development

Reservation quota: 10000   Mbit/s

Max. quota: 60,000 Mbit/s

OK   Cancel

6. Supply a name and description for the new network resource pool.

7. Define a reservation quota in Mbps or Gbps.

8. Click OK to create the new network resource pool with the values you specified.

After you have at least one user-defined network resource pool, you can map port groups to the network resource pool.

CANNOT MAP PORT GROUPS TO SYSTEM POOLS?

Port groups can be mapped to user-defined network resource pools only, not system network resource pools. This is to ensure that traffic is appropriately shared within the available bandwidth. For example, it would not be a good idea to have VM traffic in the same resource pool as critical system traffic such as Fault Tolerance or vSphere Replication.

Follow these steps to assign a port group to a user-defined network resource pool:

1. If vSphere Web Client is not already running, open a browser, connect the vSphere Web Client on your vCenter Server instance, and log on.

2. Navigate to the Networking view.

3. Select the vDS that hosts the network resource pool you would like to map to a port group.

4. Right-click the distributed port group you wish to map and select Edit Settings.

5. In the settings, select the appropriate network resource pool, as shown in Figure 11.23.

FIGURE 11.23
Users can map a distributed port group to any user-defined network resource pool, and multiple distributed port groups can be associated to a single network resource pool.

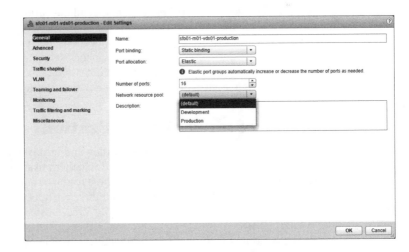

6. Click OK to save the changes and return to the Resource Allocation section.

In large environments with many distributed port groups, it may be tedious to determine which port groups are mapped to which network resource pools. To help ease this administrativ burden, vCenter Server offers an easy way to show all the port groups linked to a specific network resource pool. With a network resource pool selected, click the Distributed Port Groups tab near the bottom of the screen. The view will switch to show you the specific port groups associated with the selected network resource pool. You can see this in Figure 11.24, which show the port groups associated with the user-defined network resource pool named Production. You will also notice networking-specific details—such as VLAN ID, port binding, and the number of attached VMs—are shown in this view.

FIGURE 11.24
The vSphere Web Client provides a consolidated view of all the distributed port groups associated with a network resource pool.

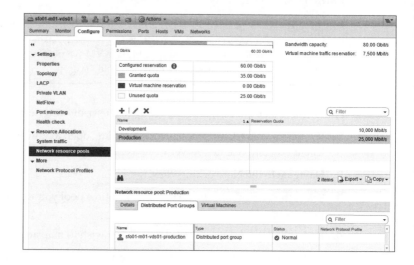

NIOC offers a powerful way to help ensure that all the various types of converged network traffic present in a vSphere environment will coexist properly, especially as organizations move to (or beyond) 10 Gbe Ethernet. Fewer faster connections means more consolidated traffic and therefore a greater need to control how that traffic coexists on the same physical medium.

We have discussed three of the four core resources and demonstrated how vSphere manages the use of and access to each. Only one resource remains: storage.

Controlling Storage I/O Utilization

For vSphere, controlling memory or CPU allocation and utilization is relatively easy. The hypervisor determines how busy the CPU is and whether physical memory has been depleted. When resource contention occurs for either of these resources, not only is it easy to detect, but it is also easy to correct. If the CPU is too busy and there are not enough CPU cycles to go around, then you do not schedule cycles for lower-priority VMs—instead, you assign more cycles to higher-priority VMs.

How is this priority determined? Recall that Shares values are the mechanism that vSphere uses to determine the priority. Likewise, if memory becomes constrained, the balloon driver is inflated in the VMs' guest OS. It then reclaims some memory or slows down the rate of allocatior to lower-priority VMs and increases the rate of allocation to higher-priority VMs. Not only does the hypervisor have complete visibility into the utilization of these resources, it also has complete control over the resources. Nothing gets scheduled on the CPU without going through the hypervisor, and nothing gets stored in memory without the hypervisor knowing about it. This complete control is what enables vSphere to offer shares as a way of establishing priority and offer reservations (guaranteed access to resources) and limits (caps on the usage of a resource). You learned about these mechanisms earlier in this chapter.

Network utilization begins to change the approach a little. The hypervisor has some visibility into the network; it can see how many Mbps are being generated and by which VMs. However, the hypervisor does not have complete control over network utilization. It can control inbound and outbound traffic, but it cannot control traffic generated somewhere else in the network. vSphere provides shares (to establish priority) and limits (to enforce a cap on the amount of network bandwidth a VM can consume). This is Network I/O Control, which we discussed in the previous section.

In many ways, resource allocation and utilization for storage is similar to networking. Other workloads are likely to be present on the shared storage (non-vSAN) vSphere requires for so many features. These other workloads will be external to vSphere and cannot be controlled or influenced in any way. Therefore, vSphere does not have complete control over the resource. Generally, the hypervisor also will not have as much visibility into the storage as it does with CPU and memory. As such, it is more difficult to detect and adjust storage resources. However, there are two metrics that vSphere can use to help determine storage utilization. The first is latency, and the second is peak throughput. Using one of these two metrics to detect contention, vSphere can offer shares (to establish priority when contention occurs) as well as limits (to ensure that a VM does not consume more than its fair share of storage resources). The feature that enables this functionality is called Storage I/O Control or SIOC.

INTRODUCTION OF STORAGE I/O CONTROL

Storage I/O Control first appeared in VMware vSphere 4.1 and supported only Fibre Channel and iSCSI datastores. In vSphere 5.0, SIOC added support for NFS.

Longtime users of vSphere are typically aware that the ability to assign Shares values to disks has been around for quite some time. The difference between that functionality and what SIOC offers is a matter of scope. Without SIOC, enabling shares on a VM virtual disk(s) is only effective for that specific host; the hosts in a cluster did not exchange information about how many shares each VM was allocated or how many shares were assigned in total. This made it virtually impossible to properly align the Shares values with the correct ratios of access to storage resources across multiple hosts.

SIOC addresses this by extending shares assignments across all hosts accessing a designated datastore. By using vCenter Server as its central information store, SIOC combines all the assigned shares across all the VMs on all the hosts and allocates storage I/O resources in the proper ratios according to the shares assignment. To make this work, SIOC has a few requirements that must be met:

◆ All datastores that are SIOC-enabled must be managed under a single vCenter Server instance. vCenter Server is the "central clearinghouse" for all the shares assignments.

♦ SIOC is supported on VMFS datastores connected via Fibre Channel (including FCoE) an‹ iSCSI. NFS datastores are also supported. Raw device mappings (RDMs) are not supported.

♦ Datastores must have only a single extent. Datastores with multiple extents are not supported.

STORAGE I/O CONTROL AND ARRAY AUTO-TIERING

If your storage array supports auto-tiering—the ability for the array to seamlessly and transparently migrate data between different tiers (SSD, FC, SAS, and SATA) of storage—be sure to double-check the VMware Compatibility Guide to verify that the array auto-tiering functionality is certified as compatible with SIOC. Also check your vendor documentation for SIOC best practices. The use of SIOC can undermine the auto-tiering built into some storage arrays.

Assuming your environment meets the requirements, you can take advantage of SIOC. Configuring SIOC is a two-step process. First, enable SIOC on one or more datastores. Then, assign shares or limits to storage I/O resources on individual VMs.

Next, we will look at how to enable SIOC a designated datastore.

Enabling Storage I/O Control

SIOC is enabled on a per-datastore basis. By default, SIOC is disabled for a datastore, meaning that you must explicitly enable SIOC to take advantage of its functionality.

DATASTORES VS. DATASTORE CLUSTERS

Although SIOC is disabled by default for individual datastores, it is enabled by default for Storage DRS–enabled datastore clusters that have I/O metrics enabled for Storage DRS. Refer to "Working with Storage DRS" in Chapter 12, "Balancing Resource Utilization," for more information on Storage DRS.

Perform the following steps to enable SIOC for a datastore:

1. If vSphere Web Client is not already running, open a browser, connect the vSphere Web Client on your vCenter Server instance, and log on.

   SIOC is available only when connected to vCenter Server, not when you are connected to an individual ESXi host with the ESXi Host Client.

2. Navigate to the Storage view.

3. Select the datastore for which you want to enable SIOC.

4. Click the Configure tab.

5. Under the Datastore Capabilities section on the General page, select Edit (Figure 11.25).

FIGURE 11.25

This dialog box allows you to manage the SIOC configuration of a specific datastore.

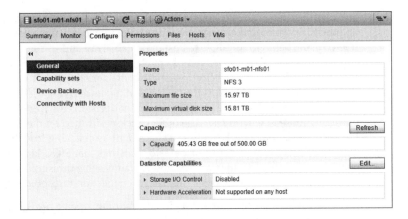

6. In the Datastore Capabilities dialog box, select the check box next to Enable Storage I/O Control.

7. Click OK.

SIOC is now enabled for the selected datastore; this is reflected in the Datastore Capabilities section of the vSphere Web Client in the Configure tab, as you can see in Figure 11.26.

FIGURE 11.26

The status of SIOC for a datastore is displayed in the vSphere Web Client.

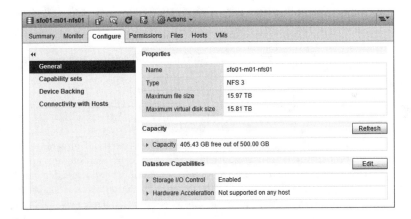

Generally, enabling SIOC using these steps is all you need to do to get started using SIOC and control use of storage I/O resources. However, in some cases, you may need to adjust the configuration of SIOC to ensure it functions properly for a specific vendor array and array configuration. Previously in this section, we discussed the two metrics in vSphere that can be used to detect contention: latency and peak throughput.

SIOC can use latency as the threshold to determine when it should activate and enforce Shares values for access to storage I/O resources. Specifically, when vSphere detects latency above a specific threshold value (measured in milliseconds), SIOC is activated. Because of the vast differences in array architectures and array performance, VMware recognized that users may need to adjust the default congestion threshold value for SIOC. After all, a specific latency measurement may indicate congestion (or contention) on some arrays and configurations but no on others. By making the congestion threshold adjustable, this allows vSphere administrators to fine-tune the behavior of SIOC to best match an array and its required configuration.

The other metric is the one that is enabled by default in vSphere 6.0: Peak Throughput. SIOC uses a tool called the IO Injector to test the characteristics of a storage array and perform two main checks. The first check is for overlaps in the underlying disk system of a datastore; this allows Storage DRS to make correct placement decisions for workload balancing, which is explained more in Chapter 12. The other check performed by the IO Injector—more relevant to this section—is the Peak Throughput check. Unlike checking for latency spikes, knowing the maximum capability of a specific datastore ensures that SIOC kicks in before congestion (or contention) occurs. Just like latency, you can adjust this threshold with a percentage setting.

Perform the following steps to adjust the congestion threshold setting for SIOC on a datastore

1. If vSphere Web Client is not already running, open a browser, connect the vSphere Web Client on your vCenter Server instance, and then log on.

2. Navigate to the Storage view.

3. Select the desired datastore from the inventory tree.

4. Select the datastore for which you want to enable SIOC.

5. Click the Configure tab.

6. Under the Datastore Capabilities section on the General page, select Edit.

   The Configure Storage I/O Control dialog box appears.

7. Enter the desired congestion threshold setting, as a percentage or in milliseconds, and then click OK.

CONGESTION THRESHOLD

When adjusting the congestion threshold setting based on latency, it is imperative that you set it properly based on your specific array, array configuration, and array vendor's recommendations. These recommendations will vary from vendor to vendor and depend on the number of drives in the array, the types of drives in the array, and whether features like array auto-tiering are enabled. In general, the following latency settings are considered reasonable guidelines for the congestion threshold:

◆ For datastores composed of flash devices, decrease to 10 ms.

◆ For datastores composed of 10K/15K FC and SAS, leave at 30 ms.

◆ For datastores composed of 7.2K SATA/NL-SAS, increase to 50 ms.

◆ For auto-tiered datastores with multiple drive types, leave at 30 ms.

Although these are reasonable guidelines, be sure to consult your vendor documentation to find the recommended values for the congestion threshold when using SIOC in conjunction with the array.

Once you have enabled SIOC on one or more datastores and you have (optionally) adjusted the congestion threshold per the storage vendor recommended values, you can start setting storage I/O resource values on your VMs.

Configuring Storage Resource Settings for a Virtual Machine

SIOC provides two mechanisms for controlling the use of storage I/O by VMs: shares and limits. These mechanisms operate in the same way here as with other resources; the Shares value establishes a relative priority as a ratio of the total number of shares assigned, and the Limit value defines the upper ceiling on the number of I/O operations per second (IOPS) that a VM may generate. As with memory, CPU, and network I/O, vSphere provides default settings for disk shares and limits. By default, every VM you create is assigned 1,000 disk shares per virtual disk and no IOPS limits.

If you need settings different from the default values, you can easily modify either the assigned storage I/O shares or the assigned storage I/O limit.

ASSIGNING STORAGE I/O SHARES

You modify the default storage I/O Shares value, open the Edit Settings for a VM, as you would when modifying memory and CPU allocation. Figure 11.27 shows the disk shares for a VM.

FIGURE 11.27
Storage I/O shares are not available in the Edit Resource Settings page of a VM. They need to be modified in the Edit Settings dialog box.

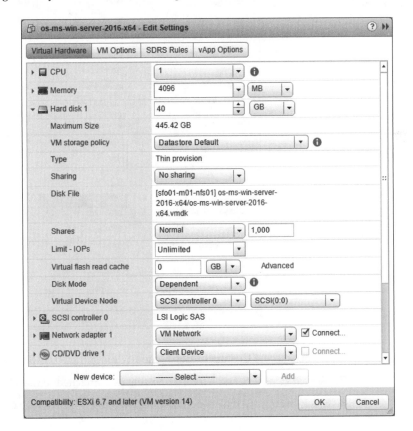

Perform the following steps to modify the storage I/O Shares value for a VM:

1. If vSphere Web Client is not already running, open a browser, connect the vSphere Web Client on your vCenter Server instance, and log on.

2. Navigate to either the Hosts And Clusters view or the VMs And Templates view.

3. Right-click the VM on which you would like to change the storage I/O settings, and selec Edit Settings from Actions menu..

4. Click the triangle next to the hard disk. This displays the dialog box shown previously in Figure 11.27.

5. For each virtual disk, click the Shares drop-down menu to change the setting from Norm to Low, High, or Custom, as shown in Figure 11.28.

FIGURE 11.28
You must change the setting to Custom if you want to assign a specific storage I/O Shares value.

6. If you selected Custom in step 5, modify the storage I/O Shares value.

7. Repeat steps 4, 5, and 6 for each virtual disk attached to the VM.

8. Click OK to save the changes and return to the vSphere Web Client.

The selected virtual disks attached to the VM will now receive a proportional allocation of storage I/O resources based on the Shares value whenever SIOC detects contention (or congestion) on the datastore. Keep in mind that vSphere can use latency or peak bandwidth, as specified in the congestion threshold described earlier, as the trigger for activating SIOC. As with all other Shares values, SIOC enforces Shares values only when contention for storage I/O resources is detected. If there is no contention—as indicated by low latency or bandwidth values for that datastore or datastore cluster—then SIOC will not be activated.

SHARES ACTIVATE ONLY ON RESOURCE CONTENTION

Shares are applicable only when there is resource contention. This is true for all the different Shares values we have discussed throughout this chapter. Regardless of whether you are setting Shares values for memory, CPU, network, or storage, vSphere will not enforce those shares until the hypervisor detects contention for the resource. Shares are not guarantees or absolute values; they establish relative priority when the hypervisor is not able to meet all the demands of its VMs.

CONFIGURING STORAGE I/O LIMITS

You can also set a limit on the number of IOPS that a VM may generate. By default, this value is unlimited. However, if you feel that you need to set an IOPS limit, you can set it in the same place as you would set storage I/O shares.

Perform these steps to set a storage I/O limit on IOPS:

1. If vSphere Web Client is not already running, open a browser, connect the vSphere Web Client on your vCenter Server instance, and log on.

2. Navigate to either the Hosts And Clusters view or the VMs And Templates view.

3. Right-click the VM on which you would like to change the storage I/O settings, and select Edit Settings from the actions.

4. Click the triangle next to the hard disk on which you would like to set an IOPS limit.

5. Click in the Limit – IOPs drop-down option, and type in a value for the maximum number of IOPS that this VM will be allowed to generate against this virtual disk.

6. Repeat steps 4 and 5 for each virtual disk attached to the VM.

7. Click OK to save the changes and return to the vSphere Web Client.

BE CAREFUL WITH IOPS LIMITS

Setting an improper IOPS limit can have a severe performance impact on a VM. Be sure you have a clear understanding of the IOPS requirements of the guest OS and the applications or services running within the guest OS before assigning an IOPS limit.

Like the limits you apply to memory, CPU, or network I/O, the storage I/O limits are absolute values. The hypervisor will enforce the assigned storage I/O limit, even when there is plenty of storage I/O available.

Setting storage I/O resource values on a per-VM basis is fine, but what about when you need to have a consolidated view of what settings have been applied to all the VMs on a datastore? The vSphere Web Client provides a way to easily see a summary of these settings.

VIEWING STORAGE I/O RESOURCE SETTINGS FOR VIRTUAL MACHINES

In the Datastores And Datastore Clusters view, you can view a list of all the datastores managed by a vCenter Server instance. You enabled SIOC from this view previously, in the section "Enabling Storage I/O Control," and here you can review the consolidated view of all the storage I/O settings applied to the VMs on a datastore.

On the VMs tab of a selected datastore in the Datastores And Datastore Clusters view, the vSphere Web Client provides a list of all the VMs resident on a datastore. If you scroll to the right using the scroll bar at the bottom of the vSphere Web Client window, you will see three SIOC-specific columns:

◆ Shares Value

◆ Limit – IOPs

◆ Datastore % Shares

Figure 11.29 shows these three columns on a datastore for which SIOC has been enabled. Note that the default values for the VMs on the selected SIOC-enabled datastore have not been modified.

FIGURE 11.29
The Virtual Machines view under the VMs tab of a datastore provides a useful summary view of storage-related information for all the VMs on that datastore.

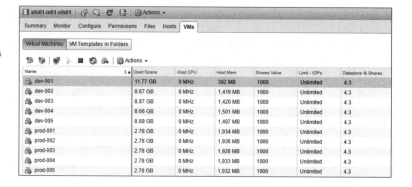

As you can see in Figure 11.29, vCenter Server has used the assigned Shares values to establish relative percentages of access to storage I/O resources in the event of contention. This consistent behavior makes the task of managing resource allocation a bit easier for vSphere administrators.

STORAGE I/O CONTROL AND EXTERNAL WORKLOADS

Storage I/O Control operates on the basis that only vSphere clusters are using the storage I/O resources managed by vCenter Server. However, this is often not the case. Modern arrays are structured so that many different workloads can all run on the same physical disks that support an SIOC-enabled datastore.

In such cases, SIOC can detect these "external workloads" and will automatically stop throttling. However, at the next latency evaluation period, SIOC will again check the latency of the datastore against the congestion threshold and see if there is a need to start throttling again, and the cycle starts again.

To resolve this issue, VMware recommends you avoid sharing physical disks across both virtual and non-virtual workloads. Because of the architecture of some arrays, this may be difficult, so check with your storage vendor for their recommendations and best practices.

Thus far, we have discussed shared storage where the features and settings are all array agnostic—Fibre Channel, iSCSI, or NFS. It does not matter how it is presented to your ESXi hosts. In the next section, we will discuss some features that are used solely with local flash-based storage.

Using Flash Storage

As physical-to-virtual ratios increase, and environments become denser, the need for faster storage grows. Flash storage has quickly become an industry standard and many servers and arrays ship with flash-based storage. Traditionally, storage arrays have used smaller portions of flash storage as caches to increase the response times to slower spindles, but as their sizes increase, so has the need for flash cache. Depending on the scenario, a more cost-effective solution can be to provision rackmount or blade servers with local flash storage.

vSphere offers two ways of using local flash-based host storage. vSphere Flash Read Cache is a feature that acts as a buffer for I/O on a per-VM basis. The other feature, Swap to Host Cache, is used to allocate local flash disks as swap space. These features are not mutually exclusive; they can be enabled at the same time and can even be backed by the same device, but they work in completely different ways.

FLASH VS. SSD

Although the industry may use different names, all flash-based storage is built on similar NAND technology. SSD, EFD, or just flash is just nonvolatile memory that retains its data even without power. The differentiator between the products is akin to traditional magnetic hard disks: latency, bandwidth, resiliency, and of course, size. And there can be very different performance and capacity characteristics depending on the model.

ENABLING VSPHERE FLASH READ CACHE FOR VIRTUAL MACHINES

vSphere Flash Read Cache (or simply flash cache) can be allocated on a per-VM basis just like CPU or memory. In fact, it can be allocated down to an individual virtual disk (VMDK) level. However, a VM does not need to have flash cache allocated to function. Just like CPU and Memory allocations, no flash cache resources are consumed and the contents of the VM cache a flushed when the VM is powered off. Also, like CPU and Memory allocation, provided you hav enough resources configured on each host in a cluster, flash cache is compatible with vSphere H and vMotion, and therefore vSphere DRS.

The following steps outline how to enable vSphere Flash Read Cache:

1. If vSphere Web Client is not already running, open a browser, connect the vSphere Web Client on your vCenter Server instance, and then log on.

2. Navigate to the Hosts And Clusters view.

3. Select a host from the Inventory tab.

4. With a host selected, click the Configure tab. Then select the Virtual Flash Resource Management page under the Virtual Flash section.

5. Click the Add Capacity button in the top-right corner of the content area.

6. Select the SSD from the list, as shown in Figure 11.30. Click OK to close the dialog box. Th SSD is now allocated to the flash resource pool.

FIGURE 11.30
You can add local SSDs to the flash resource capacity.

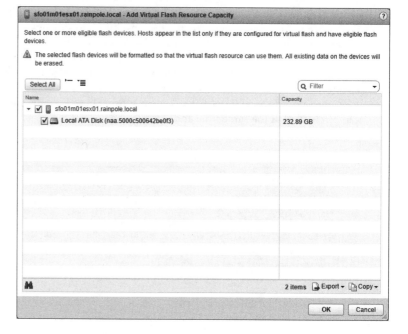

7. Navigate to the VM in the inventory that you wish to allocate flash cache resources to, select the Actions drop-down menu, and click Edit Settings.

8. In the Edit Settings dialog box, expand the Hard Disk area of the VM properties. In the Virtual Flash Read Cache, allocate an amount of desired resources in GB or MB, as shown in Figure 11.31.

FIGURE 11.31
Allocating flash cache to a VM is as easy as allocating it as you would CPU or memory.

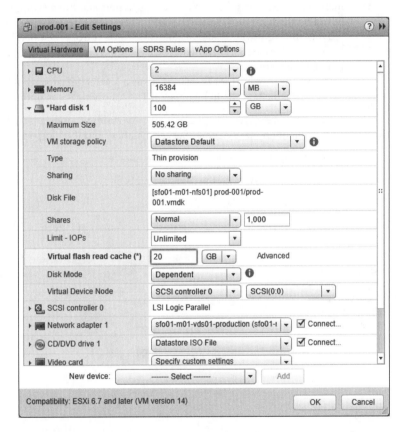

9. Click OK to close the dialog box and commit the configuration change to the VM.

As you can see, configuring and allocating flash cache is a simple task. However, it will not be so simple to determine which VM hard disks will benefit from allocating flash cache and how much to allocate. Chapter 13, "Monitoring VMware vSphere Performance," discusses monitoring vSphere Performance in detail. The use of performance graphs and `resxtop` will be of great benefit when you start to baseline workloads for flash cache inclusion. Depending on the workloads that your environment runs, you may find that flash cache is of little benefit. In a low I/O, but high memory overcommit environment, you may find that disk I/O is increasing because the hosts need to swap out memory to disk, as described earlier in this chapter. In this scenario, allocating flash-based resources to swap would be a good idea.

CONFIGURING SWAP TO HOST CACHE

Swap to Host Cache is a feature that allocates a portion of local flash storage to be the location o. a VM swap file. As discussed earlier in this chapter, the VM swap file is very different from the guest OS swap/page file.

An important point to note: this feature is beneficial only within environments that have memory contention to the point that the hypervisor must swap unreserved VM memory to disk Based on the figures explained earlier in this chapter, accessing memory swapped to disk (*even SSD*) is still significantly slower than accessing it from memory. However, if your environment fits within this category, you will realize significant performance benefits by enabling the Swap to Host Cache feature.

To configure a host for Swap to Cache, a VMFS datastore that has been identified as being backed by a flash needs to be present. The following steps outline how to enable this feature:

1. If vSphere Web Client is not already running, open a browser, connect the vSphere Web Client on your vCenter Server instance, and then log on.

2. Navigate to the Hosts And Clusters view.

3. Select a host from the Inventory tab.

4. Click the Configure tab.

5. Select Host Cache Configuration as shown in Figure 11.32.

FIGURE 11.32

The Host Cache Configuration feature is designed specifically for flash-based datastores.

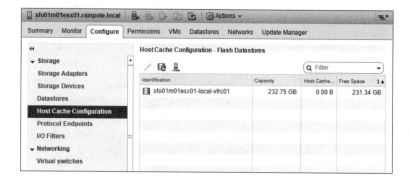

6. Highlight the appropriate flash-backed VMFS datastore and click the Edit pencil icon.

7. Ensure the Allocate Space For Host Cache option is checked. A custom size may be provided if you would like to use this datastore for other purposes.

8. Click OK to complete the configuration.

Once the Swap to Host Cache feature is enabled, the host proceeds to fill the allocated size on the datastore with .vswp files. These files will be used instead of the .vswp files typically co-located within the same datastore as the other VM files. Keep in mind that this setting must be enabled on every host within a cluster because it is not cluster aware. When a VM is vMotioned to a host that does not have the Swap to Host Cache feature enabled, the normal datastore-based swap files will be used.

MAKING THE BEST USE OF FLASH

Even though both flash cache and Swap to Host Cache can be configured on the same flash device, some thought should go into how to get the best use of this limited resource.

If your VMs have high memory contention and swap to disk often, your flash-backed datastores would be best allocated to Swap to Host Cache. However, if your VMs are I/O-constrained and experience high latency when reading or writing to disk, it would be better to allocate the flash device to flash cache.

In the end, each environment is different. Think about where your flash devices are allocated and you will be sure to get the most out of your fastest storage device.

Throughout this chapter, we have discussed how you can use reservations, shares, and limits to modify the resource allocation and resource utilization behaviors of vSphere. In the next chapter, we will discuss some additional capabilities for balancing resource utilization across groups of servers.

The Bottom Line

Manage virtual machine memory allocation.   In almost every modern virtualized datacenter, memory is the resource that typically comes under contention first. Most organizations run out of memory on their ESXi hosts before other resources become constrained. Fortunately, vSphere offers advanced memory management technologies as well as extensive controls for managing the allocation of memory and utilization of memory by VMs.

Master It   To guarantee levels of performance, your IT Director believes that all VMs must be configured with at least 8 GB of memory. However, you know that many of your applications rarely use this much memory. What might be an acceptable compromise to help ensure performance?

Master It   You are configuring a new large-scale virtual desktop infrastructure environment, but you are worried that the cluster hosts will not have enough memory to handle the expected load. Which advanced memory management technique will ensure that your virtual desktops have enough memory without having to use the swap file?

Manage CPU utilization.   In a vSphere environment, the ESXi hosts control VM access to physical CPUs. To effectively manage and scale vSphere, you must understand how to allocate CPU resources to VMs, including how to use reservations, limits, and shares. Shares help adjust the allocation of resources in a constrained environment, reservations provide guarantees to resources, and limits provide a cap on resource usage.

Master It   A fellow vSphere administrator is concerned about the use of CPU reservations. She is worried that using CPU reservations will "strand" CPU resources, preventing those reserved but unused resources from being used by other VMs. Are the concerns of the administrator well founded?

Create and manage resource pools. Managing resource allocation and usage for large numbers of VMs can create an administrative overhead. Resource pools provide a mechanism for administrators to apply resource allocation policies to groups of VMs at the same time. Resource pools use shares, reservations, and limits to control and modify resource allocation behavior, but only for memory and CPU.

Master It Your organization runs both development workloads and production workloads on the same hardware. How can you help ensure that development workloads do not consume too many resources and impact the performance of production workloads?

Control network and storage I/O utilization. Memory, CPU, network I/O, and storage I/O make up the four major resource types that vSphere administrators must effectively manage for an efficient virtualized datacenter. By applying controls to network I/O and storage I/O, you can help ensure consistent performance, meet service-level objectives, and prevent one workload from unnecessarily consuming resources at the expense of other workloads.

Master It Name two limitations of Network I/O Control.

Master It What are the requirements for using Storage I/O Control?

Chapter 12

Balancing Resource Utilization

A fundamental element of virtualization with VMware vSphere is the ability to increase the utilization of your computing resources within a single physical host. vSphere accomplishes this by letting you run multiple instances of a guest operating system (OS) on a single physical host in virtual machines (VMs). However, it is also about getting better resource utilization across multiple physical hosts, and that means workload mobility between hosts to balance the resource utilization. vSphere offers several powerful features to help administrators balance resource utilization in the modern data center.

IN THIS CHAPTER, YOU WILL LEARN TO

◆ Configure and execute vMotion

◆ Ensure vMotion compatibility across processor families

◆ Use Storage vMotion

◆ Perform combined vMotion and Storage vMotion

◆ Configure and manage vSphere Distributed Resource Scheduler

◆ Configure and manage Storage DRS

Comparing Utilization with Allocation

A fundamental but subtle difference exists between allocation and utilization. *Allocation* refers to how a resource is assigned. In a vSphere environment, allocation refers to how CPU cycles, memory, storage I/O, and network bandwidth are distributed to a virtual machine (VM) or group of VMs. *Utilization* is how those resources are used after they are allocated to the VMs from the host or hosts.

vSphere provides three mechanisms for allocation: reservations (guaranteed allocations of resources), limits (upper bound on the allocation of resources), and shares (prioritized access to resource allocation during periods of resource contention). Although these mechanisms are extraordinarily powerful and useful—as you saw in Chapter 11, "Managing Resource Allocation"—they do have their limits.

How do we address situations where a resource is highly utilized on one host and lightly utilized on another? None of the three mechanisms we have discussed thus far can balance the *utilization* of resources among ESXi hosts; they can only control the *allocation* of those resources.

VMware vSphere balances the utilization of resources in the following ways:

vMotion vMotion, commonly known as *live migration*, is used to manually balance compute resource utilization between ESXi hosts and clusters.

Storage vMotion Storage vMotion is the storage equivalent of vMotion. It is used to manually balance storage utilization between two datastores.

Cross vCenter vMotion Cross vCenter vMotion is used to manually migrate workloads between vSphere environments, such as between datacenters.

vSphere Distributed Resource Scheduler vSphere Distributed Resource Scheduler (DRS) is used to automatically balance compute resource utilization among two or more hosts in a vSphere cluster.

Storage DRS Just as Storage vMotion is the storage equivalent of vMotion, Storage DRS (SDRS) is the storage equivalent of DRS, and it is used to automatically balance storage utilization among two or more datastores within a datastore cluster before and after initial placement of VM files.

As we discuss how each of these four mechanisms balances resource utilization, we will also discuss a few related vSphere features, such as clusters and VMware Enhanced vMotion Compatibility (EVC).

Let's start the discussion with vMotion.

Exploring vMotion

The vMotion feature in vSphere provides you a mechanism to manually balance compute resource utilization between two ESXi hosts. What exactly does this mean?

vMotion can perform a live migration of a powered-on VM from one host to another without an interruption in service. This is a zero-downtime operation; network connections are not dropped, and applications or services continue to run uninterrupted. In fact, application owners and user are unaware that the VM has been migrated between the physical hosts. When vMotion is initiated to migrate a VM between hosts, the resource allocation is also migrated—CPU and memory—from one host to another. This makes vMotion an extremely effective tool for manually load-balancing VMs across hosts and eliminating "hot spots"—heavily utilized ESXi hosts—within the datacenter.

---

vMotion Over Layer 3

As of the vSphere 6.0 release, vMotion can operate over routed networks. Combined with support for up to 100 ms round-trip time (RTT) and cross vCenter Server migrations, vMotion now provides workload mobility for your VMs and the applications or services they provide the organization.

In addition to manually balancing VMs loads across ESXi hosts, vMotion provides additional benefits to an organization. If an ESXi host needs to be powered off for hardware maintenance or another event that would require it to be out of service, vMotion can be used to migrate all active

VMs to another host without waiting for a maintenance window. vMotion is a *live migration*—there is no interruption in service and no downtime—so the VMs will remain available to provide the applications and services.

Fundamentally, vMotion copies the memory content of a powered-on VM from one host to another followed by transferring the control of the VM disk files to the target host.

Let's take a closer look at how vMotion operates in the following sequence:

1. An administrator initiates a migration of a powered-on VM (VM1) from one host (sfo01m01esx01) to another (sfo01m01esx02), as shown in Figure 12.1.

FIGURE 12.1
Step 1 in a vMotion migration is invoking a migration while the VM is powered on.

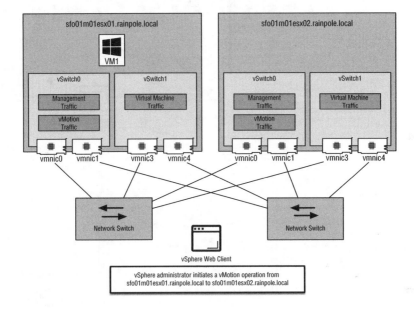

2. The source host (sfo01m01esx01) copies the active memory pages that the VM has in host memory to the destination host (sfo01m01esx02) across a VMkernel interface enabled for vMotion traffic in the *preCopy* phase. Meanwhile, the VM is still online on the source host (sfo01m01esx01). As the memory is copied from the source host to the target host, memory pages can still be changed. ESXi keeps a log of all changes that occur in the VM memory on the source host after the memory address is copied to the target host. This log is called a *memory bitmap* (see Figure 12.2). This process occurs iteratively, repeatedly copying any memory contents that have changed.

3. After the entire contents of VM memory have been transferred to the target host (sfo01m01esx02), the VM on the source host (sfo01m01esx01) is *quiesced*. The VM is still resident in memory, but it no longer services requests for data. The memory bitmap file is then transferred to the target host (sfo01m01esx02). See Figure 12.3.

4. The target host (sfo01m01esx02) reads the addresses in the memory bitmap file and requests the contents of those addresses from the source (sfo01m01esx01), as shown in Figure 12.4.

FIGURE 12.2
Step 2 in a vMotion
migration is starting the
memory copy and
adding a mem-
ory bitmap.

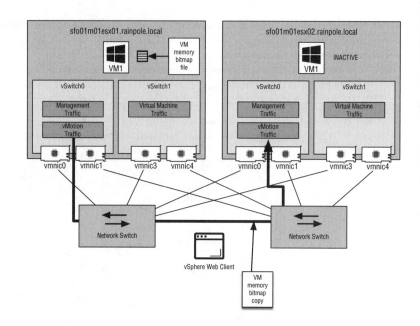

FIGURE 12.3
Step 3 in a vMotion
migration quiesces the
VM and transfers the
memory bitmap file
from the source host
to the target host.

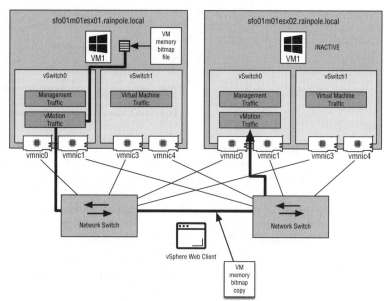

5. After the contents of the memory in the memory bitmap file are transferred to the target host, the VM starts on the host. This is *not* a reboot—the state of the VM is in memory, and the target host enables it. At this point, a Reverse Address Resolution Protocol (RARP) message is sent by the target host to register its MAC address against the physical switch ports of which the target host is connected. This process allows the physical switches to forward network packets to the appropriate host where the VM has moved.

FIGURE 12.4
In step 4 of a vMotion migration, memory listed in the bitmap file (*dirty memory*) is fetched from the source to the target.

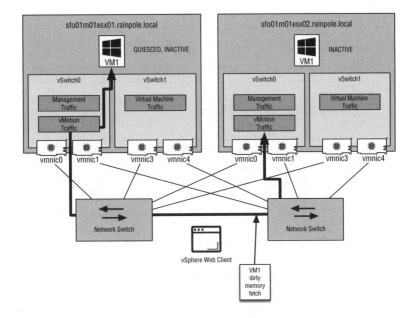

6. After the VM is successfully transferred to the target host, any memory the VM was using on the source host is deleted. This memory becomes available to the VMkernel to use as appropriate, as shown in Figure 12.5.

FIGURE 12.5
Step 6 in a vMotion migration deletes the VM memory from the source host.

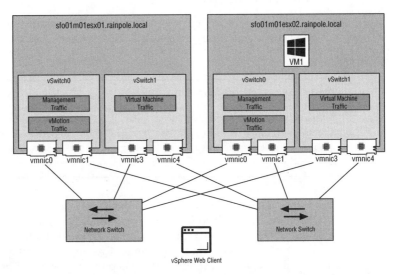

LEVERAGING MULTIPLE NICs FOR vMOTION

vMotion can take advantage of multiple NICs to assist with the transfer of memory data between hosts.

THE MEMORY BITMAP

The memory bitmap does not include the contents of the memory address that has changed; it includes only the addresses of that memory—often referred to as the *dirty memory*.

PING A VM DURING vMOTION

If you follow the previous procedure, you will see that the VM being migrated does not run for a time on either the source host or the target host. This is typically a *very short* period. A continuous ping (`ping -t` on a Windows OS) to the VM being migrated may result only in the loss of a single ping. Most applications are built to withstand the loss of more than a packet or two before any problem occurs.

Examining vMotion Requirements

Let's face it. Live migration of VMs with vMotion is amazing, and when you see it work for the first time, it is an extremely impressive bit of technology.

To enable vMotion, vCenter Server is required, and the hosts and VMs in the process must meet a specific set of requirements. Let's review these requirements.

◆ Each host must be licensed for the vMotion feature.

◆ The shared storage for VM files must be accessible by both the source and target host, such as an NFS datastore.

◆ A VMkernel port defined and enabled for vMotion traffic is enabled on each host backed by a network interface card (NIC); 1 Gbps or faster is recommended.

---

vMOTION WITHOUT SHARED STORAGE

Earlier versions of vSphere introduced the ability to perform a "shared nothing" vMotion. This feature uses vMotion in conjunction with Storage vMotion to perform a live migration of a VM across storage. We will discuss this later in the chapter, in the "Combining vMotion with Storage vMotion" section.

This VMkernel port can be on either a vSphere Standard Switch or on a vSphere Distributed Switch, but it must be enabled for the vMotion traffic type. The Gigabit Ethernet (or faster) NIC must be enabled for vMotion traffic. This can be a dedicated interface, or it can be shared with other traffic types, as necessary. In Chapter 5, "Creating and Configuring a vSphere Network," you learned the steps for creating a VMkernel port on a vSwitch. The chapter included instructions for creating a VMkernel port on either a vSphere Standard Switch or a vSphere Distributed Switch. For your convenience, we will review the steps for creating a VMkernel port on a vSphere Distributed Switch.

Perform these steps to create a VMkernel port on an existing vSphere Distributed Switch:

1. If vSphere Web Client is not already running, open a browser, and connect and log on to the vSphere Web Client on your vCenter Server.

2. Navigate to the Hosts And Clusters view.

3. From the inventory, select an ESXi host that is already participating in the vSphere Distributed Switch.

4. Select the Configure tab from the contents pane.

5. Click Networking to display the networking configuration of the host.

6. Click the VMkernel Adapters.

7. In the VMkernel Adapters content, click the Add Host Networking link to add a new VMkernel adapter.

8. Select a connection type of VMkernel Network Adapter and click Next.

9. Browse to the port group and click Next.

10. Enable the vMotion traffic and, if desired, select a specific TCP/IP stack. Click Next.

11. Specify an IP address and network mask for the VMkernel interface.

12. Review the changes for the vSphere Distributed Switch.

If all is correct, click Finish to complete adding the VMkernel interface.

In addition to the shared storage and vMotion traffic configuration requirements, a successful vMotion migration between two ESXi hosts relies on meeting all the following conditions:

◆ Prior to vSphere 6, both source and target hosts had to be configured with identical virtual switches and port groups, and vMotion-enabled VMkernel ports. If you were using a vSphere Distributed Switch, both hosts had to participate in the same vSphere Distributed Switch. vSphere 6 removed the requirement for a common distributed switch; however, it is still good practice to configure your environment consistently, since capabilities such as the Distributed Resource Scheduler (DRS) rely on consistency when automating workload migrations.

◆ Prior to vSphere 6, port groups attached to the VMs being migrated had to exist on both source and target hosts. You can specify a destination port group during the migration wizard. However, it is recommended that you ensure all port groups are available across all hosts within your cluster for DRS to operate successfully. Port group naming is case sensitive, so create identical port groups on each host, and ensure they plug into the VLANs. A virtual switch named sfo01-m01-vds01 is not the same as a virtual switch named SFO01-M01-VDS01. Remember, to prevent downtime the VM does not need to change its network address when it is live-migrated with vMotion. The VM retains its MAC address and IP address, and active connections do not need to be reestablished.

◆ Processors in both hosts must be compatible. When a VM is transferred between hosts, the VM has already detected the type of processor that it is running on when it is powered on. Because the VM is not rebooted during a vMotion operation, the guest assumes that the CPU instruction set on the target host is the same as on the source host. You can get away with slightly dissimilar processors, but in general, the processors in two hosts that perform vMotion must meet the following requirements:

◆ CPUs must be from the same vendor (Intel or AMD).

◆ CPUs must be from the same CPU family.

◆ CPUs must support the same features, such as the presence of SSE2, SSE3, and SSE4 and NX or XD (see the sidebar "Processor Instruction").

◆ For 64-bit VMs, the CPUs must have virtualization technology enabled (Intel VT or AMD-v).

We will discuss more about processor compatibility in the section "Ensuring vMotion Compatibility," later in this chapter.

PROCESSOR INSTRUCTION

Streaming SIMD Extensions 2 (SSE2) was an enhancement to the original Multimedia Extension (MMX) instruction set found in the PIII processor. The enhancement targeted the floating-point calculation capabilities of the processor by providing 144 new instructions. SSE3 instruction sets are an enhancement to the SSE2 standard targeting multimedia and graphics applications. SSE4 extensions target both the graphics and the application server.

AMD's Execute Disable (XD) and Intel's NoExecute (NX) are features of processors that mark memory pages as data only, which prevents a virus from running executable code at that address. Modern operating systems are written to take advantage of this feature.

The latest processors from Intel and AMD have specialized support for virtualization. The AMD-V and Intel Virtualization Technology (VT) must be enabled in the BIOS to create VMs that will support 64-bit guest operating systems.

In addition to the vMotion requirements for the hosts, the VM must meet the following requirements to be live-migrated:

◆ The VM must not be connected to any device physically available to only the source host. This includes disk storage and CD/DVD drives. If a VM has one of these mappings, simply deselect the Connected check box beside the offending device. For example, you will not be able to migrate a VM with a CD/DVD connected. To disconnect the drive and allow a vMotion, deselect the Connected option.

◆ The VMs must not be connected to an internal-only virtual switch.

◆ The VM must not have its CPU affinity set to a specific CPU.

◆ The VM must have all disk, configuration, log, and nonvolatile random-access memory (NVRAM) files stored on a datastore accessible from both the source and target hosts.

If you initiate a vMotion live migration and vCenter Server discovers a violation of the vMotion compatibility rules, an error message will result. In some cases, a warning, not an error, will be issued. In the case of a warning, the vMotion migration will still succeed. For instance, if you have cleared the check box on the host-attached CD/DVD, vCenter Server will alert you that there is a mapping to a host-only device that is not active. You will be prompted with a question asking whether the migration should take place anyway.

Although the vSphere requirements for vMotion include a VMkernel port backed by a network interface card, it does not have to be dedicated to vMotion traffic. When you are designing the hosts, you can dedicate a physical NIC to vMotion traffic and share it with additional VMkernel traffic types. For example, if you have two 10 Gbps NICs providing the uplinks for a vSphere Distributed Switch, you can create a dedicated VMkernel port group for Management traffic and another port group for vMotion traffic. Additional port groups can be created for additional traffic types. You can then use NIOC, as discussed in the "Regulating Network I/O Utilization" section of Chapter 11, to ensure the vMotion process can happen in an efficient manner by prioritizing the traffic.

LONG-DISTANCE vMOTION

When performing long-distance vMotion operations, the maximum supported network round-trip time (RTT) is 150 milliseconds. This RTT enables you to migrate VMs to geographical locations across longer distances. The requirement for 250 Mbps of dedicated bandwidth per concurrent vMotion session also applies.

Now that we have discussed the various prerequisites, both for ESXi hosts and VMs, let's perform a vMotion migration.

Performing a vMotion Migration Within a Cluster

After you have verified that the hosts' and VMs' requirements are in order, you are ready to perform a vMotion migration.

Perform these steps to initiate a vMotion migration of a running VM:

1. If vSphere Web Client is not already running, open a browser and connect and login to the vSphere Web Client on your vCenter Server. vMotion requires vCenter Server.

2. Navigate to either the Hosts And Clusters view or the VMs And Templates view.

3. Select a powered-on VM from the inventory. From the Actions menu, select Migrate.

4. On the Select A Migration Type page, select the Change Compute Resource Only option, and then click Next.

5. On the Select A Compute Resource page, you can select a target host, cluster, resource pool, or vApp as your target resource; Chapter 10, "Using Templates and vApps," introduced the concept of vApps. The computability section on the page will alert you if there are any potential issues with the live migration, such as an attached CD/DVD device.

   Generally, the same resource pool or cluster in which a VM resides will suffice as the target. Keep in mind that when choosing a different resource pool, it may change the VM priority for resources. Refer to Chapter 11 for a more in-depth discussion of how resource allocation is affected by placement into a resource pool.

6. Choose a target host for the VM migration. Figure 12.6 shows that you can filter the target destination by hosts, clusters, resource pools, and vApps. After you have selected the desired target host, click Next.

FIGURE 12.6
vCenter Server allows you to filter the possible destinations for your VMs.

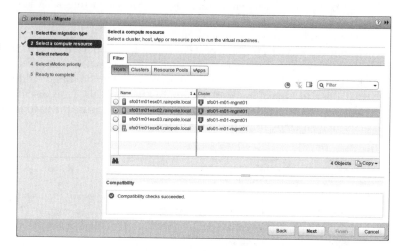

7. On the Select Networks page, select a destination port group for the VM, as shown in Figure 12.7, and click Next.

FIGURE 12.7
You can define a different destination port group as part of the vMotion process.

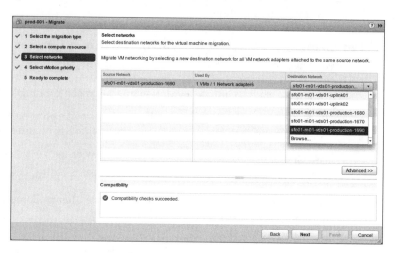

8. On the Select vMotion Priority page, select a priority with which to initiate the vMotion migration.

This setting controls the share of reserved resources allocated for migrations with vMotion. Migrations marked as Schedule vMotion With High Priority receive a reserved share of CPU resources compared to migrations marked as Schedule Regular vMotion. Migrations will proceed regardless of the resources reserved. Standard priority migrations may proceed more slowly and might even fail to complete if sufficient resources are not available. Generally, you will select Schedule vMotion With High Priority (Recommended). Click Next to continue.

9. On the Ready To Complete page, review the settings, and click Finish to initiate the VM migration with vMotion.

If there are any mistakes in the settings, simply use the Back button or the page links to step back and correct the items.

The VM should start to migrate. Often, you may observe the process pause near 14% in the Recent Tasks and then again near 65%. The pause near 14% occurs while the source and target hosts establish communications and gather the information for the pages in memory to be migrated; the pause near 65% occurs while the source VM is quiesced and the dirty memory pages are fetched from the source host.

You can monitor the progress of the vMotion operation in the Recent Tasks pane, as shown in Figure 12.8.

FIGURE 12.8
The Recent Tasks pane in the vSphere Web Client shows the progress of the vMotion operation.

---

vMOTION IS NOT A HIGH-AVAILABILITY FEATURE

vMotion is an amazing vSphere feature, but it is not a high-availability feature. While vMotion can be used to improve uptime by preventing downtime from planned maintenance, vMotion does not provide protection in the event of an unplanned host failure. For that functionality, you will need vSphere High Availability (HA) and vSphere Fault Tolerance (FT). These two features are discussed in Chapter 7, "Ensuring High Availability and Business Continuity."

ENCRYPTED vMOTION

As of vSphere 6.5, and by default, vMotion uses encryption when migrating encrypted VMs. In fact, you cannot disable encrypted vMotion on encrypted VMs. VMs that are not encrypted can use one of the encrypted vMotion options: Disabled, Required, or Opportunistic. The default is Opportunistic where encryption is used if both the source and target host support it. With the default Opportunistic option or the Required option, if the target host does not support encrypted vMotion, the migration will fail.

Encrypted vMotion supports vMotion of unencrypted VMs across vCenter Server instances. However, migration across vCenter Server instances is not supported with encrypted VMs.

vMotion is an invaluable feature of modern datacenters and their administrators. Once you have managed a datacenter with vMotion, you will wonder how you ever managed to live without it.

Over time, though, you may find yourself in a situation where you are unable to invoke a vMotion operation. As hardware manufacturers such as Intel and AMD introduce new generations of CPUs, some of your hosts may have a newer generation of CPUs than others. Remember one of the requirements for vMotion is compatible CPUs.

What happens when you perform a hardware refresh cycle or simply add more hosts to your existing infrastructure and the hosts have a newer CPU generation?

vSphere addresses this potential problem with a feature called Enhanced vMotion Compatibility (EVC).

Ensuring vMotion Compatibility

Earlier in this chapter, the section "Examining vMotion Requirements" discussed some of the prerequisites needed to perform a vMotion operation, including CPU requirements. Specifically, the CPUs must be from the same vendor, must be in the same family, and must share a common set of CPU instruction sets and features.

When source and target hosts with CPU differences exist in the same cluster, a vMotion operation between the two will fail. This is referred to as a *vMotion boundary*. In early, pre-vSphere versions, there was no fix for this issue—it was something that architects planned for and administrators simply had to endure.

However, in later versions and continuing into vSphere 6.7, vSphere supports hardware extensions from both Intel and AMD to help mitigate these CPU differences. In fact, vSphere provides a few ways to address the issue, either in part or in whole.

Using Per-Virtual-Machine CPU Masking

With vCenter Server, you can create custom CPU masks on a per-VM basis. Although this can offer a tremendous amount of flexibility in enabling vMotion compatibility, it is critically important to note that, with one exception, this function is mostly unsupported by VMware.

There is one exception. On a per-VM basis, you will find a setting that instructs the VM to show or mask the No Execute/Execute Disable (NX/XD) bit in the host CPU, and this specific instance of CPU masking is fully supported by VMware. Masking the NX/XD bit from the VM instructs it that no NX/XD bit is present. This is useful if you have two, otherwise compatible, hosts with an NX/XD bit mismatch. If the VM does not know an NX or XD bit exists on one of the hosts, it will not care if the target host has that bit if you live-migrate the VM using vMotion. The greatest vMotion compatibility is achieved by masking the NX/XD bit. If the NX/XD bit is exposed to the VM, as shown in Figure 12.9, the BIOS setting for NX/XD must match on both the source and target hosts.

For features other than the NX/XD bit, you would have to delve into custom CPU masks. This is where you step outside the bounds of VMware support. Looking at the dialog box in Figure 12.9, you will notice the Advanced link. Clicking this link opens the CPU Identification Mask dialog box, shown in Figure 12.10.

FIGURE 12.9
The option for masking the NX/XD bit is controlled on a per-VM basis.

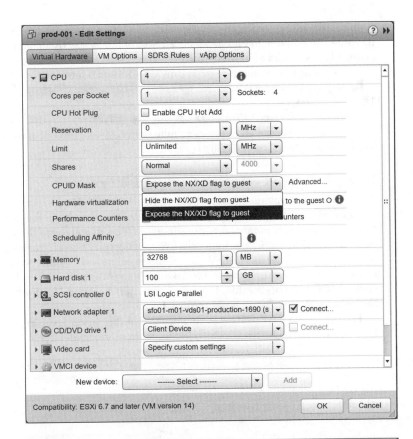

FIGURE 12.10
The CPU Identification Mask dialog box allows you to create custom CPU masks.

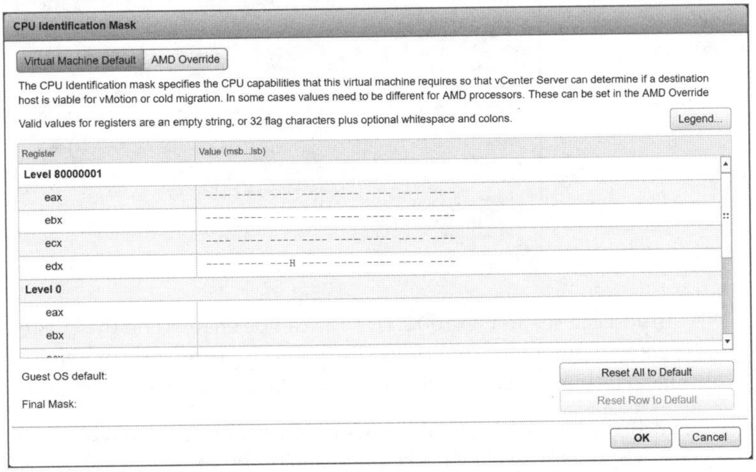

In this dialog box, you can create custom CPU masks to mark off specific bits within the CPU ID value. We will not go into detail here, because this is strictly unsupported, and it is generally not needed provided you run hardware that is on the VMware Compatibility Guide. However, Scott Lowe has two blog articles that provide additional information on the subject:

`http://blog.scottlowe.org/2006/09/25/sneaking-around-vmotion-limitations/` and

`http://blog.scottlowe.org/2007/06/19/more-on-cpu-masking/`

Fortunately, there in an easier—*and fully supported*—method of addressing this issue: Enhanced vMotion Compatibility (EVC).

Using Enhanced vMotion Compatibility

Recognizing that potential for compatibility issues with vMotion could be a significant problem, VMware worked closely with both Intel and AMD to address the issue. On the hardware side, Intel and AMD incorporated functions in their CPUs that allowed them to modify the CPU ID value returned by the CPUs. Intel calls this functionality FlexMigration; AMD simply embedded this functionality into its AMD-V virtualization extensions. On the software side, VMware created software features that would take advantage of the hardware functionality to create a common CPU ID baseline for all the servers within a cluster. This functionality is called Enhanced vMotion Compatibility (EVC).

Prior to vSphere 6.7, EVC was only enabled at the cluster level. Figure 12.11 illustrates the EVC controls for a cluster, which we'll discuss in more detail later in this section.

FIGURE 12.11
Enhanced vMotion Compatibility can be enabled and disabled at the cluster level.

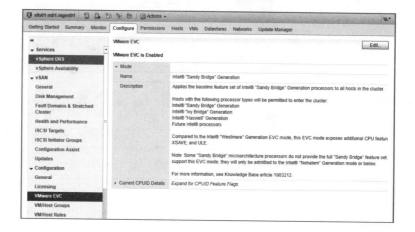

As you can see in Figure 12.11, EVC can be enabled on the cluster. This cluster contains servers with Intel "Sandy Bridge" Generation processors; therefore, EVC is using an Intel Sandy Bridge baseline. To change the baseline that EVC is using on a cluster, follow these steps:

1. If vSphere Web Client is not already running, open a browser and connect and login to the vSphere Web Client on your vCenter Server.

2. Navigate to the Hosts And Clusters view.

3. Select a cluster from the inventory. From the Actions menu, select Settings or click the Configure tab.

4. On the Configure tab, select VMware EVC.

5. Click Edit to open the Change EVC Mode dialog box.

6. On the Change EVC Mode dialog box, you can disable EVC or change the Cluster-level EVC mode baseline based on the host processor vendor, as illustrated in Figure 12.12.

FIGURE 12.12
You can enable or disable EVC as well as change the baseline it uses.

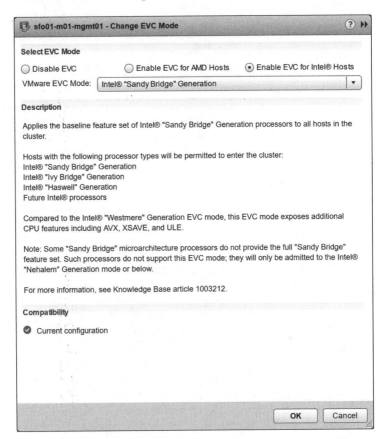

vCenter Server performs validation checks to ensure that the physical hardware can support the selected EVC mode and processor baseline. If you select a setting that the hardware cannot support, the Change EVC Mode dialog box will reflect an incompatibility. Figure 12.13 shows that an incompatible EVC mode is selected.

When you enable cluster-level EVC and set the processor baseline, vCenter Server calculates the correct CPU masks required and communicates that information to the hosts. The ESXi hypervisor then works with the underlying Intel or AMD processors to create the correct CPU ID values that will match the correct CPU mask. When vCenter Server validates vMotion compatibility by checking CPU compatibility, the underlying CPUs will return compatible CPU masks and CPU ID values.

FIGURE 12.13
vCenter Server ensures
that the selected EVC
mode is compatible with
the underlying hardware.

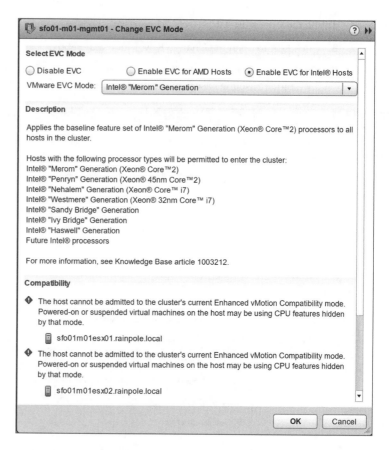

However, vCenter Server and ESXi cannot set CPU masks for VMs that currently powered on. You can verify this by opening the properties of a running VM and reviewing the CPUID Mask area on the Resources tab. You will find that all the controls are disabled when powered on.

Consequently, if you attempt to change the cluster-level EVC mode on a cluster that has powered-on VMs, vCenter Server will prevent the change, as you can see in Figure 12.14. You will have to power down all of the VMs in the cluster in order to change the cluster-level EVC mode.

When enabling cluster-level EVC mode, keep in mind that some CPU-specific features—such as newer multimedia extensions or encryption instructions—may be disabled when vCenter Server and ESXi disable them via EVC. VMs that rely on these advanced extensions may be affected by EVC. Be sure that your workloads will not be adversely affected before setting the cluster-level EVC mode.

Cluster-level EVC mode can ensure the compatibility of host CPUs in a cluster and allow live migrations of VMs with vMotion within the cluster. But what about beyond the boundaries of the cluster—other clusters across a vCenter Server instance, other vCenter Server instances, or even hybrid cloud?

vSphere 6.7 introduces the per-VM EVC feature that enables the migration beyond the cluster boundary. This new per-VM mode is managed independently of the cluster-level EVC mode.

FIGURE 12.14
vCenter Server informs the user which hosts in the cluster have powered-on or suspended VMs that are preventing the change to the cluster-level EVC mode.

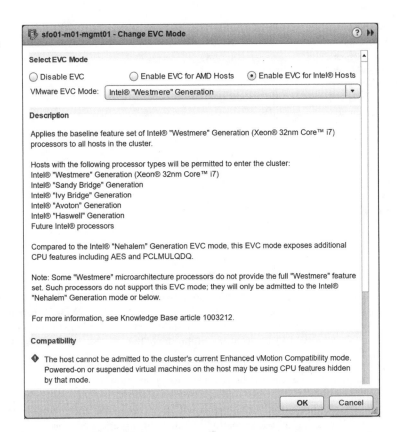

Cluster-level EVC returns the compatible CPU masks and CPU ID values a host provides to its VMs; whereas, per-VM EVC determines which CPU features a VM requires from a host to power on and to be migrated.

When a new VM is created and powered on for the first time, it inherits the CPU feature set from its parent EVC cluster or hosts. Now, in vSphere 6.7, you can raise or lower the EVC mode for a VM independently (see Figure 12.15). By lowering the per-VM EVC mode, the CPU compatibility of the VM increases.

Some key differences exist between the cluster-level EVC mode and the new per-VM EVC mode:

◆ The EVC mode on a VM can only be changed when it is powered off.

◆ Although not explicitly covered in this book, due to feature parity with the Flash-based vSphere Web Client, the per-VM EVC mode can only be configured using the HTML5 vSphere Web Client under the Configure option of the VM.

◆ Per-VM EVC mode is a VM attribute—a power cycle will not affect the compatibility of the VM. However, when a VM is migrated out of a cluster-level EVC mode cluster, a power cycle resets the EVC mode of a VM.

FIGURE 12.15
Per-VM EVC mode
determines which CPU
features a VM requires
from a host to power on
or to be migrated beyond
the cluster boundary.
This feature is only
available in the
HTML5 vSphere Web
Client under the
Configure option for a
VM when it is
powered off.

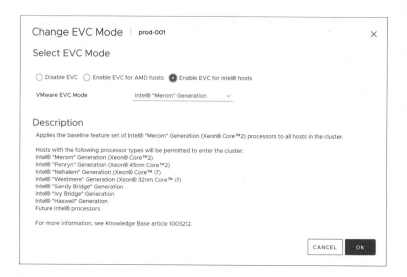

◆ Per-VM EVC mode overrides cluster-level EVC mode; however, it may not exceed the EVC mode of the cluster. This means that the per-VM CPU feature set may not contain more CPU features than the baseline feature set of the hosts in the EVC cluster. VMs with a per-VM EVC mode at a higher level than the baseline will fail to power on.

EVC is a powerful feature that assures an administrator that vMotion compatibility will be maintained over time, even as hardware generations change and as organizations expand their data center.

Traditional vMotion only helps with balancing CPU and memory load. In the next section, we will discuss a method for manually balancing storage load.

Using Storage vMotion

vMotion and Storage vMotion are like two sides of the same coin. Traditional vMotion migrates running VM from one host to another, moving the CPU and memory resource usage between hosts—but leaving the storage of the VM unchanged. vMotion enables you to manually balance the CPU and memory resource by shifting VMs from host to host. Storage vMotion, however, migrates the virtual disks of a powered on VM from one datastore to another, all while the VM continues to execute—and therefore using CPU and memory resources—on the *same* host. This feature allows you to manually balance the utilization of a datastore by shifting VM storage from datastore to datastore. Like vMotion, Storage vMotion is a live migration; the VM does not incur any downtime when migrating virtual disks from one datastore to another.

The process for Storage vMotion is relatively straightforward:

1. vSphere copies over the nonvolatile files that constitute the VM: the configuration file, VMkernel swap, log files, and snapshots.

2. vSphere starts a shadow VM on the target datastore. Because this shadow VM does not yet have a virtual disk that has not been copied over, it sits idly waiting.

3. Storage vMotion first creates the target disk. Then a mirror device—a driver that mirrors I/Os between the source and target—is inserted into the data path between the VM and the underlying storage.

4. With the I/O mirroring driver in place, vSphere makes a single-pass copy of the virtual disk(s) from the source to the target. As changes are made to the source, the I/O mirror driver ensures that those changes are also reflected to the virtual disks on the target datastore.

5. When the virtual disk copy is complete, vSphere quickly quiesces and resumes the VM to transfer control over to the shadow VM that has been created on the target datastore. As with vMotion, this generally happens so quickly that there is no disruption of service.

The files on the source datastore are deleted.

SVM MIRROR DEVICE INFORMATION IN THE LOGS

If you review the VMkernel log files on an ESXi host during and after a Storage vMotion operation, you will see log entries prefixed with *SVM*. These logs show the creation of the mirror device and provide information about the operation of the mirror device.

It is important to note that the original files are not deleted until the migration is confirmed as a successful operation; this allows vSphere to fall back to the original source location if an error occurs during the migration. This helps to prevent any data loss or unplanned VM outages if an error occurs during the Storage vMotion process.

Perform the following steps to migrate the virtual disks of a VMs using Storage vMotion:

1. If vSphere Web Client is not already running, open a browser and connect and login to the vSphere Web Client on your vCenter Server. As with vMotion, Storage vMotion is available only when hosts are managed by vCenter Server.

2. Navigate to the Hosts And Clusters view or the VMs And Templates view.

3. Select the VMs whose virtual disks you want to migrate from the inventory. From the Actions menu, select Migrate. This is the same action used to initiate vMotion.

4. On the Select A Migration Type page, select the Change Storage Only option, and then click Next.

5. On the Select Storage page, select a destination datastore or datastore cluster. We will discuss datastore clusters in the section "Working with Storage DRS," later in this chapter.

6. Select the desired virtual disk format, such as, Thick Provision Lazy Zeroed, Thick Provision Eager Zeroed, or Thin Provision.

Storage vMotion lets you change the disk format during the actual disk-migration process, so you can switch from Thick Provision Lazy Zeroed to Thin Provision, for example.

7. If you have storage policies defined in vCenter Server, select the desired policy from the VM Storage Policy drop-down box.

8. If you need to migrate the VMs configuration file and virtual hard disks separately or to separate destinations, click the Advanced option to select a target datastore per virtual disk

   Figure 12.16 shows the virtual disk format view of the Select Storage step of the Migrate Wizard and how you can choose the destination and disk formats.

FIGURE 12.16
Use the Migrate Wizard to change the virtual disk format for a VM.

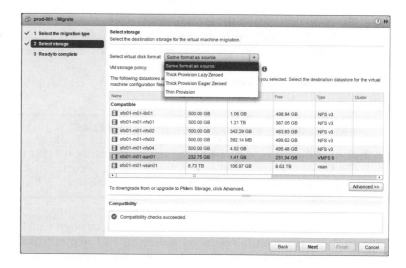

9. When you have finished making selections on the Select Storage page, click Next to continue to the Ready To Complete page.

10. Review the settings for the Storage vMotion and ensure the new settings are correct. If you need to make changes, simply use the Back button of the page links. Click Finish to initiate the Storage vMotion process.

STORAGE vMOTION WITH RAW DEVICE MAPPINGS

Be careful when using Storage vMotion with raw device mappings (RDMs). If you want to migrate only the VMDK mapping file, be sure to select Same Format As Source for the virtual disk format. If you select a different format, virtual mode RDMs will be converted into VMDKs as part of the Storage vMotion operation—physical mode RDMs are not affected. Once an RDM has been converted into a VMDK, it *cannot be* converted back into an RDM again.

Once you have initiated the Storage vMotion operation, the vSphere Web Client will show the progress of the migration in the Recent Tasks.

If a VM in the inventory has been renamed, the new name is not immediately reflected on the datastore. When you perform a Storage vMotion operation, vSphere will rename the VM files on datastores to align to the VM name that is displayed in the vSphere Web Client. On the other hand, if the VM has not been renamed since it was created or since the last Storage vMotion operation, this file renaming process will not occur. You don't have the choice to *not* rename the files—Storage vMotion renames the underlying files to adhere to the VM display name and the file-naming convention.

The following files are renamed when part of a Storage vMotion occurs to the `<VM Name>.<Extension Type>` format:

◆ `.VMX`

◆ `.VMXF`

◆ `.NVRAM`

◆ `.VMDK`

◆ `.VMSN`

There is one exception, however. If a VM has two virtual disks and Storage vMotion is only used on one of the disks, only that disk and its associated files will be renamed during the operation. If, based on the naming convention, there are two files that would receive the same filename—such as a snapshot disk—a numeric suffix is added to resolve filename conflict.

Combining vMotion with Storage vMotion

vMotion and Storage vMotion can be combined into a single operational process to produce what is often called a *shared nothing* vMotion.

Without the availability of shared storage, such as vSAN, SAN, or NAS, an administrator can move VMs from host to host regardless of the storage type. Local storage, mixed shared storage, or standard shared storage are all valid options to use when combining vMotion with Storage vMotion.

Prior to vSphere 6, the only requirement for the combined vMotion and Storage vMotion was that both hosts needed to share the same L2 (Layer 2) network. This requirement was lifted with the introduction of multiple TCP/IP stacks. You can read more about multiple TCP/IP stacks in Chapter 5. Depending on how you want this feature to work, you may need to add extra requirements. We will discuss this using examples.

Example 1

◆ Two hosts on a single vMotion network.

◆ Both hosts use local datastores.

In the first example, the two hosts are connected by a single vMotion network, but both have only local datastores, as you can see in Figure 12.17. When you migrate a VM from one host to another, there are two dataflow operations. The first flow initiated is storage. Generally, a storage transfer will take longer to complete than the memory transfer. After the storage transfer has taken place, the memory copy starts. Although there are two separate data transfers, all data flows over the same vMotion VMkernel network.

FIGURE 12.17
All data flows over the vMotion network when transferring between local datastores.

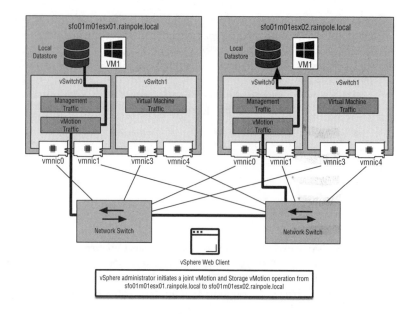

Example 2

◆ Two hosts on a single vMotion network.

◆ One host uses local datastores.

◆ One host uses SAN datastores.

In the second example, a single vMotion network connects the two hosts. One host is connected to a SAN for storage and another used local storage. In this example, not much changes with the data flow. The only difference is that the second host pushes the received data to the SAN over its storage network instead of a local datastore. You can see this in detail in Figure 12.18. Both hosts are connected to the shared storage, and that leads us to Example 3.

Example 3

◆ Two hosts on a single vMotion network.

◆ Both hosts use a shared Fibre Channel SAN datastore.

In the third example, the two hosts are typical of some larger enterprise environments—an environment where a SAN or NAS connects all ESXi hosts. In this situation, the dataflows are quite different. As usual, the vMotion network carries the memory dataflow. The difference in this example involves the shared storage component. Storage vMotion detects when both hosts can see both source and target datastores. It intelligently uses the storage network instead of the vMotion network to migrate this data even if it is a local datastore at the source. See Figure 12.19.

Perform the following steps to migrate a VM to a different host and datastore using the combined vMotion and Storage vMotion:

FIGURE 12.18
Data flows over the vMotion network and then the storage network when transferring between local and non-local datastores.

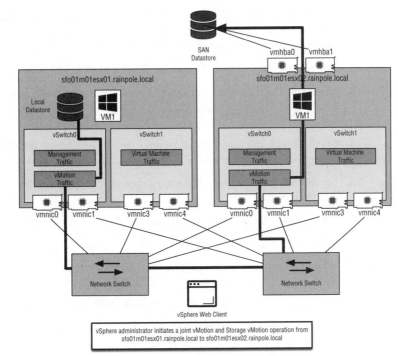

FIGURE 12.19
Even if the datastores are not the same, Storage vMotion detects whether both hosts can see the destination datastore. It uses the storage network whenever possible.

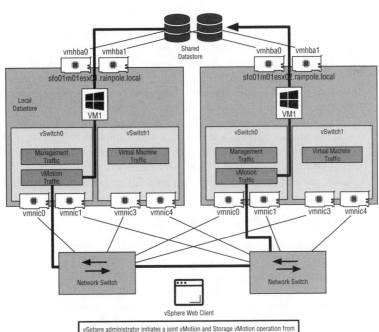

1. If vSphere Web Client is not already running, open a browser and connect and login to the vSphere Web Client on your vCenter Server. vMotion and Storage vMotion are available only when hosts are managed by vCenter Server.

2. Navigate to the Hosts And Clusters view or the VMs And Templates view.

3. Select the VM from the inventory that you wish to migrate. From the Actions menu, select Migrate. The Migrate Wizard used to initiate a vMotion and a Storage vMotion will launch.

4. On the Select The Migration Type page, select the Change Both Compute Resource And Storage option and click Next.

5. On the Select A Compute Resource page, select the destination host or cluster resource and click Next.

6. On the Select Storage page, select a target datastore or datastore cluster.

7. Select the desired virtual disk format.

8. If you have storage policies defined in vCenter Server, select the desired policy from the VM Storage Policy drop-down box. Click Next to continue.

9. On the Select Networks page, select the desired destination network.

10. On the Select vMotion Priority page, select the vMotion priority, as desired. Click Next to review the changes.

11. On the Ready To Complete page, review the changes and click Finish.

When you combine vMotion and Storage vMotion operations, the storage is the first migration to take place; the reason behind this is two-fold. First, virtual disks are both larger and slower than memory; therefore, the Storage vMotion will take significantly longer than the vMotion. Second, the rate of change to virtual disk-based storage is typically far less than memory. If the vMotion operation happened first, the memory bitmap file—discussed earlier in this chapter—would grow much larger while waiting for the Storage vMotion task to complete. This is why it makes more sense for the Storage vMotion operation to initiate first.

Like vMotion, Storage vMotion—or a combination of both—is a great approach for manually adjusting the utilization of resources. However, they are ultimately *reactive* operations. DRS and SDRS leverage vMotion and Storage vMotion to bring a level of automation and help balance cluster and datastore utilization. We will discuss both a little later in this chapter.

Cross-vCenter vMotion

Traditionally, vMotion has been an intra-cluster solution for balancing workloads. vSphere 6 pushed vMotion further, allowing you to migrate VMs across clusters, virtual standard switches, virtual distributed switches, and vCenter Servers. In addition, you can migrate between geographically dispersed environments with an RTT of 150 ms or less.

Although these capabilities provide an increase in mobility of workloads, what are the operational impacts? The good news is that the universally unique identifier (UUID) of the VM (not to be confused with the BIOS UUID) is retained during the transfer, so most of the information that you want is transferred along with the VM. vSphere HA configurations and DRS rules, events, tasks, and alarms will all move with the VM, as will any configured shares, reservations, or limits. The only downside is that performance data—which is written to the vCenter Server database—will not be migrated with the VM. (Note, however, that if each of the vCenter Server instances is monitored by the same vRealize Operations instance or cluster, you have another very powerful method to review historical performance and capacity data.)

ROUTING vMOTION TRAFFIC

One challenge in migrating workloads between geographically dispersed datacenters is that VMkernel interfaces in each site reside on different Layer 2 networks. To address that limitation, vMotion traffic is now routable, as discussed in Chapter 5. vMotion can use its own TCP/IP stack to make that process much smoother over routed Layer 3.

Examining Cross-vCenter vMotion Requirements

Although the requirements for vMotion have already been discussed, some additional requirements must be considered for cross-vCenter vMotion:

◆ vCenter Server instances participating in the migration must be a minimum of vCenter Server 6.0 and must be joined to the same Single Sign-On (SSO) domain—also known as Enhanced Linked Mode—to perform the migration using the vSphere Web Client.

◆ All hosts must be at least vSphere 6.0.

◆ The RTT between hosts must be less than 150 ms.

MAC ADDRESS HANDLING

When a VM is migrated to a new vCenter Server, its MAC address is transferred with it. To prevent conflicts, the source vCenter Server will add the MAC address of that VM to a blacklist so that it does not get assigned to another VM.

These are the requirements as defined by VMware, but there are some additional considerations when performing a vMotion beyond the boundary of the cluster it is currently a member of:

◆ Are the appropriate VLANs configured for the port group to which the VM will attach? If not, you will lose network connectivity for the VM, resulting in downtime and negating the benefit of using vMotion to perform the migration.

◆ How are your backups managed? Performing a backup over your WAN link post-migration will not be a viable option. You must also consider how your backup software determines backup policies—are you looking for VMs in a given folder? Are they defined by UUID or some other mechanism such as the Managed Object Reference ID (MoRef)?

◆ Do other objects communicate with this machine? Will migrating it to a remote datacenter impact application performance or user access?

These considerations are specific to your environment. Think about these when determining how best to make use of the new capabilities.

Performing a Cross-vCenter Motion

Once you've met the requirements for your hosts, VMs, and vCenter Servers, you can perform a cross vCenter vMotion:

1. If vSphere Web Client is not already running, open a browser and connect and login to the vSphere Web Client on your vCenter Server. vMotion is available only when hosts are managed by vCenter Server.

2. Navigate to either the Hosts And Clusters view or the VMs And Templates view.

3. Select a powered-on VM in the inventory. From the Actions menu, select Migrate.

4. On the Migration Type page, select Change Both Compute Resource And Storage, and then click Next.

   If you have a specific storage or compute requirement, you can change the default selection from Select Compute Resource First to Select Storage First. With this setting, you adjust the order in which screens appear, and you can verify that the VM is placed on the prioritized resource. For this example, leave the default selection.

5. On the Select A Compute Resource page, choose a valid compute target on another vCenter Server instance for the VM and click Next.

6. If you have any resource pools defined on the target host or target cluster, you will need to select the target resource pool or cluster. You can also select a vApp as your target resource pool (vApps were discussed in Chapter 10).

7. On the Select Storage page, select a destination datastore or datastore cluster. We will discuss datastore clusters in the section "Working with Storage DRS."

8. Select the desired virtual disk and click Next.

9. On the Select A Folder page, select the destination VM folder and click Next.

10. On the Select Network page, select the destination port group that you want the VM to join and click Next.

11. On the Select vMotion Priority page, select the priority in which you want the vMotion migration to proceed.

12. On the Ready To Complete page, review the settings, and click Finish to initiate the cross-vCenter vMotion.

    If there are any issues with the settings, use the Back button or the page links to go back and correct the settings before clicking Finish.

    The VM will begin the cross-vCenter migration. Often, the process will pause at about 14% in the progress dialog box and then again at 65% as we discussed earlier.

Although in the example, we are discussing how to migrate to compute resources within a different vCenter Server instance, you can use these same steps to migrate a VM between clusters or virtual switches within the same vCenter Server.

Exploring vSphere Distributed Resource Scheduler

When we discussed vMotion and Storage vMotion, we said that they are methods of manually balancing loads across hosts. vSphere Distributed Resource Scheduler (DRS) builds on this construct by enabling *automatic* load balancing within a cluster, which we introduced in Chapter 3, "Installing and Configuring vCenter Server," and discussed again in Chapter 7, "Ensuring High Availability and Business Continuity."

DRS is a feature of vCenter Server and has the following two main functions:

◆ To decide which host in a cluster should run a VM when it is powered on, or *intelligent placement*

◆ To evaluate the load on the cluster over time and either make recommendations for migrations or use vMotion to automatically migrate VMs and balance the cluster workloads

DRS runs as a process within vCenter Server, and therefore you must have vCenter Server to use this feature. By default, DRS checks every 5 minutes (or 300 seconds) to see if cluster workloads are well balanced. Actions within a cluster, such as adding or removing an ESXi host or changing the resource settings of a VM, will invoke DRS. When DRS is invoked, it will calculate the imbalance of the cluster, apply any resource controls (such as reservations, shares, and limits), and, if necessary, generate recommendations for migrations of VMs within the cluster. Depending on the DRS configuration, these recommendations may be applied automatically, meaning that VMs will be automatically migrated between hosts by DRS to maintain cluster balance (or, to put it another way, to minimize cluster imbalance).

VSPHERE DISTRIBUTED RESOURCE SCHEDULER ENABLES RESOURCE POOLS

DRS enables the use of resource pools when clustering vSphere ESXi hosts. If the hosts are part of an HA-enabled cluster, DRS must also be enabled to allow resource pools to be created.

If you like to retain some control over the automation level, you can set how aggressively DRS will automatically rebalance VMs in the cluster.

If you start by looking at the DRS properties which you can view by selecting a DRS-enabled cluster from the inventory, selecting the Configure tab, selecting the vSphere DRS option, and then clicking Edit—you will see that there are three DRS automation-level selections for the cluster on the Edit Cluster Settings page: Manual, Partially Automated, and Fully Automated. By clicking the triangle next to DRS Automation, you will find the Migration Threshold slider control that affects the actions of the Fully Automated setting on the cluster. These settings control the initial placement of a VM and the automatic movement of VMs between hosts in a cluster. We will examine the behavior of these automation levels in the next three sections.

Understanding Manual Automation Behavior

When a DRS cluster is set to Manual, each time you power on a VM, the cluster prompts you to selec an ESXi host where that VM should be hosted. The dialog box ranks the available hosts according to suitability at that moment in time: the lower the priority, the better the choice, as shown in Figure 12.2

FIGURE 12.20

A DRS cluster set to Manual requires you to specify where the VM should be powered on.

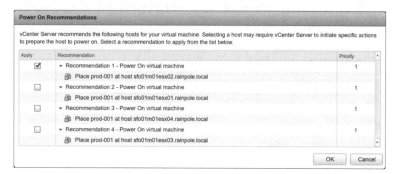

The Manual setting will also suggest vMotion migrations when DRS detects an imbalance between the hosts in the cluster. This is an averaging process that works over longer periods of time. In turn, it can be unusual to see DRS make any recommendations unless an imbalance has existed for longer than 5 minutes. You find the recommended list of migrations by selecting the cluster in the inventory, selecting the Monitor tab, followed by selecting the vSphere DRS sectio

From here, the Run DRS Now button allows you to agree with any pending DRS recommendations and initiate a migration. vMotion handles the migration automatically. Figure 12.21 shows some pending recommendations displayed on the DRS Recommendations section of a cluster that is set to the Manual DRS automation level.

FIGURE 12.21

vMotion operations must be approved by an administrator when DRS is set for Manual.

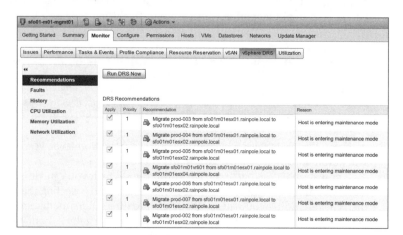

Reviewing Partially Automated Behavior

If you select the Partially Automated setting in the DRS Automation settings, DRS will make an automatic decision about which host a VM should run on when it is initially powered on. In this scenario, the placement is performed without prompting the user performing the power on task however, it will still prompt for all migrations on the migration recommendations. Thus, the partially automated configuration automatically performs the initial placement, but migrations are manually invoked.

Examining Fully Automated Behavior

The third DRS Automation level is Fully Automated. With this setting, DRS makes the decisions for initial placement and automatic vMotion decisions based on the selected automation level without user intervention.

Five positions exist for the Fully Automated slider control setting of a DRS cluster. The values of the slider control the range from Conservative to Aggressive. Conservative automatically applies recommendations ranked as priority 1 recommendations. Any other migrations are listed on the DRS tab and require administrator approval. If you move the slider bar from the most conservative setting to the next stop to the right, then all priority 1 and priority 2 recommendations are automatically applied; recommendations higher than priority 2 will wait for administrator approval. With the slider all the way over to the Aggressive setting, any imbalance in the cluster that causes a recommendation is automatically approved (even priority 5 recommendations). Be aware that this can cause additional stress in your ESXi host environment because even a slight imbalance will trigger a migration.

Calculations for migrations can change regularly. For example, assume that during a period of high activity, DRS makes a priority 3 recommendation and the automation level is set so priority 3 recommendations need manual approval, but the recommendation is not noticed or an administrator is unavailable. An hour later, the VMs that caused the recommendation in the first place have returned to operating normally. At this point, the DRS tab no longer reflects the recommendation. The recommendation has since been withdrawn. If the migration were still listed, an administrator might approve it and cause an imbalance where one did not exist.

In many cases, priority 1 recommendations have little to do with load on the cluster. Instead, priority 1 recommendations are generally the result of one of two conditions. The first condition that causes a priority 1 recommendation is when a host is placed into maintenance mode, as shown in Figure 12.22.

FIGURE 12.22
An ESXi host placed into maintenance mode cannot power on new VMs or be a target for vMotion.

Maintenance mode is a host setting that prevents an ESXi host from performing any VM-related functions. VMs running on a host being placed into maintenance mode must be migrated to another host or shut down before the host will enter maintenance mode. That is an ESXi host in a DRS-enabled cluster will automatically generate priority 1 recommendations to migrate all VMs to other hosts within the cluster. Figure 12.21 shows priority 1 recommendations generated as the result of an ESXi host being placed into maintenance mode.

The second condition that can cause a priority 1 recommendation are DRS affinity rules. This leads us to our next discussion.

A QUICK REVIEW OF DISTRIBUTED RESOURCE SCHEDULER CLUSTER PERFORMANCE

Monitoring the performance of a cluster is an important task for an administrator, particularly monitoring the CPU and memory activity of the cluster as well as the respective resource utilization of the VMs powered on within the cluster. The Summary tab for a cluster object includes information on cluster configuration as well as statistics for the current load distribution. Although resource allocation and distribution is not necessarily a direct indicator of performance, it can be a helpful metric nevertheless.

PREDICTIVE DRS

vSphere 6.5 introduced Predictive DRS as an approach to predict future demands and determine when, or where, hot spots may occur.

Dynamic thresholds are a fundamental capability of vRealize Operations. vRealize Operations collects metrics across datacenter resource objects—hosts, datastores, and VMs—throughout the day and calculates a dynamic threshold each night to determine lower and upper bounds for what is normal using its analytics algorithms.

By joining the power DRS with the analytics of vRealize Operations, DRS can now understand the workload patterns and predictively move workload *before* contention occurs.

Working with Distributed Resource Scheduler Rules

To further customize the behavior of DRS for your specific environment, vSphere lets you create DRS rules. DRS supports three types of DRS rules:

- VM affinity rules—referred to as Keep Virtual Machines Together in the vSphere Web Client

- VM anti-affinity rules—referred to as Separate Virtual Machines in the vSphere Web Clie

- Host affinity rules—referred to as Virtual Machines To Hosts in the vSphere Web Client

Figure 12.23 shows these three types of rules in the dialog box for creating new DRS rules.

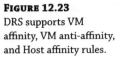

FIGURE 12.23
DRS supports VM
affinity, VM anti-affinity,
and Host affinity rules.

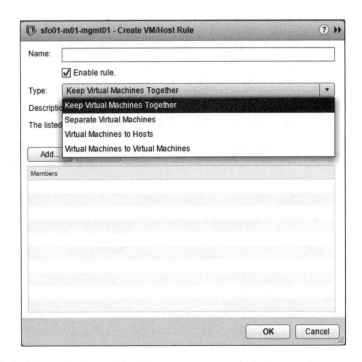

Recall from the previous section that DRS rules are the second of two conditions that will trigger a priority 1 recommendation—the first being placement of a host in maintenance mode. When DRS detects that VMs will violate DRS rules, it generates a priority 1 recommendation to migrate one or more VMs to satisfy the constraint expressed in the DRS rule.

DRS rules allow you to model the complex relationships that often exist in today's modern datacenters. Let's take a closer look at each of these three types of DRS rules.

CREATING VM AFFINITY RULES

VM affinity rules keep VMs together on a host. Consider, for example, a traditional three-tier application where you have a frontend web server, a mid-tier application server, and a backend database server. These components frequently communicate with each other and you would like for the communication to take advantage of the high-speed bus of the hosts rather than going across the network between hosts in the cluster. In this example, you could define an affinity rule—Keep Virtual Machines Together—that would ensure that these three VMs stay together on a host within the cluster. This is just an example.

Perform the following steps to create a DRS VM Affinity rule:

1. If vSphere Web Client is not already running, open a browser and connect and login to the vSphere Web Client on your vCenter Server.

DRS and DRS rules cannot be managed when connected to a specific ESXi host; you must connect to a vCenter Server instance.

2. Navigate to the Hosts And Clusters view.

3. Select a cluster from the inventory. On the Actions menu, select the Settings option or select the Configure tab in the content area.

4. Click the VM/Host Rules option.

5. Click the Add button in the VM/Host Rules page.

6. On the Create VM/Host Rule dialog box, provide a Name for the rule and select Keep Virtual Machines Together for the rule Type. By default, Enable Rule will be selected.

7. Click the Add button to add VMs as members of the VM affinity rule. Simply select the check box for the VMs you want to add as a member. Use the filter option to search for specific VMs.

8. Click OK.

9. Review the new VM/Host Rule configuration and click OK.

VM affinity rules let you specify VMs that should stay together, but what about VMs that should stay separated? This is where DRS VM anti-affinity rules can help.

CREATING VM ANTI-AFFINITY RULES

Consider, for a moment, our previous example of a traditional three-tier application. But this time, we will slightly modify. In this example, the traditional three-tier application server has grown. We now have two load-balanced frontend web servers, two load-balanced mid-tier application servers, and an active/active clustered backend database server. In this scenario, you would like to ensure that failure of a host would not have the potential to impact one or more of the tiers completely. In other words, you want to ensure that for each tier, the VMs for that tier are not on the same host in the cluster. In this example, a VM anti-affinity rule can mitigate the concern.

Perform the following steps to create a DRS VM anti-affinity rule:

1. If vSphere Web Client is not already running, open a browser and connect and login to the vSphere Web Client on your vCenter Server.

   DRS and DRS rules cannot be managed when connected to a specific ESXi host; you must connect to a vCenter Server instance.

2. Navigate to the Hosts And Clusters view.

3. Select a cluster from the inventory. On the Actions menu, select the Settings option or select the Configure tab in the content area.

4. Click the VM/Host Rules option.

5. Click the Add button in the VM/Host Rules page.

6. On the Create VM/Host Rule dialog box, provide a Name for the rule and select Separate Virtual Machines for the rule Type. By default, Enable Rule will be selected.

7. Click the Add button to add VMs as members of the VM anti-affinity rule. Simply select the check box for the VMs you want to add as a member. Use the filter option to search for specific VMs.

8. Click OK.

9. Review the new VM/Host Rule configuration and click OK.

With both VM affinity and VM anti-affinity rules, it is possible to create fallible rules, such as a Separate Virtual Machines rule that has three members, but the DRS-enabled cluster has only two hosts. In this situation, vCenter Server will generate report warnings because DRS cannot satisfy the requirements of the rule.

So far, we have discussed how to instruct DRS to keep VMs together or to keep VMs separate. But what about situations where you want to constrain VMs to a group of hosts within a cluster? This is where host affinity rules come into play.

Working with Host Affinity Rules

In addition to VM affinity and VM anti-affinity rules, DRS supports a third type of DRS rule: the host affinity rule.

Host affinity rules govern the relationships between VMs and hosts in a cluster, letting you control which hosts in a cluster can run which VMs—sometimes referred to as "sub-cluster capacity." When combined with VM affinity and VM anti-affinity rules, you can create complex rule sets to model the relationships between applications and workloads in your datacenter.

Before you can start creating a host affinity rule, you must create at least one VM DRS Group and at least one Host DRS Group. Figure 12.24 shows the VM/Host Groups. As you can see, a few groups have already been defined.

FIGURE 12.24
The DRS VM/Host Groups option allows you to create and modify both VM DRS Groups and Host DRS Groups.

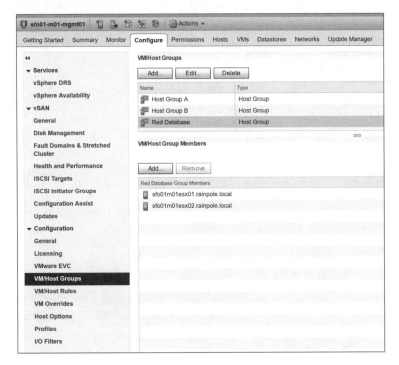

Perform the following steps to create a VM or Host DRS Group:

1. If vSphere Web Client is not already running, open a browser and connect and login to the vSphere Web Client on your vCenter Server.

   DRS VM/Host Groups cannot be managed when connected to a specific ESXi host; you must connect to a vCenter Server instance.

2. Navigate to the Hosts And Clusters view.

3. Select a cluster from the inventory. On the Actions menu, select the Settings option or select the Configure tab in the content area.

4. Click the VM/Host Groups option.

5. Click the Add button in the VM/Host Groups page.

6. On the Create VM/Host Group dialog box, provide a Name for the group.

7. Select the group Type: VM Group or Host Group.

   Depending on the type of group, click Add and select the appropriate VM or hosts members to add to the group. Use the filter option to search for VMs or hosts.

   Figure 12.25 shows two VMs added to a new VM DRS Group.

FIGURE 12.25
Use the buttons to add or remove VMs or hosts as members of a VM/Host Group. This screenshot shows VMs added to a VM DRS Group.

8. Click OK.

9. Review the new VM/Host Group configuration and click OK.

The preceding steps are the same for both VM DRS Groups and Host DRS Groups. You need to have at least one of each group rule type defined before you can create a host affinity rule.

After you have defined the VM DRS Groups and Host DRS Groups, you are ready to define the host affinity rule. This rule brings together a VM DRS Group and a Host DRS Group along with a preferred rule behavior. There are four host affinity rule behaviors:

◆ Must Run On Hosts In Group

◆ Should Run On Hosts In Group

◆ Must Not Run On Hosts In Group

◆ Should Not Run In Hosts In Group

These rules are, for the most part, self-explanatory. Each rule is either mandatory (a "Must" rule) or preferential (a "Should" rule) plus the affinity ("Run On") or anti-affinity ("Not Run On").

Mandatory host affinity rules—those with "Must"—are honored not only by DRS, but also by vSphere HA and vSphere DPM. For example, vSphere HA will not perform a failover if the failover will violate a required host affinity rule. Preferred host affinity rules—those with "Should"—may be violated. Administrators have the option of creating an event-based alarm to monitor for the violation of preferred host affinity rules. We will discuss alarms in Chapter 13, "Monitoring VMware vSphere Performance."

Figure 12.26 shows a host affinity rule coming together with a selected VM DRS Group, a rule behavior, and a selected Host DRS Group. Be careful when defining host affinity rules, especially mandatory host affinity rules like the one shown in Figure 12.26, or you could run into a situation where VMs are severely limited on where they can run, as illustrated in Figure 12.27.

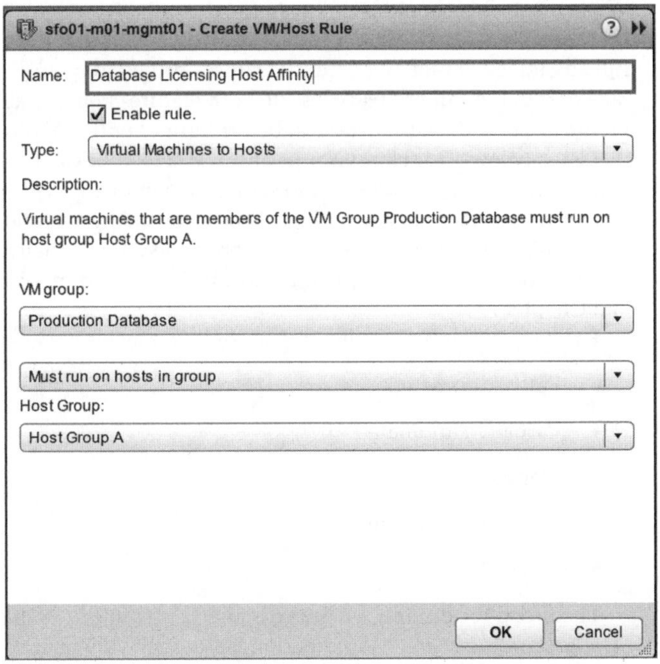

FIGURE 12.26
This host affinity rule specifies that the selected group of VMs must run on the selected group of hosts.

FIGURE 12.27
Ensure that using multiple required host affinity rules creates the desired results.

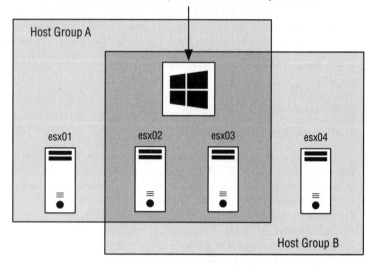

The Windows VM is in a group that is a member of two different host affinity rules. As a result, the VM can only run on hosts that satisfy both rules.

Host Group A

esx01 esx02 esx03 esx04

Host Group B

Although DRS rules provide flexibility, there may be times when you need more granularity. To satisfy this need, you can modify or disable DRS on individual VMs in a cluster.

CONFIGURING DRS VM OVERRIDES

While most VMs should be allowed to take full advantage of the DRS, on occasion you may find that some VMs are not DRS candidates. However, these VMs should remain in the cluster to take full advantage of high-availability features provided by vSphere HA. In other words, VMs will take part in HA but not DRS despite both features being enabled on the cluster. As shown in Figure 12.28, VMs in a cluster can be configured with a VM override.

Listed below VM/Host Groups and VM/Host Rules in the cluster Configure tab pane is the VM Overrides. This allows you to set HA, Component HA, and DRS settings on a per-VM basis that differ from the cluster settings. When you change settings in this way, although you can add them initially in batches of VMs, they are edited individually afterwards. If you want more information on VM restart priority, host isolation, and monitoring, HA is discussed in Chapter 3 and Chapter 7.

Focusing on DRS, the following automation levels are available:

◆ Fully Automated

◆ Partially Automated

◆ Manual

◆ Use Cluster Settings

◆ Disabled

The first three options work as discussed previously in this chapter, in the sections "Understanding Manual Automation Behavior," "Reviewing Partially Automated Behavior," an

FIGURE 12.28

Individual VMs can be prevented from participating in DRS. For example, when Fault Tolerance is enabled, an override is automatically configured for the participating VMs to disable DRS.

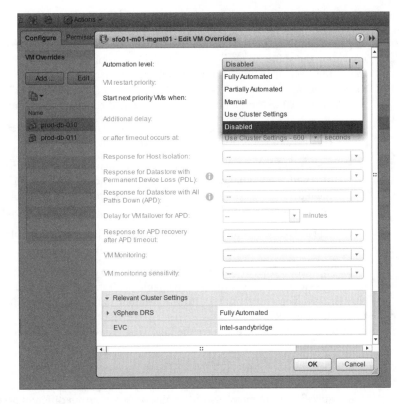

"Examining Fully Automated Behavior." The Disabled option simply turns off DRS, including the automatic host selection at startup and migration recommendations. The default Use Cluster Settings option does just that—it configures the VM to accept the automation level set on the cluster.

EXCLUDING VMs FROM DRS

Although you may be required to exclude a handful of VMs from participating in DRS, it is best not to set VMs to the Disabled option. When excluding VMs from DRS, no recommendations will be provided. A priority 2 recommendation could be provided that suggests moving a VM from a host you thought it was best suited for to an alternate host. For this reason, the Manual option is better. Be open to the possibility that a VM might perform better on a different host.

---

vSphere provides a multitude of features that make your life easier, if you understand how they operate and how to set them up properly. It might also be prudent to monitor the activities of these features to see whether a change to their configurations may be warranted over time as your environment grows. Monitoring and alarms are discussed in detail in Chapter 13.

Working with Storage DRS

Storage DRS (SDRS) builds on the functionality of Storage I/O Control and Storage vMotion, providing the ability to perform automated balancing of storage utilization. SDRS can perform this automated balancing not only based on storage capacity utilization, but also based on I/O load balancing.

Like DRS, SDRS is built on some closely related concepts and topics:

♦ Just as DRS uses clusters as a collection of hosts on which to act, SDRS uses datastore clusters as a collection of datastores on which it acts.

♦ Just as DRS can perform both initial placement and manual and ongoing balancing, SDRS also performs initial placement of VMDKs and ongoing balancing of VMDKs—as well as related VM files. The initial placement functionality of SDRS is especially appealing because it helps simplify the VM provisioning process for vSphere administrators.

♦ Just as DRS offers affinity and anti-affinity rules to influence placement recommendations, SDRS offers VMDK affinity and anti-affinity functionality.

SDRS uses the idea of a *datastore cluster*—a group of datastores treated as shared storage resources—to operate. Before you can enable or configure SDRS, you must create a datastore cluster. However, you cannot arbitrarily combine datastores into a datastore cluster; you must follow some guidelines.

Specifically, VMware provides the following guidelines for datastores that are combined into datastore clusters:

♦ Datastores of different sizes and performance characteristics can be combined in a datastore cluster. Generally, this is not a recommended practice unless you have very specific requirements. Additionally, datastores from different arrays and vendors can be combined into a datastore cluster. However, you cannot combine NFS and VMFS datastores into the same datastore cluster.

♦ You cannot combine replicated and nonreplicated datastores into an SDRS–enabled datastore cluster.

♦ Datastores shared across multiple datacenters are not supported for SDRS.

MIXED HARDWARE ACCELERATION SUPPORT

Hardware acceleration provided by supporting the vSphere Storage APIs for Array Integration (VAAI) is another factor to consider when creating datastore clusters. As a best practice, VMware recommends against mixing datastores that do support hardware acceleration with datastores that do not support hardware acceleration. All the datastores in a datastore cluster should be homogeneous and support hardware acceleration on the underlying array(s).

Along with these general guidelines, it is also a best practice to consult your storage array vendor for any additional recommendations specific to your array. Your storage vendor may have recommendations on which array-based features are, or are not, supported in conjunction with SDRS.

In the next section, we will discuss how to create and work with datastore clusters in preparation for a more in-depth look at configuring SDRS.

Creating and Working with Datastore Clusters

You are now ready to create a datastore cluster and begin exploring SDRS in more detail.

Perform these steps to create a datastore cluster:

1. If vSphere Web Client is not already running, open a browser and connect and login to the vSphere Web Client on your vCenter Server.

   SDRS and datastore clusters are possible only when you are using vCenter Server in your environment.

2. Navigate to the Storage view.

3. Select the datacenter object from the inventory where you want to create a new datastore cluster. From the Actions menu, select Storage and then select New Datastore Cluster; this launches the New Datastore Cluster Wizard.

4. On the Name And Location section of the New Datastore Cluster page, enter a Name for the datastore cluster.

5. If you want to enable SDRS for this datastore cluster, check Turn ON Storage DRS and click Next.

6. SDRS can operate in a manual mode, where it will make recommendations only, or in Fully Automated mode, where it will perform storage migrations automatically. You can also configure overrides for metrics as shown in Figure 12.29, which was introduced in vSphere 6. We will discuss these settings in closer detail in the following sections. For now, select Fully Automated on the Storage DRS Automation page and click Next.

FIGURE 12.29
SDRS automation settings can now be defined per metric.

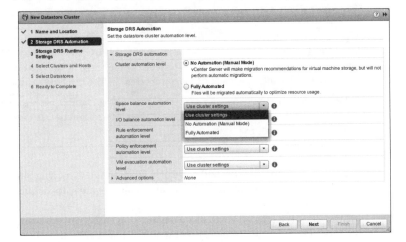

7. If you want SDRS to include I/O metrics along with space utilization as in its recommendations or migrations, select Enable I/O Metric For Storage DRS Recommendations on the Storage DRS Runtime Settings page.

   Configuring SDRS to include I/O metrics will automatically enable Storage I/O Control on the datastores that are a part of this datastore cluster.

8. You can adjust the thresholds that SDRS uses to control when it recommends or performs migrations (depending on whether SDRS is configured for manual or fully automated operation).

   The default utilized space threshold is 80%, which means when the datastore reaches 80% full, SDRS will recommend or perform a storage migration. When you are finished adjusting these values, click Next.

9. On the Select Hosts And Clusters page, select the check box next to the hosts and/or clusters for which this new datastore cluster should be added. Click Next.

10. On the Select Datastores page, select the check box next to each datastore you want added to the datastore cluster and click Next.

    Because of the nature of how SDRS works, you should leave the default Show Datastores Connected To All Hosts selection on the drop-down box. This ensures that any datastores listed are accessible from the hosts and/or clusters you selected in the previous step.

11. On the Ready To Complete page, review the settings.

    If any of the settings are incorrect or if you need to make any changes, simply use the Back button or use the page links to go back. Otherwise, click Finish.

STORAGE I/O CONTROL AND STORAGE DRS LATENCY THRESHOLDS

In Chapter 11, in the section "Enabling Storage I/O Control," we discussed adjusting the threshold for Storage I/O Control (SIOC). Note that the default I/O latency threshold for SDRS (15 ms) is well below the default for SIOC (30 ms). The idea behind these default settings is that SDRS can make a migration to balance the load (if fully automated) before throttling becomes necessary.

Check with your storage vendor for specific recommendations on SIOC latency values; you should also check with your array vendor to see if they offer recommendations for SDRS enablement and latency values.

The new datastore cluster will appear in the Storage view. The Summary tab of the datastore cluster, shown in Figure 12.30, will display the aggregate statistics about the datastores in the datastore cluster.

Once you have created a datastore cluster, you easily can add capacity to it by adding more datastores, much in the same way you would add capacity to a DRS cluster by adding new ESXi hosts.

To add a datastore to a datastore cluster, select an existing datastore cluster from the inventory. Select the Move Datastores Into option to open the Move Datastores Into Cluster Wizard,

FIGURE 12.30

The Summary tab of a datastore cluster provides overall information about total capacity, total used space, total free space, and largest free space.

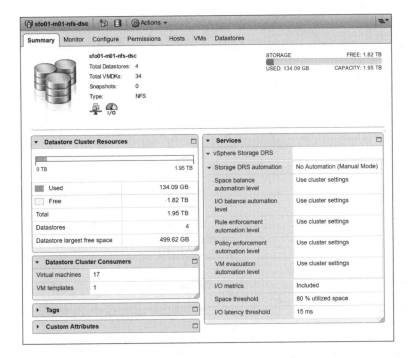

where you can select additional datastores to add to the datastore cluster. Figure 12.31 shows the Move Datastores Into Datastore Cluster Wizard, where you can see that some datastores cannot be added because not all hosts are connected to the datastore. This ensures that you do not inadvertently add a datastore to a datastore cluster and then find that an SDRS migration renders a VM VMDK unreachable by one or more hosts in the cluster.

SDRS also offers the ability to place a datastore in maintenance mode, just as DRS offers a maintenance mode option for hosts. To place a datastore into SDRS maintenance mode, select the datastore under the datastore cluster, and click Actions from the menu. Select Maintenance Mode followed by the Enter Maintenance Mode option.

Any registered VMs currently on that datastore will immediately generate migration recommendations using SDRS, as Figure 12.32 shows. If you select Cancel in the Storage DRS Maintenance Mode Migration Recommendations dialog box, you will cancel the SDRS maintenance mode request and the datastore will not be placed into maintenance mode.

No Effect on Templates and ISOs

When you place a datastore into maintenance mode through SDRS, recommendations are generated for registered VMs. However, the maintenance mode will not affect templates, unregistered VMs, or ISOs stored on that datastore.

In addition to using the Move Datastores Into Datastore Cluster Wizard you saw earlier in this section, you can use drag and drop to add a datastore to an existing datastore cluster. Note,

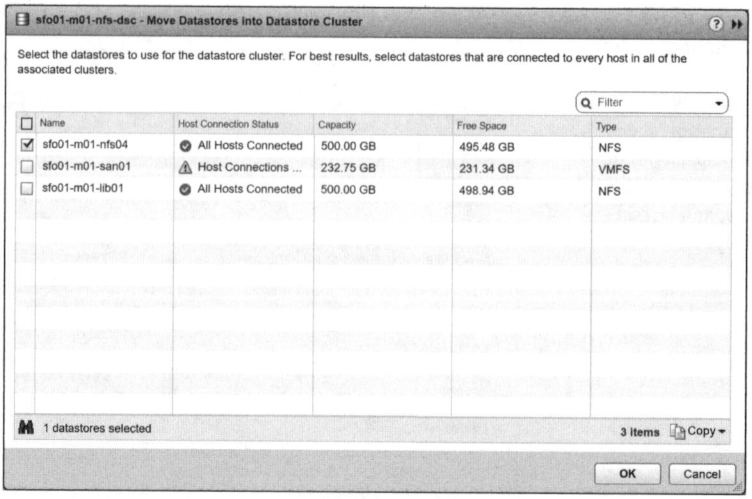

FIGURE 12.31

To add a datastore to a datastore cluster, the new datastore must be connected to all the hosts currently connected to the datastore cluster.

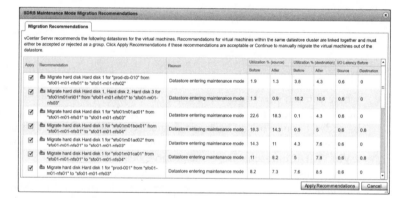

FIGURE 12.32

SDRS Maintenance Mode Migration Recommendations are provided when placing a datastore into maintenance mode.

however, that it will not warn you that you are adding a datastore that does not have connection to all the hosts that are currently connected to the datastore cluster. For this reason, we recommend that you use the Move Datastores Into Datastore Cluster Wizard shown earlier in Figure 12.31.

Now let's take a more in-depth look at configuring SDRS to work with the datastore cluster(s) that you have created.

Configuring Storage DRS

All configurations for SDRS are performed from the Configure tab. Select the Settings option from the Actions menu or click the Configure tab for a datastore cluster. Both methods have the same result. Within this view, click the Edit button on the vSphere SDRS page.

From the settings pane, you can accomplish the following tasks:

◆   Enable or disable SDRS.

◆   Configure the SDRS automation level.

◆ Change or modify the SDRS runtime rules.

◆ Configure or modify custom SDRS schedules.

◆ Create SDRS rules to influence SDRS behavior.

◆ Configure per-VM SDRS settings.

The following sections examine each of these areas in more detail.

ENABLING OR DISABLING STORAGE DRS

From the Edit dialog box, you can easily enable or disable SDRS. Figure 12.33 shows this area of the Edit dialog box. From here, you can enable SDRS by selecting Turn ON vSphere Storage DRS. If SDRS is already enabled, you can deselect Turn ON vSphere Storage DRS to disable it. If you disable SDRS, the SDRS settings are preserved. If SDRS is later re-enabled, the configuration is returned to the point where it was when it was disabled.

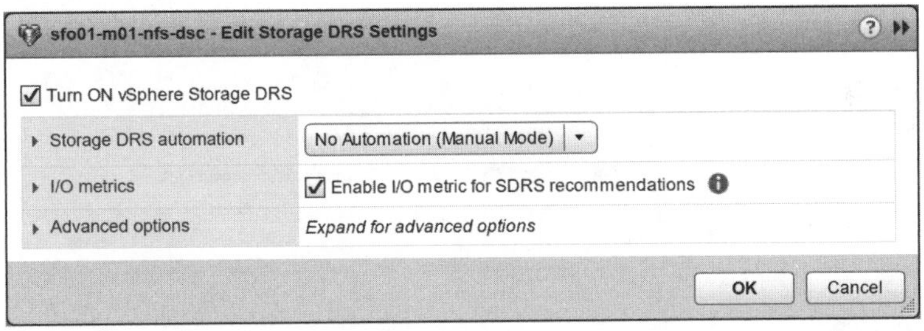

FIGURE 12.33
In addition to enabling or disabling SDRS, you can enable or disable I/O metrics for SDRS recommendations from the wizard.

CONFIGURING STORAGE DRS AUTOMATION

The SDRS automation levels are No Automation (Manual Mode) and Fully Automated, as shown in Figure 12.34.

Selecting either option would traditionally give you an "all or nothing" approach to SDRS automation. However, this is not the most flexible strategy—what if you wanted SDRS to handle space driven migrations automatically but not initiate any migration based on I/O? With many modern storage arrays providing tiering or caching functionality, this approach is not unusual. vSphere can determine whether individual metrics used by SDRS should trigger an automated or manual migration. You are provided with three options: inheriting the datastore cluster settings (manual mode or fully automated), manual mode, or fully automated. The full list of metrics is shown in Figure 12.35. When the SDRS automation level is set to No Automation (Manual Mode), SDRS will generate recommendations for initial placement and for storage migrations based on the configured space and I/O thresholds. Initial placement recommendations occur when you create a new VM with a virtual disk, add a virtual disk to an existing VM, or clone a VM or template.

Recommendations for storage migrations are noted in two different ways. First, an alarm is generated to note that an SDRS recommendation is present. You can view this alarm in the Issues option under the Monitor tab of the datastore cluster in Storage view. The alarm is shown in Figure 12.36.

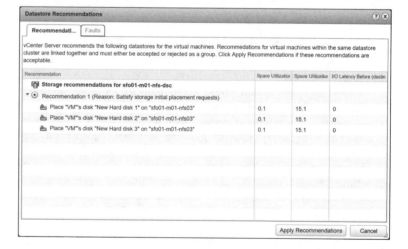

In addition, the Storage DRS section under the Monitor tab of the datastore cluster lists the current SDRS recommendations and gives you the option to apply those recommendations—that is, initiate the suggested Storage vMotion migrations. This is shown in Figure 12.37.

When SDRS is configured for Fully Automated mode, it will automatically initiate Storage vMotion migrations instead of generating recommendations for approval. In this instance, you can use the Storage DRS option under the Monitor tab of the datastore cluster to view the history

FIGURE 12.36
This alarm on the
datastore cluster
indicates that an SDRS
recommendation
is present.

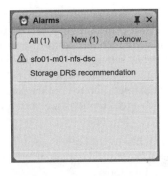

FIGURE 12.37
Click Apply
Recommendations in
the Storage DRS tab
to initiate the storage
migrations sug-
gested by SDRS.

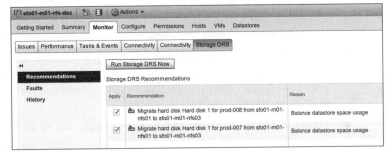

of SDRS actions by selecting the History under the Storage DRS section. Figure 12.38 shows the SDRS history for the selected datastore cluster.

FIGURE 12.38
On the Storage DRS
section of a datastore
cluster Monitor tab,
select History to review
the SDRS actions that
have taken place when
SDRS is running in
Fully Automated
mode.

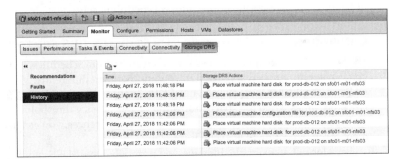

The next section describes how to modify how aggressive SDRS is when running in Fully Automated mode.

MODIFYING THE STORAGE DRS RUNTIME BEHAVIOR

When modifying the configuration of SDRS, you have several options for setting its behavior.

First, if you would like to configure SDRS runtime settings to operate only on the basis of space utilization and not I/O utilization, simply deselect Enable I/O Metric For SDRS Recommendations. This will set SDRS to recommend or perform (depending on the automation level) migrations based strictly on space utilization.

Second, the two Storage DRS Thresholds settings allow you to adjust the thresholds SDRS uses to recommend or perform migrations. By default, the Utilized Space setting is 80%, meaning that SDRS will recommend or perform a migration when a datastore reaches 80% full. The default I/O Latency setting is 15 ms—when latency measurements exceed 15 ms for a given datastore in a datastore cluster and I/O metrics are enabled, then SDRS will recommend or perform a storage migration to another datastore with a lower latency measurement.

Under the Advanced Options, you can further fine-tune the runtime behavior of Storage DRS as follows:

◆ Keep VMDKs Together By Default is somewhat self-explanatory. By default, VM disks (VMDKs) should be kept together unless there is a specific need to always separate them between datastores.

◆ The Check Imbalances Every option lets you control how often SDRS evaluates the I/O or space utilization in order to make a recommendation or perform a migration.

◆ The I/O Imbalance Threshold controls the aggressiveness of the SDRS algorithm. As the slider control is moved toward Aggressive and the counter increases, this moves up the priority of the recommendation that will be automatically acted on when SDRS is running in Fully Automated mode.

◆ Minimum Space Utilization Difference is a slider control that lets you specify how much of an improvement SDRS should look for before making a recommendation or performing a migration. The setting defaults to 5%. This means that if the target's values are 5% lower than the source's values, SDRS will make the recommendation or perform the migration.

In addition to the schedule control that controls how often SDRS evaluates I/O and space utilization, you can create more complex scheduling settings.

Configuring or Modifying the Storage DRS Schedule

The Schedule SDRS option allows you to create custom schedules. With these custom schedules, you can specify times when the SDRS should perform differently.

For example, are there times when SDRS should run with No Automation (Manual Mode)? Are there times when the space utilization or I/O latency thresholds should be adjusted? If so, and you need SDRS to adjust to these recurring differences, you can accommodate the requirement through custom SDRS schedules.

Let's look at an example. Imagine you normally have SDRS running in Fully Automated mode; however, at night, when backups are running, you do not want SDRS to automatically perform storage migrations. Using a custom SDRS schedule, you can configure SDRS to switch to manual mode during specific times of the day and days of the week. SDRS will then return to Fully Automated mode when that time period has passed.

Perform the following steps to create a custom SDRS schedule:

1. If vSphere Web Client is not already running, open a browser and connect and login to the vSphere Web Client on your vCenter Server.

2. Navigate to the Storage view.

3. Select a datastore cluster from the inventory. Select Settings in the Actions menu.

4. Select the Schedule Storage DRS option from the Configure tab. This opens the Edit Storage DRS Settings (Scheduled) Wizard.

5. On the Storage DRS Settings page, select the settings that you want to activate for this schedule. Click the Scheduling Options link to continue.

6. On the Scheduling Options page, provide a Task Name and a Task Description. Click the Change link to configure the scheduler.

7. Specify the time when this custom schedule task should be active.

For example, if you needed to change SDRS behavior while backups are running in the middle of the night, you could select Setup A Recurring Schedule For This Action and set the time to 10:00 PM weekly. Then you select the check box for every weekday and click OK to close the Scheduler.

8. Review the settings. Click OK if they are correct.

After you complete the Edit Storage DRS Settings Wizard, a new set of entries appears in the scheduling list for SDRS, as illustrated in Figure 12.39. Typically, as with this example, you will want to schedule two tasks: one for changing the setting and another for setting it back.

FIGURE 12.39
SDRS scheduling entries allow you to automatically change the settings for SDRS on certain days and at certain times.

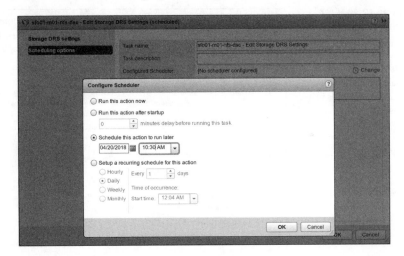

The ability to configure SDRS settings for different times or on different days is a powerful feature that will let you customize SDRS behaviors to best suit your environment. SDRS rules are another feature that provides you with more control over how SDRS handles VMs and virtual disks, as we will discuss in the next section.

CREATING STORAGE DRS RULES

Just as DRS has affinity and anti-affinity rules, SDRS allows you to create VMDK affinity and anti-affinity rules and VM anti-affinity rules. These rules modify the behavior of SDRS to ensure that specific VMDKs are always kept together (VMDK affinity rule) or separate (VMDK anti-affinity rule) or that all the virtual disks from certain VMs are kept separate (VM anti-affinity rule).

Perform these steps to create an SDRS VMDK affinity or anti-affinity or SDRS VM anti-affinity rule:

1. If vSphere Web Client is not already running, open a browser and connect and login to the vSphere Web Client on your vCenter Server.

2. Select a VM from the inventory. From the Actions menu, select Edit Settings.

3. On the Edit Setting page, select the SDRS Rules tab.

4. Click Add to add a rule.

5. In the Rule dialog box, enter a Rule Name for the rule you are creating. If VMDK Affinity is selected, the Rule Name is auto-populated.

6. From the Type drop-down box, select VMDK Affinity, VMDK Anti-Affinity, or VM Anti-Affinity, depending on which type of rule you want to create. For this example, select VMDK Anti-Affinity.

7. Select the virtual disks that you want to include in this rule, as shown in Figure 12.40, and then click OK.

FIGURE 12.40
An SDRS VMDK anti-affinity rule allows you to specify the virtual disks for a VM that should be kept on separate datastores in a datastore cluster.

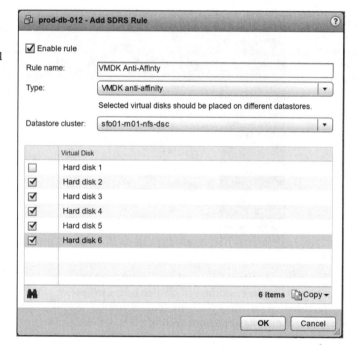

8. Click OK on the Edit SDRS Rule dialog box to complete the creation of the SDRS anti-affinity rule.

SETTING STORAGE DRS VM OVERRIDES

Just like DRS, SDRS can override cluster settings on a per-VM level through the VM Overrides feature. If you need to apply different settings on a VM or group of VMs, the VM Overrides feature gives you this granular level of control.

You can find the VM Overrides option on the Configure tab for a Datastore Cluster, or by selecting the Datastore Cluster and selecting Settings from the Actions menu. Here, you can add, edit, or delete override rules for individual VMs, as shown in Figure 12.41.

FIGURE 12.41
The per-VM Overrides area shows which VMs differ from the SDRS cluster settings.

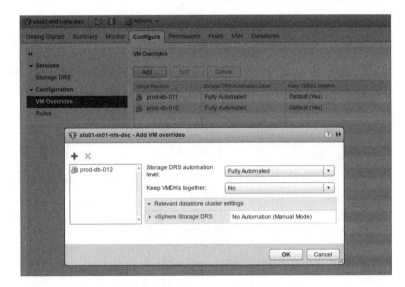

STORAGE DRS EVALUATION SCHEDULE

Normally, SDRS runs its evaluation every eight hours (this can be adjusted, as described in the section "Modifying the Storage DRS Runtime Behavior"). SDRS will include the new anti-affinity rule in the next scheduled evaluation. If you want to invoke SDRS immediately, the Storage DRS Recommendations section on the datastore cluster Monitor tab (shown in Figure 12.42) enables you to invoke SDRS immediately by clicking the Run Storage DRS Now option.

FIGURE 12.42
Run Storage DRS Now invokes SDRS on demand.

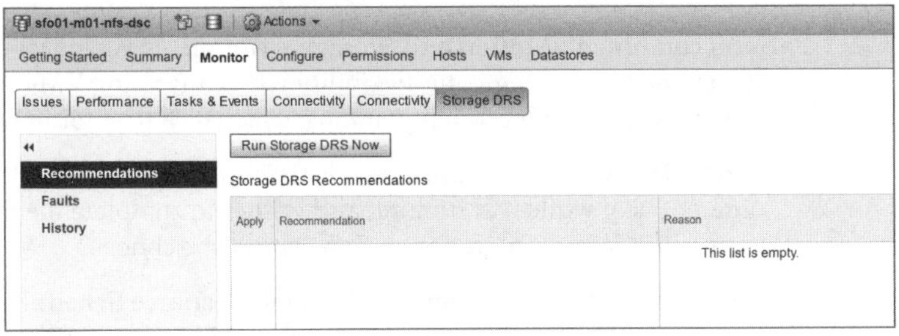

As you can see, SDRS has a tremendous amount of flexibility built into it to allow vSphere administrators to harness the power of SDRS by tailoring its behavior to best suit their specific environments.

In Chapter 13, we will discuss the tools and features that VMware vSphere offers you in the realm of performance monitoring.

The Bottom Line

Configure and execute vMotion. vMotion is a feature that allows running VMs to be migrated from one ESXi host to another without downtime to end users. To execute vMotion, you must ensure that both the ESXi hosts and the VMs meet specific configuration requirements. In addition, vCenter Server performs validation checks to ensure that vMotion compatibility rules are observed.

> **Master It** A vendor has just released a series of patches for some of the guest OSs in your virtualized infrastructure. You request an outage window from your supervisor, but your supervisor says to just use vMotion to prevent downtime. Is your supervisor correct? Why or why not?

> **Master It** Is vMotion a solution to prevent unplanned downtime?

Ensure vMotion compatibility across processor families. vMotion requires compatible CPU families on the source and target ESXi hosts to be successful. To help alleviate any potential problems resulting from changes in processor families over time, vSphere offers Enhanced vMotion Compatibility (EVC), which can mask differences between CPU families to maintain vMotion compatibility.

> **Master It** Can you change the EVC level for a cluster while there are VMs running on hosts in the cluster?

Use Storage vMotion. Just as vMotion is used to migrate running VMs from one ESXi host to another, Storage vMotion is used to migrate the virtual disks of a running VM from one datastore to another. You can also use Storage vMotion to convert between thick and thin virtual disk types.

> **Master It** Name two features of Storage vMotion that would help you cope with storage-related changes in your vSphere environment.

Perform combined vMotion and Storage vMotion. Using vMotion and Storage vMotion at the same time gives you greater flexibility when migrating VMs between hosts. Using this feature can also save time when you must evacuate a host for maintenance.

> **Master It** A fellow administrator is trying to migrate a VM to a different datastore and a different host while it is running and wishes to complete the task as quickly and as simply as possible. Which migration option should she choose?

Configure and manage vSphere Distributed Resource Scheduler. DRS enables vCenter Server to automate the process of conducting vMotion migrations to help balance the load across ESXi hosts in a cluster. You can automate DRS as you wish, and vCenter Server has flexible controls for affecting the behavior of DRS and specific VMs within a DRS-enabled cluster.

Master It You want to take advantage of DRS to provide some load balancing of virtual workloads within your environment. However, because of business constraints, you have a few workloads that should not be automatically moved to other hosts using vMotion. Can you use DRS? If so, how can you prevent these specific workloads from being affected by DRS?

Configure and manage Storage DRS. Building on Storage vMotion just as DRS builds on vMotion, SDRS automates the process of balancing storage capacity and I/O utilization. SDRS uses datastore clusters and can operate in Manual or Fully Automated mode. Numerous customizations exist—such as custom schedules, VM and VMDK anti-affinity rules, and threshold settings—to allow you to fine-tune the behavior of SDRS to your environment.

Master It Name the two ways in which an administrator is notified that an SDRS recommendation has been generated.

Master It What is a potential disadvantage of using drag-and-drop to add a datastore to a datastore cluster?

Chapter 13

Monitoring VMware vSphere Performance

The monitoring of VMware vSphere should be a combination of proactive benchmarking and reactive alarm-based actions. vCenter Server provides both methods to help you keep tabs on each of the VMs and hosts as well as the hierarchical objects in the inventory. Using both methods ensures that you aren't caught unawares of performance issues or lack of capacity.

vCenter Server provides some extensive features, such as expanded performance views and charts, for monitoring your VMs and hosts, and it greatly expands the number and types of alarms available by default. Together, these features make it much easier to manage and monitor VMware vSphere performance.

IN THIS CHAPTER, YOU WILL LEARN TO

- ◆ Use alarms for proactive monitoring
- ◆ Work with performance charts
- ◆ Gather performance information using command-line tools
- ◆ Monitor CPU, memory, network, and disk usage by ESXi hosts and VMs

Overview of Performance Monitoring

Monitoring performance is a key component of datacenter management. Fortunately, vCenter Server provides a number of ways to get insight into the behavior of the vSphere environment and the VMs running within that environment.

The first tool we'll explore is vCenter Server's alarms mechanism. Alarm definitions can be attached to just about any object within vCenter Server, and alarms offer an ideal way to proactively alert you or your datacenter staff about potential performance concerns or resource usage. We'll discuss alarms in detail in the section "Using Alarms."

Another tool is the content area on the Summary tab of ESXi clusters, ESXi hosts, and VMs. The content area contains quick "at-a-glance" information on resource usage. This information can give you a quick barometer of performance, but for more detailed performance information, you'll have to dive deeper into the vCenter tools we'll discuss later in this chapter.

Additional tools that offer an at-a-glance performance summary are the Hosts tab and the VMs tab, found on vCenter Server objects, datacenter objects, cluster objects, and ESXi hosts. Figure 13.1 shows the VMs tab of a cluster object. This tab gives an overview of general performance and resource usage for all the VMs within the cluster. This information includes CPU utilization, guest memory usage, and storage space utilized. As with the Resources pane, this information can be useful, but it is quite limited. However, keep in mind that a quick trip here might help you isolate the one VM that could be causing performance issues for the ESXi host on which it is running.

FIGURE 13.1
The VMs tab of a cluster object offers a quick look at VM CPU and memory usage.

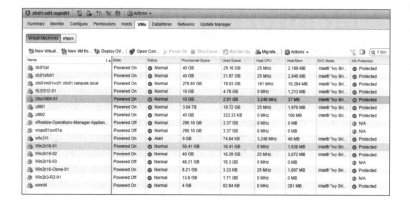

For ESXi clusters, resource pools, and VMs, another tool you can use is the Resource Allocation tab. The Resource Allocation tab gives you a picture of how CPU, memory, and storage resources are being used for the entire pool. With this high-level method of looking at resource usage, you can analyze overall infrastructure utilization. This tab also provides an easy way of adjusting individual VMs or resource pool reservations, limits, and/or shares without editing each object independently.

vCenter Server offers a powerful, in-depth tool on the Performance tab that lets you create charts that depict the resource consumption over time for a given ESXi host or VM. The charts provide historical information and can be used for trend analysis. vCenter Server has many objects and counters that allow you to analyze the performance of a single VM or host for a selected interval. The Performance tab features powerful tools for isolating performance considerations, and we discuss them in greater detail in the section "Working with Performance Charts."

VMware's esxtop gives you an in-depth view of all the counters available in vSphere to help isolate and identify problems in the hypervisor. esxtop runs from the shell of ESXi hosts directly. We'll take a look at esxtop later in this chapter in the section "Working with *esxtop*."

Finally, we'll show you how to use the various tools that we've discussed to monitor the four major resources in a vSphere environment: CPU, memory, network, and storage.

Let's get started with a discussion of alarms.

Using Alarms

In addition to using the charts and high-level information tabs, you can create alarms for VMs, hosts, networks, and datastores based on predefined triggers provided with vCenter Server. Depending on the object, these alarms can monitor resource consumption or the state of the object and alert you when certain conditions have been met, such as high resource usage or even low resource usage. These alarms can then provide an action that informs you of the condition by email or Simple Network Management Protocol (SNMP) trap. An action can also automatically run a script or offer other means to correct the problem the VM or host is experiencing.

With each revision of vSphere, VMware continues to add to the number of built-in default alarms. As you can see in Figure 13.2, the alarms that come with vCenter Server are defined at the topmost object, the vCenter Server object.

FIGURE 13.2

The default alarms for objects in vCenter Server are defined on the vCenter Server object itself.

These default alarms are usually generic in nature. Some of the predefined alarms alert you if any of the following situations occur:

◆ A host's storage status, CPU status, voltage, temperature, or power status changes.

◆ A cluster experiences a vSphere High Availability (HA) error.

◆ A datastore runs low on free disk space.

◆ A VM's CPU usage, memory usage, disk latency, or even fault tolerance status changes.

There are many more in addition to the small sampling of predefined alarms we've just described—VMware lets you create alarms on just about any object within vCenter Server. This greatly increases the ability of vCenter Server to proactively alert you to changes within the virtual environment before a problem develops.

Because the default alarms are at times too generic for your administrative needs, creating your own alarms is often necessary. Before showing you how to create an alarm, though, let's explore the concept of alarm scopes. Once we've discussed alarm scopes, we'll walk you through creating a few alarms.

Understanding Alarm Scopes

When you create alarms, one thing to keep in mind is the *scope* of the alarm. In Figure 13.2, you saw the default set of alarms available in vCenter Server. These alarms are defined at the vCenter Server object and thus have the greatest scope—they apply to all objects managed by that vCenter Server instance. It's also possible to create alarms at the datacenter level, the cluster level, the host level, or even the VM level. This allows you to create specific alarms that are limited in scope and are intended to meet specific monitoring needs.

When you define an alarm on an object, that alarm applies to all objects beneath that object in the vCenter Server hierarchy. The default set of alarms is defined at the vCenter Server object and therefore applies to all objects—datacenters, hosts, clusters, datastores, networks, and VMs—managed by that instance of vCenter Server. If you were to create an alarm on a resource pool, the alarm would apply only to VMs found in that resource pool. Similarly, if you were to create an alarm on a specific VM, that alarm would apply only to that specific VM.

Alarms are also associated with specific types of objects. For example, some alarms apply only to VMs, whereas other alarms apply only to ESXi hosts. You'll want to use this filtering mechanism to your advantage when creating alarms. If you needed to monitor a particular condition on all ESXi hosts, for instance, you could define a host alarm on the datacenter or vCenter Server object and it would apply to all ESXi hosts but not to any VMs.

HIERARCHICAL SCOPE

It's important that you keep these scoping effects in mind when defining alarms so that your new alarms work as expected. You don't want to inadvertently exclude some portion of your vSphere environment by creating an alarm at the wrong point in your hierarchy or by creating the wrong type of alarm.

Now you're ready to look at creating alarms.

Creating Alarms

As you've already learned, you can create many different types of alarms. These could be alarms that monitor resource consumption—such as how much CPU time a VM is consuming or how much RAM an ESXi host has allocated—or these alarms could monitor for specific events, such as when a specific distributed virtual port group is modified. In addition, you've learned that alarms can be created on a variety of objects within vCenter Server. Regardless of the type of alarm or the type of object to which that alarm is attached, the basic steps for creating an alarm are the same. In the following sections, we'll walk you through creating a few alarms so that you have the opportunity to see the options available to you.

CREATING A RESOURCE CONSUMPTION ALARM

First, let's create an alarm that monitors resource consumption. As discussed in Chapter 9, "Creating and Managing Virtual Machines," vCenter Server supports VM snapshots. These snapshots capture a VM at a specific point in time, allowing you to roll back (or revert) to that state later. However, snapshots require additional disk space, and monitoring disk space usage by snapshots is an important task. In vSphere, vCenter Server lets you create an alarm that monitors VM snapshot space.

Before you create a custom alarm, though, ask yourself a few questions. First, is there an existing alarm that already handles this task for you? Browsing the list of predefined alarms available in vCenter Server shows that although some storage-related alarms are present, there is no alarm that monitors snapshot disk usage. Second, if you're going to create a new alarm, where is the appropriate place within vCenter Server to create that alarm? This refers to the earlier discussion of scope: on what object should you create this alarm so that it is properly scoped and will alert you only under the desired conditions? In this particular case, you'd want to be alerted to any snapshot space usage that exceeds your desired threshold, so a higher-level object such as the datacenter object or even the vCenter Server object would be the best place to create the alarm.

YOU MUST USE vCENTER SERVER FOR ALARMS

You can't create alarms by connecting directly to an ESXi host; vCenter Server provides the alarm functionality. You must connect to a vCenter Server instance in order to work with alarms.

Perform the following steps to create an alarm that monitors VM snapshot disk space usage for all VMs in a datacenter:

1. Launch the vSphere Web Client if it is not already running, and connect to a vCenter Server instance.

2. Navigate to an inventory view or use the default Hosts And Clusters view.

3. Right-click the datacenter object (you could also choose to select a vCenter Server, a cluster or a host object) and select Alarms ➤New Alarm Definition.

4. On the General tab in the Alarm Settings dialog box, enter an alarm name and alarm description.

5. Select Virtual Machines from the Monitor drop-down list.

6. Be sure that the radio button "Monitor for specific conditions or state, for example, CPU usage, power state" is selected along with the Enable This Alarm check box. Click Next to move on to the Triggers section.

7. On the Triggers tab, click the add/plus button to add a new trigger.

8. Add the trigger type and VM Snapshot Size (GB). For this alarm, you're interested in snapshot size only, but these other triggers are available:

VM CPU Demand To Entitlement Ratio

VM CPU Ready Time

VM CPU Usage

VM Disk Aborts

VM Disk Resets

VM Disk Usage

VM Fault Tolerance Latency

VM Heartbeat

VM Max Total Disk Latency

VM Memory Usage

VM Network Usage

VM Snapshot Size

VM State

VM Total Size on Disk

9. Ensure that the Operator column is set to Is Above.

10. Change the warning and critical conditions to 10 GB and 20 GB, respectively. Click Next t
move to the Actions screen.

Figure 13.3 shows the Triggers section after changing the Warning and Critical values.

FIGURE 13.3

In the Triggers section,
define the conditions
that cause the alarm
to activate.

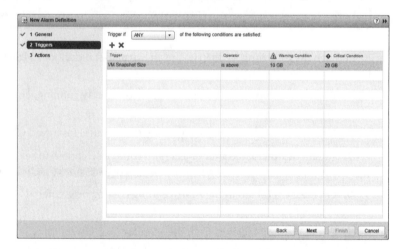

CAUTION: COUNTER VALUES WILL VARY!

The condition labelled Is Above should be selected most often for identifying a VM, host, or datastore that exceeds a certain threshold. You decide what that threshold should be and what is considered abnormal behavior (or at least interesting enough behavior to be monitored). For the most
part, monitoring across ESXi hosts and datastores will be consistent. For example, you will define a
threshold that is worthy of notification—such as CPU, memory, or network utilization—and configure an alarm across all hosts for monitoring the corresponding counter. Similarly, you may define

a threshold for datastores, such as the amount of free space available, and configure an alarm across all datastores to monitor that metric.

However, when looking at VM monitoring, you might find it difficult to come up with a single baseline that works for all VMs. Specifically, think about enterprise applications that must perform well for extended periods of time. For these types of scenarios, you will want custom alarms for earlier notifications of performance problems. This way, instead of reacting to a problem, you can proactively try to prevent problems from occurring.

For VMs with similar functions like domain controllers and DNS servers, it might be possible to establish baselines and thresholds covering all such infrastructure servers. In the end, the beauty of vCenter Server's alarms is in the flexibility to be as customized and as granular as each organization needs.

11. On the Actions tab, specify any additional actions that should be taken when the alarm is triggered.

The following actions are available:

- Send a notification email.
- Send a notification trap via SNMP.
- Change the power state on a VM.
- Migrate a VM.

If you leave the Actions tab empty, the alarm will alert you only within the vSphere Web Client. For now, leave the Actions tab empty.

CONFIGURING vCENTER SERVER FOR EMAIL AND SNMP NOTIFICATIONS

To have vCenter Server send an email for a triggered alarm, you must configure vCenter Server with an SMTP server. To configure the SMTP server, from the vSphere Web Client choose the vCenter Server from within the navigator, and then select the Manage Settings tab. Click the Edit button on the right, select Mail in the list on the left, and then supply the SMTP server and the sender account. We recommend using a recognizable sender account so that when you receive an email, you know it came from the vCenter Server computer. You might use something like vcenter-alerts@rainpole.com.

Similarly, to have vCenter Server send an SNMP trap, you must configure the SNMP receivers in the same vCenter Server Settings dialog box under SNMP receivers. You may specify from one to four management receivers to monitor for traps.

12. Click Finish to create the alarm.

The alarm is now created. To view the alarm you just created, select the datacenter object from the navigator on the left, and then click the Manage Alarm Definitions tab. You'll see your new alarm listed, as shown in Figure 13.4.

FIGURE 13.4
The Defined In column shows where an alarm was defined.

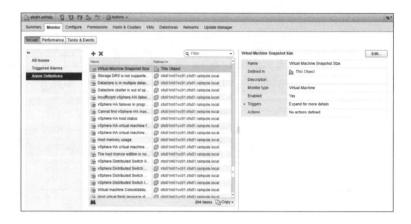

USING DURATION AND ACTION FREQUENCY WITH ALARMS

Let's create another alarm. This time you'll create an alarm that takes advantage of the parameters in the Triggers and Actions area. With the VM snapshot alarm, these parameters didn't make any sense; all you needed was just to be alerted when the snapshot exceeded a certain size. With other types of alarms, it may make sense to take advantage of these parameters.

Some triggers are simple state checks, like the VM State trigger, whereas with others you are able to specify a size, such as VM Snapshot Size. There is also a third type, which is a combination of size and time (or duration). Triggers such as VM Network Usage will activate only if the size is over (or under) the set threshold for a specified period of time.

As you may have noticed when creating the previous example alarm, alarms have two configurable states: Warning and Critical. When configuring alarm triggers, you can set the level for both warning and critical conditions; anything below these conditions is considered "Normal." The transition between these conditions then "triggers" a set of "actions" that are configured on the Actions screen. You can set actions for both transition directions at both criticality levels:

◆ Normal → Warning

◆ Warning → Critical

◆ Critical → Warning

◆ Warning → Normal

The Repeat Actions Every parameter controls the period of time during which a triggered alarm not reported again. Using the built-in VM CPU usage alarm as our example, the Frequency parameter is set, by default, to 5 minutes. This means that a VM whose CPU usage triggers the activation of the alarm won't get reported again—assuming the condition or state is still true—for 5 minutes.

With all this information in mind, let's walk through another example of creating an alarm. This time you'll use a trigger to take advantage of duration and action frequency.

Follows these steps to create an alarm that is triggered based on VM network usage:

1. Launch the vSphere Web Client if it is not already running, and connect to a vCenter Server instance.

2. Navigate to an inventory view, such as Hosts And Clusters or VMs And Templates.

3. Select the datacenter object from the navigator on the left.

4. Select the Monitor tab from the content area in the middle.

5. Select the Alarm Definitions button just below the tab bar to show alarm definitions.

6. Click the add/plus icon to create a new alarm.

7. Supply an alarm name and description.

8. Set the Monitor drop-down list to Virtual Machines.

9. Select the radio button marked "Monitor for specific conditions or state, for example, CPU usage, power state" and click Next.

10. On the Triggers screen of the Alarm Definition dialog box, click the plus/add icon to add a new trigger.

11. Add a Trigger Of VM Network Usage (kbps) type.

12. Set Condition to Is Above.

13. Set the value of the Warning column to 500, and leave the Condition Length setting at 5 minutes.

14. Set the value of the Alert column to 1000, and leave the Condition Length setting at 5 minutes.

15. On the Actions tab, click the plus/add icon and add a "Send a notification email" action.

16. For this newly created action, ensure that Normal Warning is set at Once and Warning Critical is set to Repeat.

17. Set Repeat Actions Every to 15 minutes.

18. Click Finish to create the alarm.

This alarm will now send email alerts if the VM network usage goes above 500 kbps for more than 5 minutes, but only once. If the VM network usage goes above 1,000 kbps for more than 5 minutes, an email will be sent again and then every 15 minutes advising you of this critical state until you set the alarm to green manually or the usage drops below 1,000 kbps.

ALARMS ON OTHER vCENTER SERVER OBJECTS

Although the two alarms you've created so far have been specific to VMs, the process is the same for other types of objects within vCenter Server.

Alarms can have more than just one trigger condition. The alarms you've created so far had only a single trigger condition. For an example of an alarm that has more than one trigger condition, look at the built-in alarm for monitoring host connection and power state. (Remember, all built-in alarms are defined at the vCenter Server level.) Figure 13.5 shows the two trigger conditions for this alarm. Note that *ALL* is selected in the Trigger If drop-down menu; it ensures that only powered-on hosts that are not responding will trigger the alarm.

FIGURE 13.5

You can combine multiple triggers to create more complex alarms.

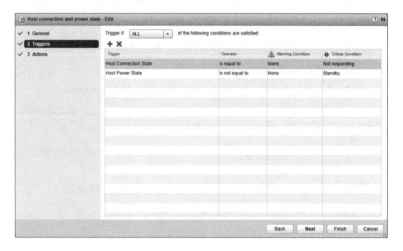

It might seem obvious, but it's important to note that you can have more than one alarm for an object.

As with any new alarm, testing its functionality is crucial to make sure you get the desired results. You might find that the thresholds you configured are not optimized for your environment and either are not activating the alarm when they should or are activating the alarm when they shouldn't. In these cases, edit the alarm to set the thresholds and conditions appropriately. Or if the alarm is no longer needed, right-click the alarm and choose Remove to delete it.

You'll be able to edit or delete alarms only if two conditions are met. First, the user account with which you've connected to vCenter Server must have the appropriate permissions granted for you to edit or delete alarms. Second, you must be editing or deleting the alarm from the object on which it was defined. Think back to the discussion on alarm scope and this makes sense. You can't delete an alarm from the datacenter object when that alarm was defined on the vCenter Server object. You must go to the object where the alarm was defined to edit or delete the alarm.

Now that you've seen some examples of creating alarms—and keep in mind that creating alarms for other objects within vCenter Server follows the same basic steps—let's take a look at managing alarms.

Managing Alarms

Several times so far in this chapter, we've directed you to the Alarm Definitions tab within the vSphere Web Client. Until now, you've been working with the definitions, looking at defined alarms. There is, however, another view to the alarms: the Triggered Alarms view. Figure 13.6 shows the Triggered Alarms view, which you access by selecting an object within the vCenter Web Client and then clicking the Monitor tab ➤ Issues ➤ Triggered Alarms.

The Monitor ➤ Issues ➤ Triggered Alarms area shows all the activated alarms for the selected object and all child objects. In the right pane of the vSphere Web Client in the Global Alarm area all alarms within vCenter are shown. In Figure 13.6, a Virtual Machine object is selected, so the Triggered Alarms view shows all activated alarms for this VM.

FIGURE 13.6
The Triggered Alarms view shows the alarms that vCenter Server has activated.

However, if only the VM had been selected, the Triggered Alarms view on the Alarms tab for that VM would show only the two activated alarms for that particular VM. This makes it easy to isolate the specific alarms you need to address.

After you are in Triggered Alarms view for a particular object, a few actions are available to you for each of the activated alarms. For alarms that monitor resource consumption (that is, the alarm definition uses the "Monitor for specific conditions or State, for example, CPU usage, power state" setting that's selected under Alarm Type on the General tab), you have the option to acknowledge the alarm. To acknowledge the alarm, right-click the alarm and select Acknowledge.

When an alarm is acknowledged, vCenter Server records the time the alarm was acknowledged and the user account that acknowledged the alarm. As long as the alarm condition persists, the alarm will remain in the Triggered Alarms view but is grayed out. When the alarm condition is resolved, the activated alarm disappears.

For an alarm that monitors events (this would be an alarm that has the option "Monitor for specific events occurring on this object, for example, VM powered on" selected under Alarm Type on the General tab), you can either acknowledge the alarm, as described previously, or reset the alarm status to green. Figure 13.7 illustrates this option.

Resetting an alarm to green removes the activated alarm from the Triggered Alarms view, even if the underlying event that activated the alarm hasn't been resolved. This behavior makes sense if you think about it. Alarms that monitor events are merely responding to an event being logged by vCenter Server; whether the underlying condition has been resolved is unknown. So, resetting the alarm to green just tells vCenter Server to act as if the condition has been resolved. Of course, if the event occurs again, the alarm will be triggered again.

Now that we've looked at alarms for proactive performance monitoring, let's move on to using vCenter Server's performance charts to view even more information about the behavior of VMs and ESXi hosts in your vSphere environment.

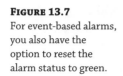

FIGURE 13.7
For event-based alarms, you also have the option to reset the alarm status to green.

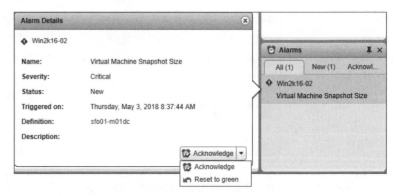

Working with Performance Charts

Alarms are a great tool for alerting you of specific conditions or events, but they don't provide t detailed information that you sometimes need, such as a resource being used that is still under a warning or critical state. This is where vCenter Server's performance charts come in. vCenter Server has many features for creating and analyzing charts. Without these charts, analyzing the performance of a VM would be nearly impossible. Installing agents inside a VM will not provid accurate details about the server's behavior or resource consumption because a VM is configure with virtual devices. Only the VMkernel knows the exact amount of resource consumption for any of those devices because it acts as the arbitrator between the virtual hardware and the physical hardware. In most virtual environments, the VM's virtual devices can outnumber the actual physical hardware devices, necessitating the complex sharing and scheduling abilities in the VMkernel.

By clicking the Monitor ➤ Performance tab for a datacenter, cluster, host, or VM, you can lear a wealth of information. Before you use these charts to help analyze resource consumption, we need to talk about performance charts and legends. We'll start by covering the two layouts available in performance charts: the Overview layout and the Advanced layout.

Overview Layout

The Overview layout is the default view when you access the Monitor Performance tab. Figure 13.8 shows you the Overview layout of the Performance tab for an ESXi host. Note the scroll bars; there's a lot more information here than the vSphere Web Client can fit in a single screen.

At the top of the Overview layout are options to change the view and the time range. The contents of the View drop-down list change depending on the object you select in the vSphere Web Client. Table 13.1 lists the options available for each object.

Next to the View drop-down list is an option to change the time range for the data currently displayed in the various performance charts. This allows you to set the time range to real time, a day, a week, a month, a year, or a custom value. The Realtime time range setting displays the las hour of data and automatically refreshes every 20 seconds, whereas the other time range setting do not automatically refresh.

Below these controls are the performance charts. The layout and the charts that are included vary based on the object selected and the option chosen in the View drop-down list. Two

FIGURE 13.8
The Overview layout provides information on a range of performance counters.

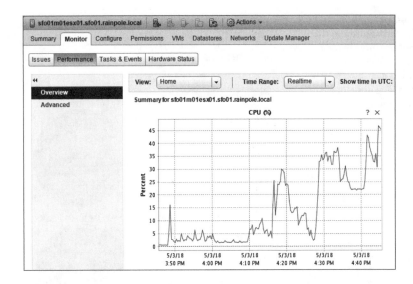

TABLE 13.1: View options in the Overview area of the Performance tab

SELECTED OBJECT	VIEW OPTIONS
Datacenter	Clusters, Storage
Cluster	Home, Resource Pools & Virtual Machines, Hosts
Resource pool	Home, Resource Pools & Virtual Machines
Host	Home, Virtual Machines
Virtual machine	Home, Storage

examples are shown in Figure 13.9 and Figure 13.10. We encourage you to explore and find the layouts that work best for your environment and, more important, layouts that clearly show you the performance information you require.

FIGURE 13.9
The Virtual Machines view of the Performance tab for an ESXi host in Overview layout offers both per-VM and summary information.

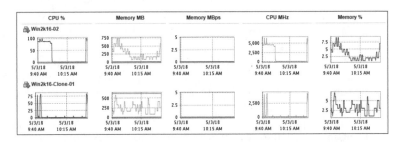

FIGURE 13.10

The Storage view of the Performance tab for a VM in Overview layout displays a breakdown of storage utilization.

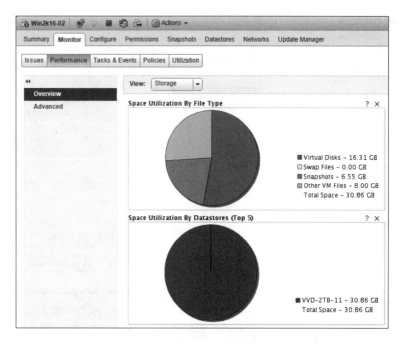

The Overview layout works well if you need a broad overview of the performance data for a datacenter, cluster, resource pool, host, or VM. But what if you need more specific data in a more customizable format? The Advanced layout is the answer, as you'll see in the next section.

Advanced Layout

Although it's called the Advanced layout, to begin with it looks somewhat simpler than the Overview layout. There is only a single chart within this view, but don't let this fool you because a significant number of configuration options exist for this performance chart alone.

Figure 13.11 shows the Advanced layout of the Performance tab for a cluster of ESXi hosts. Here in the Advanced layout is where the real power of vCenter Server's performance charts is made available to you.

At the right of the Advanced layout, you'll find a View drop-down list to quickly switch chart settings, followed by buttons that you click to refresh or export the chart. The Refresh button refreshes the data, whereas the Export button allows you to export the chart as a JPEG, PNG graphic, or CSV document. We'll discuss this functionality in the section "Exporting Performance Charts."

On each side of the chart are units of measurement. In Figure 13.11, the counters selected are measured in percentages and megahertz. Depending on the counters chosen, there may be only one unit of measurement, but there will be no more than two. Next, on the horizontal axis is the time interval. Below that, the performance chart legend provides color-coded keys to help the user find a specific object or item of interest. This area also breaks down the chart into the object being measured; the measurement being used; the units of measure; and the Latest, Maximum, Minimum, and Average measurements recorded for that object.

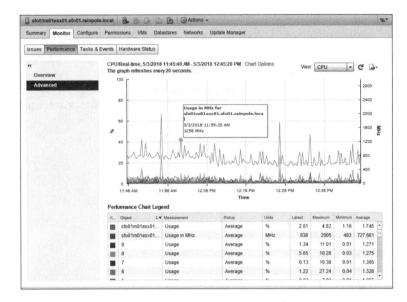

Hovering the mouse pointer over the chart at a particular recorded interval of interest displays the data points at that moment in time. Another nice feature of the charts is the ability to emphasize a specific object so that you can more easily select it from among other objects. Clicking the item in the chart legend at the bottom will emphasize that object and its representative color.

Now that you have a feel for the Advanced layout, let's take a closer look at the Chart Options link. This link exposes vCenter Server's functionality in creating highly customized performance charts and is where all the nuts and bolts are configured for this feature. Figure 13.12 shows the Chart Options dialog box. This dialog box is the central place where you will come to customize vCenter Server's performance charts; you can also just double-click the chart to display this dialog box. Here, you select the counters to view, the time ranges, and the kind of chart (Line Graph or Stacked Graph) you want to display.

FIGURE 13.12
The Chart Options
dialog box offers
tremendous flexibility to
create exactly the
performance
chart you need.

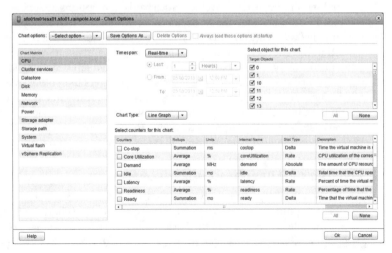

Because so much information is available in the Chart Options dialog box, we've grouped the various options and types of information into the sections that follow.

CHOOSING CHART METRICS AND COUNTERS

On the left side of the Chart Options dialog box (shown in Figure 13.12), you can choose which metric to monitor or analyze. All the available chart metrics are listed here, but only a subset of these is available:

◆ CPU

◆ Cluster Services

◆ Datastore

◆ Disk

◆ Memory

◆ Network

◆ Power

◆ Storage Adapter

◆ Storage Path

◆ System

◆ Virtual Flash

◆ Virtual Disk

◆ Virtual Machine Operations

◆ vSphere Replication

The selections available in this area change depending on the type of object that you have selected within the vCenter Web Client. That is, the options available when you're viewing the Monitor Performance tab for an ESXi host are different from the options available when you're viewing the Monitor ➤ Performance tab of a VM, a cluster, or a datacenter.

Within each of these resources, different objects and counters can be selected. Be aware that other factors affect what objects and counters are available to view; for example, in some cases the real-time interval shows more objects and counters than other intervals. A description field within the counters list explains what each counter represents. If this description does not fit within the Chart Options dialog box, simply mouse over it to view the full text. The next few sections list some of the counters available for the resource types in the Chart Options dialog box. We have not listed every available counter as there are far too many to list.

VIEWING CPU PERFORMANCE INFORMATION

If you select the CPU resource type in the Chart Options dialog box, you can choose which objects and counters you'd like to see in the performance chart. Note that the CPU resource type is not available when viewing the Performance tab of a datacenter object (DC). It is available for clusters (CL), ESXi hosts (ESXi), resource pools (RP), and individual virtual machines (VM).

Table 13.2 lists the most important objects and counters available for CPU performance information.

TABLE 13.2: Available CPU performance counters

COUNTER	CL	ESXI	RP	VM
Max Limited				X
Ready		X		X
Run				X
Swap Wait		X		X
System				X
Total	X			
Usage In MHz	X	X	X	X
Used		X		X
Usage	X			
Utilization		X		
Wait		X		X

You can view quite a bit of CPU performance information in the section "Monitoring CPU Usage." We'll discuss how to use these CPU performance objects and counters to monitor CPU usage.

VIEWING MEMORY PERFORMANCE INFORMATION

If you select the Memory resource type in the Chart Options section of the Chart Options dialog box, you can display various objects and counters. The Memory resource type is not available when viewing the Performance tab of a datacenter object. It is available for clusters, ESXi hosts, resource pools, and individual VMs.

Table 13.3 lists the most important objects and counters for memory performance information. In the section "Monitoring Memory Usage," you'll get the opportunity to use these objects and counters to monitor how ESXi and VMs are using memory.

VIEWING DISK PERFORMANCE INFORMATION

Disk performance is another key area that you need to monitor. Table 13.4 shows the most important objects and counters available for disk performance information.

Note that these counters aren't supported for datacenters, clusters, and resource pools, but they are supported for ESXi hosts and VMs. Not all counters are visible in all display intervals.

You'll use these counters in the section "Monitoring Disk Usage," later in this chapter.

TABLE 13.3:   Memory performance counters

COUNTER	CL	ESXI	RP	VM
Active		X		X
Ballooned Memory	X			
Balloon Target				X
Compressed		X		X
Consumed	X	X	X	X
Memory Saved By Zipping				X
Swap In		X		X
Swap Out		X		X
Swap Used		X		
Usage	X	X		X
Zipped Memory				X

TABLE 13.4:   Disk performance counters

COUNTER	CL	ESXI	RP	VM
Disk Bus Resets		X		X
Disk Commands Terminated		X		X
Disk Kernel Command Latency		X		X
Disk Kernel Read Latency		X		X
Disk Kernel Write Latency		X		X
Disk Maximum Queue Depth		X		X
Disk Command Latency		X		X
Disk Read Latency		X		X
Disk Write Latency		X		X
Disk Queue Command Latency		X		X

Viewing Network Performance Information

To monitor network performance, the vCenter Server performance charts cover a wide collection of performance counters. Network performance counters are available only for ESXi hosts and VMs; they are not available for datacenter objects, clusters, or resource pools.

Table 13.5 shows the most important objects and counters for network performance information.

Table 13.5: Network performance counters

Counter	CL	ESXi	RP	VM
Data Receive Rate		X		X
Data Transmit Rate		X		X
Receive Packets Dropped		X		X
Transmit Packets Dropped		X		X
Packet Receive Errors		X		
Packet Transmit Errors		X		
Packets Received		X		X
Packets Transmitted		X		X
Data Receive Rate		X		X
Data Transmit Rate		X		X
Usage		X		X

You'll use these network performance counters in the section "Monitoring Network Usage," later in this chapter.

Viewing System Performance Information

ESXi hosts and VMs also offer some performance counters in the System resource type. Datacenters, clusters, and resource pools do not support any system performance counters.

Table 13.6 lists the most important objects and counters for system performance information.

The majority of these counters are valid only for ESXi hosts, and they all center on how resources are allocated or how the ESXi host itself is consuming CPU resources or memory.

Viewing Datastore Performance Information

Monitoring datastore performance allows you to see the performance of the whole datastore instead of using disk counters per VM. Datastore performance counters are available only for ESXi hosts and VMs; they are not available for datacenter objects, clusters, or resource pools.

TABLE 13.6: System performance counters

COUNTER	CL	ESXI	RP	VM
Resource CPU Active (1 Min Average)		X		
Resource CPU Active (5 Min Average)		X		
Resource CPU Maximum Limited (1 Min)		X		
Resource CPU Maximum Limited (5 Min)		X		
Resource CPU Running (1 Min Average)		X		
Resource CPU Running (5 Min Average)		X		
Resource CPU Usage (Average)		X		
Resource Memory Shared		X		
Resource Memory Swapped		X		
Uptime		X		X

Table 13.7 shows the most important objects and counters for datastore performance information.

TABLE 13.7: Datastore performance counters

COUNTER	CL	ESXI	RP	VM
Storage I/O Control Aggregated IOPS		X		
Storage I/O Control Datastore Maximum Queue Depth		X		
Storage DRS Datastore Normalized Read Latency		X		
Storage DRS Datastore Normalized Write Latency		X		
Highest Latency		X		X
Average Read Requests Per Second		X		X
Average Write Requests Per Second		X		X
Storage I/O Control Normalized Latency		X		
Read Latency		X		X
Write Latency		X		X

VIEWING STORAGE PATH PERFORMANCE INFORMATION

Storage Path is one of the new categories of performance counters. As the name suggests, these counters can help you troubleshoot storage path problems. Storage path counters are available only for ESXi; they are not available for datacenter objects, clusters, VMs, or resource pools.

Table 13.8 shows the objects and counters for storage path performance information.

TABLE 13.8:   Storage path performance counters

COUNTER	CL	ESXi	RP	VM
Average Commands Issued Per Second		X		
Highest Latency		X		
Average Read Requests Per Second		X		
Average Write Requests Per Second		X		
Read Rate		X		
Storage Path Throughput Usage		X		
Read Latency		X		
Write Latency		X		
Write Rate		X		

VIEWING OTHER PERFORMANCE COUNTERS

The following performance counter types are also available:

◆ ESXi hosts participating in a cluster also have a resource type of Cluster Services, with two performance counters: CPU Fairness and Memory Fairness. Both of these counters show the distribution of resources within a cluster.

◆ The datacenter object contains a resource type marked as Virtual Machine Operations. This resource type contains performance counters that monitor the number of times a particular VM operation has occurred. These include VM Power-On Events, VM Power-Off Events, VM Resets, vMotion Operations, and Storage vMotion Operations.

SETTING A CUSTOM INTERVAL

Just as with the Overview layout, within each of the resource types you have a choice of intervals to view. Some objects offer a Real-Time option; this option shows what is happening with that resource right now, with a historical view over the past hour, and the charts automatically refresh every 20 seconds. The others are self-explanatory in their time span, but note that they do not refresh automatically. The Custom option allows you to specify exactly what you'd like to see on the performance chart. For example, you could specify that you'd like to see performance data for the last 8 hours. Having all of these interval options allows you to choose exactly the right interval necessary to view the data you're seeking.

MANAGING CHART SETTINGS

Let's look at one more area of the Chart Options dialog box: the Chart Options drop-down and Save Options As button along the top.

After you've gone through and selected the resource type, display interval, objects, and performance counters that you'd like to see in the performance chart, you can save that collection of chart settings using the Save Options As button. The vCenter Web Client prompts you to enter a name for the saved chart settings. After a chart setting is saved, you can easily access it again from the drop-down list at the top of the performance chart's Advanced layout. Figure 13.13 shows the View drop-down list, with two custom chart settings: CPU-8hr View and MEM - Overhead. By selecting either of these from the View drop-down list, you can quickly switch to those settings. This allows you to define the performance charts that you need to see and then quickly switch between them.

FIGURE 13.13

You can access saved chart settings from the View drop-down list.

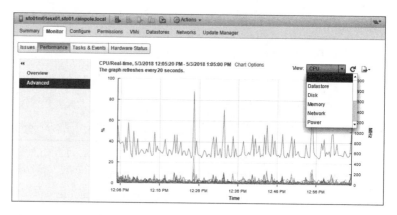

If you have a custom chart saved, the Chart Options dialog box allows you to delete chart settings you've saved but no longer need.

In addition to offering you the option of saving the chart settings, vCenter Server allows you to save the chart.

EXPORTING PERFORMANCE CHARTS

When we first introduced you to the Advanced layout view of the Performance tab, we briefly mentioned the Export button. This button, found in the upper-right corner of the Advanced layout, allows you to save the results of the performance chart to an external file for long-term archiving, analysis, or reporting.

When you click the Export button, a standard Save dialog box appears. You have the option of choosing where to save the resulting file as well as the option of saving the chart either as a graphic file or as a comma-separated value (CSV) file. If you are going to perform any additional analysis, the option to save the chart data as a Microsoft Excel spreadsheet is quite useful. The graphics options are useful when you need to put the performance data into a report.

There's a lot of information exposed via vCenter Server's performance charts. We'll revisit the performance charts again in the sections on monitoring specific types of resources later in this chapter. We'll now explain the last tools in the toolbox, esxtop, and then show you how to combine all the tools to keep your environment in top condition.

Working with *esxtop*

In addition to alarms and performance charts, VMware provides esxtop to help you monitor performance and resource usage. A great reason to use esxtop is the immediate feedback it gives you. Using esxtop, you can monitor all four major resource types (CPU, disk, memory, and network) on a particular ESXi host. Also, when using esxtop, you don't need vCenter Server to be able to monitor performance and resource usage. Figure 13.14 shows some sample output from esxtop.

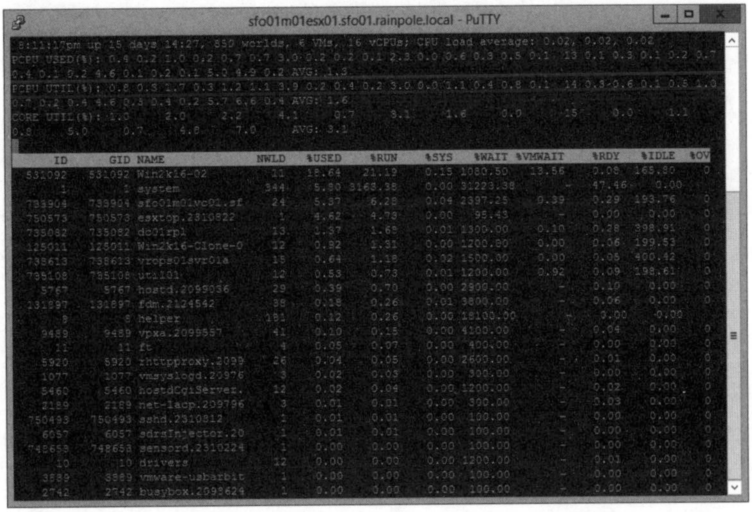

FIGURE 13.14
esxtop shows real-time information on CPU, disk, memory, and network utilization.

To run esxtop, you will need to enable SSH on your ESXi host and connect to the secure shell. Once you are logged in, it can be started by simply entering **esxtop**. Once esxtop is running, you can use single-letter commands to switch among the various views.

Upon launch, esxtop defaults to showing CPU utilization. At the top of the screen are summary statistics; below that are statistics for specific VMs and VMkernel processes. To show only VMs, press V. Be aware that esxtop, like many Linux commands, is case sensitive, so you'll need to be sure to use an uppercase V in order to toggle the display of VMs only.

Monitoring CPU Usage with C   Two CPU counters of interest to view with esxtop are the CPU Used (%USED) and Ready Time (%RDY) counters. You can also see these counters in the VM charts, but with esxtop, they are calculated as percentages. The %RDY counter is also helpful in determining whether you have overallocated CPU resources to the VM. This might be the case if, for example, you've allocated two vCPUs to a VM that really needs only a single vCPU. While in CPU mode, you can also press the lowercase e to expand a VM's CPU statistics so that you can see the components that are using CPU time on behalf of a VM. This helps you determine what components of a VM may be taking up CPU capacity.

If you switch away to another resource, press C (uppercase or lowercase) to come back to the CPU counters display. At any time when you are finished with esxtop, you can simply press q (lowercase only) to exit the utility and return to the vMA command prompt.

ESXTOP SHOWS SINGLE HOSTS ONLY

Remember, esxtop shows only a single ESXi host. In an environment where vMotion, vSphere Distributed Resource Scheduler (DRS), and vSphere High Availability (HA) have been deployed, VMs may move around often. It is possible that while you are monitoring a VM, it can be suddenly moved off the host by a vMotion action. Also be aware of this when capturing performance in batch mode.

Monitoring Memory Usage with M   Memory is one of the most important components of your ESXi host because this resource is usually one of the first to get exhausted.

To monitor memory usage with esxtop, press m (lowercase only). This gives you real-time statistics about the ESXi host's memory usage in the top portion and the VM's memory usage in the lower section. As with CPU statistics, you can press V (uppercase only) to show only VMs. This helps you weed out VMkernel resources when you are trying to isolate a problem with a VM. The %ACTV counter, which shows current active guest physical memory, is a useful counter, as are the %ACTVS (slow-moving average for long-term estimates), %ACTVF (fast-moving average for short-term estimates), %ACTVN (prediction of %ACTV at next sampling), and SWCUR (current swap usage) counters.

Monitoring Network Statistics with N   Networking in a vSphere environment is often taken for granted, but while your environment grows, you'll learn that keeping an eye on network performance is essential.

To monitor network statistics about the virtual machine network interface cards (vmnics), individual VMs, or VMkernel ports used for iSCSI, VMotion, and NFS, press n (lowercase only). The columns showing network usage include packets transmitted and received and megabytes transmitted and received for each vmnic or port. Also shown in the DNAME column are the vSwitches or dvSwitches and, to the left, what is plugged into them, including VMs, VMkernel, and Service Console ports. If a particular VM is monopolizing the vSwitch, you can look at the amount of network traffic on a switch and the individual ports to see which VM is the culprit. Unlike in other esxtop views, you can't use V (uppercase only) here to show only VMs.

Monitoring Disk I/O Statistics with D   Memory and disk I/O are considered the most important components in your vSphere environment. Although memory is important because it gets exhausted first, disk I/O is often overlooked even though bad disk performance will directly impact the VMs performance.

To monitor disk I/O statistics about each of the disk adapters, press d (lowercase only), press u (lowercase only) for disk devices, and v (lowercase only) for disk VM. As with some other views, you can press V (uppercase only) to show only VMs. The columns labeled READS/s, WRITES/s, MBREAD/s, and MBWRTN/s are most often used to determine disk loads. Those columns show loads based on reads and writes per second and megabytes read and written per second.

The esxtop command also lets you view CPU interrupts by pressing i. This command will show you the device(s) using the interrupt and is a great way to identify VMkernel devices, such as a vmnic, that might be sharing an interrupt with the Service Console. This sort of interrupt sharing can impede performance.

Another great feature of esxtop is the ability to capture performance data for a short period of time and then play back that data. Using the command vm-support, you can set an interval and duration for the capture.

Perform the following steps to capture data to be played back on esxtop:

1. Using PuTTY (Windows) or a terminal window (Mac OS X or Linux), open an SSH session to an ESXi host. Note that this requires enabling the ESXi shell and SSH, both of which are disabled by default.

2. Enter the **su -** command to assume root privileges.

3. While logged in as root or after switching to the root user, change your working directory to /tmp by issuing the command **cd /tmp.**

4. Enter the command **vm-support -p -i 10 -d 180.** This creates an esxtop snapshot, capturing data every 10 seconds, for the duration of 180 seconds.

5. The resulting file is a tarball and is compressed with gzip. You must extract it with the command **tar -xzf esx*.tgz**. This creates a vm-support directory that is called in the next command.

6. Run **esxtop -R /vm-support*** to replay the data for analysis.

Now that we've shown you the various tools (alarms, performance charts, and esxtop) that you will use to monitor performance in a vSphere environment, let's go through the four major resources—CPU, RAM, network, and disk—and see how to monitor the usage of these resources.

Monitoring CPU Usage

When monitoring a VM, it's always a good starting point to keep an eye on CPU consumption. Many VMs started out in life as underperforming physical servers. One of VMware's most successful sales pitches was being able to take all those lackluster physical boxes that are not busy and convert them to VMs. Once they are converted, virtual infrastructure managers tend to think of these VMs as simple, lackluster, and low-utilization servers with nothing to worry over or monitor. The truth, though, is quite the opposite.

When the server was physical, it had an entire box of hardware to itself. Now it must share its resources with many other workloads. In aggregate, they represent quite a load, and if some or many of them become somewhat busy, they contend with each other for the finite capabilities of the ESXi host on which they run. Of course, they don't know they are contending for resources because the VMkernel tries to make sure they get the resources they need. Virtual CPUs need to be scheduled, and ESXi does a remarkable job given that there are more VMs than physical processors most of the time. Still, the hypervisor can do only so much with the resources it has, and invariably there comes a time when the applications running in a VM may need more CPU time than the host can give.

When this happens, it's usually the application owner who notices first and raises the alarm with the system administrators. Now the vSphere administrators have the task of determining why this VM is underperforming. Fortunately, vCenter Server provides a number of tools that make monitoring and analysis easier. These are the tools you've already seen: alarms, performance charts, and esxtop.

Let's begin with a hypothetical scenario. A help desk ticket has been submitted indicating that an application owner isn't getting the expected level of performance on a particular server, which in this case is a VM. As the vSphere administrator, you need to first delve deeper into the problem and ask as many questions as necessary to discover what the application owner needs to be satisfied with performance. Some performance issues are subjective, meaning some users might complain about the slowness of their applications, but they have no objective benchmark for such a claim. Other times, this is reflected in a specific benchmark, such as the number of transactions by a database server or throughput for a web server. In this case, our issue revolves around benchmarking CPU usage, so our application is CPU intensive when it does its job.

ASSESSMENTS, EXPECTATIONS, AND ADJUSTMENTS

If an assessment was done prior to virtualizing a server, there might be hard numbers you can look at to give some details as to what was expected with regard to minimum performance or a service-level agreement (SLA). If not, you need to work with the application's owner to make more CPU resources available to the VM when needed.

When working with customers in the past, we tried to have conversations with application (or server) owners, to ensure we knew what their expectations were. Expectation management is key when dealing with performance levels. Talking to the customer about the assessment results (if it was done) or their understanding of the current performance requirements saved many future headaches for everyone involved.

---

vCenter Server's charts, which you have explored in great detail, are the best way to analyze usage, both short and long term. In this case, let's assume the help desk ticket describes a slowness issue in the last hour. As you've already seen, you can easily create a custom performance chart to show CPU usage over the last hour for a particular VM or ESXi host.

Perform the following steps to create a CPU chart that shows data for a VM from the last hour:

1. Connect to a vCenter Server instance with the vSphere Web Client.

2. Navigate to the Hosts And Clusters or VMs And Templates view.

3. In the navigator, select a virtual machine.

4. Select the Monitor ➤ Performance tab from the contents pane on the right, and then change the view to Advanced.

5. Click the Chart Options link.

6. In the Chart Options dialog box, select CPU from the Resource Type list. Select the Custom interval for the time span.

7. Leave the interval to Realtime (this shows the previous hour).

8. Set the chart type to Line Graph.

9. Select the VM from the list of objects.

10. From the list of counters, select Usage In MHz (Average) and Ready.

11. Click OK to apply the chart settings.

CPU READY

CPU Ready is a very important metric you should understand when monitoring the CPU performance of your VMs. It shows how long a VM is waiting to be scheduled on a logical processor. A VM waiting many thousands of milliseconds to be scheduled on a processor might indicate that the ESXi host is overloaded, a resource pool has too tight a limit, or the VM has too few CPU shares (or, if no one is complaining, nothing at all). Be sure to work with the server or application owner to determine an acceptable amount of CPU Ready for any CPU-intensive VM.

The chart in Figure 13.15 shows CPU utilization for the selected VM, but it won't necessarily help you get to the bottom of why this particular VM isn't performing as well as expected. In this scenario, we would fully expect the CPU Usage In MHz (Average) counter to be high; this simply tells you that the VM is using all the CPU cycles it can get. Unless the CPU Ready counters are also high, indicating that the VM is waiting on the host to schedule it onto a physical processor, you still haven't uncovered the cause of the slowness that triggered the help desk ticket. Instead, you'll need to move to monitoring host CPU usage.

Monitoring a host's overall CPU usage is fairly straightforward. Keep in mind that other factors usually come into play when looking at spare CPU capacity. Add-ons such as vMotion, vSphere DRS, and vSphere HA directly impact whether there is enough spare capacity on a server or a cluster of servers.

FIGURE 13.15
Understanding the metrics is important when building custom advanced performance graphs.

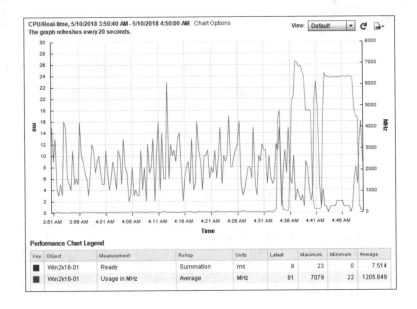

Key	Object	Measurement	Rollup	Units	Latest	Maximum	Minimum	Average
■	Win2k16-01	Ready	Summation	ms	9	23	0	7.514
■	Win2k16-01	Usage in MHz	Average	MHz	81	7079	22	1205.849

Perform the following steps to create a real-time chart for a host's CPU usage:

1. Launch the vSphere Web Client if it is not already running, and connect to a vCenter Server instance.

2. Navigate to the Hosts And Clusters or VMs And Templates view.

3. In the navigator, select a host. This shows you the Summary tab.

4. Select the Monitor ➤ Performance tab, and then switch to Advanced view.

5. Click the Chart Options link.

6. In the Chart Options dialog box, select the CPU resource type and the Real-Time display interval.

7. Set Chart Type to Stacked Graph (Per VM).

8. Select all objects.

9. You should see a separate object for each VM hosted on the selected ESXi host.

10. Select the Usage (Average) performance counter.

11. Click OK to apply the chart settings and return to the Performance tab.

As you can see in Figure 13.16, the chart shows the use of all the VMs on the selected ESXi host in a stacked fashion. From this view, you should be able to determine whether there is a specific VM or group of VMs consuming abnormal amounts of CPU capacity.

FIGURE 13.16
The CPU utilization of an ESXi host can be seen spread between each VM that hosts.

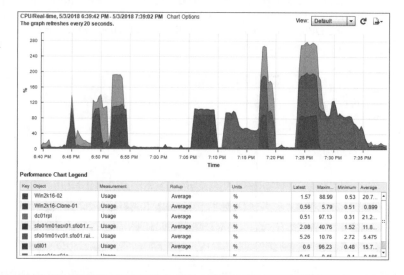

VMKERNEL BALANCING ACT

Always remember that on an oversubscribed ESXi host, the VMkernel will load-balance the VMs based on current loads, reservations, and shares represented on individual VMs and/or resource pools.

In this scenario, we identified the application within the VM as CPU bound, so these two performance charts should clearly identify why the VM isn't performing well. In all likelihood, the ESXi host on which the VM is running doesn't have enough CPU capacity to satisfy the requests of all the VMs. Your solution, in this case, would be to use the resource allocation tools described in Chapter 11, "Managing Resource Allocation," to ensure that this specific application receives the resources it needs to perform at acceptable levels.

Monitoring Memory Usage

Monitoring memory usage, whether on a host or a VM, can be challenging. The monitoring itself is not difficult; it's the availability of the physical resource that can be a challenge. Of the four resources, memory can be oversubscribed without much effort. Depending on the physical form factor chosen to host VMware ESXi, running out of physical RAM is easy to do. Although the blade form factor creates a very dense consolidation effort, the blades are sometimes constrained by the amount of physical memory and network adapters that can be installed. But even with other regular form factors, having enough memory installed comes down to how much the physical server can accommodate and your budget.

If you suspect that memory usage is a performance issue, the first step is to isolate whether this is a memory shortage affecting the host (you've oversubscribed physical memory and need to add more memory) or whether this is a memory limit affecting only that VM (meaning you need to allocate more memory to this VM or change resource allocation policies). Normally, if the ESXi host is suffering from high memory utilization, the predefined vCenter Server alarm will trigger and alert the vSphere administrator. However, the alarm doesn't allow you to delve deeper into the specifics of how the host is using memory. For that, you'll need a performance chart.

Perform the following steps to create a real-time chart for a host's memory usage:

1. Connect to a vCenter Server instance with the vSphere Web Client.

2. Navigate to Hosts And Clusters view.

3. In the navigator, click an ESXi host. This shows you the Summary tab.

4. Click the Monitor tab, and the Performance sub-tab. Then switch to Advanced view.

5. Click the Chart Options link.

6. In the Chart Options dialog box, select the Memory resource type and the Real-Time display interval.

7. Select Line Graph as the chart type. The host will be selected as the only available object.

8. In the Counters area, select the Active (Average), Consumed (Average), Overhead Consumed (Average), Swap Consumed (Average), and VMkernel Consumed counters.

   As you can see in Figure 13.17, this should give you a fairly clear picture of how much memory the ESXi host is using.

9. Click OK to apply the chart options and return to the Performance tab.

FIGURE 13.17
An ESXi host can show where all its memory is allocated down to a very granular level.

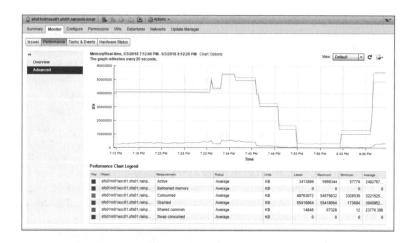

COUNTERS, COUNTERS, AND MORE COUNTERS

As with VMs, you can use a plethora of counters with a host to monitor memory usage. Which ones you select will depend on what you're looking for. It is common to monitor straight memory usage, but don't forget that there are other counters that could be helpful, such as Ballooning, Unreserved, VMkernel Swap, and Shared, just to name a few. The ability to assemble the appropriate counters for finding the right information comes with experience and depends on what is being monitored.

These counters, in particular the Memory Swap Used (Average) counter, will give you an idea of whether the ESXi host is under memory pressure. If the ESXi host is not suffering from memory pressure and you still suspect a memory problem, then the issue likely lies with the VM. Perform the following steps to create a real-time chart for a VM's memory usage:

1. Use the vSphere Web Client to connect to a vCenter Server instance.

2. Navigate to either the Hosts And Clusters or the VMs And Templates view.

3. In the navigator, click a virtual machine. This shows you the Summary tab.

4. Click the Monitor tab, and the Performance sub-tab. Then switch to Advanced view.

5. Click the Chart Options link.

6. In the Chart Options dialog box, select the Memory resource type and the Real-Time display interval.

7. Select Line Graph as the chart type.

8. In the list of counters, select to show the Overhead Consumed (Average), Consumed (Average), and Granted (Average) counters. This shows memory usage, including usage relative to the amount of memory configured for the VM.

9. Click OK to apply the chart options and return to the Performance tab.

From this performance chart, you will be able to tell how much of the memory configured for the VM is actually being used. This might reveal to you that the applications running inside that VM need more memory than the VM has been assigned and that adding more memory to the VM—assuming that there is sufficient memory at the host level—might improve performance.

Memory, like CPU, is just one of several factors that can impact VM performance. Network usage is another area that can affect performance, especially perceived performance.

Monitoring Network Usage

vCenter Server's charts provide a wonderful tool for measuring the network usage of a VM or a host.

Monitoring network usage requires a slightly different approach than monitoring CPU or memory. With either CPU or memory, reservations, limits, and shares can dictate how much of these two resources can be consumed by any one VM. Network usage cannot be constrained by these mechanisms. Because VMs plug into a VM port group, which is part of a vSwitch on a single host, how the VM interacts with the vSwitch can be manipulated by the virtual switch's or port group's policy. For instance, if you need to restrict a VM's overall network output, you would configure traffic shaping on the port group to restrict the VM to a specific amount of outbound bandwidth. Unless you are using vSphere Distributed Switches or the Nexus 1000V third-party distributed virtual switch, there is no way to restrict VM inbound bandwidth on ESXi hosts.

VM ISOLATION

Certain VMs may indeed need to be limited to a specific amount of outbound bandwidth. Servers such as FTP, file and print, web and proxy servers, or any server whose main function is to act as a file repository or connection broker may need to be limited or the traffic may need to be shaped to an amount of bandwidth that allows it to meet its service target but not monopolize the host it runs on. Isolating any of these VMs to a vSwitch of its own is probably a better solution, but it requires the appropriate hardware configuration.

To get an idea of how much network traffic is being generated, you can measure outgoing and incoming network traffic from a VM or host using the charts in vCenter Server. The charts can provide accurate information on the actual usage or ample information that a particular VM is monopolizing a virtual switch, especially using the Stacked Graph chart type.

Perform the following steps to create a real-time chart for a stacked graph of transmitted network usage by each VM on an ESXi host:

1. Launch the vSphere Web Client if it is not already running, and connect to a vCenter Server instance.

2. Navigate to either the Hosts And Clusters view or the VMs And Templates view.

3. In the navigator, click an ESXi host. This shows you the Summary tab.

4. Click the Monitor tab, and the Performance sub-tab. Then switch to Advanced view.

5. Click the Chart Options link.

6. From the Chart Options dialog box, select the Network resource type and the Real-Time display interval in the Chart Options area.

7. Select a chart type of Stacked Graph (Per VM).

8. In the objects list, be sure all the VMs are selected.

9. In the list of counters, select the Data Transmit Rate counter.

   This gives you an idea of how much network bandwidth each VM is consuming outbound on this ESXi host.

10. Click OK to apply the changes and return to the Performance tab.

What if you wanted a breakdown of traffic on each of the network interface cards (NICs) in the ESXi host instead of by VM? That's fairly easily accomplished by another trip back to the Chart Options dialog box.

Follow these steps to create a real-time chart for a host's transmitted network usage by NIC:

1. Connect to a vCenter Server instance with the vSphere Web Client.

2. Navigate to the Hosts And Clusters view.

3. In the navigator, select an ESXi host. This will show you the Summary tab in the content area to the right.

4. Click the Monitor tab, and the Performance sub-tab. Then switch to Advanced view.

5. Click the Chart Options link.

6. Under Chart Options in the Chart Options dialog box, select the Network resource type and the Real-Time display interval.

7. Set the chart type to Line Graph.

8. In the objects list, select the ESXi host as well as all the specific NICs.

9. Select the Data Transmit Rate and Packets Transmitted counters.

10. Click OK to apply the changes and return to the Performance tab.

As with the previous example for a VM, the two counters shown in Figure 13.18 will give you a window into how much network activity is occurring on this particular host in the outbound direction for each physical NIC. This is especially relevant if you want to see different rates of usage for each physical network interface, which, by definition, represent different virtual switches.

Now that you've examined how to monitor CPU, memory, and network usage, there's only one major area left: monitoring disk usage.

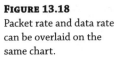

FIGURE 13.18
Packet rate and data rate can be overlaid on the same chart.

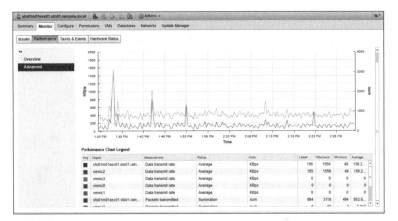

Monitoring Disk Usage

Monitoring a host's controller or VM's virtual disk usage is similar in scope to monitoring network usage. This resource, which represents a controller or the storing of a VM's virtual disk on a type of supported storage, isn't restricted by CPU or memory mechanisms like reservations, limits, or shares. The only way to restrict a VM's disk activity is to assign shares on the individual VM, which in turn may have to compete with other VMs running from the same storage volume. vCenter Server's charts come to our aid again in showing actual usage for both ESXi hosts and VMs.

Perform the following steps to create a host chart showing disk controller utilization:

1. Use the vSphere Web Client to connect to a vCenter Server instance.

2. Navigate to the Hosts And Clusters view.

3. In the navigator, select an ESXi host.

   This shows you the Summary tab in the Details section on the right.

4. Click the Monitor tab, and the Performance sub-tab. Then switch to Advanced view.

5. Click the Chart Options link. This opens the Chart Options dialog box.

6. Under Chart Options, choose the Real-Time display interval for the disk resource type.

7. Set the chart type to Line Graph.

8. Selecting an object or objects—in this case, an NFS datastore device—and a counter or counters lets you monitor for activity that is interesting or necessary to meet service levels. Select the objects that represent the ESXi host and one of the disks or datastores.

9. In the counters list, select Read Rate and Write Rate, to get an overall view of the activity for the selected disk / datastore object.

10. Click OK to return to the Performance tab.

The performance chart shown in Figure 13.19 will give you an idea of the activity on the selected disk. But what if you want to see disk activity for the entire host by each VM? In this case, a Stacked Graph view can show you what you need.

FIGURE 13.19

The read and write statistics for an NFS datastore are shown over the past hour.

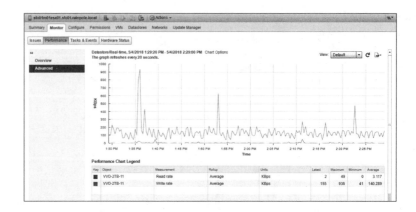

STACKED VIEWS

A stacked view is helpful in identifying whether one particular VM is monopolizing a volume. Whichever VM has the tallest stack in the comparison may be degrading the performance of other VMs' virtual disks.

Now let's switch to the virtual machine view. Looking at individual VMs for insight into their disk utilization can lead to some useful conclusions. File and print VMs, or any server that provides print queues or database services, will generate some disk-related I/O that needs to be monitored. In some cases, if the VM is generating too much I/O, it may degrade the performance of other VMs running out of the same volume. Let's take a look at a VM's chart.

Follow these steps to create a VM chart showing real-time disk controller utilization:

1. Launch the vSphere Web Client if it is not already running, and connect to a vCenter Server instance.

2. Navigate to either the Hosts And Clusters view or the VMs And Templates view.

3. In the navigator, click a virtual machine.

   This shows you the Summary tab in the Details section on the right.

4. Click the Monitor tab, and the Performance sub-tab. Then switch to Advanced view.

5. Click the Chart Options link to open the Chart Options dialog box.

6. Under Chart Options, select the Virtual Disk resource type and the Real-Time display interval.

7. Set the chart type to Line Graph.

8. Set both objects listed in the list of objects.

9. In the list of counters, select Read Rate, Write Rate (Average/Rate).

10. Click OK to apply these changes and return to the Performance tab.

With this chart, you should have an informative picture of this VM's disk I/O behavior. This VM is busy generating reads and writes for its application. Does the chart show enough I/O to meet a service-level agreement, or does this VM need some help? The charts allow administrators to make informed decisions, usually working with the application owners, so that any adjustments to improve I/O will lead to satisfied VM owners.

In addition, by looking at longer intervals of time to gain a historical perspective, you may find that a VM has become busier or fallen off its regular output. If the amount of I/O is just slightly impaired, then adjusting the VM's shares may be a way to prioritize its disk I/O ahead of other VMs sharing the volume. The administrator may be forced to move the VM's virtual disk(s) to another volume or LUN if share adjustments don't achieve the required results. You can use Storage VMotion, described in Chapter 6, "Creating and Configuring Storage Devices," to perform this sort of LUN-based load balancing without any disruption to the end users.

PERFORMANCE MONITORING FROM THE INSIDE AND THE OUTSIDE

It's important to remember that the very nature of how virtualization operates means that it is impossible to use performance metrics from within a guest OS as an indicator of overall resource utilization. Here's why.

In a virtualized environment, each guest OS "sees" only its slice of the hardware as presented by the VMkernel. A guest OS that reports 100% CPU utilization isn't reporting that it's using 100% of the physical server's CPU but rather that it's using 100% of the CPU capacity given to it by the hypervisor. A guest OS that is reporting 90% RAM utilization is really using only 90% of the RAM made available to it by the hypervisor.

Does this mean that performance metrics gathered from within a guest OS are useless? No, but these metrics cannot be used to establish overall resource usage—only relative resource usage. You must combine any performance metrics gathered from within a guest OS with matching metrics gathered from outside the guest OS. By combining the metrics from within the guest OS with metrics from outside the guest OS, you can create a more complete view of how a guest OS is using a particular type of resource and therefore get a better idea of what steps to take to resolve any resource constraints.

For example, if a guest OS is reporting high memory utilization but the vCenter Server resource management tools are showing that the physical system has plenty of memory available, this tells you that the guest OS is using everything available to it and might perform better with more memory allocated to it.

Monitoring resources can be tricky, and it requires a good knowledge of the applications running in the VMs in your environment. If you are a new vSphere administrator, it's worth spending some time using vCenter Server's performance charts to establish some baseline behaviors. This helps you become much more familiar with the normal operation of the VMs so that when something unusual or out of the ordinary does occur, you'll be more likely to spot it.

Once you are familiar with the counters, and what each counter means, it can often be quickest to look at the Utilization sub-tab found under the Monitor tab for Cluster and VM objects. As shown in Figure 13.20, you can get a quick look at the CPU and Memory being used by the object.

FIGURE 13.20

The Utilization area can provide an overview of some current, point-in-time CPU and Memory statistics without the need to delve into performance charts.

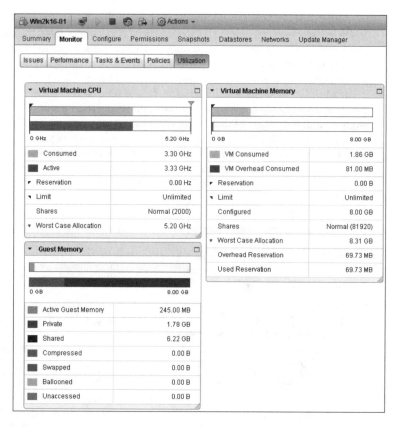

If you have a particular interest in the ongoing monitoring of resources and the performance management of your environment, it may be worthwhile to take a look at VMware vRealize Operations Manager (vROps). Built entirely for the purpose of monitoring, vROps integrates tightly with VMware's suite of products and provides even more in-depth metrics and intelligent analytics.

The Bottom Line

Use alarms for proactive monitoring.   vCenter Server offers extensive alarms for alerting vSphere administrators to excessive resource consumption or potentially negative events. You can create alarms on virtually any type of object found within vCenter Server, including datacenters, clusters, ESXi hosts, and VMs. Alarms can monitor for resource consumption or for the occurrence of specific events. Alarms can also trigger actions, such as running a script, migrating a VM, or sending a notification email.

Master It   What are the questions you should ask before creating a custom alarm?

Work with performance charts.   vCenter Server's detailed performance charts are the key to unlocking the information necessary to determine why an ESXi host or VM is performing poorly. The performance charts expose a large number of performance counters across a variety of resource types, and vCenter Server offers functionality to save customized chart settings, export performance graphs as graphic figures or Excel workbooks, and view performance charts in a separate window.

Master It You find yourself using the Chart Options link in the Advanced layout of the Performance tab to set up the same chart over and over again. Is there a way to save yourself some time and effort so that you don't have to keep re-creating the custom chart?

Gather performance information using command-line tools. VMware supplies a few command-line tools that are useful in gathering performance information. For VMware ESXi hosts, esxtop provides real-time information about CPU, memory, network, or disk utilization. Finally, the vm-support tool can gather performance information that can be played back later using esxtop.

Master It Explain how to run esxtop from the shell of an ESXi host.

Monitor CPU, memory, network, and disk usage by ESXi hosts and VMs. Monitoring usage of the four key resources—CPU, memory, network, and disk—can be difficult at times. Fortunately, the various tools supplied by VMware within vCenter Server can lead the vSphere administrator to the right solution. In particular, using customized performance charts can expose the right information that will help you uncover the source of performance problems.

Master It A junior vSphere administrator is trying to resolve a performance problem with a VM. You've asked this administrator to see if it is a CPU problem, and the junior administrator keeps telling you that the VM needs more CPU capacity because the CPU utilization is high within the VM. Is the junior administrator correct, based on the information available to you?

Chapter 14

Automating VMware vSphere

The role of a VMware vSphere administrator has become more demanding as the features and capabilities of the platform are enhanced and integrated with adjacent solutions. VMware continues to ensure that these features are quickly consumable for an administrator, as you have seen throughout this book. However, new features often lead to additional responsibilities, more opportunities for errors or inconsistencies, and lower tolerances for outages of critical and complex workloads.

As a vSphere administrator, you will often need to perform repetitive tasks with increasingly more touch points. Examples include creating multiple virtual machines (VMs) from a template, changing the network configuration on a group of VMs or hosts, migrating VMs to new data-stores with Storage vMotion, and gathering information about an environment for internal and external audits. Automation can help you complete these tasks much more quickly, provide greater consistency, and ultimately save your organization money by reducing the risk of errors and unplanned outages. Automation can benefit every administrator and every organization that adopts vSphere in their environment and the benefits can be realized regardless of scale or previous experience.

IN THIS CHAPTER, YOU WILL LEARN TO

- Identify automation available for vSphere

- Install PowerCLI on Windows, macOS, and Linux

- Get started with PowerCLI scripting

- Perform some more-advanced PowerCLI scripting

- Access and contribute to the community

Why Use Automation?

You may ask yourself, "Why should I use automation?" The simple, but obvious, answer is that you are only one person. An individual can perform only a finite amount of work manually in any given hour, day, or week. With automation, modern datacenter administrators can increase their efficiency, accuracy, and capacity.

Efficiency Automation enables you to complete repeated tasks with less effort. Scripts and workflows do not get distracted by a colleague or a meeting, causing it to miss a step or not complete its work in a timely manner.

Accuracy Automation delivers consistency across repetitive and mundane tasks. Configuration changes, reports, and process workflows can be automated with high confidence that errors will not occur.

Capacity: Automation can often increase productivity. Tasks that would often take hours manually can now be completed in minutes or seconds with automation.

These benefits apply to any modern data center environment. The increase of business requirements and expectations means that we must find ways to extend our finite abilities and ensure we consistently deliver outcomes. In this chapter, you will learn how to continue to invest and innovate to deliver vSphere automation capabilities to administrators of various needs and backgrounds.

vSphere Automation Options

VMware continues to make significant improvements in the automation capabilities and options it offers. These advancements provide vSphere administrators with options from which to choose to accomplish their automation goals, regardless of skill level or requirements. This section briefly outlines the various vSphere automation tools and the existing experience that best aligns with them

---

OTHER AUTOMATION AND ORCHESTRATION PRODUCTS

This chapter does not discuss non-VMware developed tools—such as, Ansible, Terraform, and Puppet—that are available to automate vSphere environments. These tools take advantage of the same vSphere APIs that the VMware automation tools leverage.

In our experience, the most widely adopted automation tool to manage and automate vSphere i PowerCLI. Built on PowerShell, PowerCLI is a multi-platform, command-line and scripting tool th appeals to Windows and Linux users alike. Providing more than 600 cmdlets for not only vSphere, but also adjacent solutions such as, vSAN, NSX-T, vRealize Operations Manager, vCloud Director, VMware Cloud on AWS, and VMware Horizon, it is often the vSphere automation tool of choice.

VMware PowerCLI is covered in this chapter based on common usage in the virtualization industry and the relative learning curve. Our intention is to demonstrate how you can begin to automate tasks within your environments, regardless of little or no automation experience.

What are some additional vSphere automation tools provided by VMware?

The vSphere Automation SDKs include the libraries for programmatically accessing features available via the API, such as virtual machine (VM) and vCenter Server appliance management. In addition, the SDKs contain samples for interoperating with vSphere APIs.

vRealize Orchestrator is an orchestration engine that is included with vSphere licensing entitlements. It provides the ability to use the out-of-the-box workflows or design and deploy custom, scalable workflows to automate vSphere processes. The adoption of vRealize Orchestrator is increasingly more common as it has become tightly integrated in the vRealize Automation where it can automate management and operational tasks across both VMware and third-party solutions, such as NSX and service management systems.

AUTOMATION AND ESXI FREE VERSION

It's no secret that testing scripts and workflows in a production environment is a bad idea. As an administrator, you will want to test and learn more about the various automation tools outlined in this chapter, and perhaps other third-party solutions as well. It is important to note that there are some limitations when using the free vSphere Hypervisor. Automation tools like PowerCLI and the SDKs are limited to read-only functionality with the free vSphere Hypervisor. Full capabilities are available by taking advantage of VMware's 60-day trial periods.

Another, often overlooked, resource to learn and test automation solutions is the VMware Hands-on Labs (HOL). VMware provides free access to time-limited labs that enable you to learn about products and features in a sandboxed environment on their cloud—in fact, some labs are dedicated to delving into specific automation topics. From a browser, you can log on and launch a fully functional lab in a matter of moments, and then use the lab to learn a topic or practice and experiment with an automation solution. Once you are done, simply log out, and the lab is destroyed and the resources are returned to the cloud for the next lab. Learn more at `https://labs.hol.vmware.com`.

Automating with PowerCLI

Generally considered the tool of choice for automating vSphere, PowerCLI provides the ability to easily manage nearly all components in a vSphere environment.

People with Windows administration backgrounds generally have some familiarity with PowerShell and find adopting PowerCLI more natural than adopting the other tools. Individuals who are comfortable with console administration will find PowerCLI easy to pick up and use.

In the following sections, we will introduce you to PowerShell, walk you through the initial configuration of PowerCLI on multiple platforms, examine essential PowerCLI cmdlets, demonstrate how to build more scripts that use the functionality of PowerCLI, and discuss the new features found in PowerCLI 10.

PowerShell and PowerCLI

PowerCLI would not be possible were it not for PowerShell. Based on the .NET Framework, PowerShell is a command-line and scripting language developed by Microsoft. As a standard Microsoft automation platform, PowerShell has shipped natively with Microsoft Windows since Windows 7 and Server 2008, although it has been available for much longer. PowerShell has tremendous capabilities for managing a wide range of Windows systems and applications. Microsoft Exchange and SQL Server administrators have been using PowerShell for years because those products were among the earliest solutions in which Microsoft made PowerShell the management tool of choice. A growing percentage of vendors and partners have developed modules and snap-ins for PowerShell to help manage their applications and hardware.

In 2018, Microsoft expanded the platform and enabled administrators to automate the administration of multiple operating systems with PowerShell Core 6.0. Adding support for Windows, macOS, and Linux, these operating systems and application processes running on each can now be managed and rapidly automated.

In this section, we will briefly discuss some key PowerShell concepts that will help you g started with PowerCLI.

POWERSHELL IS OPEN SOURCED

The Microsoft PowerShell Team has forked and open-sourced the PowerShell base code to GitHub for community contributions. However, contributions made in the repository are not automatically made to Windows PowerShell. Learn more at github.com/powershell/powershell.

CMDLETS

The first PowerShell term that needs defining is *cmdlets* (pronounced "command-lets"), which are compiled .NET classes that perform a single action on an object. PowerShell cmdlets follow a `<verb>-<singular noun>` syntax followed by a set of parameters. For the most part, cmdlets are simple to use because they do not attempt to do too much all at once. With an established naming convention, you can often find the cmdlet you need by simple intuition. For example, to get today's date, you would execute `Get-Date` in PowerShell, or to get all VMs in a vCenter Server instance, you would simply execute `Get-VM` in PowerCLI. This is intuitive by design.

OBJECTS

PowerShell is built on the Microsoft .NET Framework, and as such, objects are a critical component to understand and be successful with PowerCLI. Simply put, an object is a container of properties and methods. When you execute the PowerCLI cmdlet `Get-VM` while connected to a vCenter Server instance, the information that is returned is a collection of VM objects. Each VM can be treated as its own object that contains unique information for that VM. The information for VM-1 and VM-2 will be different, but they will be the same type of object or container. This means you can filter or compare properties of each object because they share the same format. To do this, it helps to understand what properties are available. We will discuss the various ways you can quickly retrieve general and detailed information from an object.

GETTING THE MOST OUT OF THIS SECTION

The information in this section will be more meaningful once you have installed VMware PowerCLI and connected to your environment. We recommend returning to this section and trying out the steps listed next.

General information can be gained by simply entering the cmdlet and reviewing the output. The default output has been programmed into PowerCLI to return the most-common properties sought for the given object. For instance, running the `Get-VM` cmdlet will return *all* of the VMs in the vCenter Server inventory with the attributes for the VM name, power state, number of CPUs, and memory (MB). You can specify which information you want to return using the `Select-Object` cmdlet in the pipeline as follows:

```
Get-VM | Select-Object Name, PowerState
```

To return all information associated with all of the VMs, you execute the following command, with the second option demonstrating the very common `Select-Object` alias `Select`:

```
Get-VM | Select-Object *
```

Or:

```
Get-VM | Select *
```

You will notice that the output is likely to fill up and scroll the console rather quickly. In such a situation, you can export the result set to a .CSV file by piping to the `Export-CSV` cmdlet:

```
Get-VM | Select * | Export-CSV -Path C:\Mastering vSphere 6.7\AllVMs.csv -
NoTypeInformation
```

As we discussed earlier, you can get more detailed information about objects. Using `Select *` gives you a full output of all property values, but there is an easier way to identify what properties are available. Using the `Get-Member` cmdlet, you can return a list of the available properties and methods of an object type. Try both of the following examples, where the second example uses GM, an alias for `Get-Member`:

```
Get-VM | Get-Member
```

And then:

```
Get-VM | GM
```

Before we discuss additional PowerShell terms, we have one more tip. If you have a large inventory and want things to run faster while you learn, you can use the `Select-Object` cmdlet to select only the first few returned objects. In the following example, the command will return only the first three VM objects in your inventory:

```
Get-VM | Select -First 3
```

We will discuss additional functionality in this chapter, but for now, this should give you an idea of how simple it is to select properties that you are interested in and a better understanding of the structure of objects in PowerShell/PowerCLI.

VARIABLES

Variables are not unique to PowerShell; they are used in many programming and scripting languages. In PowerShell, variables begin with a $ followed by alphanumeric characters. There are both global and user-defined variables, and we will touch on examples of each.

Think of a variable as an empty container where you can store objects within PowerShell. The most common use cases for variables are to collect results of a script or to store information that will be used later in a script. Building on the example in the Objects section, imagine that you want to store a list of all VM objects in a variable for later use:

```
$vm = Get-VM | Select-Object Name, PowerState
```

The variable $vm now contains the same data produced when you ran the longer command earlier. Now, you can simply type **$vm** into the PowerCLI console for the current session and you will see the same results. This means you can do a variety of things with the variable later in the console or script:

```
$vm | Export-CSV -Path C:\Test\VMs.csv -NoTypeInformation
$vm | Where-Object{$_.PowerState -eq "PoweredOn"}
```

Keep in mind that there are also global variables already in use with PowerShell and PowerCLI. You can return a full listing of them with the `Get-Variable` cmdlet. However, keep in mind that $host variable is already in use by the system and cannot be set within your scripts. It is common to use `$vm` and `$vmhost` instead. You will learn about `$DefaultVIserver` later in this chapter, in the "Connecting to vCenter Server and ESXi Hosts" section.

Never Use the Same Variable Twice in a Script

You'll see the use of variables used throughout this chapter and in community code examples. Always be careful not to use the same variable twice in your script. Name variables so that it is easy to discern what information is stored in the variable.

Pipeline

Fundamental to PowerShell's capability is the *pipeline*. Those administrators with a Linux or Unix background are well versed in the concept of a pipeline. However, PowerShell took the traditional pipeline and kicked it up a notch. In the past, pipelines were a means to pass text from one command to another, simplifying the syntax of a given operation. In PowerShell, pipelines are a means to pass entire objects from one cmdlet to another. This ability increased the power of the pipeline while simplifying its capacity to accomplish almost any administrative action. In short, this means that as you use PowerCLI cmdlets, you will be able to pass a Cluster object through the pipeline and retrieve all the hosts within a cluster. In the following example, we will do this and then check each `Get-VMHost` object so that you return only those that are in maintenance mode:

```
Get-Cluster <cluster name> | Get-VMHost |`
Where-Object{$_.ConnectionState -eq "Maintenance"}
```

In the next example, return only the hosts in the cluster that are running ESXi 6.7.0:

```
Get-Cluster <cluster name> | Get-VMHost |`
Where-Object{$_.Version -eq "6.7.0"}
```

Continuing Pipeline over Multiple Lines

When using PowerShell and the pipeline, you may have lines that do not fit cleanly on the screen or your editor. This book uses the ` symbol to indicate that the code continues onto the next line. This symbol is recognized by PowerShell as continuing the current pipeline even though it is written on a separate line. Every attempt is made with each use to make the break logical to maintain the readability of the code.

Alternatively, you could check each of your clusters for hosts in maintenance mode. Doing so means that you pass a collection of all Cluster objects in inventory through the pipeline and then gather the `Get-VMHosts` that are in maintenance mode:

```
Get-Cluster | Get-VMHost |`
Where{$_.ConnectionState -eq "Maintenance"}
```

Notice that the `Where-Object` cmdlet is now using the `Where` alias, and is collecting the `Get-VMHosts` objects to check for the `ConnectionState` property value. This is just a touch of what the pipeline can provide as you pass objects through. You will see many more examples of the pipeline throughout this chapter, and hopefully the concepts of objects and the pipeline will become second nature to you.

What's New in PowerCLI 10

Each version of PowerCLI has included new cmdlets to take advantage of the many new features provided in vSphere—and other VMware products. As such, the product name has transformed from the vSphere PowerCLI naming to VMware PowerCLI.

In 2017, PowerCLI removed the need for a Windows .MSI installer package. The management of the PowerCLI modules transitioned the PowerShell Gallery. Now, by using the PowerShell default cmdlets for working with modules in the PowerShell Gallery, PowerCLI can be installed and updated with ease. We will explore these steps in the next section.

In early 2018, PowerCLI hit a milestone and celebrated its tenth anniversary and was aptly iterated to VMware PowerCLI 10. But there is a bigger story. With the name change, support for more than vSphere, and the transition to the PowerShell Gallery, PowerCLI was removed from the lockstep versioning with vSphere—allowing it to integrate faster to deliver new features and capabilities across not only vSphere but also across the VMware stack.

Following the Microsoft PowerShell Team open-sourcing of the PowerShell base code and the release of PowerShell 6.0, PowerCLI 10 introduced multi-platform support by adding macOS and Linux support with PowerShell Core. This is huge—you can now use PowerShell *and* PowerCLI on Windows, macOS, or Linux!

PowerCLI 10.1.0, which was released shortly after the general availability of vSphere 6.7, added support for this vSphere release.

Installing and Configuring PowerCLI on Windows

To install PowerCLI 10 on Windows, you must have a compatible Microsoft Windows operating system (OS) (Table 14.1) along with compatible .NET and PowerShell engine versions (Table 14.2).

TABLE 14.1:   Supported Windows operating systems and versions for PowerCLI 10

OS TYPE	VERSIONS
Server	Windows Server 2016
	Windows Server 2012 R2
	Windows Server 2008 R2 Service Pack 1
Workstation	Windows 10
	Windows 8.1
	Windows 7 Service Pack 1

For the best experience and support for the latest features, consider upgrading to PowerShell 5.1.

TABLE 14.2: Required components and compatible versions for PowerCLI 10 on Windows

COMPONENT	VERSIONS
.NET Framework	4.5
	4.5.x
	4.6
	4.6.x
	4.7.x
PowerShell	3.0
	4.0
	5.0
	5.1

Installing PowerCLI involves installing two different components:

PowerShell   Powershell has been a core component of Microsoft Windows since Windows 7. As previously suggested, for the best experience and support for the latest Windows Management Framework features, consider upgrading to PowerShell 5.1. Windows Management Framework 5.1 is available for download from the Microsoft website at microsoft.com/download.

PowerCLI   PowerCLI is available from the PowerShell Gallery.

Before installing PowerCLI, you need to do the following:

◆   Uninstall PowerCLI 6.5 R1 or earlier.

◆   Verify access to the Internet.

◆   Register PowerShell Gallery as a local repository.

NOTE   In this example, a fresh install of Microsoft Windows 10, April 2018 (1803) Update is used.

Perform the following steps to install PowerCLI on a system with PowerShell 5.1;

1. Launch the PowerShell console with Run-As Administrator.

2. Run the following command to install all official PowerCLI modules:

```
Install-Module VMware.PowerCLI -Scope CurrentUser
```

The modules are installed to $home\Documents\WindowsPowerShell\Modules.

3. If prompted that the "NuGet Provider is required to continue," type **Y** and press Enter to continue. PowerShellGet will download and import the NuGet provider.

4. If prompted with "Untrusted Repository," type **Y** and press Enter to continue with the repository. The PowerCLI modules will be downloaded and installed from the PowerShell Gallery.

To avoid this prompt, prior to installing PowerCLI, run the following command to change the installation policy for the PowerShell Gallery:

```
Set-Repository -Name PSGallery`-InstallationPolicy Trusted`-SourceLocation
https://www.powershellgallery.com/api/v2
```

5. PowerShell will download and install the PowerCLI modules for the current user. Once that process is completed, verify the status of the modules by running the following command:

```
Get-Module VMware* -ListAvailable
```

The command will return a list of the modules.

At any time, run the following command to update to the latest version of PowerCLI from the PowerShell Gallery.

```
Update-Module -Name VMware.PowerCLI
```

That's it! You have now successfully installed PowerCLI on Microsoft Windows. However, you still need to modify the script execution policy of PowerShell. As of PowerShell v4, the default execution policy is Remote Signed on Windows Server 2012 R2 and later.

Follow these steps to set the PowerShell script execution policy on operating systems other than Windows Server 2012 R2 and later:

1. Launch the PowerShell console with Run-As Administrator.

2. Run the following command to set the execution policy:

```
Set-ExecutionPolicy RemoteSigned
```

3. Type **Y** and press Enter to continue. The PowerShell script execution policy will be set to RemoteSigned.

4. To verify the script execution policy setting, run the following cmdlet:

```
Get-ExecutionPolicy
```

The cmdlet should return RemoteSigned.

5. Type **Exit** and press Enter to close the PowerShell session.

Now when you relaunch PowerShell, you can begin to use PowerCLI modules. Unlike older versions of PowerCLI, there is no need to load these new modules into a PowerShell session. Once the modules are loaded into the module folder, PowerShell will automatically register the cmdlets with the PowerShell session.

However, unlike prior versions of PowerCLI, a shortcut to PowerCLI will not be created. Although it is not required in order for you to use the PowerCLI modules, you may wish to create a shortcut. To do this, perform the following steps:

1. Right-click the Desktop and select New ➤ Shortcut.

2. In the Create Shortcut Wizard, enter the following for the location, and then click Next.

```
C:\Windows\System32\WindowsPowerShell\v1.0\powershell.exe -noe -c
"Import-Module VMware.PowerCLI"
```

3. Type **PowerCLI** for the Name and click Finish.

4. Right-click on the new PowerCLI shortcut and select Properties. In the Start In field, type **C:** as shown in Figure 14.1. Then click OK.

5. Right-click on the shortcut (Figure 14.2) and select Run As Administrator. When prompted by User Account Control to allow the program to make changes to the device, click Yes.

You are greeted with several excellent starting cmdlets, such as `Connect-VIServer`, `Get-VIcommand`, `Get-PowerCLIHelp`, and `Get-PowerCLICommunity` (Figure 14.3). These suggestions are important, especially since `Connect-VIServer` is a required first cmdlet for connecting to your virtual infrastructure. You are now ready to get started with PowerCLI on Windows.

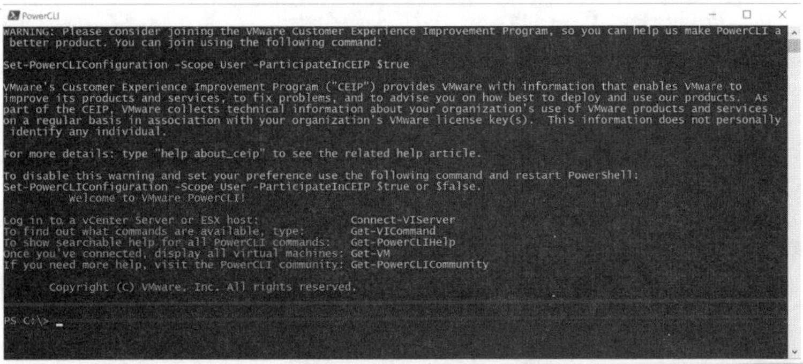

FIGURE 14.3 The PowerCLI startup screen provides quick tips on a few useful commands.

> **POWERSHELL SCRIPT EXECUTION POLICY**
>
> Through the PowerShell script execution policy, you can manage which scripts can be run on your computer. By default, in versions prior to PowerShell v4 on Windows 2012 R2, PowerShell runs as *Restricted*, which means that no scripts can be run, and PowerShell can run only in interactive console mode. This also includes PowerCLI. The recommended setting is *RemoteSigned*, which allows scripts that you write as well as those signed by a trusted publisher, such as VMware. You will likely see recommendations to set the execution policy to *Unrestricted*, which will allow you to run all Windows PowerShell/PowerCLI scripts. This certainly makes things easier for troubleshooting, but you should consider the security of the system before setting the execution policy to Unrestricted. Unrestricted allows even malicious scripts to run.

Installing and Configuring PowerCLI on macOS

To install PowerCLI 10 on macOS, you must have a compatible macOS OS (Table 14.3) along with compatible PowerShell Core engine version (Table 14.4).

TABLE 14.3: Supported macOS OS and version for PowerCLI 10

OS TYPE	VERSION
Workstation	macOS 10.12+

TABLE 14.4: Required component and compatible version for PowerCLI 10 on macOS

COMPONENT	VERSION
PowerShell Core	6.0.2

Installing PowerCLI on macOS involves installing two different components:

PowerShell Core   Powershell Core can be installed using the Homebrew package manager, or by downloading the installation PKG package from the releases page on Github at `github` `.com/powershell/powershell/releases`.

PowerCLI   PowerCLI is available from the PowerShell Gallery after invoking PowerShell Core.

Before you begin the process of installing PowerCLI on macOS, verify that you have access to the Internet.

NOTE   In this walkthrough, a fresh install of macOS 10.13.3 High Sierra is used. Homebrew is the preferred method for installing PowerShell Core and is described here.

Perform the following steps to install PowerShell Core on macOS:

1. Open `Terminal.app` and type **brew**. If a "command not found" message is returned, run the following command to install the Homebrew package manager for macOS:

   ```
   /usr/bin/ruby -e "$(curl -fsSL
   https://raw.githubusercontent.com/Homebrew/install/master/install)".
   ```

2. Once Homebrew is installed, install Homebrew-Cask, so you can install more packages:

   ```
   brew tap caskroom/cask
   ```

3. Once Homebrew-Cask is installed, PowerShell Core can be installed. To begin installing PowerShell Core 6, run the following command:

   ```
   brew cask install powershell
   ```

4. Once the PowerShell Core package is installed, launch PowerShell by running the following command:

   ```
   pwsh
   ```

When a new version of PowerShell Core is released, simply update Homebrew and install the PowerShell Core update by running the following commands:

```
brew update
brew cask upgrade powershell
```

Once PowerShell Core is installed, you can perform the following steps to install PowerCLI on macOS:

1. Open `Terminal.app` and invoke PowerShell Core with the following command:

   ```
   pwsh
   ```

2. Run the following command to install all official PowerCLI modules:

   ```
   Install-Module VMware.PowerCLI -Scope CurrentUser
   ```

   The modules are installed to /Users/<username>/.local/share/powershell/Modules.

3. If prompted with "Untrusted Repository," type **Y** and press Enter to continue with the repository. The PowerCLI modules will be downloaded and installed from the PowerShell Gallery.

4. Once the download and installation process is completed, verify the status of the modules by running the following command:

```
Get-Module VMware* -ListAvailable
```

The command will return a list of the PowerCLI modules.

At any time, run the following command to update to the latest version of PowerCLI from the PowerShell Gallery.

```
Update-Module -Name VMware.PowerCLI
```

You are now ready to get started with PowerCLI on macOS (Figure 14.4.)

FIGURE 14.4
PowerCLI on macOS

Installing and Configuring PowerCLI on Linux

To install PowerCLI 10 on Linux, you must have a compatible Linux OS (Table 14.5) along with compatible PowerShell Core engine version (Table 14.6).

Installing PowerCLI on Linux involves installing two different components:

PowerShell Core   PowerShell Core is published to a package repository for simple installation and updates. This is the preferred method. It can also be downloaded from the releases page on Github at `github.com/powershell/powershell/releases`.

TABLE 14.5:   Supported Linux OS and version for PowerCLI 10

OS TYPE	VERSION
Workstation	Ubuntu Linux 16.04

TABLE 14.6:   Required component and compatible version for PowerCLI 10 on Linux

COMPONENT	VERSION
PowerShell Core	6.0.2

PowerCLI   PowerCLI is available from the PowerShell Gallery after invoking PowerShell Core.

Before you begin the process of installing PowerCLI on Ubuntu, verify that you have access to the Internet.

NOTE   In this walkthrough, a fresh install of Ubuntu Desktop 16.04 LTS is used. The package repository is the preferred method for installing PowerShell Core and is described here.

Perform the following steps to install PowerShell Core on Ubuntu:

1. On the Desktop, open the Terminal application.

2. Run the following command to import the repository GPG keys:

```
curl https://packages.microsoft.com/keys/microsoft.asc | sudo apt-key add -
```

3. Run the following command to register the Microsoft Repository for Ubuntu 16.04:

```
sudo curl -o /etc/apt/sources.list.d/microsoft.list
https://packages.microsoft.com/config/ubuntu/16.04/prod.list
```

4. Run the following command to update the product list on Ubuntu Linux:

```
sudo apt-get update
```

5. Run the following command to install PowerShell Core on Ubuntu Linux:

```
sudo apt-get install -y powershell
```

6. Once the PowerShell Core package is installed, launch PowerShell by running the following command:

```
pwsh
```

Perform the following steps to install PowerCLI on Ubuntu:

1. Open a Terminal and invoke PowerShell Core with the following command:

```
pwsh
```

2. Run the following command to install all official PowerCLI modules:

```
Install-Module VMware.PowerCLI -Scope CurrentUser
```

The modules are installed to /home/<username>/.local/share/powershell/Modules.

3. If prompted with "Untrusted Repository," type **Y** and press Enter to continue with the repository. The PowerCLI modules will be downloaded and installed from the PowerShell Gallery for the current user.

4. Once completed, verify the status of the modules by running the following command:

```
Get-Module VMware* -ListAvailable
```

The command will return a list of the PowerCLI modules.

At any time, run the following command to update to the latest version of PowerCLI from the PowerShell Gallery:

```
Update-Module -Name VMware.PowerCLI
```

You are now ready to get started with PowerCLI on Ubuntu (Figure 14.5).

FIGURE 14.5
PowerCLI on Ubuntu

Additional PowerCLI Capabilities

VMware PowerCLI provides over 600 cmdlets for managing and automating more than just vSphere. It also supports vCloud Director, vRealize Operations, vSAN, NSX-T, VMware Cloud on AWS, and VMware Horizon.

Additionally, PowerNSX—a community developed PowerCLI module for NSX for vSphere (NSX-v)—is also available to manage and automate NSX-v implementations. Learn more at powernsx.github.io.

SNAP-INS, BE GONE!

If you have used PowerShell in the past, you may remember that PowerShell v1 required the use of snap-ins to extend the shell or add features and capabilities to PowerShell. Written in .NET, these snap-ins had to be assembled before being released. Once a user downloaded a snap-in, that snap-in would need to be installed and registered on the user's system. In addition, snap-ins lacked the ability to explicitly define dependencies, which could cause issues for PowerCLI, which consists of several components.

In PowerShell v2, Microsoft introduced modules to address these concerns. Both .NET and PowerShell can be used to develop PowerShell modules that are mobile and no longer require registrations. By simply downloading the modules—as you saw previously when importing PowerCLI from the PowerShell Gallery—these modules can be immediately consumed once placed into the proper directory path or by specifying the directory path on a system.

PowerCLI Backward Compatibility

VMware has done an excellent job of making the newest version of PowerCLI backward-compatible with previous versions of vSphere. Always check the release notes of the latest version of PowerCLI to ensure that your scripts will run properly against your environment. PowerCLI 10 supports vSphere 5.5 and later. For up-to-date details on the interoperability of VMware PowerCLI, see the VMware Product Interoperability Matrixes at vmware.com/go/interop.

Note that general support for vSphere 5.5 ended on September 19, 2018.

Getting Started with PowerCLI

The first and most important thing to remember about PowerCLI is that the PowerShell's <verb>-<noun> nomenclature for cmdlets makes it easy to read and easy to find the right cmdlet for the job. In the following sections, we will discuss the basic starting points of PowerCLI. By the end of this discussion, you will be able to connect PowerCLI to your vSphere resources, locate the cmdlet you need, get information about how to use any cmdlet, and start creating one-liner scripts. These are the first steps to automating vSphere with PowerCLI.

FINDING CMDLETS

VMware PowerCLI provides a special cmdlet, Get-VICommand, that helps you find the cmdlet you need. Get-VICommand is similar to PowerShell's Get-Command, but it is specific to the PowerCLI-provided cmdlets. Imagine that you are looking for available cmdlets to manage your logs. Using the following command in PowerCLI will return a list of all available log cmdlets:

```
Get-VICommand *log*
```

Alternatively, you could use the Get-Command cmdlet and narrow your search criteria to only the <noun> portion of the cmdlet name:

```
Get-Command -Noun *log*
```

You will notice that the Get-Command cmdlet returns more results than Get-VICommand. Why is this? The Get-Command cmdlet will return all PowerShell cmdlets that contain log in the

<noun> position of cmdlet name, whereas `Get-VICommand` will return only PowerCLI cmdlets that contain `log` in the <noun> position of the cmdlet name.

If you are using PowerShell version 3 or later on Windows, you can use the `Show-Command` cmdlet to launch a visual of the cmdlet and its parameters. You can also input values into the parameters and then run or copy the PowerCLI syntax.

PowerShell, and therefore PowerCLI, provides tab completion for all cmdlets. This means that if you type **Get-VM** and press Tab, PowerCLI will cycle through all available cmdlets that begin with `Get-VM`, starting with `Get-VM` and then `Get-VMGuest`. Usually, this is not the fastest method to find the cmdlet you are looking for, but it certainly works when you are in a pinch. Tab completion also works within the cmdlet. Pressing the spacebar after a cmdlet and then pressing Tab repeatedly will cycle you through the list of parameters for which you can specify values. For example, if you type **Get-VM -D** and press Tab, PowerCLI will cycle through all available parameters for the cmdlet that begin with D, starting with `Datastore` and then `DistributedSwitch`. However, tab completion only cycles through each cmdlet name or parameter in PowerShell/PowerCLI on Windows with each press of Tab. For macOS and Linux, the first press of Tab will return a complete list of the available options and retain your previous commands.

GETTING HELP

Regardless of how long you have been working with PowerShell or PowerCLI, there will always be times when you need help. PowerShell provides a useful cmdlet for just this occasion: `Get-Help`. The `Get-Help` cmdlet can provide helpful information about cmdlets or topics within PowerShell. Simply type the cmdlet in your console and press Enter for a breakdown of its capabilities. In the context of PowerCLI, we will show you how to get more information from the cmdlets you located earlier using `Get-VIcommand`.

Once you identify the cmdlet you need, you can use `Get-Help` to find out more about it, like the parameters or parameter sets, a description of how it is used, and examples of how to use it. For example, try the following:

```
Get-Help Get-Log
```

The command will return a brief synopsis of `Get-Log` cmdlet capabilities, the syntax for usage, a more detailed description, and links associated with the cmdlet. If you are looking for examples to get you started with the cmdlet, use the `-examples` parameter as follows:

```
Get-Help Get-Log -examples
```

There are several other parameters to choose from under the Remarks section, such as `-full` and `-online`. The `-full` parameter will return a full text-based reference for the cmdlet to the session, whereas, using the `-online` parameter will open the default browser to the PowerCLI Reference on VMware {code} at https://code.vmware.com. For example:

```
Get-Help Get-Log -online
```

CONNECTING TO VCENTER SERVER AND ESXI HOSTS

The first cmdlet that any PowerCLI user must know is `Connect-VIServer`. This cmdlet has many features that make connecting to your vCenter Server or ESXi hosts easy. We will discuss a few of those features in this section. If you would like to see the full capabilities of `Connect-VIServer`, you can check the PowerCLI help by entering the following:

```
Get-Help Connect-VIServer -full
```

Connecting to a vCenter Server is the most common use of `Connect-VIServer`. To connect, you must provide, at a minimum, the vCenter Server name, a username, and a password:

```
Connect-VIServer -Server <vCenter Server FQDN or IP>`
-User <username> -password <password>
```

This works well, but it is certainly not something you would want to do with someone peering over your shoulder or as part of a script. Including a password in plaintext is simply asking for trouble. On Windows, PowerCLI can natively use the user's domain credentials for the system login. If the account you are logged into has vCenter access, no credentials are required. Many organizations follow the practice of separate administrative accounts and, as such, it is important to demonstrate ways to protect credentials. To solve this problem, you can securely prompt for credentials in your scripts and store them encrypted in a variable using the `Get-Credential` cmdlet. When you call `Get-Credential` in a script, it will prompt for a username and password. It stores them in the `PSCredential` object, which can then be used by `Connect-VIServer` as follows:

```
$credential = Get-Credential
Connect-VIServer -Server <vCenter Server FQDN or IP>`
-Credential $credential
```

Aside from the security benefits, the best part of this method is that the `$credential` variable information remains for the duration of the PowerCLI session or until you update the variable with new information. This means you can have the same variable set to different credentials in different PowerCLI sessions. This is ideal for running multiple scripts simultaneously on the same system and protects your credentials from prying eyes.

You can also connect to multiple vCenter Server instances or ESXi hosts in the same session by separating them with a comma.

In the following example, we're connecting to two vCenter Server instances:

```
Connect-VIServer -Server`
sfo01m01vc01.rainpole.local,sfo01m01vc02.rainpole.local `
-Credential $credential
```

In the next example, we're connecting directly to two ESXi hosts:

```
Connect-VIServer -Server`
sfo01m01esx01.rainpole.local,sfo01m01esx02.rainpole.local `
-Credential $credential
```

If you are running multiple vCenter Server instances with Enhanced Linked Mode or Embedded Linked Mode, here is one final, and handy, tip for the `Connect-VIServer` cmdlet. If your account has common permissions across vCenter Server instances in linked mode, you can connect to all instances with PowerCLI using the `-AllLinked` parameter like this:

```
Connect-VIServer -Server sfo01m01vc01.rainpole.local`
-Credential $credential -AllLinked:$true
```

Before we leave the `Connect-VIServer` cmdlet, it is important for you to know about its counterpart: `Disconnect-VIServer`. If you run `Disconnect-VIServer` by itself in the PowerCLI console, you will be prompted for verification that you want to disconnect from the vCenter Server instance. You can press Enter, and it will disconnect from the active server (identified by

$VIServer). If you are connected to multiple systems, by default this command will not disconnect from all of them. You can accomplish this by specifying the name of the systems you wish to disconnect from or by using a wildcard *. Use the -Confirm parameter to prevent being prompted to disconnect.

In the following example, we specify the vCenter Server instances that will be disconnected in the session:

```
Disconnect-VIServer -Server`
sfo01m01vc01.rainpole.local,sfo01m01vc02.rainpole.local`
-Confirm:$false
```

And in the next example, we use a wildcard (*) to disconnect all vCenter Server instances in the session:

```
Disconnect-VIServer * -Confirm:$false
```

At times, you may wish to verify any vCenter Server instances or ESXi hosts you are connected to. To do this, simply type the variable **$DefaultVIServers** in PowerCLI. You can also identify the current default system by typing **$DefaultVIServer**. The default server will be disconnected if no server is specified when using the Disconnect-VIServer cmdlet.

POWERCLI AND INVALID CERTIFICATE HANDLING

Another notable feature in PowerCLI 10 includes a change to the way certificates are handled. Previously, if you connected to a vCenter Server instance or ESXi host with an invalid certificate—self-signed or otherwise—PowerCLI would return a warning and continue. The handling has been updated to be secure by returning a warning and stopping the connection. If you are using an invalid certificate—such as a default self-signed certificate—you can bypass the warning with the Set-PowerCLIConfiguration' cmdlet by setting InvalidCertificateAction to Ignore. The available settings include Fail, Warn, Ignore, Prompt, and Unset.

For example, to ignore invalid certificate warnings, run the following:

```
Set-PowerCLIConfiguration -InvalidCertificateAction Ignore
```

YOUR FIRST ONE-LINER: REPORTING

One of the most common uses of PowerCLI is reporting. You can gather tremendous amounts of data about an environment in a short period of time. Previously, in the discussion about the pipeline, we mentioned how you can quickly identify the hosts in your environment that are in maintenance mode. That small script is often called a "one-liner". One-liners are scripts that can be written out and executed in a single line using the pipeline to pass information. Let's combine a few things we have discussed and see how you can quickly generate reports for your environment.

Since ESXi does not store logs for an extended period, your hosts should redirect their syslog data to an external location. Failure to do so results in logs being lost at reboot. How can you quickly determine which hosts are configured and which are not? Using PowerCLI, you can return the information in moments:

```
Get-VMHost | Get-VMHostSyslogServer |`
Export-CSV C:\Mastering vSphere\Reports\Syslog.csv`
-NoTypeInformation
```

This one-liner gathers a collection of all ESXi hosts in inventory and then collects the syslog server settings for each. The final pipeline takes that syslog server information and exports it to a CSV file. You may note that this script does not tell you *which* host has what configuration!

You can fix this by creating a parameter for the Get-VMHost object in the pipeline. This is an intermediate PowerShell technique, but one that we want to show you because it is helpful with cmdlets like Get-VMHostSyslogServer and Get-VMHostNTPServer:

```
Get-VMHost |`
Select Name, @{N="SyslogServer";E={$_ |Get-VMHostSyslogServer}} |`
Export-CSV C:\Mastering vSphere\Reports\Syslog.csv`
-NoTypeInformation
```

Now that you have this information, what do you do if you have multiple ESXi hosts with the incorrect syslog settings? Write a one-liner to update them, of course!

YOUR FIRST ONE-LINER: CONFIGURATION CHANGE

PowerCLI is not just for reporting. You can also modify the environment, assuming you have the appropriate privileges. In the previous section, you identified systems that did not have the correct syslog settings. To update these hosts, you need to identify the supporting cmdlet. In situations like this, where a Get- verb is used in a cmdlet, it is common that a Set- verb is also available. In this instance, you will want to use the Set-VMHostSyslogServer cmdlet. Running Get-Help Set-VMHostSyslogServer -full returns the syntax and tells you that you will need to specify the -SysLogServer parameter, and perhaps the -SysLogServerPort parameter if the syslog collector endpoint is listening on a specific port. Assume in this scenario that you are sending your logs to a vRealize Log Insight cluster with hostname sfo01vrli01.rainpole.local. Go ahead and specify port 514:

```
Get-VMHost | Set-VMHostSyslogServer -SysLogServer`
sfo01vrli01.rainpole.local -SysLogServerPort 514
```

You may have noticed that this one-liner does more than set the correct syslog server settings on the systems that had the incorrect settings. It sets the settings on all the VMHosts collected with Get-VMHost. Although this is not necessarily a problem, it could take quite some time to run in large environments. Let's assume that you want to change only those that are not correct.

If you have a small environment, we recommend just running the previous one-liner to update all systems with each pass. If, however, you have a large environment or a strong desire to update only the incorrect settings, let's move forward. We are going to build on what we have discussed earlier and use some additional PowerShell techniques. Let's identify the hosts with the incorrect setting and update them with a single one-liner:

```
Get-VMHost | Select Name, @{N="SyslogServer";E={$_ |Get-VMHostSyslogServer}} |`
Where{$_.SyslogServer -notlike "sfo01vrli01.rainpole.local:514"} |`
Set-VMHostSyslogServer -SysLogServer sfo01vrli01.rainpole.local
SysLogServerPort 514
```

If you are following along, you will notice that this one-liner throws an error. We wanted to show you how this method has changed the VMHost object type, which Set-VMHostSyslogServer cannot accept through the pipeline. One way to fix this is by using a ForEach loop (using the % alias) so that you process each VMHost, and changing its object type back to something that Set-VMHostSyslogServer can use.

```
Get-VMHost | Select Name, @{N="SyslogServer"; E={$_ |Get-VMHostSyslogServer}} |`
Where{$_.SyslogServer -notlike "sfo01vrli01.rainpole.local:514"} |`
%{Set-VMHostSyslogServer -VMhost (Get-VMHost -Name $_.Name)`
-SysLogServer sfo01vrli01.rainpole.local -SysLogServerPort 514}
```

Thanks for following along. You had to do a few new things there to accomplish something relatively simple. We wanted to go through this exercise to demonstrate the value of the pipeline, the importance of understanding objects, and how much can be done with a single line of PowerCLI scripting.

You should now have enough exposure to start branching beyond one-liners into multiline PowerCLI scripts.

Building PowerCLI Scripts

You have seen that one-liners are nothing more than a series of PowerCLI cmdlets strung into a series of PowerShell pipelines. Scripts can often be as straightforward as a one-liner saved to a text file with a .ps1 filename extension for future reuse. Often, as you have seen, multiple steps are necessary to accomplish your automation goal. This is where you begin to tie together all the topics discussed. With that in mind, we will discuss a few more examples of how PowerCLI can make your work easier.

MIGRATING ALL VIRTUAL MACHINES ON A HOST

In the first example, you will build a simple pipeline using multiple PowerCLI cmdlets. By combining cmdlets in a pipeline, you can build more complex commands, such as the following:

```
Get-VMHost <FirstHost> | Get-VM | Move-VM`
-Destination (Get-VMHost <SecondHost>)
```

This command relocates all VMs on the ESXi host specified by <FirstHost> to the ESXi host represented by <SecondHost>. This includes both running VMs, which are moved with vMotion, as well as powered-off VMs. Notice that we use parentheses when defining the destination VMHost. PowerShell will run the content within the parentheses first and use the result for the -Destination parameter. This is like a mathematical order of operations.

You could also perform this action by storing the source and destination VMHost in a variable:

```
$SourceHost = Get-VMHost <FirstHost>
$DestinationHost = Get-VMHost <SecondHost>
Get-VMHost $SourceHost | Get-VM | Move-VM -Destination $DestinationHost
Set-VMHost $SourceHost -State Maintenance
```

Suffice it to say, there are always many ways to accomplish the same outcome.

MANIPULATING VIRTUAL MACHINE SNAPSHOTS

Let's look at a second scenario, where you will use PowerCLI to work with VM snapshots.

In this example, imagine you need to perform an application upgrade for a workload that consists of multiple VMs. It may be useful to create a snapshot for all the VMs associated with the application, which you have organized in a VM folder within the inventory. This one-liner would quickly accomplish the task for you:

```
Get-Folder <Folder Name> | Get-VM | New-Snapshot`
-Name "Pre-Upgrade"
```

Once the application upgrade is completed and operationally verified, you can use the Remove-Snapshot cmdlet to delete the snapshot created on each VM:

```
Get-Folder <Folder Name> | Get-VM | Get-Snapshot`
-Name "Pre-Upgrade" | Remove-Snapshot
```

Finally, you can use the Get-Snapshot cmdlet to list all snapshots so that you could be sure you had created or deleted them:

```
Get-Folder <Folder Name> | Get-VM | Get-Snapshot
```

(Remember, snapshots are not backups!)

This command would return a list of any snapshot objects for all the VMs in the specified VM folder.

RECONFIGURING VIRTUAL MACHINE NETWORKING

In this third example, imagine that you want to move all the VMs currently connected to one port group to a different port group. This is possible with a one-line command in PowerCLI:

```
Get-VM | Get-NetworkAdapter | Where-Object {$_.NetworkName`
-like "OldPortGroupName"} |`
Set-NetworkAdapter -NetworkName "NewPortGroupName"`
-Confirm:$false
```

A few new concepts are introduced here in this script, so we will break it down a little bit:

◆ The Get-VM cmdlet returns the VM objects.

◆ The VM objects are passed to the Get-NetworkAdapter cmdlet, which returns virtual NIC objects for all VMs.

◆ The virtual NIC objects are parsed using the Where-Object cmdlet to include only those virtual NICs where the NetworkName property is like the "OldPortGroupName" string.

◆ The parsed list of virtual NICs is passed to the Set-NetworkAdapter cmdlet, which sets the NetworkName property to the "NewPortGroupName" value.

◆ The Confirm parameter instructs PowerShell not to ask the user for confirmation of each operation.

MOVING VIRTUAL MACHINES BETWEEN RESOURCE POOLS

In this example, we will use PowerCLI to move a group of VMs from one resource pool to another. However, we want to move only a subset of the VMs from the source resource pool. Only the VMs that are running a Microsoft Windows guest OS should be moved.

We will build this example in steps. First, as you have probably guessed, we can use the Get-ResourcePool, Get-VM, and Get-VMGuest cmdlets to create a list of VM guest OS objects in the resource pool:

```
Get-ResourcePool <ResourcePoolName> | Get-VM | Get-VMGuest
```

Next, we need to filter the output to return only those objects identified as Microsoft Windows guest OSs. As you saw in a previous example, we can use the `Where-Object` cmdlet to filter the output list in a pipeline:

```
Get-ResourcePool <ResourcePoolName> | Get-VM | Get-VMGuest |` Where-Object {
$_.OSFullName -Match "^Microsoft Windows*"}
```

This should do it, right? To finish the command, you should be able to add the `Move-VM` cmdlet and move the VMs to the destination resource pool. Unfortunately, that will not work. You are working with objects with PowerShell, and a VM guest OS object—which is what is being returned by the `Get-VMGuest` cmdlet—is not an object that the `Move-VM` cmdlet will accept as input.

Instead, you will have to use a multiline script for this, as shown in Listing 14.1.

LISTING 14.1:   A PowerCLI script that selectively moves VMs to a new resource pool

```
$VMs = Get-VM -Location (Get-ResourcePool Development)
foreach ($vm in $VMs) {
$vmguest = Get-VMGuest -VM $vm
if ($vmguest.OSFullName -match "^Microsoft Windows*") {
Move-VM -VM $vm -Destination (Get-ResourcePool "Production") } }
```

Again, we will break down the script so that it is easier to understand:

♦ Line 1 uses the `Get-VM` and `Get-ResourcePool` cmdlets to retrieve a list of VM objects in the specified resource pool. That list of VM objects is stored in the `$VMs` variable.

♦ Line 2 creates a loop that operates for each of the objects in the `$VMs` variable. Each individual VM object is stored as `$vm`.

♦ Line 3 uses the `Get-VMGuest` cmdlet with the `$vm` variable to retrieve the guest OS object for that VM object and store the result in the `$vmguest` variable.

♦ Line 4 tests to see whether the `OSFullName` property of the `$vmguest` object matches a string starting with `"Microsoft Windows"`.

♦ Line 5 executes only if the test on the fourth line was successful; if it executes, it uses the `Move-VM` and `Get-ResourcePool` cmdlets to move the VM object represented by the `$vm` variable to the resource pool named Production.

If you were to save the script in Listing 14.1 as `MoveWindowsVMs.ps1`, then you could run it in PowerCLI like this:

```
PS C:\>.\<Path to Script>\MoveWindowsVMs.ps1
```

SETTING A BASELINE HOST CONFIGURATION WITH POWERCLI AND JSON

In this example, we will kick things up a notch and use PowerCLI in conjunction with a JSON configuration to automate the baseline configuration of several freshly installed ESXi hosts.

Imagine that you are establishing—or resetting—the infrastructure for a lab environment. In this scenario, eight hosts have been installed with the ESXi hypervisor and have their hostname, management IP address, netmask, and gateway configured—four hosts for a management cluster and four hosts for a workload cluster. A vCenter Server instance will be deployed on a management host; then the datacenter and cluster objects for management and workload will be created, and the hosts will be added and prepared for use.

Instead of manually configuring each host with some baseline settings so that the vCenter Server instance can be deployed, the hosts can be added quickly, and avoid manual misconfigurations, you have decided to script a portion of the setup process (*although you could certainly automate more than just this*).

You have decided to automate the configuration of the following settings on each host based on its use—management or workload.

◆   NTP Servers

◆   DNS Servers

◆   DNS suffix

◆   VMkernel for NFS storage traffic with jumbo frames

◆   Port groups for management, storage, and VM traffic

◆   Mount 2 NFS datastores

◆   Enable SSH

In Listing 14.2, we have created a JSON configuration with the host, network, and datastore objects for the hosts based on a management or workload classification. JSON is a minimal and readable format to structure data in simple key/value pairs.

LISTING 14.2:   A JSON file to set a baseline host configuration

```
{
"hosts": [
  {
    "tag": "management",
    "hostname": "sfo01m01esx01",
    "fqdn": "sfo01m01esx01.rainpole.local",
    "ip": "172.28.11.101",
    "username": "root",
    "password": "VMware1!",
    "storageVmk": "192.168.106.25",
    "storageVmkNetmask": "255.255.252.0",
    "ntpServer0": "0.ntp.rainpole.local",
    "ntpServer1": "1.ntp.rainpole.local",
    "dnsServer0": "172.28.11.5",
    "dnsServer1": "172.28.11.4",
    "dnsSuffix0": "rainpole.local"
  },{
```

```
    "tag": "management",
    "hostname": "sfo01m01esx02",
    "fqdn": "sfo01m01esx02.rainpole.local",
    "ip": "172.28.11.102",
    "username": "root",
    "password": "VMware1!",
   "storageVmk": "192.168.106.26",
   "storageVmkNetmask": "255.255.252.0",
   "ntpServer0": "0.ntp.rainpole.local",
   "ntpServer1": "1.ntp.rainpole.local",
   "dnsServer0": "172.28.11.5",
   "dnsServer1": "172.28.11.4",
   "dnsSuffix0": "rainpole.local"
},{
   "tag": "management",
   "hostname": "sfo01m01esx03",
   "fqdn": "sfo01m01esx03.rainpole.local",
   "ip": "172.28.11.103",
   "username": "root",
   "password": "VMware1!",
   "storageVmk": "192.168.106.27",
   "storageVmkNetmask": "255.255.252.0",
   "ntpServer0": "0.ntp.rainpole.local",
   "ntpServer1": "1.ntp.rainpole.local",
   "dnsServer0": "172.28.11.5",
   "dnsServer1": "172.28.11.4",
   "dnsSuffix0": "rainpole.local"
},{
   tag": "management",
   "hostname": "sfo01m01esx04",
   "fqdn": "sfo01m01esx04.rainpole.local",
   "ip": "172.28.11.104",
   "username": "root",
   "password": "VMware1!",
   "storageVmk": "192.168.106.28",
   "storageVmkNetmask": "255.255.252.0",
   "ntpServer0": "0.ntp.rainpole.local",
   "ntpServer1": "1.ntp.rainpole.local",
   "dnsServer0": "172.28.11.5",
   "dnsServer1": "172.28.11.4",
   "dnsSuffix0": "rainpole.local"
},{
   "tag": "workload",
   "hostname": "sfo01w01esx01",
   "fqdn": "sfo01w01esx01.rainpole.local",
   "ip": "172.28.21.101",
   "username": "root",
   "password": "VMware1!",
```

```
      "storageVmk": "192.168.106.29",
      "storageVmkNetmask": "255.255.252.0",
      "ntpServer0": "0.ntp.rainpole.local",
      "ntpServer1": "1.ntp.rainpole.local",
      "dnsServer0": "172.28.11.5",
      "dnsServer1": "172.28.11.4",
      "dnsSuffix0": "rainpole.local"
    },{
      "tag": "workload",
      "hostname": "sfo01w01esx02",
      "fqdn": "sfo01w01esx02.rainpole.local",
      "ip": "172.28.21.102",
      "username": "root",
      "password": "VMware1!",
      "storageVmk": "192.168.106.30",
      "storageVmkNetmask": "255.255.252.0",
      "ntpServer0": "0.ntp.rainpole.local",
      "ntpServer1": "1.ntp.rainpole.local",
      "dnsServer0": "172.28.11.5",
      "dnsServer1": "172.28.11.4",
      "dnsSuffix0": "rainpole.local"
    }
  ],
  "networks": [
    {
      "tag": "management",
      "mgmtPortgroupName": "Management Network",
      "mgmtVlanID": "3511",
      "vmPortgroupName": "VM Network",
      "vmVlanId": "3511",
      "StoragePortgroupName": "Storage",
      "StorageVlanId": "3104",
      "StorageMtu": "9000"
    },{
      "tag": "workload",
      "mgmtPortgroupName": "Management Network",
      "mgmtVlanID": "3521",
      "vmPortgroupName": "VM Network",
      "vmVlanId": "3521",
      "StoragePortgroupName": "Storage",
      "StorageVlanId": "3104",
      "StorageMtu": "9000"
    }
  ],
  "nfs": [
    {
      "tag": "management",
      "NfsServer": "192.168.104.251",
```

```
        "DatastoreName0": "sfo01-m01-nfs00",
        "Share0": "/lab/nfs/m01/00",
        "DatastoreName1": "sfo01-m01-nfs01",
        "Share1": "/lab/nfs/m01/01"
    },{
        "tag": "workload",
        "NfsServer": "192.168.104.251",
        "DatastoreName0": "sfo01-w01-nfs00",
        "Share0": "/lab/nfs/w01/00",
        "DatastoreName1": "sfo01-w01-nfs01",
        "Share1": "/lab/nfs/w01/01
    }
    ]
    }
```

VISUAL STUDIO CODE: A LIGHTWEIGHT, MULTI-PLATFORM, AND EXTENSIBLE SOURCE CODE EDITOR

As an administrator, you likely have an editor in your resource kit to write code and scripts or to simply take notes in markdown. There can often be a lively debate on which editor is better and which one has the better widgets, but in our experience, Visual Studio Code is quickly becoming the editor of choice—especially for PowerShell/PowerCLI scripting.

Visual Studio Code is an open source, lightweight, and extensible source code editor developed by Microsoft and distributed under a proprietary license. Like PowerShell and PowerCLI, Visual Studio Code is multi-platform and can run on Windows, Linux, and macOS. Its extensibility provides support for an embedded shell, debugging, Git source control, syntax highlighting for many languages, intelligent code completion, and third-party extensions. It's fully customizable, allowing you to set up your environment to meet your needs with a variety of extensions and themes, keyboard shortcuts, and preferences.

Learn more at `code.visualstudio.com`.

Now that we have populated a JSON configuration file with the hosts, networks, and datastore objects that represent what we want to configure in the environment, we can now write a PowerCLI script to ingest the key/value pairs and configure the hosts to the specification.

In Listing 14.3, we have created a PowerCLI script that will consume the JSON specification and begin to iterate through each object and take action. Unlike our previous scripts, this one includes additional helpful, onscreen outputs as it runs to provide an update for each step of the procedure using the `Write-Host` cmdlet along with a `-ForegroundColor` option. For example, look at the following line:

```
Write-Host "Successfully created $NetworksStoragePortgroupName Portgroup with
VLAN $NetworksStorageVlanId on vSwitch0 for $HostFQDN" -ForegroundColor Green
```

It could result in the following being displayed onscreen in green:

```
Successfully created Storage Portgroup with VLAN 3104 on vSwitch0 for
sfo01m01esx01.rainpole.local
```

LISTING 14.3: A PowerCLI Script that sets a baseline host configuration

```
<#
  .EXAMPLE
  PS C:\>.\Mastering vSphere\Configure-Hosts.ps1 Lab.json
#>
# Check for .json for import.
Param($InputJSON=$(throw "Please specify the .json for import."))

# Import .json configuration file. e.g. Lab.json
Clear-Host
$HostsJson = (Get-Content -Raw $InputJSON) | ConvertFrom-Json

# Load Host Information
ForEach ($hosts in $HostsJson.hosts){
  $HostFQDN = $Hosts.fqdn
  $HostIP = $Hosts.ip
  $HostUsername = $Hosts.username
  $HostPassword = $Hosts.password
  $HostStorageVmk = $Hosts.storageVmk
  $HostStorageVmkNetmask = $Hosts.storageVmkNetmask
  $HostTag = $Hosts.tag
  $HostNTPServer0 = $Hosts.ntpServer0
  $HostNTPServer1 = $Hosts.ntpServer1
  $HostDNSServer0 = $Hosts.dnsServer0
  $HostDNSServer1 = $Hosts.dnsServer1
  $HostdnsSuffix0 = $Hosts.dnsSuffix0

  # Load Network Information
    if ($HostTag -eq "management"){
      ForEach ($Networks in $HostsJson.networks){
        $NetworksTag = $Networks.tag
        if ($NetworksTag -eq "management"){
          $NetworksmgmtPortgroupName = $Networks.mgmtPortgroupName
          NetworksmgmtVlanId = $Networks.mgmtVlanID
          $NetworksvmPortgroupName = $Networks.vmPortgroupName
          $NetworksvmVlanId = $Networks.vmVlanId
          $NetworksStoragePortgroupName = $Networks.StoragePortgroupName
          $NetworksStorageVlanId = $Networks.StorageVlanId
          $NetworksStorageMtu = $Networks.StorageMtu
        }
      }
    }
    elseif ($HostTag -eq "workload"){
      ForEach ($networks in $HostsJson.networks){
        $NetworksTag = $Networks.tag
        if ($NetworksTag -eq "workload"){
```

```
          $NetworksmgmtPortgroupName = $Networks.mgmtPortgroupName
          $NetworksmgmtVlanId = $Networks.mgmtVlanID
          $NetworksvmPortgroupName = $Networks.vmPortgroupName
          $NetworksvmVlanId = $Networks.vmVlanId
          $NetworksStoragePortgroupName = $Networks.StoragePortgroupName
          $NetworksStorageVlanId = $Networks.StorageVlanId
          $NetworksStorageMtu = $Networks.StorageMtu
        }
      }
    }

# Load NFS Information
    if ($HostTag -eq "management"){
      ForEach ($Nfs in $HostsJson.nfs){
        $NfsTag = $Nfs.tag
        if ($NfsTag -eq "management"){
          $NfsDatastoreName0 = $Nfs.DatastoreName0
          $NfsShare0 = $Nfs.Share0
          $NfsDatastoreName1 = $Nfs.DatastoreName1
          $NfsShare1 = $Nfs.Share1
          $NfsServer = $Nfs.NfsServer
        }
      }
    }
    elseif ($HostTag -eq "workload"){
      ForEach ($Nfs in $HostsJson.nfs){
        $NfsTag = $Nfs.tag
        if ($NfsTag -eq "workload"){
          $NfsDatastoreName0 = $Nfs.DatastoreName0
          $NfsShare0 = $Nfs.Share0
          $NfsDatastoreName1 = $Nfs.DatastoreName1
          $NfsShare1 = $Nfs.Share1
          $NfsServer = $Nfs.NfsServer
        }
      }
    }
    Try {
      Clear-Host
      Write-Host "Connecting to $HostFQDN at $HostIP" -ForegroundColor Yellow
      Connect-VIServer $HostIP -user $HostUsername -pass $HostPassword
      $TargetHost = Get-VMHost | Where-Object { $_.name -eq $HostIp }
      Write-Host "Successfully connected to $HostFQDN at $HostIP" -
        ForegroundColor Green
      Write-Host "Step 1 - Creating $NetworksStoragePortgroupName Portgroup
        with VLAN $NetworksStorageVlanId on vSwitch0 for $HostFQDN" -
        ForegroundColor Yellow
      [string]$ExistPortGroup = Get-VMHost $HostIP | Get-VirtualPortGroup |
        Where-Object {$_.Name -eq $NetworksStoragePortgroupName} # Check for
        existence of portgroup
```

```
      if ($ExistPortGroup -eq $NetworksStoragePortgroupName){
        Write-Host "The $NetworksStoragePortgroupName Portgroup already
      exists on vSwitch0 for $HostFQDN" -ForegroundColor Magenta
        }
      else {
        Get-VMHost $HostIP | Get-VirtualSwitch -Name "vSwitch0" | New-
      VirtualPortGroup -Name $NetworksStoragePortgroupName -VLanId
      $NetworksStorageVlanId | Out-Null
          Write-Host "Successfully created $NetworksStoragePortgroupName
      Portgroup with VLAN $NetworksStorageVlanId on vSwitch0 for $HostFQDN"
      -ForegroundColor Green
        }
  Write-Host "Step 2 - Creating a VMKernel on the
      $NetworksStoragePortgroupName Portgroup for $HostFQDN" -
      ForegroundColor Yellow
  [string]$ExistStorageVmk = Get-VMHost $HostIP | Get-
      VMHostNetworkAdapter -VMKernel | Where-Object {$_.PortgroupName -eq
      $NetworksStoragePortgroupName} # Check existence of vmkernel on
      the portgroup
      if ($ExistStorageVmk -eq "vmk1"){
        Write-Host "A VMKernel already exist on the
      $NetworksStoragePortgroupName Portgroup for $HostFQDN"
      -ForegroundColor Magenta
        }
      else {
        New-VMHostNetworkAdapter -VMHost $HostIP -PortGroup "Storage" -
      VirtualSwitch vSwitch0 -IP $HostStorageVmk -SubnetMask
      $HostStorageVmkNetmask -Mtu $NetworksStorageMtu | Out-Null
          Write-Host "Successfully created a VMKernel on the
      $NetworksStoragePortgroupName Portgroup for $HostFQDN" -
      ForegroundColor Green
        }
  Write-Host "Step 3 - Mounting $NfsDatastoreName0 Datastore to
      $HostFQDN" -ForegroundColor Yellow
  [string]$ExistDatastore0 = Get-VMHost -Name $HostIP | Get-Datastore |
      Where-Object {$_.Name -eq $NfsDatastoreName0} # Check existence of
      the datastore
      if ($ExistDatastore0 -eq $NfsDatastoreName0){
        Write-Host "$NfsDatastoreName0 already mounted to $HostFQDN" -
      ForegroundColor Magenta
        }
      else {
        Get-VMHost -Name $HostIP | New-Datastore -NFS -Path $NfsShare0
      -NfsHost $NfsServer -Name $NfsDatastoreName0 | Out-Null
        Write-Host "Successfully mounted $NfsDatastoreName0 to $HostFQDN" -
      ForegroundColor Green
        }
```

```
Write-Host "Step 4 - Mounting $NfsDatastoreName1 Datastore to
  $HostFQDN" -ForegroundColor Yellow
[string]$ExistDatastore1 = Get-VMHost -Name $HostIP | Get-Datastore |
  Where-Object {$_.Name -eq $NfsDatastoreName1} # Check existence of
  the datastore
if ($ExistDatastore1 -eq $NfsDatastoreName1){
  Write-Host "$NfsDatastoreName0 already mounted to $HostFQDN" -
  ForegroundColor Magenta
  }
  else {
    Get-VMHost -Name $HostIP | New-Datastore -NFS -Path $NfsShare1
  -NfsHost $NfsServer -Name $NfsDatastoreName1 | Out-Null
    Write-Host "Successfully mounted $NfsDatastoreName1 to $HostFQDN" -
  ForegroundColor Green
  }
Write-Host "Step 5 - Setting VLAN $NetworksvmVlanId on the
  $NetworksvmPortgroupName portgroup for $HostFQDN" -
  ForegroundColor Yellow
$NetworksvmPortgroupName = "VM Network"
$CurrentvmPortgroupName = Get-VMHost $HostIP | Get-VirtualPortGroup
  -Name $NetworksvmPortgroupName
Set-VirtualPortGroup -VirtualPortGroup $CurrentvmPortgroupName -VLanId
  $NetworksvmVlanId | Out-Null
Write-Host "Successfully set VLAN $NetworksvmVlanId on the
  $NetworksvmPortgroupName porgroup for $HostFQDN"
  -ForegroundColor Green
Write-Host "Step 6 - Enabling SSH and setting an auto-start policy on
  $HostFQDN" -ForegroundColor Yellow
Get-VMHostService | Where-Object {$_.key -eq 'TSM-SSH'} | Start-
  VMHostService -Confirm:$false | Out-Null # Starting the TSM-
  SSH Service
Set-VMHostService -HostService (Get-VMHostservice | Where-Object
  {$_.key -eq "TSM-SSH"}) -Policy "On" | Out-Null # Setting the TSM-SSH
  Service start and stop with host
$shellWarning = Get-VMHost | Get-AdvancedSetting | Where-Object
  {$_.Name -eq "UserVars.SuppressShellWarning"} # Suppressing the
  warning for the SSH service
if($shellWarning){
  if($shellWarning.Value -ne "1"){
    Set-AdvancedSetting -AdvancedSetting $shellWarning -Value "1"
  -Confirm:$false
  }
} else {
Get-VMHost | New-AdvancedSetting -Name "UserVars.SuppressShellWarning"
  -Value "1" -Force:$true -Confirm:$false # Adding an advanced setting
  to suppress the SSH warning.
}
```

```
    Write-Host "Successfully configured SSH settings on $HostFQDN"
      -ForegroundColor Green
    Write-Host "Step 7 - Configuring NTP and setting an auto-start policy
      on $HostFQDN" -ForegroundColor Yellow
    Get-VMHostService | Where-Object {$_.key -eq 'ntpd'} | Stop-
      VMHostService -Confirm:$false | Out-Null # Stopping the NTP Service
    $CurrentNTPServerList = Get-VMHostNtpServer
    if ($CurrentNTPServerList){
      Remove-VMHostNtpServer -NtpServer $CurrentNTPServerList
      -Confirm:$false | Out-Null # Deleting any existing ntp servers
    }
    Add-VMHostNtpServer -NtpServer $HostNTPServer0 -Confirm:$false |
      Out-Null # Updating the first NTP Server
    Add-VMHostNtpServer -NtpServer $HostNTPServer1 -Confirm:$false |
      Out-Null # Updating the second NTP Server
    Get-VMHostService | Where-Object {$_.key -eq 'ntpd'} | Start-
      VMHostService -Confirm:$false | Out-Null # Starting the NTP Service.
    Set-VMHostService -HostService (Get-VMHostservice | Where-Object
      {$_.key -eq "ntpd"}) -Policy "On" | Out-Null # Setting NTP Service to
      start and stop with host
    Write-Host "Successfully configured NTP settings on $HostFQDN" -
      ForegroundColor Green
    Write-Host "Step 8 - Configuring DNS settings on $HostFQDN"
      -ForegroundColor Yellow
    Get-VMHostNetwork -VMHost $HostIP | Set-VMHostNetwork -DomainName
      $HostdnsSuffix0 -SearchDomain $HostdnsSuffix0 -DNSAddress
      $HostdnsServer0 , $HostdnsServer1 -Confirm:$false | Out-Null
    Write-Host "Successfully configured DNS settings on $HostFQDN"
      -ForegroundColor Green
    Write-Host "Disconnecting from $HostFQDN." -ForegroundColor Yellow
    Disconnect-viserver -Server $TargetHost.Name -Force -Confirm:$false
      -WarningAction SilentlyContinue
    Write-Host "Successfully disconnected from $HostFQDN"
      -ForegroundColor Green
    }
      Catch {
        $ErrorMessage = $_.Exception.Message
        Write-Host "An error occurred while processing host "$HostFQDN"
      with error message: "$ErrorMessage"." -ForegroundColor Red
        Write-Host ""
        Write-Host "Disconnecting from $HostFQDN" -ForegroundColor Magenta
        Disconnect-VIServer $HostIP -Force -Confirm:$false -WarningAction
      SilentlyContinue
      }
    }
```

Next, let's look at what is happening through the script execution.

If you were to save the configuration file in Listing 14.2 as `Lab.json` and the script in Listing 14.3 as `Configure-Hosts.ps1` into `C:\Mastering vSphere\`, then you could run it in PowerCLI like this:

```
PS C:\>.\Mastering vSphere\Configure-Hosts.ps1 Lab.json
```

First, notice that we are passing the JSON configuration file as a parameter for the script so that we can select the JSON file we want to use for this run. The script and the specification are separate entities. so that we can update the configuration without changing the script. If the JSON file is not provided, the script will present a message that the parameter must be provided.

Next, the `Get-Content` and the `ConvertFrom-JSON` cmdlets read the specifications into PowerCLI and begin a loop through each host, setting the variables that need to be defined and called during the execution, such as the networking and datastore settings based on a `"management"` or `"workload"` tag. Once the variables are set for the first host in the loop, PowerCLI will initiate a connection to the hosts with the `Connect-VIServer` cmdlet using the username and password from the configuration file. It then loops through to configure and report its progress as follows:

◆ Step 1: Creates the storage port group on the host with the name and VLAN from the specification.

◆ Step 2: Creates the VMkernel for NFS storage traffic on the host with the IP, netmask, and MTU from the specification.

◆ Step 3: Mounts the first NFS datastore on the host with the datastore in the specification.

◆ Step 4: Mounts the second NFS datastore on the host with the datastore in the specification.

◆ Step 5: Creates the VM Network port group on the host with the name and VLAN from the specification.

◆ Step 6: Enables SSH and configures the auto-start policy.

◆ Step 7: Configures the NTP settings on each host using the NTP servers in the specification.

◆ Step 8: Configures the DNS settings on each host using the DNS servers in the specification.

Once the first host is completed, the script disconnects from the current host with the `Disconnect-VIServer` cmdlet and continues the loop for the remaining hosts in the JSON specification example.

There is so much more that you can do with PowerShell and PowerCLI—these examples just scratch the surface. In the next section, we will discuss some of the advanced capabilities available to automate vSphere with PowerCLI.

PowerCLI Advanced Capabilities

You should now have a good understanding of the many possibilities for automating a vSphere environment with PowerCLI. Next, we will demonstrate some advanced functionality that directly leverage the vSphere vCenter API.

PowerCLI users are not limited to just the cmdlets included in PowerCLI. VMware extends the capabilities of PowerCLI by allowing users to access various methods and information with the vSphere API. The Get-View cmdlet gives PowerCLI users the ability to call these methods a part of their PowerCLI scripts or directly from the PowerShell console.

Listing 14.4 shows a situation where an administrator recognized functionality in the vCente Server that was not natively available in the PowerCLI cmdlets. Specifically, when attempting t vMotion a VM, vCenter Server would perform checks to verify that the prerequisites for vMotio to that host were met. If something was found to be incorrect, vCenter Server would notify the administrator that vMotion could not be performed and generally identify the root cause. The purpose was to check every VM in a cluster prior to a scheduled maintenance window, allowin the administrator to identify any issues prior to the scheduled maintenance and address them t minimize delays or the need for rollback.

LISTING 14.4:   A PowerCLI function that tests vMotion capabilities of VMs

```
Function Test-vMotion{
param( [CmdletBinding()]
[Parameter(ValueFromPipeline=$true,Position=0,Mandatory=$false,`
HelpMessage="Enter the Cluster to be checked.")] [PSObject[]]$Cluster,
[Parameter(ValueFromPipeline=$false,Position=1,Mandatory=$false,`
HelpMessage="Enter the virtual machine to migrate.")] [PSObject[]]$VM,
[Parameter(ValueFromPipeline=$false,Position=2,Mandatory=$false,`
HelpMessage="Enter the destination host.")] [PSObject[]]$VMHost,
[Parameter(ValueFromPipeline=$false,Position=3,Mandatory=$false,`
HelpMessage="Set to false to Turn off console writing for use in
        Scheduled Tasks.")]
[Boolean]$Console=$true
)
$report = @()
#Sets information based on type of work being done.
#Whole cluster or single VM.
If($Cluster -ne $null){
If($VM -ne $null){
If($Console = $true){
Write-Host "VM value $VM cannot be used`
when using -Cluster parameter. Value is being set to null."
}
$VM = $null
}
If($VMHost -ne $null){
$DestHost = Get-VMHost $VMHost
If(($DestHost.ConnectionState -ne "Connected") -or`
($DestHost.PowerState -ne "PoweredOn")){
Return "You must provide a destination host that is powered on and`
not in Maintenance Mode or Disconnected>"
}
}
```

```
$singlevm = $false
$targetcluster = Get-Cluster $Cluster
$vms = $targetcluster | Get-VM | `
Where{$_.PowerState -eq "PoweredON"} | Sort-Object
$vmhosts = $targetcluster | Get-VMHost | `
Where{($_.ConnectionState -eq "Connected") -and `
($_.PowerState -eq "PoweredOn")}
If ($vmhosts.Count -lt 2){
Return "You must provide a target host that is not`
the source host $sourcehost"
}
$count = $vms.Count
If($Console = $true){
Write-Host ?Checking $count VMs in cluster $cluster"
}
} ELSE {
$vms = Get-VM $VM
If($VMHost -eq $null){
$DestHost = Get-Cluster -VM $vms | Get-VMHost | `
Where{($_.ConnectionState -eq "Connected") -and `
($_.PowerState -eq "PoweredOn")} | Get-Random | Where{$_ -ne $vms
.VMhost}
} ELSE {
$DestHost = Get-VMHost $VMHost
}
$singlevm = $true
}
#Functional Loop
foreach($v in $vms) {
If($Console = $true){
Write-Host "------------------------"
Write-Host "Checking $v ..."
}
$SourceHost = $v.VMhost
If($singlevm -eq $false){
While(($DestHost -eq $null) -or ($DestHost -eq $SourceHost)){
#Select random host from the cluster if Source
#and Destination are the same or Destination is Null.
$DestHost = $vmhosts | Get-Random | Where{($_ -ne $SourceHost)`
-and ($_ -ne $null)}
}
}
If($Console = $true){
Write-Host "from $SourceHost to $DestHost"
}
#Set Variables needed for CheckMigrate Method
$pool = ($v.ResourcePool).ExtensionData.MoRef
$vmMoRef = $v.ExtensionData.MoRef
```

```
$hsMoRef = $DestHost.ExtensionData.MoRef
$si = Get-View ServiceInstance -Server $global:DefaultVIServer
$VmProvCheck = get-view $si.Content.VmProvisioningChecker
$result = $VmProvCheck.CheckMigrate( $vmMoRef, $hsMoRef, $pool,
    $null, $null )
#Organize Output
$Output = "" | Select VM, SourceHost, DestinationHost,`
Error, Warning, CanMigrate
$Output.VM = $v.Name
$Output.SourceHost = $SourceHost
$Output.DestinationHost = $DestHost.Name
#Parse Error and Warning messages
If($result[0].Warning -ne $null){
$Output.Warning = $result[0].Warning[0].LocalizedMessage
$Output.CanMigrate = $true
If($Console = $true){
Write-Host -ForegroundColor Yellow`
"$v has warning but can still migrate"
}
}
If($result[0].Error -ne $null){
$Output.Error = $result[0].Error[0].LocalizedMessage
$Output.CanMigrate = $False
If($Console = $true){
Write-Host -ForegroundColor Red "$v has error and cannot migrate"
}
}Else {
$Output.CanMigrate = $true
If($Console = $true){
Write-Host -ForegroundColor Green "$v is OK"
}
}
$report += $Output
#This resets the Destination Host to the preferred host
#in case it had to be changed.
If($VMHost -ne $null){
$DestHost = Get-VMHost $VMHost
}
}
Return $report
# End Function
}
```

To accomplish this, the administrator must identify the method used in the vSphere API. VMware publishes the API documentation at www.vmware.com/support/pubs/sdk_pubs html. You can also use the API documentation by using the VMware {code} API Explorer at code.vmware.com/apis to browse, search, and inspect the APIs.

In the API documentation, you can locate the `CheckMigrate` method. The documentation outlines the required information to invoke the method. In the script (Listing 14.4) we collect the components, the VM, the destination host, and the resource pool as variables in the script prior to calling the `CheckMigrate` method. The entirety of the script revolves around the small amount of code seen below. Most of the script works on setting the required variables to use the `CheckMigrate` method and then handling the output of that method as follows:

```
# Set Variables needed for CheckMigrate Method
$pool = ($v.ResourcePool).ExtensionData.MoRef
$vmMoRef = $v.ExtensionData.MoRef
$hsMoRef = $DestHost.ExtensionData.MoRef
$si = Get-View ServiceInstance -Server $global:DefaultVIServer
$VmProvCheck = get-view $si.Content.VmProvisioningChecker
$result = $VmProvCheck.CheckMigrate($vmMoRef,$hsMoRef,$pool,$null,$null)
```

You should note that this script is built as a PowerShell function. This means it is designed to be loaded into a PowerShell console session and used like a cmdlet. For example, once you have loaded the function, you can call this command as follows:

```
Get-Cluster "ClusterName" | Test-vMotion
```

LOADING POWERSHELL FUNCTIONS

When you receive functions from trusted sources such as VMware or trusted community contributors, you will need to load them into your PowerCLI/PowerShell session. This is done by "dot-sourcing" the function. You simply need to type a period, followed by a space, followed by the complete path to the function. Unless you add the function to your PowerShell profile, you will need to reload it for each new session of PowerCLI, as in this example:

```
PS C:\>.\Mastering vSphere\Test-vMotion.ps1
```

You should now have a solid understanding of the vast capabilities of PowerCLI and how to get started. We have provided you with the essential information to help you start the journey towards automating vSphere.

Additional Resources

As you get started with PowerCLI, and even as you dive into more advanced scripting, remember that there are many resources to help enable and support you in your journey. Let's look at some of these.

First and foremost are the VMware PowerCLI product pages on VMware {code} and the PowerShell Gallery. You can get the latest documentation and reference material for the most recent versions of PowerCLI from the following sources:

◆ VMware PowerCLI on VMware {code}: `code.vmware.com/web/dp/tool/vmware-powercli/`

◆ VMware PowerCLI in the PowerShell Gallery: `powershellgallery.com/packages/VMware.PowerCLI/`

You can also make use of the vibrant VMware community to get help. The VMware Community forums, the VMware PowerCLI blog, and the VMware {code} Sample Exchange a excellent resources to browse and download code samples directly from VMware as well as cc samples contributed by the VMware community. You can also submit requests for new sample or contribute your own scripts to the community. Use the VMware {code} API Explorer to star learning, modeling, and using the vSphere API though PowerCLI.

- VMware Communities: `vmware.com/go/powercli`
- VMware PowerCLI blog: `blogs.vmware.com/powercli`
- VMware {code} Sample Exchange: `code.vmware.com/samples`
- VMware {code} API Explorer: `code.vmware.com/apis`
- VMware PowerCLI posters: `vmware.com/go/posters`

We also highly recommend the book *VMware vSphere PowerCLI Reference: Automating vSphe Administration, 2nd Edition* (Sybex, 2016). It contains a wealth of information and detailed explanations of PowerCLI capabilities. And remember to always look to the community forun and bloggers for assistance as you navigate PowerCLI.

Happy automating!

The Bottom Line

Identify automation solutions for VMware vSphere.   With over 600 cmdlets, the most widely adopted automation tool to manage and automate vSphere is PowerCLI. Some additional vSphere automation tools provided by VMware include the vSphere Automatio SDKs with libraries for programmatically accessing features available via the API. vRealize Orchestrator provides the ability to use the out-of-the-box workflows or design and deploy custom, scalable workflows to automate vSphere processes.

> **Master It**   Explore these and additional options for vSphere automation tools by VMw and third-party providers that leverage the vSphere Automation SDKs.

Use PowerCLI on multiple platforms.   PowerCLI 10 introduced multi-platform support b adding macOS and Linux support with PowerShell Core after the Microsoft PowerShell Tea open-sourced the PowerShell base code with the release of PowerShell 6.0. PowerShell and PowerCLI can now run on Windows, macOS, and Linux.

> **Master It**   Practice installing PowerShell and VMware PowerCLI on each platform. Fro each OS, grow your scripting to more complex scenarios to make common, repetitive, a often error-prone tasks a breeze. Use Microsoft Visual Code with an integrated shell and plug-ins for a common development interface.

Create PowerCLI scripts to automate common tasks.   VMware PowerCLI builds on the Power of the PowerShell scripting language to provide you with a simple yet powerful way automate tasks within the vSphere environment and the ability to do so from your platform of choice. It is easy to get started with your first one-liner and grow your scripting to more complex scenarios to make common, repetitive, and often error-prone tasks a breeze.

Master It   If you are familiar with other scripting languages, what would be the biggest hurdle in learning to use PowerShell and PowerCLI, other than syntax?

Appendix A

The Bottom Line

Chapter 1: Introducing VMware vSphere 6.7

Identify the role of each product in the vSphere product suite. The VMware vSphere product suite contains VMware ESXi and vCenter Server. ESXi provides the base virtualization functionality and enables features like Virtual SMP. vCenter Server provides management for ESXi and enables functionality like vMotion, Storage vMotion, vSphere Distributed Resource Scheduler (DRS), vSphere High Availability (HA), and vSphere Fault Tolerance (FT). Storage I/O Control and Network I/O Control provide granular resource controls for VMs. The vStorage APIs for Data Protection (VADP) provide a backup framework that allows for the integration of third-party backup solutions into a vSphere implementation.

> **Master It** Which products are licensed features within the VMware vSphere suite?

> **Master It** Which two features of VMware ESXi and VMware vCenter Server together aim to reduce or eliminate downtime due to unplanned hardware failures?

> **Solution** vSphere HA and vSphere FT are designed to reduce (vSphere HA) and eliminate (vSphere FT) the downtime resulting from unplanned hardware failures.

Recognize the interaction and dependencies between the products in the vSphere suite. VMware ESXi forms the foundation of the vSphere product suite, but some features require the presence of vCenter Server. Features like vMotion, Storage vMotion, vSphere DRS, vSphere HA, vSphere FT, SIOC, and NIOC require ESXi as well as vCenter Server.

> **Master It** Name three features that are supported only when using vCenter Server along with ESXi.

> **Solution** All of the following features are available only with vCenter Server: vSphere vMotion, Storage vMotion, vSphere DRS, Storage DRS, vSphere HA, vSphere FT, SIOC, and NIOC.

> **Master It** Name two features that are supported without vCenter Server but with a licensed installation of ESXi.

> **Solution** Features that are supported by VMware ESXi without vCenter Server include core virtualization features like virtualized networking, virtualized storage, vSphere vSMP, and resource allocation controls.

Understand how vSphere differs from other virtualization products. VMware vSphere's hypervisor, ESXi, uses a Type 1 bare-metal hypervisor that handles I/O directly within the hypervisor. This means that a host operating system, like Windows or Linux, is not required in order for ESXi to function. Although other virtualization solutions are listed as "Type 1 bare-metal hypervisors," most other Type 1 hypervisors on the market today require the presence of a "parent partition" or "dom0" through which all VM I/O must travel.

Master It   One of the administrators on your team asked whether he should install the standard Red Hat Linux (RHEL) deployment on the new servers you purchased for ESXi. What should you tell him, and why?

Solution   VMware ESXi is a bare-metal hypervisor that does not require the installation of a general-purpose host operating system. Therefore, it's unnecessary to install Linux on the equipment that was purchased for ESXi.

Chapter 2: Planning and Installing VMware ESXi

Understand ESXi compatibility requirements.   Unlike traditional operating systems like Windows or Linux, ESXi has much stricter hardware compatibility requirements. This helps ensure a stable, well-tested product line that can support even the most mission-critical applications.

Master It   You have some older servers onto which you'd like to deploy ESXi. They aren't on the Compatibility Guide. Will they work with ESXi?

Solution   They might, but they won't be fully supported by VMware. In all likelihood, the CPUs in these older servers don't support some of the hardware virtualization extensions or don't support 64-bit operation, both of which would directly impact the ability of ESXi to run on that hardware. You should choose only hardware that is on the Compatibility Guide.

Plan an ESXi deployment.   Deploying ESXi will affect many different areas of your organization—not only the server team but also the networking team, the storage team, and the security team. There are many issues to consider, including server hardware, storage hardware, storage protocols or connection types, network topology, and network connections. Failing to plan properly could result in an unstable and unsupported implementation.

Master It   Name three areas of networking that must be considered in a vSphere design.

Solution   Among other things, networking areas that must be considered include VLAN support, link aggregation, network speed (1 Gbps or 10 Gbps), load-balancing algorithms, and the number of NICs and network ports required.

Master It   What are some of the different types of storage that ESXi can be installed on?

Solution   By far the most common way to boot ESXi is the Local/Direct attached disks, but also supported are USB / SD storage, an isolated SAN boot LUN, and using iSCSI.

Deploy ESXi.   ESXi can be installed onto any supported and compatible hardware platform. You have three different ways to deploy ESXi: install it interactively, perform an unattended installation, or use vSphere Auto Deploy to provision ESXi as it boots up.

Master It   Your manager asks you to provide a copy of the unattended installation script that you will be using when you roll out ESXi using vSphere Auto Deploy. Is this something you can give?

Solution   No. When using vSphere Auto Deploy, there is no installation script. The vSphere Auto Deploy server streams an ESXi image to the physical host as it boots up. Redeployment of an ESXi host with vSphere Auto Deploy can be as simple as a reboot.

Master It   Name two advantages and two disadvantages of using vSphere Auto Deploy to provision ESXi hosts.

Solution   Some advantages include fast provisioning, fast reprovisioning, and the ability to quickly incorporate new ESXi images or updates into the provisioning process. Some disadvantages include additional complexity and dependency on additional infrastructure.

Perform post-installation configuration of ESXi.   Following the installation of ESXi, some additional configuration steps may be required. For example, if the wrong NIC is assigned to the management network, the server won't be accessible across the network. You'll also need to configure time synchronization.

Master It   You've installed ESXi on your server, but the welcome web page is inaccessible, and the server doesn't respond to a ping. What could be the problem?

Solution   More than likely, the wrong NIC was selected for use with the management network or the incorrect VLAN was selected. You'll need to use the Direct Console User Interface (DCUI) directly at the physical console of the ESXi host in order to reconfigure the management network and restore network connectivity.

Use the vSphere Host Client.   ESXi is managed using the vSphere Host Client, a HTML5-based web UI that provides the functionality to manage the virtualization platform.

Master It   Can you use the VMware installable vSphere client to manage your new ESXi 6.7 hosts?

Solution   No. vSphere 6.7 can not be managed by the legacy installable vSphere clients.

Chapter 3: Installing and Configuring vCenter Server

Understand the components and role of vCenter Server.   vCenter Server plays a central role in the management of ESXi hosts and VMs. Key features such as vMotion, Storage vMotion, vSphere DRS, vSphere HA, and vSphere FT are all enabled and made possible by vCenter Server. vCenter Server provides scalable authentication and role-based administration based on integration with Active Directory.

Master It   Specifically with regard to authentication, what are three key advantages of using vCenter Server?

Solution   First, vCenter Server centralizes the authentication so that user accounts don't have to be managed on a per-host basis. Second, vCenter Server eliminates the need to share the root password for hosts or to use complex configurations to allow administrators to perform tasks on the hosts. Third, vCenter Server brings role-based administration for the granular management of hosts and VMs while also providing additional roles above and beyond what stand-alone ESXi offers.

Plan a vCenter Server deployment. Planning a vCenter Server deployment includes selecting a backend database engine, choosing an authentication method, sizing the hardwa appropriately, and providing a sufficient level of high availability and business continuity. You must also decide whether you will run vCenter Server as a VM or on a physical system Finally, you must decide whether you will use the Windows Server–based version of vCent Server or deploy the vCenter Server virtual appliance.

Master It What are some of the advantages and disadvantages of running vCenter Server as a VM?

Solution Some of the advantages include the ability to easily clone the VM for backup o disaster-recovery purposes, the ability to take snapshots to protect against data loss or dat corruption, and the ability to leverage features such as vMotion or Storage vMotion. Some the disadvantages include the inability to cold-clone the vCenter Server VM, cold-migrate the vCenter Server VM (because vCenter needs to be online to clone or migrate VMs), or edit the virtual hardware of the vCenter Server VM. It can also add additional recovery complexity if an outage occurs on the infrastructure running the vCenter Server VM.

Master It What are some of the advantages of using the vCenter Server virtual appliance?

Solution Some of the advantages are a potentially much easier deployment (just use t vCenter Deploment Tool and perform post-deployment configuration instead of installi Windows Server, installing prerequisites, and finally, installing vCenter Server), more services available with a single deployment, and no Windows Server licensing requirements.

Install and configure a vCenter Server database. vCenter Server supports several enterprise- grade database engines, including Oracle and Microsoft SQL Server. Depending on th database in use, there are specific configuration steps and specific permissions that must be applied in order for vCenter Server to work properly.

Master It Why is it important to protect the database engine used to support vCenter Server?

Solution Although vCenter Server uses Microsoft Active Directory for authentication, the majority of the information managed by vCenter Server is stored in the backend database. The loss of the backend database would mean the loss of significant amounts data that are crucial to the operation of vCenter Server. Organizations should take adequate steps to protect the backend database accordingly.

Install and configure the Platform Services Controller. The Platform Services Controller i an architectural change in vCenter Server 6. Along with SSO, it allows the vSphere Client to present multiple solutions interfaces within a single console provided the authenticated use has access.

Master It After installing vCenter 6.7 and all the appropriate components, you cannot log into the vCenter Server Web Client with your local credentials and gain access to vCenter. What could be missing from the configuration of SSO?

Solution   When configuring SSO, you have the ability to link it to an external directory service such as Active Directory. The other option is to manually configure local accounts within SSO itself. These are local to SSO, not local to the server that SSO is installed on.

Install and configure vCenter Server.   vCenter Server is installed using the VMware vCenter Server Appliance Installer. You can install vCenter Server as a stand-alone instance or join a linked mode group for greater scalability.

Master It   When preparing to install multiple vCenter Servers, are there any concerns about using a single Platform Services Controller versus multiple? Can this be handled later?

Solution   When installing vCenter on Windows, the account just needs administrative permissions on the computer where vCenter Server is being installed. In previous versions, if you were using Microsoft SQL Server with Windows authentication, you had to log on to the computer that was going to run vCenter Server by using the account previously configured with the appropriate permissions on the SQL server and the SQL database. This is because the earlier versions of the vCenter Server Installer did not provide the ability to choose which account to use; it used the currently logged-on account. This is no longer the case for vCenter Server 5.0 and above.

Use vCenter Server's management features.   vCenter Server provides a wide range of management features for ESXi hosts and VMs. These features include scheduled tasks, host profiles for consistent configurations, tags for metadata, and event logging.

Master It   Your department just merged vSphere environments with another department, and your manager has asked for you to find a way of easily tracking both departments' virtual machines. How would you go about accomplishing that task?

Solution   Provided you have vCenter Server configured with the appropriate tags and categories, a simple search on his requirements should provide enough information for your manager.

Provide Visibility into vCenter Server's settings.   vCenter Server Appliance Management Interface provides insight into its health, configuration, and settings.

Master It   Your manager has asked you why the vCenter Server recently came back on an audit report saying that SSH is enabled. What section in vCenter Server's VAMI will help you in this task?

Solution   The VAMI Access menu has controls to enable or disable SSH logins, the DCUI, the Console CLI, and the Bash Shell.

Master It   You recently added a few more Active Directory domain controllers within your environment after a recent refresh and configured them to replace your older time server. How can you update the NTP servers on your vCenter Servers and Platform Services Controllers?

Solution   The PSC and vCenter VAMI interfaces can be used to configure NTP settings under the Time menu.

Chapter 4: vSphere Update Manager and the vCenter Support Tools

Determine which ESXi hosts or VMs need to be patched or upgraded. Baselines are the "measuring sticks" whereby VUM knows whether an ESXi host or VM instance is up-to-date. VUM compares the ESXi hosts or VMs to the baselines to determine whether they need to be patched and, if so, what patches need to be applied. VUM also uses baselines to determine which ESXi hosts need to be upgraded to the latest version or which VMs need to have their VM hardware upgraded. VUM comes with some predefined baselines and allows administrators to create additional baselines specific to their environments. Baselines can be fixed—the contents remain constant—or they can be dynamic, where the contents of the baseline change over time. Baseline groups allow administrators to combine baselines and apply them together.

Master It In addition to ensuring that all your ESXi hosts have the latest critical and security patches installed, you need to ensure that all your ESXi hosts have another specific patch installed. This additional patch is noncritical and therefore doesn't get included in the critical patch dynamic baseline. How do you work around this problem?

Solution Create a baseline group that combines the critical patch dynamic baseline with a fixed baseline that contains the additional patch you want installed on all ESX/ESXi hosts. Attach the baseline group to all your ESX/ESXi hosts. When you perform remediation, VUM will ensure that all the critical patches in the dynamic baseline plus the additional patch in the fixed baseline are applied to the hosts.

Use VUM to upgrade VM hardware or VMware Tools. VUM can detect VMs with outdated VM hardware versions and guest OSs that have outdated versions of VMware Tools installed. VUM comes with predefined baselines that enable this functionality. In addition, VUM has the ability to upgrade VM hardware versions and upgrade VMware Tools inside guest OSs to ensure that everything is kept up-to-date. This functionality is especially helpful after upgrading your ESXi hosts to version 6.7 from a previous version.

Master It You've just finished upgrading your virtual infrastructure to VMware vSphere. What two additional tasks should you complete?

Solution Upgrade VMware Tools in the guest OSs and then upgrade the virtual machine hardware to version 14.

Apply patches to ESXi hosts. Like other complex software products, VMware ESXi needs software patches applied from time to time. These patches might be bug fixes or security fixes. To keep your ESXi hosts up-to-date with the latest patches, you can have VUM apply patches to your hosts on a schedule of your choosing. In addition, to reduce downtime during the patching process or perhaps to simplify the deployment of patches to remote offices, VUM can stage patches to ESXi hosts before the patches are applied.

Master It How can you avoid VM downtime when applying patches (for example, remediating) to your ESXi hosts?

Solution VUM automatically leverages advanced VMware vSphere features like Distributed Resource Scheduler (DRS). If you make sure that your ESX/ESXi hosts are in a fully automated DRS cluster, VUM will leverage vMotion and DRS to move VMs to other ESX/ESXi hosts, avoiding downtime to patch the hosts.

Upgrade hosts and coordinate large-scale datacenter upgrades. Upgrading hosts manually, with each host having dozens of VMs on it, is burdensome and doesn't scale well once you have more than a handful to deal with. Short outage windows, host reboots, and VM downtime mean that coordinating upgrades can involve complex planning and careful execution.

Master It Which VUM functionality can simplify the process of upgrading vSphere across a large number of hosts and their VMs?

Solution VUM can take care of these interactions in an automated fashion with what is known as an orchestrated upgrade. An orchestrated upgrade combines several baseline groups that include updates for the hosts and subsequent updates for the VMs' hardware and VMware Tools. Virtual appliance upgrade baselines can also be included. When combined with fully automated DRS clusters and sufficient redundant capacity, potentially an entire vCenter's host inventory can be upgraded in one orchestrated task.

Use alternative approaches to VUM updates when required. VUM presents the simplest and most efficient method to upgrade your vSphere hosts. However, sometimes VUM may not be available. For example, VUM is reliant on vCenter, so if the host isn't connected to a licensed vCenter, an alternate method to upgrade the host must be used.

Master It Without using VUM, how else can you upgrade an existing host?

Solution You can grab the CD install media and run an interactive upgrade on the host. You can also use the inherent command-line tool on the hosts' themselves: esxcli software vib update (see VMware Knowledge Base article 2008939 for full details) or esxcli software vib install to patch them with individual VIBs.

Configure hosts for centralized logging. To make use of the ESXi Dump Collector, you must configure each host to point to the centralized loggers.

Master It You have just started a new job as the vSphere administrator at a company. The company hasn't previously centralized the hosts' core dumps and you decide you want to collect them, and so you want to setup the ESXi Dump Collector tool. How do you go about setting this up on the company's vCSA instance?

Solution The Syslog Collector and ESXi Dump Collector are already included in vCSA and enabled by default. You should log into the vCSA console and check that the services are running. Also, ensure you adjust the core dump's repository so it's large enough for their environment.

Chapter 5: Creating and Configuring a vSphere Network

Identify the components of virtual networking. Virtual networking is a blend of virtual switches, physical switches, VLANs, physical network adapters, VMkernel adapters, uplinks, NIC teaming, virtual machines, and port groups.

Master It What factors contribute to the design of a virtual network and the components involved?

Solution Many factors contribute to a virtual network design: the number of physical network adapters in each ESXi host, using vSphere Standard Switches versus vSphere Distributed Switches, the presence or use of VLANs in the environment, the existing network topology, requirements for the support of LACP or port mirroring, and the connectivity needs of the VMs in the environment are all factors that will play a role in the final network design. These are some common questions to ask while designing the network:

◆ Do you have or need a dedicated network for management traffic, such as for the management of physical switches?

◆ Do you have or need a dedicated network for vMotion traffic?

◆ Are you using 1 Gb Ethernet or 10 Gb Ethernet?

◆ Do you have an IP storage network? Is this IP storage network a dedicated network? Are you running iSCSI or NAS/NFS?

◆ Do you need extremely high levels of fault tolerance for VMs?

◆ Is the existing physical network composed of VLANs?

◆ Do you want to extend the use of VLANs into the virtual switches?

Create virtual switches and distributed virtual switches.   vSphere supports both vSphere Standard Switches and vSphere Distributed Switches. vSphere Distributed Switches bring new functionality to the vSphere networking environment, including private VLANs and a centralized point of management for ESXi clusters.

Master It   You've asked a fellow vSphere administrator to create a vSphere Distributed Switch for you, but the administrator can't complete the task because he can't find out how to do this with an ESXi host selected in the vSphere Client. What should you tell this administrator?

Solution   vSphere Distributed Switches aren't created on a per–ESXi host basis but instead span multiple ESXi hosts at the same time. This is what enables the centralized configuration and management of distributed port groups. Tell the administrator to navigate to the Distributed Switches area of the vSphere Client to create a new vSphere Distributed Switch.

Create and manage NIC teaming, VLANs, and private VLANs.   NIC teaming allows virtual switches to have redundant network connections to the rest of the network. Virtual switches also provide support for VLANs, which provide logical segmentation of the network, and private VLANs, which provide added security to existing VLANs while allowing systems to share the same IP subnet.

Master It   You'd like to use NIC teaming to make the best use of physical uplinks for both greater redundancy and improved throughput, even under network contention. Which load-balancing policy on the distributed switch should you use?

Solution   Route Based on Physical NIC load ensures that the physical uplinks are utilized efficiently under contention.

Master It   How do you configure both a vSphere Standard Switch and a vSphere Distributed Switch to pass VLAN tags all the way up to a guest OS?

Solution   On a vSphere Standard Switch, you configure Virtual Guest Tagging (VGT, the name of this particular configuration) by setting the VLAN ID for the VM's port group to 409

Configure virtual switch security policies. Virtual switches support security policies for allowing or rejecting Promiscuous mode, allowing or rejecting MAC address changes, and allowing or rejecting forged transmits. All of the security options can help increase Layer 2 security.

Master It You have a networking application that needs to see traffic on the virtual network that is intended for other production systems on the same VLAN. The networking application accomplishes this by using Promiscuous mode. How can you accommodate the needs of this networking application without sacrificing the security of the entire virtual switch?

Solution Because port groups (or distributed port groups) can override the security policy settings for a virtual switch, and because there can be multiple port groups/distributed port groups that correspond to a VLAN, the best solution involves creating another port group that has all the same settings as the other production port group, including the same VLAN ID. This new port group should allow Promiscuous mode. Assign the VM with the networking application to this new port group, but leave the remainder of the VMs on a port group that rejects Promiscuous mode. This allows the networking application to see the traffic it needs to see without overly compromising the security of the entire virtual switch.

Master It Another vSphere administrator on your team is trying to configure the security policies on a distributed switch but is having some difficulty. What could be the problem?

Solution On a vSphere Distributed Switch, all security policies are set at the distributed port group level, not at the distributed switch level. Tell the administrator to modify the properties of the distributed port group(s), not the distributed switch itself. She can also use the Manage Distributed Port Groups command on the Actions menu in the vSphere Client to perform the same task on multiple distributed port groups at the same time.

Chapter 6: Creating and Configuring Storage Devices

Differentiate and understand the fundamentals of shared storage. vSphere depends on shared storage for advanced functions, cluster-wide availability, and the aggregate performance of all the VMs in a cluster. Designing a high-performance and highly available shared storage infrastructure is possible on Fibre Channel, FCoE, and iSCSI SANs and is possible using NAS; in addition, it's available from midrange to enterprise storage architectures. Always design the storage architecture to meet the performance requirements first, and then ensure that capacity requirements are met as a corollary.

Master It Identify examples where each of the protocol choices would be ideal for different vSphere deployments.

Solution iSCSI would be a good choice for a customer with no existing Fibre Channel SAN and getting started with vSphere. Fibre Channel would be a good choice for a customer with an existing Fibre Channel infrastructure or for those that have VMs with high-bandwidth (200 MBps+) requirements (not in aggregate but individually). NFS would be a good choice where there are many VMs with a low-bandwidth requirement individually (and in aggregate) that is less than a single link's worth of bandwidth.

Master It Identify the three storage performance parameters and the primary determinant of storage performance and how to quickly estimate it for a given storage configuration.

Solution The three factors to consider are bandwidth (MBps), throughput (IOPS), and latency (ms). The maximum bandwidth for a single datastore (or RDM) for Fibre Channel is the HBA speed times the number of HBAs in the system (check the fan-in ratio and number of Fibre Channel ports on the array). The maximum bandwidth for a single datastore (or RDM) for iSCSI is the NIC speed times the number of NICs in the system, up to about 9 Gbps (check the fan-in ratio and number of Ethernet ports on the array). The maximum bandwidth for a single NFS datastore for NFS is the NIC link speed (across multiple datastores, the bandwidth can be balanced across multiple NICs). In all cases, the throughput (IOPS) is primarily a function of the number of spindles (assuming no cache benefit and no RAID loss). A quick rule of thumb is that the total number of IOPS = IOPS × the number of that type of spindle. Latency is in milliseconds, though it can get to tens of milliseconds in cases where the storage array is overtaxed.

Understand vSphere storage options. vSphere has four fundamental storage presentation models: vSAN, VMFS on block, RDM, and NFS. The most flexible configurations use all four predominantly via a shared-container model and selective use of RDMs.

Master It Characterize use cases for vSAN, VMFS datastores, NFS datastores, and RDMs.

Solution vSAN, VMFS and NFS datastores are shared-container models; they store virtual disks together. VMFS is governed by the block storage stack, and NFS is governed by the network stack. NFS is generally (without use of 10 GbE LANs) best suited to large numbers of low bandwidth (any throughput) VMs. VMFS is suited for a wide range of workloads. RDMs should be used sparingly for cases where the guest must have direct access to a single LUN.

Master It If you're using VMFS and there's one performance metric to track, what would it be? Configure a monitor for that metric.

Solution The metric to measure is queue depth. Use esxtop or the Web Client Performance Charts to monitor. The datastore-availability or used-capacity managed datastore alerts are good nonperformance metrics to use.

Configure storage at the vSphere layer. After a shared storage platform is selected, vSphere needs a storage network configured. The network (whether Fibre Channel or Ethernet based) must be designed to meet availability and throughput requirements, which are influenced by protocol choice and vSphere fundamental storage stack (and in the case of vSAN and NFS, the network stack) architecture. Proper network design involves physical redundancy and physical or logical isolation mechanisms (SAN zoning and network VLANs). With connectivity in place, configure LUNs and VMFS datastores and/or NFS exports/NFS datastores using the predictive or adaptive model (or a hybrid model). Use Storage vMotion to resolve hot spots and other non-optimal VM placement.

Master It What would best identify an oversubscribed VMFS datastore from a performance standpoint? How would you identify the issue? What is it most likely to be? What would be two possible corrective actions you could take?

Solution An oversubscribed VMFS datastore is best identified by evaluating the queue depth and would manifest as slow VMs. The best way to track this is with ESXTOP, using the QUED (the Queue Depth column). If the queue is full, take any or all of these courses of action: make the queue deeper and increase the Disk.SchedNumReqOutstanding advanced parameter to match; vacate VMs (using Storage vMotion); or add more spindles to the LUN so that it can fulfill the requests more rapidly or move to a faster spindle type.

Master It A VMFS volume is filling up. What are three possible nondisruptive corrective actions you could take?

Solution The actions you could take are as follows:

◆ Use Storage vMotion to migrate some VMs to another datastore.

◆ Grow the backing LUN, and grow the VMFS volume.

◆ Add another backing LUN, and add another VMFS extent.

Master It What would best identify an oversubscribed NFS volume from a performance standpoint? How would you identify the issue? What is it most likely to be? What are two possible corrective actions you could take?

Solution The workload in the datastore is reaching the maximum bandwidth of a single link. The easiest way to identify the issue would be using the vCenter performance charts and examining the VMkernel NIC's utilization. If it is at 100 percent, the only options are to upgrade to 10 GbE or to add another NFS datastore, add another VMkernel NIC, follow the load-balancing and high-availability decision tree to determine whether NIC teaming or IP routing would work best, and finally, use Storage vMotion to migrate some VMs to another datastore (remember that the NIC teaming/IP routing works for multiple datastores, not for a single datastore). Remember that using Storage vMotion adds additional work to an already busy datastore, so consider scheduling it during a low I/O period, even though it can be done live.

Configure storage at the VM layer. With datastores in place, create VMs. During the creation of the VMs, place VMs in the appropriate datastores, and employ selective use of RDMs but only where required. Leverage in-guest iSCSI where it makes sense but understand the impact to your vSphere environment.

Master It Without turning the machine off, convert the virtual disks on a VMFS volume from thin to thick (eager zeroed thick) and back to thin.

Solution Use Storage vMotion and select the target disk format during the Storage vMotion process.

Master It Identify where you would use a physical compatibility mode RDM and configure that use case.

Solution One use case would be a Microsoft Windows cluster. You should download the VMware Microsoft clustering guide and follow that use case. Other valid answers are a case where virtual-to-physical mobility of the LUNs is required or one where a Solutions Enabler VM is needed.

Leverage best practices for shared storage with vSphere. Read, follow, and leverage key VMware and storage vendors' best practices and solutions guide documentation. Don't oversize up front, but instead learn to leverage VMware and storage array features to monitor performance, queues, and backend load, and then nondisruptively adapt. Plan for performance first and capacity second. (Usually capacity is a given for performance requirements to be met.) Spend design time on availability design and on the large, heavy I/O VMs, and use flexible pool design for the general-purpose VMFS and NFS datastores.

Master It Quickly estimate the minimum usable capacity needed for 200 VMs with an average VM size of 40 GB. Make some assumptions about vSphere snapshots. What would be the raw capacity needed in the array if you used RAID 10? RAID 5 (4+1)? RAID 6 (10+2)? What would you do to nondisruptively cope if you ran out of capacity?

Solution Using rule-of-thumb math, 200 × 40 GB = 8 TB × 25 percent extra space (snapshots, other VMware files) = 10 TB. Using RAID 10, you would need at least 20 TB raw. Using RAID 5 (4+1), you would need 12.5 TB. Using RAID 6 (10+2), you would need 12 TB. If you ran out of capacity, you could add capacity to your array and then add datastores and use Storage vMotion. If your array supports dynamic growth of LUNs, you could grow the VMFS or NFS datastores, and if it doesn't, you could add more VMFS extents.

Master It Using the configurations in the previous question, what would the minimum amount of raw capacity need to be if the VMs are actually only 20 GB of data in each VM, even though they are provisioning 40 GB and you used thick on an array that didn't support thin provisioning? What if the array did support thin provisioning? What if you used Storage vMotion to convert from thick to thin (both in the case where the array supports thin provisioning and, in the case where it doesn't)?

Solution If you use thick virtual disks on an array that doesn't support thin provisioning, the answers are the same as for the previous question. If you use an array that does support thin provisioning, the answers are cut down by 50 percent: 20 TB for RAID 10, 6.25 TB for RAID 5 (4+1), and 6 TB for RAID 6 (10+2). If you use Storage vMotion to convert to thin on the array that doesn't support thin provisioning, the result is the same, just as it is if you do thin on thin.

Master It Estimate the number of spindles needed for 100 VMs that drive 200 IOPS each and are 40 GB in size. Assume no RAID loss or cache gain. How many if you use 500 GB SATA 7200 RPM? 300 GB 10K Fibre Channel/SAS? 300 GB 15K Fibre Channel/SAS? 160 GB consumer-grade SSD? 200 GB enterprise flash?

Solution This exercise highlights the foolishness of looking just at capacity in the server use case. 100 × 40 GB = 4 TB usable × 200 IOPS = 20,000 IOPS. With 500 GB 7200 RPM, that's 250 drives, which have 125 TB raw (non-optimal). With 300 GB 10K RPM, that's 167 drives, which have 50 TB raw (non-optimal). With 15K RPM, that's 111 drives with 16 TB raw (getting closer). With consumer-grade SSD, that's 20 spindles and 3.2 TB raw (too little). With EFD, that's 4 spindles and 800 GB raw (too little). The moral of the story is that the 15K RPM 146 GB drive is the sweet spot for this workload. Note that the extra space can't be used unless you can find a workload that doesn't need any performance at all; the spindles are working as hard as they can. Also note that the 4 TB requirement was usable, and I was calculating the raw storage capacity. Therefore, in this case, RAID 5, RAID 6, and RAID 10 would all have extra usable capacity in the end. It's unusual to have all VMs with a common workload, and 200 IOPS (as an average) is relatively high. This exercise also shows why it's efficient to have several tiers and several datastores for different classes of VMs (put some on SATA, some on Fibre Channel, some on EFD or SSD)—because you can be more efficient.

Chapter 7: Ensuring High Availability and Business Continuity

Understand Windows clustering and the different types of clusters.   Windows clustering plays a central role in the design of any high-availability solution for both virtual and physical servers. Windows clustering gives us the ability to have application failover to the secondary server when the primary server fails.

> **Master It**   Specifically with regard to Windows clustering in a virtual environment, what are three different types of cluster configurations that you can have?
>
> **Solution**   The first is a cluster in a box, which is mainly used for testing or in a development environment where both nodes of a Windows cluster run on the same ESXi host. The second is the cluster across boxes, which is the most common form of clustering in a virtual environment. In this configuration, you can use Windows clustering on VMs that are running on different physical hosts. The third is the physical-to-virtual configuration, where you have the best of both the physical and virtual worlds by having a Windows clustering node on both a physical server and a virtual server.
>
> **Master It**   What is the key difference between NLB clusters and Windows failover clusters?
>
> **Solution**   Network load balancing (NLB) clusters are used primarily for scaling performance. Windows failover clusters are primarily used for high availability and redundancy.

Use vSphere's built-in high-availability functionality.   VMware Virtual Infrastructure has high-availability options built in and available to you out of the box: vSphere High Availability (HA) and vSphere Fault Tolerance (FT). These options help you provide better uptime for your critical applications.

> **Master It**   What are the two types of high-availability options that VMware provides in vSphere, and how are they different?
>
> **Solution**   VMware provides two forms of high availability in vSphere. vSphere HA provides a form of high availability by giving you the ability to restart any VMs that were running on a host that crashes. vSphere SMP Fault Tolerance (FT) uses Checkpoint technology to send the result of processed inputs to a secondary VM on another host in the cluster. Failover from the primary VM to the secondary VM is without any downtime. vSphere HA restarts the VM in the event of failure; vSphere SMP-FT does not need to restart the VM because the secondary VM is kept in sync with the primary and can take over immediately in the event of a failure.

Recognize differences between high-availability solutions.   A high-availability solution that operates at the application layer, like Oracle Real Application Cluster (RAC), is different in architecture and operation from an OS-level clustering solution like Windows failover clustering. Similarly, OS-level clustering solutions are very different from hypervisor-based solutions such as vSphere HA or vSphere FT. Each approach has advantages and disadvantages, and today's administrators will likely need to use multiple approaches in their datacenter.

Master It   Name one advantage of a hypervisor-based high-availability solution over an OS-level solution.

Solution   Because a hypervisor-based solution would operate beneath the guest OS level, it would operate independently of the guest OS and could therefore potentially support any number of different guest OSs. Depending on the implementation, hypervisor-based solutions might be simpler than OS-level solutions. For example, vSphere HA is generally less complex and easier to set up or configure than Windows failover clustering.

Understand additional components of business continuity.   There are other components of ensuring business continuity for your organization. Data protection (backups) and replication of your data to a secondary location are two areas that can help ensure that business continuity needs are satisfied, even in the event of a disaster.

Master It   What are three methods to replicate your data to a secondary location, and what is the golden rule for any continuity plan?

Solution   First, you have the backup and restore method from tape. It is a best practice to keep backup tapes off site and, when they are needed after a disaster, have them shipped to the secondary site. Second, you can replicate your data by using replication at the SAN level. This gives you the ability to replicate data over both short and long distances. Third, you can use a disk-to-disk backup appliance, such as vSphere Replication, that also offers offsite replication to another location. This method offers shorter backup windows as well as the benefits of offsite backups. Finally, the golden rule for any successful continuity design is to test, test, and test again.

Chapter 8: Securing VMware vSphere

Configure and control authentication to vSphere.   Both ESXi and vCenter Server have authentication mechanisms, and both products can utilize local users or users defined in external directories. Authentication is a basic tenet of security; it's important to verify that users are who they claim to be. You can manage local users on your ESXi hosts using either the traditional vSphere Client or the command-line interface (such as the vSphere Management Assistant). Both the Windows-based and the Linux-based virtual appliance versions of vCenter Server can leverage Active Directory, OpenLDAP, or local SSO accounts for authentication as well.

Master It   You've asked an administrator on your team to create some accounts on an ESXi host. The administrator is uncomfortable with the command line and is having a problem figuring out how to create the users. Is there another way for this administrator to perform this task?

Solution   Yes, the administrator can use the web based vSphere Client UI and connect directly to the ESXi hosts on which the accounts need to be created.

Manage roles and access controls.   Both ESXi and vCenter Server possess a role-based access control system that combines users, groups, privileges, roles, and permissions. vSphere administrators can use this role-based access control system to define very granular permissions that define what users are allowed to do with the vSphere Client against an ESXi host or the vSphere Client against a vCenter Server instance. For example, vSphere administrators can limit users to specific actions on specific types of objects within the vSphere Client. vCenter Server ships with some sample roles that help provide an example of how you can use the role-based access control system.

Master It   Describe the differences between a role, a privilege, and a permission in the ESXi/vCenter Server security model.

Solution   A role is a combination of privileges; a role is assigned to a user or group. Privileges are specific actions (like power on a VM, power off a VM, configure a VM's CD/DVD drive, and take a snapshot) that a role is allowed to perform. You combine privileges into a role. Permissions are created when you assign a role (with its associated privileges) to an inventory object within ESXi or vCenter Server.

Control network access to services on ESXi hosts.   ESXi provides a network firewall that you can use to control network access to services on your ESXi hosts. This firewall can control both inbound and outbound traffic, and you have the ability to further limit traffic to specific source IP addresses or subnets.

Master It   Describe how you can use the ESXi firewall to limit traffic to a specific source IP address.

Solution   In the Firewall Properties dialog box, click the Firewall button and specify a source IP address or source IP subnet.

Integrate with Active Directory.   All the major components of vSphere—the ESXi hosts and vCenter Server (both the Windows Server–based version and the Linux-based virtual appliance) as well as the vSphere Management Assistant—support integration with Active Directory. This gives vSphere administrators the option of using Active Directory as their centralized directory service for all major components of vSphere 5.5.

Master It   You've just installed a new ESXi host into your vSphere environment and you are trying to configure the host to enable integration with your Active Directory environment. For some reason, though, it doesn't seem to work. What could be the problem?

Solution   A couple different issues could be at work here. First, the ESXi host needs to be able to resolve the domain name of the Active Directory domain via DNS. The ESXi host also needs to be able to locate the Active Directory domain controllers via DNS. This usually involves configuring the ESXi host to use the same DNS servers as the domain controllers. Second, there could be network connectivity issues; verify that the ESXi host has connectivity to the Active Directory domain controllers. If there are any firewalls between the ESXi host and the domain controllers, verify that the correct ports are open between the ESXi host and the domain controllers.

Get familiar with KMS in your vSphere environment. Having a KMS infrastructure in your environment enables a multitude of features within vSphere, including VSAN and VM encryption, as well as vTPM2.0 devices for virtual machines. This gives you, the administrator, multiple tools at your disposal to secure your environment based on the available technologies presented and requirements given.

Master It You've been tasked by your boss with deploying vTPM2.0 devices to all of your Windows 10 workloads for the upcoming updates being pushed from Microsoft. What prerequisites do you need to have in place before you can start adding these devices to your workloads?

Solution The following must be configured before adding vTMP2.0

◆ A Key Management Server (KMS) must be configured.

◆ Each VM must be turned off to add vTPM2.0.

◆ The ESXi hosts running in your environment must be ESXi 6.7 or later.

◆ The virtual machine must use EFI firmware.

Chapter 9: Creating and Managing Virtual Machines

Create a virtual machine. A VM is a collection of virtual hardware pieces, like a physical system—one or more virtual CPUs, RAM, video card, SCSI devices, IDE devices, floppy drives, parallel and serial ports, and network adapters. This virtual hardware is virtualized and abstracted from the underlying physical hardware, providing portability to the VM.

Master It Create two VMs, one intended to run Windows Server 2012 and a second intended to run SLES 11 (64-bit). Make a list of the differences in the configuration that are suggested by the Create New Virtual Machine Wizard.

Solution vCenter Server suggests 1 GB of RAM, an LSI Logic parallel SCSI controller, and a 16 GB virtual disk for 64-bit SLES 11; for Windows Server 2012, the recommendations are 4 GB of RAM, an LSI Logic SAS controller, and a 40 GB virtual disk.

Install a guest operating system. Just as a physical machine needs an operating system, a VM also needs an operating system. vSphere supports a broad range of 32-bit and 64-bit operating systems, including all major versions of Windows Server, Windows 10, Windows 7, XP, and Windows 2000 as well as various flavors of Linux, macOS, FreeBSD, Novell NetWare, and Solaris

Master It What are the three ways in which a guest OS can access data on a CD/DVD, and what are the advantages of each approach?

Solution The three ways to access a CD/DVD are as follows:

◆ Client device: This has the advantage of being very easy to use; VMware administrators can put a CD/DVD into their local workstation and map it into the VM.

◆ Host device: The CD/DVD is physically placed into the optical drive of the ESXi host. This keeps the CD/DVD traffic off the network, which may be advantageous in some situations.

◆ An ISO image on a shared library/datastore: This is the fastest method and has the advantage of being able to have multiple VMs access the same ISO image at the same time. A bit more work may be required up front to create the ISO image.

Install VMware Tools. For maximum performance of the guest OS, it needs to have virtualization-optimized drivers that are specially written for and designed to work with the ESXi hypervisor. VMware Tools provides these optimized drivers as well as other utilities focused on better operation in virtual environments.

Master It A fellow administrator contacts you and is having a problem installing VMware Tools. This administrator has selected the Install/Upgrade VMware Tools command, but nothing seems to be happening inside the VM. What could be the cause of the problem?

Solution There could be any number of potential issues. First, a guest OS must be installed before VMware Tools can be installed. Second, if the VM is running Windows, AutoPlay may have been disabled. Finally, it's possible—although unlikely—that the source ISO images for VMware Tools installation have been damaged or deleted and need to be replaced on the host.

Manage virtual machines. Once a VM has been created, the vSphere Client makes it easy to manage. Virtual floppy images and CD/DVD drives can be mounted or unmounted as necessary. vSphere provides support for initiating an orderly shutdown of the guest OS in a VM, although this requires that VMware Tools be installed. VM snapshots allow you to take a point-in-time "picture" of a VM so that administrators can roll back changes if needed.

Master It What is the difference between the Shut Down Guest command and the Power Off command?

Solution The Shut Down Guest command uses VMware Tools to initiate an orderly shutdown of the guest OS. This ensures that the guest OS file system is consistent and that applications running in the guest OS are properly terminated. The Power Off command simply "yanks" the power from the VM, much like pulling the power cord out of the back of a physical system.

Modify virtual machines. vSphere offers a number of features to make it easy to modify VMs after they have been created. Administrators can hot-add certain types of hardware, like virtual hard disks and network adapters, and some guest OSs also support hot-adding virtual CPUs or memory, although this feature must be enabled first.

Master It Which method is preferred for modifying the configuration of a VM: editing the VMX file or using the vSphere Client?

Solution Although it is possible to edit the VMX file to make changes, that method is error prone and is not recommended. Using the vSphere Client is the recommended method.

Master It Name the types of hardware that cannot be added while a VM is running.

Solution The following types of virtual hardware cannot be added while a VM is running: serial port, parallel port, floppy drive, CD/DVD drive, vTMP, and PCI device.

Chapter 10: Using Templates and vApps

Clone a VM. The ability to clone a VM is a powerful feature that dramatically reduces the amount of time to get a fully functional VM with a guest OS installed and running. vCenter Server provides the ability to clone VMs and to customize VMs, ensuring that each VM is unique. You can save the information to customize a VM as a customization specification and then reuse that information over and over again. vCenter Server can even clone running VMs.

Master It Where and when can customization specifications be created in the vSphere Client?

Solution You can create customization specifications using the Customization Specification Manager, available from the vSphere Client home screen. You can also create customization specifications while cloning VMs or deploying from templates by supplying answers to the Guest Customization Wizard and saving those answers as a customization specification.

Master It A fellow administrator comes to you and wants you to help streamline the process of deploying Solaris x86 VMs in your VMware vSphere environment. What do you tell him?

Solution You can use cloning inside vCenter Server to help clone VMs that are running Solaris x86, and that will help speed up the process of deploying new VMs. However, the Solaris administrator(s) will be responsible for customizing the configuration of the cloned VMs because vCenter Server is unable to customize a Solaris guest OS installation as part of the cloning process.

Create a VM template. vCenter Server's templates feature is an excellent complement to the cloning functionality. With options to clone or convert an existing VM to a template, vCenter Server makes it easy to create templates. By creating templates, you ensure that your VM master image doesn't get accidentally changed or modified. Then, once a template has been created, you can use vCenter Server to clone VMs from that template, customizing them in the process to ensure that each one is unique.

Master It Of the following tasks, which are appropriate to be performed on a VM running Windows Server 2016 that will eventually be turned into a template?

a. Align the guest OS's file system to a 64 KB boundary.

b. Join the VM to Active Directory.

c. Perform some application-specific configurations and tweaks.

d. Install all patches from the operating system vendor.

Solution The answers are as follows:

a. Yes. This is an appropriate task but unnecessary because Windows Server 2016 installs already aligned to a 64 KB boundary. Ensuring alignment ensures that all VMs then cloned from the template will also have their file systems properly aligned.

b. No. This should be done by the vSphere Client Guest Customization Wizard or a customization specification.

c. No. Templates shouldn't have any application-specific files, tweaks, or configurations unless you are planning on creating multiple application-specific templates.

d. Yes. This helps reduce the amount of patching and updating required on any VMs cloned from this template.

Deploy new VMs from a template. By combining templates and cloning, VMware vSphere administrators have a powerful way to standardize the configuration of VMs being deployed, protect the master images from accidental change, and reduce the amount of time it takes to provision new guest OS instances.

Master It Another VMware vSphere administrator in your environment starts the wizard for deploying a new VM from a template. She has a customization specification she'd like to use, but there is one setting in the specification she wants to change. Does she have to create an all-new customization specification?

Solution No. She can select the customization specification she wants to use and then select Use The Customization Wizard To Customize This Specification to supply the alternate values she wants to use for this particular VM deployment. She also has the option of cloning the existing customization specification and then changing the one setting within this new clone. This can be a useful option if these alternate parameters will be used on other clones or templates in the future.

Deploy a VM from an Open Virtualization Format (OVF) template. Open Virtualization Format (OVF) templates provide a mechanism for moving templates or VMs between different instances of vCenter Server or even entirely different and separate installations of VMware vSphere. OVF templates combine the structural definition of a VM along with the data in the VM's virtual hard disk and can exist either as a folder of files or as a single file. Because OVF templates include the VM's virtual hard disk, OVF templates can contain an installation of a guest OS and are often used by software developers as a way of delivering their software preinstalled into a guest OS inside a VM.

Master It A vendor has given you a zip file that contains a VM they are calling a *virtual appliance*. Upon looking inside the zip file, you see several VMDK files and a VMX file. Will you be able to use vCenter Server's Deploy OVF Template functionality to import this VM? If not, how can you get this VM into your infrastructure?

Solution You will not be able to use vCenter Server's Deploy OVF Template feature; this requires that the virtual appliance be provided with an OVF file that supplies the information that vCenter Server is expecting to find. However, you can use vCenter Converter to perform a V2V conversion to bring this VM into the VMware vSphere environment, assuming it is coming from a compatible source environment.

Export a VM as an OVF template. To assist in the transport of VMs between VMware vSphere installations, you can use vCenter Server to export a VM as an OVF template. The OVF template will include the configuration of the VM as well as the data found in the VM.

Master It You are preparing to export a VM to an OVF template. You want to ensure that the OVF template is easy to transport via a USB key or portable hard drive. Which format is most appropriate, OVF or OVA? Why?

Solution   The OVA format is probably a better option here. OVA distributes the entire OVF template as a single file, making it easy to copy to a USB key or portable hard drive for transport. Using OVF would mean keeping several files together instead of working with only a single file.

Organize templates and media.   Organizing and synchronizing templates and media around larger environments can be troublesome. Content Libraries (instead of SAN-based replication), scheduled copy scripts, and "sneaker net" can be used to ensure the right templates and files are in the right places.

Master It   List the file types that cannot be added to Content Libraries for synchronization.

Solution   Any file type can be uploaded to a Content Library. All files will be synchronized as configured without changes. VM templates not in OVF format will be converted to OVF format as they are being uploaded, however.

Work with vApps.   vSphere vApps leverage OVF as a way to combine multiple VMs into a single administrative unit. When the vApp is powered on, all VMs in it are powered on, in a sequence specified by the administrator. The same goes for shutting down a vApp. vApps also act a bit like resource pools for the VMs contained within them.

Master It   Name two ways to add VMs to a vApp.

Solution   There are four ways to add VMs to a vApp: create a new VM in the vApp, clone an existing VM into a new VM in the vApp, deploy a VM into the vApp from a template, and drag and drop an existing VM into the vApp.

Chapter 11: Managing Resource Allocation

Manage virtual machine memory allocation.   In almost every modern virtualized datacenter, memory is the resource that typically comes under contention first. Most organizations run out of memory on their ESXi hosts before other resources become constrained. Fortunately, vSphere offers advanced memory management technologies as well as extensive controls for managing the allocation of memory and utilization of memory by VMs.

Master It   To guarantee levels of performance, your IT Director believes that all VMs must be configured with at least 8 GB of memory. However, you know that many of your applications rarely use this much memory. What might be an acceptable compromise to help ensure performance?

Solution   One way would be to configure the VMs with 8 GB of RAM and specify a reservation of only 2 GB. VMware ESXi will guarantee that every VM will get 2 GB of RAM, including preventing additional VMs from being powered on if there isn't enough RAM to guarantee 2 GB of RAM to that new VM. However, RAM greater than 2 GB is not guaranteed and, if it is not being used, will be reclaimed by the host for use elsewhere. If plenty of memory is available to the host, the ESXi host will grant what is requested; otherwise, it will arbitrate the allocation of that memory according to the share values of the VMs.

Master It You are configuring a new large-scale virtual desktop infrastructure environment, but you are worried that the cluster hosts will not have enough memory to handle the expected load. Which advanced memory management technique will ensure that your virtual desktops have enough memory without having to use the swap file?

Solution Transparent page sharing (TPS) ensures that if you have multiple VMs with the same blocks of memory, you allocate it only once. This can almost be thought of as "de-duplication for RAM." Within virtual desktop environments, many VMs are run as "clones" with their operating system and applications all identical—a perfect case for TPS to take advantage of.

Manage CPU utilization. In a vSphere environment, the ESXi hosts control VM access to physical CPUs. To effectively manage and scale vSphere, you must understand how to allocate CPU resources to VMs, including how to use reservations, limits, and shares. Shares help adjust the allocation of resources in a constrained environment, reservations provide guarantees to resources, and limits provide a cap on resource usage.

Master It A fellow vSphere administrator is concerned about the use of CPU reservations. She is worried that using CPU reservations will "strand" CPU resources, preventing those reserved but unused resources from being used by other VMs. Are the concerns of the administrator well founded?

Solution For CPU reservations, no. Although it is true that VMware must have enough unreserved CPU capacity to satisfy a CPU reservation when a VM is powered on, reserved CPU capacity is not "locked" to a VM. If a VM has reserved but unused capacity, that capacity can and will be used by other VMs on the same host. The other administrator's concerns could be valid, however, for memory reservations.

Create and manage resource pools. Managing resource allocation and usage for large numbers of VMs can create an administrative overhead. Resource pools provide a mechanism for administrators to apply resource allocation policies to groups of VMs at the same time. Resource pools use shares, reservations, and limits to control and modify resource allocation behavior, but only for memory and CPU.

Master It Your organization runs both development workloads and production workloads on the same hardware. How can you help ensure that development workloads do not consume too many resources and impact the performance of production workloads?

Solution Create a resource pool and place all the test/development VMs in that resource pool. Configure the resource pool to have a CPU limit and a lower CPU shares value. This ensures that the test/development VMs will never consume more CPU time than specified in the limit and that, in times of CPU contention, the test/development environment will have a lower priority on the CPU than production workloads.

Control network and storage I/O utilization. Memory, CPU, network I/O, and storage I/O make up the four major resource types that vSphere administrators must effectively manage for an efficient virtualized datacenter. By applying controls to network I/O and storage I/O, you can help ensure consistent performance, meet service-level objectives, and prevent one workload from unnecessarily consuming resources at the expense of other workloads.

Master It Name two limitations of Network I/O Control.

Solution Network I/O Control works only with vSphere Distributed Switches and it requires vCenter Server in order to operate. Another limitation is that system network resource pools cannot be assigned to user-created port groups.

Master It What are the requirements for using Storage I/O Control?

Solution All datastores and ESXi hosts that will participate in Storage I/O Control must be managed by the same vCenter Server instance. In addition, raw device mappings (RDMs) are not supported. Datastores must have only a single extent; datastores with multiple extents are not supported.

Chapter 12: Balancing Resource Utilization

Configure and execute vMotion. vMotion is a feature that allows running VMs to be migrated from one ESXi host to another without downtime to end users. To execute vMotion, you must ensure that both the ESXi hosts and the VMs meet specific configuration requirements. In addition, vCenter Server performs validation checks to ensure that vMotion compatibility rules are observed.

Master It A vendor has just released a series of patches for some of the guest OSs in your virtualized infrastructure. You request an outage window from your supervisor, but your supervisor says to just use vMotion to prevent downtime. Is your supervisor correct? Why or why not?

Solution Your supervisor is incorrect. vMotion can be used to move running VMs from one physical host to another, but it does not address outages within a guest OS because of reboots or other malfunctions. If you had been requesting an outage window to apply updates to the host, the supervisor would have been correct—you could use vMotion to move all the VMs to other hosts within the environment and then patch the first host. There would be no end-user downtime in that situation.

Master It Is vMotion a solution to prevent unplanned downtime?

Solution No. vMotion is a solution to address planned downtime of the ESXi hosts on which VMs are running, as well as to manually load-balance CPU and memory utilization across multiple ESXi hosts. Both the source and destination ESXi hosts must be up and running and accessible across the network in order for vMotion to succeed.

Ensure vMotion compatibility across processor families. vMotion requires compatible CPU families on the source and target ESXi hosts to be successful. To help alleviate any potential problems resulting from changes in processor families over time, vSphere offers Enhanced vMotion Compatibility (EVC), which can mask differences between CPU families to maintain vMotion compatibility.

Master It Can you change the EVC level for a cluster while there are VMs running on hosts in the cluster?

Solution No, you cannot. Changing the EVC level means that you must calculate and apply new CPU masks. CPU masks can be applied only when VMs are powered off, so you can't change the EVC level on a cluster when there are powered-on VMs in that cluster.

Use Storage vMotion. Just as vMotion is used to migrate running VMs from one ESXi host to another, Storage vMotion is used to migrate the virtual disks of a running VM from one datastore to another. You can also use Storage vMotion to convert between thick and thin virtual disk types.

Master It Name two features of Storage vMotion that would help you cope with storage-related changes in your vSphere environment.

Solution You can use Storage vMotion to facilitate no-downtime storage migrations from one storage array to a new storage array, greatly simplifying the migration process. Storage vMotion can also migrate between different types of storage (FC to NFS, iSCSI to FC or FCoE), which helps you cope with changes in how the ESXi hosts access the storage. Finally, Storage vMotion allows you to convert VMDKs between thick and thin, to give you the flexibility to use whichever VMDK format is most effective for you.

Perform combined vMotion and Storage vMotion. Using vMotion and Storage vMotion at the same time gives you greater flexibility when migrating VMs between hosts. Using this feature can also save time when you must evacuate a host for maintenance.

Master It A fellow administrator is trying to migrate a VM to a different datastore and a different host while it is running and wishes to complete the task as quickly and as simply as possible. Which migration option should she choose?

Solution Storage vMotion, like vMotion, can operate while a VM is running. However, choosing to perform both migrations together will not only allow the VM to stay powered on, it also turns what is regularly a two-step process into a single step.

Configure and manage vSphere Distributed Resource Scheduler. DRS enables vCenter Server to automate the process of conducting vMotion migrations to help balance the load across ESXi hosts in a cluster. You can automate DRS as you wish, and vCenter Server has flexible controls for affecting the behavior of DRS and specific VMs within a DRS-enabled cluster.

Master It You want to take advantage of DRS to provide some load balancing of virtual workloads within your environment. However, because of business constraints, you have a few workloads that should not be automatically moved to other hosts using vMotion. Can you use DRS? If so, how can you prevent these specific workloads from being affected by DRS?

Solution Yes, you can use DRS. Enable DRS on the cluster, and set the DRS automation level appropriately. For those VMs that should not be automatically migrated by DRS, configure a VM Override set to Manual. This will allow DRS to make recommendations on migrations for these workloads but it will not actually perform the migrations.

Configure and manage Storage DRS. Building on Storage vMotion just as DRS builds on vMotion, SDRS automates the process of balancing storage capacity and I/O utilization. SDRS uses datastore clusters and can operate in Manual or Fully Automated mode. Numerous customizations exist—such as custom schedules, VM and VMDK anti-affinity rules, and threshold settings—to allow you to fine-tune the behavior of SDRS to your environment.

Master It Name the two ways in which an administrator is notified that an SDRS recommendation has been generated.

Solution On the Storage DRS tab of a datastore cluster, the recommendation(s) will be listed with an option to apply the recommendations. In addition, on the Alarms tab of the datastore cluster, an alarm will be triggered to indicate that a Storage DRS recommendation exists.

> **Master It**   What is a potential disadvantage of using drag-and-drop to add a datastore to a datastore cluster?

> **Solution**   When you use drag-and-drop to add a datastore to a datastore cluster, the user is not notified if the datastore isn't accessible to all the hosts that are currently connected to the datastore cluster. This introduces the possibility that one or more ESXi hosts could be "stranded" from a VM's virtual disks if Storage DRS migrates them onto a datastore that is not accessible from that host.

Chapter 13: Monitoring VMware vSphere Performance

Use alarms for proactive monitoring.   vCenter Server offers extensive alarms for alerting vSphere administrators to excessive resource consumption or potentially negative events. You can create alarms on virtually any type of object found within vCenter Server, including datacenters, clusters, ESXi hosts, and VMs. Alarms can monitor for resource consumption or for the occurrence of specific events. Alarms can also trigger actions, such as running a script, migrating a VM, or sending a notification email.

> **Master It**   What are the questions you should ask before creating a custom alarm?

> **Solution**   You should ask yourself several questions before you create a custom alarm:

> ◆ Does an existing alarm meet my needs?

> ◆ What is the proper scope for this alarm? Do I need to create it at the datacenter level so that it affects all objects of a particular type within the datacenter or at some lower point?

> ◆ What are the values this alarm needs to use?

> ◆ What actions, if any, should this alarm take when it is triggered? Does it need to send an email or trigger an SNMP trap?

Work with performance charts.   vCenter Server's detailed performance charts are the key to unlocking the information necessary to determine why an ESXi host or VM is performing poorly. The performance charts expose a large number of performance counters across a variety of resource types, and vCenter Server offers functionality to save customized chart settings, export performance graphs as graphic figures or Excel workbooks, and view performance charts in a separate window.

> **Master It**   You find yourself using the Chart Options link in the Advanced layout of the Performance tab to set up the same chart over and over again. Is there a way to save yourself some time and effort so that you don't have to keep re-creating the custom chart?

> **Solution**   Yes. After using the Chart Options dialog box to configure the performance chart to show the desired counters, use the Save Chart Settings button to save these settings for future use. The next time you need to access these same settings, they will be available from the Switch To drop-down list on the Advanced view of the Performance tab.

Gather performance information using command-line tools. VMware supplies a few command-line tools that are useful in gathering performance information. For VMware ESXi hosts, `esxtop` provides real-time information about CPU, memory, network, or disk utilization. Finally, the `vm-support` tool can gather performance information that can be played back later using `esxtop`.

Master It Explain how to run `esxtop` from the shell of an ESXi host.

Solution On the ESXi shell, Enter the command vm-support -p -i 10 -d 180. This creates a resxtop snapshot, capturing data every 10 seconds, for the duration of 180 seconds.

Monitor CPU, memory, network, and disk usage by ESXi hosts and VMs. Monitoring usage of the four key resources—CPU, memory, network, and disk—can be difficult at times. Fortunately, the various tools supplied by VMware within vCenter Server can lead the vSphere administrator to the right solution. In particular, using customized performance charts can expose the right information that will help you uncover the source of performance problems.

Master It A junior vSphere administrator is trying to resolve a performance problem with a VM. You've asked this administrator to see if it is a CPU problem, and the junior administrator keeps telling you that the VM needs more CPU capacity because the CPU utilization is high within the VM. Is the junior administrator correct, based on the information available to you?

Solution Based on the available information, not necessarily. A VM may be using all of the cycles being given to it, but because the overall ESXi host is CPU constrained, the VM isn't getting enough cycles to perform acceptably. In this case, adding CPU capacity to the VM wouldn't necessarily fix the problem. If the host is indeed constrained, migrating VMs to other hosts or changing the shares or the CPU limits for the VMs on this host may help alleviate the problem.

Chapter 14: Automating VMware vSphere

Identify automation solutions for VMware vSphere. With over 600 cmdlets, the most widely adopted automation tool to manage and automate vSphere is PowerCLI. Some additional vSphere automation tools provided by VMware include the vSphere Automation SDKs with libraries for programmatically accessing features available via the API. vRealize Orchestrator provides the ability to use the out-of-the-box workflows or design and deploy custom, scalable workflows to automate vSphere processes.

Master It Explore these and additional options for vSphere automation tools by VMware and third-party providers that leverage the vSphere Automation SDKs.

Solution For SDK and API examples, browse: **https://code.vmware.com**.

Use PowerCLI on multiple platforms. PowerCLI 10 introduced multi-platform support by adding macOS and Linux support with PowerShell Core after the Microsoft PowerShell Team open-sourced the PowerShell base code with the release of PowerShell 6.0. PowerShell and PowerCLI can now run on Windows, macOS, and Linux.

Master It   Practice installing PowerShell and VMware PowerCLI on each platform. From each OS, grow your scripting to more complex scenarios to make common, repetitive, and often error-prone tasks a breeze. Use Microsoft Visual Code with an integrated shell and plug-ins for a common development interface.

Solution   PowerCLI 10 introduced multi-platform support by adding macOS and Linux support with PowerShell Core after the Microsoft PowerShell Team open-sourced the PowerShell base code with the release of PowerShell 6.0. PowerShell and PowerCLI can now run on Windows, macOS, and Linux.

Create PowerCLI scripts to automate common tasks.   VMware PowerCLI builds on the Power of the PowerShell scripting language to provide you with a simple yet powerful way to automate tasks within the vSphere environment and the ability to do so from your platform of choice. It is easy to get started with your first one-liner and grow your scripting to more complex scenarios to make common, repetitive, and often error-prone tasks a breeze.

Master It   If you are familiar with other scripting languages, what would be the biggest hurdle in learning to use PowerShell and PowerCLI, other than syntax?

Solution   Everything in PowerShell and PowerCLI is object based. Thus, when a command outputs results, those results are objects. This means you have to be careful to properly match object types between the output of one command and the input of the next command.

Index

W

X-Y-Z